READINGS IN PSYCHOLOGY: RESEARCH AND APPLICATIONS

Edited by

JOHN NEIL BOHANNON

Butler University

Allyn and Bacon

Boston   London   Sydney   Toronto

Series Editor: John-Paul Lenney
Series Editorial Assistant: Susan Brody
Production Administrator: Lorraine Perrotta

ISBN 0–205–11978–6

Printed in the United States of America

10 9 8 7 6 5 4 3 2   93 92 91 90 89

CONTENTS

"How People Make Their Own Environments: A Theory of Genotype Æ Environmental Effects," by Sandra Scarr and Kathleen McCartney. Reprinted with permission from Child Development, Vol. 54, 1983, pp. 424–435. Copyright © 1983 The Society for Research in Child Development, Inc.

"Behavioral Study of Obedience," by Stanley Milgram. From Journal of Abnormal and Social Psychology, 1963. Copyright 1963 by the American Psychological Association.

"When Bystanders Just Stand There," by R. Lance Shotland. Reprinted with permission from Psychology Today Magazine. Copyright © 1985 (P. T. Partners, L. P.)

"The Three Faces of Love," by Robert J. Trotter. Reprinted with permission from Psychology Today Magazine. Copyright © 1986 (P. T. Partners, L. P.)

"Are Criminals Made or Born?" by Richard J. Herrnstein and James Q. Wilson. Reprinted by permission from The New York Times. Copyright © 1985 by The New York Times Company.

"Acceptance of Personality Interpretations: The 'Barnum Effect' and Beyond," by C.R. Snyder, Randee Jae Shenkel, and Carol R. Lowery. From Journal of Consulting and Clinical Psychology, Vol. 45, 1977. Copyright 1977 by the American Psychology Association.

"The Myth of Mental Illness," by Thomas S. Szasz. From American Psychologist, Vol. 15, 1960. Copyright 1960 by the American Psychological Association.

"Adolescent Eating Disorder: Bulimia," by Rolf E. Muuss. From Adolescence, Vol. 21, 1986, pp. 257–267. Copyright © 1986 Rolf E. Muuss.

"From Rationalization to Reason," by Seymour S. Kety. The American Journal of Psychiatry, Vol. 131, 1974, pp. 957–963. Copyright 1974, The American Psychiatric Association.

"Biofeedback and the Placebo Effect," by Jerome D. Frank. Reprinted by permission from Biofeedback and Self-Regulation, Vol. 7, 1982, pp. 449–460. Copyright © 1982 Plenum Publishing Corporation.

"On Being Sane in Insane Places," by David L. Rosenhan. Reprinted by permission from Science, Vol. 179, 1973, pp. 250–258. Copyright © 1973 American Association for the Advancement of Science.

Chapter 14   Applied Psychology   **403**

PREFACE

All too often students are first exposed to psychology in huge lecture sections, where they are part of a crowd—anonymous and passive recipients of information. Moreover, the breadth of content to which they are exposed in a typical introductory psychology course is too vast to consider a coherent body of knowledge. Students report feeling like they "are drinking from a fire hose." They do not have enough time to grapple with any single issue long enough to truly understand its nature, or its relevance to their lives. For these reasons, some instructors have tried to break away from the use of large lecture sections, at least in part. For example, some large introductory classes break up into small discussion sections for one period a week for the purpose of discussion, demonstration, or both. Although such discussion sections are an ideal forum for this book, the readings can also be used to enliven the general class sessions as well as foster student understanding of the text and lecture contents.

This book is designed to supplement a basic introductory text, *not* replace one. Each chapter contains papers on basic theory or research, and its applications. The number of selections has been kept relatively small so that each can be addressed in a typical fifty-minute class period. There are discussion issues, homework questions, or both included in each chapter. They can serve as the basis for discussion or as a point of departure for the instructor's own line of inquiry.

The editor of this volume has used most of these selections in sixty-plus discussions sections with over 2,000 students per year for the past four years. The benefits derive from reducing the students' feelings of anonymity, exposing them to original research and applications in psychology, and encouraging them to express their own ideas about the issues raised by their reading. Both the context (small versus large class) and the mode of instruction (interactive versus passive) have led to a superior degree of retention of the material. Therefore, as students are given their "bicycle tour of the Louvre" in their introductory psychology classes, this book may give them the feeling that they stopped once or twice to appreciate a point of interest.

TO THE STUDENT

This book is a supplement to the textbook chosen for your class. The readings should be addressed *after* you read the relevant sections and chapter from your textbook. For example, before reading Chapter 1 on methods, you should find the methodology section in your textbook, usually in the first chapter or in the back as an appendix, and read it. The readings were selected, and the homework questions written, under the assumption that the reader knows the basics of the area. The first page of each chapter has enough room to write your answers to the homework questions.

With these instructions aside, there are some general principles of which you should be aware. First, psychology is a vigorous science in which new discoveries occur almost daily. This makes writing a definitive textbook a difficult task. Your introductory text in psychology, even if it is up-to-date, will probably not present facts and theories that are set in stone, but only "the state of the art." The readings selected for this book are similarly chosen. Some are "classics", such as the Milgram paper (Chapter 10), whose importance endures; but others, such as Sternberg's theory of love (Chapter 10), are brand new. Twenty years ago, Sternberg's theory did not exist, nor did much of the entire area of cognitive psychology. Thus, as you read, it is important to understand that some authority is not presenting you with the immutable truth, but with facts and their theoretical interpretations and implications as they are presently constituted. It is necessary to continue to ask if the research data and the methods used to gather them justify the conclusions of the theorists.

The spirit of healthy skepticism is important in psychology. Because of the sheer volume of research being performed, some isolated instances of facile thinking occur. This happens when people discover an intriguing fact about psychology and rush to apply it before seriously researching all its parameters. The result is the misapplication of a valid research finding. One must be especially wary of those whose purpose is to promote some aspect of behavioral control (see Chapter 13 on psychotherapy).

With these guidelines in mind, you may enjoy seeing psychology at work, both the research and its applications. Try to determine what research or theories from your introductory text are the basis for the articles in your reader. The purpose of the reader is to supply you with more concrete material you can analyze and discuss with your instructor. The more you actively confront the issues and ideas presented in the readings, the more you will know about psychology at the end of your introductory course.

ACKNOWLEDGMENTS

I would like to think the following reviewers, who offered comments on both the content and format of this book. Their suggestions were constructive and insightful, and greatly aided in the development of the manuscript:

Robert A. Baron
Rensselaer Polytechnic Institute

William Calhoun
University of Tennessee at Knoxville

Paul D. Cherulnik
Southeast Missouri State University

John M. Davis
Southwest Texas State University

Don Devers
Northern Virginia Community College

Richard L. Floyd
California State University at Hayward

David A. Griese
State University of New York at Farmingdale

Stephen B. Klein
Fort Hays State University

Lester A. Lefton
University of South Carolina at Columbia

Ronald Murdoff
San Joaquin Delta Community College

Raymond R. Shrader
University of Tennessee at Knoxville

Arno F. Wittig
Ball State University

I would also like to thank my editor, John-Paul Lenney, and his assistant, Susan Brody, for their help with the development of the manuscript. Finally, special thanks must go to Lorraine Perrotta for making the production of this book possible.

Chapter 1

Methods

CHAPTER 1: METHODS

One of the least understood aspects of psychology is the nature of good behavioral research. People often think that research in psychology is either a form of the "Freudian" clinical interview or a matter of running rats in mazes. Although good research may involve either of these techniques, it is certainly much more varied. Further, behavioral research often requires more caution than research in other sciences. For example, in chemistry there is no reason to think an experiment with a particular batch of carbon should lead to any different results from that obtained with another batch of carbon. But, people and animals differ—from person to person, and animal to animal—even within subspecies. You also don't have to worry about mistreating carbon or having to deceive it for your experiment to work properly; whereas people and animals have the right not to be mistreated, and there is some question about the ethics of deceiving human subjects during experiments. These are among the problems that arise in doing research in behavior. The three articles selected for this section address important aspects of these problems. Students should try to ascertain from each paper what might constitute a good research study.

1a. Huff, D. (1954). The sample with the built in bias. In *How to Lie with statistics*. New York: Norton, pp. 11–26.

This article addresses one of the most important aspects of psychological research—sample selection. Too often, research ignores the possibility of bias in the selection of subjects, despite the fact that bias can make the resulting data meaningless. After reading this paper, do you think the typical psychological study (which uses college freshmen and sophomores) could generalize to everybody? Why or why not? Make sure you argue your point with information from the article.

1b. King, F. (1984). Animals in research: The case for experimentation. *Psychology Today*, Sept., 56–58.

About seven years ago, two former caretakers of a lab in Hawaii freed two dolphins who had undergone three years of language training. What do you think should happen to caretakers who do such things? Assume that the care for these animals was humane, but the research was "basic"—that is, not designed to have any practical human applications.

Is there anything that would justify hurting animals, or taking their lives? At what point should researchers be prohibited from performing a specific study? Imagine that you are chairperson of a university's animal research committee. Write at least three rules or guidelines for making such judgments. Be prepared to explain and defend your rules.

1c. Milgram, S. (1977). Subject reaction: The neglected factor in the ethics of experimentation. *Hastings Center Report*, 7, Oct.

This selection discusses some of the controversy over using humans in social psychology experiments. Imagine that you are serving as a subject in a social psychology study. During the course of the study you "go along" with the group or "obey" a figure of authority. In doing so, you find out something about yourself that you don't like, and are troubled by it. Say the study involved the use of "deception"; based on the material in the article, is deception justified? Can you sue for damages? What is the basis for the claim that the experimenter harmed you? What would be the important arguments of your suit? Be prepared to argue your case.

The Sample with the Built in Bias

Darrell Huff and Irving Geis

"The average Yaleman, Class of '24," *Time* magazine noted once, commenting on something in the New York *Sun*, "makes $25,111 a year."

Well good for him!

But wait a minute. What does this impressive figure mean? Is it, as it appears to be, evidence that if you send your boy to Yale you won't have to work in your old age and neither will he?

Two things about the figure stand out at first suspicious glance. It is surprisingly precise. It is quite improbably salubrious.

There is small likelihood that the average income of any far-flung group is ever going to be known down to the dollar. It is not particularly probable that you know your own income for last year so precisely as that unless it was all derived from salary. And $25,000 incomes are not often all salary; people in that bracket are likely to have well-scattered investments.

Furthermore, this lovely average is undoubtedly calculated from the amounts the Yale men *said* they earned. Even if they had the honor system in New Haven in '24, we cannot be sure that it works so well after a quarter of a century that all these reports are honest ones. Some people when asked their incomes exaggerate out of vanity or optimism. Others minimize, especially, it is to be feared, on income-tax returns; and having done this may hesitate to contradict themselves on any other paper. Who knows what the revenuers may see? It is possible that these two tendencies, to boast and to understate, cancel each other out, but it is unlikely. One tendency may be far stronger than the other, and we do not know which one.

We have begun then to account for a figure that common sense tells us can hardly represent the truth. Now let us put our finger on the likely source of the biggest error, a source that can produce $25,111 as the "average income" of some men whose actual average may well be nearer half that amount.

This is the sampling procedure, which is the heart of the greater part of the statistics you meet on all sorts of subjects. Its basis is simple enough, although its refinements in practice have led into all sorts of by-ways, some less than respectable. If you have a barrel of beans, some red and some white, there is only one way to find out exactly how many of each color you have: Count 'em. However, you can find out approximately how many are red in much easier fashion by pulling out a handful of beans and counting just those, figuring that the proportion will be the same all through the barrel. If your sample is large enough and selected properly, it will represent the whole well enough for most purposes. If it is not, it may be far less accurate than an intelligent guess and have nothing to recommend it but a spurious air of scientific precision. It is sad truth that conclusions from such samples, biased or too small or both, lie behind much of what we read or think we know.

The report on the Yale men comes from a sample. We can be pretty sure of that because reason tells us that no one can get hold of all the living members of that class of '24. There are bound to be many whose addresses are unknown twenty-five years later.

And, of those whose addresses are known, many will not reply to a questionnaires, particularly a rather personal one. With some kinds of mail questionnaire, a five or ten per cent response is quite high. This one should have done better than that, but nothing like one hundred per cent.

So we find that the income figure is based on a sample composed of all class members whose addresses are known and who replied to the questionnaire. Is this a representative sample? That is, can this group be assumed to be equal in income to the unrepresented group, those who cannot be reached or who do not reply?

Who are the little lost sheep down in the Yale rolls as "address unknown"? Are they the big-income earners–the Wall Street men, the corporation directors, the manufacturing and utility executives? No; the addresses of the rich will not be hard to come by. Many of the most prosperous members of the class can be found through *Who's Who in America* and other reference volumes even if they have neglected to keep in touch with the alumni office. It is a good guess that the lost names are those of the men who, twenty-five years or so after becoming Yale bachelors of arts, have not fulfilled any shining promise. They are clerks, mechanics, tramps, unemployed alcoholics, barely surviving writers and artists . . . people of whom it would take half a dozen or more to add up to an income of $25,111. These men do not so often register at class reunions, if only because they cannot afford the trip.

Who are those who chucked the questionnaire into the nearest wastebasket? We cannot be so sure about these, but it is at least a fair guess that many of them are just not making enough money to brag about. They are a little like the fellow who found a note clipped to his first pay check suggesting that he consider the amount of his salary confidential and not material for the interchange of office confidences. "Don't worry," he told the boss. "I'm just as ashamed of it as you are."

It becomes pretty clear that the sample has omitted two groups most likely to depress the average. The $25,111 figure is beginning to explain itself. If it is a true figure for anything it is one merely for that special group of the class of '24 whose addresses are known and who are willing to stand up and tell how much they earn. Even that requires an assumption that the gentlemen are telling the truth.

Such an assumption is not to be made lightly. Experience from one breed of sampling study, that called market research, suggests that it can hardly ever be made at all. A house-to-house survey purporting to study magazine readership was once made in which a key question was: What magazines does your household read? When the results were tabulated and analyzed it appeared that a great many people loved *Harper's* and not very many read *True Story*. Now there were publishers' figures around at the time that showed very clearly that *True Story* had more millions of circulation than *Harper's* had hundreds of thousands. Perhaps we asked the wrong kind of people, the designers of the survey said to themselves. But no, the questions had been asked in all sorts of neighborhoods all around the country. The only reasonable conclusion then was that a good many of the respondents, as people are called when they answer such questions, had not told the truth. About all the survey had uncovered was snobbery.

In the end it was found that if you wanted to know what certain people read it was no use asking them. You could learn a good deal more by going to their houses and saying you wanted to buy old magazines and what could be had? Then all you had to do was count the *Yale Reviews* and the *Love Romances*. Even that dubious device, of course, does not tell you what people read, only what they have been exposed to.

Similarly, the next time you learn from your reading that the average American (you hear a good deal about him these days, most of it faintly improbable) brushes his teeth 1.02 times a day—a figure I have just made up, but it may be as good as anyone else's—ask yourself a question. How can anyone have found out such a thing? Is a woman who has read in countless advertisements that non-brushers are social offenders going to confess to a stranger that she does not brush her teeth regularly? The statistic may have meaning to one who wants to know only what people say about tooth-brushing but it does not tell a great deal about the frequency with which bristle is applied to incisor.

A river cannot, we are told, rise above its source. Well, it can seem to if there is a pumping station concealed somewhere about. It is equally true that the result of a sampling study is no better than the sample it is based on. By the time the data have been filtered through layers of statistical manipulation and reduced to a decimal-pointed average, the result begins to take on an aura of conviction that a closer look at the sampling would deny.

Does early discovery of cancer save lives? Probably. But of the figures commonly used to prove it the best that can be said is that they don't. These, the records of the Connecticut Tumor Registry, go back to 1935 and appear to show a substantial increase in the five-year survival rate from that year till 1941. Actually those records were begun in 1941, and everything earlier was obtained by tracing back. Many patients had left Connecticut, and whether they had lived or died could not be learned. According to the medical reporter Leonard Engel, the built-in bias thus created is "enough to account for nearly the whole of the claimed improvement in survival rate."

To be worth much, a report based on sampling must use a representative sample, which is one from which every source of bias has been removed. That is where our Yale figure shows its worthlessness. It is also where a great many of the things you can read in newspapers and magazines reveal their inherent lack of meaning.

A psychiatrist reported once that practically everybody is neurotic. Aside from the fact that such use destroys any meaning in the word "neurotic," take a look at the man's sample. That is, whom has the psychiatrist been observing? It turns out that he has reached this edifying conclusion from studying his patients, who are a long, long way from being a sample of the population. If a man were normal, our psychiatrist would never meet him.

Give that kind of second look to the things you read, and you can avoid learning a whole lot of things that are not so.

It is worth keeping in mind also that the dependability of a sample can be destroyed just as easily by invisible sources of bias as by these visible ones. That is, even if you can't find a source of demonstrable bias, allow yourself some degree of skepticism about the results as long as there is a possibility of bias somewhere. There always is. The presidential elections in 1948 and 1952 were enough to prove that, if there were any doubt.

For further evidence go back to 1936 and the *Literary Digest's* famed fiasco. The ten million telephone and *Digest* subscribers who assured the editors of the doomed magazine that it would be Landon 370, Roosevelt 161 came from the list that had accurately predicted the 1932 election. How could there be bias in a list already so tested? There was a bias, of course, as college theses and other post mortems found: People who could afford telephones and magazine subscriptions in 1936 were not a cross section of voters. Economically they were a special kind of people, a sample biased because it was loaded with what turned out to be Republican voters. The sample elected Landon, but the voters thought otherwise.

The basic sample is the kind called "random." It is selected by pure chance from the "universe," a word by which the statistician means the whole of which the sample is a part. Every tenth name is pulled from a file of index cards. Fifty slips of paper are taken from a hatful. Every twentieth person met on Market Street is interviewed. (But remember that this last is not a sample of the population of the world, or of the United States, or of San Fransisco, but only of the people on Market Street at the time. One interviewer for an opinion poll said that she got her people in a railroad station because "all kinds of people can be found in a station." It had to be pointed out to her that mothers of small children, for instance, might be underrepresented there.)

The test of the random sample is this: Does every name or thing in the whole group have an equal chance to be in the sample?

The purely random sample is the only kind that can be examined with entire confidence by means of statistical theory, but there is one thing wrong with it. It is so difficult and expensive to obtain for many uses that sheer cost eliminates it. A more economical substitute, which is almost universally used in such fields as opinion polling and market research, is called stratified random sampling.

To get this stratified sample you divide your universe into several groups in proportion to their known prevalence. And right there your trouble can begin: Your information about their proportion may not be correct. You instruct your interviewers to see to it that they talk to so many Negroes and such-and-such a percentage of people in each of several income brackets, to a specified number of farmers, and so on. All the while the group must be divided equally between persons over forty and under forty years of age.

That sounds fine—but what happens? On the question of Negro or white the interviewer will judge correctly most of the time. On income he will make more mistakes. As to farmers—how do you classify a man who farms part time and works in the city too? Even the question of age can pose some problems which are most easily settled by choosing only respondents who obviously are well under or well over forty. In that case the sample will be biased by the virtual absence of the late-thirties and early-forties age groups. You can't win.

On top of all this, how do you get a random sample within the stratification? The obvious thing is to start with a list of everybody and go after names chosen from it at random; but that is too expensive. So you go into the streets—and bias your sample against stay-at-homes. You go from door by day—and miss most of the employed people. You switch to evening interviews—and neglect the movie-goers and night-clubbers.

The operation of a poll comes down in the end to a running battle against sources of bias, and this battle is conducted all the time by all the reputable polling organizations. What the reader of the reports must remember is that the battle is never won. No conclusion that "sixty-seven per cent of the American people are against" something or other should be read without the lingering question, Sixty-seven per cent of which American people?

So with Dr. Alfred C. Kinsey's "female volume." The problem, as with anything based on sampling, is how to read it (or a popular summary of it) without learning too much that is not necessarily so. There are at least three levels of sampling involved. Dr. Kinsey's samples of the population (one level) are far from random ones and may not be particularly representative, but they are enormous samples by comparison with anything done in this field before and his figures must be accepted as revealing and important if not necessarily on the nose. It is possibly more it important to remember that any questionnaire is only a sample (another level) of the possible questions and that the answer the lady gives is no more than a sample (third level) of her attitudes and experiences on each question.

The kind of people who make up the interviewing staff can shade the result in an interesting fashion. Some years ago, during the war, the National Opinion Research Center sent out two staffs of interviewers to ask three questions of five hundred Negroes in a Southern city. White interviewers made up one staff, Negro the other.

One question was, "Would Negroes be treated better or worse here if the Japanese conquered the U.S.A.?" Negro interviewers reported that nine per cent of those they asked said "better." White interviewers found only two per cent of such responses. And while Negro interviewers found only twenty-five per cent who thought Negroes would be treated worse, white interviewers turned up forty-five per cent.

When "Nazis" was substituted for "Japanese" in the question, the results were similar.

The third question probed attitudes that might be based on feelings revealed by the first two. "Do you think it is more important to concentrate on beating the Axis, or to make democracy work better here at home?" "Beat Axis" was the reply of thirty-nine per cent, according to the Negro interviewers; of sixty-two per cent, according to the white.

Here is bias introduced by unknown factors. It seems likely that the most effective factor was a tendency that must always be allowed for in reading poll results, a desire to give a pleasing answer. Would it be any wonder if, when answering a question with connotations of disloyalty in wartime, a Southern Negro would tell a white man what sounded good rather than what he actually believed? It is also possible that the different groups of interviewers chose different kinds of people to talk to.

In any case the results are obviously so biased as to be worthless. You can judge for yourself how many other poll-based conclusions are just as biased, just as worthless—but with no check available to show them up.

You have pretty fair evidence to go on if you suspect that polls in general are biased in one specific direction, the direction of the *Literary Digest* error. This bias is toward the person with more money, more education, more information and alertness, better appearance, more conventional behavior, and more settled habits than the average of the population he is chosen to represent.

You can easily see what produces this. Let us say that you are an interviewer assigned to a street corner, with one interview to get. You spot two men who seem to fit the category you must complete: over forty, Negro, urban. One is in clean overalls, decently patched, neat. The other is dirty and he looks surly. With a job to get done, you approach the more likely-looking fellow and your colleagues all over the country are making similar decisions.

Some of the strongest feeling against public-opinion polls is found in liberal or left-wing circles, where it is rather commonly believed that polls are generally rigged. Behind this view is the fact that poll results so often fail to square with the opinions and desires of those whose thinking is not in the conservative direction. Polls, they point out, seem to elect Republicans even when voters shortly thereafter do otherwise.

Actually, as we have seen, it is not necessary that a poll be rigged—that is, that the results be deliberately twisted in order to create a false impression. The tendency of the sample to be biased in this consistent direction can rig it automatically.

Animals in Research:
The Case for Experimentation

Frederick A. King

The Mobilization for Animals Coalition (MFA) is an international network of more than 400 animal-protectionist organizations that address themselves to a variety of issues, including hunting, trapping, livestock protection, vegetarianism and pets. Their primary concern, however, is an adamant opposition to animal research. Some groups within the movement want to severely curtail research with animals, but the most visible and outspoken faction wants to eliminate it.

The astonishing growth of this activist movement during the past three years has culminated this year in an intense attack on the use of animals in psychological research. This past spring, John McArdle of the Humane Society of the United States charged that torture is the founding principle and fundamental characteristic of experimental psychology, and that psychological experimentation on animals among all the scientific disciplines is "the ideal candidate for elimination. No major scientific endeavor would suffer by such an act." A recent pamphlet published by the MFA stated, "Of all these experiments, those conducted in psychology are the most painful, pointless and repulsive."

The following specific allegations have been made by the MFA: Animals are given intense, repeated electric shocks until they lose the ability even to scream in pain; animals are deprived of food and water and allowed to suffer and die from hunger and thirst; animals are put in isolation until they are driven insane or die from despair and terror; animals are subjected to crushing forces that smash their bones and rupture their internal organs; the limbs of animals are mutilated or amputated to produce behavioral changes; animals are the victims of extreme pain and stress, inflicted out of idle curiosity, in nightmarish experiments designed to make healthy animals psychotic.

Such irresponsible accusations of research cruelty have consistently characterized the publications of the MFA. However, a recent study by psychologist D. Caroline Coile and Neal E. Miller of Rockefeller University counters these charges. Coile and Miller looked at every article (a total of 608) appearing in the past five years in journals of the American Psychological Association that report animal research. They concluded that none of the extreme allegations made by the MFA could be supported.

Coile and Miller admit that charges of cruelty may have gone unreported or been reported elsewhere but, they say, if such studies did occur, "they certainly were infrequent, and it is extremely misleading to imply that they are typical of experimental psychology."

Furthermore, there are standards and mechanisms to ensure that research animals are treated in a humane and scientifically sensible way, These mechanisms include the Federal Animal Welfare Act of 1966 (amended in Congress in 1970, 1976 and 1979); periodic inspection of all animal-research facilities by the Department of Agriculture; visits by federal agencies that fund animal research and are increasingly attentive to the conditions of animal care and experimental procedures that could cause pain or distress; and a comprehensive document, "Guide for the Care and Use of Laboratory Animals," prepared by the National Academy of Sciences. In addition, virtually every major scientific society whose members conduct animal research distributes guidelines for such research. Above and beyond all of this, most universities and research institutes have animal-care committees that monitor animal research and care.

THE UNITED STATES PUBLIC HEALTH SERVICE IS REVISING ITS GUIDELINES TO REQUIRE INSTITUTIONS THAT DO RESEARCH WITH ANIMALS TO DESIGNATE EVEN CLEARER LINES OF AUTHORITY AND RESPONSIBILITY FOR ANIMAL CARE.

This will include detailed information about how each institution complies with the new regulations as well as a requirement that animal-research committees include not only the supervising laboratory veterinarian and scientists but also a nonscientist and a person not affiliated with the institution. These committees will review programs for animal care, inspect all animal facilities and review and monitor all research proposals before they are submitted to agencies of the United States Public Health Service. The committees will also have the power to disapprove or terminate any research proposal.

This is not to say that research scientists are perfect. There will be occasional errors, cases of neglect and instances of abuse—as is the case with any human endeavor, whether it be the rearing of children, the practicing of a trade or profession or the governing of a nation. But a high standard of humane treatment is maintained.

The choice of psychological research for special attack almost certainly stems from the fact that such research is viewed as more vulnerable than are studies of anatomy, physiology or microbiology. In the minds of many, psychology is a less well-developed science than the biological sciences and the benefits that have accrued from psychological research with animals are less well known. Hence, it is more difficult to grasp the necessity for animal research in behavioral studies than it is in biomedical studies.

Anyone who has looked into the matter can scarcely deny that major advances in medicine have been achieved through basic research with animals. Among these are the development of virtually all modern vaccines against infectious diseases, the invention of surgical approaches to eye disorders, bone and joint injuries and heart disease, the discovery of insulin and other hormones and the testing of all new drugs and antibiotics.

The benefits to humans of psychological research with animals may be less well known than those of medical research but are just as real. Historically, the application of psychological research to human problems has lagged considerably behind the applied use of medical research. Mental events and overt behavior, although controlled by the nervous system and biology of an organism, are much more difficult to describe and study than are the actions of tissues or organ systems. To describe the complex interplay of perceptions, memories, cognitive and emotional processes with a physical and social environment that changes from moment to moment, elaborate research designs had to be developed. Since even a single type of behavior, such as vocalization, has so many different forms, a wide variety of ways of measuring the differences had to be developed. Finally, because much psychological research makes inferences from behavioral observations about internal states of an organism, methods were needed to insure that the interpretations were valid. Such complexities do not make the study of animal or human behavior less scientific or important than other kinds of research, but they do make it more difficult and slow its readiness for clinical applications.

BASIC PSYCHOLOGICAL RESEARCH WITH ANIMALS HAS LED TO IMPORTANT ACHIEVEMENTS IN THE INTEREST OF HUMAN WELFARE.

Examples include the use of biofeedback, which had its origin in studies of behavioral conditioning of neuromuscular activities in rats and other animals. Today, biofeedback can be used to control blood pressure and hypertension and help prevent heart attacks. In the case of paralyzed patients, it can be used to elevate blood pressure, enabling those who would otherwise have to spend their lives lying down to sit upright. Biofeedback techniques also are used in the reduction and control of severe pain and as a method of neuromuscular control to help reverse the process of scoliosis, a disabling and disfiguring curvature of the spine. Biofeedback can also be a cost-effective alternative to certain medical treatments and can help avoid many of the complications associated with long-term drug use.

Language studies with apes have led to practical methods of teaching language skills to severely retarded children who, prior to this work, had little or no language ability. Patients who have undergone radiation therapy for cancer can now take an interest in nutritious foods and avoid foods that have little nutritional value, thanks to studies of conditioned taste aversion done with animals. Neural and behavioral studies of early development of vision in cats and primates—studies that could not have been carried out with children—have led to advances in pediatric ophthalmology that can prevent irreversible brain damage and loss of vision in children who have cataracts and various other serious eye problems.

Behavioral modification and behavioral therapy, widely accepted techniques for treating alcohol, drug and tobacco addiction, have a long history of animal studies investigating learning theory and reward systems. Programmed instruction, the application of learning principles to educational tasks, is based on an array of learning studies in animals. These are but a few examples of the effectiveness and usefulness for humans of psychological research with animals.

Those opposed to animal research have proposed that alternatives to animal research, such as mathematical and computer models and tissue cultures, be used. In some cases, these alternatives are both feasible and valuable. Tissue cultures, for example, have been very effective in toxicological studies that formerly required live animals. For psychological studies, however, it is often necessary to study the whole animal and its relationship to the environment. Visual problems, abnormal sexual behavior, depression and aggression, for example, are not seen in tissue cultures and do not lend themselves to computer models. When human subjects cannot be used for such studies, animals are necessary if the research is to be done at all.

EXTREMISTS WITHIN THE ANIMAL MOVEMENT TAKE THE POSITION THAT ANIMALS HAVE RIGHTS EQUAL TO OR GREATER THAN THOSE OF HUMANS.

It follows from this that even if humans might benefit from animal research, the cost to animals is too high. It is ironic that despite this moral position, the same organizations condone—and indeed sponsor—activities that appear to violate the basic rights of animals to live and reproduce. Each year 10,000,000 dogs are destroyed by public pounds, animal shelters and humane societies. Many of these programs are supported and even operated by animal-protectionist groups. Surely there is a strong contradiction when those who profess to believe in animal rights deny animals their right to life. A similar situation exists with regard to programs of pet sterilization, programs that deny animals the right to breed and to bear offspring and are sponsored in many cases by antivivisectionists and animal-rights groups. Evidently, animal-rights advocates sometimes recognize and subscribe to the position that animals do not have the same rights as humans. However, their public posture leaves little room for examining these subtleties or applying similar standards to animal research.

Within the animal-protectionist movement there are moderates who have confidence in scientists as compassionate human beings and in the value of research. Their primary aims are to insure that animals are treated humanely and that discomfort in animal experimentation is kept to a minimum. It is to this group that scientists and scientific organizations have the responsibility to explain what they do, why and how they do it and what benefits occur.

I believe that the values guiding contemporary animal research represent prevailing sentiment within the scientific community and, indeed, within society at large. And I believe that these values are congruent with those of the moderates within the animal-protectionist movement. As articulated by ethicist Arthur Caplan, rights, in the realistic sense, are granted by one group to another based on perceived similarities between the groups. Plainly, animals lack those characteristics that would allow them to share in the rights we grant to humans. We do not grant domestic animals the right to go where they wish or do what they want because they are obviously unable to comprehend the responsibilities and demands of human society. In fact, we do not as a society even grant all domestic animals and pets the right to live.

This does not mean, however, that we do not have a moral responsibility to animals. I behave, along with Caplan and the scientific research community at large, that we hold a moral stewardship for animals and that we are obliged to treat them with humane compassion and concern. Many animal forms can and do feel pain and are highly aware of their environment. This awareness makes them worthy of our respect and serious concern. Caplan is certainly correct when he says that this moral obligation ought to be part of what it means to be a scientist today.

SCIENCE MUST PROCEED. THE OBJECTIVE QUEST FOR KNOWLEDGE IS A TREASURED ENTERPRISE OF OUR HERITAGE AND CULTURE.

Scientific inquiry into the nature of our living world has freed us from ignorance and superstition. Scientific understanding is an expression of our highest capacities—those of objective observation, interpretive reasoning, imagination and creativity. Founded on the results of basic research, often conducted with no goal other than that of increased understanding, the eventual practical use of this knowledge has led to a vastly improved well-being for humankind.

Extremists in the animal-rights movement probably will never accept such justifications for research or assurances of humane treatment. They may reject any actions, no matter how conscientious, that scientists take in realistically and morally reconciling the advance of human welfare with the use of animals. But, fortunately, there are many who, while deeply and appropriately concerned for the compassionate treatment of animals, recognize that human welfare is and should be our primary concern.

Frederick A. King is director of the Yerkes Regional Primate Research Center of Emory University and chair of the American Psychological Association's Committee on Animal Research and Experimentation.

Subject Reaction: The Neglected Factor in the Ethics of Experimentation

Stanley Milgram

Social psychology is concerned with the way in which individual behavior, thoughts, and actions are affected by the presence of other people. Although experimentation is not the only way of garnering knowledge in the discipline, it is a major tool of inquiry. As experiments in social psychology typically involve human subjects, they necessarily raise ethical issues, some of which I will discuss here.

Informed Consent

Many regard informed consent as the cornerstone of ethical practice in experimentation with human subjects. Yet social psychology has until now been unable to assimilate this principle into its routine experimental procedures. Typically, subjects are brought into an experiment without being informed of its true purpose. Indeed, sometimes subjects are misinformed. Is such a procedure ever justifiable?

Herbert Kelman[1] has distinguished two quite different explanations for not informing the potential subject of the nature of the experiment in which he is to take part. We might term the first the motivational explanation; that is, if one told the subject what the experiment was to be like, he might refuse to participate in it. Misinforming people to gain their participation appears to be a serious violation of the individual's rights, and cannot routinely constitute an ethical basis for subject recruitment.

The second, more typical, reason for not informing a subject is that many experiments in social psychology cannot be carried out if the subject knows about the experiment beforehand.

Consider in this connection Solomon Asch's classic study[2] of group pressure and conformity. The subject is told that he is to take part in a study on the perception of lines. He is asked to make a judgment as to which of three lines is equivalent in length to a standard line, but he does so in the presence of other individuals who, unknown to him, are working for the experimenter and give wrong answers. The experimenter's purpose is to see whether the subject will go along with the erroneous group information or resist the group and give the correct answer.

Clearly the subject is misinformed in several respects. He is told that he is to take part in an experiment on perception rather than group pressure. He is not informed that the others present are working for the experimenter, but is led to believe that they have the same relationship to the experimenter as he. It is apparent that if a subject were informed of the true purpose before participating in the study, he could not experience the psychological conflict that is at the crux of Asch's study. The subject is not denied the information because the experimenter team fears he would not participate in the study, but for strictly epistemological reasons, that is, for somewhat the same reason the author of a murder mystery does not reveal to the reader who the culprit is: to do so would undermine the psychological effects of the reading experience.

A majority of the experiments carried out in social psychology use some degree of misinformation. Such practices have been denounced as "deception" by critics, and the term "deception experiment" has come to be used routinely, particularly in the context of discussions concerning the ethics of such procedures. But in such a context, the term "deception" somewhat biases the issue. It is preferable to use morally neutral terms such as "masking," "staging," or "technical illusions" in describing such techniques, because it is not possible to make an objective ethical judgment on a practice unless it is described in terms that are not themselves condemnatory.

Is the use of technical illusions ever justified in experiments? The simplest response, and the one that is most socially and ethically comfortable, is to assert unequivocally that they are not. We all know that honesty and a fully informed relationship with the subject is highly desirable and should be implemented whenever possible. The problem is that many also believe strongly in the value of inquiry in social psychology, of its potential to enlighten us about human social behavior, and ultimately to benefit us in important ways, Admittedly, this is a faith, but one which impels us to carefully examine whether the illusions and misinformation required by experiments have any claim to legitimacy. We know that illusions are accepted in other domains without affronting our moral sensibilities. To use a simple-minded example, on radio programs, sound-effects of prancing horses are typically created by a sound-effects man who uses split coconut shells; rainfall is created by sand failing on metal sheets, and so forth. A certain number of listeners know about this, some do not; but we do not accuse such programs of deceiving their listeners. Rather we accept the fact that these are technical illusions used in support of a dramatic effort.

Most experiments in social psychology, at least the good ones, also have a dramatic component. Indeed, in the best experiments the subjects are brought into a dramaturgical situation in which the script is only partially written: it is the subjects' actions that complete the script, providing the information sought by the investigator. Is the use of technical illusions to be permitted in radio programs, but not scientific inquiry?

There are many instances in everyday life in which misinformation is tolerated or regarded as legitimate. We do not cringe at the idea of giving children misinformation about Santa Claus, because we feel it is a benign illusion, and common sense tells us it is not harmful. Furthermore, the practice is legitimized by tradition. We may give someone misinformation that takes him to a surprise party. The absolutists may say that this is an immoral act, that in doing so one has lied to another person. But it is more important to focus on the person who is the recipient of this information. Does he find it a demeaning experience, or a delightful treat?

One thing is clear: masking and technical illusions ought never to be used unless they are indispensable to the conduct of an inquiry. Honesty and openness are the only desirable bases of transaction with people generally. This still leaves open the question of whether such devices are permissible when they cannot be avoided in a scientific inquiry.

There is another side to this issue. In the exercise of virtually every profession there may be some exemption from general moral practice which permits the profession to function. For example, although a citizen who has witnessed a murder has a moral obligation to come forth with this information, lawyers have a right—indeed an obligation—of "privileged communication." A lawyer may know that his client has committed a murder, and is obligated not to tell the authorities. In other words, a generally accepted moral obligation is suspended and transformed in the case of legal practice, because in the long run we consider this exemption beneficial to society.

Similarly, it is generally impermissible to examine the genitals of strange women. But it is a technical requirement for the practice of obstetrics and gynecology. Once again, for technical reasons, we suspend a general moral rule in the exercise of a profession, because we believe the profession is beneficial to society.

The question arises: is there any comparable exemption due the social scientist because of technical requirements in the kind of work he does, which in the long run, we believe will benefit society? It is true that most often the individual participant in an experiment is not the beneficiary. Rather it is society as a whole that benefits, or at least, that is the supposition of scientific inquiry.

Still another side to the use of staging by social psychologists is frequently overlooked. The illusions employed in most experiments are usually short-term. They are sustained only insofar as they are required for the purpose of the experiment. Typically, the subject is informed of the experiment's true character immediately after he has participated in it. If for thirty minutes the experimenter holds back on the truth, at the conclusion he reaffirms his confidence in the subject by extending his trust to him by a full revelation of the purpose and procedures of the experiment. It is odd how rarely critics of social psychology experiments mention this characteristic feature of the experimental hour.

From a formal ethical standpoint, the question of misinformation in social psychology experiments is important, because dissimulation subverts the possibility of informed consent. Indeed, the emphasis on "deception" has virtually preempted discussion of ethics among social psychologists. Some feel it is a misplaced emphasis. Support is given to this view by a recent study by Elinor Mannucci.[3] She questioned 192 laymen concerning their reaction to ethical aspects of psychology experiments, and found that they regard deception as a relatively minor issue. They were far more concerned with the quality of the experience they would undergo as subjects. For example, despite the "deceptive" elements in the Asch experiment the great majority of respondents in Mannucci's study were enthusiastic about it, and expressed admiration for its elegance and significance. Of course, the layman's view need not be the final word, but it cannot be disregarded, and a general argument is that far more attention needs to be given to the experiences and views of those who actually serve as subjects in experiments.

Negative Effects

Is an experiment that produces some sort of negative, aversive, or stressful effect in the subject ever justified? In this matter, two parameters seem critical: first, the intensity of the negative experience, and second, its duration. Clearly, the discussion that follows refers to effects that do not permanently damage a subject, and which most typically do not exceed in intensity experiences which the subject might encounter in ordinary life.

One thing is clear. If we assert categorically that negative emotions can never ethically be created in the laboratory, then it follows that highly significant domains of human experience are excluded from experimental study. For example, we would never be able to study stress by experimental means; nor could we implicate human subject in experiments involving conflict. In other words, only experiments that aroused neutral or positive emotions would be considered ethical topics for experimental investigation. Clearly, such a stricture would lead to a very lopsided psychology, one that caricatured rather than accurately reflected human experience.

Moreover, historically, among the most deeply informative experiments in social psychology are those that examine how subjects resolve conflicts, for example: Asch's study of group pressure studies the conflict between truth and conformity; Bibb Latané and John Darley's bystander studies[4] create a conflict as to whether the subject should implicate himself in other peoples' troubles or not get involved; my studies of obedience[5] create a conflict between conscience and authority. If the experience of conflict is categorically to be excluded from social psychology, then we are automatically denying the possibility of studying such core human issues by experimental means. I believe that this would be an irreparable loss to any science of human behavior.

My own studies of obedience were criticized because they created conflict and stress in some of the subjects. Let me make a few comments about this. First, in this experiment I was interested in seeing to what degree a person would comply with an experimental authority who gave orders to act with increasing harshness against a third person. I wanted to see when the subject would refuse to go on with the experiment. The results of the experiment showed first that it is more difficult for many people to defy the experimenter's authority than was generally supposed. The second finding is that the experiment often places a person in considerable conflict. In the course of the experiment subjects sometimes fidget, sweat, and break out in nervous fits of laughter. I have dealt with some of the ethical issues of this experiment at length elsewhere,[6] but let me make a few additional remarks here.

Subject Reaction: A Neglected Factor

To my mind, the central moral justification for allowing my experiment is that it was judged acceptable by those who took part in it. Criticism of the experiment that does not take account of the tolerant reaction of the participants has always seemed to me hollow. I collected a considerable amount of data on this issue, which shows that the great majority of subjects accept this experiment, and call for further experiments of this sort. The table below shows the overall reaction of participants to this study, as indicated in responses to a questionnaire. On the whole, these data have been ignored by critics, or even turned against the experimenter, as when, critics claim that "this is simply cognitive dissonance. The more subjects hated the experiment, the more likely they are to say they enjoyed it." It becomes a "damned-if-they-like-it and damned-if-they-don't" situation. Critics of the experiment fail to come to grips with what the subject himself says. Yet, I believe that the subject's viewpoint is of extreme importance, perhaps even paramount. Below I shall present some approaches to ethical problems that derive from this view.

Excerpt from Questionnaire Used in a Follow-up Study of the Obedience Research

Now that I have read the report, and all things considered...	Defiant	Obedient	All
1. I am very glad to have been in the experiment	40.0%	47.8%	43.5%
2. I am glad to have been in the experiment	43.8%	35.7%	40.2%
3. I am neither sorry nor glad to have been in the experiment	15.3%	14.8%	15.1%
4. I am sorry to have been in the experiment	0.8%	0.7%	0.8%
5. I am very sorry to have been in the experiment	0.0%	1.0%	0.5%

Some critics assert that an experiment such as mine may indicate a negative insight on the subject. He or she may have diminished self-esteem because he has learned he is more submissive to authority than he might have believed. First, I readily agree that the investigator's responsibility is to make the laboratory session as constructive an experience as possible, and to explain the experiment to the subject in a way that allows his performance to be integrated in an insightful way. But I am not at all certain that we should hide truths from subjects, even negative truths. Moreover, this would set experimentation completely apart from other life experiences. Life itself often teaches us things that are less than pleasant, as when we fail an examination or do not succeed in a job interview. And in my judgment, participation in the obedience experiment had less effect on a participant's self-esteem than the negative emotions engendered by a routine school examination. This does not mean that the stress of taking an examination is good, any more than the negative effects of the obedience experiments are good. It does mean that these issues have to be placed in perspective.

I believe that it is extremely important to make a distinction between biomedical interventions and those that are of a purely psychological character, particularly the type of experiment I have been discussing. Intervention at the biological level *prima facie* places a subject "at risk." The ingestion of a minute dose of a chemical or the infliction of a tiny surgical incision has the potential to traumatize a subject. In contrast, in all of the social psychology experiments that have been carried out, there is no demonstrated case of resulting trauma. And there is no evidence whatsoever that when an individual makes a choice in a laboratory situation—even the difficult choices posed by the conformity or obedience experiments—any trauma, injury, or diminution of well-being results. I once asked a government official, who favored highly restrictive measures on psychology experiments, how many cases of actual trauma or injury he had in his files that would call for such measures. He indicated that not a single such case was known to him. If this is true, then much of the discussion about the need to impose government restrictions on the conduct of psychology experiments is unrealistic.

Of course, one difficulty in dealing with negative effects is the impossibility of proving their nonexistence. This is particularly true of behavioral or psychological effects. It seems that no matter what procedures one follows—interviewing, questionnaires, or the like—there is always the possibility of unforeseen negative effects, even if these procedures do not uncover them. Therefore, in an absolute sense, one can never establish the absence of negative effects. While this is logically correct, we cannot use this as a basis for asserting that such effects necessarily follow from psychological experimentation. All we can do is rely on our best judgment and assessment procedures in trying to establish the facts, and to formulate our policies accordingly.

Is Role-Playing a Solution?

Given these problems and the particular requirements of experiments in social psychology, is there any way to resolve these issues so that the subject will be protected, while allowing experimentation to continue? A number of psychologists have suggested that role playing be substituted for any experiment that requires misinformation. Instead of bringing the subject into a situation whose true purpose and nature were kept   from him, the subject would be fully informed that he was about to enter a staged situation, but he would be told to act *as if it* were real. For example, in the obedience experiment subjects would be told: "pretend you are the subject performing an experiment and you are giving shocks to another person." The subject would enter the situation knowing the "victim" was not receiving shocks, and he would go through his paces.

I do not doubt that role playing has a certain utility. Indeed, every good experimenter employs such role playing when he is first setting up his laboratory situation. He and his assistants often go through a dry run to see how the procedure flows. Thus, such simulation is not new, but now it is being asked to serve as the end point, rather than the starting point of an experimental investigation. However, there is a major scientific problem. Even after one has had a subject role play his way through an experimental procedure, we still must wonder whether the observed behavior is the same as that which a genuine subject would produce. So we must still perform the crucial experiment to determine whether role-played behavior corresponds to nonrole-played behavior.

Nor is role playing free of ethical problems. A most striking simulation in social psychology was carried out by Philip Zimbardo at Stanford University.[7] Volunteers were asked to take part in a mock prison situation. They were to simulate either the role of prisoner or guard with the roles chosen by lot. They were picked up at their homes by local police cars, and delivered to Zimbardo's mock prison. Even in the role-playing version of prison, the situation became rather ugly and unpleasant, and mock guards acted cruelly toward the mock prisoners. The investigator called off the simulation after six days, instead of the two weeks for which it had been planned. Moreover, the simulation came under very heavy ethical criticism. The ethical problems that simulation was designed to solve did not all disappear. The more closely role-playing behavior corresponds to real behavior, the more it generates real emotions, including aversive states, hostile behavior, and so on. The less real emotions are present, the less adequate the simulations. From the standpoint of the aversive emotions aroused in a successful simulation, ethical problems still exist.

Kelman aptly summarized the state of simulation research when he stated that simulation is not so useless a tool of investigation as its critics first asserted, nor as free of ethical problems as its proponents believed.[8]

Presumptive Consent

Recall that the major technical problem for social psychology research is that if subjects have prior knowledge of the purposes and details of an experiment they are often, by this fact, disqualified from participating in it. Informed consent thus remains an ideal that cannot always be attained. As an alternative, some psychologists have attempted to develop the doctrine of *presumptive consent*. The procedure is to solicit the view of a large number of people on the acceptability of an experimental procedure. These respondents would not themselves serve in the experiment, having been "spoiled" in the very process of being told the details and purposes of the experiment. But we could use their expressed views about participation as evidence of how people in general would react to participation. Assuming the experiment is deemed acceptable, new subjects would be recruited for actual participation. Of course, this is, ethically, a far weaker doctrine than that which relies on informed consent of the participant, Even if a hundred people indicate that they would be willing to take part in an experiment, the person actually chosen for participation might find it objectionable. Still, the doctrine of the "presumed consent of a reasonable person" seems to me better than no consent at all. That is, when for epistemological purposes the nature of a study cannot be revealed beforehand, one would try to determine in advance whether a reasonable person would consent to being a subject in the study and use that as a warrant either for carrying out the investigation or as a basis for modifying it.

Perhaps a more promising solution is to obtain *prior general consent* from subjects in advance of their actual participation. This is a form of consent that would be based on subjects' knowing the general types of procedures used in psychological investigations, but without their knowing what specific manipulations would be employed in the particular experiment in which they would take part. The first step would be to create a pool of volunteers to serve in psychology experiments. Before volunteering to join the pool people would be told explicitly that sometimes subjects are misinformed about the purposes of an experiment, and that sometimes emotional stresses arise in the course of an experiment. They would be given a chance to exclude themselves from any study using deception or involving stress *if they so wished*. Only persons who had indicated a willingness to participate in experiments involving deception or stress would, in the course of the year, be recruited for experiments that involved these elements. Such a procedure might reconcile the technical need for misinformation with the ethical problem of informing subjects.

Finally, since I emphasize the experience of the person subjected to procedures as the ultimate basis for judging whether an experiment should continue or not, I wonder whether participants in such experiments might not routinely be given monitoring cards which they would fill out and submit to an independent monitoring source while an experiment is in progress. An appropriate monitoring source might be a special committee of the professional organization, or the human subjects' committee of the institution where the experiment is carried out. Such a procedure would have the advantage of allowing the subject to express reactions about an experiment in which he has just participated, and by his comments the subject himself would help determine whether the experiment is allowable or not. In the long run, I believe it is the subject's reaction and his experience that needs to be given its due weight in any discussion of ethics, and this mechanism will help achieve this aim.

References

1 Herbert Kelman, "Remarks made at the American Psychological Association," New Orleans, 1974.
2 Solomon E. Asch, *Social Psychology* (New York: Prentice Hall, 1952).
3 Elinor Mannucci, *Potential Subjects View Psychology Experiments: An Ethical Inquiry*. Unpublished Doctoral Dissertation. The City University of New York, 1977.
4 Bibb Latane and John Darley, *The Unresponsive Bystander: Why Doesn't He Help?* (New York: Appleton, 1970).
5 Stanley Milgram, *Obedience to Authority: An Experimental View* (New York: Harper and Row, 1974).
6 Stanley Milgram, "Issues in The Study of Obedience: A Reply to Baumrind," *American Psychologist* 19 (1964), 848–52.
7 Philip Zimbardo, "The Mind is a Formidable Jailer: A Pirandellian Prison," *The New York Times Magazine* (April 8, 1973), p. 38.
8 Kelman, "Remarks."

The Obedience Experiments

In order to take a close look at the act of obeying, I set up a simple experiment at Yale University. Eventually, the experiment was to involve more than a thousand participants and would be repeated at several universities, but at the beginning, the conception was simple. A person comes to a psychological laboratory and is told to carry out a series of acts that come increasingly into conflict with conscience. The main question is how far the participant will comply with the experimenter's instructions before refusing to carry out the actions required of him.

But the reader needs to knows a little more detail about the experiment. Two people come to a psychology laboratory to take part in a study of memory and learning. One of them is designated as a "teacher" and the other a "learner." The experimenter explains that the study is concerned with the effects of punishment on learning. The learner is conducted into a room, seated in a chair, his arms strapped to prevent excessive movement, and an electrode attached to his wrist. He is told that he is to learn a list of word pairs; whenever he makes an error, he will receive electric shocks of increasing intensity.

The real focus of the experiment is the teacher. After watching the learner being strapped into place, he is taken into the main experimental room and seated before an impressive shock generator. Its main feature is a horizontal line of thirty switches, ranging from 15 volts to 450 volts, in 15-volt increments. There are also verbal designations which range from SLIGHT SHOCK to DANGER—SEVERE SHOCK. The teacher is told that he is to administer the learning test to the man in the other room. When the learner responds correctly, the teacher moves on to the next item; when the other man gives an incorrect answer, the teacher is to give him an electric shock. He is to start at the lowest shock level (15 volts) and to increase the level each time the man makes an error, going through 30 volts, 45 volts, and so on.

The "teacher" is a genuinely naïve subject who has come to the laboratory to participate in an experiment. The "learner," or victim, is an actor who actually receives no shock at all. The point of the experiment is to see how far a person will proceed in a concrete and measurable situation in which he is ordered to inflict increasing pain on a protesting victim. At what point will the subject refuse to obey the experimenter?

Conflict arises when the man receiving the shock begins to indicate that he is experiencing discomfort. At 75 volts, the "learner" grunts. At 120 volts he complains verbally; at 150 he demands to be released from the experiment. His protests continue as the shocks escalate, growing increasingly vehement and emotional. At 285 volts his response can only be described as an agonized scream.

Observers of the experiment agree that its gripping quality is somewhat obscured in print. For the subject, the situation is not a game; conflict is intense and obvious. On the one hand, the manifest suffering of the learner presses him to quit. On the other, the experimenter, a legitimate authority to whom the subject feels some commitment, enjoins him to continue. Each time the subject hesitates to administer shock, the experimenter orders him to continue. To extricate himself from the situation, the subject must make a clear break with authority. The aim of this investigation was to find when and how people would defy authority in the face of a clear moral imperative.

From *Obedience to authority: An experimental view* by Stanley Milgram (New York: Harper & Row, 1974), pp. 3–4.

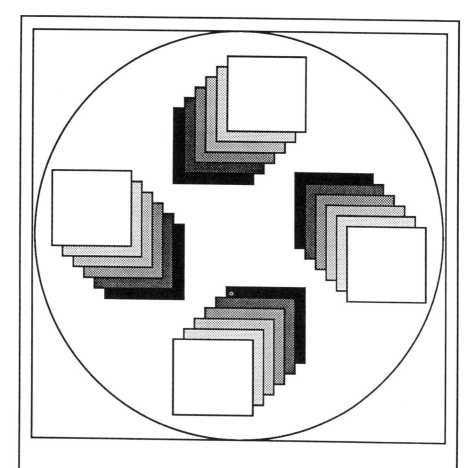

Chapter 2

Biobases

CHAPTER 2: BIOBASES

Every behavior of every organism is ultimately controlled by neural activity, which is in turn controlled by other biological factors (genetics and neural chemistry). For example, humans speak and listen, whereas no other species we know of can communicate with similar ease and complexity. Humans have specialized parts of their brains and throats that allow for this extraordinary behavior. The development of these specialized organs is controlled by specific genetic information that allows humans, but not monkeys or any other animal, to learn and use language in this way. Exactly what biological mechanisms underlie various behaviors and how they operate are appropriate subjects for research and speculation in psychology. The three papers included in this chapter address interesting applications of genetic theory and physiological psychology to human behavior.

2a. Gold, P. (1986). Sweet memories. *American Scientist, 75,* 151–155.

A psychologist, Karl Lashely, spent his entire career searching for the physiological basis of learning. He never could pin down how or where the brain stored experience. After reading the Gold article, what external and internal conditions do you think might facilitate learning? Which of these could you use to improve your memory for exams?

2b. Hardyck, C., & Haapanen, R. (1979). Educating both halves of the brain: Educational breakthrough or neuromythology. *Journal of School Psychology, 17,* 219–230.

The application to education of the theory of right brain–left brain dichotomy has aroused controversy. Imagine that the elementary school your children are attending is currently debating the adoption of new educational curricula. One of these teaching systems is based on the "two brain" system. Prepare a position paper arguing for the adoption or rejection of this system. Be sure to use facts from your reading to justify your position.

2c. Wilson, E. O. (1975). Human decency is animal. *The New York Times Magazine.* Oct. 12.

The basic assumption of sociobiology is that all behavior has some genetic basis. Sociobiologists use the hypotheses about social altruism and homosexuality to support their point. Take the concept of religion and apply the same sociobiological reasoning and methods. Support or deny the possibility that there are "genes" for religion.

Sweet Memories

Paul E. Gold

You can probably remember fairly easily where you parked your car in the lot at work today. But most likely you cannot recall the spot in which you parked last Tuesday. Similarly, you probably remember what you had for dinner last night, but it is less likely that you remember your dinner fare last week. Not all memories are as fragile as these. You are far more likely to remember where you parked last week if you observed another car hitting yours (Fig. 1). You probably also can recall the foods you ate long ago on those fortunately rare occasions when you experienced severe intestinal disorders; indeed, many of us regularly avoid foods that precipitated such disorders.

Figure 1. You may wonder what is sweet about seeing someone back into your car in a parking lot, but recent research indicates that the adrenaline released on such stressful occasions increases the level of glucose in the blood, regulating the formation and storage of memories. (Photograph by R. Paul Andersen.)

Other events can also be printed relatively indelibly in our memories. For example, depending on your age, you may recall vividly where you were when you heard about the Pearl Harbor attack, the assassination of John Kennedy, or the space shuttle tragedy. People can also have excellent memories of events at the times of major positive experiences, such as marriage or the birth of a child. Evidently we remember important events, and often the circumstances surrounding those events, better than other events, even if the latter occurred more recently.

For the science of the biology of memory, it is not enough to say that important events are remembered better than trivial events. There is a "why" which must be addressed. Recent work in this field has identified a physiological system that appears to determine which memories will be stored best. This article reviews the current evidence and suggests some of the likely directions and consequences of research dealing with physiological regulation of memory storage.

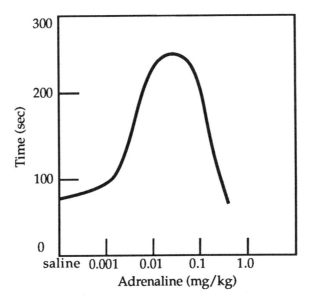

Figure 2. One of the leading approaches to the study of the biology of memory concentrates on the role played by hormonal responses to experience. Chief among the hormones under investigation is adrenaline. Researchers have found that an injection of adrenaline immediately after training increases rats' memory of what they have been taught, in this case to avoid a very mild footshock administered while they were drinking from a waterspout. Memory was assessed 24 hours later. Strength of memory is indicated by the time an animal hesitates to return to the waterspout. Note that adrenaline enhanced memory storage when administered at intermediate doses. (After Gold and van Buskirk 1975.)

As recently as twenty-five years ago, there was no evidence showing that brains were biologically altered by experience. The best indications that such changes occurred were based on the fact that humans and animals learned and remembered; it was accepted as an article of faith that the behavioral changes must be represented by some type of modifications in the brain. In the 1960s, the first papers appeared which indicated that rats raised in "enriched" environments, complete with toys and other rats, had brains heavier than those of animals raised in standard individual cages (reviewed by Rosenzweig 1984). Clearly, this important discovery meant that brains could be changed by experience. On the other hand, changes in brain weight had such vague meaning for brain function that their importance for learning and memory was obscure.

More recent findings reveal that the brain can exhibit relatively precise changes in its fine anatomy, changes which occur not only when animals are reared in different environments but also when they receive specific types of training (Greenough 1984). The changes appear in the extent of dendritic branching of certain cell populations. The dendrites are a major source of incoming information to the neurons, and the findings indicate that transmission of information between cells may be modified by these structural changes. There is also a substantial amount of evidence showing relatively long-lasting physiological and biochemical changes in neurons after training (Lynch et al.)1984; Weinberger et al. 1985).

Whether one or several of these changes provide the biological basis for memory is not yet known. However, the findings are encouraging in the sense that changes like these are quite likely to mediate memory storage in the brain. Even if we take these modifications as the basis for memory, we do not yet know why they occur or what determines the probability that they will occur. This returns us to the issue with which we began. Why are some events more likely to be remembered than others? What is the difference between important and trivial events that promotes the storage of the former and permits (or promotes) forgetting the latter?

Studies of the physiological control of memory storage began with examinations of conditions which impair memory. Many forms of acute brain trauma, for example seizures or concussions, produce a relatively specific form of impairment, a loss of memory of experiences which occurred between a few days and several minutes before the trauma. This phenomenon is termed retrograde amnesia because of the time-dependent nature of the memory deficit.

Comparable findings were readily obtained in animals as well. In a typical study, rats or mice receive training followed at various intervals by the administration of a treatment, such as a drug or electrical stimulation of the brain. The animals then are tested for memory a day or more later. The results of studies like this show that treatments which produce amnesia are more effective when administered shortly after. As the time between training and treatment increases, the extent of the amnesia decreases. The maximal length of time after training at which a given treatment still effectively impairs memory is termed the retrograde amnesia gradient. The length of the temporal gradient varies substantially with several known factors, including intensity or site of brain stimulation, drug dose, type of training, and circadian rhythms. The major rule underlying the phenomenon of retrograde amnesia is that, in all cases, recent memories are more susceptible to disruption than older memories.

It was also discovered that some treatments could accomplish the reverse of this phenomenon: many stimulant drugs enhance memory storage when administered soon after training, but not at longer intervals (McGaugh 1983). Indeed, it appears likely that most treatments which act on memory storage can both enhance and impair memory, depending on such factors as dose and the specific nature of the training situation.

Hormones and memory

With this background, researchers began to examine the neural mechanisms by which the various treatments enhanced or impaired memory. Some selected specific treatments, such as using protein synthesis inhibitors to try to determine whether protein synthesis was necessary for memory storage. Both types of research were based on the premise that if one could determine the mechanisms of memory modification, one might learn an important characteristic of memory storage itself.

There is another way to look at the same early findings, however; this is the rationale that has guided the work in my laboratory and several other laboratories for the past ten years or so. We began by looking carefully at the major features of amnesia and memory enhancement. The principal general finding was that recent memories exhibit a remarkable sensitivity to a wide range of apparently disparate treatments. Why might that be the case? In an evolutionary sense, what advantage is there in a brain in which experiences establish a memory that is readily modified?

Here at last we come to the crux of the matter. The most obvious advantage is that the brain can receive additional information defining whether the recent events are worthy of storage—that is, whether the events were important or trivial. If the events were important, the additional information can then direct the brain to store the new memories. We call this directive process memory modulation or regulation (Gold and Zornetzer 1983; Gold 1984).

Arousal appears to be the major contributor of additional information telling the brain to make new memories. The realization that arousal levels interact with learning and memory is not at all new. A psychological law developed at the turn of the century states that the relationship between arousal and performance follows an inverted-U curve in which low and high arousal levels are related to poor learned performance and moderate arousal levels are linked to good performance (Yerkes and Dodson 1908). However, although the relationship appears to hold true in a wide variety of circumstances, it is difficult to study arousal as a mechanism for the neurobiology of memory regulation, in part because arousal cannot be measured with certainty and in part because the relationship itself is tautological: important events are arousing and trivial events are boring.

It should nonetheless be possible to identify physiological responses to experiences which contribute to memory regulation. In other words, some physiological concomitants of arousal should follow important events and regulate the storage of information contained in those events. Likely candidates include hormones, particularly those often associated with stress (high arousal). As the reader will soon see, there is now a great deal of evidence suggesting that some of the endocrine responses to experiences do indeed regulate memory storage.

The evidence for hormonal regulation of memory storage is best illustrated by describing a typical laboratory experiment in which rats are the subjects. This one-trial behavioral training procedure is performed in a rectangular box with a well-lit white compartment separated by a door from a dimly lit black compartment. The black compartment has a metal floor through which a brief, mild electric shock can be administered. The animals are placed in the white compartment, and after a few seconds, the door is opened. Generally, the rats cross into the black compartment after only a few seconds. As soon as they have fully entered, the door is closed and the animals receive a footshock. They are then returned to their home cages for a day before they are tested for memory. Each rat is placed in the white compartment as before, and the door is opened. If the rats remember what happened to them before, they demonstrate that memory by being reluctant to enter the black compartment. The reluctance to enter is then an indication of the strength of an animal's memory, which is measured by the length of time the animal hesitates before crossing into the black compartment.

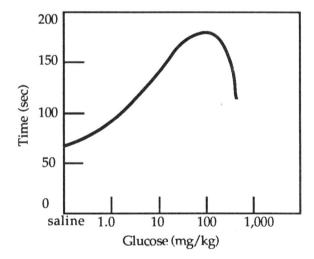

Figure 3. Like adrenaline, glucose injected immediately after training enhances memory tested the next day. The dose-response curve is an inverted U, as it was for adrenaline. It appears that plasma adrenaline may trigger an increase in glucose, which in turn regulates storage of memories in the central nervous system. (After Gold 1986.)

Not surprisingly, an animal's reluctance depends on the intensity and duration of the shock it received in training. However, the issue here is whether there are differences in the hormonal responses to differing training conditions that contribute to later differences in memory: is the increase in memory after more forceful training dependent not only on the immediate sensory aspects of the shock level employed but also, in part, on a stronger hormonal response to the shock? To test the latter possibility, we train rats using a very mild footshock and inject a hormone which would have been released by a more intense footshock. In such an experiment, then, we artificially create a physiological situation in which the animal receives a mild footshock during training but has the hormonal consequences of a stronger footshock. When the animal is tested the next day, it behaves as if it had received a more intense footshock during training—that is, the animal shows greater reluctance to enter the black compartment than it would without the hormone injection.

How adrenaline regulates memory storage

Several hormones, such as adrenaline, adrenocorticotropic hormone (ACTH), and maybe vasopressin, have effects like those just described. Of the hormones tested, we know the most about adrenaline, but it would be misleading to convey the impression that adrenaline is the most important hormone for memory storage. We have more evidence for adrenaline in large part because there are better methods for measuring this hormone than for measuring the others and also because there is a wealth of specific drugs with which to test adrenaline actions. As the technology for studying other hormones improves, we will undoubtedly gain further insights into the mechanisms by which they too act on memory.

Adrenaline is a hormone which is very responsive to stressors and changes in the environment. It is released into plasma from the adrenal medulla when, for instance, an animal is put in a cold place or when it receives a mild footshock. Therefore, as an initial candidate for a hormone which might regulate memory formation, adrenaline meets the basic requirement that it be released normally during experiences that involve learning. More importantly, as we have seen, an injection of adrenaline into a rat or mouse immediately after training enhances memory on later tests. The specific dose is critical to the phenomenon. A typical dose response curve is shown in Figure 2. The important feature is that the shape of the curve is an inverted U, just as one would expect from the Yerkes-Dodson law.

It is one thing to show that a drug, here adrenaline, has effects on memory. It is quite another to try to show that the hormone acts normally on memory storage. What we want to show is that animals trained with a stronger footshock, which therefore have better memory for the immediately preceding experience, release more adrenaline than do animals trained with a mild footshock. Furthermore, the optimal adrenaline dose for enhancing memory should, if we are truly mimicking the natural situation, produce plasma levels comparable to those in animals trained with a stronger footshock. Our experiments have indeed fulfilled these expectations: we have found that plasma adrenaline levels reach about 1,500 pg/ml after the higher footshock intensity, and the optimal dose for memory enhancement also results in plasma levels which are about 1,500 pg/ml.

Additional evidence also indicates that adrenaline plays an important role in regulating memory storage. For example, adrenaline enhances memory for many different kinds of tasks, including tasks which train animals using rewards as well as those which use punishment. Adrenaline also can be used to ameliorate memory under a variety of conditions in which memory would otherwise be poor. In one study, we found that animals could even learn under deep anesthesia if first injected with adrenaline (Weinberger et al. 1984). A tone was presented to anesthetized rats, simultaneously with an electric shock. The rats were tested several days after training by playing the tone while they were drinking water; our expectation was that the animals which remembered that the tone preceded a shock would stop drinking. Those rats which had received saline prior to the training under anesthesia showed no evidence of fear when the tone came on, However, the animals which had received adrenaline ceased drinking, and in the most dramatic instances went to the corner of the cage farthest from the speaker and froze in one position throughout the minute the tone was sounded.

Adrenaline also appears to enhance memory in very young and very old rats and mice. Juvenile animals exhibit rapid forgetting of new responses, a phenomenon called infantile amnesia. (The same rapid forgetting is seen in children as well. How early is your first memory?) One explanation for the failure to store and to retain new memories in the brains of young organisms is that the memory processes are immature and cannot "hold" the information. Our experiments suggested another possibility: that the memory processes might be ready but the hormonal modulators are not engaged. When testing this hypothesis, we obtained initial results like those seen by many researchers. Young animals—for example, 16-day-old rats—remembered an avoidance response for about one hour after training but showed no evidence of memory when tested the next day. However, if injected with adrenaline immediately after training, the young animals showed significant memory the next day. Results such as these illustrate one more condition under which adrenaline appears to promote memory storage and, in addition, suggest that storage processes apparently mature before the hormonal responses which regulate those processes.

We have obtained similar results when testing the memory of aged rodents (Gold et al. 1981). Like humans, old rats (and monkeys, mice, and sea slugs) appear to forget new information much more rapidly than do young adult members of the species. A substantial amount is already known about age-related changes in anatomical, physiological, and biochemical aspects of the brain. These changes, appearing collectively as they do, must underlie the changes in cognitive functions seen in aging organisms. Some are likely to produce problems which cannot now be ameliorated. However, there are changes in hormonal responsiveness for which it may be possible to apply compensatory treatments. Again, we find that studies of adrenaline may explain some of the deficits in memory storage.

After training in a one-trial avoidance task (as described above), aged rats (two years old) show excellent memory when tested one hour after training, some memory when tested one day after training, but severely impaired memory on tests given one week or more later. In studies of responsiveness of adrenaline to training, the plasma levels are much lower than those found in younger rats. We have found that an injection of adrenaline given immediately after training, however, enhances memory retention in the aged rats so that they now show good memory one week after training (Sternberg et al. 1985). Such results point to the exciting possibility that there may be pharmacological treatments which can alleviate the memory loss that comes with age. Unfortunately, because adrenaline has a variety of cardiovascular and other effects which are undesirable, especially in older people, we need to study the specific mechanisms by which adrenaline acts before such drugs can be developed.

Glucose and memory

The finding that adrenaline regulates memory storage indicates that one of the hormone's actions must be to modify brain processes. However, for a long time it has been clear that the hormone itself does not pass from blood into brain cells, at least not in measurable amounts. We are faced with an apparent paradox: the hormone has large effects on brain function but does not act on the brain—at least not directly. How then can adrenaline accomplish its role in regulating memory information?

Over the past year, we tested the possibility that one of the hormone's actions outside the brain might be responsible for modulation of memory storage processing. One of the consequences of adrenaline release in an animal responding to stress is hyperglycemia, an increase in plasma glucose levels. We therefore examined the effects of glucose on memory in rats. The results, shown in Figure 3, demonstrate that glucose too can enhance memory. The dose-response curve is again an inverted U. The effects are time-dependent, injections delayed by an hour after training have no effect on retention and performance. These are all features in common with the effects of adrenaline: the doses of glucose or adrenaline most effective in enhancing memory also result in plasma glucose levels comparable to the natural response to good training conditions.

Additional evidence for glucose regulation of memory storage is actually based on negative findings: the memory-enhancing and impairing effects of adrenaline and most other treatments are blocked in animals treated with adrenergic antagonists, drugs which block peripheral adrenaline receptors (Gold and Sternberg 1978), but the antagonists have no effect on memory enhancement produced by glucose

(Gold et al. 1986). These results are as they should be if glucose release is a memory-modulation step subsequent to the release of adrenaline. Because the antagonists block the receptors by which adrenaline acts, they would be expected to block the effects of adrenaline and those treatments which act through adrenaline to regulate memory. However, the effects of glucose on memory, acting beyond the relevant adrenaline receptors, should remain intact—and they do. Furthermore, because glucose injected directly into the brain can enhance memory, we tentatively behave that plasma glucose may act directly on the brain to modulate memory storage.

Unlike adrenaline, glucose is a very safe drug with which to study memory in humans. We are now completing a study of just this type examining the effects of glucose on memory in 70-year-old people. The subject in this study were quite healthy, showing no signs of dementia such as accompanies Alzheimer's disease. Still, there is a substantial literature, as well as a wealth of anecdotal information, showing that at this age memory is not what it used to be. Our findings were consistent with this idea: our elderly subjects had poorer memory than the college students we tested at the same time.

The elderly subjects were asked to drink a glass of lemonade which had been prepared with either saccharin or glucose. A variety of memory tests administered soon after yielded preliminary evidence that glucose may improve memory. We also found that those elderly individuals who had poor regulation of blood glucose were the people with poor memory (Hall et al., unpubl.). These early results point to a significant new direction for ameliorating memory impairments with pharmacological agents. It should be noted that, although we believe that adrenaline acts on memory by raising plasma glucose levels, we do not yet have any information about the mechanism by which glucose acts. It is the answer to this question that may provide us with the insights necessary for the development of appropriate pharmacological agents.

References

Gold, P. E. 1984. Memory modulation: Neurobiological contexts. In *Neurobiology of Learning and Memory*, ed. G. Lynch, J. L. McGaugh, and N. M. Weinberger, pp. 374–82. Guilford Press.

_____. 1986. Glucose Modulation of memory storage processing. *Beh. Neural Biol.* 45:342–49.

Gold, P. E., J. L. McGaugh, L. L. Hankins, R. P. Rose, and B. J. Vasquez. 1981. Age-dependent changes in retention in rats. *Experimental Aging Res.* 8:53–58.

Gold, P. E., and D. B. Sternberg. 1978. Retrograde amnesia produced by several treatments: Evidence for a common neurobiological mechanism. *Science* 201:367–69.

Gold, P. E., and R. B. van Buskirk. 1975. Facilitation of time-dependent memory processes with posttrial epinephrine injections. *Beh. Biol.* 13:145–53.

Gold, P. E., J. Vogt, and J. L. Hall. 1986. Posttraining glucose effects on memory: Behavioral and pharmacological characteristics. *Beh. Neural Biol.* 46:145–55.

Gold, P. E., and S. F. Zornetzer. 1983. The mnemon and its juices: Neuromodulation of memory processes. *Beh. Neural Biol.* 38:151–89.

Greenough, W. T. 1984. Possible structural substrates of plasma neural phenomena. In *Neurobiology of Learning and Memory*, ed. G. Lynch, J. L. McGaugh, and N. M. Weinberger, pp. 370–478. Guilford Press.

Hall, J. L., J. Vogt, L. Gonder-Frederick, and P. E. Gold. Unpubl. Glucose effects on memory in college-age and elderly subjects.

Lynch, G., J. L. McGaugh, and N. M. Weinberger, eds. 1984. *Neurobiology of Learning and Memory*. Guilford Press.

McGaugh, J. L. 1983. Hormonal influences on memory. *Ann. Rev. Psychol.* 34:297–323.

Rosenzweig, M. R. 1984. Experience, memory, and the brain. *Am. Psychol.* 39:365–76.Sternberg, D. B., J. Martinez, J. L. McGaugh, and P. E. Gold. 1985. Age-related memory deficits in rats and mice: Enhancement with peripheral injections of epinephrine. *Beh. Neural Biol.* 44:213–20.

Weinberger, N. M., P. E. Gold, and D. B. Sternberg 1984. Epinephrine enables Pavlovian fear conditioning under general anesthesia. *Science* 233:605–07,

Weinberger, N. M., J. L. McGaugh, and G. Lynch, eds. 1985. *Memory Systems of the Brain*. Guilford Press.

Yerkes; R. M., and J. D. Dodson. 1908. The relation of strength of stimulus to rapidity of habit-formation. *J. Comp. Neurol. Psychol.* 18:458–82.

Educating Both Halves of the Brain:
Educational Breakthrough or Neuromythology

Curtis Hardyck and Randy Haapanen

Summary: The increasing popularity of the idea that the two hemispheres of the human cerebral cortex carry on different modes of thinking has resulted in an accelerating social and commercial pressure to organize school curricula, teaching, and testing to conform to a right brain-left brain dichotomy. Evidence gathered from commissurotomy (spilt-brain) patients and right hemisphere-left hemisphere studies on normal intact humans is reviewed and evaluated. Conclusions from this review are (a) the commissurotomy patients are not a suitable group on which to base generalizations about cortical functioning in the normal intact human; (b) the right-left hemisphere differences reported in many experiments on normal subjects are small and can be found only in an extremely narrow experimental context; and (c) there is no scientific basis in this work for any reorganization of curricular, teaching, or testing programs within contemporary educational practice.

A concept currently in vogue and the subject of considerable attention within some areas of education is the belief that the two hemispheres of the human cerebral cortex function very differently and in an almost noninteractive manner. A popular account of this belief can be found in an article by Maya Pines in the *New York Times Magazine* for September 9, 1973, entitled "We are Left-Brained or Right-Brained." Her opening sentence is both a candid statement of the concept and an expression of belief in its validity.

"Two very different persons inhabit our heads, residing in the left and right hemispheres of our brains, the twin shells that cover the central brain stem. One of them is verbal, analytic, dominant. The other is artistic but mute and almost totally mysterious." (p. 32)

Extreme simplification is probably unavoidable in an account designed for popular consumption. Unfortunately, accounts within the field of education do not seem too much improved. There are currently several academic roadshows on tour with titles such as "Educating Both Halves of the Brain." Promotional literature for these symposia state that attendance will give the educational administrator, the school psychologist, or the teacher some new insights into educating the "whole mind." Any educator under the impression that current educational practice was "whole mind" oriented is quickly disabused. Statements are made bluntly that contemporary systems of education teach to only that half of the brain which is verbal and analytic and completely ignore the "creative" other half.

As an idea, hemispheric specialization is intriguing, if somewhat startling in its implications for educational practice. The American educational system is oriented toward verbal proficiency and geared to stimulate analytical thinking. If such processes are carried out in only half the brain, perhaps there is some merit to this idea. Unfortunately, the implications conveyed by promoters of this idea are not only those of neglect, but of wrongdoing. The nonverbal, nonanalytic half of the brain is said to be artistic and creative. Thus, by failing to teach the whole mind, creativity is being stifled, probably producing generations of uninspired, uncreative lackluster drudges.

If the above conclusion seems a bit overblown, a sample quotation illustrative of the more extreme forms of speculation about hemisphere differences may be instructive. The closing remarks of Crinella, Beck, and Robinson (1971) in their study of laterality and neuropsychological integrity serves as an interesting example of the extent to which such speculation can be carried.

"While most Americans have become too sophisticated to insist upon right-handed performance in their offspring, there seems to be little doubt that our educational system is characterized by heavily "left-brained" (or right-winged) (sic) philosophy, valuing the acquisition and manipulation of language and symbols foremost, at the expense of self-awareness, spatial schemata, music and the fine arts. In the light of current crises in identity (both individual and group), near ecological disaster, and growing shallowness in artistic expression, it is tempting to speculate that we are witnessing the demise of a culture which had 'educated the hemisphere that wields the sword'." (p. 2052)

Any educator with even the remotest shadow of self-doubt would probably be able to generate a certain amount of guilt after considering the speculations of Crinella et al. In fact, such a reaction is becoming more and more common in public schools. As assertions about the duality of cerebral processes have filtered through educational systems, elementary and secondary teachers have begun to request help from school psychologists in developing programs and curricula for teaching the "other" half of the brain—another topic added to the already overwhelming list of items on which the school psychologist is considered the expert.

If there is merit to these assertions about the duality of mental processes, then it is evident that some drastic revision of current educational practices is necessary. However, before we discard the bulk of contemporary educational practice and leave its bones to bleach in the sun, it seems worthwhile to carefully examine the evidence for the two hemisphere formulations. If teaching curricula are to be revised, a great deal of money spent on new materials and new tests (since we can be quite sure that the implications of a new idea for education will be only light-seconds ahead of attempts to commercially exploit it), it would be wise to know that proceedings are on a sound scientific basis with reliable information. To do this, it is instructive to examine the accumulated evidence, anatomical, behavioral, and conceptual. supporting the belief that our hemispheres function so differently and so separately.

Evidence for Specialized Processing by the Cerebral Hemispheres

To begin, a conservative summary of basic knowledge about hemisphere specialization seems appropriate.

1. In the great majority of individuals, verbal processes are apparently located in the left cerebral hemisphere. Damage to the left hemisphere most frequently produces the varieties of verbal dysfunction known as the aphasias. Such processes as form recognition (including faces), color recognition, and spatial abilities are not often affected by left hemisphere damage.[1] Correspondingly, damage to the right hemisphere frequently leaves verbal processes intact, but produces disturbances of form recognition, color perception, and spatial abilities.

These formulations are not new. Paul Broca in 1861 first provided definite proof of the relationships between specific brain lesions and language disorders. The accumulated medical literature of several wars and almost a century of investigation support these differences in hemisphere functions.

2. The concept of the two cerebral hemispheres somehow leading lives of their own stems from the work of Roger Sperry and his students on a small group of epilepsy patients who were unresponsive to medication normally effective in controlling epileptic seizures. (Epileptic seizures originate from damage to brain tissue.) In these patients, seizures were increasing in intensity and duration, and were life endangering. As a means of limiting the extent of the seizures, a drastic surgical intervention was attempted in which a majority of the fibers of the corpus callosum—the structure connecting the two hemispheres of the brain—were surgically severed. The surgery was successful in limiting the seizures, but left the two hemispheres of these individuals with essentially no communicative linkage. The systematic behavioral study of nine of these patients over a period of several years by Sperry and his students (Sperry, 1968a, 1968b, 1970, 1973; Sperry, Gazzaniga, & Bogen, 1969) led to the development of the concept of separate functioning of the cerebral hemispheres.

3. The evidence is compelling that in these patients there were striking hemisphere differences. These differences have been summarized by Sperry (1973).

"Very early in the postoperative examination of these subjects it became apparent that the disconnected left hemisphere processing information from the right hand and the right half visual field is the hemisphere that does essentially all the talking, reading, writing, and mathematical calculation in these right-handed subjects (Gazzaniga, Bogen, & Sperry, 1967). The disconnected right hemisphere on the other hand remains essentially mute, alexic, agraphic, and unable to carry out calculations beyond simple additions to sums under 20. In other words, thinking that deals with information processed through the left hand, the left half visual field, the right nostril or with any other information processed entirely within the right hemisphere, remains cut off from the centers for language and calculation located in the left hemisphere. These test results added up to a striking confirmation of hemispheric lateralization with respect to language in general . . . .

The disconnected minor hemisphere, lacking language like the animal brain and thus unable to communicate what it is thinking or experiencing, is much less accessible to investigation, and accordingly the nature and quality of the inner mental life of the silent right hemisphere have remained relatively obscure." (pp. 212–213)

The Validity of Cerebral Bisection Data in Interpreting Normal Functioning

[1]These statements are true for the majority of humans. There are individuals who have speech functions apparently located in the right hemisphere and visual-spatial processes in the left, although such individuals are relatively rare. Some individuals, notably the familial left-handed, show a bilaterality of cerebral organization, having both verbal and visual-spatial processes in both hemispheres. Although the evidence suggests a genetic basis for such differences, functional factors cannot be eliminated. The ability of the cerebral cortex to functionally reorganize during the early childhood years, following injury, is well documented. See Smith and Sugar (1975) for an interesting case history of functional reorganization.

There is extensive documentation (for a review, see Trevarthen, 1974) of the behavioral differences reported by Sperry, and there seems little question about the value of these contributions. However, questions remain concerning the extent to which this information can be generalized to normally functioning humans. Is it appropriate to infer normal human cortical functioning on the basis of data gathered from individuals suffering such severe cortical damage that radical surgery was deemed necessary to sustain life? To answer this question, it is necessary to assess similarities and differences in the functioning of intact humans and commissurotomy patients.

Central to this question is evidence on recovery of function following damage to brain tissue. The topic is best described in terms of cortical reorganization, since central nervous system tissue does not regenerate, once damaged. Cortical reorganization may be said to have occurred when there is no detectable loss of function, even though areas of the brain known to be associated with certain functions (language, for example) are damaged or destroyed.

The topic of brain reorganization is, to some extent, controversial. Reviews of cortical damage at different ages such as that of Lenneberg (1967) suggest that functional cortical reorganization is possible until approximately age 13. Lunneberg's conclusions have been challenged by Krashen (Note 1), who argues that functional reorganization of the brain is not possible after age 5. However, there is little disagreement concerning the idea that reorganization, especially in early childhood, is possible. A notable example of such reorganization was recently presented by Smith and Sugar (1975), who reported test results on an individual 25 years after complete removal of the left cerebral hemisphere at age 5 1/2. This person's performance on the Wechsler Adult Intelligence Scale is above average with a full scale IQ of 116, a performance IQ of 98, and verbal IQ of 126. The discrepancy between verbal and performance scores are approximately what would be expected given the educational achievements. Academic performance through school has been consistently above average. Currently, this individual is enrolled in college, carrying a full academic load, and working part time. There is no evidence of any loss of function, despite the complete absence of the entire left cerebral hemisphere.

Given the impressive evidence for functional reorganization, it is appropriate to ask if such cerebral reorganization may have occurred in the commissurotomy patients prior to surgical intervention. If these patients had epileptic seizures shortly after birth or prior to age 5, the possibility of functional reorganization cannot be eliminated. However, if the disorder is of relatively late onset, such as late adolescence or early adulthood, then it is reasonable to assume that cortical organization is within normal limits.

This question has been recently reviewed in detail by Whitaker and Ojeman, who examined a majority of the published research literature on the commissurotomy patients. They concluded that for a majority of these patients, the probability of major functional reorganization is quite high, since the disorder had been present from early childhood. For six of the patients, seizures were present from birth or appeared in early childhood.

"It should first be emphasized that all of these patients suffered from intractable epileptic seizures which could not be controlled by drug therapy: seizures arise from lesions in brain tissue especially cortex. Sometimes the damage is focal and sometimes diffuse. Consequently, in these patients, prior to thc operation, either the RH (right hemisphere) or the LH (left hemisphere), or both, are damaged and do not function normally. In all the patients for which information is published, the seizure had been present for a long period of time; in six of the patients, injury was sustained either at birth or in early childhood. All these facts point to a maximal opportunity for the brain to functionally re-organize (plasticity). Particularly in the case of the six patients with early injury, we can expect a significant degree of transfer of functions to other brain areas."

To summarize, Whitaker and Ojeman offer a convincing argument that hemisphere differences as assessed in the commissurotomy patients are inappropriate models of functioning for the normal human, since the possibility of drastic cortical reorganization cannot be eliminated.

In addition to these searching criticisms, Whitaker and Ojeman go on to point out that it is impossible to know, in the commissurotomy patients, the extent of trauma or damage caused by the surgery. To cut the corpus callosum it is necessary to retract the medial surface of one hemisphere, thus running considerable risk of damage to the opposite hemisphere. Since a majority of the commissurotomy patients had retraction of the right hemisphere, it is impossible to know whether differences in hemisphere functioning are due to the differential location of epileptic foci (with consequent possible reorganization in the case of early onset), surgical damage due to retraction, or both.

Given these limitations, it seems appropriate to exercise caution in generalizing from commissurotomized human to intact human. In fact, the safest course of action might be to conclude that data on commissurotomy patients is valid only for those patients.

Processing Versus Memory Differences Between the Cerebral Hemispheres

Dichotic Listening. An additional body of data needs to be evaluated. By now there are a large number of studies on normal intact human subjects reporting right-left hemisphere differences. Studies of normal subjects have been done through use of dichotic listening techniques (Kimura, 1967) in which differing auditory stimuli are presented simultaneously to the right and left ears. The sensory connections from the ears to Heschl's Gyrus are illustrated in Figure 1. Electrophysiological studies (Rosenzweig, 1951) indicated that contralateral nerve fibers take functional precedence over ipsilateral fibers when both are simultaneously stimulated. From this finding it is expected that when verbal stimuli are used, there should be a right ear advantage, since the fibers from the right ear take precedence in reaching the left hemisphere where language functions are located.

Such results have been reported for digits (Kimura, 1967, 1973), consonant-vowel monosyllables (Berline, Lowe-Bell, Cullen, Thompson, & Loovis, 1973; Bryden, 1975; Shankweiler & Studdert-Kennedy, 1967), words (McGlone & Davidson, 1973), and sentences (Zurif, 1974). While some clinical studies support the use of the technique in determining language lateralization (Kimura, 1967), problems of reliability of measurement (Blumstein, Goodglass, & Tartter, 1975; Bryden, 1975) are such that interpretations of dichotic results must be made cautiously.

Visual Half-Field Studies. Visual testing of hemisphere differences has been done using tachistoscopic presentations of stimuli into visual half-fields. In this technique the subject is required to focus on a reference point displayed in a tachistoscope or on a projection screen. When the subject fixates the reference point, a stimulus projected to the right or left of the fixation point for a time period not exceeding 150 milliseconds will be registered on nerve paths leading to only one hemisphere, depending on placement of the stimulus. Retinal connections to the visual cortex are shown in Figure 2.

Since the nasal hemiretina of the left eye and the temporal hemiretina of the right eye receive information from the left visual projecting to the right hemisphere (cf. Figure 2), a stimulus shown only in the left visual field will be registered only in the right hemisphere; similarly, the right nasal hemiretina and the left temporal hemiretina register information in the right visual field projecting to the left hemisphere. (For a detailed discussion of this technique, see Kimura, 1973).

Studies using this technique have generally found a left hemisphere advantage for verbal stimuli, including words (McKeever & Huling, 1971), single letters (Bryden, 1965, 1973; Kimura, 1966, Rizzolati, Umilta, & Berlucchi, 1971), and digits (Geffen, Bradshaw, & Wallace, 1971). Right hemisphere advantages have been reported for face recognition (Geffen. Bradshaw, & Wallace, 1971; Rizzolati, Umilta, & Berlucchi, 1971) and depth perception (Dumford & Kimura, 1971).

Visual half-field tachistoscopic testing is also subject to methodological problems, as White (1969, 1972) has pointed out in some detail. Methodological evaluations of hemisphere difference experiments have tended to focus on the experimental methodology per se, and not on the larger evaluative framework. The questions remain as to (a) whether these observed differences in hemisphere function exist in a context outside of the laboratory procedures used to study them, and (b) whether these results have any implications for educational practice.

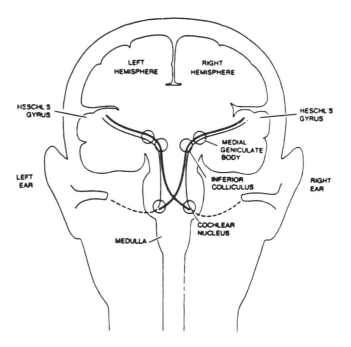

Figure 1. Auditory pathways from the ears to the cerebral auditory receiving areas in the right and left hemispheres are partially crossed. Although each hemisphere can receive input from both ears, the neural connections from one ear to the hemisphere on the opposite side are stronger than the connections to the hemisphere on the same side. When ipsilateral (same side) and contralateral (opposite side) inputs compete in the auditory neural system, it is thought that the stronger conralateral input inhibits or occludes the ipsilateral signals.

With regard to the experimental context of hemisphere differences, it is instructive to review the recent work of Hardyck, Tzeng, and Wang (1978) on semantic judgments across two languages. Using the tachistoscopic technique of visual half-field presentations, they presented pairs of stimuli in two languages—Chinese and English. Previous work on same/different judgments to verbal stimuli shown tachistoscopically in one language frequently found no differences in right and left hemisphere ability. Such a result is inconsistent with the generally accepted belief that the left hemisphere processes language, but has usually been resolved by the argument that right hemisphere judgments are done using a pattern matching strategy, while left hemisphere judgments are done on a semantic basis.

In their first experiment, Hardyck et al. had subjects fluent in reading Chinese and English make judgments of meaning (same/different) to a Chinese character and an English word shown simultaneously within either the right visual field leading to the left hemisphere (RVF-LH), the left visual field leading to the right hemisphere (LVF-RH) or with one member of each pair in each visual field (EVF).

The use of two languages with such marked structural orthographic differences eliminates pattern matching as a possibility, allowing an examination of hemisphere differences in language ability on a purely semantic basis.

The results of this first experiment, using 96 Chinese-English pairs, each presented once for 150 msec., were quite surprising. There were no hemisphere differences present either in accuracy of judgment or in speed of response (reaction time). An analysis of errors by hemisphere over all subjects revealed a total of 46 errors in the LVF-RH, 47 in the RVF-LH, and 19 in the EVF.

These results are simply not reconcilable with an interpretive framework which states that language processing occurs in the left hemisphere. Specialization of the left hemisphere for such a task suggests that material requiring a semantic judgment presented to the left hemisphere should (a) be judged more accurately (b) in a shorter time. In these results accuracy and speed of response did not differ, the only difference present being reduced errors when stimuli were shown with one member of each pair in a visual field (EVF). Judgments of same/different under such conditions requires interhemispheric communication, suggesting that people do much better using both hemispheres, or, put another way, the whole brain.

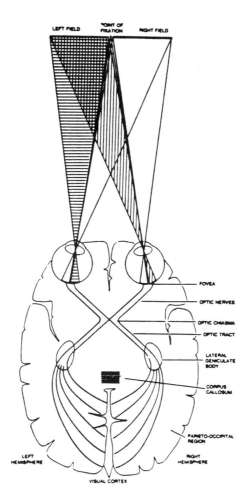

Figure 2. Visual pathways are completely crossed, so that when the eyes are fixated on a point, all of the field to the left of the fixation point (crosshatched area) excites the visual cortex in the right hemisphere and stimuli from the right visual field excite the left visual cortex. The visual cortexes can communicate via the corpus callosum, which connects the two hemispheres.

Hardyck, Tzeng, and Wang carried out a second experiment to see if the results of the first study could be replicated and to see if a combination of pattern matching and semantic matching produced hemisphere differences. In this experiment subjects fluent in reading Chinese and English were shown 90 pairs of stimuli, 30 Chinese-Chinese, 30 English-English, and 30 Chinese-English (15 stimuli were semantically the same and 15 semantically different). Results of this experiment were very similar to those found in the first experiment, with no hemisphere differences present in accuracy or reaction time.

However, in a second part of the experiment, a hemisphere difference was found. At the close of the experiment, the subjects were asked to write down all the words (Chinese and English) they could remember from the tachistoscopic presentations. Analysis of these data revealed that subjects remembered significantly more words shown in the right visual field leading to the left hemisphere. Such a result suggests that the left hemisphere may contain long-term memory storage for language. Given this possibility, it is feasible to entertain the idea that hemisphere differences may be differences in memory rather than thinking.

As a first stage in evaluating, this idea, a detailed analysis was done of published reports of hemisphere function differences. Results of this analysis indicated that a majority of the experiments reporting significant hemisphere differences, whether right or left hemisphere, used a small number of stimuli shown for a large number of trials. Those experiments reporting no hemisphere differences either used new information on each trial (as did the Chinese-English bilingual experiments) or had a relatively large ratio of stimuli to trials.

An illustration of each type of experiment can be provided. The work of Rizzolati et al. (1971) is frequently cited as evidence for the right-left specialization of the cerebral hemispheres. They reported, in two separate experiments, that subjects responded more quickly in making same/different judgments of verbal material when stimuli were presented in the right visual field leading to the left hemisphere. Twelve subjects participated in this experiment making judgments of 1 out of 4 possible letters in relation to a reference letter for 630 trials. In a separate experiment, Rizzolati et al. reported that judgments of same/different of human faces are made more quickly when the face is shown in the left visual field leading to the right hemisphere. As in their first experiment, 12 subjects made judgments of 1 out of 4 possible faces in relation to a reference face for 700 trials.

By contrast, in an experiment reporting no hemisphere differences, Dimond, Gibson, and Gazzaniga (1972) made tachistoscopic presentations of four letter words. A word was presented, followed by a 3-second delay and then a second word. Subjects were asked to make same/different judgments of the words. Dimond et al. found no hemisphere differences in accuracy, but a slightly higher error rate when the second word appeared in the visual field other than that of the initial presentation. Of particular interest here is the fact that they used 200 four letter words, with no repetitions.

It seems reasonable to argue that the experiments of Rizzolati et al. and Dimond et al. are not comparable. The cognitive processes appropriate to same/different judgments over constantly changing stimuli are not necessarily the same as those utilized in making same/different judgments of four simple stimuli for 700 trials. It would be difficult to argue that automatic, stereotyped responses are not present in the Rizzolati et al. experiments by the time 100 responses are completed and certainly by the time the subject has finished his 700th response.

Such a formulation is experimentally testable. If subjects show no hemisphere differences in judgments of stimuli where new information is presented on every trial, but show hemisphere differences in a small subset of such material when it is repeated over a great many trials, the arguments for both differing cognitive strategies and the limitations of hemisphere differences are considerably strengthened.

In two additional experiments Hardyck et al. tested such a formulation. In the first experiment, monolingual English-speaking subjects made judgments of same/different of the 30 English-English and 30 Chinese-Chinese word pairs used in their second bilingual experiment. The subjects were as accurate at the Chinese-Chinese (pattern matching) as at the English-English (semantic matching and pattern matching) and showed no hemisphere differences in either accuracy or reaction time, where each stimulus item was shown once, with no repetitions.

In a final experiment, a small set of English-English and Chinese-Chinese word pairs was selected—three terms in each language, allowing a maximum of six combinations within each language—three same and three different. These combinations were shown tachistoscopically to monolingual English-speaking subjects for 200 trials. When an analysis of reaction time by blocks of 5 trials each was carried out, it was found that by the 40th trial subjects were responding more quickly to English-English when presented to the left hemisphere and more quickly to Chinese-Chinese when presented to the right hemisphere. These differences continued to increase over trials until stabilizing after approximately 150 trials.

In evaluating the results of these last two experiments, it is necessary to keep in mind that the differences found in the last experiment are exactly what would have been expected by a researcher working on the hypothesis that the left hemisphere is specialized for language processing and the right hemisphere for pattern recognition, but who is unaware of the narrow context within which such differences can be detected. It is also clear that a great deal of work remains to be done in this area. However, the following conclusions seem reasonable on the basis of the accumulated data.

1. Right-left brain differences are not detectable when new information is present on every trial or measure. If the left hemisphere processes verbal material, it should be able to do so equally well with new and constantly changing information as with a miniscule number of verbal stimuli shown for a large number of trials. There is simply no analogue to the Rizzolati et al. experiments in real life—in our speech, our communicative acts, our reading, we do not encounter such limited amounts of information and make such simple judgments. Although admittedly an extreme point of view, it is possible to argue that hemisphere differences we found because the investigative tasks are so simple that they can easily be done with half a brain.

2. Although the evidence for lateralization of thinking is questionable, the results of the Chinese-English bilingualism experiments suggest that there are consistent memory differences between hemispheres that are in accord with existing findings of both experimental research and studies of brain lesion effects. The idea of differential memories for language and visual-spatial material seems reasonable and consistent with current research findings, even if some reinterpretaionn is necessary.

3. If the concept of differential memory storage within hemispheres is reasonable, then the question of thinking in ongoing cognitive processing has to be faced. While it does not seem possible at

this time to identify the specific location of a central processor or thinking unit, the possibility should be considered that some areas common to both hemispheres carry out this task, calling for appropriate information from memory as needed. Such a system is considerably more sophisticated than a left brain for one kind of thinking, and a right brain for another kind, but seems much more able to account for the kinds of cognitive processes we all carry out rather effortlessly as part of normal life.

Implications for Educational Practice

What implications do these conclusions have for educational systems? In answering this question, it is important to keep in mind that public education was established to promote widespread literacy in the form of reading, writing, and quantitative skills. Its purpose was to give individuals the tools to help them structure their experience, to gain knowledge and experience through the written word, and to improve communication with others. Even though schools have emphasized such language-related skills, only a small part of a child's oral language development can be attributed to the classroom curriculum. A similar argument can be made with regard to a child's experience with spatial relations skills. Doing such things as puzzles, taking apart toys, clocks, and engines (and hopefully, putting them back together) occurs in many contexts not related to school settings.

A closing comment seems obvious. Before reorganizing the curriculum, buying new right and left brain tests, or learning to think in "right brain" or "left brain" terminology, we should ask for more evidence that these differences really exist outside a narrow experimental context unrepresentative of either the educational process or the course of daily life. Before trying to educate both halves of the brain, we should ask for more evidence concerning the reality of this distinction other than that supplied by isolated cases of severe brain damage. Finally, before developing too much guilt over stressing "linear, analytic" thought over "holistic mentation and intuition," we should have more proof that these distinctions really exist in the functioning of the human brain.

Reference Note

1. Krashen, S. Language and the left hemisphere. UCLA Working Papers in Phonetics, No. 24. October, 1972 (mimeo). Available from UCLA Department of Linguistics, Los Angeles, California 90024.

References

Berlin, C. I., Lowe-Bell, S. S., Cullen, J. K., Thompson, C. L., & Loovis, C. F. Dichotic speech perception: An interpretation of right ear advantage and temporal offset effects. *Journal of the Acoustical Society of America*, 1973, *53*, 699–709.

Blumstein, S., Goodglass, H., & Tartter, V. The reliability of ear advantage in dichotic listening. *Brain and Language*, 1975, *2*, 226–236.

Broca, P. Remarques sur le siege de la faculte du langage articule, suivi d'une observation d'apheme. *Bulletin Societe Anthropologie*, 1961, *6*, 330–357.

Bryden, M. P. Tachistoscopic recognition, handedness, and cerebral dominance. *Neuro-psychologia*, 1965, *3*, 1–8.

Bryden, M. P. Perceptual asymmetry in vision: Relation to handedness, eyedness, and speech lateralization. *Cortex*, 1973, *9*, 419–435.

Bryden, M. P. Speech lateralization in families. A preliminary study using dichotic listening. *Brain and Language*, 1975, *2*, 201–211.

Crinella, F. M., Beck, F. W., & Robinson, J. W. Unilateral dominance is not related to psychological integrity. Child Development, 1971, *42*, 2033–2054.

Dimond, S. J., Gibson, A. R., & Gazzaniga, M. S. Cross field and within field integration of visual information. *Neuropsychologia*, 1972, *10*, 379–381.

Durnford, M., & Kimura, D. Right hemisphere specialization for depth perception reflected in visual field differences. *Nature*, 1971, *231*, 394–395.

Gazzaniga, M. S., Bogen, J. E., & Sperry, R. W. Dyspraxia following division of the cerebral commissures. *Journal of Nervous and Mental Disease* 1967, *16*, 606–612.

Geffen, G., Bradshaw, J. L. , & Wallace, G . Interhemispheric effects on reaction time to verbal and non-verbal visual stimuli. *Journal of Experimental Psychology*, 1971, *87*, 415–422.

Hardyck, C. Tzeng, O. J. L.. & Wang, W. S-Y. Lateralization of function and bilingual judgments: Is thinking lateralized? *Brain and Language*, 1978, *5*, 56–71.

Kimura, D. Dual function asymmetry of the brain in visual perception. *Neuropsychologia*, 1966, *4*, 275–285.

Kimura, D. Functional asymmetry of the brain in dichotic listening. *Cortex*, 1967, *3*, 163–178.

Kimura, D. The asymmetry of the human brain. *Scientific American*, 1973, *228*(3), 70–78.

Lenneberg, E. *Biological foundations of language*. New York: John Wiley and Sons, 1967.

McGlone. J., & Davidson, W. The relation between cerebral speech laterality and spatial ability with special reference to sex and hand preference. *Neuropsychologia*, 1973, *11*, 105–113.

McKeever, W. F., & Huling, M. Bilateral tachistoscopic word recognition as a function of hemisphere stimulated and interhemispheric transfer time. *Neuropsychologia*, 1971, *9*, 281–288.

Pines, M. We are right-brained or left-brained. *New York Times Magazine*, 1973, 32–33, 127–138.

Rizzolati, G., Umilta, C., & Berlucchi, G. Opposite superiorities of the right and left cerebral hemispheres in discriminative reaction time to physiognomical and alphabetic material. *Brain*, 1971, *94*, 431–442.

Rosenzweig, M. R. Representation of the two ears at the auditory cortex. *American Journal of Physiology*, 1951, *167*, 147–158.

Shankweiler, D., & Studdert-Kennedy, M. Identification of consonants and vowels presented to left and right ears. *Quarterly Journal of Experimental Psychology*, 1967, *19*, 59–63.

Smith, A., & Sugar, O. Development of above normal language and intelligence 21 years after left hemispherectomy. *Neurology*, 1975, *25*, 813–818.

Sperry, R. W. Mental unity following surgical disconnection of the cerebral hemispheres. *The Harvey lectures*, Series 62. New York: Academic Press, 1968. (a)

Sperry, R. W. Hemisphere deconnection and unity in conscious awareness. *American Psychologist*, 1968, 23(10), 723–733. (b)

Sperry, R. W. Perception in the absence of the neocortical commissures. *The Association for Research in Nervous and Mental Disease*, 1970, 48.

Sperry. R. W. Lateral specialization of cerebral function. In F. J. McGuigan arid R. A. Schoonover (Eds.). *The psychophysiology of thinking*. New York: Academic Press, 1973.

Sperry, R. W. Gazzaniga, M. S.. & Bogen, J. E. Interhemispheric relationships: The neocortical commissures; syndromes of hemisphere disconnection. In P. J. Vinken and G. W. Bruyn (Eds.), *Handbook of clinical neurology* (Vol. 4). Amsterdam: North Holland Publishing Co., 1969.

Trevanthen, C. Analysis of cerebral activities that generate and regulate consciousness in commissurotomy patients. In S. J. Dimond and J. G. Beaumont (Eds.), *Hemisphere function in the human brain*. New York, John Wiley & Sons, 1974.

Whitaker, H. A., & Ojeman, G. A. Lateralization of higher cortical functions: A critique. In S. J. Dimond and D. A. Blizard (Eds.), *Evolution and lateralization of the brain*. New York: New York Academy of Sciences.

White, M. J. Laterality differences in perception: A review. *Psychological Bulletin*, 1969, *72*, 387–405.

White, M. J. Hemispheric asymmetries in tachistoscopic information-processing. *British Journal of Psychology*, 1972, *63*, 497–508.

Zurif, E. B. Auditory lateralization: Prosodic and syntactic factors, *Brain and Language*, 1974, *1*, 391–404.

We thank Nadine Lambert for her helpful comments and W. H. Freeman and Company for permission to reprint Figures 1 and 2 from "The asymmetry of the human brain" by Doreen Kimura, *Scientific American*, March 1973.

Human Decency Is Animal

Edward O. Wilson

During the American wars of this century, a large percentage of Congressional Medals of Honor were awarded to men who threw themselves on top of grenades to shield comrades, aided the rescue of others from battle sites at the price of certain death to themselves, or made other, often carefully considered but extraordinary, decisions that led to the same fatal end. Such altruistic suicide is the ultimate act of courage and emphatically deserves the country's highest honor. It is also only the extreme act that lies beyond the innumerable smaller performances of kindness and giving that bind societies together. One is tempted to leave the matter there, to accept altruism as simply the better side of human nature. Perhaps, to put the best possible construction on the matter, conscious altruism is a transcendental quality that distinguishes human beings from animals. Scientists are nevertheless not accustomed to declaring any phenomenon off limits, and recently there has been a renewed interest in analyzing such forms of social behavior in greater depth and as objectively as possible.

Much of the new effort falls within a discipline called sociobiology, which is defined as the systematic study of the biological basis of social behavior in every kind of organism, including man, and is being pieced together with contributions from biology, psychology and anthropology. There is of course nothing new about analyzing social behavior, and even the word "sociobiology" has been around for some years. What is new is the way facts and ideas are being extracted from their traditional matrix of psychology and ethology (the natural history of animal behavior) and reassembled in compliance with the principles of genetics and ecology.

In sociobiology, there is a heavy emphasis on the comparison of societies of different kinds of animals and of man, not so much to draw analogies (these have often been dangerously misleading, as when aggression is compared directly in wolves and in human beings) but to devise and to test theories about the underlying hereditary basis of social behavior. With genetic evolution always in mind, sociobiologists search for the ways in which the myriad forms of social organization adapt particular species to the special opportunities and dangers encountered in their environment.

A case in point is altruism. I doubt if any higher animal, such as a hawk or a baboon, has ever deserved a Congressional Medal of Honor by the ennobling criteria used in our society. Yet minor altruism does occur frequently, in forms instantly understandable in human terms, and is bestowed not just on offspring but on other members of the species as well. Certain small birds, robins, thrushers and titmice, for example, warn others of the approach of a hawk. They crouch low and emit a distinctive thin, reedy whistle. Although the warning call has acoustic properties that make it difficult to locate in space, to whistle at all seems at the very least unselfish; the caller would be wiser not to betray its presence but rather to remain silent and let someone else fall victim.

When a dolphin is harpooned or otherwise seriously injured, the typical response of the remainder of the school is to desert the area immediately. But, sometimes, they crowd around the stricken animal and lift it to the surface, where it is able to continue breathing air. Packs of African wild dogs, the most social of all carnivorous mammals, are organized in part by a remarkable division of labor. During the denning season, some of the adults, usually led by a dominant male, are forced to leave the pups behind in order to hunt for antelopes and other prey. At least one adult, normally the mother of the litter, stays behind as a guard. When the hunters return, they regurgitate pieces of meat to all that stayed home. Even sick and crippled adults are benefited, and as a result they are able to survive longer than would be the case in less generous societies.

Other than man, chimpanzees may be the most altruistic of all mammals. Ordinarily, chimps are vegetarians, and during their relaxed foraging excursions they feed singly in the uncoordinated manner of other monkeys and apes. But, occasionally, the males hunt monkeys and young baboons for food. During these episodes, the entire mood of the troop shifts toward what can be characterized as a manlike state. The males stalk and chase their victims in concert; they also gang up to repulse any of the victims' adult relatives which oppose them. When the hunters have dismembered the prey and are feasting, other chimps approach to beg for morsels. They touch the meat and the faces of the males, whimpering and hooing gently, and hold out their hands—palms up—in supplication. The meat eaters sometimes pull away in refusal or walk off. But, often, they permit the other animal to chew directly on the meat or to pull off small pieces with its hands. On several occasions, chimpanzees have actually been observed to tear off pieces and drop them into the outstretched hands of others—an act of generosity unknown in other monkeys and apes.

Adoption is also practiced by chimpanzees. Jane Goodall has observed three cases at the Gombe Stream National Park in Tanzania. All involved orphaned infants taken over by adult brothers and sisters. It is of considerable interest, for more theoretical reasons to be discussed shortly, that the altruistic behavior was displayed by the closest possible relatives rather than by experienced females with children of their own, females who might have supplied the orphans with milk and more adequate social protection.

In spite of a fair abundance of such examples among vertebrate creatures, it is only in the lower animals and in the social insects particularly, that we encounter altruistic suicide comparable to man's. A large percentage of the members of colonies of ants, bees and wasps are ready to defend their nests with insane charges against intruders. This is the reason that people move with circumspection around honeybee hives and yellow jacket burrows, but can afford to relax near the nests of solitary species such as sweet bees and mud daubers.

The social stingless bees of the tropics swarm over the heads of human beings who venture too close, locking their jaws so tightly onto tufts of hair that their bodies pull loose from their heads when they are combed out. Some of the species pour a burning glandular secretion onto the skin during these sacrificial attacks. In Brazil, they are called *cagafogos* ("fire defecators"). The great entomologist William Morton Wheeler described an encounter with the "terrible bees," during which they removed patches of skin from his face, as the worst experience of his life.

Honeybee workers have stings lined with reversed barbs like those on fishhooks. When a bee attacks an intruder at the hive, the sting catches in the skin; as the bee moves away, the sting remains embedded, pulling out the entire venom gland and much of the viscera with it. The bee soon dies, but its attack has been more effective than if it withdrew the sting intact.   The reason is that the venom gland continues to leak poison into the wound, while a banana like odor emanating from the base of the sting incites other members of the hive into launching Kamikaze attacks of their own at the same spot. From the point of view of the colony as a whole, the suicide of an individual accomplishes more than it loses. The total worker force consists of 20,000 to 80,000 members, all sisters born from eggs laid by the mother queen. Each bee has a natural life span of about 50 days, at the end of which it dies of old age. So to give a life is only a little thing, with no genes being spilled in the process.

My favorite example among the social insects is provided by an African termite with the orotund, technical name *Globitermes sulfureus*. Members of this species' soldier caste are quite literally walking bombs. Huge paired glands extend from their heads back through most of their bodies. When they attack ants and other enemies, they eject a yellow glandular secretion through their mouths; it congeals in the air and often fatally entangles both the soldiers and their antagonists. The spray appears to be powered by contractions of the muscles in the abdominal wall. Sometimes, the contractions become so violent that the abdomen and gland explode, spraying the defensive fluid in all directions.

Sharing a capacity for extreme sacrifice does not mean that the human mind and the "mind" of an insect (if such exists) work alike. But it does not mean that the impulse need not be ruled divine or otherwise transcedental, and we are justified in seeking a more conventional biological explanation. One immediately encounters a basic problem connected with such an explanation: Fallen heroes don't have any more children. If self-sacrifice results in fewer descendants, the genes, or basic units of heredity, that allow heroes to be created can be expected to disappear gradually from the population. This is the result of the narrow mode of Darwinian natural selection: Because people who are governed by selfish genes prevail over those with altruistic genes, there should be a tendency over many generations for selfish genes to increase in number and for the human population as a whole to become less capable of responding in an altruistic manner.

How can altruism persist? In the case of the social insects, there is no doubt at all. Natural selection has been broadened to include a process called kin selection. The self-sacrificing termite soldier protects the rest of the colony, including the queen and king which are the soldier's parents. As a result, the soldier's more fertile brothers and sisters flourish, and it is they which multiply the altruistic genes that are shared with the soldier by close kinship. One's own genes are multiplied by the greater production of nephews and nieces. It is natural, then, to ask whether the capacity for altruism has also evolved in human beings through kin selection. In other words, do the emotions we feel, which on occasion in exceptional individuals climax in total self-sacrifice, stem ultimately from hereditary units that were implanted by the favoring of relatives during a period of hundreds or thousands of generations? This explanation gains some strength from the circumstance that during most of mankind's history the social unit was the immediate family and a tight network of other close relatives. Such exceptional cohesion, combined with a detailed awareness of kinship made possible by high intelligence, might explain why kin selection has been more forceful in human beings than in monkeys and other mammals.

To anticipate a common objection raised by many social scientists and others, let me grant at once that the intensity and form of altruistic acts are to a large extent culturally determined. Human social evolution is obviously more cultural than genetic. The point is that the underlying emotion, powerfully manifested in virtually all human societies, is what is considered to evolve through genes. This sociobiological hypothesis does not therefore account for differences among societies, but it could explain why human beings differ from other mammals and why, in one narrow aspect, they more closely resemble social insects.

In cases where sociobiological explanations can be tested and proved true, they will, at the very least, provide perspective and a new sense of philosophical ease about human nature. I believe that they will also have an ultimately moderating influence on social tensions. Consider the case of homosexuality. Homophiles are typically rejected in our society because of a narrow and unfair biological premise made about them: Their sexual preference does not produce children; therefore, they cannot be natural. To the extent that this view can be rationalized, it is just Darwinism in the old narrow sense: Homosexuality does not directly replicate genes. But homosexuals can replicate genes by kin selection, provided they are sufficiently altruistic toward kin.

It is not inconceivable that in the early, hunter-gatherer period of human evolution, and perhaps even later, homosexuals regularly served as a partly sterile caste, enhancing the lives and reproductive success of their relatives by a more dedicated form of support than would have been possible if they produced children of their own. If such combinations of interrelated heterosexuals and homosexuals regularly left more descendants than similar groups of pure heterosexuals, the capacity for homosexual development would remain prominent in the population as a whole. And it has remained prominent in the great majority of human societies, to the consternation of anthropologists, biologists and others.

Supporting evidence for this new kin-selection hypothesis does not exist. In fact, it has not even been examined critically. But the fact that it is internally consistent and can be squared with the results of kin selection in other kinds of organisms should give us pause before labeling homosexuality an illness. I might add that if the hypothesis is correct, we can expect homosexuality to decline over many generations. The reason is that the extreme dispersal of family groups in modern industrial societies leaves fewer opportunities for preferred treatment of relatives. The labor of homosexuals is spread more evenly over the population at large, and the narrower form of Darwinian natural selection was against the duplication of genes favoring this kind of altruism.

A peacemaking role of modern sociobiology also seems likely in the interpretation of aggression, the behavior at the opposite pole from altruism. To cite aggression as a form of social behavior is, in a way, contradictory; considered by itself, it is more accurately identified as antisocial behavior. But, when viewed in a social context, it seems to be one of the most important and widespread organizing techniques. Animals use it to stake out their own territories and to establish their rank in the pecking orders. And because members of one group often cooperate for the purpose of directing aggression at competitor groups, altruism and hostility have come to be opposite sides of the same coin.

Konrad Lorenz, in his celebrated book "On Aggression," argued that human beings share a general instinct for aggressive behavior with animals, and that this instinct must somehow be relieved, if only through competitive sport. Erich Fromm, in "The Anatomy of Human Destructiveness," took the still dimmer view that man's behavior is subject to a unique death instinct that often leads to pathological aggression beyond that encountered in animals. Both of these interpretations are essentially wrong. A close look at aggressive behavior in a variety of animal societies, many of which have been carefully studied only since the time Lorenz drew his conclusions, shows that aggression occurs in a myriad of forms and is subject to rapid evolution.

We commonly find one species of bird or mammal to be highly territorial, employing elaborate, aggressive displays and attacks, while a second, otherwise similar, species shows little or no territorial behavior. In short, the case for a pervasive aggressive instinct does not exist.

The reason for the lack of a general drive seems quite clear. Most kinds of aggressive behavior are perceived by biologists as particular responses to crowding in the environment. Animals use aggression to gain control over necessities—usually food or shelter—which are in short supply or likely to become short at some time during the life cycle. Many species seldom, if ever, run short of these necessities; rather, their numbers are controlled by predators, parasites or emigration. Such animals are characteristically pacific in their behavior toward one another.

Mankind, let me add at once, happens to be one of the aggressive species. But we are far from being the most aggressive. Recent studies of hyenas, lions and langur monkeys, to take three familiar species, have disclosed that under natural conditions these animals engage in lethal fighting, infanticide and even cannibalism at a rate far above that found in human beings. When a count is made of the number of murders committed per thousand individuals per year, human beings are well down the list of aggressive creatures, and I am fairly confident that this would still be the case even if our episodic wars were to be averaged in. Hyena packs even engage in deadly pitched battles that are virtually indistinguishable from primitive human warfare. Here is some action in the Ngorongoro Crater as described by Hans Kruuk of Oxford University:

"The two groups mixed with an uproar of calls, but within seconds the sides parted again and the Mungi hyenas ran away, briefly pursued by the Scratching Rock hyenas, who then returned to the carcass. About a dozen of Scratching Rock hyenas, though, grabbed one of the Mungi males and bit him wherever they could—especially in the belly, the feet and the ears. The victim was completely covered by his attackers, who proceeded to maul him for about ten minutes while their clan fellows were eating the wildebeest. The Mungi male was literally pulled apart, and when I later studied the injuries more closely, it appeared that his ears were bitten off and so were his feet and testicles, he was paralyzed by a spinal injury, had large gashes in the hind legs and belly, and subcutaneous hemorrages all over . . . . The next morning, I found a hyena eating from the carcass and saw evidence that more had been there: about one-third of the internal organs and muscles had been eaten. Cannibals! "

Alongside ants, which conduct assassinations, skirmishes and pitched battles as routine business, men are all but tranquil pacifists. Ant wars, incidentally, are especially easy to observe during the spring and summer in most towns and cities in the Eastern United States. Look for masses of small blackish brown ants struggling together on sidewalks or lawns. The combatants are members of rival colonies of the common pavement ant, *Tetramorium caespitum*. Thousands of individuals may be involved, and the battlefield typically occupies several square feet of the grassroots jungle.

Although some aggressive behavior in one form or another is characteristic of virtually all human societies (even the gentle !Kung Bushmen until recently had a murder rate comparable to that of Detroit and Houston), I know of no evidence that it constitutes a drive searching for an outlet. Certainly, the conduct of animals cannot be used as an argument for the widespread existence of such a drive.

In general, animals display a spectrum of possible actions, ranging from no response at all, through threats and feints, to an all-out attack; and they select the action that best fits the circumstances of each particular threat. A rhesus monkey, for example, signals a peaceful intention toward another troop member by averting its gaze or approaching with conciliatory lip-smacking. A low intensity of hostility is conveyed by an alert, level stare. The hard look you receive from a rhesus when you enter a laboratory or the primate building of a zoo is not simple curiosity—it is a threat.

From that point onward, the monkey conveys increasing levels of confidence and readiness to fight by adding new components one by one, or in combination: The mouth opens in an apparent expression of astonishment, the head bobs up and down, explosive ho's! are uttered and the hands slap the ground. By the time the rhesus is performing all of these displays, and perhaps taking little forward lunges as well, it is prepared to fight. The ritualized performance, which up to this point served to demonstrate precisely the mood of the animal, may then give way to a shrieking, rough-and-tumble assault in which hands, feet and teeth are used as weapons. Higher levels of aggression are not exclusively directed at other monkeys.

Once, in the field, I had a large male monkey reach the hand-slapping stage three feet in front of me when I accidentally frightened an infant monkey which may or may not have been a part of the male's family. At that distance, the male looked like a small gorilla. My guide, Professor Stuart Altmann of the University of Chicago, wisely advised me to avert my gaze and to look as much as possible like a subordinate monkey.

Despite the fact that many kinds of animals are capable of a rich, graduated repertory of aggressive actions, and despite the fact that aggression is important in the organization of their societies, it is possible for individuals to go through a normal life, rearing offspring, with nothing more than occasional bouts of play-fighting and exchanges of lesser hostile displays. The key is the environment: Frequent intense display and escalated fighting are adaptive responses to certain kinds of social stress which a particular animal may or may not be fortunate enough to avoid during its lifetime. By the same token, we should not be surprised to find a few human cultures, such as the Hopi or the newly discovered Mindanao, in which aggressive interactions are minimal. In a word, the evidence from comparative studies of animal behavior cannot be used to justify extreme forms of aggression, bloody drama or violent competitive sports practiced by man.

This brings us to the topic which, in my experience, causes the most difficulty in discussions of human sociobiology: the relative importance of genetic vs. environmental factors in the shaping of behavioral traits. I am aware that the very notion of genes controlling behavior in human beings is scandalous to some scholars. They are quick to project the following political scenario: Genetic determinism will lead to support for the status quo and continued social injustice. Seldom is the equally plausible scenario considered: Environmentalism will lead to support for authoritarian mind control and worse injustice. Both sequences are highly unlikely, unless politicians or ideologically committed scientists are allowed to dictate the uses of science. Then anything goes.

That aside, concern over the implications of sociobiology usually proves to be due to a simple misunderstanding about the nature of heredity. Let me try to set the matter straight as briefly but fairly as possible. *What the genes prescribe is not necessarily a particular behavior but the capacity to develop certain behaviors and, more than that, the tendency to develop them in various specified environments.* Suppose that we could enumerate all conceivable behavior belonging to one category—say, all the possible kinds of aggressive responses—and for convenience label them by letters. In this imaginary example, there might be exactly 23 responses, which we designate A through W. Human beings do not and cannot manifest all the behaviors; perhaps all societies in the world taken together employ A through P.

Furthermore, they do not develop each of these with equal facility; there is a strong tendency under most possible conditions of child-rearing for behaviors A through G to appear, and consequently H through P are encountered in very few cultures. It is this *pattern* of possibilities and probabilities that is inherited.

To make such a statement wholly meaningful, we must go on to compare human beings with other species. We note that hamadryas baboons can perhaps develop only F through J, with a strong bias toward F and G, while one kind of termite can show only A and another kind of termite only B. Which behavior a particular human being displays depends on the experience received within his own culture, but the total array of human possibilities, as opposed to baboon or termite possibilities, is inherited. It is the evolution of this pattern which sociobiology attempts to analyze.

We can be more specific about human patterns. It is possible to make a reasonable inference about the most primitive and general human social traits by combining two procedures. First, note is made of the most widespread qualities of hunter-gatherer societies. Although the behavior of the people is complex and intelligent, the way of life to which their cultures are adapted is primitive. The human species evolved with such an elementary economy for hundreds of thousands of years; thus, its innate pattern of social responses can be expected to have been principally shaped by this way of life. The second procedure is to compare the most widespread hunter-gatherer qualities with similar behavior displayed by the species of langurs, colobus, macaques, baboons, chimpanzees, gibbons and other Old World monkeys and apes that, together, comprise man's closest living relatives.

Where the same pattern of traits occurs in man—and in most or all of the primates—we conclude that it has been subject to relatively little evolution. Its possession by hunter-gatherers indicates, (but does not prove), that the pattern was also possessed by man's immediate ancestors; the pattern also belongs to the class of behaviors least prone to change even in economically more advanced societies. On the other hand, when the behavior varies a great deal among the primate species, it is less likely to be resistant to change.

The list of basic human patterns that emerges from this screening technique is intriguing: (1) The number of intimate group members is variable but normally 100 or less; (2) some amount of aggressiveness and territorial behavior is basic, but its intensity is graduated and its particular forms cannot be predicted from one culture to another with precision; (3) adult males are more aggressive and are dominant over females; (4) the societies are to a large extent organized around prolonged maternal care and extended relationships between mothers and children, and (5) play, including at least mild forms of contest and mock-aggression, is keenly pursued and probably essential to normal development.

We must then add the qualities that are so distinctively ineluctably human that they can be safely classified as genetically based: the overwhelming drive of individuals to develop some form of a true, semantic language, the rigid avoidance of incest by taboo and the weaker but still strong tendency for sexually bonded women and men to divide their labor into specialized tasks.

In hunter-gatherer societies, men hunt and women stay at home. This strong basis persists in most agricultural and industrial societies and, on that ground alone, appears to have a genetic origin. No solid evidence exists as to when the division of labor appeared in man's ancestors or how resistant to change it might be during the continuing revolution for women's rights. My own guess is that the genetic bias is intense enough to cause a substantial division of labor even in the most free and most egalitarian of future societies.

As shown by research recently summarized in the book "The Psychology of Sex Differences," by Eleanor Emmons Maccoby and Carol Nagy Jacklin, boys consistently show more mathematical and less verbal ability than girls on the average, and they are more aggressive from the first hours of social play at age 2 to manhood. Thus, even with identical education and equal access to all professions, men are likely to continue to play a disproportionate role in political life, business and science. But that is only a guess and, even if correct, could not be used to argue for anything less than sex-blind admission and free personal choice.

Certainly, there are no a priori grounds for concluding that the males of the predatory species must be a specialized hunting class. In chimpanzees, males are the hunters; which may be suggestive in view of the fact that these apes are by a wide margin our closest living relatives. But, in lions, the females are the providers, typically working in groups with their cubs in tow. The stronger and largely parasitic males hold back from the chase, but rush in to claim first share of the meat when the kill has been made. Still another pattern is followed by wolves and African wild dogs: Adults of both sexes, which are very aggressive, cooperate in the hunt.

The moment has arrived to stress that there is a dangerous trap in sociobiology, one which can be avoided only by constant vigilance. The trap is the naturalistic fallacy of ethics, which uncritically concludes that what is, should be. The "what is" in human nature is to a large extent the heritage of a Pleistocene hunter-gatherer existence. When any genetic bias is demonstrated, it cannot be used to justify a continuing practice in present and future societies. Since most of us live in a radically new environment of our own making, the pursuit of such a practice would be bad biology; and like all bad biology, it would invite disaster. For example, the tendency under certain conditions to conduct warfare against competing groups might well be in our genes, having been advantageous to our Neolithic ancestors, but it could lead to global suicide now. To rear as many healthy children as possible was long the road to security; yet with the population of the world brimming over, it is now the way to environmental disaster.

Our primitive old genes will therefore have to carry the load of much more cultural change in the future. To an extent not yet known, we trust—we insist—that human nature can adapt to more encompassing forms of altruism and social justice. Genetic biases can be trespassed, passions averted or redirected, and ethics altered; and the human genius for making contracts can continue to be applied to achieve healthy and freer societies. Yet the mind is not infinitely malleable. Human sociobiology should be pursued and its findings weighed as the best means we have of tracing the evolutionary history of the mind. In the difficult journey ahead, during which our ultimate guide must be our deepest and, at present, least understood feelings, surely we cannot afford an ignorance of history.

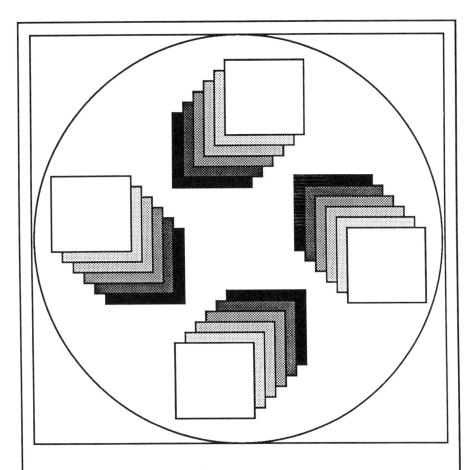

Chapter 3

Sensation and Perception

CHAPTER 3: SENSATION AND PERCEPTION

Most textbooks define sensation as the physical capacity of a receptor to react to a stimulus. Thus, human eyes can "sense" the light of a candle at a distance of a mile. Perception, on the other hand, is what we make of the sensations and what they mean to us. Pygmies living in African rain forests can see or sense a line drawing of a tree with a smaller elephant in the background, but they "perceive" the elephant not merely as distant but as remarkably small; due to the rainforest environment they lack the opportunity to see distance. Although both sensation and perception are topics for psychological research, the area of perception concerns how one's culture and experience influence our responses to sensations. So intertwined are the two that some sensations are extremely difficult to measure without also addressing the issue of perception. The papers in this chapter examine forms of perception that are different from the more common topics of vision and audition—the perception of emotion in others and the influence of intrauterine experience on later, extrauterine speech perception.

3a. McDermott, J. (1986). Face to face: It's the expression that bears the message. *Smithsonian*, March.

The capacity to perceive how those around us feel is an important one. According to the article, is this ability learned or does it seem to be innate? Back up your argument with facts from the article.

3b. DeCasper, A. J., & Spence, M. J. (1986). Prenatal maternal speech influences newborn's perception of speech sounds. *Infant Behavior and Development, 9,* 133–150.

One way scientists sought to establish that behavior is inherited was to deny an immature organism experience and see if typical behavior developed anyway. Based on the DeCasper and Spence article, what experiment or condition should be examined to determine the "innateness" of language perception in humans? Why?

Face to Face:
It's the Expression that Bears the Message

Jeanne McDermott

Paul Ekman has a funny face. It is not the long mouth, the black eyebrows or the broad furrowed forehead, but the way his face tumbles and contorts into an unabashed exhibition of expressions. After practicing before the mirror for several years, Ekman has learned how to control each individual muscle in his face, a dexterity few mimes and actors will claim. "Most people can't do this," he says, snapping into the odd grin that became Charlie Chaplin's trademark. "When I was a kid, my mother said 'Stop making all those crazy expressions on your face,' " he recalls. The odd expression softens into one of bemused contentment. "Now I'm making a living at it."

As an experimental psychologist, Ekman has devoted his entire career to discovering what is in a face. His quest and curiosity are hardly novel. In Helen of Troy's time, there was enough mystique to launch a thousand ships. Even in faces without memorable beauty (which studies of beauty-contest winners suggest is only the idealization of the species' juvenile characteristics), there is plenty. Nothing that we see, no other object in the world, possesses such hypnotic fascination, such wealth of meaning or such power in its confluence of expression and identity.

So rich is the face that each generation of artists has revealed something new about the way we see it. According to Gertrude Stein, Picasso painted faces the way they might appear to a newborn baby: flat, without dimension, features straying off course. With calligraphic brushstrokes, Henri Matisse made quick sketches of his friend, the poet Louis Aragon, capturing how much the face changes from one moment to the next. And with the technology of the 20th century, New York City artist Nancy Burson creates faces that belong to the horizon of dream and imagination.

The woman in one of Burson's photographs looks like a Vogue model, today's image of a natural beauty (p.115). But look again. There is nothing natural about this face. It belongs to no one who has ever existed or ever will. Rather, it is a chimera, a composite created by camera and computer. For more than a decade, Burson has been developing the software that allows her to merge two or more faces into one believable and utterly impossible composite. When a plastic surgeon told Burson that people came to him with a list of ten things they wanted—"like Audrey Hepburn's nose"—it stimulated her interest in the notion of what we call beautiful. Rather than making a patchwork of the desired features, she superimposed the faces of five icons from the 1950s: Grace Kelly, Sophia Loren, Bette Davis, Audrey Hepburn and Marilyn Monroe. Then she blended the faces of today's icons: Brooke Shields, Jacqueline Bisset, Diane Keaton, Jane Fonda and Meryl Streep. Alone, each composite face is a ghost of beauty. Together, they remind us that our ideal face, and Hollywood's, changes with time.

Darwin's overlooked theory of faces

Like artists, scientists have also been drawn to faces as a subject of study. Some contemporary scientists see the face as a key to understanding how we communicate, how we see and how we remember emotional experience. For the first time, and with the usual loose ends and debates, they are tendering some precise answers to many long-standing questions. Charles Darwin was the first to subject the nature of facial expressions to modern scientific analysis. In *The Expression of the Emotions in Man and Animals*, a best-seller in 1872, he argued that the expressions of the face are, in large measure, universal and innate. But despite Darwin's clout and the common sense in his argument, the book had little impact in the late 19th century's flux of ideas. The public still believed in phrenology, divining a person's character from the bumps on his head, and physiognomy, divining a person's character from the features on his face (*Smithsonian*, November 1980). The infant science of psychology, the study of the mind, was breaking off from philosophy and from physiology, the study of the body. Out of this turmoil came the conviction that universal expressions of the face did not exist, a belief later reinforced by the behaviorists and cultural anthropologists in the 20th century.

Only in the mid-1960s did Paul Ekman, along with Carroll Izard, also a psychologist, resurrect Darwin's ideas, which they had both encountered in Silvan Tomkins' book, *Affect, Imagery, Consciousness*. In appearance and style, the two offer a contrast. Ekman is broad-shouldered and works in a mask-filled clutter on the fog-cool San Francisco campus of the University of California. Izard is thin to the point of gauntness with a superclean desk at the University of Delaware. But you cannot help noticing that both possess very expressive faces.

Although individuals can read nearly infinite shades of meaning into a face, Ekman and Izard wanted to know if any expressions carry the same meaning, regardless of the observer, the word we attach to it, the culture or the context. Ekman, who was initially skeptical and Izard, who was not, used photographs of faces that a large number of people in this country agreed depicted one and only one simple emotion. On what Ekman now calls the "universals expedition," he and Izard found the same responses among literate people in Europe, South America, Africa and Japan. Ekman then showed these photos to tribespeople in Borneo and New Guinea who did not read or write and who had never been exposed to modern media. When asked which face illustrated a story, such as "she is angry and about to fight," the tribespeople judged the faces in the same way we do. While each culture used different words to label the emotions, all associated the same expressions with the same feelings. Around the world, brows lowered and drawn together, tightened lower eyelids and pressed lips mean anger; a wrinkled nose signals disgust. For fear, happiness, sadness and surprise, they also discovered universal expressions of the face. Izard in his travels in literate areas identified three more—contempt, interest and shame.

Once identified, Ekman and Izard spent the 1970s describing the six universals and their myriad variations by videotaping and analyzing hundreds, if not thousands, of faces. Slow-motion videotaping led Ekman to discover what he calls microexpressions. While an average expression lasts from one to one-and-a-half seconds, these flash across the face in a fraction of a second too fast for anyone to register consciously. They are fully formed expressions at distinct odds with whatever shows on the person's face. Ekman found them when a patient had attempted suicide only shortly after doctors had granted her leave from a psychiatric hospital. Perplexed, the doctors said she had given them no clue to her despair. Only by replaying a videotape of her last session in slow motion did Ekman catch the fleeting microexpressions of sadness mingled with her otherwise happy face.

Ekman's technique for analyzing the face is based on the underlying muscles. "Unlike other mammals, humans have only facial muscles attached to the skin," he says. "While a horse can flip a fly from its flank, you can only flip a fly off your forehead." Ekman remapped the face's muscles, uncovering ones that anatomists had overlooked. In total, he found 44, assigned each a number and then spent many years with a mirror learning which muscles contract to form what expressions. He has found more than 10,000 possible anatomical combinations and now speaks of faces in terms of numbers. "That's a 13," he says of the Chaplin smile. Only one expression has no number, "A neutral face is one without any muscular contraction evident. But you can read anything into a neutral face, which is what we do," he says, deadpan.

Only a short time after Ekman and Izard gave the scientific community powerful tools for analyzing the face, researchers trooped off to the nursery to find out if the universals are also innate, present from birth. Just how and when and why these expressions emerge is being hotly debated now. Newborns lack the use of only one facial muscle that adults possess, Number 13, in fact. We are born to communicate with the face.

No one believes this as strongly as Tiffany Field, psychologist at the University of Miami Medical School. "We work a lot with newborns, just playing. The tendency is to make funny faces at them. And their tendency is to make funny faces back," she says. When Field did a systematic study of this playing, she found that babies only 36 hours old can and do imitate happy, sad and surprised expressions on the face. Even prematurely born babies were able to do it.

Newborns were once thought to be blind at birth and are now believed to have limited perception of depth and visual acuity; how can they see a face well enough to mimic it? Many scientists are highly skeptical, and Field herself admits that "the imitative behavior is surprising." Is it a reflex? How much voluntary control does the infant have? Field believes that newborns have an innate ability to compare what they can perceive with what they can do, a built-in resonance to faces and their expressions. Half-jokingly, she says this may explain why smiles are contagious.

The earlier work of Andrew Meltzoff, psychologist at the University of Washington in Seattle, inspired Field's research (p. 118).

He looked at actions like sticking the tongue out and opening the mouth. Under conditions that optimized a newborn's ability to see, he found it would readily imitate the adult. But like many scientists, Meltzoff gets wary when it comes to making claims about emotion. "My work is about the imitation of basic facial actions," he says, "not about complex facial patterns like emotional displays."

What babies may be doing in the first weeks of life is the facial equivalent of babbling, testing the "equipment," so to speak. Since infants seem to be sensitive to faces almost from birth, it is a fair assumption that the "equipment" includes nerve cells in the brain that are attuned to faces. Robert Emde, psychiatrist at the University of Colorado Medical School in Denver, has been studying what newborns can do with this basic equipment. Although Emde has a sleek, Scandinavian style analyst's couch in his office, he has been interested since graduate-student days in what infants and children communicate without words. From the day of birth, perhaps even before, babies smile. Family folklore says it is a gas pain, or more poetically that the child is smiling at the angels. Emde says that the first smiles are associated with REM, the rapid eye movement stage of brain activity that occurs in adults during the dreaming stage of sleep. In infant, REM occurs 50 percent of the time, when the infant is both awake and asleep. The mother has no control over the REM smiles. "That so violates our intuitive understanding of the principles of communication that some mothers say the smile must be caused by gas or the deities," he says. As the infant ages, the smiling associated with the REM stage changes, paralleling a growth spurt in the brain. By three weeks infants smile, irregularly, to changes in the environment. By two months, infants smile at faces, anybody's face, and soon after, to the caregiver's face more than any other.

Long before children speak or understand language, they speak and understand a powerful language of the face. While working on her doctoral thesis several year ago, Denver psychologist Mary Klinnert discovered a process now known as "social referencing." Watching a session in a camera-lined laboratory-playroom, she noticed how strongly the mother's facial expressions influenced the baby's actions. So she invited toddlers, 12 and 18 months old, to play with scary toys like Incredible Hulk and a remote-controlled spiderlike robot. Before making a beeline for the toy, some children hesitated and checked the mother's face for guidance. Klinnert had carefully trained the mothers in the expressions of approval or apprehension. When the mother smiled serenely, the child went ahead and played. But when the mother grimaced or showed fear, most children backed off and some cried. Not a word was required to keep the dubious infant away from uncertainty. All it took was a convincing expression on the mother's face. Klinnert explains: "The child learns ways of seeing the world from other people's expressions."

In the early days of Klinnert's study, however, the children's response was not always as clear-cut. Sometimes, instead of backing off in fear, they began to laugh. When Klinnert played the videotapes in slow motion, she saw what the children had seen: the mothers of laughing babies had changed their posed expression of fear ever so slightly. Rather than lifting the eyebrows, they let them relax. Rather than dropping the corners of the mouth, they began to raise them. The expression of surprise was creeping into that of their fear and the babies, who were attuned to peekaboo games, sensed the very subtle difference. The problem was solved by placing a wireless microphone in the mother's ear and coaching her to keep a fearful look.

If the infant's face is initially a pure medium of expression, then only with time does it become a mask, molded by what the family believes are proper ways to show feeling. "By the age of one, kids are learning enormous amounts about rules for the expression of emotion," says Emde who is studying faces for clues to how different families teach these rules. At this age, children first learn not to show emotion, particularly anger, and they learn to put on expressions, particularly smiles. The tight coupling between a facial expression and the feeling itself begins to stretch.

While the bond between what the face reveals and what the person feels may loosen, it is never truly severed. Ekman studied actors trained in the Stanislavsky method, which teaches them to physically become the characters they play. When asked to assume certain facial expressions, these actors reported feeling the emotion that accompanies the expression—and by such objective physical indicators as heart rate and skin temperature, they did. Izard had earlier obtained similar results when, on a sabbatical in Moscow, he tested actors trained at several institutes following Stanislavsky. If the physical action triggers the emotional sensation, does that mean you will feel happy if you put on a happy face? Not with a smile, says Ekman, but he has found a close connection with the emotions of anger, depression, fear and sadness. Feigning those expressions can trigger corresponding internal sensations and physiological changes, he says.

By the age of two, the face is not only a medium and mask for communication but it also becomes the locus of identity. Children learn how to recognize their own faces as reflections of themselves at this age, and then all through childhood they become increasingly adept at recognizing other people's faces. Curiously, this ability momentarily falters around ages 11 through 14, which MIT psychologist Susan Carey attributes to the hormonal and cognitive reshuffling of puberty. But in the midteens, it snaps back and by adulthood, the number of faces that we are able to recognize is as boundless as the universe of possibilities. "We are all Einsteinian physicists when it comes to recognizing faces," Carey says.

For scientists who study how we see and remember, the process of recognizing faces is an enigma. "It's impossible to say in detail how we do it," says Alvin Goldstein, psychologist at the University of Missouri, Columbia. As an object of perception, the face is in a class by itself. Nothing in the environment gives so much information essential to survival. Is the other friend or foe? Kin or outsider? The answer is in the face. And despite the transformation brought by aging, no other object is probably recognized so automatically and on the basis of such slender clues.

When the Defense Advanced Research Projects Agency (DARPA) decided to fund research in teleconferencing, MIT's Media Technology

Laboratory initiated an investigation called Transmission of Presence. The question came up: What is needed to carry on a face-to-face conversation between people at remote places? Susan Brennan, now a researcher at Hewlett-Packard Labs, proposed the caricature as one answer. For her master's thesis, she developed software that transforms faces into caricatures. Her system starts with a realistic line drawing, which it compares with an "average" face composed of all the other faces stored in the computer's memory. An operator exaggerates the differences between the line drawing and the average until an acceptable likeness is found. Then the caricature is automatically animated and driven by speech over ordinary telephone lines.

Caricatures proved more acceptable to teleconferencers than another approach to the MIT project called Lipsync, which borrowed from the traditions of puppetry. Looking vaguely like an advertisement for the Rocky Horror Picture Show, it animated a digitized photograph of the face with only the lips moving in synchrony to the person's words. One reason for the caricature's relative success (it has yet to be used commercially) is that it may be a visual shortcut, a potent distillation of the eye and brain's own strategy for recognizing faces. From the exaggerated lines of a caricature emerge a likeness that just isn't there in the equally simple but more faithful lines of a silhouette. The caricaturist knows that the face is not merely the sum of its features, but something whole—an arrangement of three-dimensional relationships. Unlike a silhouette artist, the caricaturist takes information from several points of view and compresses and distorts them onto a flat page. A caricature does not simply distort the face's features but makes that distortion relative to a tacit understanding of what is unusual about the face and what is not. While Richard Nixon and Alfred Hitchcock made easy targets for caricature, Gerald Ford did not. His face looked too "average."

With the exception of such famous faces, the "average" faces that people carry in their minds for reference vary with experience. Cognitive psychologists believe that we may recognize people by learning the range of variations possible within a group of faces and by unconsciously flagging the ways each individual falls within the range. The well-known fact that people of one race have trouble distinguishing people of another reflects the segregation of society more than any biological predisposition. The white child without black friends will not learn about the range of variations in black faces, and thus what makes one face distinctive relative to others.

While no one knows how to describe just what we recognize, the memory for faces is both durable and flexible. A famous study done at Ohio Wesleyan University in the 1970s found that we can recognize the faces of high-school classmates (without necessarily remembering the names) even 50 years after graduation. And they are hardly the same faces. After the bones and cartilage of the face stop growing, time and gravity take over, until the skin begins to sag around the jaw, neck and eyes, and wrinkles, creases and crow's-feet make their appearance.

Although the face does not age in easily predictable ways, computer artist Nancy Burson has developed the means to electronically simulate the aging process. In 1969, she first imagined a computer-screen version of *The Picture of Dorian Gray*—Oscar Wilde's tale of a portrait that grows old and ugly on canvas. Computer scientists told her at that time that it could not be done. But Burson was tenacious. By the late 1970s, the technology had caught up with her and she was able to apply a realistic mask of wrinkles to anyone's face. After using it initially to see what celebrities like the Royal Family and Brooke Shields would look like as senior citizens, she turned her attention to the aging of missing children. For the case of Etan Patz, a New York City child who disappeared seven years ago on his way to the school bus, Burson interviewed the family and asked them to decide whom Etan most resembled. She blended one of his last photographs with a recent one of his older sibling. While the child has not yet been found, the FBI has expressed interest in using Burson's approach with other cases.

A person who can't recognize her own face

The answer to why most people never forget a face may eventually come from people who do. Nowhere is the process of facial recognition so disturbed as in people with a very strange disorder called prosopagnosia. Antonio Damasio, neurologist at the University of Iowa's College of Medicine and this country's expert, sees only about one case a year. It develops only after a stroke or accident injures the tiny section of the brain involved in processing information about the face. Once-familiar faces no longer appear familiar. In one case, according to Damasio, "a 60-year-old woman suddenly noted that she could no longer recognize the faces of her husband and daughter. To her amazement, she could not even recognize herself in the mirror, nor could she recognize the faces of her neighbors. Yet she always knew that a face was a face." By showing patients photographs of people they knew and monitoring their automatic (or unconscious) responses with skin electrodes, Damasio found that his patients actually did recognize the faces—unconsciously. But this recognition had somehow slipped away from their conscious control.

As Damasio has pointed out, prosopagnosics fail to recognize more than faces, an observation that may lead to a more global understanding of the structure of the brain's memory. Boston neurologist Michael Alexander has one patient, an electrician, who finds wiring panels as confusing now as the faces of his three daughters. Another patient is a dermatologist who is no longer able to distinguish skin diseases. Alexander speculates that "at a very young age, some basic neurological mechanism for recognizing faces develops and we may use this feature to distinguish other meaningful objects."

Alexander's speculation raises an intriguing possibility. Does this innate framework for facial recognition also serve as a foundation for an esthetic sense? "Our notion of beauty may well originate in the face," says Joseph Campos, director of the Infant Development Laboratory of the University of Denver. "A baby may first scrutinize the face and then generalize it to other objects." The face contains all the qualities artists traditionally celebrate—symmetry, proportion, contrast. And these qualities, in turn, may also explain why the face proves to be such an enduring and irresistible subject for artists.

Like the artists before them, scientists with many different perspectives are converging on the face. It took Ekman's and Izard's "universals expeditions" and their tools for analysis to make the face a respectable thing to study. By and large, Ekman shrugs off his pioneering role. Credit belongs to many. But then he says playfully, "I've never been able to understand why everybody doesn't study the face." Actually, most of us do. We just don't get paid for it.

Prenatal Maternal Speech Influences Newborns' Perception of Speech Sounds[*]

Anthony J. DeCasper and Malanie J. Spence
University of North Carolina at Greensboro

ABSTRACT

Pregnant women recited a particular speech passsage aloud each day during their last 6 weeks of pregnancy. Their newborns were tested with an operant-choice procedure to determine whether the sounds of the recited passage were more reinforcing than the sounds of a novel passage. The previously recited passage was more reinforcing. The reinforcing value of the two passages did not differ for a matched group of control subjects. Thus, third-trimester fetuses experience their mothers' speech sounds and that prenatal auditory experience can influence postnatal auditory preferences.

Introduction

Human newborns do not act like passive and neutral listeners. They prefer their own mothers' voices to those of other females, female voices to male voices, and intrauterine heartbeat sounds to male voices, but they do not prefer their fathers' voices to those of other males (Brazelton , 1978; DeCasper & Fifer, 1990; DeCasper & Prescott, 1984; Fifer, 1980; Panneton & DeCasper, 1984; Wolff, 1963). Why should newborns prefer some sounds over others? One hypothesis is that their auditory preferences are influenced by prenatal experience with their mothers' speech and heartbeats (DeCasper & Prescott, 1984). Several considerations suggest this hypothesis is plausible.

Third-trimester fetuses hear, or are behaviorally responsive to, sound (e.g., Bernard & Sontag, 1947; Birnholz & Benacerraf, 1983; Crimwade, Walker, Bartlett, Gordon, & Wood, 1971; Johansson, Wedenberg, & Westin, 1964; Sontag & Wallace, 1935). Intrauterine recordings taken near term indicate that maternal speech and heartbeats are audible in utero (Querleu & Renard, 1981; Querleu, Renard, & Crepin, 1981; Walker, Grimwade, & Wood, 1971).

[*] This research was supported by a Research Council Grant from the University of North Carolina at Greensboro and a generous equipment loan by Professor Michael D. Zeiler. We wish to thank the medical and administrative staff of Moses H. Cone Hospital, Greensboro, NC and, especially, the mothers and their infants for making this research possible. Thanks also to G. Gottlieb, R. Harter, R. Hunt, R. Panneton, K. Smith, and, especially, W. Salinger for their helpful comments on drafts of the manuscript. Portions of this paper were presented at the Third Biennial International Conference on Infant Studies. March 1982, Austin, TX.

Correspondence and requests for reprints should be addressed to Anthony J. DeCasper, Department of Psychology, University of North Carolina at Greensboro, Greensboro, NC 27412.

Nonmaternal speech, for example male speech, is less audible because of attenuation by maternal tissue and/or masking by intrauterine sounds (Querleu & Renard, 1981; Querleu et al., 1981).

The newborns' preference for their own mothers' voices required that they had some prior experience with her voice, but there is no evidence that the necessary experience occurred after birth. Fifer (1980) failed to find any relation between maternal-voice preference and postnatal age, whether the newborns roomed with their mother or in a nursery, or whether they were breast fed or bottle fed. Since the maternal voice is audible in utero, and since third-trimester fetuses can hear, perhaps the necessary experience occurred before birth. In contrast, newborns show no preference for their own fathers' voices, even if they had explicit postnatal experience with his voice. Since male voices are not very audible in utero, perhaps the absence of a paternal-voice preference indicates the absence of prenatal experience with his voice (DeCasper & Prescott, 1984). The correlations between the presence or absence of specific-voice sounds before birth, and the presence or absence of specific-voice preferences after birth suggest that prenatal auditory experiences influence the earliest voice preferences.

Consider that complex auditory stimuli can function as positive reinforcers, neutral stimuli, or negative reinforcers of newborn behavior. Known reinforcers include vocal-group singing, solo female singing, prose spoken by a female, synthetic speech sounds, and intrauterine heartbeat sounds (Butterfield & Cairns, 1974; Butterfield & Siperstein, 1972; DeCasper, Butterfield & Cairns, 1976; DeCasper & Carstens, 1981; DeCasper & Sigafoos, 1983). On the other hand, male speech and instrumental music lack reinforcing value, while white noise and faster-than-normal heartbeat sounds are aversive (Butterfield & Siperstein, 1972; DeCasper & Prescott, 1984; Salk, 1962). The differential reinforcing effectiveness of these sounds seems to convey more with their similarity to sounds that were present in utero than with any general acoustic characteristic(s), which further suggests that prenatal auditory experience influences postnatal auditory perception.

Finally, prenatal auditory experience has been shown to cause postnatal auditory preferences in a variety of infrahuman species (e.g.. Gottlieb, 1981; Vince, 1979; Vince, Armitage, Walser, & Reader, 1982).

The hypothesis implies that prenatal experience with maternal speech sounds causes some property of the sounds to be differentially reinforcing after birth. Speech sounds enable at least two kinds of discriminations; some speech cues allow discrimination or language-relevant sounds, per se, or what is said, and some allow discrimination of the speaker or source of the speech sounds (Bricker & Pruzansky, 1976; Studdert-Kennedy, 1982). Thus, the prenatal experience hypothesis implies that newborns prefer their own mothers' voices, regardless of what she says, because of prenatal experience with her voice-specific cues. This implication, however, cannot be directly tested for obvious ethical and practical reasons. The hypothesis also implies that newborns will prefer the acoustic properties of a particular speech passage if their mothers repeatedly recite that passage while they are pregnant.

We directly tested the latter implication in the following way. First, pregnant women tape-recorded three separate prose passages. Then, they recited one of the passages, their target passage, aloud each day during the last 6 weeks of pregnancy. After birth their infants were observed in an operant learning task where recordings of the target passage and a novel passage, one their mothers had recorded but had not recited, were both available as reinforcers. Then their relative reinforcing effectiveness was evaluated. If the prenatal experience with the target passage increases its reinforcing value, then (a) the acoustic properties of the target passage will be more reinforcing than those of a novel passage; (b) the differential reinforcing value of the target passage should be carried by its language-relevant cues and, thus, should not require the presence of the infant's own mother's voice cues; and (c) the reinforcing values of the target and novel passages should not differ for control newborns who had never been exposed to either passage.

Method

Prenatal Phase

Pregnant Subjects. Thirty-three healthy women approximately 7 1/2 months pregnant were recruited from childbirth preparation classes after being informed about the project. All were experiencing uncomplicated pregnancies.

Prenatal Procedures. After becoming familiar with three short children's stories they tape-recorded all three. Recordings were made in a quiet room on an Akai 4000 stereophonic tape recorder. The tapes would be used as reinforcers in a postnatal learning task. Each woman was then assigned one of the stories as her target story. Assignment was made after all three had been recorded to prevent them from biasing the recording of their target, for example, by exaggerated intonation.

The women were instructed to read their target story aloud "two times through each day when you feel that your baby (fetus) is awake" and to "read the story in a quiet place so that your voice is the only sound that your baby can hear." They maintained a log of their daily recitations and were occasionally checked by the researchers.

Story Materials. The stories were *The King, the Mice, and the Cheese* (Gurney & Gurney, 1965), the first 28 paragraphs of *The Cat in the Hat* (Seuss, 1957), and a story we called *The Dog in The Fog*, which was the last 28 paragraphs of *The Cat in The Hat* with salient nouns changed. The three stories were about equally long, they contained 579, 611, and 642 words, respectively. Each could be comfortably recited in about 3 min. Each was also composed from equal size vocabularies of 152, 142, and 154 words, respectively. Salient, high-frequency nouns common to at least two stories were changed. For example, cat and hat in *The Cat* became dog and fog in *The Dog*, and cat and dog from those stories became turtle and zebra in *The King. The Cat* contained 46 unique words (i.e., words that appeared only in *The Cat*), which accounted for 22% of the total word count; *The Dog* contained 57 unique words, which accounted for 22% of the total word count; and *The King* contained 85 unique words, which accounted for 44% of the total word count. All three stories contained common high-frequency words. For example, a, all, and, did, do, he, I, in, like, not, now, of, said, that, the, to, with, and you occurred at least three times in each. The common high-frequency words accounted for 43% of *The Cat*, 38% of the *The Dog*, and 36% of *The King*. The remaining words occurred at least once in at least two of the stories. The stories also differed in prosodic qualities, such as patterns of syllabic beats. Thus, they differed in the acoustic properties of individual words as well as in prosody. *The Cat* and *The Dog* sounded more similar to each other than either did to *The King*, but we could readily identify the origin of short (several seconds) segments from all three.

Postnatal Phase

Experienced Newborns. Sixteen of the 33 fetal subjects completed testing as newborns. The 16 had been prenatally exposed to their target story an average of 67 times or for about 3.5 hours in all. They were tested at an average age of 55.8 hours (SD = 10). Each had to have had an uncomplicated full-term gestation and delivery, a birth weight between 3500–3900 grams, and APGAR scores of 8, 9, or 10 at 1 and 5 min. after birth. If a subject was circumcised, he was not tested until at least 12 hours afterward. Parents gave informed consent for the testing and were invited to observe.

Seventeen infants were not tested or did not complete a test session: 5 because their mothers failed to return their logs, 4 because they encountered intrapartum or postpartum difficulties, 5 failed to meet state criteria at the time of testing or cried, and 3 subjects' sessions were unavoidably interrupted.

Apparatus. Sessions occurred in a quiet, dimly lit room adjacent to the nursery. The infants lay supine in their bassinets and wore TDH-39 earphones, which were suspended from a flexible rod. They sucked on a regular feeding nipple with the hole enlarged to 1 mm. Rubber tubing connected the nipple to a Statham P23AA pressure transducer that was connected to a Grass polygraph and solid state programming and recording components. Each infant heard a tape recording of his/her target story and a tape recording of a novel story, one of the others their mother had recorded but not recited. Both stories were recorded by the same woman, and each was played on separate channels of the stereo recorder. The tape ran continuously, and sound was electronically gated to the earphones by the automated programming equipment. Intensities averaged 70 dB SPL at the earphones.

Testing Procedures. Sessions began about 2.5 hours after a scheduled feeding in order to maximize the chance of obtaining an awake, alert, and cooperative infant (Cairns & Butterfield, 1974). Each infant was brought to a quiet-alert slate before testing could begin (Wolff, 1966) and had to visually fixate and follow an experimenter's face when he/she spoke to the infant. (If the infant was not and did not fixate or follow, he/she was returned to the nursery, and another attempt was made after a later feeding.) The infant was then placed supine in the bassinet and the earphones were locked in place. One researcher who could not be seen by the infant and who was blind to the exact experimental condition in effect, held the nonnutritive nipple loosely in the infant's mouth. Another monitored the equipment. The infant was then allowed 2 min. to adjust to the situation and had to emit sucks having negative pressures of at least 20-mm Hg, a pressure normally exceeded by healthy infants. (If the infant failed to suck adequately, he/she was returned to the nursery, and another attempt was made after a later feeding.)

Testing began with 5 min. of baseline sucking during which no voices were presented over the earphones. Unconstrained nonnutritive sucking occurs as groups or bursts of individual sucks separated by interburst intervals of several seconds. A sucking burst was defined as a series of individual sucks separated from one another by less than 2 s; when 2 s elapsed without a suck the equipment registered the end of the burst. Thus, interburst intervals (IBIs) began 2 s after the last suck of one burst and ended with the onset of the first suck of the next burst. This criterion accurately captures the burst-pause pattern of newborns' nonnutritive sucking (see Figure 1). IBIs tend to be unimodally distributed for individual infants, and modal values vary between infants. The baseline was used to estimate the distributors and median value of each infant's IBIs just before reinforcement began. Differential reinforcement of IBIs began after baseline had been established. (Hereafter, if the infant stopped sucking for any reason, he/she was returned to the nursery and not tested again.)

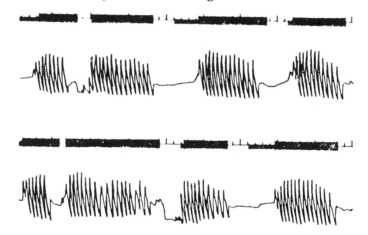

Figure 1. Polygraph record of a newborn's nonnutritive sucking. Wide horizontal marks indicate the onset and offset of a sucking burst. The time between the end of one burst and the beginning of the next denotes an interburst interval. Onset of the narrow event mark denotes that the time criterion, 1 second, has elapsed since the end of the last burst. Vertical lines indicate time in seconds.

Reinforcement Contingencies. For eight randomly selected infants sucking bursts that terminated IBIs equal to or greater than the infants' baseline medians (1) produced the recording of a woman's voice reciting the target story. Bursts terminating IBIs less than the baseline median were reinforced with the same woman's recording of a novel story. Thus, only one of the two stories was presented binaurally with the first suck of a burst and remained on until the burst ended. Reinforcement contingencies were completely controlled by the solid-state equipment. Reinforcement contingencies were reversed for the other eight newborns, to control for the effects of any response bias that might arise from either of the contingencies or from changes in the behavioral dispositions of the infants, for example, arousal or fatigue. Differential reinforcement lasted about 20 min.

The same differential reinforcement procedures were used in earlier voice preference studies (DeCasper & Fifer, 1980; DeCasper & Prescott, 1984). The rationale is based on well established reinforcement procedures that differentiate the temporal properties of behavior: Differentially reinforcing a range of IBIs causes the shorter differentially reinforced IBIs to increase in frequency (see newborn studies by DeCasper & Fifer, 1980; DeCasper & Sigafoos, 1983; as well as animal studies by Anger, 1956; Catania, 1970; DeCasper & Zeiler, 1977; Malott & Cumming, 1964).

Subject Controls. Twelve control newborns matched to a prenatally experienced counterpart on sex, race, and median interburst interval of baseline were also tested. They met the same selection criteria and were tested under exactly the same conditions as their counterparts, but their mothers had never recited any of the three stories.

Other Experimental Controls. The influence of mother-specific voice cues on the reinforcing effects of the target stories was controlled by having nine newborns reinforced with recordings made by their own mother and seven with recordings made by some other infant's mother. Both stories heard by an infant were recorded by the same woman to insure that their reinforcing value could not be unequally influenced by the speaker's voice characteristics. The acoustic properties of any one story could not systematically influence the reinforcing value of the target because each of the three stories had served as the target at least four times. No particular combination of target/novel pairings could systematically influence the reinforcing value of the target because five of the six possible target/novel pairings occurred at least twice. Unpredictable subject loss prevented precise counterbalancing of voices and target/novel pairings (see Table 1).

Table 1

| | Story | | | Experienced Subjects | | | | Control Subjects | | | |
| | | | | Target | | Novel | | Target | | Novel | |
Sex	Target/Novel	Criteria for Target	Voice	C.P. Base	C.P. Rein.	C.P. Base	C.P. Rein.	C.P. Base	C.P. Rein.	C.P. Base	C.P. Rein.
F	Cat/Dog	<5	M	.11	.06	.18	.21				
F	Dog/Cat	<6	M	.06	.26	.26	.32				
F	Dog/King	<3	M	.12	.10	.18	.13	.16	.10	.06	.16
M	King/Dog	<6	M	.10	.16	.33	.28	.06	.05	.32	.11
F	Cat/King	<3	O	.14	.16	.33	.06	.04	.07	.19	.13
F	Dog/King	<4	O	.02	.15	.10	.07	.08	.10	.20	.23
M	Dog/King	<4	O	.09	.12	.19	.21	.10	.17	.21	.16
M	King/Dog	<6	O	.03	.09	.19	.11	.06	.04	.24	.11
M	Cat/Dog	≥3	M	.29	.37	.12	.13				
M	Dog/Cat	≥5	M	.23	.21	.06	.05				
F	Dog/King	≥3	M	.16	.17	.13	.11	.08	.22	.12	.13
M	King/Dog	≥3	M	.26	.32	.17	.18	.63	.35	.09	.16
M	Cat/King	≥5	M	.17	.31	.09	.10	.49	.16	.12	.07
F	King/Dog	≥3	O	.06	.08	.17	.08	.26	.05	.10	.05
M	Dog/King	≥3	O	.03	.20	.24	.29	.13	.12	.14	.19
F	Cat/King	≥6	O	.23	.28	.06	.18	.31	.16	.14	.03

Data Analysis. Interburst intervals were read off the polygraph records. Times between the event marks signalling the end of one burst and the beginning of the next burst were measured and rounded down to the nearest whole second (see Figure 1). Thus, the scorers (AJD and MJS), who were highly practiced, did not have to make detailed judgments about IBI values that might bias the data. Interscorer reliability approached 100%.

Next, each subject's IBIs from the baseline and reinforcement phases were converted to a proportion of their time criterion (t). For example, if t = 4 s then all 2-s IBIs had the value 0.5t, and if t = 6 s then 2-s IBIs had the value of 0.33t. Converted IBIs were grouped into bins that were 0.21 s wide; Bin 1 contained IBIs between 0.0t and 0.2t s, Bin 2 contained IBIs between 0.2t and 0.4t s, and Bin 10 contained IBIs between 1.8t and 2.0t s. Bin 11 contained all IBIs greater than 2.0t s. IBIs were assumed to be equally distributed within a bin. The conversion equates the relative size of IBIs across subjects and allows averaging over subjects.

Results

Experienced Newborns

The hypothesis asserts that in utero exposure to the acoustic properties of the target story will make it more reinforcing than the novel story. If so, the relative frequency of short IBIs should increase over baseline when reinforced by the target stories in the IBI > t condition and the relative frequency of IBIs slightly longer than the baseline median should increase when reinforced by target stories in the IBI > t condition.

Baseline IBI distributions were examined first in order to determine whether they differed between reinforcement contingencies. They did not differ: A mixed ANOVA of the relative frequencies of baseline IBIs, with Contingencies (< t vs. > i) and Bin (1–10) as factors, indicated a significant effect of Bin, F(9, 126) = 13.3, p < .001. The effect merely confirms that the IBIs were unimodally distributed. Most important, there was no contingency effect, F(1,14)p < 1.0, and no Contingency x Bin interaction, F(9, 126) = 1.67, p > .10.

The predictions of the hypothesis were first assessed by examining file differences between the relative frequencies of IBIs that occurred during baseline and those that occurred during reinforcement. Difference scores were entered into a mixed ANOVA with Contingencies (t vs. > t) and Bin (1–10) as factors. There was no effect of Contingency, F(1, 14) < 1.0, and a significant effect of Bin, F(9, 126) = 5.48, p < .025. Most important, there was a significant Contingency x Bin interaction F(1, 126) = 2.07, p < .05. Planned tests of simple effects confirmed that the interaction occurred because with the IBI < t contingency the relative frequency of short IBIs increased over baseline levels, while those of all other IBIs either decreased or did not change. With the IBI < t contingency the relative frequency of IBIs slightly greater than > t seconds increased, while those of the others decreased or did not change. Any IBI between 0 and t seconds would have produced the target story under the IBI < t contingency, and any IBI > t seconds would have produced it under the IBI > t contingency. But only the relative frequencies of the shorter IBIs reinforced by the targets systematically increased.

The differential reinforcement effects are more clearly revealed in the analysis of IBIs between 0.0t and 0.4t (the shorter IBIs) and those between 1.0t and 1.4t (IBIs slightly longer than 1 second). Conditional probabilities of baseline and reinforced IBIs in these classes were obtained by dividing the relative frequency of IBIs in each class by the relative frequency of that class and all longer IBIs (see Table 1). This is a sensitive measure of temporally differentiated responding because: (a) it adjusts the inherently unequal opportunity for infants to emit equal numbers of short and long IBIs in a limited period of time; (b) it measures the probability that an infant will emit a particular class of IBIs given the opportunity to do so (cf. Anger, 1956; DeCasper & Fifer, 1980); and (c) it renders the conditional probabilities of IBIs between 0.0t and 0.4t, and those between 1.0t and 1.4t, arithmetically independent of one another. The dependent variables for the target story and for the novel story were their reinforcement ratios: (conditional probabilities of IBIs during reinforcement) divided by (conditional probability of IBIs during reinforcement) plus (conditional probability of IBIs during baseline).

The average values of baseline conditional probabilities of target-story IBIs and novel-story IBIs did not differ, $t(15) - 1.37$, $p > .10$. However, their reinforcement ratios differed as expected. A mixed ANOVA with Contingency (< t vs. > t) and Interval (0.0t–0.4t vs. 1.0t–1.4t as factors, revealed no effect of Contingency, $F(1,14) < 1.0$, and no effect of Interval, $F(1,14) = 1.59$, $p > .20$, but a significant Contingency x Interval interaction, $F(1,14) = 6.65$, $p < .025$ (Figure 2). Target-story reinforcement ratios were larger than novel-story reinforcement ratios, independent of the contingency and of the interval. The fact that 13 of the 16 infants had larger target ratios than novel ratios ($p = .011$ by the binomial test) and 13 of the 16 had target-story ratios greater than .50 indicates this result was typical. The individual-subject consistency implies that maternal voice cues were not necessary for producing the differential reinforcement effect. Neither the target-story reinforcement ratios nor the difference between the target ratios and novel ratios differed between the 9 infants who heard their own mothers' voices and the 7 who heard unfamiliar voices, p-values of both t-tests > .10.

Control Subjects

The following analysis of control-subject performances parallels that of the experienced subjects. The relative frequency distributions of baseline IBIs did not differ between reinforcement contingency conditions. A mixed ANOVA with Contingency (< t vs. > t) and Bin (1–

10) as factors revealed a marginal effect of Bin, F(9,90) = 1.90, .10 < p > .05, but effect of Contingency, F(1, 10) < 1.0, or of the Contingency x Bin interaction, F(9,90) = 1.38 p > .10. The subsequent mixed ANOVA on the difference scores of IBIs that occurred during the baseline and reinforcement phases revealed no effect of Contingency, F(1,10) < 1.0, a significant effect of Bin, F(9,90) = 5.19, p < .001, and a significant Contingency x Bin interaction, F(9,90) = 3.48, p < .005. However, none of the follow-up tests or simple effects were statistically reliable; the interaction seemed to result from unsystematic variation in the difference scores of the two contingency conditions in Bins 1–5.

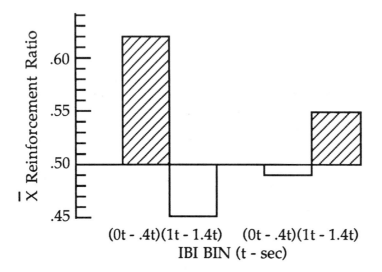

Figure 2. Mean reinforcement ratios of the target (hatched bars) and novel (open bars) stories for Experienced Infants in the IBIs < t condition (left side) and in IBIs > t condition (right side). The means are based on a total of 400 baseline and 1040 reinforced interburst intervals.

Subsequent analysis of conditional probabilities confirmed that the preceding interaction did not result from systematic effects of target-story reinforcement. The baseline conditional probabilities of target and novel stories did not differ, t(11) < 1.0; neither did their reinforcement ratios computed for the intervals 0.0t–0.4t and 1.0t–1.4t. The mixed ANOVA with Contingency and Interval as factors revealed no reliable effects whatever, p values of all F statistics > .10 (Figure 3).

A comparison of the reinforcement ratios of matched-subject pairs re vealed that experienced newborns had larger target-story ratios than their matched naive counterparts, t(11) = 2.68, p < .05, but that their novel-story ratios did not differ, t(11) < 1.0.

Discussion

Three implications of the prenatal-experience hypothesis were confirmed: (1) For experienced subjects the target story was more reinforcing than the novel story when both were concurrently available; (2) the greater reinforcing value of the target story was independent of who recited the story; and (3) for matched-control infants the target story was no more reinforcing than the novel story. The only experimental variable that can systematically account for these findings is whether the infants' mothers had recited the target story while pregnant. Subject characteristics also seem unable to account for the results; the differential-reinforcement effect did not occur within the matched-control group, and the differential-reinforcing value of the target story differed between matched subjects, but the reinforcing effect of the novel story did not. The results also cannot be attributed to individual-subject and subgroup differences in baseline patterns of responding. The most reasonable conclusion is that the target stories were the more effective reinforcers, that is, were preferred, because the infants had heard them before birth. The conclusion is consistent with earlier, independent evidence that hearing becomes functional during the third trimester and that maternal speech attains audible in utero levels during this time. Thus, the study provides the first direct evidence that prenatal auditory experience with a particular maternally generated speech stimulus influences the reinforcing value of that stimulus after birth.

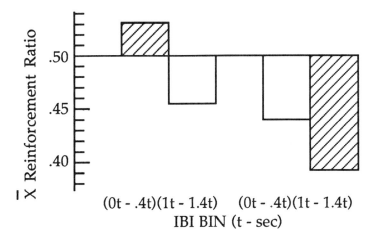

Figure 3. Mean reinforcement ratios of the target (hatched bars) and novel (open bars) stories for Control infants in the IBI < t condition (left side) and in the IBI > t condition (right side). The means are based on 300 baseline and 800 reinforced interburst intervals.

The conclusion implies that the fetuses had learned and remembered something about the acoustic cues which specified their particular target passage (e.g., prosodic cues such as syllabic beat, the voice-onset-time of consonants, the harmonic structure of sustained vowel sounds, and/or the temporal order of these sounds). Recall also that newborns prefer their mothers' voices over that of another female, when both speak the same novel material (DeCasper & Fifer, 1980; Fifer, 1980). The present results add to the evidence indicating that the maternal-voice preference also originated in utero. If so, then fetuses also register some specific information about their mothers' voices (e.g., spectra of nasals and vowels, glottal frequency and spectrum, and/or the temporal characteristics of pitch, intensity, and formants) (Bricker & Pruzansky, 1976). The specific acoustic cues that register in utero and which influence subsequent perception of speech and voice sounds are not known at present. However, whether language-relevant cues or voice-specific cues play an active role in newborns' perception has now been shown to depend upon: (a) which class of cues are differentially available, (b) the infants' prenatal experience with the cues, and (e) the circumstances attending postnatal perception (e.g., behavioral contingencies, infant state, or the presence or absence of other sounds).

The present study suggests noninvasive, ethically acceptable methods to further study the effects of prenatal auditory stimulation on postnatal auditory function and development, especially the development of speech perception. Such research might also benefit clinical treatment of the perinate, for example, by aiding in the diagnosis of fetal condition and by providing information for designing environments of preterm infants.

Some Post Hoc Considerations

Learning is generally and most satisfactorily inferred from a change in performance rather than from absolute measures of performance. However, change scores—the difference scores and reinforcement ratios used in this study—are almost always inversely related to prelearning performance, the baseline probabilities of responding (cf. Glass & Stanley, 1970, p. 182). The present discussion focuses on the extent to which the preceding inferences about differential reinforcement effects were influenced by the relation between baseline levels of performance and the difference scores and reinforcement ratios. The issue is salient here because the hypothesis asserts that reinforcement would differentially affect specific IBIs whose baseline probabilities varied considerably.

The abscissa of Figure 4 shows the mean conditional probabilities of baseline IBIs for each of the eight subconditions represented in Table 1. The mean baseline conditional probabilities of IBIs between 0.0t and 0.4t (subconditions 1–4 in Figure 4) are lower than the mean baseline conditional probabilities of IBIs between 1.0t and 1.4t (subconditions 5–8). They differ simply because baseline IBIs between 0.0t and 0.4t come from the left of a unimodal distribution and IBIs between 1.0t and 1.4t come from near the median of the distribution. The primary means of experimentally controlling for the influence of these baseline differences was to counterbalance the reinforcers associated with the

IBI < t and IBI > t contingencies: As Figure 4 suggests. and as reported earlier, when the values of baseline probabilities are pooled over IBIs < t and the IBI > t contingencies (1 with 6; 2 with 5; 3 with 8; 4 with 7) the average baseline probabilities do not differ.

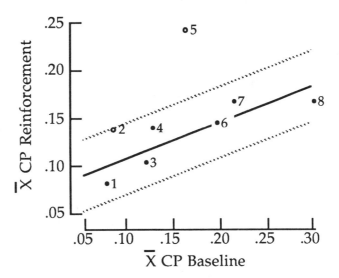

Figure 4. Mean conditional probability that subjects in the eight subconditions would emit IBIs between 0.0t–0.4t and between 1.0t–1.4t during reinforcement as a function of the mean conditional probability that they would do so during baseline. Open circles refer to Experienced subjects reinforced by the target story with IBI < t (2) and with IBI > t (5). Filled circles refer to Experienced subject reinforced by the novel story with IBI < t (4) and with IBI > t (7); to Control subjects reinforced by the novel story, with IBI < t (3) and with IBI > t (8); and to Control subjects reinforced by the novel story with IBI < t (1) and with IBI > t (6) . The solid line represents the regression equation (.07 + .38 [baseline probability] for the six control subconditions (filled circles) and the dashed lines represent the 95% confidence interval around the regression line.

Figure 4 also shows the empirical relation between the mean baseline probabilities and the mean probabilities occurring with reinforcement for each subcondition. The solid line represents the regression equation relating the baseline and reinforcement probabilities for the six subconditions in which no differential-rcinforccr effect was expected (filled symbols), r = .89, p < .02, For these six subconditions the probability of responding during reinforcement is almost completely determined by the prior baseline probability. Their reinforcement probabilities do not increase over baseline probabilities, but instead become increasingly smaller than baseline as the baseline probability increases. Figure 5 shows that when reinforcement ratio (a change score) is substituted for reinforcement probability (the absolute score), the strong linear relation between baseline performance and reinforced performance is preserved, but for statistical and mathematical reasons, the correlation is negative, $r = -.93$, $p < .01$.

Since the means of the subcondition baselines were not equal to these, correlations raise an important question. Might the reinforcement probabilities and reinforcement ratios that resulted when Experienced newborns were reinforced with their target story be determined simply by their baseline probabilities? That is, do the differences in the subgroups' terminal performances, as measured by reinforcement probabilities or difference scores and reinforcement ratios, reflect differential reinforcement effects or just the fact that the subgroups began with different baseline probabilities?

Figure 4 shows that the mean baseline probabilities of the two conditions where Experienced subjects were reinforced with their target story (open symbols) are well within the range of baseline probabilities entailed in the correlation. Significantly, however, the mean probabilities that occur with reinforcement by the target story are both above their baseline levels and above the 95% confidence interval of the regression line ($p < .0006$). Similarly, both reinforcement ratios are well above .50 and also above the 95% confidence interval of the regression line of Figure 5. Thus, the possibility that the reinforcement probabilities and reinforcement ratios occurring when Experienced subjects were reinforced with their target story were determined by or could be predicted by their baseline probabilities can be rejected. The favored alternative hypothesis, of course, is that prenatal experience increased the reinforcing effectiveness of their target stories: The effect of prenatal experience with the reinforcer was to increase the conditional probability of reinforced responding by 40% over the level predicted by baseline in the IBI < t condition and by 76% in the IBI > t condition. Reinforcement ratios were increased by 20% and 26% over the levels predicted by baseline performance.

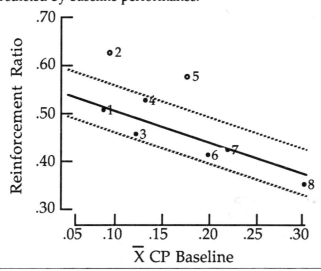

Figure 5. Reinforcement ratio as a function of baseline conditional probability for the eight subconditions described in Figure 4. This regression equation is (.57 – .63 [baseline probability]) for the control subconditions and the dashed lines represent the 95% confidence interval.

It may still be argued, however, that the preceding analysis was based on subgroup means and that the pattern of individual-subject baseline probabilities within the subgroups was biased toward producing difference scores and reinforcement ratios that supported the prenatal hypothesis. That is, if the baseline probability of each Experienced subject reinforced with the target story had been the same as the baseline of a control subject, then their reinforcement probabilities and reinforcement ratios might not differ.

The following analyses addressed this possibility by comparing selected groups of subjects after matching individual infants on baseline probabilities. Subject matching was accomplished by applying the following three rules: (1) baseline probabilities had to be within +.02 of each other; (2) if possible, the subjects were to have the same reinforcement contingency; and (3) if more than one match was possible, pairs were matched so as to minimize the difference between conditional probabilities that occurred with reinforcement. No other factors were considered.

In the first comparison, 10 of the 16 baseline probabilities produced by Experienced infants in the conditions where they were reinforced with the target story were matched to the baseline probabilities of 10 of the 16 Experienced subjects in the conditions where they were reinforced with the novel story. The 10 baseline pairs were: (.06/.06), (.06/.06), (.09/.09), (.10/.10), (.12/.12) (.14/.13), (.16/.17), (.17/.17), (.23/.24), and (.26/.26). The mean baseline probability for each group was .14. The mean probability occurring with reinforcement by the target-story (.20) was greater than that occurring with reinforcement by the novel story (.13), $t(9) = 2.61$, $p < .01$ (1-tail t test); $T = 4.5$, $p < .025$ (Wilcoxen test). The mean probability of responding with target-story reinforcement was greater than the baseline mean, $t(9) = 2.99$, $p < .005$;. $T = 3$, $p < .01$, but the mean probability of responding with novel-story reinforcement did not differ from baseline, $t(9) = .58$; $T = 22.5$. In addition, the mean occurring with target-story reinforcement was well above the 95% confidence interval of Figure 4, but the mean occurring with novel-story reinforcement was well within the interval. The reinforcement ratio of the target story was well above the 95% confidence interval of Figure 5, but the reinforcement ratio for the novel-story was within the interval.

Six infants from each reinforcement condition could not be matched. The mean of the unmatched baselines for the target-story condition was .12; the mean occurring with reinforcement was .18. For the novel-story infants these means were .22 and .17, respectively. The reinforcement mean and reinforcement ratio occurring with target-story reinforcement were above the 95% confidence intervals of Figures 4 and 5, but the analogous measures resulting from reinforcement with the novel-story were well within the confidence intervals.

Next, baselines of Experienced subjects who were reinforced with the target story were matched to baselines of Control subjects reinforced with the target story. Nine pairs could be identified: (.03/.04),

(.06/.06), (.06/.06), (.09/.08), (.10/.10). (.14/.13), (.16/.16), (.26/.26), and (.29/.31). The baseline mean of each group was .13. The mean reinforcement probability for the Experienced subjects (.19) was greater than that of Control infants (.10),1(8) = 2.58, p < .01; T = 1, p < .005. The Experienced subjects' reinforcement probabilities were larger than baseline probabilities, t(8) = 2.94, p < .005; T = 0, p < .005, but the Control subjects' were not, t(8) = 1.19, p > .10; T = 15. Here, too, the Experienced subject's mean reinforcement probability and reinforcement ratio were both well above the 95% confidence intervals of Figures 4 and 5. The reinforcement probability of the Control group was within the interval of Figure 4. Their reinforcement ratio, however, fell below the 95% confidence interval of Figure 5, even though the members of the group had exactly the same baseline probabilities as their Experienced counterparts.

Seven Experienced subjects' and three Control subjects' baselines could not be matched. The baseline means of these subjects are .13 and .40, respectively. Their respective means occurring with reinforcement by the target story were .19 and .20. The reinforcement mean and reinforcement ratio of the Experienced subjects both lay well above the 95% confidence intervals of Figures 4 and 5. Analogous scores for Control subjects were within the intervals.

Finally, Experienced subjects reinforced with the novel story were matched to Control subjects who were also reinforced with the novel story. The mean pairs of baseline probabilities were: (.06/.06), (.09/.09), (.10/.10), (.12/.12), (.13/.13), (. 19/.20), (.19/.19). (.24/.24), and (.33/.32). The mean for each group was .16. Neither the between-group difference nor the changes from baseline were statistically reliable (all t values < 1.0; all T values > 16). All reinforcement means and reinforcement ratios fell within the confidence intervals of Figures 4 and 5. Seven Experienced infants and three Control infants could not be matched. Their respective baseline means were .19 and .16, and their respective reinforcement means were .18 and .13. All reinforcement means and reinforcement ratios were within the confidence intervals of Figures 4 and 5.

After equating the baseline probability of IBIs of individual infants in specific conditions, the only consistent finding was that the target story was the more effective reinforcer for Experienced infants. In sum, the results of this study cannot be accounted for by differences in the baseline values of subconditions or individual subjects. The previous conclusion can be retained: The postnatal reinforcing value of a speech passage is increased by prenatal experience with the passage.

References

Anger, D. (1956). The dependence of interresponse times upon the relative reinforcement of different interresponse times, *Journal of Experimental Psychology, 52*, 145–161.

Bernard, J., & Sontag, L.W. (1947). Fetal reactivity to tonal stimulation: A preliminary report, *Journal of Genetic Psychology, 70*, 205–210.

Birnholz, J.C., & Benacerraf, B.R. (1983). The development of human fetal hearing. *Science, 222*, 517–519.

Brazelton, T.R. (1978). The remarkable talents of the newborn. *Birth & Family Journal 5*, 4–10.

Bricket, P.D., & Pruzansky, S. (1976). Speaker recognition. In N.J. Lass (Ed.), *Contemporary issues in experimental phonetics.* New York: Academic.

Butterfield, E.C., & Cairns, O.F. (1974). Whether infants perceive linguistically is uncertain, and if they did its practical importance would be equivocal. In R.L. Scheifelbush & L.L. Lloyd (Eds.), *Language perspectives: Acquisition, retardation, and intervention.* Baltimore, MD: University Park Press.

Butterfield, E.C., & Siperstein, G.N. (1972). Influences of contingent auditory stimulation upon nonnutritional sucking. In J. Bosma (Ed.), *Oral sensation and perception: The mouth of the infant.* Springfield. IL, Charles C. Thomas.

Cairns, G., & Butterfield, E.C. (1974). Assessing infants' auditory functioning. In B.Z. Friedlander, G.M. Sterritt, & G.C. Kirk (Eds.), *Exceptional infant*: Vol 3. New York: Brunner/Mazel.

Catania. C.C. (1970). Reinforcement schedules and psychophysical judgments: A study of some temporal properties or behavior. In W.N. Schoenfeld (Ed.), *The theory of reinforcement schedules.* New York: Appleton-Century-Crofts.

DeCasper, A.J., Butterfield, E.C., & Cairns, G.F (1976) The role of contingency relations in speech discrimination by newborns. Paper presented at the Fourth Biennial Conference on Human Development Nashville, TN.

DeCasper, A.J., & Carstens, A.A. (1981). Contingencies of stimulation: Effects on learning and emotion in neonates. *Infant Behavior and Development, 4*, 19–35.

DeCasper, A.J., & Fifer, W.P. (1980) Of human bonding: Newborns prefer their mother's voices. *Science, 208*, 1174–1176.

DeCasper, A. J., & Prescott, P.A. (1984). Human newborns' perception of male voices: Preference, discrimination and reinforcing value, *Developmental Psychobiology, 17*, 481–491.

DeCasper, A.J., & Sigafoos. A.D. (1983). The intrauterine heartbeat: A potent reinforcer for newborns. Infant Behavior and Development, *6*, 19–25.

DeCasper, A.J., & Zeiler, M.D. (1977). Time limits for completing fixed ratios: IV. Components of the ratio. *Journal of the Experimental Analysis of Behavior, 27*, 235–244.

Fifer, W.P. (1980). Early attachment: Maternal voice preferences in one- and three-day old infants. Unpublished doctoral dissertation, University of North Carolina at Greensboro.

Glass, G.V, & Stanley, J.C. (1970). *Statistical methods in education and psychology.* Englewood Cliffs, NJ: Prentice-Hall.

Gottlieb, G.G. (1981). Roles of Early Experience in species-specific perceptual development, In R.N. Aslin, J.R. Alberts, & M.R. Petersen (Eds.), *Development of perception.* New York: Academic.

Grimwade, J.C., Walker, D.W., Bartlett, M., Cordon, S., & Wood, C. (1971). Human fetal heart rate change and movement in response to sound and vibration. *American Journal of Obstetrics and Gynecology, 109*, 86–90.

Gurney, N. & Gurney, E. (1965). *The king, the mice, and the cheese.* New York: Beginner Books/Random House.

Johannsson, B., Wedenberg, E., & Westlin, B. (1964). Measurement of tone response by the human fetus: A preliminary report. *Acta Otolaryngologica, 57*, 188–192.

Malott, R.W., & Cumming, W.W. (1964). Schedules of interresponse time reinforcement. *Psychological Record, 14*, 211–252.

Panneton, R.K., & DeCasper, A.J. (1984). Newborns prefer intrauterine heartbeat sounds to male voices. Paper presented at the International Conference on Infant Studies, New York.

Querleu, D., & Renard. K. (1981). Les perceptions auditives du foetus humain. *Medicine & Hygiene, 39*, 2102–2110.

Querleu, D., Renard, K., & Crepin, G. (1981). Perception auditive et reactivite foetale aux stimulations sonores. *Journal de Gynecologie Obstetrique et Biologie de la Reproduction, 10*, 307–314.

Salk, L,. (1962). Mothers' heartbeat as an Imprinting stimulus. *Transactions of the New York Academy of Science, 24*, 753–763.

Seuss, D. (1957). *The cat in the hat.* New York: Beginner Books/Random House.

Sontag. L.W., & Wallace, R. (1935). The movement response of the human fetus to sound stimuli. *Child Development, 6*, 253–258.

Studdert-Kennedy, M. (1992). The beginnings of speech. In K. Immelmann, G.W. Barlow, Petrinovich, & M. Main (Eds.), *Behavioral development.* Cambridge: Cambridge University Press.

Vince, M.A. (1979). Postnatal effects of prenatal sound stimulation in the guinea pig. *Animal Behavior, 27*, 908–919.

Vince, M.A., Armitage, S.E., Walser, E.S., & Reader, M. (1982). Postnatal consequence of prenatal sound stimulation in the sheep. *Behavior, 81*, 128–139.

Walker, D., Grimwade, J., & Wood, C. (1971). Intrauterine noise: A component of the fetal environment. *American Journal of Obstetrics and Gynecology, 109*, 91–95.

Wolff, P.H. (1963). Observations on the early development of smiling. In B.M. Foss (Ed.), *Determinants of infant behavior* (Vol. 2). New York: Wiley.

Wolff, P.H. (1966). The causes, controls and organization of behavior in the neonate. *Psychological Issues, 5* (1, Monograph No. 1).

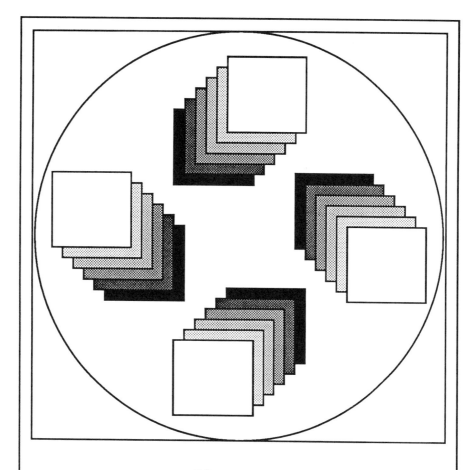

Chapter 4

Development

CHAPTER 4: DEVELOPMENT

When humans deal with pets, they often anthropomorphize the pets' activities. Humans often grant their pets human emotion and intentions; for example, they say things such as "Rover knows he shouldn't have done that on the floor—see how *guilty* he looks?". Similarly, adults often misinterpret their children's behavior, not realizing how differently from them small children or infants think and act. Old people are also often misunderstood because of biases and preconceptions. However, developmental psychologists know only too well that childhood and old age are qualitatively different from any other time of life. Thanks to our growing knowledge of the developmental process, we can make more intelligent and knowledgeable decisions about people across the entire life span. The articles selected for this chapter highlight some of the ways children and older adults differ from each other, and more specifically, how children differ from adults' stereotyped expectations of them.

4a. Harlow, F. (1958). The nature of love. *American Psychologist*, 673–682.

The bonding between parents and children may be one of the most important psychological phenomena in childhood. Prior to Harlow's work with monkeys, how did psychologists think this happened? How does Harlow account for it? Explain what relevance this may have for humans.

4b. Englund, S. (1974). Birth without violence. *The New York Times Magazine*, Dec. 8.

Otto Rank, a neo-freudian psychoanalyst, thought all human problems and fears could be traced back to the "trauma of birth." How do the concepts behind the Leboyer birth method parallel this idea? Does the selection relate any data that support the validity of Leboyer's method? (Hint—see the first article on sample selection and generalizability.) What kind of people might choose the Leboyer method?

4c. Meer, J. (1986). The reason of age. *Psychology Today, 20*, 60–64.

A recent court case tried to decide when airline pilots could be forced to retire. After reading this article, write a pro or con opinion based on research regarding this case. Then make a list of at least five jobs that should not have an age limit, five that should have a limit, and provide justification for each.

The Nature of Love

Harry F. Harlow

Love is a wondrous state, deep, tender, and rewarding. Because of its intimate and personal nature it is regarded by some as an improper topic for experimental research. But, whatever our personal feelings may be, our assigned mission as psychologists is to analyze all facets of human and animal behavior into their component variables. So far as love or affection is concerned, psychologists have failed in this mission. The little we know about love does not transcend simple observation, and the little we write about it has been written better by poets and novelists. But of greater concern is the fact that psychologists tend to give progressively less attention to a motive which pervades our entire lives. Psychologists, at least psychologists who write textbooks, not only show no interest in the origin and development of love or affection, but they seem to be unaware of its very existence.

The apparent repression of love by modern psychologists stands in sharp contrast with the attitude taken by many famous and normal people. The word "love" has the highest reference frequency of any word cited in Bartlett's book of *Familiar Quotations*. It would appear that this emotion has long had a vast interest and fascination for human beings, regardless of the attitude taken by psychologists; but the quotations cited, even by famous and normal people, have a mundane redundancy. These authors and authorities have stolen love from the child and infant and made it the exclusive property of the adolescent and adult.

Thoughtful men, and probably all women, have speculated on the nature of love. From the developmental point of view, the general plan is quite clear: The initial love responses of the human being are those made by the infant to the mother or some mother surrogate. From this intimate attachment of the child to the mother, multiple learned and generalized affectional responses are formed.

Unfortunately, beyond these simple facts we know little about the fundamental variables underlying the formation of affectional responses and little about the mechanisms through which the love of the infant for the mother develops into the multifaceted response patterns characterizing love or affection in the adult. Because of the dearth of experimentation, theories about the fundamental nature of affection have evolved at the level of observation, intuition, and discerning guesswork, whether these have been proposed by psychologists, sociologists, anthropologists, physicians, or psychoanalysts.

The position commonly held by psychologists and sociologists is quite clear: The basic motives are, for the most part, the primary drives—particularly hunger, thirst, elimination, pain, and sex—all other motives, including love or affection, are derived or secondary drives. The mother is associated with the reduction of the primary drives—particularly hunger, thirst, and pain—and through learning, affection or love is derived.

It is entirely reasonable to believe that the mother through association with food may become a secondary-reinforcing agent, but this is an inadequate mechanism to account for the persistence of the infant-maternal ties. There is a spate of researches on the formation of secondary reinforcers to hunger and thirst reduction. There can be no question that almost any external stimulus can become a secondary reinforcer if properly associated with tissue-need reduction, but the fact remains that this redundant literature demonstrates unequivocally that such derived drives suffer relatively rapid experimental extinction. Contrariwise, human affection does not extinguish when the mother ceases to have intimate association with the drives in question. Instead, the affectional ties to the mother show a lifelong, unrelenting persistence and, even more surprising, widely expanding generality.

Oddly enough, one of the few psychologists who took a position counter to modern psychological dogma was John B. Watson, who believed that love was an innate emotion elicited by cutaneous stimulation of the erogenous zones. But experimental psychologists, with their peculiar propensity to discover facts that are not true, brushed this theory aside by demonstrating that the human neonate had no differentiable emotions, and they established a fundamental psychological law that prophets are without honor in their own profession.

The psychoanalysts have concerned themselves with the problem of the nature of the development of love in the neonate and infant, using ill and aging human beings as subjects. They have discovered the overwhelming importance of the breast and related this to the oral erotic tendencies developed at an age preceding their subjects' memories. Their theories ran from a belief that the infant has an innate need to achieve and suckle at the breast to beliefs not unlike commonly accepted psychological theories. There are exceptions, as seen in the recent writings of John Bowlby, who attributes importance not only to food and thirst satisfaction, but also to "primary object-clinging," a need for intimate physical contact, which is initially associated with the mother.

As far as I know, there exists no direct experimental analysis of the relative importance of the stimulus variables determining the affectional or love responses in the neonatal and infant primate. Unfortunately, the human neonate is a limited experimental subject for such researches because of his inadequate motor capabilities. By the time the human infant's motor responses can be precisely measured, the antecedent determining conditions cannot be defined, having been lost in a jumble and jungle of confounded variables.

Many of these difficulties can be resolved by the use of the neonatal and infant macaque monkey as the subject for the analysis of basic affectional variables. It is possible to make precise measurements in this primate beginning at two to ten days of age, depending upon the maturational status of the individual animal at birth. The macaque infant differs from the human infant in that the monkey is more mature at birth and grows more rapidly; but the basic responses relating to affection, including nursing, contact, clinging, and even visual and auditory exploration, exhibit no fundamental differences in the two species. Even the development of perception, fear, frustration, and learning capability follows very similar sequences in rhesus monkeys and human children.

Three years' experimentation before we started our studies on affection gave us experience with the neonatal monkey. We had separated more than 60 of these animals from their mothers 6 to 12 hours after birth and suckled them on tiny bottles. The infant mortality was only a small fraction of what would have obtained had we let the monkey mothers raise their infants. Our bottlefed babies were healthier and heavier than monkey-mother-reared infants. We know that we are better monkey mothers than are real monkey mothers thanks to synthetic diets, vitamins, iron extracts, penicillin, chloromycetin, 5% glucose, and constant, tender, loving care.

During the course of these studies we noticed that the laboratory-raised babies showed strong attachment to the cloth pads (folded gauze diapers) which were used to cover the hardware-cloth floors of their cages. The infants clung to these pads and engaged in violent temper tantrums when the pads were removed and replaced for sanitary reasons. Such contact-need or responsiveness bad been reported previously by Gertrude van Wagenen for the monkey and by Thomas McCulloch and George Haslerud for the chimpanzee and is reminiscent of the devotion often exhibited by human infants to their pillows, blankets, and soft, cuddly stuffed toys. Responsiveness by the one-day-old infant monkey to the cloth pad is shown in Figure 1, and an unusual and strong attachment of a six-month-old infant to the cloth pad is Illustrated in Figure 2. The baby, human or monkey, if it is to survive, must clutch at more than a straw.

We had also discovered during some allied observational studies that a baby monkey raised on a bare wire-mesh cage floor survives with difficulty, if at all, during the first five days of fife. If a wire-mesh cone is introduced, the baby does better; and, if the cone is covered with terry cloth, husky, healthy, happy babies evolve. It takes more than a baby and a box to make a normal monkey. We were impressed by the possibility that, above and beyond the bubbling fountain of breast or bottle, contact comfort might be a very important variable in the development of the infant's affection for the mother.

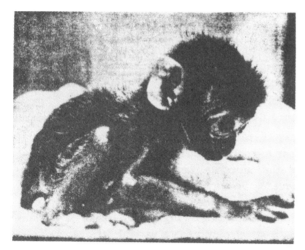

FIG. 1. Response to cloth pad by one-day-old monkey.

FIG. 3. Cloth mother surrogate.

FIG. 2. Response to gauze pad by six-month-old monkey
used in earlier study.

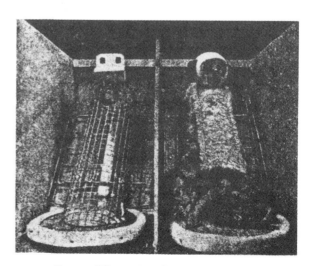

FIG. 4. Wire and cloth mother surrogates.

At this point we decided to study the development of affectional responses of neonatal and infant monkeys to an artificial, inanimate mother, and so we built a surrogate mother which we hoped and believed would be a good surrogate mother. In devising this surrogate mother we were dependent neither upon the capriciousness of evolutionary processes nor upon mutations produced by chance radioactive fallout. Instead, we designed the mother surrogate in terms of modern human-engineering principles (Figure 3). We produced a perfectly proportioned, streamlined body stripped of unnecessary bulges and appendices. Redundancy in the surrogate mother's system was avoided by reducing the number of breasts from two to one and placing this unibreast in an upper-thoracic, sagittal position, thus maximizing the natural and known perceptual-motor capabilities of the infant operator. The surrogate was made from a block of wood, covered with sponge rubber, and sheathed in tan cotton terry cloth. A light bulb behind her radiated heat. The result was a mother, soft, warm, and tender, a mother with infinite patience, a mother available twenty-four hours a day, a mother that never scolded her infant and never struck or bit her baby in anger. Furthermore, we designed a mother-machine with maximal maintenance efficiency since failure of any system or function could be resolved by the simple substitution of black boxes and new component parts. It is our opinion that we engineered a very superior monkey mother, although this position is not held universally by the monkey fathers.

Before beginning our initial experiment we also designed and constructed a second mother surrogate, a surrogate in which we deliberately built less than the maximal capability for contact comfort. This surrogate mother is illustrated in Figure 4. She is made of wire-mesh, a substance entirely adequate to provide postural support and nursing capability, and she is warmed by radiant heat. Her body differs in no essential way from that of the cloth mother surrogate other than in the quality of the contact comfort which she can supply.

In our initial experiment, the dual mother-surrogate condition, a cloth mother and a wire mother were placed in different cubicles attached to the infant's living cage as shown in Figure 4. For four newborn monkeys the cloth mother lactated and the wire mother did not; and, for the other four, this condition was reversed. In either condition the infant received all its milk through the mother surrogate as soon as it was able to maintain itself in this way, a capability achieved within two or three days except in the case of very immature infants. Supplementary feedings were given until the milk intake from the mother surrogate was adequate. Thus, the experiment was designed as a test of the relative importance of the variables of contact comfort and nursing comfort. During the first 14 days of life the monkey's cage floor was covered with a heating pad wrapped in a folded gauze diaper, and thereafter the cage floor was bare. The infants were always free to leave the heating pad or cage floor to contact either mother, and the time spent on the surrogate mothers was automatically recorded. Figure 5 shows the total time spent on the cloth and wire mothers under the two conditions of feeding. These data make it obvious that contact comfort is a variable of overwhelming importance in the development of affectional responses, whereas lactation is a variable of negligible importance. With age and opportunity to learn, subjects with the lactating wire mother showed decreasing responsiveness to her and increasing responsiveness to the nonlactating cloth mother, a finding completely contrary to any interpretation of derived drive in which the mother-form becomes conditioned to hunger-thirst reduction. The persistence of these differential responses throughout 165 consecutive days of testing is evident in Figure 6.

One control group of neonatal monkeys was raised on a single wire mother, and a second control group was raised on a single cloth mother. There were no differences between these two groups in amount of milk ingested or in weight gain. The only difference between the groups lay in the composition of the feces, the softer stools of the wire-mother infants suggesting psychosomatic involvement. The wire mother is biologically adequate but psychologically inept.

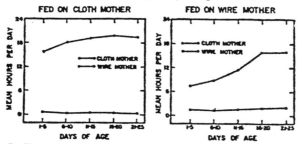

Fig. 5. Time spent on cloth and wire mother surrogates.

We were not surprised to discover that contact comfort was an important basic affectional or love variable, but we did not expect it to overshadow so completely the variable of nursing; indeed, the disparity is so great as to suggest that the primary function of nursing as an affectional variable is that of insuring frequent and intimate body contact of the infant with the mother. Certainly, man cannot live by milk alone. Love is an emotion that does not need to be bottle- or spoon-fed, and we may be sure that there is nothing to be gained by giving lip service to love.

A charming lady once heard me describe these experiments; and, when I subsequently talked to her, her face brightened with sudden insight: "Now I know what's wrong with me," she said, "I'm just a wire mother." Perhaps she was lucky. She might have been a wire wife.

We believe that contact comfort has long served the animal kingdom as a motivating agent for affectional responses. Since at the present time we have no experimental data to substantiate this position, we supply information which must be accepted, if at all, on the basis of face validity.

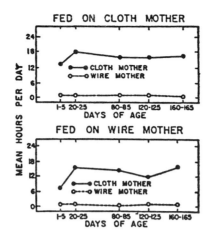

Fig. 6. Long-term contact time on cloth and wire mother surrogates.

Fig. 7. Typical fear stimulus.

One function of the real mother, human or sub-human, and presumably of a mother surrogate, is to provide a haven of safety for the infant in times of fear and danger. The frightened or ailing child clings to its mother, not its father; and this selective responsiveness in times of distress, disturbance, or danger may be used as a measure of the strength of affectional bonds. We have tested this kind of differential responsiveness by presenting to the infants in their cages, in the presence of the two mothers, various fear-producing stimuli such as the moving toy bear illustrated in Figure 7. A typical response to a fear stimulus is shown in Figure 8, and the data on differential responsiveness are presented in Figure 9. It is apparent that the cloth mother is highly preferred over the wire one, and this differential selectivity is enhanced by age and experience. In this situation, the variable of nursing appears to be of absolutely no importance: the infant consistently seeks the soft mother surrogate regardless of nursing condition.

Fig. 8. Typical response to cloth mother surrogate in fear test.

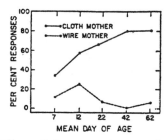

Fig. 9. Differential responsiveness in fear tests.

Similarly, the mother or mother surrogate provides its young with a source of security, and this role or function is seen with special clarity when mother and child are in a strange situation. At the present time we have completed tests for this relationship on four of our eight baby monkeys assigned to the dual mother-surrogate condition by introducing them for three minutes into the strange environment of a room measuring six feet by six feet by six feet (also called the "open-field test") and containing multiple stimuli known to elicit curiositymanipulatory responses in baby monkeys. The subjects were placed in this situation twice a week for eight weeks with no mother surrogate present during alternate sessions and the cloth mother present during the others. A cloth diaper was always available as one of the stimuli throughout all sessions. After one or two adaptation sessions, the infants always rushed to the mother surrogate when she was present and clutched her, rubbed their bodies against her, and frequently manipulated her body and face. After a few additional sessions, the infants began to use the mother surrogate as a source of security, a base of operations. As is shown in Figures 10 and 11, they would explore and manipulate a stimulus and then return to the mother before adventuring again into the strange new world. The behavior of these infants was quite different when the mother was absent from the room. Frequently they would freeze in a crouched position, as is illustrated in Figures 12 and 13. Emotionality indices such as vocalization, crouching, rocking, and sucking increased sharply, as shown in Figure 14. Total emotionality score was cut in half when the mother was present. In the absence of the mother some of the experimental monkeys would rush to the center of the room where the mother was customarily placed and then run rapidly from object to object, screaming and crying all the while. Continuous, frantic clutching of their bodies was very common, even when not in the crouching position. These monkeys frequently contacted and clutched the cloth diaper, but this action never pacified them. The same behavior occurred in the presence of the wire mother. No difference between the cloth-mother-fed and wire-mother-fed infants was demonstrated under either condition. Four control infants never raised with a mother surrogate showed the same emotionality scores when the mother was absent as the experimental infants showed in the absence of the mother, but the controls scores were slightly larger in the presence of the mother surrogate than in her absence.

Figure 10. Response to cloth mother in the open-field test.

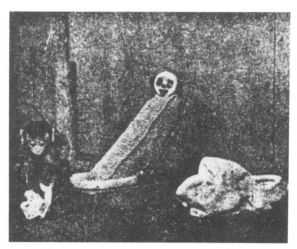

Figure 11. Object exploration in presence of cloth mother.

Some years ago Robert Butler demonstrated that mature monkeys enclosed in a dimly lighted box would open and reopen a door hour after hour for no other reward than that of looking outside the box. We now have data indicating that neonatal monkeys show this same compulsive visual curiosity on their first test day in an adaptation of the Butler apparatus which we call the "love machine," an apparatus designed to measure love. Usually these tests are begun when the monkey is 10 days of age, but this same persistent visual exploration has been obtained in a three-day-old monkey during the first half-hour of testing. Butler also demonstrated that rhesus monkeys show selectivity in rate and frequency of door-opening to stimuli of differential attractiveness in the visual field outside the box. We have utilized this principle of response selectivity by the monkey to measure strength of affectional responsiveness in our infants in the baby version of the Butler box. The test sequence involves four repetitions of a test battery in which four stimuli—cloth mother, wire mother, infant monkey, and empty box—presented for a 30-minute period on successive

Figure 12.   Response in the open-field test in the
absence of the mother surrogate.

Figure 13. Response in the open-field test in the absence of the mother surrogate.

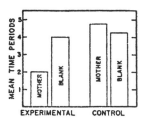

Figure 14. Emotionality index with and without the presence of the cloth mother.

Figure 15. Visual exploration apparatus.

days. The first four subjects in the dual mother-surrogate group were given a single test sequence at 40 to 50 days of age, depending upon the availability of the apparatus, and only their data are presented. The second set of four subjects is being given repetitive tests to obtain information relating to the development of visual exploration. The apparatus is iilustrated in Figure 15. The data obtained from the first four infants raised with the two mother surrogates are presented in the middle graph of Figure 16 and show approximately equal responding to the cloth mother and another infant monkey, and no greater responsiveness to the wire mother than to an empty box. Again, the results are independent of the kind of mother that lactated, cloth or wire. The same results are found for a control group raised, but not fed, on a single cloth mother these data appear in the graph on the right. Contrariwise, the graph on the left shows no differential responsiveness to cloth and wire mothers by a second control group, which was not raised on any mother surrogate. We can be certain that not all love is blind.

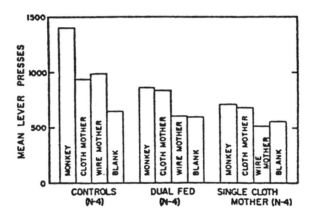

Fig. 16. Differential responses to visual exploration.

The first four infant monkeys in the dual mother-surrogate group were separated from their mothers between 165 and 170 days of age and tested for retention during the following 9 days and then at 30-day intervals for six successive months. Affectional retention as measured by the modified Butler box is given in Figure 17. In keeping with the data obtained on adult monkeys by Butler, we find a high rate of responding to any stimulus, even the empty box. But throughout the entire 185-day retention period there is a consistent and significant difference in response frequency to the cloth mother contrasted with either the wire mother or the empty box, and no consistent difference between wire mother and empty box.

Affectional retention was also tested in the open field during the first 9 days after separation and then at 30-day intervals, and each test condition was run twice at each retention interval. The infant's behavior differed from that observed during the period preceding separation. When the cloth mother was present in the post-separation period, the babies rushed to her, climbed up, clung tightly to her, and rubbed their heads and faces against her body. After this initial embrace and reunion, they played on the mother, including biting and tearing at her cloth cover; but they rarely made any attempt to leave her during the test period, nor did they manipulate or play with the objects in the room, in contrast with their behavior before maternal separation. The only exception was the occasional monkey that left the mother surrogate momentarily, grasped the folded piece of paper (one of the standard stimuli in the field), and brought it quickly back to the mother. It appeared that deprivation had enhanced the tie to the mother and rendered the contact-comfort need so prepotent that need for the mother overwhelmed the exploratory motives during the brief, three-minute test session. No change in these behaviors was observed throughout the 185-day period. When the mother was absent from the open field, the behavior of the infants was similar in the initial retention test to that during the preseparation tests; but they tended to show gradual adaptation to the open-field situation with repeated testing and, consequently, a reduction in their emotionality scores.

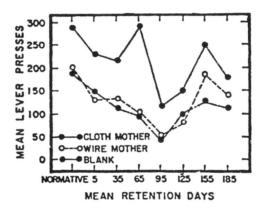

Fig. 17. Retention of differential visual-exploration responses.

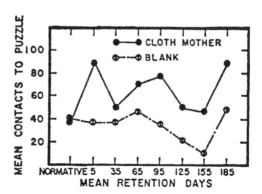

Fig. 18. Retention of puzzle manipulation responsiveness.

In the last five retention test periods, an additional test was introduced in which the surrogate mother was placed in the center of the room and covered with a clear Plexiglas box. The monkeys were initially disturbed and frustrated when their explorations and manipulations of the box failed to provide contact with the mother. However, all animals adapted to the situation rather rapidly. Soon they used the box as a place of orientation for exploratory and play behavior, made frequent contacts with the objects in the field, and very often brought these objects to the Plexiglas box. The emotionality index was slightly higher than in the condition of the available cloth mother, but it in no way approached the emotionality level displayed when the cloth mother was absent. Obviously, the infant monkeys gained emotional security by the presence of the mother even though contact was denied.

Affectional retention has also been measured by tests in which the monkey must unfasten a three-device mechanical puzzle to obtain entrance into a compartment containing the mother surrogate. All the trials are initiated by allowing the infant to go through an unlocked door, and in half the trials it finds the mother present and in half, an empty compartment. The door is then locked and a ten minute test conducted. In tests given prior to separation from the surrogate mothers, some of the infants had solved this puzzle and others had failed. The data of Figure 18 show that on the last test before separation there were no differences in the manipulation under mother-present and mother-absent conditions, but striking differences exist between the two conditions throughout the post-separation test periods. Again, there is no interaction with conditions of feeding.

The over-all picture obtained from surveying the retention data is unequivocal. There is little, if any, waning of responsiveness to the mother throughout this five-month period as indicated by any measure. It becomes perfectly obvious that this affectional bond is highly resistant to forgetting and that it can be retained for very long periods of time by relatively infrequent contact reinforcement. During the next year, retention tests will be conducted at 90-day intervals, and further plans are dependent upon the results obtained. It would appear that affectional responses may show as much resistance to extinction as has been previously demonstrated for learned fears and learned pain, and such data would be in keeping with those of common human observation.

The infant's responses to the mother surrogate in the fear tests, the open-field situation, and the baby Butler box and the responses on the retention tests cannot be described adequately with words. For supplementary information we turn to the motion picture record. (At this point a 20-minute film was presented illustrating and supplementing the behaviors described thus far in the address.)

We have already described the group of four control infants that had never lived in the presence of any mother surrogate and had demonstrated no sign of affection or security in the presence of the cloth mothers introduced in test sessions. When these infants reached the age of 250 days, cubicles containing both a cloth mother and a wire mother were attached to their cages. There was no lactation in these mothers, for the monkeys were on a solid-food diet. The initial reaction of the monkeys to the alterations was one of extreme disturbance. All the infants screamed violently and made repeated attempts to escape the cage whenever the door was opened. They kept a maximum distance from the mother surrogates and exhibited a considerable amount of rocking and crouching behavior, indicative of emotionality. Our first thought was that the critical period for the development of maternally directed affection had passed and that these macaque children were doomed to live as affectional orphans. Fortunately, these behaviors continued for only 12 to 48 hours and then gradually ebbed, changing from indifference to active contact on, and exploration of, the surrogates. The home-cage behavior of these control monkeys slowly became similar to that of the animals raised with the mother surrogates from birth. Their manipulation and play on the cloth mother became progressively more vigorous to the point of actual mutilation, particularly during the morning after the cloth mother had been given her daily change of terry covering. The control subjects were now actively running to the cloth mother when frightened and had to be coaxed from her to be taken from the cage for formal testing.

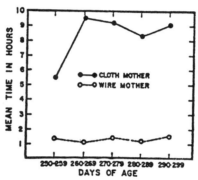

Figure 19. Differential time spent on cloth and wire mother surrogates by monkeys started at 250 days of age.

Objective evidence of these changing behaviors is given in Figure 19, which plots the amount of time these infants spent on the mother surrogates. Within 10 days mean contact time is approximately nine hours, and this measure remains relatively constant throughout the next 30 days. Consistent with the results on the subjects reared from birth with dual mothers, these late-adopted infants spent less than one and one-half hours per day in contact with the wire mothers, and this activity level was relatively constant throughout the test sessions. Although the maximum time that the control monkeys spent on the cloth mother was only about half that spent by the original dual mother-surrogate group, we cannot be sure that this discrepancy is a function of differential early experience. The control monkeys were about three months older when the mothers were attached to their cages than the experimental animals had been when their mothers were removed and the retention tests begun. Thus, we do not know what the amount of contact would be for a 250-day-old animal raised from birth with surrogate mothers. Nevertheless, the magnitude of the differences and the fact that the contact-time curves for the mothered-from-birth infants had remained constant for almost 150 days suggest that early experience with the mother is a variable of measurable importance.

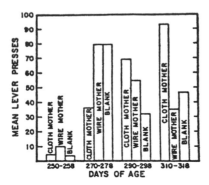

Fig. 20. Differential visual exploration of monkeys started at 250 days of age.

The control group has also been tested for differential visual exploration after the introduction of the cloth and wire mothers; these behaviors are plotted in Figure 20. By the second test session a high level of exploratory behavior had developed, and the responsiveness to the wire mother and the empty box is significantly greater than that to the cloth mother. This is probably not an artifact since there is every reason to believe that the face of the cloth mother is a fear stimulus to most monkeys that have not had extensive experience with this object during the first 40 to 60 days of life. Within the third test session a sharp change in trend occurs, and the cloth mother is then more frequently viewed than the wire mother or the blank box; this trend continues during the fourth session, producing a significant preference for the cloth mother.

Before the introduction of the mother surrogate into the home-cage situation, only one of the four control monkeys had ever contacted the cloth mother in the open-field tests. In general, the surrogate mother not only gave the infants no security, but instead appeared to serve as a fear stimulus The emotionality scores of these control subjects were slightly higher during the mother-present test sessions than during the mother-absent test sessions. These behaviors were changed radically by the fourth post-introduction test approximately 60 days later. In the absence of the cloth mothers the emotionality index in this fourth test remains near the earlier level, but the score is reduced by half when the mother is present, a result strikingly similar to that found for infants raised with the dual mother-surrogates from birth. The control infants now show increasing object exploration and play behavior, and they begin to use the mother as a base of operations, as did the infants raised from birth with the mother surrogates. However, there are still definite differences in the behavior of the two groups. The control infants do not rush directly to the mother and clutch her violently; but instead they go toward, and orient around, her, usually after an initial period during which they frequently show disturbed behavior, exploratory behavior, or both.

That the control monkeys develop affection or love for the cloth mother when she is introduced into the cage at 250 days of age cannot be questioned. There is every reason to believe, however, that this interval of delay depresses the intensity of the affectional response below that of the infant monkeys that were surrogate-mothered from birth onward. In interpreting these data it is well to remember that the control monkeys had had continuous opportunity to observe and hear other monkeys housed in adjacent cages and that they had had limited opportunity to view and contact surrogate mothers in the test situations, even though they did not exploit the opportunities.

During the last two years we have observed the behavior of two infants raised by their own mother. Love for the real mother and love for the surrogate mother appear to be very similar. The baby macaque spends many hours a day clinging to its real mother If away from the mother when frightened, it rushes to her and in her presence shows comfort and composure. As far as we can observe, the infant monkey's affection for the real mother is strong, but no stronger than that of the experimental monkey for the surrogate cloth mother, and the security that the infant gains from the presence of the real mother is no greater than the security it gains from a cloth surrogate. Next year we hope to put this problem to final, definitive, experimental test. But, whether the mother is real or a cloth surrogate, there does develop a deep and abiding bond between mother and child. In one case it may be the call of the wild and in the other the McCall of civilization, but in both cases there is "togetherness."

In spite of the importance of contact comfort, there is reason to believe that other variables of measurable importance will be discovered. Postural support may be such a variable, and it has been suggested that, when we build arms into the mother surrogate, 10 is the minimal number required to provide adequate child care. Rocking motion may be such a variable, and we are comparing rocking and stationary mother surrogates and inclined planes. The differential responsiveness to cloth mother and cloth-covered inclined plane suggests that clinging as well as contact is an affectional variable of importance. Sounds, particularly natural, maternal sounds, may operate as either unlearned or learned affectional variables. Visual responsiveness may be such a variable, and it is possible that some semblance of visual imprinting may develop in the neonatal monkey. There are indications that this becomes a variable of importance during the course of infancy through some maturational process.

John Bowlby has suggested that there is an affectional variable which he calls "primary object following," characterized by visual and oral search of the mother's face. Our surrogate-mother-raised baby monkeys are at first inattentive to her face, as are human neonates to human mother faces. But by 30 days of age ever-increasing responsiveness to the mother's face appears—whether through learning, maturation, or both—and we have reason to believe that the face becomes an object of special attention.

Our first surrogate-mother-raised baby had a mother whose head was just a ball of wood since the baby was a month early and we had not had time to design a more esthetic head and face. This baby had contact with the blank-faced mother for 180 days and was then placed with two cloth mothers, one motionless and one rocking, both being endowed with painted, ornamented faces. To our surprise the animal would compulsively rotate both faces 180 degrees so that it viewed only a round, smooth face and never the painted, ornamented face. Furthermore, it would do this as long as the patience of the experimenter in reorienting the faces persisted. The monkey showed no sign of fear or anxiety, but it showed unlimited persistence. Subsequently it improved its technique, compulsively removing the heads and rolling them into its cage as fast as they were returned. We are intrigued by this observation, and we plan to examine systematically the role of the mother face in the development of infant-monkey affections. Indeed, these observations suggest the need for a series of ethological-type researches on the two-faced female.

Although we have made no attempts thus far to study the generalization of infant-macaque affection or love, the techniques which we have developed offer promise in this uncharted field. Beyond this, there are few if any technical difficulties in studying the affection of the actual, living mother for the child, and the techniques developed can be utilized and expanded for the analysis and developmental study of father-infant and infant-infant affection.

Since we can measure neonatal and infant affectional responses to mother surrogates, and since we know they are strong and persisting, we are in a position to assess the effects of feeding and contactual schedules; consistency and inconsistency in the mother surrogates; and early, intermediate, and late maternal deprivation. Again, we have here a family of problems of fundamental interest and theoretical importance.

If the researches completed and proposed make a contribution, I shall be grateful; but I have also given full thought to possible practical applications. The socioeconomic demands of the present and the threatened socioeconomic demands of the future have led the American woman to displace, or threaten to displace, the American man in science and industry. If this process continues, the problem of proper child-rearing practices faces us with startling clarity. It is cheering in view of this trend to realize that the American male is physically endowed with all the really essential equipment to compete with the American female on equal terms in one essential activity: the rearing of infants. We now know that women in the working classes are not needed in the home because of their primary mammalian capabilities; and it is possible that in the foreseeable future neonatal nursing will not be regarded as a necessity, but as a luxury—to use Veblen's term—a form of conspicuous consumption limited perhaps to the upper classes. But whatever course history may take, it is comforting to know that we are now in contact with the nature of love.

[1] Address of the President at the sixty-sixth Annual Convention of the American Psychological Association, Washington, D. C, August 31, 1958.

The researches reported in this paper were supported by funds received by Grant No. M-722, National Institutes of Health, by a grant from the Ford Foundation and by funds received from the Graduate School of the University of Wisconsin.

Birth without Violence

Steven Englund

"I believe that birth is too important an event to be left to the obstetricians, that a newborn and his mother need a loving artist's attention, not the impersonal manipulation of a highly trained engineer." These are the words of Fredrick Leboyer, a French obstetrician who has perceived and practiced a controversial new method of child delivery that many people believe has had a profoundly beneficial effect on children he has delivered. Leboyer, 56, who graduated from the Faculte de Medecine in the Universite de Paris in 1937 as an advanced scholar and later attained the rank of *chef de clinique* with teaching privileges before he set up his private practice, has brought an estimated 1,000 children into the world by this radical technique. His critics regard it as, at best, foolish, at worst, dangerous; his followers think it may well be an important new contributing factor to good human health.

By the Leboyer method, the first moments of life are strikingly different from those of the traditional childbirth though the differences are achieved with utmost simplicity, by three particularly nontechnical innovations. First, the delivery chamber is kept shadowy and dim, as an unlit room at twilight, and silence is maintained by everyone present. In this way the baby's eyes are not blinded by the sudden onslaught of harsh surgical lights, and its ears are not suddenly violated by strident sounds. Second, when the baby is born, it is not picked up by the heels and slapped on the behind, but instead, laid softly on the mother's stomach —umbilical still unsevered—where for the next four or five minutes it is tenderly massaged. Finally, at the end of this peaceful time, the cord is cut and for another few minutes, the baby is gently bathed in a basin of warm water. And that is all. Nothing more to it. Neither during the nine months preceding delivery nor afterwards is the fetus or baby treated any differently than in standard medical procedure.

In January, Leboyer described his method and, to him, more important, the unscientific attitudes behind it, in a book called, "Birth Without Violence," which is a kind of prose poem dedicated to what he regards as the light that has come to him from India and the East. The book was a best seller in France, has been translated into a dozen languages and is due to appear in the United States in March. It reads like Dante's "Inferno," and Milton's "Paradise Regained" set side by side, a tale of horror of what Leboyer thinks most deliveries are actually like, and a poem of beauty about how they can be.

His fundamental thesis is that babies are people, not tiny nonentities, with a full complement of sensory and psychological vulnerabilities. Indeed in many ways Leboyer's book is an extended anthropomorphization of the birth trauma; a few excerpts from the *Inferno* portion:

Yes, hell exists. It is not a fairy tale. One indeed burns there. This hell is not at the end of life. It is here. At the beginning Hell is what the infant must experience before he gets to us. . . . This tragic brow, these closed eyes, eyebrows raised and knotted. This howling mouth, this head which rolls back and tries to escape. These hands which stretch out, implore, beg, then rise to the head in a gesture of calamity. These feet which kick furiously, legs which bend in to protect a tender stomach. This flesh which is but a mass of spasms, starts, and shakes. He doesn't speak, the newborn? Why his entire being shouts out, Don't touch me! Don't touch me!' . . . This is birth. This is the torture, the Calvary.

From this sort of premise, it is easy to see how Leboyer's method follows. The infant's whole psychic future may depend upon how hastily the surgeon cuts the umbilical cord. To do it too early "is an act of the greatest cruelty whose negative effect one can hardly measure." The newborn cannot with impunity leap from the state of "unity" in which he lived in the womb to the "independence" of this world. Leaving the cord intact for four or five minutes (until it stops pulsating) may require a virtual "re-education" of profit-minded obstetricians eager to run off to the next delivery, but it is the only way, says Leboyer, to permit the baby to "graduate" peacefully from prelife to life. During the bathing, "the child floats!" Leboyer says in "Birth Without Violence": *Once again immaterial. Light. And free as in the distant good old days of pregnancy when he could play, move around freely in a boundless ocean . . . . What might have remained of fear, stiffness, tension now melts away like snow in the sunshine. Everything in the baby's body which was still anxious, rigid, and blocked starts to live to dance . . . . Beyond any possible doubt, a human being is there. Who was hiding behind fear. And we realize that it was terror which had kept his eyes closed.*

To help get across his message, Leboyer has made a 21 minute black and white film, called simply "Birth." It is not a cinematographic record of a single Leboyer delivery, as it seems, but rather a work of art filmed during many deliveries. Like the book, it depends upon its artistic imagery to strike a resonant chord in the viewer, especially the female. There are no speaking parts, the "narrative" is simply occasional printed passages projected on the screen. The background music, not surprisingly, is a Japanese flute played by a Zen monk. The entire effect—the chiaroscuro images, the hypnotic music and above all the infant wreathed in smiles, or lying peacefully on his mother's stomach—is indeed impressive as art or reality, for that matter.

Virtually the entire medical Establishment, however, is distinctly not impressed. Substantively speaking, Leboyer's changes hardly constitute a major advance in obstetrics on a par with the development of the forceps by Dr. William Smellie in the seventeen-fifties or the childbirth techniques of Dick-Read in Britain and Lamaze in France. Leboyer's method hardly amounts to more than a gentle set of loving hands. And yet his unusual vocabulary and concepts, along with their implications for science and medicine, have produced a polarization of refractory, passionate and often exaggerated opinion.

His critics accuse him of everything from shamanism and mysticism to outright quackery. To some, clearly, his chief sin is against the Establishment itself, in failing to show it sufficient reverence, or at least in failing to worship properly the gods of science. To others he is guilty of more serious offenses. Prof. Claude Sureau of Paris's Hospital St. Vincent de Paul maintains that some of what Leboyer advocates is dangerous, and that what there is of value is not new. "Many infants are born calm and beautiful without Leboyer's help," he says, adding that most modem delivery rooms are kept reasonably quiet. Furthermore, infants are kept under infrared lamps to keep them warm and "Leboyer's ideas about bathing are romantic, almost old-fashioned. Lifting the baby in and out of the water became a game, and that's a bit silly."

As for the dimly lighted rooms, Sureau scoffs: "What if difficulties arise? We have to be able to see the baby's color." He also favors cutting the umbilical cord rather early: " You cannot leave it there forever. There is a risk of infection." The stroking of the baby on the mother's stomach is acceptable, says Sureau, "but it should not last long. A baby's contact with his mother cannot be eternal. It is unhealthy to want to associate children to all their mothers' activities." Lastly, the professor, "like most of my colleagues," believes " a good hearty scream" is important to hear from the baby to make certain he is breathing forcefully.

Dr. Claudine Escoffier-Lambiotte, medical columnist for Le Monde, is favorable to "any ideas which humanize or personalize medicine." But she nevertheless feels Leboyer has gone too far. "He is a mystic who believes that the outdated notion of the birth trauma is at the center of humanity's problems." The attacks from other prestigious obstetricians are numerous; *"He's absurd . . . . We have enough problems without having to invoke a lot of incantatory reveries . . . If the high number of accidents at birth in France is to be diminished, it is important to train a larger number of gynecologists and obstetricians and midwives, and I don't think that standing in a shadowy room, preparing a warm bath, and making 'maternal love' to the infant would be the proper first stage . . . . The most painful moment of birth is the period of uterine contractions—not the moment of first cry or breath . . . No obstetrician enjoys torturing the newborn but there are necessary rules of security . . . . Everyone knows that on the quality of fetal oxygenation in the first minute of life will depend the 'quality' of a future human being. At 16 years of age, it is better to have been delivered properly oxygenated and screaming than anoxic and caressed. 'Village idiots' are often smiling after all.*

There are no figures on village idiots or on how many babies were lost in Leboyer's years of practice, but it is unlikely that the man could have practiced in a major city with enormous success for many years if his method was producing dead fetuses or retarded children. Even his most unrelenting critics have not hinted that this is the case—only that it could be.

Some of Leboyer's colleagues are not above *ad hominem* reflections on the controversy. "Everyone knows he is out to make money," says one obstetrician who wishes to remain unidentified. "He is the grocer of obstetrics and well-known for it. Moreover he has published no important scientific papers." In fact Leboyer has been retired for well over a year from all clinical work; but even while he was in practice, his fees were no higher than those of any other successful obstetrician. And, in fact, since his time-consuming method permitted fewer deliveries at a time, he made rather less money than some of his assembly-line colleagues. Furthermore, as in the United States, private practitioners in France almost never pursue research or publish papers.

I asked about some of the specific points of criticism made by others in his profession. "They mock me," he says, "by pushing my method to the extremes. And they pretend that much of what I do is not new when in fact it is *very* new—just take a look at the gleaming impersonality of their delivery rooms and styles. Of course I don't work in a pitch black room. Certainly I am attentive to a baby's coloring. Of course if there is the slightest complication or emergency, I use all the resources of modern medicine. But this is all beside the point. Their *real* complaints are unspoken. They know it and I know it. At the heart of the matter is the fact that I am not simply offering another method or two, a new wrinkle or two in post-modern scientific obstetrics, but am challenging their whole world view. I am offering an alternative means of conceptualizing not just birth, but self, life, others. . . .

"If a baby is born with his umbilicus wrapped around his neck, it is obvious that we don't sing a mystical song. We cut it. If a baby's life is in danger because he has difficulty in breathing, we reanimate him immediately, of course. And we turn the lights on. And if a baby is seen to spit up heavy mucus substances, naturally we suck them out with a probe. What we do not do is to employ all these instruments as a *matter of routine* as other doctors do, just in case.' All this technical monkey business during birth represents only our own fears of being inadequate should trouble arise. This is selfish because the baby is highly sensitive in the first hours after birth to all these fears which we and our instruments and anxiety project onto him. . . . I don't go into the delivery looking for opportunities to display and use my technical wares. Other things on other planes are more important."

What about cardiac surveillance during labor? "No of course I'm not against it as such, but I disapprove of the *attitude to technology* that it represents. This is research for research's sake without a moments' concern for how the baby feels, how his mind registers. . . . What some of my colleagues have a resistance against is that my ideas have nothing to do with technique. They change nothing on *that level*. But it is precisely that level which is least interesting and least important once we are sure the baby is breathing and healthy."

Isn't it important to get the baby breathing strongly at once? "It is important, and I agree that his first hearty cry is also vital. What we are trying to avoid is that he should carry on crying and screaming at length. That means the baby is suffering. Nobody wants to admit this simple fact. It is too humiliating to admit something so simple."

What's the purpose of the bathing? Leboyer looked very moved as he answered: "Bathing is so simple and yet it makes *such a difference*. I hope people are going to accept the idea soon. It is not just a question of getting the child used to the idea of changing from the liquid environment of the womb which he knew as a fetus, but also of getting rid of those tensions in the spinal cord which are responsible for so many later deformities in our bodies, like teeth that stick out or ears, though admittedly these are relatively minor."

Odile Herdner, an anesthetist who used to work with Dr. Leboyer during many of his deliveries, also addressed herself to the criticisms. "All I can say is that everything is interesting and nothing is categorical. Before the baby is presented, everything is done in the normal way with the latest equipment, and that often includes surveillance. You can add fantasies and play the games afterwards, even sing mystical songs. It's a matter of choice and can be very interesting and helpful under certain circumstances. It's really a matter of personal choice. If problems arise, we switch on the lights and act as any team would in an emergency."

Mlle. Herdner is clearly a believer, but she says, "Mothers should not necessarily be encouraged to ask for a 'Leboyer method' delivery. Of course it can be a good thing, but it is highly personal and every mother is a special case. If she reads his book or sees his film and feels, 'This is for me,' then she should look into it. Some deliveries run quiet smoothly and calmly without using Leboyer's method, while other babies have been seen to scream during one of his deliveries. I can only repeat that *everything is interesting with Leboyer and nothing is categorical.*"

In the world of Leboyer mothers, opinions run just about as strongly and uniformly as in the medical Establishment, only in the opposite direction. Here he is revered as elsewhere he is reviled. Marie-France Han, 33, a sales manager for a French film company, met him at a dinner party in 1971. She shared his interest in things Oriental (she is married to a Chinese), and she found his ideas on childbirth congenial. When, a short time later, she became pregnant with her first child, "it seemed natural to put myself in his hands."

"During the months of pregnancy, Dr. Leboyer treated me no differently from the way my friends were treated by their obstetricians. I enrolled in a class of natural birth techniques, and Dr. Leboyer did advise me that if I chose to, it might be a good idea to study yoga. I ageed and did so. But this was definitely not a 'must.' " Her delivery, said Mme. Han, was "just like the film version. And in fact seeing the film made me want to do it over again."

"I lay in the delivery room quite conscious and aware. The room was dim, but it was dawn and you could see the sun coming through the window. The atmosphere Dr. Leboyer created was quiet and meditative, like a church. Things were serious but joyous. I felt as though a ritual were going to take place. The doctor was marvelously helpful during labor, but at the moment of birth he became just as interested in my baby as in me. When I cried out in happiness and excitement, he quickly calmed me because it is not good for the newborn to hear loud noises. I must be serene and quiet to welcome my baby, he told me.

"Then he put my daughter on my stomach for as long as the umbilical cord continued to function. He massaged the baby and he let me help with my own hands. During the whole time Dr. Leboyer was singing a soft , repetitive Indian melody of some kind. Gradually I could feel my baby relax under his soothing massage and became calmer. She cried only a little bit. Then he gave her a long bath in warm water. The delivery was one of the most important, happiest moments in my life. I'll be so sad if I can't go back to Dr. Leboyer when I'm pregnant again someday."

Marie-France Han's daughter is now nearly two years old. Her mother, a strong believer in the significance of the birth trauma, believes much of the infant's "sweetness of disposition" is due to Leboyer's handling at her birth. She and her husband are very impatient with the "raking over" which the obstetrician has received from his peers. "I won't claim that all children who are born via this method will grow up perfectly," says Mme. Han, "but I guarantee Leboyer's way is as safe and secure as any other, and far more beautiful. I found his book beautiful but totally unscientific. It's a poem on birth and his colleagues just aren't poets, I guess."

Another "Leboyer mother" was a working woman of humble origins whose first childbirth six years ago was so traumatic for her as well as the baby that she resolved never again to have another child. When she became pregnant a second time, it took weeks for her friends to persuade her not to have an abortion. Without knowing Leboyer beforehand, she ageed reluctancy to be delivered by him. The results were a replica of Mme. Han's experience, even to the extent of "wishing I could have more children delivered by Dr. Leboyer." Rather more significant is the fact that she and her husband as well as all their friends and a clinical psychologist have remarked on the "dramatic difference" between their two children: the elder one is tense and insecure, moody and often hard to get along with; the younger is gay, open and easily satisfied.

A clinical child psychologist, Dr. Danielle Rapoport, who teaches at the Sorbonne, has undertaken a follow-up study of a sampling of 50 Leboyer-delivered babies ranging in age from 8 months to 4 years. Though several years away from completing her report, Dr. Rapoport was willing to share some of her tentative discoveries and conclusions. "There is no question in my mind, these children *are* noticeably different from others who were delivered in the 'classical' way," was how she summarized her finding.

"The children I have studied have been spared nearly all of the major and minor psychopathologies—of eating, sleeping, maternal relations, etc.—of infancy. They show a markedly greater precocity of interest in the world and in people. They use their intelligence in more positive and socially adaptive ways than other babies do." She gave the older children in her sampling a French version of the Gesell Baby Test which measures "adaptivity" and they scored significantly higher than average.

Rather neutral in the Leboyer controversy, Danielle Rapoport feels that "Leboyer's problem is that he tries to antagonize his colleagues and makes himself disliked by taking stands and using language which are incomprehensible, if not inimical, to the medical world." Escoffier-Lambiotte, Sureau and others are fighting battles for fundamental improvements and humanization of medicine, notes Rapoport, and Leboyer's mystical vocabulary—his (to them) archaic and "unscientific" attachment to Freudian notions like the birth trauma—strike them as ridiculous and obscurantist. On the other hand, says the clinical psychologist, many obstetricians are simply "threatened by Leboyer's disavowal of the accepted goals and style of medicine" and react "in a childish and malicious way."

Leboyer himself thinks he has been "excommunicated" but not disproved. He lives in simplicity now in Montmartre, having sold his luxurious 16th Arrondissement house, is writing a book in collaboration with a swami, about Indian music and is thinking of moving to India. Despite his protestations, it is clear that he has been hurt by the campaign against him. "I tried to transform births into nativities," he said as he showed a guest prints of El Greco, Rembrandt, Raphael and La Tour nativities. "See how the light shines from the Infant Christ's face?" he asks. "There is no reason why that cannot happen for all babies. But first we must stop treating them as mere squalling digestive tracts."

There is something profoundly dissatisfying to the Anglo-Saxon mind about a story of a controversy, especially a *medical* controversy, where there is finally no right or wrong, just different views and levels and styles of explanation. Many of us still believe unquestioningly in the ethos of science and technology, and in their empirical testability. For these people, Leboyer is retrograde. Others may have come to doubt the omniscience of medicine and science and to search beyond for intuitive, psychological or spiritual truths. For them, Leboyer may speak a healing, helping word.

Ultimately perhaps Mlle. Herdner, Leboyer's assistant, was probably correct when she said that the doctor's "method," is right for some, but not for all, mothers. But right for whom? Only the would-be mystics among them? Several of the women interviewed for this article are not the "spiritual type," do not know the first thing about Oriental philosophy or religion, and in general tend to accept what Leboyer would call "the scientific myths" of our time. And yet these same women were profoundly impressed by the doctor-artist's manner and methods, and would happily go back to him a second time if they could.

Certainly it would be unnerving for a prospective mother to read the unanimously and often mockingly critical reactions of Leboyer's colleagues. But the problem is the men who make them do not themselves subscribe to the basic *sine qua non* behind "Birth Without Violence": the existence and significance of the birth trauma and the belief that a newborn baby is *mentally* a human being. If you do not accept this, then Leboyer's ideas are so much superfluous mumbo-jumbo. If you do, then you don't have to be an Orientalist or a mystic to support or make use of his methods.

In sum, a prospective mother is well-advised to read extensively about Leboyer's method before requesting it. In any case, there will be little chance of her getting her request because her obstetrician is not likely to realign his views and change his practice—unless the poetry, the concepts, philosophy and, in small though intriguing degree, the results of "Birth Without Violence" persuade him or others to carry on where Frederick Leboyer left off.

The Reason of Age

WE LOSE SOME MENTAL SPEED
WITH THE YEARS, BUT WE CAN OFTEN
SUBSTITUTE EXPERIENCE FOR QUICKNESS.

By Jeff Meer

The golden years are making a comeback. As researchers spend less time looking at what we lose as we get older and more at what we keep or gain, aging is looking better.

Consider Andres Segovia, still giving acclaimed concerts on the classical guitar at age 92 . . . Claude Pepper, who came in with the 20th century and has served in Congress for most of the past 50 years . . . Bob Hope, entertaining and golfing his way around the world 82 years after his birth in Eltham, England.

But aren't these people exceptions? Of course they are. Men and women with unusual abilities are always exceptions, whatever their age. Ability and activity vary among people in their 70s, 80s and 90s just as they do earlier in life.

Evidence is piling up that most of our mental skills remain intact as long as our health does, if we keep mentally and physically active. Much of our fate is in our own hands, with "use it or lose it" as the guiding principle. We are likely to slow down in some ways, but there is evidence that healthy older people do a number of things better than young people.

Psychologist James Birren, dean of the Andrus Gerontological Center at the University of Southern California, is one of many researchers who show that older people perform tasks more slowly, from cutting with a knife and dialing a telephone to remembering lists. There are numerous theories about what body changes are responsible but no conclusive answers.

More important, slowing down doesn't make much difference in most of what we do. Slower reflexes are certainly a disadvantage in driving an automobile, but for many activities speed is not important. And when it is, there are often ways to compensate that maintain performance at essentially the same level. "An awful lot of what we can measure slows down," says psychologist Timothy Salthouse of the University of Missouri at Columbia, "but it isn't clear that this actually affects the lives of the people we study in any significant way."

As an example, Salthouse cites an experiment in which he tested the reaction time and typing skills of typists of all ages. He found that while the reactions of the older typists were generally slower than those of younger ones, they are just as fast. It could be that the older typists were even faster at one time and had slowed down. But the results of a second test lead Salthouse to believe that another factor was at work.

When he limited the number of characters that the typists could look ahead, the older typists slowed greatly, while the younger ones were affected much less. "There may be limits, but I'm convinced that the older typists have learned to look farther ahead in order to type as quickly as the younger typists," Salthouse says.

A similar substitution of experience for speed may explain how older people maintain their skills in many types of problem-solving and other mental activity. Because of this, many researchers have come to realize that measuring one area of performance in the laboratory can give only a rough idea of a person's ability in the real world.

As an example, psychologist Neil Charness of the University of Waterloo in Ontario gave bridge and chess problems to players of all ages and ability levels. When he asked the bridge players to bid and the chess players to choose a move or remember board positions, the older players took longer and could remember fewer of the chess positions. But the bids and the moves they chose were every bit as good as those of younger players. "I'm not sure exactly what the compensatory mechanisms are," Charness says, "but at least until the age of 60, the special processes that the older players use enable them to make up for what they have lost in terms of speed and memory ability."

Many researchers now believe that one reason we associate decline with age is that we have asked the wrong questions. "I suspect that the lower performance of older people on many of the tasks we have been testing stems from the fact that they have found that these things are unimportant, whereas young people might enjoy this kind of test because it is novel," says psychologist Warner K. Schaie of Pennsylvania State University. Relying on their experience and perspective, he says, older people "can selectively ignore a good many things."

Memory is probably the most thoroughly studied area in the relationship between age and mental abilities. Elderly men and women do complain more that they can't remember their friends' names, and they seem to lose things more readily than young people. In his book *Enjoy Old Age*, B.F. Skinner mentions trying to do something that one learned to do as a child—folding a piece of paper to make a hat, for example—and not remembering how. Such a failure can be especially poignant for an older person.

But the fact is that much of memory ability doesn't decline at all. "As we get older, old age gets blamed for problems that may have existed all along," says psychologist Ilene Siegler of the Duke University Medical Center. "A 35-year-old who forgets his hat is forgetful," she says, "but if the same thing happens to grandpa we start wondering if his mind is going." If an older person starts forgetting things, it's not a sure sign of senility or of Alzheimer's disease. The cause might be incorrect medication, simple depression or other physical or mental problems that can be helped with proper therapy.

Psychologists divide memory into three areas, primary, secondary and tertiary. Primary or immediate memory is the kind we use to remember a telephone number between the time we look it up and when we dial it. "There is really little or no noticeable decline in immediate memory," according to David Arenberg, chief of the cognition section at the Gerontology Research Center at the National Institute on Aging. Older people may remember this type of material more slowly, but they remember it as completely as do younger people.

Secondary memory, which, for example, is involved in learning and remembering lists, is usually less reliable as we get older, especially if there is a delay between the learning and the recall. In experiments Arenberg has done, for example, older people have a difficult time remembering a list of items if they are given another task to do in between.

Even with secondary memory, however, where decline with age is common, the precise results depend on exactly how memory is tested. Psychologist Gisela Labouvie-Vief of Wayne State University in Detroit has found that older people excel at recalling the metaphoric meaning of a passage. She asked people in their early 20s and those in their 70s to remember phases such as "the seasons are the costumes of nature." College students try to remember the text as precisely as they can. Older people seem to remember the meaning through metaphor. As a result, she says, "they are more likely to preserve the actual meaning, even if their reproduced sentence doesn't exactly match the original." In most situations, understanding the real meaning of what you hear or read is more important than remembering the exact words.

Part of the problem with tests of memory is that most match older people against students. "As long as we accept students as the ideal, older people will look bad," Labouvie-Vief says. Students need to memorize every day, whereas most older people haven't had to cram for an exam in years. As an example of this, psychologist Patricia Siple and colleagues at Wayne State University found that older people don't memorize as well as young students do. But when they are matched against young people who are not students, they memorize nearly as well.

The third kind of memory, long-term remembrance of familiar things, normally decreases little or not at all with age. Older people do particularly well if quickness isn't a criterion. Given time and the right circumstances they may do even better than younger men and women. When psychologist Roy Lachman of the University of Houston and attorney Janet Lachman tested the ability to remember movies, sports information and current events, older people did much better, probably because of their greater store of information. Since they have more tertiary memory to scan, the Lachmans conclude, older people scan that kind of memory more efficiently.

Psychologist John Horn of the University of Denver and other researchers believe that crystallized knowledge such as vocabulary increases throughout life. Horn, who has studied the mental abilities of hundreds of people for more than 20 years, says, "If I were to put together a research team, I'd certainly want some young people who might recall material more quickly, but I'd also want some older crystallized thinkers for balance."

Researchers often echo the "use it or lose it" idea. When psychologist Nancy Denney of the University of Wisconsin-Madison uses the game "20 questions" in experiments, she finds that the needed skills are not lost. "The older people start off by asking inefficient questions," she says, "but we know that the abilities are still there because once they see the efficient strategy being used by others, they learn it very quickly."

Psychologist Liz Zelinski of the University of Southern California makes a similar point when she tests the ability to read and understand brief passages. People in their 70s and 80s show no significant decline in comprehension. "Our tests don't involve the kind of questions that require older people to store information temporarily in memory," she cautions. "Tests like that might show declines." Zelinski has also found that older men and women read her tests just as fast as younger people do. "It is a good guess that they maintain the ability to read quickly because they do it all the time," she says.

Even when skills atrophy through disuse, many people can be trained to regain them. Schaie and psychologist Sherry Willis of Pennsylvania State University recently reported on a long-term study with 4,000 people, most of whom were older. Using individualized training, the researchers improved spatial orientation and deductive reasoning for two-thirds of those they studied. Nearly 40 percent of those whose abilities had declined returned to a level they had attained 14 years earlier.

Mnemonics is another strategy that can help people memorize something as simple as a shopping list. Arenberg has found that older people are much better at remembering a 16-item list if they first think of 16 locations in their home or apartment and then link each item with a location. With practice, they master this technique very easily, Arenberg says, "and become very effective memorizers."

When it comes to aging's effect on general intelligence, as measured by standard IQ tests, the same questions of appropriateness, accuracy and motivation complicate the findings. Psychologist Paul Costa, chief of the laboratory of personality and cognition of the Gerontology Research Center at the National Institute on Aging in Baltimore, points out that many early studies on aging tested older people and younger people at the same time, instead of testing the same people over a period of years. These studies were, in effect, measuring the abilities of older people, largely lower-income immigrants, against the generations of their children and grandchildren. "The younger people enjoyed a more comfortable life-style, were better educated and didn't face the same kind of life stresses," he says, "so comparisons were mostly inappropriate."

Most researchers today are uncomfortable with the idea of using standard intelligence tests for older people. "How appropriate is it to measure the scholastic aptitude of a 70-year old?" asks University of Michigan psychologist Marion Perlmutter.

She and others, including Robert Sternberg at Yale, believe that aspects of adult functioning, such as social or professional competence and the ability to deal with one's environment ought to be measured along with traditional measures of intelligence. "We are really in the beginning stages of developing adequate measures of adult intelligence and in revising what we think of as adult intelligence," Perlmutter says. "If we had more comprehensive tests including these and other factors, I suspect that older people would score at least as well and probably better than younger people."

Erroneous ideas about automatic mental deterioration with age hit particularly hard in the workplace. Although most jobs require skills unaffected by age, many employers simply assume that older workers should be phased out. Psychologists David Waldman and Bruce Alvolio of the State University of New York at Binghamton recently reviewed 13 studies of job performance and found little support for deterioration of job performance with increasing age. Job performance, measured objectively, increased as employees, especially professionals, grew older. The researchers also discovered, however, that if supervisors' meetings were used as the standard, performance seemed to decline slightly with age. Expectation became reality.

Despite all the experiments and all the talk about gains and losses with age, we should remember that many older people don't want to be compared, analyzed or retrained, and they don't care about being as fast or as nimble at problem solving as they once were. "Perhaps we need to redefine our understanding of what older people can and cannot do," Perlmutter says. Just as children need to lose some of their spontaneity to become more mature, perhaps "some of what we see as decline in older people may be necessary for their growth." While this does not mean that all age-related declines lead to growth or can be ignored, it does highlight a bias in our youth-oriented culture. Why do we so often think of speed as an asset and completely ignore the importance of patient consideration?

Special Cases: The Oldest

One group of particular interest to researchers on aging is those more than 85 years old. There are at least two million Americans in this category, more than 1 percent of the population, and growing faster than any other segment.

Depending upon whom you talk to, this group is called the old old, the oldest old or the extreme aged. More than half live independently, by themselves or with a spouse. And many do more than just live. History and current headlines tell us of extraordinary individuals who have done important work in their ninth decade (see "The Art of Aging," *Psychology Today*, January 1984). Mystery writer Agatha Christie, statesman Konrad Adenauer and cellist Pablo Casals are only three well-known examples.

Other less famous but equally industrious men and women of similar advanced age contribute in their own fields. During the 1950s, gerontologist S.L. Pressey studied the lives of 313 people more than 80 years old whose names he found in newspaper clippings, nursing home records and other random sources. He learned that most were working at least part-time. Two men past the age of 90 were presidents of small-town banks and one nonagenarian woman ran an insurance business. If people are given the opportunity to continue making contributions,

Pressey concluded—especially if they work in professional fields or are self-employed—they are likely to do so.

Psychologist Marion Perlmutter has begun to study a group of 80-year-olds to see what keeps them going and what we can learn from them to help others. The first interviews suggest that the abilities to be open to new situations and cope with challenges distinguish people who grow during adulthood from people who stabilize or decline. "One reason to study these people is because they're successes. If you make it to 80, you must be doing something right."

Jeff Meer, 26, is an assistant editor at *Psychology Today,* whose grandparents are the wisest people he knows.

Chapter 5

Learning

CHAPTER 5: LEARNING

For the first fifty or sixty years of this century, American psychologists have believed that an organism's ability to learn is the central and most powerful psychological phenomenon. Psychologists, such as Thorndike and Skinner, thought that if *all* the principles of learning could be discovered, then they could explain *all* behavior. Psychologists were so convinced of the preeminence of learning processes that they thought it was the same among all animals, including humans (see Harlow's article in chapter 4). Indeed, without a clear understanding of how all behavior changes with experience, accurate predictions of behavior could not be made. On the other hand, some behaviors—such as attachment in babies—are so important to the organism's survival that they might be either innate or learned very quickly. In short, learning *is* a powerful and pervasive phenomenon in psychology, but not every behavior in every species can be explained by a few learning mechanisms. The articles selected for this chapter highlight both the limitations of learning and its power.

5a. Breland, K., & Breland, M. (1961). The misbehavior of organisms. *American Psychologist, 16,* 682–684.

Many psychologists realize that to gain a fuller understanding of behavior, a broad range of animals must be studied. Obviously, horses can't fly without wings but might they be trained to retrieve objects? Can you teach animals almost any trick they have the physical capacity to perform? Back up your answer with facts from this article. Based on reading it, how would you house train a puppy?

5b. Poulos, C., Hinson, R., & Siegel, S. (1981). The role of Pavlovian processes in drug tolerance and dependence. *Addictive Behaviors, 6,* 205–211.

Many people consider alcoholics and others with chemical dependencies to be weak because their dependencies are so difficult to break. After reading this article, suggest some guidelines that doctors should consider when putting together a treatment program. Use information from the article to support and document your guidelines.

The Misbehavior of Organisms

Keller Breland and Marian Breland

There seems to be a continuing realization by psychologists that perhaps the white rat cannot reveal everything there is to know about behavior. Among the voices raised on this topic, Beach (1950) has emphasized the necessity of widening the range of species subjected to experimental techniques and conditions. However, psychologists as a whole do not seem to be heeding these admonitions, as Whalen (1961) has pointed out.

Perhaps this reluctance is due in part to some dark precognition of what they might find in such investigations, for the ethologists Lorenz (1950, p. 233) and Tinbergen (1951, p. 6) have warned that if psychologists are to understand and predict the behavior of organisms, it is essential that they become thoroughly familiar with the instinctive behavior patterns of each new species they essay to study. Of course, the Watsonian or neobehavioristically oriented experimenter is apt to consider "instinct" an ugly word. He tends to class it with Hebb's (1960) other "seditious notions" which were discarded in the behavioristic revolution, and he may have some premonition that he will encounter this bete noir in extending the range of species and situations studied.

We can assure him that his apprehensions are well grounded. In our attempt to extend a behavioristically oriented approach to the engineering control of animal behavior by operant conditioning techniques, we have fought a running battle with the seditious notion of instinct.[1] It might be of some interest to the psychologist to know how the battle is going and to learn something about the nature of the adversary he is likely to meet if and when he tackles new species in new learning situations.

Our first report (Breland & Breland, 1951) in the *American Psychologist*, concerning our experiences in controlling animal behavior, was wholly affirmative and optimistic, saying in essence that the principles derived from the laboratory could be applied to the extensive control of behavior under nonlaboratory conditions throughout a considerable segment of the phylogenetic scale.

When we began this work, it was our aim to see if the science would work beyond the laboratory, to determine if animal psychology could stand on its own feet as an engineering discipline. These aims have been realized. We have controlled a wide range of animal behavior and have made use of the great popular appeal of animals to make it an economically feasible project. Conditioned behavior has been exhibited at various municipal zoos and museums of natural history and has been used for department store displays, for fair and trade convention exhibits, for entertainment at tourist attractions, on television shows,

---

[1] In view of the fact that instinctive behaviors may be common to many zoological species, we consider species specific to be a sanitized misnomer, and prefer the possibly spent adjective "instinctive."

and in the production of television commercials. Thirty-eight species, totaling over 6,000 individual animals, have been conditioned, and we have dared to tackle such unlikely subjects as reindeer, cockatoos, raccoons, porpoises, and whales.

Emboldened by this consistent reinforcement, we have ventured further and further from the security of the Skinner box. However, in this cavalier extrapolation, we have run afoul of a persistent pattern of discomfiting failures. These failures, although disconcertingly frequent and seemingly diverse, fall into a very interesting pattern. They all represent breakdowns of conditioned operant behavior. From a great number of such experiences, we have selected, more or less at random, the following examples.

The first instance of our discomfiture might be entitled, What Makes Sammy Dance? In the exhibit in which this occurred, the casual observer sees a grown bantam chicken emerge from a retaining compartment when the door automatically opens. The chicken walks over about 3 feet, pulls a rubber loop on a small box which starts a repeated auditory stimulus pattern (a four-note tune). The chicken then steps up onto an 18-inch, slightly raised disc, thereby closing a timer switch, and scratches vigorously, round and round, over the disc for 15 seconds, at the rate of about two scratches per second until the automatic feeder fires in the retaining compartment. The chicken goes into the compartment to eat, thereby automatically shutting the door. The popular interpretation of this behavior pattern is that the chicken has turned on the "juke box" and "dances."

The development of this behavioral exhibit was wholly unplanned. In the attempt to create quite another type of demonstration which required a chicken simply to stand on a platform for 12–15 seconds, we found that over 50% developed a very strong and pronounced scratch pattern, which tended to increase in persistence as the time interval was lengthened. (Another 25% or so developed other behaviors—pecking at spots, etc.) However, we were able to change our plans so as to make use of the scratch pattern, and the result was the "dancing chicken" exhibit described above.

In this exhibit the only real contingency for reinforcement is that the chicken must depress the platform for 15 seconds. In the course of a performing day (about 3 hours for each chicken) a chicken may turn out over 10,000 unnecessary, virtually identical responses. Operant behaviorists would probably have little hesitancy in labeling this an example of Skinnerian "superstition" (Skinner, 1948) or "mediating" behavior, and we list it first to whet their explanatory appetite.

However, a second instance involving a raccoon does not fit so neatly into this paradigm. The response concerned the manipulation of money by the raccoon (who has "hands" rather similar to those of the primates). The contingency for reinforcement was picking up the coins and depositing them in a 5-inch metal box.

Raccoons condition readily, have good appetites, and this one was quite tame and an eager subject. We anticipated no trouble. Conditioning him to pick-up the first coin was simple. We started out by reinforcing him for picking up a single coin. Then the metal container was introduced, with the requirement that he drop the coin into the container. Here we ran into the first bit of difficulty: he seemed to have a great deal of trouble letting go of the coin. He would rub it up against the inside of the container, pull it back out, and clutch it firmly for several seconds. However, he would finally turn it loose and receive his food reinforcement. Then the final contingency: we put him on a ratio of 2, requiring that he pick up both coins and put them in the container.

Now the raccoon really had problems (and so did we). Not only could he not let go of the coins, but he spent seconds, even minutes, rubbing them together (in a most miserly fashion), and dipping them into the container. He carried on this behavior to such an extent that the practical application we had in mind—a display featuring a raccoon putting money in a piggy bank—simply was not feasible. The rubbing behavior became worse and worse as time went on, in spite of nonreinforcement.

For the third instance, we return to the gallinaceous birds. The observer sees a hopper full of oval plastic capsules which contain small toys, charms, and the like. When the S_D (a light) is presented to the chicken, she pulls a rubber loop which releases one of these capsules onto a slide, about 16 inches long, inclined at about 30 degrees. The capsule rolls down the slide and comes to rest near the end. Here one or two sharp, straight pecks by the chicken will knock it forward off the slide and out to the observer, and the chicken is then reinforced by an automatic feeder. This is all very well—most chickens are able to master these contingencies in short order. The loop pulling presents no problems; she then has only to peck the capsule off the slide to get her reinforcement.

However, a good 20% of all chickens tried on this set of contingencies fail to make the grade. After they have pecked a few capsules off the slide, they begin to grab at the capsules and drag them backwards into the cage. Here they pound them up and down on the floor of the cage. Of course, this results in no reinforcement for the chicken, and yet some chickens will pull in over half of all the capsules presented to them.

Almost always this problem behavior does not appear until after the capsules begin to move down the slide. Conditioning is begun with stationary capsules placed by the experimenter. When the pecking behavior becomes strong enough, so that the chicken is knocking them off the slide and getting reinforced consistently, the loop pulling is conditioned to the light. The capsules then come rolling down the slide to the chicken. Here most chickens, who before did not have this tendency, will start grabbing and shaking.

The fourth incident also concerns a chicken. Here the observer sees a chicken in a cage about 4 feet long which is placed alongside a miniature baseball field. The reason for the cage is the interesting part. At one end of the cage is an automatic electric feed hopper. At the other is an opening, through which the chicken can reach and pull a loop on a bat. If she pulls the loop hard enough the bat (solenoid operated) will swing, knocking a small baseball up the playing field. If it gets past the miniature toy players on the field and hits the back fence, the chicken is automatically reinforced with food at the other end of the cage. If it does not go far enough, or hits one of the players, she tries again. This results in behavior on an irregular ratio. When the feeder sounds, she then runs down the length of the cage and eats.

Our problems began when we tried to remove the cage for photography. Chickens that had been well conditioned in this behavior became wildly excited when the ball started to move. They would jump up on the playing field, chase the ball all over the field, even knock it off on the floor and chase it around, pecking it in every direction, although they had never had access to the ball before. This behavior was so persistent and so disruptive, in spite of the fact that it was never reinforced, that we had to reinstate the cage.

The last instance we shall relate in detail is one of the most annoying and baffling for a good behaviorist. Here a pig was conditioned to pick up large wooden coins and deposit them in a large "piggy bank." The coins were placed several feet from the bank and the pig required to carry them to the bank and deposit them, usually four or five coins for one reinforcement. (Of course, we started out with one coin, near the bank.)

Pigs condition very rapidly, they have no trouble taking ratios, they have ravenous appetites (naturally), and in many ways are among the most tractable animals we have worked with. However, this particular problem behavior developed in pig after pig, usually after a period of weeks or months, getting worse every day. At first the pig would eagerly pick up one dollar, carry it to the bank, run back, get another, carry it rapidly and neatly, and so on, until the ratio was complete. Thereafter, over a period of weeks the behavior would become slower and slower. He might run over eagerly for each dollar, but on the way back, instead of carrying the dollar and depositing it simply and cleanly, he would repeatedly drop it, root it, drop it again, root it along the way, pick it up, toss it up in the air, drop it, root it some more, and so on.

We thought this behavior might simply be the dilly-dallying of an animal on a low drive. However, the behavior persisted and gained in strength in spite of a severely increased drive—he finally went through the ratios so slowly that he did not get enough to eat in the course of a day. Finally it would take the pig about 10 minutes to transport four coins a distance of about 6 feet. This problem behavior developed repeatedly in successive pigs.

There have also been other instances: hamsters that stopped working in a glass case after four or five reinforcements, porpoises and whales that swallow their manipulanda (balls and inner tubes), cats that will not leave the area of the feeder, rabbits that will not go to the feeder, the great difficulty in many species of conditioning vocalization with food reinforcement, problems in conditioning a kick in a cow, the failure to get appreciably increased effort out of the ungulates with increased drive, and so on. These we shall not dwell on in detail, nor shall we discuss how they might be overcome.

These egregious failures came as a rather considerable shock to us, for there was nothing in our background in behaviorism to prepare us for such gross inabilities to predict and control the behavior of animals with which we had been working, for years.

The examples listed we feel represent a clear and utter failure of conditioning theory. They are far from what one would normally expect on the basis of the theory alone. Furthermore, they are definite, observable; the diagnosis of theory failure does not depend on subtle statistical interpretations or on semantic legerdemain—the animal simply does not do what he has been conditioned to do.

It seems perfectly clear that, with the possible exception of the dancing chicken, which could conceivably, as we have said, be explained in terms of Skinner's superstition paradigm, the other instances do not fit the behavioristic way of thinking. Here we have animals, after having been conditioned to a specific learned response, gradually drifting into behaviors that are entirely different from those which were conditioned. Moreover, it can easily be seen that these particular behaviors to which the animals drift are clear-cut examples of instinctive behaviors having to do with the natural food getting behaviors of the particular species.

The dancing chicken is exhibiting the gallinaceous birds' scratch pattern that in nature often precedes ingestion. The chicken that hammers capsules is obviously exhibiting instinctive behavior having to do with breaking open of seed pods or the killing of insects, grubs, etc. The raccoon is demonstrating so-called "washing behavior." The rubbing and washing response may result, for example, in the removal of the exoskeleton of a crayfish. The pig is rooting or shaking-behaviors which are strongly built into this species and are connected with the food getting repertoire.

These patterns to which the animals drift require greater physical output and therefore are a violation of the so-called "law of least effort." And most damaging of all, they stretch out the time required for reinforcement when nothing in the experimental setup requires them to do so. They have only to do the little tidbit of behavior to which they were conditioned—for example, pick up the coin and put it in the container—to get reinforced immediately. Instead, they drag the process out for a matter of minutes when there is nothing in the contingency which forces them to do this. Moreover, increasing the drive merely intensifies this effect.

It seems obvious that these animals are trapped by strong instinctive behaviors, and clearly we have here a demonstration of the prepotency of such behavior patterns over those which have been conditioned.

We have termed this phenomenon "instinctive drift." The general principle seems to be that wherever an animal has strong instinctive behaviors in the area of the conditioned response, after continued running the organism will drift toward the instinctive behavior to the detriment of the conditioned behavior and even to the delay or preclusion of the reinforcement. In a very boiled-down, simplified form, it might be stated as "learned behavior drifts toward instinctive behavior."

All this, of course, is not to disparage the use of conditioning techniques, but is intended as a demonstration that there are definite weaknesses in the philosophy underlying these techniques. The pointing out of such weaknesses should make possible a worthwhile revision in behavior theory.

The notion of instinct has now become one of our basic concepts in an effort to make sense of the welter of observations which confront us. When behaviorism tossed out instinct, it is our feeling that some of its power of prediction and control were lost with it. From the foregoing examples, it appears that although it was easy to banish the Instinctivists from the science during the Behavioristic Revolution, it was not possible to banish instinct so easily.

And if, as Hebb suggests, it is advisable to reconsider those things that behaviorism explicitly threw out, perhaps it might likewise be advisable to examine what they tacitly brought in—the hidden assumptions which led most disastrously to these breakdowns in the theory.

Three of the most important of these tacit assumptions seem to us to be: that the animal comes to the laboratory as a virtual *tabula rasa*, that species differences are insignificant, and that all responses are about equally conditionable to all stimuli.

It is obvious, we feel, from the foregoing account, that these assumptions are no longer tenable. After 14 years of continuous conditioning and observation of thousands of animals, it is our reluctant conclusion that the behavior of any species cannot be adequately understood, predicted, or controlled without knowledge of its instinctive patterns, evolutionary history, and ecological niche.

In spite of our early successes with the application of behavioristically oriented conditioning theory, we readily admit now that ethological facts and attitudes in recent years have done more to advance our practical control of animal behavior than recent reports from American "learning labs."

Moreover, as we have recently discovered, if one begins with evolution and instinct as the basic format for the science, a very illuminating viewpoint can be developed which leads naturally to a drastically revised and simplified conceptual framework of startling explanatory power (to be reported elsewhere).

It is hoped that this playback on the theory will be behavioral technology's partial repayment to the academic science whose impeccable empiricism we have used so extensively.

References

Beach, F. A. The snark was a boojum. *Amer. Psychologist*, 1950, *5*, 115–124.

Breland, K., & Breland, M. A field of applied animal psychology. *Amer. Psychologist*, 1951, *6*, 202–204.

Hebb, D. O. The American revolution. *Amer. Psychologist*, 1960, *15*, 735–74S.

Lorenz, K. Innate behavior patterns. In *Symposia of the Society for Experimental Biology*. No. 4. Physiological mechanisms in animal behavior. New York: Academic Press, 1950.

Skinner, B. F. Superstition in the pigeon. *J. Exp. Psychol*, 1948, *38*, 168–172.

Tinbergen, N. *The study of instinct*. Oxford: Clarendon, 1951.

Whalen, R.E. Comparative psychology. *Amer. Psychologist*, 1961, *16*, 84.

The Role of Pavlovian Processes in Drug Tolerance and Dependence

Constantine X. Poulos, Riley E. Hinson, and Shepard Siegel

ABSTRACT

Evidence for the crucial role of Pavlovian conditional compensatory responses in tolerance to opiates and alcohol is presented. Furthermore, an analysis of the motivational role of Pavlovian conditional compensatory responses to craving and relapse is discussed, and supportive experimental and epidemiological evidence are presented. Given the role ascribed to Pavlovian processes in tolerance, craving, and relapse, it is proposed that extinction of cues which elicit conditional compensatory responses is an essential factor for treatment. Additionally, it is suggested that by virtue of prior Pavlovian conditioning, stress and depression may serve as cues to elicit conditional compensatory responses and attendant craving and these cues can also be extinguished by Pavlovian procedures. Finally, it is suggested that explication of this conditioning analysis to the patient may itself be an important cognitive adjunct to treatment.

An accumulated body of research (cf. Siegel, 1979) demonstrates that tolerance is not the inevitable consequence of repeated drug stimulation. Rather, the manifestation of tolerance is modulated by the associative history of the situational cues coincident with drug administration. Results of other experiments, and epidemiological studies, indicate that evidence of withdrawal distress is also related to the occurrence of situational stimuli previously associated with drug administration (e.g., Ludwig, Cain, Wikler, Taylor, & Bendfeldt, 1977; Robins, Helzer, & Davis, 1975).

The contribution of stimuli previously related to drug administration on drug effects has been analyzed using principles of Pavlovian conditioning (Siegel, 1975; Wikler, 1973). This analysis is based on the suggestion by Pavlov (1927) that the administration of a drug constitutes a conditioning trial, where the conditional stimulus (CS) consists of the administration procedures and rituals accompanying drug administration, and the unconditional stimulus (UCS) consists of the actual pharmacological stimulation. According to the conditioning analysis, it should be possible to observe drug-based conditional responses (CRs) by presenting the usual drug administration ritual in the absence of the drug. The results of a number of such studies have demonstrated CRs which are opposite in direction to the acute effects of the drug. For example, animals with a history of morphine injections, with its analgesic effect, evidence a conditional hyperalgesic reaction during placebo testing (Siegel, 1975; Krank, Hinson, & Siegel, in press) and animals which have repeatedly experienced alcohol-induced hypothermia, evidence a conditional hyperthermic reaction when administered saline where they have previously received alcohol (Crowell, Hinson, & Siegel, 1981; Lê, Poulos, & Cappell, 1979). Many other examples of such drug-compensatory CRs have been described (see Obál, 1966; Siegel, 1979; Wikler, 1973).

Drug-compensatory CRs and drug tolerance

Drug CRs, elicited by the usual predrug cues in anticipation of drug stimulation, would be expected to interact with the actual drug effect. When the drug CR is opposite in direction to the effect of the drug, the net result of this interaction should be an attenuation of the drug effect. With repeated administration of the drug in conjunction with the same situational stimuli, the drug-opposite CRs would be expected to grow stronger, thereby more completely attenuating the drug effect. Such a decreased response to a drug over the course of repeated administrations defines tolerance.

On the basis of the conditioning analysis of tolerance, environmental stimuli previously associated with the systemic effects of the drug should be crucial for the display of tolerance. Such stimuli enable the organism to make adaptive drug-compensatory CRs in anticipation of the effects of the drug. In accordance with this conditioning model, many experiments indicate that tolerance to effects of morphine is maximally displayed only in the context of cues previously paired with the drug (see review by Siegel, 1979). Indeed, it has been found that rats, while demonstrably tolerant in an environment previously associated with morphine, will evidence nontolerant behavior when morphine is administered in an environment not previously associated with the drug (Siegel, 1976). Similar findings have also been reported with respect to alcohol tolerance (Crowell et al., 1981 ; Lê et al., 1979; Mansfield & Cunningham, 1980).

Additional evidence for the role of conditioning factors in drug effects comes from studies which have shown that Pavlovian procedures known to affect conditioning similarly affect tolerance. For example, partial reinforcement and preconditioning exposure to the CS retard Pavlovian conditioning. In line with the conditioning model, the development of morphine tolerance is similarly retarded by both these procedures (Siegel, 1978, 1979).

A procedure of particular interest in regard to treatment implications is extinction which is known to decrement established conditional responses. If tolerance is attributable (at least in part) to a drug-based conditional response, it should be extinguishable. In other words, repeated presentation of predrug conditional stimuli, without the drug, should diminish the tolerant response. As expected on the basis of the conditioning model, tolerance to effects of alcohol and morphine are subject to extinction. Indeed, in some of these experiments, placebo administrations eliminated tolerance. That is, the extinguished animal responded to the drug with the completely nontolerant response seen in the drug-naive animal (e.g., Cappell & Poulos, 1978; Crowell et al., 1981; Siegel, 1975).

A compensatory conditioning analysis of craving and dependence

Withdrawal distress and craving. It has been suggested that the drug-compensatory CRs which partially mediate tolerance also partially mediate withdrawal distress and relapse. Just as the display of drug tolerance may depend upon the occurrence of drug-associated environmental stimuli, so too may the display of many of the symptoms of drug dependence depend upon the presence of such predrug cues (cf. Hinson & Siegel, 1980). This conditioning analysis is consistent with the observation of a high correlation commonly noted between tolerance and dependence (Goldstein, Aranow, & Kalman, 1974, p. 510; Kalant, 1973, p. 5), and the observation that many withdrawal symptoms are characterized as opposite to the acute effects of the drug (Barry, 1977; Marx, 1976; Kalant, 1973).

According to the conditioning theory of tolerance, conditional compensatory responses serve to adaptively attenuate the pharmacological assault when the drug is delivered. Consider the situation in which the anticipated drug is not delivered; that is, no drug is available, but the individual is in an environment where he or she has frequently used a drug, or it is the time of day when the drug is typically administered, or it is the usual number of hours since the last drug administration, or any of a variety of other drug associated stimuli occur. In such circumstances, the drug-compensatory CRs elicited by these environmental cues, which are unaltered by any drug effects, may constitute an aspect of so-called withdrawal symptoms. According to this analysis, for such instances a better term than withdrawal symptoms may be "preparation symptoms." That is, the individual is displaying responses that would tend to cancel the pharmacologically-induced homeostatic imbalance usually experienced in these circumstances. However, since the pharmacological stimulation is absent, the result of the preparatory responding is a homeostatic imbalance of a different sort, which may be generally characterized as responses opposite to those induced by the drug. Such drug preparatory responding may be an important aspect of craving. Ludwig and Wikler (1974) have similarly suggested that craving represents "the psychological or cognitive correlate of a 'subclinical conditioned withdrawal syndrome' " (p. 114).

Drug-related affective states and craving. There are a number of terms which can be used in describing the positive affective attributes of drug; with alcohol, for example, terms such as "euphoria" and "happy"come quickly to mind. Whether tolerance occurs to these properties of drugs is as yet an unresolved empirical question (Cappell & LeBlanc, in press). However, if tolerance does occur to the affective properties of drugs and is governed by compensatory conditioning processes, then in the absence of the drug, predrug cues should elicit negative affective states which are opposite to the positive ones produced by the drug. The conditional elicitation of such negative affective states would operate to increase the incentive value or craving for the drug. The increase in incentive value of a drug which would result from the conditional elicitation of a negative affective state may be likened to the increase in incentive value of a "warm" sweater in the context of being cold. The notion that drug-related negative affective states may be an important motivational component in drug taking is familiar from the work of Solomon and Corbit (1974). The conditioning analysis of the possible contribution of such negative affective states to drug use makes the important suggestion that such affective states may be conditioned to reliable predrug cues, and that the conditional elicitation of such negative affective states may directly increase the disposition to consume a drug.

Evidence for conditioning factors in craving and dependence

The preceding formulations provide possible mechanisms by which conditional drug compensatory responses produce an increased disposition to administer a drug. We cannot at present be more conclusive as to exactly how conditional compensatory responses lead to craving. Nevertheless, the important assumption for the conditioning analysis is that the elicitation of compensatory responses and disposition to consume the drug are causally related. Empirically, evidence for the above would come from demonstrations of common operational specifications in that experimental determinants of compensatory responses will also lead to increased desire for a drug.

There is a considerable amount of data indicating that this is the case for both alcohol and opiates. One way to determine if environmental stimuli associated with drug administration are effective in eliciting symptoms of withdrawal and craving is simply to ask former addicts. Several investigators have done just this. Ludwig and Stark (1974) reported that about 56% of a sample of 60 alcoholic patients reported that their craving for alcohol increased when they were in places where alcohol was likely to be found. Matthew, Claghorn and Largen (1979) found that 48% of a group of 46 abstinent alcoholics reported that external events related to alcohol drinking elicited craving. On the basis of these, and other data, these authors concluded that "craving, to a large extent, is a conditioned response to environmental cues" (p. 606). O'Brien (1976) and Teasdale (1973) have reported similar results indicating that environmental stimuli, which subjects have previously experienced in conjunction with heroin self-administration, are capable of eliciting both subjective reports of craving and some observable withdrawal symptoms.

A clearly reliable signal for the central effects of alcohol is the taste of the alcoholic beverage. On the basis of the conditioning model, then, it is not surprising that a potent elicitor of craving in alcoholics is the taste of alcohol. Ludwig and Stark (1974) reported that approximately 93% of their sample of 60 alcoholic patients reported craving increased after sampling alcoholic beverages. According to the conditioning analysis of the role of the taste-cue in craving, there should be less of an effect of ingested alcohol on craving if the taste of alcohol is masked than if it is unaltered. In agreement with this expectation, Merry (1966) found that a priming dose of vodka was ineffective in eliciting craving when the taste of the alcohol was disguised.

Further evidence that withdrawal distress and craving are controlled by drug administration cues is provided by studies which have experimentally manipulated the degree to which stimuli presented to addicts have been associated with drug effects. Teasdale (1973) showed opiate addicts slides depicting drug-related material (e.g., scenes of a syringe beside a vein) or illustrating nondrug-related material (e.g., a bottle of milk). On the basis of a variety of measures, he concluded that drug-related slides induced more emotional responding and evidence of withdrawal distress than nondrug-related slides. Similarly, Sideroff and Jarvik (1980) showed heroin addicts videotapes of activities associated with heroin use (e.g., injecting the drug) or of activities not typically associated with heroin use. The addicts who viewed heroin-related activities responded with changes in heart rate and respiration similar to those seen during withdrawal. Furthermore, addicts viewing heroin related videotapes were observed to yawn, sniff, and generally appear fatigued at the end of the experiment. Sideroff and Jarvik (1980) concluded that the conditioned responses demonstrated in this report are similar to those associated with withdrawal (p. 535).

The tendency for environmental signals of alcohol to elicit craving has been demonstrated in an experiment by Ludwig et al. (1977). Alcoholic patients rated their craving and were given the opportunity to obtain small amounts of alcohol in one of two environments. One environment was a "drinking" environment, i.e., a mock barroom interior (see Ludwig et al., 1977, for details). The second environment was a "nondrinking" environment, i.e., a general experimental laboratory room. Subjects who were "heavy drinkers" rated their craving for alcohol higher and pressed an alcohol-delivery button more frequently in the drinking environment than in the "nondrinking" one. Ludwig, Wikler, and Stark (1974) have reported similar results showing that in detoxified alcoholics, alcohol-related cues elicit withdrawal sickness, subjective reports of craving, and tendency towards relapse more than nonalcohol-related cues. Results of an investigation of differences in drinking behavior in a barroom compared to a laboratory setting (Strickler, Dobbs, & Maxwell, 1979) also indicate that alcohol-associated stimuli influence craving and alcohol acquisitive behavior.

In summary, observations and results from laboratory and naturalistic studies indicate that environmental stimuli, previously associated with drug receipt, are capable of eliciting reports of craving, drug-directed behavior, and, in some cases, physiological and behavioral symptoms of withdrawal.

The nature of stimuli which may serve as CSs for drugs

The conditioning analysis emphasizes the importance of stimuli which signal drug effects in influencing the organism's response, both when the drug is administered and when the drug is not received. The research summarized so far in this paper in support of this suggestion has identified predrug cues as involving physical stimuli associated with drugs. (e.g., the accoutrements of the barroom, syringes, taste of alcohol, etc.), and in fact, much research demonstrates that such stimuli are elicitors of withdrawal discomfort and craving. However, much research indicates that other events, such as emotional states, also serve as potent elicitors of withdrawal and craving. Ludwig and Stark (1974) reported that over 75% of their sample of patients experienced craving for alcohol when "depressed," "nervous" or "under stress." Similarly, Matthew et al. (1979) found that about 85% of their group of patients reported that "nonalcohol events of an unpleasant nature" precipitated craving. In short, emotional states such as stress and depression, can elicit withdrawal and craving. While one can plausibly relate the psychodynamics of stress and depression to drug use, the conditioning analysis can parsimoniously analyze the situation in terms of an associative process. If stress has been reliably associated with abusive drinking for a particular individual, then stress can function as a conditional stimulus for the elicitation of compensatory responses and craving. The important point of this analysis is the indication that many different types of exteroceptive and interoceptive cues (e.g., emotional states, physical objects) may serve as CSs for drug effects, and that such events may subsequently influence drug use by eliciting conditional drug-compensatory responses and craving.

A role of drug-associated stimuli in relapse

One aim of treatment programs is the prevention of the resumption of excessive drug use. Typically, following a period of detoxification, patients will no longer display withdrawal distress and no longer report craving. Following such subjective reports (and objective evidence) of cure, when patients are released and return to environments where they previously used drugs, they display withdrawal distress, report craving, and relapse.

Given the evidence of cure which typically precedes completion of a treatment program, why might former addicts relapse? One factor contributing to relapse may be that the capacity of drug-associated stimuli to elicit craving and withdrawal distress has not been reduced during treatment. Research reported in the previous sections demonstrates that environmental stimuli associated with drug use can elicit craving and withdrawal long after the termination of drug use. Hence, relapse may occur in part because former addicts experience drug-compensatory CRs when they are confronted with drug-associated stimuli upon return to their drug-taking environment.

According to the conditioning analysis, readdiction should occur more rapidly in the context of stimuli previously associated with drug consumption than in the context of stimuli not previously occurring during drug receipt. The findings of an animal experiment by Thompson and Ostlund (1965) provides direct evidence for this. Initially rats were orally addicted to a morphine solution, and, following this they underwent a period of abstinence in which water replaced the morphine. Finally, morphine was reintroduced, either in the original addiction environment or in a nondrug environment. The results showed that rats initiated consumption more rapidly and consumed larger quantities of the morphine solution in the context of the original addiction environment than in the nondrug environment. Analogous results have been obtained in another animal experiment by Weeks and Collins (1968).

The importance of environmental cues in relapse is indicated by epidemiological data. These data suggest that the prognosis for successful and lasting drug abstinence is much better if substantial environmental changes occur subsequent to detoxification (see Reynolds & Randall, 1957, p. 141). For example, the very low relapse rate of United States veterans addicted to heroin while in Vietnam, compared to a civilian addict population, has been well-documented by Robins and her colleagues (e.g., Robins et al., 1975); the military addicts, in contrast to the civilian addicts, were returned to an environment very different from that associated with drug use. Similarly, Saunders and Kershaw (1979) recently reported that the vast majority of successfully remitted alcoholics made substantial environmental changes in conjunction with treatment (e.g., marriage and/or job change).

The likelihood of relapse should, according to the conditioning analysis, be reduced if drug-associated stimuli are prevented from eliciting craving and withdrawal distress. It should be possible to reduce craving and withdrawal distress by repeated presentation of the usual drug cues with no drug or, with less than the usual amount of the drug. A study by Blakey and Baker (1980) is to the point. These investigators first analyzed the drinking history of six male alcoholics in terms of the antecedent events or stimuli which "triggered" bouts of drinking. Although these antecedent stimuli varied for the different patients, they generally involved stimuli normally coincident with alcohol consumption (i.e., smell of drink, travelling home by a particular pub, being in a pub, being with male friends, etc). Treatment consisted of systematic exposure to these stimuli without allowing drinking, and patients were asked to rate their desire to drink during this treatment. Five of the six patients maintained abstinence and reported progressively diminished desire to drink over the course of successive cue exposure. Similar results have been reported in a single-case study by Hodgson and Rankin (1976) demonstrating that the desire to drink and withdrawal discomfort elicited by a single drink of alcohol (40 ml of 65.5% vodka) can be extinguished.

Overview of treatment implications

We have suggested that conditional compensatory responses provide an important motivational component in drug use, and by extension, in drug relapse. The primary implication of a conditioning model is that treatment programs must incorporate procedures which lead to the extinction of cues associated with drug use. A client may well report little desire for a drug in an insular treatment environment, not because he is cured, but rather because there are few relevant cues to activate drug craving. When, however, the client is returned to his pretreatment environment which contains strong drug-associated cues, drug-compensatory CRs and craving would be manifest.

In the previously described animal literature, the extinction of drug-induced conditional compensatory responses was simple and almost mechanical: Following repeated drug exposure in a distinctive environment, the animal is merely repeatedly reexposed to the same distinctive environment and the drug withheld for extinction of the conditional responses. We will hasten to point out that this use of a parallel extinction procedure with a highly cognitive organism who has a long history of drug use about which we have no direct knowledge will be far from simple or mechanical. It follows that a situational analysis of the individual patient's previous drinking history is necessary for the development of an appropriate extinction program (see Blakey & Baker, 1980).

Social contexts in which alcohol is easily available would generally be a common example where frequent drinking previously occurred. Hence the extinction of such alcohol-related social situations would presumably be important for the typical patient.

As indicated previously, stress and depression are often powerful determinants of craving and relapse (Ludwig & Stark, 1974; Mathew et al., 1979). With little effort we can document drinking histories where specific factors such as job or affiliational problems produced stress and depression which reliably led to alcohol abuse. We have already indicated how stress, depression, etc. may act to elicit craving and drug use from the conditioning point of view. The extinction of stress as a conditional cue for drug effects should occur just as the extinction of a distinctive environment for drug effects occurs. This would seem to be an area in which current inpatient treatment programs may be particularly lacking since many of the patients' usual stress situations are precluded.

When controlled drinking is the treatment goal, many patients report that they wish to maintain social drinking albeit within a specified boundary. From a conditioning view, a history of "noncontrolled" drinking can be analyzed in terms of the initial drinks serving as potent conditional cues for the subsequent binge. From conditioning principles, the conditional cue aspect of initial drinks can be extinguished (see Hodgson & Rankin, 1976).

Finally, the explication of this conditioning analysis to the patient may itself be an important factor for effective treatment programs. First, it permits the patient to use extinction procedures for himself and also provides a coherent conceptual framework for the patient to alert himself to particularly vulnerable situations. Finally, it provides a cognitive framework for the patient to experience craving as a temporary and reversible effect rather than as a symptom of a "weak" will or an irreversible "disease."

References

Blakey, R., & Baker, R. An exposure approach to alcohol abuse. *Behavior Research and Therapy*, 1980, *18*, 319–325.

Cappell, H., & LeBlanc, A.E. Tolerance and physical dependence: Do they play a role in alcohol and drug self-administration? In Y. Israel, F. Glaser, H. Kalant, R.E. Popham, W. Schmidt, & R.G. Smart (Eds.), *Research advances in alcohol and drug problems* (Vol. 6). New York: Plenum Press, in press.

Cappell, H., & Poulos, C.X. *Associative factors in tolerance to morphine: Dose-response determination.* Paper presented at Annual Meeting of American Psychological Association, Toronto, Canada, 1978.

Crowell, C.R., Hinson, R.E., & Siegel, S. The role of conditional drug responses in tolerance to the hypothermic effects of ethanol. *Psychopharmacology*, 1981, *73*, 51–54.

Goldstein, A., Aranow, L., & Kalman, S.M. *Principles of drug action: The basics of pharmacology* (2nd ed.). New York: Wiley, 1974.

Hinson, R.E., & Siegel, S. The contribution of Pavlovian conditioning to ethanol tolerance and dependence. In H. Rigter & J.C. Crabbe (Eds.), *The behavioral pharmacology of alcohol tolerance, dependence, and addiction: A research handbook.* Elsevier/North Holland Biomedical Press, 1980.

Hodgson, R.J., & Rankin, H.J. Modification of excessive drinking by cue exposure. *Behavior Research and Therapy*, 1976, *14*, 305–307.

Kalant, H. Biological models of alcohol tolerance and physical dependence. In M.M. Gross (Ed.). *Alcohol intoxication and withdrawal: Experimental studies.* New York: Plenum Press, 1973.

Krank, M.D., Hinson, P., & Siegel, S. Conditional hyperalgesia is elicited by environmental signals of morphine. Behavioral and Neural Biology, in press.

Lê, A.D., Poulos, C.X., & Cappell, H. Conditioned tolerance to the hypothermic effect of ethyl alcohol. *Science*, 1979, *206*, 1109–1110.

Ludwig, A.M., Cain, R.B., Wikler, A., Taylor, R.M., & Bendfeldt, F. Physiological and situational determinants of drinking behavior. In M.M. Gross (Ed.), *Alcohol intoxication and withdrawal (Vol. IIIb): Studies in alcohol dependence.* New York: Plenum Press, 1977.

Ludwig, A.M., & Stark, L.H. Alcohol craving: Subjective and situational aspects. *Quarterly Journal of Studies on Alcohol*, 1974, *35*, 899–905.

Ludwig, A.M. & Wikler, A. Craving and relapse to drink. *Quarterly Journal of Studies on Alcohol*, 1974, *35*, 108–130.

Ludwig, A.M., Wikler, A., & Stark, L.H. The first drink: Psychobiological aspects of craving. *Archives of General Psychiatry*, 1974, *30*, 539–547.

Mansfield, J.E., & Cunningham, C.L. Conditioning and extinction of tolerance to the hypothermic effect of ethanol in rats. *Journal of Comparative and Physiological Psychology*, 1980, *94*, 962–969.

Mathew, R.J., Claghorn, J.L., & Largen, J. Craving for alcohol in sober alcoholics. *American Journal of Psychiatry*, 1979, *136*, 603–606.

Merry, J. The "loss of control" myth. *Lancet*, 1966, *1*, 1257–1258.

Obál, F. The fundamentals of the central nervous control of vegetative homeostasis. *Acta Physiology Academy of Science, Hungary*, 1966, *30*, 15–29.

O'Brien, C.P. Experimental analysis of conditioning factors in human narcotic addiction. *Pharmacological Reviews*, 1976, *27*, 533–543.

Pavlov, I. P. *Conditioned reflexes* (G.V. Anrep. Trans.). London: Oxford, 1927.

Reynolds, A. K., & Randall, L.O. *Morphine and allied drugs*. Toronto: University of Toronto Press, 1957.

Robins, L.N., Helzer, J. E., & Davis, P.H. Narcotic use in Southeast Asia and afterwards. *Archives of General Psychiatry*, 1975, *32*, 955–961.

Saunders, W.M., & Kershaw, P.W. Spontaneous remission from alcoholism—A community study. *British Journal of Addiction*, 1979, *74*, 251–265.

Sideroff, S.I., & Jarvik, M.E. Conditioned responses to a videotape showing heroin related stimuli. *International Journal of the Addictions*, 1980, *15*, 529–536.

Siegel, S. Evidence from rats that morphine tolerance is a learned response. *Journal of Comparative Physiological Psychology*, 1975, *89*, 498–506.

Siegel, S. Morphine analgesic tolerance: Its situation specificity supports a Pavlovian conditioning model. *Science*, 1976, *193*, 323–325.

Siegel, S. A Pavlovian conditioning analysis of morphine tolerance. In N.A. Krasnegor (Ed.), *Behavioral tolerance: Research and treatment implication* (NIDA Monograph No. 18, U.S. Department of Health, Education and Welfare Publication No. ADM 78-551). Washington: U.S. Government Printing Office, 1978, 27–53.

Siegel, S. The role of conditioning in drug tolerance and addiction. In J.D. Keehn (Ed.), *Psychopathology in animals: Research and treatment implications*. New York: Academic Press, 1979.

Solomon, R.L., & Corbit, J.D. An opponent-process theory of motivation. *Psychological Reviews*, 1974, *81*, 119–145.

Strickler, D.P., Dobbs, S.D., & Maxwell, W.A. The influence of setting on drinking behaviors. The laboratory vs the barroom. *Addictive Behaviors*, 1979, *4*, 339–344.

Teasdale, J.D. Conditioned abstinence in narcotic addicts. *International Journal of Addictions*, 1973, *8*, 273–292.

Thompson, T., & Ostlund, W., Jr. Susceptibility to readdiction as a function of the addiction and withdrawal environments. *Journal of Comparative and Physiological Psychology*, 1965, *60*, 388–392.

Weeks, J.R., & Collins, R.J. Patterns of intravenous self-injection by morphine-addicted rats. In A.H. Wikler (Ed.), *The addictive states*. Baltimore: Williams and Wilkins, 1968.

Wikler, A. Conditioning of successive adaptive responses to the initial effects of the drug. *Conditioned Reflex*, 1973, *8*, 193–210.

Chapter 6

Motivation and Emotion

CHAPTER 6: MOTIVATION AND EMOTION

One of the first scientific subjects of behavioral research concerned the various mechanisms involved in emotional expression. In the late nineteenth century, Darwin applied his new evolutionary theory to behavioral similarities across animals and humans. He noticed some striking behavioral analogies between angry cats, dogs, and humans. For example, all of them bare their teeth and threaten with open mouths. Of course, our knowledge of how emotions affect behavior has advanced significantly since then. We now know that we still have remnants of our ancestors' aggression, and that many aspects of memory are influenced by our current emotional state. One theorist who attempted to summarize our various levels of emotions and desires was Maslow. The articles presented in this chapter are a cross-section of research in this fascinating area.

6a. Leonard, G. (1983). Abraham Maslow and the new self. *Esquire*, Dec.

This selection discusses Maslow's theories within the context of his life and personal development. After reading it, summarize Maslow's need hierarchy and present examples from your own life where a more basic need conflicted with a higher one. According to Maslow, why did this happen? What resolution occurred? How were your needs met?

6b. Pines, M. (1985). Aggression: The violence within. *Science Digest*, July.

The Pines selection deals with important physiological and social questions about aggression. What, according to Pines, is the primary causal factor of aggression? Imagine that you are on a jury dealing with a manslaughter case in which someone died due to the nonpremeditated aggression of the defendant. Based on reading this article, what factors would you consider important in mitigating the defendant's responsibility for the crime. Then, explain your answer in terms of Pines's theory of aggression.

6c. Bower, G. (1981). Mood and memory. *Psychology Today*, June 1981.

This selection discusses the interrelationship between emotion and memory. To what extent do emotions affect our ability to remember? Back up your answer with research from the article, and make recommendations regarding memory and emotion to students studying for exams.

Abraham Maslow and the New Self

by George Leonard

To him, man was not a mass of neuroses but a wealth of potential

Humanistic Psychology

He wrote with none of the dark grandeur of a Freud or the learned grace of an Erik Erikson or the elegant precision of a B.F. Skinner. He was not a brilliant speaker; in his early years he was so shy he could hardly bring himself to mount the podium. He traveled little; Brooklyn was his home for nearly half his life. The branch of psychology he founded has not achieved a dominant position in the colleges and universities. He died in 1970, but a full scale biography remains to be written.

And yet, Abraham Maslow has done more to change our view of human nature and human possibilities than has any other American psychologist of the past fifty years. His influence, both direct and indirect, continues to grow, especially in the fields of health, education, and management theory, and in the personal and social lives of millions of Americans.

Maslow confronts us with paradoxes. He started out as a behaviorist, a skilled experimenter, and then went on to demonstrate the crippling limitations of just that kind of psychology in the study of human affairs. He coauthored a textbook on abnormal psychology, a classic in its field, and then went on to investigate, not the pathological, but the exceptionally healthy person. Considering himself a Freudian, he went on to take Freudian psychology out of the basement of warring drives and inevitable frustration, up into the spacious previously unexplored upper stories of the human personality, where entirely different, non-Freudian rules seemed to prevail.

Working ten to twelve hours a day in the shadow of a heart condition that was to kill him at sixty-two, Maslow produced a rich and varied body of work, one that has altered our way of thinking about human needs and motivations, neurosis and health, experience and values. Some of his theories are still controversial, especially in their particulars, but no one can deny that this dogged and daring explorer has radically revised our picture of the human species and has created a vastly expanded map of human possibilities.

Abraham H. Maslow was born on April 1, 1908, in a Jewish slum in Brooklyn, the first of seven children. His father, a cooper by trade, had come to America from Kiev, then had sent for a hometown cousin to join him as his wife. Young Maslow's childhood was generally miserable. He was alienated from his mother ("a pretty woman, but not a nice one," he later told English writer Colin Wilson) and afraid of his father ("a very vigorous man, who loved whiskey and women and fighting"). His father's business succeeded, and when Abe was nine the family moved out of the slums and into the first of a series of lower middle-class houses, each slightly more comfortable than the one preceding it. But these moves took the family into Italian and Irish neighborhoods and made Abe the victim of terrifying anti-Semitism. He was not only Jewish but also, by his own account, a peculiar-looking child, so underweight that the family doctor feared he might get tuberculosis. "Have you ever seen anyone uglier than Abe?" his father mused aloud at a family gathering.

Reading was his escape, the library his magic kingdom. And when he chose to go to Brooklyn Borough High School, an hour-and-a-half's journey from his home, Abe got his first taste of success. He became a member of the chess team and of the honor society Arista. He edited the Latin magazine and the physics magazine, for which, in 1923, at the age of fifteen, he wrote an article predicting atom-powered ships and submarines. In terms of sheer, raw intelligence, Maslow was a true prodigy. Tested years later by the psychologist Edward L. Thorndike, he registered an IQ of 195, the second highest Thorndike ever encountered.

At eighteen, Maslow enrolled in New York's City College. It was free and his father wanted Abe to study law. But Maslow found the school impersonal and the required courses dull. He skipped classes, made poor grades, and was put on probation for the second semester.

No matter. Maslow was intoxicated with the rich artistic and intellectual life of New York City in the vintage year of 1927. He discovered the music of Beethoven and the plays of Eugene O'Neil. He went to two concerts a week at Carnegie Hall and sold peanuts to get into the theater. He attended lectures by Will Durant and Bertrand Russell and Reinhold Niebuhr. Like most young American intellectuals of that period, he became a socialist and an atheist.

But if Maslow was in love with the life of the mind, he was even more in love—blissfully, hopefully—with his cousin Bertha. And it was during the year he was nineteen that he experienced two of the great moments of life, the kinds of moments he was later to call "peak experiences." The first came when he read William Graham Sumner's *Folkways*, a book that introduced him to the idea of cultural evolution, forever disabused him of the assumption that his own society was the "fixed truth from which everything else was a foolish failing away," and triggered a lifelong interest in anthropology. By his own account, he was never again the same.

The second peak experience of that year came when he kissed Bertha. Previously, he had never dared to touch her. His frustration was indeed so painful that it drove him to leave New York City for a semester at Cornell. When he returned, Bertha's sister Anna took matters into her own hands by literally pushing him into Bertha's arms. "I kissed her," Maslow later told Colin Wilson, "and nothing terrible happened—the heavens didn't fall, and Bertha accepted it, and that was the beginning of a new life . . . . I was accepted by a female. I was just deliriously happy with her. It was a tremendous and profound and total love affair."

By now it was clear that Maslow would not become a lawyer, and he went away to the University of Wisconsin to study psychology in earnest. A few lonely, frustrated months later, Abe wired Bertha that they were going to get married. The wedding took place in New York during the December holidays of 1928. Bertha returned to Wisconsin with him and enrolled as a student.

Thus began Abraham Maslow's life as a psychologist. It was a life that would be graced with an extraordinary succession of mentors, distinguished scholars who were somehow drawn to this shy, brilliant young man and wanted him to work with them; they invited him to meals, drove him to meetings, helped get him jobs. One might say that these mentors served an emotional function as surrogate mothers and fathers, but if the Fates had conspired to choose ideal professional influences, they could not have done a better job.

As an undergraduate, Maslow became a lab assistant to William H. Sheldon, who later was to achieve fame with his theory of constitutional types (endomorph, mesomorph, ectomorph). Sheldon and other professors provided a solid grounding in classical laboratory research. Professor Harry Harlow, the noted primate researcher, eventually became Maslow's chief mentor at Wisconsin. In 1932 Harlow shared authorship of a paper on the intelligence of primates with Maslow, and the twenty-four-year-old undergraduate was so inspired by seeing his name in print in the *Journal of Comparative Psychology* that he spent all of his next summer vacation, helped by Bertha, repeating the experiment with every primate in the Bronx Park Zoo.

As a graduate student at Wisconsin, Maslow came up with a truly original line of research. He discovered that the incessant mounting behavior of primates, which involved males mounting males, females mounting females, and females mounting males, as well as the "conventional" mounting of females by males, had more to do with dominance than with sexuality. This activity was, in fact, a means of sorting out the hierarchy of the primate horde. What's more, he learned that the ferocity involved in dominance behavior tends to fade away as one goes up the primate intelligence scale: the monkey uses its dominance position to tyrannize; the chimpanzee, to protect.

Maslow moved from Wisconsin to Columbia University as the eminent behaviorist Edward Thorndike's research associate. And he continued his work on dominance and sexuality, going from simple dominance in animals to dominance-feeling in humans to the relationship between self-esteem and sexuality. In 1936, while still at Columbia, he began doing Kinsey-type interviews with female college students, possibly inspiring Kinsey's own work, which began some two years later. Maslow's interviews showed that highly dominant women, regardless of their sex drives, are more likely to be sexually active and experimental than are less dominant women. But he also found—and this is important in terms of his later work—that "any discussion of dominance must be a discussion of insecure people, that is, of slightly sick people. . . . Study of carefully selected psychologically secure individuals indicates clearly that their sexual lives are little determined by dominance-feeling." Here was a hint, a seed: there seems to exist a state of psychological health that transcends at least one lower drive.

During this period of inspired excitement and feverish work, Maslow continued to collect mentors. One, of them was Alfred Adler, an early disciple of Freud who eventually broke with his master.

Maslow also sat at the feet of such eminent psychologists and anthropologists as Erich Fromm, Kurt Goldstein, Karen Horney, and Margaret Mead—some of them refugees from the Nazi terror. It was the late Thirties and New York was both an exciting and a sobering place for a Jewish intellectual.

Of all his mentors, Ruth Benedict, the anthropologist, and Max Wertheimer, the founder of the European Gestalt school of psychology, had the greatest influence on Maslow's life. Both became good friends and often came to dinner with him and Bertha at their modest Brooklyn home. Maslow admired Benedict and Wertheimer inordinately. Not only were they giants in their fields, but they were also, to put it simply, wonderful human beings. He began making notes on these exceptional people. Nothing he had learned in psychology equipped him to understand them. How could they be what they so clearly were in a world of savage, repressed Freudian drives and Nazi horrors? Who was the real human species-type, Hitler or Benedict and Wertheimer?

These questions helped set the stage for the major turning point in Maslow's life, one that was to change psychology and our view of the human personality for all time. The year, as best as it can be reconstructed, was 1942; the place, New York City. By now, though not a great lecturer, Maslow was a beloved teacher, so popular that the college newspaper characterized him as the Frank Sinatra of Brooklyn College. He was working very hard, sometimes teaching nights as well as days for the extra income. He adored his daughters, who were now two and four; their innocence and potential in a darkening world sometimes moved him to tears. And the war was always in the back of his mind. He was too old to be drafted for military service but he wanted to make his contribution in the fight against Hitler. He wanted somehow to enlist himself in the larger enterprise of helping create a world in which there would be no Hitlers, in which "good people" would prevail.

It was in that emotional climate that he happened upon a parade of young American servicemen on their way to combat duty. And he was overcome by the evils of war, the needless suffering and death, the tragic waste of human potential. He began weeping openly. Against the backdrop of those times, the conventional, step-by step psychology he had been doing was entirely inadequate. He knew he would have to change his life and career. It would have been easy enough to stay on his present course. His research credentials were finally established. His recently published *Principles of Abnormal Psychology*, coauthored with Bela Mittelmann, was being well received. Maslow was undoubtedly on his way to a successful career in mainstream psychology. But now, tears streaming down his cheeks, he determined to take a more difficult, more uncertain course.

The direction of his exploration was set by a flash of insight that came to him while he was musing over his notes on Ruth Benedict and Max Wenheimer, trying to puzzle out the pattern that made these two people so very different from the neurotic, driven people who are usually the subject of psychological study. As he wrote years later, "I realized in one wonderful moment that their two patterns could be generalized. I was talking about a kind of person, not about two noncomparable individuals. There was a wonderful excitement in that. I tried to see whether this pattern could be found elsewhere, and I did find it elsewhere, in one person after another."

Like many historic breakthroughs, this one, in retrospect, seems obvious, so simple a child might have hit upon it: Up until that time, the field of psychology had by and large concentrated on mental illness, neglecting or entirely ignoring psychological *health*. Symptoms had been relentlessly pursued, abnormalities endlessly analyzed. But the normal personality continued to be viewed primarily as a vague, gray area of little interest or concern. And *positive* psychological health was terra incognita.

From the moment of the turning point at the parade in New York City, Maslow would devote his life and his thought to the exploration of this unknown land, of what he called in his last book "the farther reaches of human nature." In this exploration, he would find it necessary to leave his mentors behind. Though he would go on to form his own network of colleagues and supporters, he would find himself increasingly alone out on the frontiers of human knowledge. He was to become, in his words, "a reconnaissance man, a Daniel Boone," one who enjoys being "first in the wilderness."

Maslow stayed at Brooklyn College until 1951, then went to Brandeis University, in Waltham, Massachusetts, where he became chairman of the psychology department. In 1969 he moved to Menlo Park, California. A special fellowship set up by an industrialist would give him unlimited time for writing. But time was short; he died a year later. Still, in the twenty-seven years after the turning point in his career, he published close to a hundred articles and books that add up to a great synthesis, a bold and original psychological theory.

Maslow's theory is built upon his finding that human needs can be arranged in a hierarchy, beginning with the physiological needs for oxygen, water, food, and the like, then moving up through the needs for safety, belongingness, love, and esteem. Each lower need is, in Maslow's term, "prepotent" to the one above it. A very hungry person, for example, will quickly forget hunger if deprived of oxygen. Generally, each of the lower needs must be met before the one above it emerges. Taken this far, his "hierarchy of needs" is a useful but not particularly shattering formulation. For one thing, it avoids the twists and turns in the Freudian notion that all so-called higher feelings and actions are merely disguised versions of the primary drives of sex and ego-need; tenderness, for example, is seen by Freud as nothing more than "aim-inhibited sexuality." But Maslow goes even further: After all of the "deficiency-needs" listed above are fairly well satisfied, then a need for "self-actualization" emerges. This "being-need" is just as real, just as much a part of human nature as are the deficiency-needs.

The concept of self-actualization crystalized during Maslow's moment of insight about Ruth Benedict and Max Wertheimer, but it evolved and developed through years of studying exceptionally healthy and successful individuals. Self-actualization is, in short, the tendency of every human being—once the basic deficiency-needs are adequately fulfilled—to *make real* his or her full potential, to become everything he or she can be. The self-actualizing person is the true human species-type; a Max Wertheimer is a more accurate representation of the human species than is a Hitler. For Maslow, the self-actualizing person is not a normal person with something added, but a normal person with nothing taken away. In a "synergic" society— the term is Benedict's—what is good for the development and well-being of the individual is also good for the development and well-being of the society. Our type of society is obviously not synergic, which accounts for the rarity of self-actualizing people. Though the physiological needs of most of our citizens are fulfilled, the safety needs are hardly to be taken for granted, what with the prevalence of dog-eat-dog competition and crime. And many lives are lacking in an adequate supply of belongingness, love, and esteem. Maslow sees these lacks, these "holes" in the development of a person, as a prime cause of mental illness. Indeed, for Maslow, neurosis can be viewed largely as a deficiency disease. Thus, the Maslovian thesis cries out against the injustice that deprives so many people of their most basic needs and suggests major reforms in our ways of relating, especially in the family.

For those people who somehow transcend the deficiency-needs, self-actualization becomes a growth process, an unfolding of human nature as it potentially could be. Maslow defines this "true" human nature in terms of the characteristics of self-actualizing people, using not just personal interviews but also the study of such historical figures as Thomas Jefferson, Albert Einstein, Eleanor Roosevelt, Albert Schweitzer, and Jane Addams.

One of the most striking characteristics of these people is that they are strongly focused on problems outside of themselves. They generally have a mission in life; they delight in bringing about justice, stopping cruelty and exploitation, fighting lies and untruth. They have a clear perception of reality, along with a keen sense of the false, the phony. They are spontaneous and creative, sometimes displaying what might be called a mature childlikeness, a "second naiveté." They are autonomous, not bound tightly to the customs and assumptions of their particular culture. Their character structure is highly democractic, so that their friendships tend to cut across the dividing lines of class, education, politics, and ethnic background. At the same time, they are marked by a certain detachment and a need for privacy; they generally limit themselves to a relatively small circle of close friends. Significantly, they do not lump people or ideas in the usual categories but rather tend to see straight through "the man-made mass of concepts, abstractions, expectations, beliefs and stereotypes that most people confuse with the world. "

Self-actualizing people, Maslow discovered, are far more likely than others to have peak experiences—that is, episodes of delight and heightened clarity and even revelation, during which all things seem to flow in perfect harmony. Through numerous interviews and questionnaires, he found that even ordinary people take on self-actualizing qualities during peak experiences. He also comes very close to saying that such experiences provide a glimpse into the realm of Being, into ultimate reality itself.

Here is another paradox: Maslow the self-proclaimed atheist insisting upon the importance of a class of human experience that includes the experiences of the greatest religious figures back through the ages. But he himself was always filled to the brim with a religious wonder, with a profound sense of what Rudolf Otto calls *das Heilige*, "the holy"; and he never shrank from presenting the transcendent realm of Being forcefully, even if he did so in a secular, psychological context. At the turn of the century William James had written eloquently about the mystic experience, but most psychologists ignored this entire aspect of human life or dismissed it as some kind of compensation mechanism. For Freud, who confessed he had never had such an experience, the "oceanic feeling" is mere infantile regression. Maslow's courage in bringing the peak experience out of the closet has since been validated by several studies and polls showing its universality and value.

When people reach the stage of self-actualization, according to Maslow, many of the assumptions of conventional psychology are overturned. For example, human motivation prior to Maslow was generally treated in terms of tension reduction, and impulses were considered to be dangerous. But Maslow points out that this is true only in the realm of the lower needs. The "growth-needs" of the self-actualizing person are not mere itches to be relieved by scratching. The higher tensions (problems to be solved, human relations to be deepened) can be pleasurable. Creative impulses, then, are to be welcomed and trusted.

By opening up the previously hidden area of psychological health, Maslow provides a new kind of guidance for the human journey. Self-actualizing people, he argues, are good choosers. When given an opportunity, they gravitate toward what is good for them and, in his view, good for the human race. "So far as human value theory is concerned," Maslow writes in his 1962 book, *Toward a Psychology of Being*, "no theory will be adequate that rests simply on the statistical description of the choices of unselected human beings. To average the choices of good and bad choosers, of healthy and sick people, is useless. Only the choices and tastes and judgment of healthy human beings will tell us much about what is good for the human species in the long run."

In the 1950s Maslow began to see his work as part of a Third Force in psychology, representing a decisive, positive move beyond standard Freudian psychology with its sickness-oriented view of humankind, and beyond behaviorism, which tends to treat the individual as a mere point between stimulus and response. With his generous, inclusive spirit, Maslow viewed Third Force psychology as large enough to hold Adlerians, Rankians, Jungians, Rogerians, neo-Freudians, Talmudic psychologists, Gestaltists, and many others. In 1961 his mailing list, which had long been used to circulate papers and ideas, became the basis for the *Journal of Humanistic Psychology*, whose founding members included Charlotte Buhler, Kurt Goldstein, David Riesman, Henry Murray, and Lewis Mumford. Two of the most influential founders were Rollo May, who was instrumental in introducing

European existential psychology to the U.S., and Carl Rogers, whose humanistic, client-centered approach to psychotherapy and counseling has since spread throughout the world.

The summer of 1962 was to see two events that would play a major role in Maslow's influence on the culture. The first involved his appointment as a visiting fellow to Non-Linear Systems, a high-tech plant in Del Mar, California. Here, Maslow first realized that his theories could be applied to management. He discovered that there were just as many self-actualizing people in industry—perhaps more than in the universities, and he got the idea that a humane, enlightened management policy devoted to the development of human potential could also be the most effective. He called this concept "eupsychian management," which became the title of his 1965 book on the subject. As it turned out, Maslow's ideas foreshadowed those that are now associated with the best of Japanese management, and it is hard to find a book on management theory today that does not give a prominent place to Abraham Maslow.

The second event of that summer was synchronistic—to use a word coined by Jung to describe coincidences that are more than just that. Abe and Bertha were driving down California's Highway 1 for a holiday, and their progress was slower than anticipated on that spectacular and tortuous coast road. Looking for a place to spend the night, they saw a light and drove off the road down a steep driveway toward what they took to be a hotel. They were astonished to find that almost everybody there was reading the recently published *Toward a Psychology of Being* and enthusiastically discussing Maslovian ideas.

The Maslows had stumbled upon what was to become Esalen Institute on the eve of its opening to the public. The institute's cofounder, Michael Murphy,. had just bought a dozen copies of the book and given them to the members of his staff. Later, Maslow and Murphy became close friends and Maslow became a major influence on Esalen and on the entire counterculture of the 1960s.

This association was to raise some eyebrows among Maslow's conservative colleagues. The first press reports on the newly minted human-potential movement were, to be as charitable as possible, sensationalized and uninformed, and a less courageous man might have pulled back. But Maslow was not one to flinch under fire. "Esalen's an experiment," he told Bertha. "I'm glad they're trying it." And later, in public symposia, Maslow called Esalen "potentially the most important educational institution in the world."

Maslow's influence on America, transmitted through this lineage, can hardly be overstated. What has happened is that the counterculture of the 1960s has become a major and influential segment of the mainstream culture of the 1980s. This development has been largely ignored by the established journals of opinion but is clearly seen in the surveys of Louis Harris and Daniel Yankelovich, in the sophisticated Trend Reports of John Naisbitt, and in Naisbitt's recent best seller, *Megatrends*.

It is also becoming clear that while the quest for self-actualization might lead some people to a narrow preoccupation with the self, the number who go to this extreme is small, and the "me first" stage is generally temporary, a way station on the journey to social consciousness. This is seen in the Values and Lifestyles (VALS) Program of SRI International, a California-based research and consulting organization, which has adapted Maslow's hierarchy of needs to an analysis of the U.S. population and which numbers some of the nation's most successful corporations among its subscribers. The VALS study shows that the "Inner-Directeds," those who might be said to be on the path toward self-actualization, now make up 21 percent of all Americans and represent the fastest-growing segment of the population. Of this 21 percent, only 3 percent are in the self-centered, narcissistic "I-am-me" category. The Inner-Directeds, for the most part, tend to move inexorably toward social consciousness, service to others, and personal integration—which should come as no surprise to anyone who has given Maslow more than a cursory reading.

Critics argue that Maslow did not adequately- deal with the problem of evil, with humanity's darker side, and there is something to this criticism. But Maslow himself was aware that he had much more work to do, "at least two hundred years' worth," he told Bertha shortly before his death. True, Maslow's theory might not be complete, but it never fails to challenge us with a spine-tingling vision of individual potential and health and of a synergic society.

Despair is often comfortable, in some circles even fashionable, and it is easy enough to dismiss or even ridicule Maslow's challenge. After all, nothing is more difficult or painful than to look clearly at your own wasted potential, then start doing something about it. But ever-increasing numbers of Americans are taking the challenge. For example, the fastest growing movement in health management today involves the field of holistic, health-oriented approaches to the physical that Maslow applied to the psychological. If anything can solve the crisis of medical depersonalization and rising costs, it is this classically Maslovian shift: more and more people working against a pathogenic environment and society while taking personal responsibility for their own positive good health.

In spite of his unorthodox views, Maslow was elected to the presidency of the American Psychological Association in 1967, and now, more than twelve years after his death, his voice is still being heard, even if indirectly, even if by people who barely know his name. Warren Bennis, professor of management at USC, recalls it as "that incredibly soft, shy, tentative, and gentle voice making the most outrageous remarks." Bennis also remembers Maslow for "a childlike spirit of innocence and wonder—always wearing his eyebrows (as Thomas Mann said about Freud) continually raised in a constant expression of awe."

Still, it takes another characteristic to join the shyness, the outrageousness, and the awe into a complete human being, and that is courage, which is the essence of Abraham Maslow's story. Psychologist James F.T. Bugental, who served as the first president of the Association for Humanistic Psychology, lived near Maslow during the last year of his life. "Abe used to go for his walks," Bugental recalls, "and he'd come by our house. We had this myth that one of the cans of beer in the refrigerator was his, and he'd always say, 'Is my beer cold?'

"And he'd drink his beer and get a little sentimental and sometimes show us pictures of his granddaughter and weep because she was so beautiful and innocent and would have to lose her innocence. And sometimes he would talk about the time in his childhood when he'd have to go through a tough Irish neighborhood to get to the library, and about how he would plan his route and sometimes get chased and sometimes get beat up. But he never let that stop him. He went to the library even though he might have to get beat up.

"That's the way I see his life. He never stopped doing what he thought he had to do, even though he might get beat up. He had courage, just plain courage."

Dossier

Abraham Maslow was born on April 1, 1908, in Brooklyn. The eldest of seven children, he remembered "clinging" to his father. "I have no memory," he wrote, "of expecting anything from my mother." He later called his mother a "schizophrenogenic . . . one who makes crazy people. . . . I was awfully curious to "find out why I didn't go insane."

In elementary school he met anti-Semitism and a teacher he later described as a "horrible bitch." Challenging his reputation as the class's best speller, the teacher made Maslow stand up and spell one word after another. When he finally missed one—parallel—the teacher publicly concluded, "I knew you were a fake."

Throughout his adolescence he was intensely shy and, he recalled, "terribly unhappy, lonely, isolated, self-rejecting." A loving uncle, his mother's brother, looked after him. "He may have saved my life, psychically," Maslow said.

He left New York for Cornell University partly because of his strong passion for his cousin Bertha: "I had not yet touched Bertha. . . And this was getting kind of rough on me—sexually, because I was very powerfully sexed . . . ."

At the University of Wisconsin his professors accepted him as a colleague. Still, he was amazed when one day in a men's room, a professor stepped up to the urinal next to his. "How did I think that professors urinated?" he later marveled. "Didn't I know they had kidneys?"

At Columbia University he found the initial research he conducted for psychologist E. L. Thorndike boring. He wrote Thorndike a note saying so—even though he stood to lose his job during the Depression. Far from firing Maslow, Thorndike respected his opinion.

For all his popularity with students, Maslow was terrified of public speaking until he was over fifty. In 1925 a paper he wrote never got published because he fled a conference rather than read it. In 1959 he delivered a talk, then for days afterward stayed in bed recovering from it.

He suffered his first heart attack in 1945 and never again was completely healthy. He had an arthritic hip, and though he was always tired, he had trouble sleeping. Only in the year before his death did a doctor discover that Maslow's chronic fatigue was a form of hypoglycemia. For years the ailment had made him crabby, inhibited his work, and stifled his sex life.

Until the age of thirty he considered himself a socialist—"Fabian rather than Marxist." He said he dropped socialism after Franklin Roosevelt put "our whole socialist programme. . . into law" and he didn't see "any great miracles occur."

After his bar mitzvah, at thirteen, he became "a fighting atheist." Yet later in fife, when offers came to teach at other universities, he would not leave his teaching job at Brandeis. "Why?" he asked himself "Partly it's the Jewish business. I have been so proud of the great Jewish university—I didn't realize how much—and I feel like a rat deserting the sinking ship. . . just the way I did when I left Brooklyn and abandoned the poor Jewish students whom nobody loved but me. The guilt of upward mobility."

In 1954 he wrote: "Human nature is not nearly as bad as it has been thought to be. . . . In fact it can be said that the possibilities of human nature have customarily been sold short. . . . "

He enjoyed art museums, shopping, and reading science fiction. He admired J. D. Salinger. (". . .read *Fanny and Zooey*. . . . He says in his way what I've been trying to say. The novelist can be so much more effective.") He also liked Betty Friedan's *The Feminine Mystique*, which discusses his views on sex and dominance. ("A passionate book— I was swept along unintentionally.")

In 1969 the White House invited him to join a committee to define national goals, but he was too sick to attend. He was miffed by the popular press's indifference to his work: "A new image of man. . . a new image of nature, a new philosophy of science, a new economics, a new everything, and they just don't notice it."

Still, at fifty-six he wrote: "With my troubles about insomnia and bad back and conflict over my role in psychology and. . . in a certain sense, *needing* psychoanalysis, if anyone were to ask me 'Are you a happy man?' I'd say 'yes, yes!' Am I lucky?. . . The darling of fortune? Sitting as high up as a human being ever has? Yes!"

Five years later, on June 8, 1970, he died of a heart attack. *The New York Times* published no obituary.

Aggression: The Violence Within

Maya Pines

About the Author

Maya Pines has been writing on the brain since research in the field really took off in the 1970s. Her book *The Brain Changers: Scientists and the New Mind Control*, which described research on the two hemispheres and on mind-altering drugs, won the National Media Award of the American Psychological Association in 1974. She has also written a book on retarded children and one on the enormous potential of the very young child.

When his supervisor made a sarcastic comment about the latest production delay, the young engineer said nothing. But he could feel his blood boil. On the way home he had a few drinks to calm down.

That didn't help much. He was not bearing the blame well. At home, he took some Valium. Then he got into an argument with his wife. Suddenly he exploded and punched her. He then smashed a chair, stormed out of the house and got into his car, taking off at top speed. Going out of control, he crashed into another car and wrecked it. The collision broke the other driver's neck.

As the incident illustrates, aggression is not confined to the New York City subways (see Vigilantism, p. 161). It lurks in suburban streets and sometimes invades our homes. The so-called civilized world is riddled with violence, both sanctioned and unsanctioned. At a time when more and more people have access to atomic weapons, a single person's aggressive impulses—or perhaps a nation's—could be the most dangerous force on Earth.

Today, we are all at risk of becoming the targets or accidental victims of some kind of violence. Cars driven by aggressive people can be the instruments of suicide or murder. Stabbings, shootings and rapes are now so commonplace that most newspapers don't bother to report them. Law-enforcement agencies reported a total of 1.2 million violent crimes in 1983; probably at least as many other episodes went unrecorded. More than 50,000 Americans are murdered or commit suicide annually.

In the hope of finding ways to prevent or reduce aggression, psychiatrists, brain researchers and behavioral scientists are now making a determined effort to understand its causes. They are not concerned with the kind of drive that fuels ambition and makes people stand up for their rights, nor with aggressive thoughts, but with physical aggression—outright attacks that result in injuries or death. Among some recent findings:

• Harsh punishment produces aggressive behavior in children. So does the example of violence, at home or on television.

• Extremely impulsive and aggressive people of both sexes have unusually low levels of a brain chemical that inhibits the firing of nerve cells.

• Men who are highly aggressive have higher levels of the male hormone testosterone.

• Treatment with lithium reduces aggressive behavior in highly impulsive and violent people.

While much of the research on the biology of aggression has been carried out on animals, it is known that human beings can resist their biological drives more efficiently than other creatures, because their neocortex—the thinking part of the brain—is more highly developed.

"By the time the human brain matures, the normal individual is controlled very largely by social norms," says Estelle Ramey, a professor of physiology and biophysics at the Georgetown University School of Medicine. "Men don't urinate on the living-room floor, even when they're in agony; they wait until they get to the bathroom. Although urination is a normal, instinctive biological drive, it's very quickly brought under control. Similarly, young men learn quickly who it's safe to be aggressive toward. A man may be a meek and mild Caspar Milquetoast in the office, and kowtow to his boss, and then go home and beat up his wife. Is he an aggressive male?" She answers her own question: "He's aggressive when it's safe for him to be aggressive."

Much depends, therefore, on the level of aggression that is acceptable in a particular society at a particular time. Cultural change is possible, argued John Paul Scott of Bowling Green State University at a recent session on evolutionary theory and warfare. Warlike habits can give way to very peace-loving ones. Although Scandinavian culture spawned the Vikings, for instance, it is now represented by people who are "among the most pacific in the world."

Much depends on one's early training. Extreme aggression tends to run in families—a finding that has set off a furious debate over the cause. In the nature-versus-nurture controversy, strong proponents cite genetic causes while others claim children learn from their parents' example.

Last winter, a team of researchers reported on an extraordinary study of aggressive behavior that was made by tracking three generations. It revealed how much children are influenced by their parents' aggression. Led by L. Rowell Huesmann and Leonard Eron of the University of Illinois at Chicago, the team began in 1960 by testing 870 third-graders, who were asked to rate one another on such questions as "who pushes and shoves children?" Their parents were interviewed as well. The researchers then followed up more than 600 of these children and their parents for 22 years—by which time many of the original children had children of their own, who then also became subjects of the study.

The researchers found that the children who most frequently pushed, shoved, started fights and were considered more aggressive by their classmates at age 8 turned into the more aggressive adults. These men were very likely to have criminal records by the age of 30. If their behavior did not land them in jail, they were apt to get into fights, smash things when angry, drive while drunk and abuse their wives. Many of their own children already showed signs of the same type of aggressive behavior.

At the beginning of their study, the team had learned that the more aggressive children had parents who punished them far more severely than the less aggressive children. Now the pattern was repeating itself as these aggressive adults severely punished their own children. The most likely explanation for this repetition, the researchers concluded, was that children learn to be aggressive by copying what their parents do to them and to others.

In their report, they said it was most impressive that "the children who are nominated as more aggressive by their third-grade classmates on the average commit more serious crimes as adults." They also found that the degree of aggressiveness in the third-graders was, 22 years later, even more strongly related to the aggressiveness of their children than it was to their own aggressiveness as adults. In short, the study concluded that the aggressive child is father to the aggressive child.

Once aggression is established as a child's "characteristic way of solving social problems," it becomes a relatively stable and self-perpetuating behavior, the researchers emphasized. And by the time this behavior comes to the attention of society, "it is not readily amenable to change."

The idea, then, is to prevent such behavior from becoming fixed before adolescence. One approach is to limit the amount of violence to which children are exposed. Children are copycats, and when they see repeated violence on television, they tend to imitate it. The evidence for this is so strong that the American Academy of Pediatrics is now warning parents about the effects of TV violence and urging them to limit—as well as monitor—what their children watch.

Another approach is to put clear limits on children's aggressive behavior at an early age. Psychologist Gerald Patterson, of the Oregon Social Learning Center in Eugene, and others have found that one of the most effective means of stopping excessive aggression is to isolate children in a room for about five minutes before the child's behavior becomes extreme. Patterson calls this a time-out procedure—a nonpunitive way of saying "that's not acceptable behavior."

If the pattern of violence is not broken before adulthood, little can be done by psychological means. Highly aggressive adults generally resist psychotherapy, according to Gerald Brown, a psychiatrist at the National Institute of Mental Health (NIMH), although behavior therapy is sometimes helpful. Anybody who thinks he or she can reform one of these volatile and violent men through love "is in for a lot of trouble," Brown says. "That idea has brought a lot of grief into marriages. These people can idealize you one minute and attack you the next."

Generally these highly aggressive people are men. Men, in fact, commit about 90 percent of all violent crimes in the United States. This is in part the result of social conditioning. As children grow up, they learn that "it's socially unacceptable for women to become aggressive, but if a man throws his weight around, that's *manly!*" points out Estelle Ramey. But there are also biological reasons for the higher level of aggression in males, as indicated by studies involving certain brain chemicals and male sex hormones.

One chemical that seems to play a key role in preventing or releasing aggression is serotonin, which carries inhibitory messages from cell to cell in the brain. Serotonin is difficult to measure directly, but a substance called 5-HIAA, which is a breakdown product of serotonin, can now be measured in spinal fluid. Several experiments have shown that highly aggressive people have lower levels. This holds true for both men and women, but on the average, men have less 5-HIAA.

Because research involving 5-HIAA requires sometimes painful spinal taps, few studies have been conducted. At the National Naval Medical Center in Bethesda, Maryland, 26 marines and sailors, aged 17 to 32, who had come to the attention of psychiatrists because of their histories of repeated assault, agreed to undergo taps.

"They were the kind of people who'd had temper tantrums as small children and lots of fights in grade school and who would go into bars and tear up the place," says Brown, the NIMH psychiatrist who directed the spinal-fluid study. "They had a very short fuse—they'd be provoked by things others would not find provoking."

Predictable Aggression

Although aggression is highly valued in the military, Brown points out that "it must be controlled and predictable aggression. If people are too unpredictable and keep getting into trouble, they're not suitable for the service." In fact, the young men under study were being examined by a board of officers who were to decide whether they should be discharged from the Navy.

The laboratory that analyzed their spinal fluid found that 14 of the young men had low levels of 5-HIAA, while the rest had nearly double the amount. The first group included the men who had the worst records for impulsive acts of aggression, and 12 were discharged.

"We could have looked at their spinal fluid and predicted with eighty-five percent accuracy which people would be removed," declares Brown.

The results of this study complement earlier research in which scientists lowered the level of serotonin in animals' brains through chemicals or brain surgery and saw a dramatic increase in the animals' aggressive behavior—at least in the kind of aggression characterized by explosive attacks.

Brain researchers have known for decades that there are at least two unrelated kinds of aggression. In the 1920s, the Swiss physiologist Walter Hess, who later won a Nobel prize, described the cat's characteristic "bad-tempered aggression": With dilated pupils and bristling hair, the cat hisses, spits and growls. By contrast, "predatory aggression" is more cold-blooded and deliberate, as when the cat stalks a mouse, kills it quietly and eats it. Only the first variety seems to involve low levels of serotonin.

Testosterone has long been associated with aggression. A time-honored method of making male animals less aggressive is to castrate them—a procedure that eliminates the source of testosterone. When male mice are castrated at birth, for instance, they do not begin to fight each other at one or two months of age, as normal mice do upon reaching sexual maturity, but giving these castrated mice injections of testosterone makes them fight as if they had not been altered.

"Testosterone increases the biological intensity of stress, so that more adrenaline is released," explains Ramey. This produces a state of anxiety and irritability but also damages the lining of blood vessels and may lead to heart disease. That's why male animals generally die earlier than females, she says—unless they have been castrated, in which case they tend to live as long as females.

In one study, blood from hockey players rated by coaches and teammates as particularly aggressive was found to contain relatively high levels of testosterone. In another study, involving prisoners jailed for violent crimes, the men who were most aggressive toward other prisoners had twice as much testosterone in their blood as those who were not.

While the effects of such biological differences should not be underestimated, researchers emphasize that biology can only set the stage for aggressive acts or make such acts more likely. Biological forces can produce rage or the urge to attack, but they cannot dictate whether an attack will actually take place.

Even dogs react differently when annoyed by their masters, whom they seldom bite, and when annoyed by strangers, whom they will attack with much less provocation. They are particularly lenient toward young children.

In certain circumstances, such as self-defense, any of us may become violent. But when previously unaggressive people suddenly become violent for no apparent reason, they may have had too much alcohol or taken drugs such as PCP (angel dust), both of which often trigger aggression. Psychologist Claude Steele, of the University of Washington, recently found that alcohol accelerates aggressive behavior to an extreme level because, when in a state of conflict, a person using alcohol tends to lessen inhibitions by blocking thoughts of negative consequences.

Most of the violence in the United States comes from people who are chronically aggressive. Some of them simply earn their living from crime. Others have such a short fuse that aggression has become a way of life. For these impulsive people, a new kind of treatment now appears possible in some cases: the use of lithium, a drug that is generally prescribed to treat manic-depressives.

Lithium seems to affect the activity of several brain chemicals, including serotonin, preventing both highs and lows. Scientists don't yet understand exactly how it works, but it has been shown to reduce aggression in rats, mice and fish. On this basis, several psychiatrists have tried it on prison inmates with histories of repeated impulsive assaults. Joe Tupin, a professor of psychiatry at the University of California, Davis, gave lithium to 27 particularly aggressive male prisoners in a maximum-security prison in California. "More than two-thirds of them responded to the lithium," he reports. "It removed the explosive quality of their violence."

The men who responded best were those who would become extremely angry after trivial provocations. Their violence was not only inappropriate but very rapid, Tupin explains. "Between the provocation and the violence, these people didn't think—as if they didn't have the capacity to," he says. "They didn't stop for half a second of internal review during which they could think 'Gee, it was just an accident'; they didn't look at the possible consequences of their acts; they went totally out of control, with no in-between stages."

During the nine months that they were treated with lithium, these men became more reflective and had fewer violent episodes, Tupin says. The drug did not stop them from attacking their fellow prisoners deliberately from time to time, but it did prevent many hair-trigger explosions.

A number of psychiatrists are now giving lithium to patients of this impulsive type. According to Tupin, lithium is "a good choice" for this kind of patient; however, it would be ineffective with people who commit calculated, predatory violence or with psychotics, who are aggressive because of their delusions.

Controlling Behavior

Ideally, psychiatrists agree, highly aggressive behavior should be dealt with in childhood, by psychological means and by improving the economic and social conditions in which children grow up. But inevitably—either because of their brain chemistry or the way they were raised—a small percentage of people will go on being extremely aggressive ·and dangerous throughout their adult lives. If further research shows that lithium or other drugs are truly effective in such cases, does society have the right to prescribe them to control these people's behavior?

"I certainly wouldn't try to answer that question," says Gerald Brown. "But it is something the public will have to start thinking about, just as it is now thinking about the wisdom of putting mechanical hearts into people." Sooner or later, he says, society will have to decide what is the most humane and rational way to deal with people who keep on hurting others through uncontrolled aggression.

Vigilantism by Andrea Dorfman

When Bernhard Goetz drew his gun and shot four youths who, he claims, were harassing him on a New York City subway, he captured the nation's imagination. Not since the days of the Wild West and lynch mobs in the South had people been so preoccupied with a so-called vigilante: A *Washington Post*-ABC News poll found that nearly half of those interviewed supported Goetz. Was his personal crime-fighting crusade an isolated incident, or did it presage a national trend?

"There's a lot of rage and frustration in our society about the ineffectiveness of law enforcement," says Ralph Slovenko, a professor of law and psychiatry at Wayne State University, in Detroit. "Crime is a very safe profession. Only two percent of the people who commit serious crimes are actually sentenced."

A prior mugging victim who had seen his assailants get off easy, Goetz was hardly a vigilante in the traditional sense: Rather than pursuing a specific target in order to right perceived wrongs, he was ready to lash out at the next person who went after him.

"I believe strongly that Mr. Goetz was a man whose emotional state deteriorated in the time after his previous victimization," says psychologist Morton Bard, of the Center for Social Research at the City University of New York, "He was acting out a revenge fantasy that virtually all crime victims have."

What is particularly disturbing is that Bernhard Goetz may be a harbinger of things to come. Everyone agrees that conventional law enforcement is becoming less and less effective; the court system is slow, trial costs are high, and overcrowded prisons mean an increasing reliance on what's known as turnstile justice.

As yet, vigilantism is a predominantly urban phenomenon, fueled by the crowded, alienating environment. The self-styled Army of God is systematically bombing abortion clinics nationwide. A Massachusetts man wounded a teenager as revenge for hitting his car. Abroad, crime-fighting citizens patrol Amsterdam's streets at night, and squads in Dublin combat a growing drug problem. But rural areas can be affected, too: Two men in backwoods Arkansas recently castrated a man charged with rape.

"The American public is fed up," notes James Turner, a clinical psychologist at the University of Tennessee Center for the Health Sciences, in Memphis. "The system no longer protects them. It protects the guilty and punishes the innocent—the victims." He is now writing a book, called *Victims to Vigilantes*, that will document this progression in public opinion.

Researchers have only just begun to consider the effects of crime on the victim. Bard, who recently chaired an American Psychological Association task force on the victims of crime and violence, believes these studies are long overdue. "Victims should have services available to help them deal with the emotional and physical trauma of crime," he says. "Until now, there has been little sensitivity to victims and their 'invisible wounds.'"

Sociologist Emilio Viano, at American University's School of Justice, thinks better treatment of victims will forestall future Bernhard Goetzes. "Victims have been ignored and abused, used only as sources of information. The failure of the court system has weakened the fabric of society. People have nowhere to turn for help. If they want anything done, they feel they must do it themselves."

James Turner is investigating various nonlethal means of self-defense. "We must teach people how to deal with violence, or they will become victims," he says. "Basic police classes are moderately effective; karate needs to be practiced in order to be useful. Mace can make an attacker even angrier, and it's illegal in many major cities."

Turner is now reviewing a "stun gun" that uses electronic pulses to temporarily override an attacker's neuromuscular system, causing him to collapse in a daze.

Mood & Memory

Gordon H. Bower

About the Author

Gordon H. Bower is chairman of the psychology department at Stanford University. An experimental psychologist, he specializes in human learning and memory, and is coauthor, with Ernest Hilgard, of the textbook *Theories of Learning* (Prentice-Hall), now in its fifth edition. Bower, a member of the National Academy of Sciences, describes his studies of the impact of emotion on learning as a recent sideline. This article is adapted from his Distinguished Scientific Contributions Award address given last year at a meeting of the American Psychological Association. The full address first appeared in the *American Psychologist.*

An American soldier in Vietnam blacked out as he stared at the remains of his Vietnamese girlfriend, killed by Vietcong mortar fire. Vowing revenge, he plunged into the jungle. Five days later an American patrol discovered him wandering aimlessly, dazed, disoriented. His memory of the preceding week was a total blank. He had no idea where he'd been or what he'd been doing for that period. Even after his return to the U.S., he could not recall the blackout period.

Several years later, a psychiatrist treating him for depression put him under hypnosis and encouraged him to reconstruct events from his combat days, both before and during the blackout. He calmly recalled earlier events, but when he neared the traumatic episode, he suddenly became very agitated, and more memories came pouring out. He began to relive the trauma of seeing his girlfriend's body and felt again the revulsion, outrage, and lust for revenge. Then, for the first time, he remembered what had happened after the mortar attack. He had commandeered a jeep, traveled alone for days deep into Vietcong territory, stalked Vietcong in the jungles, and set scores of booby traps with captured weapons before stumbling upon the American patrol. Curiously, after awakening from his hypnotic trance, the patient could remember only a few incidents singled out by the psychiatrist. But further treatments, described in the book *Trance and Treatment* by psychiatrists Herbert and David Spiegel, enabled him to bring more details into consciousness.

This case illustrates an extreme memory dissociation; the blackout events could be recalled in one state (of hypnotic agitation) but not in another (normal consciousness). Hypnosis helped the person return to the psychic state he was in when the blackout started; at that point, the emotional feelings returned, as did memories of the details of the blacked-out events. Psychoanalysts might call this a case of severe repression, which refers to the avoidance of anxiety-provoking memories. I believe such a label equates an observation with an explanation that may or may not be correct. Instead, I believe the soldier's case is an example of state-dependent memory, a more encompassing theory that refers to people's difficulty in recovering during one psychological state any memories acquired in a different state. State-dependency and repression are competing theories of forgetting. Each offers an explanation of why the soldier's blacked-out memories returned as he relived his trauma. But repression could not explain why a happy person can find happy memories easier to recover than sad ones.

The idea of studying the efficiency of memory during different psychological states—for example, while in hypnosis, under the influence of drugs, or after sensory deprivation—has been around for more than 50 years. However, previous investigations have been limited both in method and scope. While many clinical examples of state-dependency occur—for instance, violent "crimes of passion" are often blocked out but hypnotically recoverable by the assailant—such cases are really too rare, inconvenient, and complex for an adequate scientific analysis. In an earlier article in *Psychology Today* ("I Can't Remember What I Said Last Night, But It Must Have Been Good," August 1976), Roland Fischer described several examples and conjectured that memories are bound up with specific levels of physiological arousal. But my research shows that arousal level is not nearly as critical as the type of emotion felt—whether fear, depression, anger, or happiness. The most common laboratory method in previous studies of state-dependency used rats, learning with or without an injection of a drug like Amytal and later tested in either a drugged or nondrugged state.

As an experimentalist, I was challenged to produce state-dependent memory in the laboratory, using normal people and trying to evoke commonly occurring emotions as "states." Two of my students, Steve Gilligan and Ken Monteiro, and I were especially interested in trying to produce such learning using different emotions, such as depression, joy, fear, and anger. This turned into a more ambitious project when we found evidence not only of state-dependent memory but also of related emotional influences on thinking, judging, and perceiving, First, I'll describe our work on state-dependent memory.

The technique we employed for inducing moods used our subjects' imaginations, guided by hypnotic suggestion. College students who were very hypnotizable volunteered for our study. After hypnotizing them, we asked them to get into a happy or sad mood by imagining or remembering a scene in which they had been delightfully happy or grievously sad. Often the happy scene was a moment of personal success or of close intimacy with someone; the sad scenes were often of personal failure or the loss of a loved one. We told them to adjust the intensity of their emotion until it was strong but not unbearable—it was important for them to function well enough to learn. After getting into a mood state, the subjects performed a learning experiment for 20 or 30 minutes, after which they were returned to a pleasantly relaxed state before debriefing. (These procedures are harmless and our subjects have willingly volunteered for further experiments.)

After some pilot work, we found that strong mood state-dependent memory could be produced by teaching people two sets of material (such as word lists)—one while happy, the other while sad—and then asking them to remember one set in a happy or a sad mood. In one study, groups of hypnotized subjects learned List A while happy or sad, then learned List B while happy or sad, and then recalled the List A while happy or sad. The lists were 16 words long; memory was always tested by free recall. The groups can be classified into three conditions. In the first, control subjects learned and recalled both lists in a single mood, happy for half of them and sad for the other half. In the second condition, the subjects learned List A in one mood, learned List B in a different mood, and recalled List A in their original mood; these subjects should have recalled more than the control subjects because their different learning moods helped them to isolate the two lists, thus reducing confusion and interference from List B when they tried to recall List A. The third interference condition was just the reverse; those students tried to recall List A when they were in their second, List B mood. Their recall of List A should have suffered, because the recall mood evokes memories of the wrong List B rather than the target List A.

When we returned subjects to their original moods, we did so by having them call up scenes different from their original ones. For example, if a woman originally induced happiness by reliving a scene of herself scoring the winning goal in a soccer match, we would instruct her to return to the happy mood by imagining a different scene, such as riding a horse along the beach. We had subjects use a second imagined situation so that any memory advantage obtained for same-mood testing would be due to overlap of moods, not to overlap of imaginary scenes.

A person's retention score was calculated as the percentage of originally learned items that were recalled on the later test. The results are in the chart on page 64; there is an obvious state-dependent effect. People who were sad during recall remembered about 80 percent of the material they had learned when they were sad, compared with 45 percent recall of the material they had learned when they were happy. Conversely, happy recallers remembered 78 percent of their happy list, versus 46 percent of their sad list. The state-dependent memory effect shows up in the crossover of these lines on the chart. A good metaphor for this is to suppose that you have one bulletin board for happy moods and another for sad moods. On each board you post the messages you learn while in that mood. You will be able to read off your messages from the happy bulletin board best if you first get into a happy mood, and the messages on the sad bulletin board best when you get into a sad mood.

Aside from the state-dependent effect, I am often asked whether people learn better when they are happy or when they are sad. Others have found that clinically depressed patients are often poor learners. However, in all of our experiments with word lists, we never have found a difference in overall learning rate or later retention that was due to the subject's mood. I suspect this reflects our control over the hypnotic subjects' motivation to do as well as possible in the learning task despite their happy or sad feelings.

Mood and Word Recall

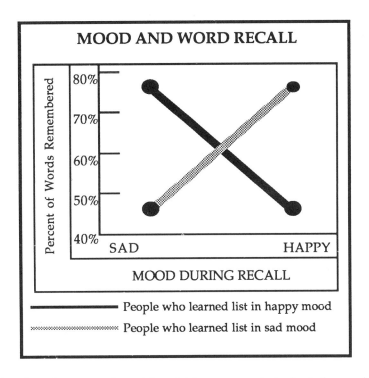

Results of an experiment in which groups of students learned a list of words while in one mood and later tried to recall as many as they could while in the same mood or a different mood. They were able to remember a much larger percentage when their learning mood matched their recall mood. This "state-dependency" effect is seen in the big difference between scores in the two recall situations, dramatized by the steep incline of the two lines connecting them. (The black dots show average percentages for both groups.)

We next addressed the issue of whether state-dependency would occur for recall of actual events drawn from a person's emotional life. We enlisted some volunteers who agreed to record such emotional events in a daily diary for a week. We gave these subjects a booklet for recording emotional incidents and discussed what we meant by an emotional incident. Examples would be the joy they experienced at a friend's wedding or the anger they experienced in an argument at work. For each incident they were to record the time, place, participants, and gist of what happened and to rate the incident as pleasant or unpleasant on a 10-point intensity scale.

Conscientious diary-keeping is demanding, and we dropped nearly half of our subjects because they failed to record enough incidents in the proper manner consistently over the week. We collected usable diaries from 14 subjects and scheduled them to return a week later. At that one-week interval they were hypnotized; half were put into a pleasant mood and the other half into an unpleasant mood, and all were asked to recall every incident they could remember of those recorded in their diaries the week before.

The percentages of recall showed the expected results: people in a happy mood recalled a greater percentage of their recorded pleasant experiences than of their unpleasant experiences; people in a sad mood recalled a greater percentage of their unpleasant experiences than of their pleasant experiences.

Remember that when subjects originally recorded their experiences, they also rated the emotional intensity of each experience. These intensity ratings were somewhat predictive: recall of more intense experiences averaged 37 percent, and of less intense experiences 25 percent. The intensity effect is important, and I will return to it later.

After subjects had finished recalling, we asked them to rate the current emotional intensity of the incidents they recalled. We found that they simply shifted their rating scale toward their current mood: if they were feeling pleasant, the recalled incidents were judged as more pleasant (or less unpleasant); if they were feeling unpleasant, the incidents were judged more unpleasant (or less pleasant) than originally. That should be familiar—here are the rose-colored glasses of the optimist and the somber, gray outlook of the pessimist.

Is it possible that recording incidents in a diary and rating them as pleasant or unpleasant encourages subjects to label their experiences in this manner and in some way gives us the results we want. Perhaps. To avoid such contaminants, in our next experiment we simply asked people to recall childhood incidents. We induced a happy or sad mood in our subjects and asked them to write brief descriptions of many unrelated incidents of any kind from their pre-high school days. Subjects were asked to "hop around" through their memories for 10 minutes, describing an incident in just a sentence or two before moving on to some unrelated incident.

The next day, we had the subjects categorize their incidents as pleasant, unpleasant, or neutral while unhypnotized and in a normal mood (so that their mood would not influence how pleasant or unpleasant they rated an event). The few neutral incidents recalled were discarded, and the chart below shows the main results. Happy subjects retrieved many more pleasant than unpleasant memories (a 92 percent bias); sad subjects retrieved slightly more unpleasant than pleasant memories (a 55 percent bias in the reverse direction).

What the subjects reported was enormously dependent on their mood when recalling. That is state-dependent memory: the subjects presumably felt pleasant or unpleasant at the time the incidents were stored, and their current mood selectively retrieves the pleasant or the unpleasant memories.

What kind of theory can explain these mood-state dependent effects? A simple explanation can be cast within the old theory that memory depends upon associations between ideas. All we need to assume is that an emotion has the same effect as an "active idea unit" in the memory system. Each distinct emotion is presumed to have a distinct unit in memory that can be hooked up into the memory networks. The critical assumption is that an active emotion unit can enter into association with ideas we think about, or events that happened, at the time we are feeling that emotion. For instance, as the ideas recording the facts of a parent's funeral are stored in memory, a powerful association forms between these facts and the sadness one felt at the time.

Retrieval of some contents from memory depends upon activating other units or ideas that are associated with those contents. Thus, returning to the scene of a funeral, the associations activated by that place may cause one to reexperience the sadness felt earlier at the funeral. Conversely, if a person feels sad for some reason, activation of that emotion will bring into consciousness remembrances of associated ideas—most likely other sad events.

This theory easily explains state-dependent retrieval. In the first experiment, for example, the words of List A became associated both with the List A label and with the mood experienced at that time. Later, the words from List A can be retrieved best by reinstating the earlier List A mood, since that mood is a strongly associated cue for activating their memory. On the contrary, if a person had to recall List A while feeling in a different (List B) mood, that different mood would arouse associations that competed with recall of the correct items, thus reducing the memory scores. The same reasoning explains how one's current mood selectively retrieves personal episodes associated originally with pleasant or unpleasant emotions.

Beyond state-dependent memory, the network theory also helps to explain a number of influences of emotion on selective perception, learning, judgment, and thinking. When aroused, an emotion activates relevant concepts, thoughts, and frameworks for categorizing the social world. We have confirmed, for example, that people who are happy, sad, or angry produce free associations that are predominantly happy, sad, or angry, respectively. Similarly, when asked to fantasize or make up an imaginative story to pictures of the Thematic Apperception Test (TAT), they produce happy, sad, or hostile fantasies, depending on their emotional state. If asked for top-of-the-head opinions about their acquaintances, or the performance of their car or TV, they give highly flattering or negative evaluations, according to their mood. Also, their mood causes them to be optimistic or pessimistic in prognosticating future events about themselves and the nation. These influences can be seen as veiled forms of state-dependent retrieval of either the positive or negative memories about the person, event, or object.

Mood-Dependent Childhood Memories

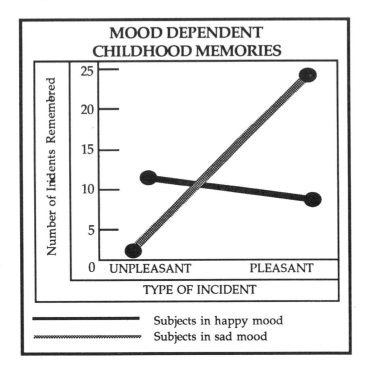

Another experiment showing the state-dependency effect. Groups of students were put into a sad or a happy mood and then asked to remember incidents from childhood. Later, they labeled the incidents as either pleasant or unpleasant. Happy subjects recalled far more pleasant than unpleasant incidents. Sad subjects retrieved slightly more unpleasant memories. (The black dots show averages for both groups.)

Mood affects the way we "see" other people. Social interactions are often ambiguous, and we have to read the intentions hidden behind people's words and actions. Is that person being steadfast in arguing his position or is he being pigheaded and obstructive? Was his action courageous or reckless? Was that remark assertive or aggressive? In reading others' intentions the emotional premise from which we begin strongly influences what we conclude. Thus the happy person seems ready to give a charitable, benevolent interpretation of social events, whereas the grouch seems determined to find fault, to take offense, or to take the uncharitable view. We find that these effects appear just as strongly when people are judging themselves on competence or attractiveness as well as when they're judging others. For example, when our subjects were in a depressed mood, they tended to judge their actions moment-by-moment in a videotaped interview as inept, unsociable, and awkward; but if they were in a happy mood, they judged their behaviors as confident, competent, and warmly sociable. Thus, social "reality" is constructed in the eye of the beholder, and that eye is connected to the emotions.

The network theory further predicts that an emotion should act as a selective filter in perception, letting in signals of a certain emotional wavelength and filtering out others. The emotional state adjusts the filter so that the person will attend more to stimulus material that agrees with or supports the current emotion. An analogy is that our feelings are like a magnet that selects iron filings from a heap of dust, attracting to itself whatever incoming material it can use.

Emotional effects can be demonstrated in attention and perception as well as learning. Thus, a sad person will look at pictures of sad faces more than happy faces; a happy person will dwell longer on happy faces. People who are happy from having just succeeded at an intelligence task have lower thresholds for seeing "success" words; subjects who've failed have lower thresholds for "failure" words.

The main work we've done on this salience effect concerns selective learning. In one of our experiments, subjects were made happy or sad by a posthypnotic suggestion as they read a brief story about two college men getting together and playing a friendly game of tennis. Andre is happy—everything is going well for him; Jack is sad—nothing is going well for him. The events of the two men's lives and their emotional reactions are vividly described in the story, which is a balanced, third-person account. When our subjects finished reading the story, we asked them to tell us who they thought the central character was and who they identified with. We found that readers who were happy identified with the happy character, thought the story was about him, and thought the story contained more statements about him; readers who were sad identified with the sad character and thought there were more statements about him.

Our subjects tried to recall the text the next day while in a neutral mood. Eighty percent of the facts remembered by the sad readers were about the sad character; 55 percent of the facts remembered by the happy readers were about the happy character. This is a mood-congruity effect; readers attend more to the character whose mood matches their own. Since all recallers were in a neutral mood, their differing recall results from their selective learning; it is not a state-dependent effect, since that requires varying subjects' mood during recall as well as during learning.

How is the mood-congruity effect explained? Why is mood-congruent material more salient and better learned? Two explanations seem worth considering.

The first hypothesis is that when one is sad, a sad incident in a story is more likely than a happy incident to remind one of a similar incident in one's life; vice versa, when one is happy. (Note that this is simply the state-dependent retrieval hypothesis.) An additional assumption is that the reminding is itself an event that enhances memory of the prompting event. This may occur because the old memory allows one to elaborate on the prompting event or to infuse it with greater emotion. In other studies, we have found that people remember descriptions of events that remind them of a specific incident in their lives far better than they recall descriptions that don't cause such reminiscence. To summarize, this hypothesis states that the mood-congruity effect is produced by selective reminding.

The second hypothesis, which complements the first, is that the mood-congruity effect comes from the influence of emotional intensity on memory. We demonstrated this idea in a study in which subjects were put in a sad or happy mood during hypnosis and then asked to read a story that went from a happy incident to a sad incident to a happy incident, and so on. Although our hypnotized subjects in several experiments tried to maintain steady moods, they reported that a mood's intensity would wane when they read material of the opposite quality. Thus happy subjects would come down from their euphoria when they read about a funeral or about unjust suffering; those topics intensified the sad subjects' feelings.

But why are intense emotional experiences better remembered? At present, there are many explanations. One is that events that evoke strong emotional reactions in real life are typically events involving personally significant goals, such as attaining life ambitions, elevating self-esteem, reducing suffering, receiving love and respect, or avoiding harm to oneself or loved ones. Because of their central importance, those goal-satisfying events are thought about frequently and become connected to other personal plans and to one's self-concept.

Intense experiences may also be remembered better because they tend to be rare. Because they are distinctive, they are not easily confused with more numerous, ordinary experiences; they tend to be insulated from interference.

The explanation of the mood-congruity effect that fits our lab results best is that mood-congruous experiences may be rehearsed more often and elaborated or thought about more deeply than experiences that do not match our mood. Thus sad people may be quickly able to embroider and elaborate upon a sad incident, whereas they don't elaborate on happy incidents. Because their sad incidents are elaborated and processed more deeply, sad people learn their sad incidents better than their happy ones. The same principle explains why happy people learn happy incidents better.

Having reviewed some evidence for mood-congruity and mood-dependency effects, let me speculate a bit about the possible implications for other psychological phenomena.

One obvious phenomenon explained by mood dependency is mood perpetuation—the tendency for a dominant emotion to persist. A person in a depressed mood will tend to recall only unpleasant events and to project a bleak interpretation onto the common events of life. Depressing memories and interpretations feed back to intensify and prolong the depressed mood, encouraging the vicious circle of depression. One class of therapies for depression aims at breaking the circle by restructuring the way depressed people evaluate personal events. Thus patients are taught to attend to and rehearse the positive, competent aspects of their lives and to change their negative evaluations.

State-dependent memory helps us to interpret several other puzzling phenomena. One is the impoverished quality of dream recall shown by most people. Most people forget their dreams, which is surprising considering that such bizarre, emotionally arousing events would be very memorable had they been witnessed in the waking state.

But the sleep state (even the REM state of dreaming) seems psychologically distinct from the waking state, and dream memories may thus not be easily transferred from one state to the other.

State-dependent retention may also explain the fact that people have very few memories from the first year or two of their lives. In this view, as infants mature, their brains gradually change state, so that early memories become inaccessible in the more mature state. The problem with this hypothesis is that it leads to no novel predictions to distinguish it from the plethora of competing explanations of infantile amnesia, which generally range from Freud's repression theory to the theory that the infant's and adult's "languages of thought" mismatch so badly that adults can't "translate" records of infant memories.

State-dependent memory has been demonstrated previously with psychoactive drugs like marijuana, alcohol, amphetamines, and barbiturates. For example, after taking amphetamines, subjects remember material they have learned while high on the drug in the past better than when they are not high on it. Since such substances are also mood-altering drugs, a plausible hypothesis is that they achieve their state-dependent effect by virtue of their impact on mood.

To summarize, we have now found powerful influences of emotional states upon selective perception, learning, retrieval, judgments, thought, and imagination. The emotions studied have been quite strong, and their temporary psychological effects have been striking. What is surprising to me is that the emotional effects on thinking uncovered so far seem understandable in terms of relatively simple ideas—the notion that an aroused emotion can be viewed as an active unit in an associative memory and that it stimulates memories, thoughts, perceptual categories, and actions. Perhaps this is as it should be— that theories developed in one field (memory) aid our understanding of phenomena in another field (for example, emotional fantasies in the psychiatric clinic). Certainly that is the goal of all basic science.

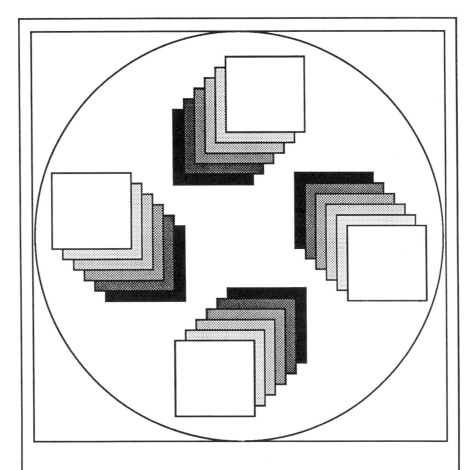

Chapter 7

Cognition and Memory

CHAPTER 7: COGNITION AND MEMORY

This area of psychology addresses aspects of learning that are more complex than the simple associative mechanisms addressed in Chapter 4. Some find that the increase in the complexity of the processes to be studied makes them more interesting. Yet, as psychological mechanisms become more complex, there are more and greater opportunities for errors and naive preconceptions increase proportionately. These selections concern the basic trust the judicial system places in people's memories, and whether or not this is warranted. This chapter also addresses the possibility that some of the basic memory research done in labs may not be as important to judicial decisions as previously thought.

7a. Loftus, E. (1984). Eyewitnesses: Essential but unreliable. *Psychology Today*, Feb., 22–26.

7b. Winograd, E. (1980). Face-saving memory. *Psychology Today*, Feb.

7c. McCloskey, M., & Egeth, H. Eyewitness identification: What can a psychologist tell a jury? *American Psychologist, 38*(5), May, 550–563.

Loftus presents the current status of eyewitness testimony in the United States, and how scientific knowledge of memory mechanisms might influence a jury's decision. Imagine that you are part of a rape trial, and a police officer has identified the defendent as the perpetrator. From the information supplied in these three articles, write a brief position paper to present to a judge, in which you either support or deny the motion to allow a memory psychologist to testify.

Eyewitnesses: Essential but Unreliable

Elizabeth F. Loftus

The ladies and gentlemen of William Bernard Jackson's jury decided that he was guilty of rape. They made a serious mistake, and before it was discovered, Jackson had spent five years in prison. There he suffered numerous indignities and occasional attacks, until the police discovered that another man, who looked very much like Jackson, had committed the rapes.

If you had been on the jury, you would probably have voted for conviction too. Two women had positively identified Jackson as the man who had raped them in September and October of 1977. The October victim was asked on the witness stand, "Is there any doubt in your mind as to whether this man you have identified here is the man who had the sexual activity with you on October 3, 1977?" She answered "No doubt." "Could you be mistaken?" the prosecutor asked. "No, I am not mistaken," the victim stated confidently. Jackson and other defense witnesses testified that he was home when the rapes occurred. But the jury didn't believe him or them.

This is just one of the many documented cases of mistaken eyewitness testimony that have had tragic consequences. In 1981, Steve Titus of Seattle was convicted of raping a 17-year-old woman on a secluded road; the following year he was proven to be innocent. Titus was luckier than Jackson; he never went to prison. However, Aaron Lee Owens of Oakland, California, was not as fortunate. He spent nine years in a prison for a double murder that he didn't commit. In these cases, and many others, eyewitnesses testified against the defendants, and jurors believed them.

One reason most of us, as jurors, place so much faith in eyewitness testimony is that we are unaware of how many factors influence its accuracy. To name just a few: what questions witnesses are asked by police and how the questions are phrased; the difficulty people have in distinguishing among people of other races; whether witnesses have seen photos of suspects before viewing the lineup from which they pick out the person they say committed the crime; the size, composition and type (live or photo) of the lineup itself.

I know of seven studies that assess what ordinary citizens believe about eyewitness memory. One common misconception is that police officers make better witnesses than the rest of us. As part of a larger study, my colleagues and I asked 541 registered voters in Dade County, Florida, "Do you think that the memory of law enforcement agents is better than the memory of the average citizen?" Half said yes, 38 percent said no and the rest had no opinion. When A. Daniel Yarmey of the University of Guelph asked judges, lawyers and policemen a similar question, 63 percent of the legal officials and half the police agreed that "The policeman will be superior to the civilian" in identifying robbers.

This faith in police testimony is not supported by research. Several years ago, psychologists A. H. Tinkner and E. Christopher Poulton showed a film depicting a street scene to 24 police officers and 156 civilians. The subjects were asked to watch for particular people in the film and to report instances of crimes, such as petty theft. The researchers found that the officers reported more alleged thefts than the civilians but that when it came to detecting actual crimes, the civilians did just as well.

More recently, British researcher Peter B. Ainsworth showed a 20-minute videotape to police officers and civilians. The tape depicted a number of staged criminal offenses, suspicious circumstances and traffic offenses at an urban street corner. No significant differences were found between the police and civilians in the total number of incidents reported. Apparently neither their initial training nor subsequent experience increases the ability of the police to be accurate witnesses.

Studies by others and myself have uncovered other common misconceptions about eyewitness testimony. They include:

• *Witnesses remember the details of a violent crime better than those of a nonviolent one.* Research shows just the opposite: The added stress that violence creates clouds our perceptions.

• *Witnesses are as likely to underestimate the duration of a crime as to overestimate it.* In fact, witnesses almost invariably think a crime took longer than it did. The more violent and stressful the crime, the more witnesses overestimate its duration.

• *The more confident a witness seems, the more accurate the testimony is likely to be.* Research suggests that there may be little or no relationship between confidence and accuracy, especially when viewing conditions are poor.

The unreliability of confidence as a guide to accuracy has been demonstrated outside of the courtroom, too; one example is provided by accounts of an aircraft accident that killed nine people several years ago. According to *Flying* magazine, several people had seen the airplane just before impact, and one of them was certain that "it was heading right toward the ground, straight down." This witness was profoundly wrong, as shown by several photographs taken of the crash site that made it clear that the airplane hit flat and at a low enough angle to skid for almost 1,000 feet.

Despite the inaccuracies of eyewitness testimony, we can't afford to exclude it legally or ignore it as jurors. Sometimes, as in cases of rape, it is the only evidence available, and it is often correct. The question remains, what can we do to give jurors a better understanding of the uses and pitfalls of such testimony? Judges sometimes give the jury a list of instructions on the pitfalls of eyewitness testimony. But this method has not proved satisfactory, probably because, as studies show, jurors either do not listen or do not understand the instructions.

Another solution, when judges permit, is to call a psychologist as an expert witness to explain how the human memory works and describe the experimental findings that apply to the case at hand. How this can affect a case is shown by a murder trial in California two years ago. On April 1, 1981, two young men were walking along Polk Street in San Francisco at about 5:30 in the evening. A car stopped near them, and the driver, a man in his 40s, motioned one of the men to get in, which he did. The car drove off. Up to this point, nothing appeared unusual. The area was known as a place where prostitutes hang out; in fact, the young man who got in the car was there hustling for "tricks." Three days later, he was found strangled in a wooded area some 75 miles south of San Francisco.

Five weeks later, the victim's friend was shown a six-person photo lineup and picked out a 47-year-old I'll call D. The quick selection of D's photograph, along with the strong emotional reaction that accompanied it (the friend became ill when he saw the photo), convinced the police that they had their man. D was tried for murder.

At his trial, the defense lawyer introduced expert testimony by a psychologist on the factors that made accurate perception and memory difficult. For example, in the late afternoon of April 1, the witness had been using marijuana, a substance likely to blur his initial perceptions and his memory of them. Furthermore, just before viewing the lineup, the witness had seen a photograph of D on a desk in the police station, an incident that could have influenced his selection. During the five weeks between April 1 and the time he saw the photographs, the witness had talked about and been questioned repeatedly about the crime, circumstances that often contaminate memory.

In the end, the jury was unable to reach a verdict. It is difficult to assess the impact of any one bit of testimony on a particular verdict. We can only speculate that the psychologist's testimony may have made the jury more cautious about accepting the eyewitness testimony. This idea is supported by recent studies showing that such expert testimony generally increases the deliberation time jurors devote to eyewitness aspects of a case.

Expert testimony on eyewitness reliability is controversial. It has its advocates and enemies in both the legal and psychological professions. For example, several judicial arguments are used routinely to exclude the testimony. One is that it "invades the province of the jury," meaning that it is the jury's job, not an expert's, to decide whether a particular witness was in a position to see, hear and remember what is being claimed in court. Another reason judges sometimes exclude such testimony is that the question of eyewitness reliability is "not beyond the knowledge and experience of a juror" and thus is not a proper subject matter for expert testimony.

In virtually all the cases in which a judge has prohibited the jury from hearing expert testimony, the higher courts have upheld the decision, and in some cases have driven home the point with negative comments about the use of psychologists. In a recent case in California, *People v. Plasencia*, Nick Plasencia Jr. was found guilty of robbery and other crimes in Los Angeles County. He had tried to introduce the testimony of a psychologist on eyewitness reliability, but the judge refused to admit it, saying that "the subject matter about which (the expert) sought to testify was too conjectural and too speculative to support any opinion he would offer." The appellate court upheld Plasencia's conviction and made known its strong feelings about the psychological testimony:

"Since our society has not reached the point where all human conduct is videotaped for later replay, resolution of disputes in our court system depends almost entirely on the testimony of witnesses who recount their observations of a myriad of events.

"These events include matters in both the criminal and civil areas of the law. The accuracy of a witness's testimony of course depends on factors which are as variable and complex as human nature itself. . . . The cornerstone of our system remains our belief in the wisdom and integrity of the jury system and the ability of 12 jurors to determine the accuracy of witnesses' testimony. The system has served us well. . . .

"It takes no expert to tell us that for various reasons, people can be mistaken about identity, or even the exact details of an observed event. Yet to present these commonly accepted and known facts in the form of an expert opinion, which opinion does nothing more than generally question the validity of one form of traditionally accepted evidence, would exaggerate the significance of that testimony and give a 'scientific aura' to a very unscientific matter.

"The fact remains, in spite of the universally recognized fallibility of human beings, persons do, on many occasions, correctly identify individuals. Evidence that under contrived test conditions, or even in real-life situations, certain persons totally unconnected with this case have been mistaken in their identification of individuals is no more relevant than evidence that in other cases, witnesses totally unconnected with this event have lied.

"It seems beyond question that the identifications in this case were correct. We find no abuse of discretion in the trial court's rejecting the proffered testimony."

Quite the opposite view was expressed by the Arizona Supreme Court in *State v. Chapple*. At the original trial, defendant Dolan Chapple had been convicted of three counts of murder and two drug-trafficking charges, chiefly on the testimony of two witnesses who identified him at the trial. Earlier they had selected him from photographs shown them by the police more than a year after the crime.

Chapple's lawyer tried to introduce expert psychological testimony on the accuracy of such identification. The judge refused to permit it on the grounds that the testimony would pertain only to matters "within the common experience" of jurors. The high court disagreed, maintaining that expert testimony would have provided scientific data on such pertinent matters as the accuracy of delayed identification, the effect of stress on perception and the relationship between witness confidence and accuracy. "We cannot assume," the court added, "that the average juror would be aware of the variables concerning identification and memory" about which the expert would have testified. Chapple's conviction was reversed, and he has been granted a new trial.

Like lawyers and judges, psychologists disagree on whether expert testimony is a good solution to the eyewitness problem. Two of the most outspoken critics are Michael McCloskey and Howard Egeth of The Johns Hopkins University. These experimental psychologists offer four reasons why they believe that expert testimony on eyewitness reliability is a poor idea. They say that there is no evidence that such testimony is needed, that there is no evidence that it does any good or that it can provide much beyond the intuitions of ordinary experience; that the data base on which the expert must rely is not sufficiently well-developed; and that conflicting public testimony between experts would tarnish the profession's image. Given this sorry state of affairs, they argue, psychologists may do more harm than good by intruding into judicial proceedings.

Obviously, many psychologists disagree with this assessment and believe that both the law and psychology gain from mutual interaction. In the area of eyewitness testimony, information supplied by psychologists to lawyers has stimulated responses that have suggested a number of important ideas for future research.

For example, psychologists need to learn more about the ideas that the rest of us have about the operation of human perception and memory. When these ideas are wrong, psychologists need to devise ways to educate us so that the judgments we make as jurors will be more fully informed and more fair. Only through this give-and-take, and occasional biting controversy, will progress be made. It is too late to help William Jackson, or Steve Titus, or Aaron Lee Owens, but it is not yet too late for the rest of us.

Face-Saving Memory

Eugene Winograd

The ability to recognize faces is not just an important social skill, it is absolutely essential for people in many occupations. The policeman and the politician, the doorman of an apartment building, the receptionist and the bank teller all come in contact with vast numbers of people and must be able to sort out the familiar face from the strange one.

Not all people have this ability to the same degree. Still, most of us are good enough at it to remember those we encounter frequently and to avoid embarrassment (the only exception being victims of certain forms of brain damage, usually from stroke, who exhibit a condition called prosopagnosia in which all faces appear unfamiliar as in a bad dream). For those who would like to improve their memory for faces, mnemonic-improvement books propose a few strategies. But recently, behavioral scientists have begun to clarify the cognitive processes that are involved and have proposed more effective learning methods.

Studies by Elizabeth Warrington at the National Hospital in London, Gordon Bower at Stanford, and my own studies at Emory University in Georgia suggest that one of the best strategies when meeting a person for the first time is to ask yourself a particular kind of question such as, "Would I buy a used car from this man?" The purpose is not to associate the face with positive or negative feelings about the person. You can get equally good recall by asking if the person looks like a teacher, or if he or she appears to be shy, or a host of other such questions. Nor does it matter whether the answer is yes or no. People are equally likely to recall faces they regard as trustworthy or not trustworthy, intelligent or lacking in intelligence. It's not the answer but the question that counts: the very processes needed to judge a face in this way also seem to increase recognition.

How does this method differ from older, standard techniques? The most common strategy is one that is often taught to policemen, perhaps the only professional group that receives special training in remembering faces in order to improve their capacity to describe criminal suspects. In Atlanta, for example, policemen are taught to note certain physical features of the suspect: shape of head, color and type of hair, and distinguishing marks, such as scars. To assess the methods that such seasoned observers use, we tested a group of experienced police officers at the Atlanta Police Academy. We showed them a series of 50 photographs of unfamiliar people and asked them to try to remember as many as they could. Although we did not instruct them to use any particular strategy, most of the officers informed us later that they had studied the features that their training emphasized. What we discovered suggests that their strategy was not of much use. For, when they were shown 30 of the same faces again mingled randomly with 30 new ones, the officers recognized about the same proportion of them as did a group of college students given the same test who had received no training and used no special strategy.

In our own work at Emory, we have used a more elaborate experimental procedure based on Warrington's method. We divide our volunteer subjects into three groups and show them 50 photographs of people they have never seen (in one case, pictures of male British actors taken from a casting directory). In the first group, subjects are asked to judge each face for a specific personality trait: for instance, whether or not it appears friendly, or whether or not it seems intelligent. We call these subjects the trait group. A second group, the physical features group, is asked one question about each face: for example, whether it has a big nose, or a square jaw, or, perhaps, bushy eyebrows. Those in a third group, the control group, are simply told to try to remember the faces and are left to their own devices. After the volunteers in all three groups are given the opportunity to peruse each of the 50 faces for eight seconds, they are shown an assortment of 100 photographs with the same 50 mixed randomly among faces they have never seen before and asked to pick out those that appeared in the first batch.

Common sense might predict that those who pay attention to specific features will come out best. However, in this case, common sense would be wrong. Subjects who judge faces on trait dimensions, such as friendliness or intelligence, remember 10 to 15 percent more faces on the average than do subjects who look at a physical feature specified by the experimenter beforehand. People who are simply told to remember the faces without any instructions in strategy do about as well on these tests as those who attend to physical features.

Why do trait judgments lead to better memory for faces? A currently influential theory of memory developed by F. I. M. Craik and Robert Lockhart at the University of Toronto starts with the premise that memory for any event is directly related to how deeply it was registered in the mind at the time it happened. Thus, for example, studies have shown that people who associate meanings with unfamiliar words or phrases recall them better than those who take note only of their sounds or of the physical pattern of letters on the page.

By analogy, some psychologists have assumed that for faces, deeper "encodings" of this sort occur when people are required to associate a face with personality traits and not just with specific physical features. While that line of argument is seductive, I prefer a less qualitative and more quantitative hypothesis, which says that memory for a face or for any visual pattern is a function of the amount of information the observer has extracted from it. The more characteristics of a face we register, the more likely we are to remember that face. At this point, the problem for the researcher is to come up with an experiment that can produce different outcomes for the depth-of-processing and the number-of-features hypotheses.

I have conducted such an experiment, this time comparing three groups: a traits group and a physical features group, both instructed exactly as before, plus a new group, which I called the distinctive features group. People in this new group were asked to tell us what they thought was the most prominent or distinctive feature of each face. The group would thus be examining physical features, like the second group, but with attention to many more of them, to find distinguishing characteristics on their own.

Surprisingly, the memory for faces of those in the distinctive features group was as good as that of those in the traits group. Both did better than those in the physical features group. These findings offer little support for the depth-of-processing position. After all, making a personality judgment should lead to more meaningful, deeper processing than searching for a prominent physical feature. Yet, the two conditions yielded equivalent performances on the memory test.

The findings are more in line with the hypothesis that memory for faces increases in direct relation to the number of features encoded. Personality judgments are effective, according to this hypothesis, simply because they lead to more information about the face being stored in memory. Similarly, the distinctive features strategy (one recommended by several books on memory skills) is effective because one has to scan the face, registering all of its characteristics, in order to decide which feature is most prominent. By contrast, in the physical features group, subjects' attention is directed to only one feature per face, that one is preselected by the investigator. These subjects necessarily encode less information.

What accounts for the evident individual differences among people in their memory for faces? My hunch is that some people unconsciously make extensive analyses of new faces, while others habitually encode fewer features. This line of argument would be on firmer ground if we could predict what types of people are likely to be good at it and what types are not. Our only attempt to do so was an experiment with college students in which Steven Nowicki, Barbara Millard, and I tried to determine whether recall for faces was influenced by two personality dimensions: anxiety and "locus of control," or how much control a person feels he has over his life.

Locus of control refers to the extent to which people perceive society's reward system as contingent on their own behavior. At one extreme, people with an external locus of control ("externals," for short) believe that how things work out depends mostly on luck, fate, or circumstance. Typical of an external is the view that whether you get an A or a C grade depends more on whether or not the teacher likes you than on how hard you work. "Internals," on the other hand, see a cause-and-effect relation between their behavior and what happens to them. We found that for male subjects, internals tended to remember faces better than externals did, but that anxiety was unrelated to facial memory. For female subjects, the relationship was different: the less anxious the subject, the more faces she recognized, but locus of control was not related to memory.

These results are too complex to point to any firm conclusions, but they do suggest that there may be some interesting relationships between personality and the memory for faces that should be pursued. By developing psychological profiles of those who perform best on this particular skill, we may get answers to larger questions of how memory works.

Eyewitness Identification:
What Can a Psychologist Tell a Jury?

Michael McCloskey
Howard E. Egeth

ABSTRACT: Psychologists have long been concerned about the use of eyewitness testimony in the courtroom. Recently, it has been suggested that experimental psychologists should testify as expert witnesses in cases involving eyewitnesses to inform the jury about problems with eyewitness testimony. In this article we examine the arguments offered in favor of the use of expert testimony about eyewitnesses. We suggest that contrary to strong claims made recently by several psychologists and lawyers, it is by no means clear that expert psychological testimony about eyewitnesses would improve jurors' ability to evaluate eyewitness testimony. In fact, it is even possible that this sort of expert testimony would have detrimental effects. We suggest that experimental psychologists should carefully consider the issues raised in this article when deciding whether to offer expert testimony.

Imagine the following scene. An experimental psychologist is sitting in his or her office, lost in thought, when the phone rings. An attorney is calling.

Psychologist: Hello.
Attorney: Hello, Dr. Smith, this is Joe Doaks; I'm an attorney. I've been retained by a man who has been charged with armed robbery. The prosecution's case does not look very impressive to me except for one point—at a lineup my client was positively identified by an eyewitness to the crime.

What I'm calling about is to ask if you'd be willing to serve as an expert witness for the defense to explain to the jury the problems with eyewitness testimony.

Psychologist: Well, I don't know. I don't think I'd be comfortable going into a courtroom and impugning the testimony of a witness.

Attorney: No, no, of course not. I would not want you to try to tell the jury whether or not the eyewitness is right. The judge would never allow such testimony anyway. All I would like you to do is talk in fairly general terms about the problems in perception and memory that can occur when a person observes a crime. I mean, the whole thing took place very quickly, the witness was very frightened, and the lineup didn't take place until 10 days after the crime. And on top of that, my client is black and the witness is white. These factors all can affect the accuracy of an eyewitness identification.

Psychologist: You seem to be quite knowledgeable about eyewitness testimony yourself; what do you need me for?

Attorney: Basically, I can only ask questions. I'm not permitted to lecture the jury about psychology. But you can. You would not be the first psychologist to give expert testimony about problems with eyewitnesses. Many of your colleagues have testified as experts in cases involving eyewitnesses, and many more probably will in the near future. Judges sometimes don't allow this sort of expert psychological testimony, but in many cases they do admit it.

Psychologist: This sounds very interesting, but I don't want to rush into it. Let me think about it for a few days and do some reading.

Attorney: Very good. I'll get back to you in a few days. Goodbye.

Psychologist: Goodbye.

What should the psychologist do? What considerations should inform the decision to testify or not to testify? In the following pages, we discuss several basic questions that we think the psychologist should consider in the process of reaching his or her decision. It should be made clear at the outset that this article has been written by and (largely) for experimental psychologists. The content is psychological. We have made no effort to consider legal aspects of the problem, such as laws affecting the admissibility of psychological testimony in various jurisdictions (such discussions are provided by Ellison & Buckout, 1981; Gass, 1979; Loftus & Monahan, 1980; Woocher, 1977).

A basic premise of our discussion is that intervention in the workings of the justice system should not be undertaken lightly. In particular, we take the position that expert psychological testimony about perception and memory in eyewitnesses[1] should be offered only if there is clear evidence that such testimony has salutary effects. As we discuss in greater detail below, the use of expert psychological testimony in the absence of clear evidence of its utility would carry substantial risks both for the system of justice and for the psychological profession. Consequently, in the following evaluation of arguments that have been offered in favor of the use of expert psychological testimony, we ask not, Does this claim seem plausible? or Might this assumption be valid? but rather, What does the available evidence say about this argument?

The final decision about whether to testify is up to the individual psychologist. However, we suggest that contrary to the claims of several psychologists and lawyers (e.g., Addison, 1978; Ellison & Buckhout, 1981; Loftus, 1979; Loftus & Monahan, 1980; Lower, 1978; Starkman, 1979; Woocher, 1977) the available evidence fails to demonstrate the general utility of expert psychological testimony and in fact does not even rule out the possibility that such testimony may have detrimental effects.

---

[1] We will henceforth use the phrase "expert psychological testimony" as a convenient shorthand for the more cumbersome "expert psychological testimony about perception and memory in eyewitnesses." It should be understood that we are referring only to expert testimony about eyewitnesses and not to other sorts of expert psychological testimony.

Rationales for the Use of Expert Psychological Testimony

Two major rationales have been offered for the use of expert psychological testimony. First, the *discrimination* rationale asserts that jurors cannot discriminate adequately between accurate and inaccurate eyewitnesses (Lindsay, Wells, & Rumpel, 1981; Loftus, 1979; Loftus & Monahan, 1980; Wells, Lindsay, & Ferguson, 1979; Wells, Lindsay, & Tousignant, 1980). Consequently, the argument continues, jurors often disbelieve accurate witnesses and believe inaccurate witnesses. According to this view, expert psychological testimony could improve juror discrimination by informing jurors about factors known to influence witness accuracy and by cautioning against reliance on irrelevant factors.

The second rationale for the use of expert psychological testimony asserts that jurors are in general too willing to believe eyewitness testimony (Ellison & Buckhout, 1981; Lindsay et al., 1981; Loftus, 1974, 1979; Loftus & Monahan, 1980; Wall, 1965; Wells et al., 1980). According to this *overbelief* rationale, an expert witness could increase juror skepticism to a more appropriate level by discussing research demonstrating the unreliability of eyewitness testimony and by pointing out aspects of the case at hand (e.g., stress experienced by the witness) that might have led to witness inaccuracy. Loftus (1979) provides a strong statement of the overbelief claim: "Since jurors rarely regard eyewitness testimony with any skepticism, the expert testimony will increase the likelihood of this happening. This is its value" (p. 197).

Both the discrimination and the overbelief rationales make two fundamental claims: (a) Jurors need help in evaluating eyewitness testimony and (b) expert psychological testimony can provide this help. In the following sections we examine these claims.

Do Jurors Need Help?

Overbelief. Consider first the claim that jurors are too willing to believe eyewitnesses. Several arguments have been advanced in support of this claim. One argument that is frequently implicit in discussions of juror evaluation of eyewitness testimony (e.g., Ellison & Buckhout, 1981; Loftus, 1979; Woocher, 1977) is that the conclusion of juror overbelief follows from research showing that eyewitness testimony is often unreliable. An important but unstated assumption here is that jurors are not aware of the unreliability of eyewitnesses and consequently are too willing to believe eyewitness testimony. However, there is virtually no empirical evidence that people are unaware of the problems with eyewitness testimony. Further, there appears to be no reason to assume a priori that people are not cognizant of these problems. Cases of mistaken identification are often widely publicized and wrongful conviction on the basis of mistaken or perjured eyewitness testimony is a rather common theme in fiction. In addition, there is no consensus within the legal community that jurors are unaware of the unreliability of eyewitnesses and consequently give too much credence to eyewitness testimony. For example, in ruling against the admission of expert psychological testimony, the trial judge in the case of *People v. Guzman*[2] stated: "It is something that everyone knows about, the problems of identification. The jurors here were well questioned regarding their experience . . . with having mistakenly identified people. Everyone knows these things happen." Thus, in the absence of evidence that jurors are unaware of the unreliability of eyewitness testimony, the conclusion that jurors are too willing to believe eyewitnesses cannot legitimately be drawn from research demonstrating that eyewitnesses are often inaccurate.

A second argument asserts that juror overbelief is demonstrated by the existence of documented cases in which defendants were wrongfully convicted on the basis of eyewitness testimony later shown to be mistaken. The implicit assumption here seems to be that if jurors were appropriately skeptical, wrongful convictions based upon erroneous identifications would never occur. But this is not a tenable position. It must be borne in mind that the degree of skepticism jurors exhibit toward eyewitnesses will affect not only the likelihood that an innocent defendant will be convicted but also the likelihood that a guilty defendant will not be convicted. Thus, an increase in juror skepticism toward eyewitness testimony would decrease convictions of the guilty as well as convictions of the innocent, and a degree of skepticism that eliminated wrongful conviction on the basis of eyewitness testimony would also eliminate any role of eyewitnesses in the conviction of the guilty. In signal-detection terms, it is unfortunate but true that except in situations involving very high signal-to-noise ratios, one cannot eliminate false alarms without also eliminating hits merely by shifting one's decision criterion. Consequently, some wrongful convictions must be accepted as the unavoidable price for convicting guilty defendants. As Rembar (1980) puts it, "A system of justice that has no miscarriages of justice is not a workable system of justice" (p. 95).

To demonstrate juror overbelief in eyewitnesses, one must show not merely that erroneous convictions based on eyewitness testimony sometimes occur but that the ratio of conviction of the innocent to conviction of the guilty is unacceptably high. However, documented cases of wrongful conviction resulting from mistaken eyewitness testimony obviously represent only a small fraction of 1% of the cases in which defendants were convicted at least in part on the basis of eyewitness testimony. Thus, although we cannot say what should be considered an acceptable ratio of conviction of the innocent to conviction of the guilty, it would seem to be difficult to argue that documented cases of wrongful conviction establish that the ratio is unacceptably high. Consequently, the known cases of erroneous convictions fail to demonstrate that jurors are too willing to believe eyewitness testimony (Pachella, 1981).

---

2 People v. Guzman, 47 Cal. App. 3rd 380, 121 Cal. Rptr. 69 (1975).

Our point here is not that the frequency of wrongful conviction is acceptably low but merely that known cases of erroneous conviction fail to establish that the frequency is unacceptably high. Thus, our argument is not affected by the possibility that documented cases of wrongful conviction represent only the tip of the iceberg. In the absence of a means of estimating the number of undocumented cases of wrongful conviction, these undocumented cases cannot be used as evidence that erroneous conviction on the basis of eyewitness testimony occurs too often.

A third argument offered in favor of the overbelief claim is based on an experiment by Loftus (1974, 1979; see also Cavoukian, Note 1). In this experiment, university students read a very brief summary of evidence presented at a robbery-murder trial and voted individually for conviction or acquittal. In the no-eyewitness condition, the trial description mentioned only physical evidence against the defendant (e.g., money found in the defendant's room). Only 18% of the subjects in this condition voted for conviction. In the eyewitness condition, the trial description mentioned the physical evidence and also indicated that an eyewitness had identified the defendant as the robber. In this condition, 72% of the students voted to convict. Finally, in the discredited eyewitness condition, subjects were told about the physical evidence and the eyewitness identification. However, they were also informed that the defense attorney "claimed the witness had not been wearing his glasses the day of the robbery, and since he had vision poorer than 20/400, he could not possibly have seen the face of the robber from where he stood" (Loftus, 1979, p. 117). In this condition, 68% of the students voted to convict. The high percentage of subjects voting for conviction in the eyewitness condition and the lack of difference between the eyewitness and discredited-eyewitness conditions, it is argued, indicate that people give too much credence to eyewitness testimony.

Several recent studies, however, cast doubt on this conclusion. First, an experiment was recently conducted in our laboratory in which subjects read detailed summaries (4,000–6,500 words) of a fictitious bank robbery trial and voted individually for conviction or acquittal (McKenna, Mellott, & Webb, Note 2). The bank teller who was robbed chose the defendant from a lineup two days after the robbery and positively identified him during the trial. In addition, the prosecution demonstrated that an amount of money closely matching that stolen from the bank was found in the defendant's possession.

The defense consisted of the testimony of the defendant's mother. She stated that the money found in the defendant's possession was a loan from her so that the defendant could buy a car and that the defendant had followed his normal routine the day of the robbery, coming home from his night job in the morning, going to sleep, and getting up at 5 p.m. On cross-examination, the defendant's mother admitted that she could not be sure that the defendant was at home at the time of the robbery, as his door was closed.

Part of our original purpose in conducting this study was to examine the impact of expert psychological testimony. Hence, the experiment included a no-expert-testimony condition, in which only the testimony described above was presented, and an expert-testimony condition, in which the trial summary included testimony of an experimental psychologist concerning factors (e.g., stress) that may lead to inaccurate eyewitness identifications.

In spite of the teller's positive identification of the defendant, guilty verdicts were obtained from only 2 of the 24 subjects (8%) in the no-expert-testimony condition and 3 of the 48 subjects (6%) in the condition involving expert testimony. Examination of the subject explanations for their verdicts revealed that many, including those in the no-expert testimony condition, felt that although the defendant may well have been guilty, it was possible that the teller had made an erroneous identification. Consequently, they were not certain enough of the defendant's guilt to vote for conviction. In subsequent experiments, we have replicated these results using adults from the Baltimore community as subjects and with a trial scenario in which the defense case in a robbery-murder trial consisted solely of the defendant's testimony that he was at home alone at the time of the crime.

Similar findings have been obtained by Hosch, Beck, and McIntyre (1980). In their study, subjects serving in eight six-person juries viewed a trial in which an eyewitness positively identified the defendant. Four of the juries heard expert psychological testimony; the other four juries did not. After deliberating, all eight juries voted unanimously for acquittal. These results are somewhat difficult to reconcile with Loftus's claim that jurors rarely regard eyewitness testimony with any skepticism.

Other studies have examined the claim that jurors will believe even a discredited eyewitness. In an experiment in which subjects made individual guilty/not guilty decisions after reading a detailed summary of a robbery-murder trial, we found that the subjects disregarded a prosecution eyewitness who was convincingly discredited (McCloskey, Egeth, Webb, Washburn, & McKenna, Note 3). Hatvany and Strack (1980) and Weinberg and Baron (1982) have obtained similar results.

Thus, studies using methodologies similar to that of the Loftus (1974, 1979) experiment have shown that (a) a high percentage of subjects do not routinely vote guilty when an eyewitness has positively identified the defendant and (b) when a witness is convincingly discredited, his or her testimony is disregarded. Although definite conclusions about the behavior of jurors in actual trials cannot readily be drawn from these studies, the results clearly suggest that the Loftus study should not be taken as strong support for the juror overbelief argument.[3]

---

[3] One question of interest at this point is, What are the reasons for the differences in results between the Loftus experiment and later studies? Results we have obtained (McCloskey et al., Note 3) suggest that Loftus obtained high percentages of guilty verdicts whereas subjects in our study and in that of Hosch et al. (1980) rarely voted guilty because subjects in the latter two studies, but not in the Loftus experiment, received judges' instructions on the *beyond a reasonable doubt* criterion for voting guilty. However the reasons for the discrepancies between the Loftus study and other experiments in regard to the effects of discrediting manipulations are not clear (see Weinberg & Baron, 1982).

A final argument in favor of the claim that jurors overbelieve eyewitnesses stems from a recent series of experiments by Wells, Lindsay, and their colleagues (Lindsay et al., 1981; Wells et al., 1980). In these experiments, subjects serving as witnesses viewed a staged crime and then attempted to identify the criminal from an array of photographs. Witnesses who made accurate identifications as well as witnesses who identified the wrong person were then videotaped as they answered questions about the viewing conditions, the appearance of the criminal, and so forth. Additional subjects serving as jurors watched videotapes of witnesses and judged for each whether the witness had made an accurate identification. Under some witnessing conditions, the percentage of jurors believing a witness was higher than the percentage of witnesses who made accurate identifications. For example, in one situation 50% of the witnesses made an accurate identification. However, jurors viewing videotapes believed witnesses from that condition 66% of the time. Lindsay et al. (1981) and Wells et al. (1980) argue on the basis of these results that jurors are too willing to believe eyewitness testimony.

Although the Wells and Lindsay argument seems plausible, it is not entirely valid. The logic of the argument appears to be as follows: The finding that juror belief rates exceed witness accuracy rates implies that jurors overestimate the probability that an eyewitness is accurate, and this in turn implies that jurors are too willing to believe eyewitnesses.

There are some difficulties with the first step in this argument, because the finding that the percentage of jurors believing a witness was higher than the percentage of witnesses who were accurate does not necessarily imply that the jurors overestimated the probability that the witness was accurate.[4] However, even if we ignore this problem and assume that in some situations jurors overestimate the probability that an eyewitness is accurate, the conclusion that jurors are too willing to believe eyewitnesses does not follow. As we discussed earlier, to say that jurors are too willing to believe eyewitnesses means that jurors are too willing to *convict* on the basis of eyewitness testimony (or, more technically, that the weight given by jurors to eyewitness testimony results in an unacceptably high ratio of number of innocent defendants convicted to number of guilty defendants convicted).

Although we would expect the likelihood of conviction to increase monotonically with jurors' degree of belief in a prosecution eyewitness, data suggesting that jurors overestimate the probability that eyewitnesses are accurate do not necessarily imply that jurors are overly willing to convict on the basis of eyewitness testimony. The reasonable doubt criterion, among other things, intervenes between

---

[4] A simple example serves to make this point. Consider a situation in which 90% of witnesses make an accurate identification. If jurors accurately estimate the probability that a witness was accurate at .9, all jurors will probably make *believe* decisions, and the juror belief rate (100%) will exceed the witness accuracy rate (90%).

judging the likelihood that a witness is accurate and voting to convict or to acquit. In our research, we have frequently seen subjects, who read trial summaries and arrived at verdicts, vote not guilty in spite of a stated belief that an eyewitness who identified the defendant was probably correct. These subjects generally say that although they believe the defendant is probably guilty, they are not certain beyond a reasonable doubt. Thus, if the criterion for convict decisions is sufficiently stringent, juror overestimates of witness accuracy need not result in an overwillingness to convict on the basis of eyewitness testimony. More generally, our point here is that in the absence of data concerning jurors' criteria for convict/acquit decisions, we cannot determine from juror estimates of witness accuracy (or, more specifically, from the believe/disbelieve judgments collected by Wells et al. and Lindsay et al.) whether jurors are insufficiently likely, just likely enough, or too likely to convict on the basis of eyewitness testimony.

One other point should be made regarding the Wells et al. and Lindsay et al. results. In considering whether jurors overbelieve eyewitnesses, we have focused on the question of whether juror evaluation of eyewitness testimony results in an acceptable ratio of number of innocent defendants convicted to number of guilty defendants convicted. However, one may also ask whether jurors give eyewitness testimony appropriate weight relative to other sorts of evidence (e.g., the defendant's fingerprints found at the scene of the crime, money found in the defendant's possession, alibi evidence). If it could be determined that jurors give eyewitness testimony too much weight relative to some other types of evidence, it might be argued that at least in some sense jurors overbelieve eyewitness testimony. (Of course, if in this situation juror evaluation of eyewitnesses produced appropriate conviction rates, it might more reasonably be concluded that the other evidence was underbelieved.)

Unfortunately, the question of whether jurors give eyewitness testimony too much weight relative to other sorts of evidence is difficult to answer, for at least two reasons. First, there are few studies comparing the weight given to eyewitness testimony with that accorded other types of evidence. Second, and most important, it is difficult to determine how much weight various sorts of evidence should be given relative to each other. Thus, we have little to say about juror evaluation of eyewitnesses relative to other types of evidence. However, we should point out that the Wells et al. and Lindsay et al. findings suggesting that subject-jurors may sometimes overestimate the probability that an eyewitness identification was accurate do not imply that jurors overvalue eyewitness testimony relative to other sorts of evidence. It is certainly conceivable that studies using the Wells-Lindsay paradigm, with other kinds of evidence substituted for eyewitness testimony, might show that jurors "overbelieve" (in the Wells-Lindsay sense) those other kinds of evidence as well. (Although, as we mentioned earlier, this sort of overbelief would not necessarily imply an overwillingness to convict.) Thus, the Wells et al. and Lindsay et al. findings demonstrate neither that jurors are overly willing to convict on the basis of eyewitness testimony nor that eyewitness testimony is overvalued relative to other sorts of evidence.

Finally, in discussing juror overbelief we should mention two recent studies of actual trial outcomes that cast doubt on the claim that jurors rarely regard eyewitness testimony with any skepticism. Chen (1981) tabulated the outcomes of all criminal cases in the Los Angeles County system from July 1977 through December 1978. Other factors partialed out, the ratio of convictions in cases with at least one eyewitness identification of the defendant to convictions in cases without identification was 1.1 to 1. Similarly, Myers (1979) examined the 201 criminal cases tried by jury in Marion County, Indiana, between January 1974 and June 1976. She found that convictions were no more likely in cases involving identification of the defendant by a victim or other eyewitness(es) than in cases where there was no eyewitness identification. These sorts of results are, of course, not definitive. For example, the prosecution may have brought otherwise weaker cases to trial when an eyewitness was available than when there was no eyewitness. Nevertheless, the Chen and Myers findings cast doubt on the claim that jurors rarely regard eyewitness testimony with any skepticism. A dramatic illustration of this point is provided by the case of a man who was arrested 13 times and tried 5 times in an 18-month period for a series of crimes that were later confessed to by another man. What is noteworthy about this is that he was acquitted in all five trials, even though one or more eyewitnesses testified against him in each (Shoemaker, 1980).

In summary, the available evidence fails to show that jurors are overly willing to believe eyewitness testimony. This does not mean that jurors exhibit an appropriate degree of skepticism toward eyewitness testimony. Our point is simply that contrary to the claims of many psychologists and lawyers (e.g., Ellison & Buckhout, 1981; Lindsay et al., 1981; Loftus, 1974, 1979; Loftus & Monahan, 1980; Wells et al., 1980; Woocher, 1977), juror overbelief in eyewitnesses has not been demonstrated. Consequently, it is by no means clear that there is a need for expert psychological testimony to make jurors more skeptical.

Discrimination. The discrimination rationale asserts that regardless of whether jurors are generally skeptical or generally, credulous of eyewitness testimony, they cannot distinguish well between accurate and inaccurate eyewitnesses. According to this view, expert psychological testimony could improve juror discrimination.

The claim that jurors cannot readily discriminate accurate from inaccurate eyewitnesses appears to be well founded. Cases of wrongful conviction based on mistaken eyewitness testimony demonstrate that juror discrimination is not perfect, and the recent studies of Wells, Lindsay, and their colleagues suggest that jurors' ability to distinguish accurate and inaccurate eyewitnesses may indeed be quite poor. As we mentioned above, these researchers conducted a series of studies in which subjects serving as jurors judged whether witnesses to staged crimes made an accurate or inaccurate identification of the perpetrator. They found that within a given crime situation, jurors were as likely to believe inaccurate witnesses as they were to believe accurate witnesses (Lindsay et al., 1981; Wells et al., 1979, 1980).

Although these results are clearly very disturbing, the situation is perhaps not as bleak as it first appears. In the Lindsay et al. (1981) study, the witnesses viewed a staged crime under either good, moderate, or poor viewing conditions (in the *poor* condition, for example, the criminal was visible for only 12 seconds and wore a hat that completely covered his hair, whereas in the *good* condition the criminal's head was uncovered and he was visible for 20 seconds). Accurate identification of the criminal was made by 33%, 50%, and 74% of the witnesses in the poor, moderate, and good viewing conditions, respectively. Jurors in the study (see also Wells et al., 1980) were just as likely to believe inaccurate as accurate witnesses *within a given viewing condition*. (For example, inaccurate witnesses from the good viewing condition were believed as often as accurate witnesses from the same condition.) However, jurors were less likely to believe witnesses, the less favorable the viewing conditions. Specifically, juror belief rates were 77%, 66%, and 62%, for witnesses in the good, moderate, and poor viewing conditions, respectively. These results suggest that jurors weighing eyewitness testimony are able to take into account at least some factors that influence witness accuracy. Nevertheless, it seems clear that jurors' ability to discriminate accurate from inaccurate witnesses is far from perfect.

Can Psychologists Provide the Needed Help?

Our conclusions above are that (a) it is by no means clear that jurors need expert testimony to make them appropriately skeptical but that (b) there is room for improvement in the ability of jurors to discriminate accurate from inaccurate witnesses. In this section, we consider the possible effects of expert psychological testimony on jurors.

Three recent studies suggest that expert psychological testimony may serve to make jurors more skeptical of eyewitness testimony (Hosch et al, 1980; Loftus, 1980; Wells et al., 1980). For example, Wells et al. found that expert psychological testimony reduced the likelihood that a subject would believe that an eyewitness to a staged crime made an accurate identification, and Loftus reported that subjects who read brief trial summaries were less likely to vote guilty when the summaries included expert psychological testimony than when no such testimony was included. It is not a straightforward matter to extrapolate the results of these studies to the verdicts of real juries. However, even if we accept the findings at face value, we are left with the following question: Given the absence of clear evidence that jurors overbelieve eyewitnesses, is it really appropriate for psychologists to offer expert testimony that serves to reduce jurors' overall level of belief in eyewitnesses?

If we turn now to the possible effects of expert psychological testimony on jurors' ability to discriminate accurate from inaccurate eyewitnesses, we find only one relevant study (Wells et al., 1980). This study employed the basic Wells-Lindsay paradigm described above, in which subjects serving as jurors judged whether or not witnesses to a staged crime accurately identified the perpetrator. In the Wells et al. (1980) study, half of the "jurors" received expert psychological advice before judging the credibility of witnesses, and the remaining "jurors" received no expert advice. The expert testimony emphasized two general points. The first was that eyewitness identification in criminal cases is quite different from recognizing one's friends and associates, in that research using staged crimes has shown that, depending on conditions, 15% to 85% of eyewitnesses may choose the wrong person from a lineup. The second major point was that there is considerable evidence to show that witness confidence may have little or no relationship to witness accuracy. The psychologist also mentioned that jurors should pay attention to situational factors that might affect witness accuracy.

"Jurors" in the expert-advice and no-expert advice conditions viewed videotapes of witnesses and made believe/disbelieve judgments. The videotapes were taken from the Lindsay et al. (1981) study in which witnesses observed a staged crime under poor, moderate, and good viewing conditions (resulting in 33%, 50%, and 74% accurate identifications, respectively).

As mentioned above, the expert psychological testimony reduced the jurors' overall willingness to believe eyewitnesses. However, the expert testimony had absolutely no effect on jurors' ability to discriminate accurate from inaccurate witnesses.

In summary, the available evidence suggests that there may be a rather ironic mismatch between the type of help needed by jurors and the possible effects of expert psychological testimony. Specifically, jurors clearly need help in discriminating accurate from inaccurate eyewitnesses but may not need to be made more skeptical overall. Expert testimony, on the other hand, may serve to increase juror skepticism but not to improve juror discrimination.

Of course, firm conclusions at this point would be premature. This is especially true with regard to the effects of expert psychological testimony on juror discrimination. As we have seen, only one study relevant to this issue has been conducted (Wells et al., 1980). Furthermore, the expert testimony used in that study may not have been optimal for improving juror discrimination. Aside from the negative advice to ignore witness confidence, jurors were told only to examine "situational factors." It is certainly conceivable that expert testimony that provided a detailed discussion of specific factors that affect witness accuracy would result in better juror discrimination. Nevertheless, we must conclude that at present there is no evidence that expert psychological advice improves juror evaluation of eyewitness testimony.

Expert Psychological Testimony and the Factors Affecting Witness Accuracy

At this point, an advocate of the use of expert psychological testimony might argue as follows: "Although the Wells et al. (1980)

study failed to show an improvement in juror discrimination of accurate and inaccurate witnesses as a result of expert advice, this failure probably reflects, as mentioned above, the vagueness of the expert's remarks. There is every reason to believe that more specific expert testimony would improve juror discrimination. Empirical research has identified many variables that affect witness accuracy in ways that are not obvious to the lay juror. Expert testimony that discusses these factors in detail would, and in practice does, increase jurors' ability to distinguish accurate from inaccurate eyewitnesses."

The validity of this argument can be assessed only through additional research. We suggest, however, that there is less reason than might be supposed for optimism about the effects of expert psychological testimony on juror discrimination. The claim that detailed expert testimony would improve juror discrimination rests on the assumption that there are many variables for which both of the following are true: (a) The relationship between the variable and eyewitness accuracy is known to psychologists as the result of empirical research, and (b) jurors do not understand how the variable is related to witness accuracy. However, it turns out to be surprisingly difficult to find variables of this sort. In other words, for many (if not most) variables that have been listed as suitable topics for expert testimony, either the effects of the variable on witness accuracy are not well documented, or these effects are probably obvious to the juror. A few examples will illustrate this point.

For a variable such as exposure duration, the well-documented effects are probably obvious to jurors. It is difficult to imagine that jurors are not aware of the fact that longer exposures lead to increased witness accuracy.

For retention interval, the situation is slightly more complex. Since the time of Ebbinghaus (1885/1913), the verbal-learning literature has quite consistently shown that retention declines as a function of the delay between the learning experience and the subsequent test. For face recognition, there are fewer studies, and the available data are not entirely consistent. Many studies show run-of-the-mill retention losses. For example, Shepherd and Ellis (1973) measured recognition performance a few minutes, 6 days, or 35 days after exposure. Performance declined from 87% correct to 71% over that period. However, others have failed to find performance declining over time. For example, Goldstein and Chance (1971) found accuracy to be unaffected by delay over the range 0-48 hours. Similarly, Laughery, Fessler, Lenorovitz, and Yoblick (1974) found no difference in recognition performance among the six retention intervals they studied (4 minutes, 30 minutes, 1 hour, 4 hours, 1 day, and 1 week). Finally, it is worth noting that Carr, Deffenbacher, and Leu (Note 4; see also Deffenbacher, Carr, & Leu, 1981) actually found a reminiscence effect— recognition of faces was slightly better 2 weeks after original viewing than 2 minutes after. This pattern of results did not obtain for the other classes of stimuli that were tested (concrete nouns, pictures of common objects, and pictures of landscapes).

There are two ways in which this situation can be assessed. First, one could conclude that at present the effects of retention interval on face recognition are not sufficiently well understood to be discussed in expert testimony. Alternatively, one could argue that the available evidence on memory in general overwhelmingly supports the generalization that retention declines with delay between acquisition and test. According to this view, the face recognition studies showing no effect of retention interval, or reminiscence, would be said to fail to reflect the true state of affairs. If this latter position is taken, however, it follows that the true effects of retention interval on face recognition probably match jurors' beliefs about these effects and consequently, that expert testimony about retention interval may be unnecessary.

Consider now the cross-racial identification effect. Several studies have shown that cross-racial identification (e.g., white witness black defendant) is more difficult than within-racial identification (e.g., black witness–black defendant; Malpass & Kravitz, 1969). The result is often discussed (e.g., Loftus, 1979) as if it were not obvious to the lay juror. However, the claim that jurors are unaware of the difficulty of cross-racial identification is questionable at best. For example, the cliche "they all look alike to me" used in reference to members of another race suggests that there may be a general awareness of the difficulty of cross-racial identification. In fact, the Devlin (1976) report describes studies of cross-racial identification as "support for what is widely accepted on the basis of common intuition" (p. 73).

Loftus (1979; see also Deffenbacher & Loftus, 1982; Yarmey & Jones, 1983), in a study of beliefs about factors affecting witness accuracy, found that only, 55% of the subjects correctly answered a four-alternative multiple-choice question concerning cross-racial identification. However, this result probably should not be taken too seriously as evidence that people do not understand the difficulty of cross-racial identification, because Loftus's question was extremely complex and difficult to understand:

Two women are walking to school one morning, one of them an Asian and the other white. Suddenly, two men, one black and one white, jump into their path and attempt to grab their purses. Later, the women are shown photographs of known purse snatchers in the area. Which statement best describes your view of the women's ability to identify the purse snatchers?

(a) Both the Asian and the white woman will find the white man harder to identify than the black man.
(b) The white woman will find the black man more difficult to identify than the white man.
(c) The Asian woman will have an easier time than the white woman making an accurate identification of both
(d) The white woman will find the black easier to identify than the white man. (p. 172)

In a similar study, Deffenbacher and Loftus (1982) asked subjects their opinion of the cliche "they all look alike to me." The answer Deffenbacher and Loftus deemed correct, "it is true," was chosen by only about 20% of the subjects. However, this result should not be taken to indicate that people are unaware of the difficulty of cross-racial identification because "they all look alike to me" is obviously a gross overstatement. Thus, many people may judge this statement to be technically false even though they feel that there is a kernel of truth in it.

At present, then, it is by no means clear that jurors are unaware of the difficulty of cross-racial identification.

Finally, for several variables that purportedly have nonobvious effects on accuracy and consequently are cited as appropriate topics for expert testimony, there is in fact little empirical evidence about how (or even if) these variables affect new performance. Consider, for example, weapon focus, which is the alleged tendency of a person threatened with a weapon to focus on the weapon and consequently pay little attention to the appearance of his or her assailant. Although weapon focus is frequently cited as an important factor in assessing eyewitness accuracy and has been discussed in expert testimony (see Loftus, 1979, pp. 223–224), there is virtually no evidence that the phenomenon actually occurs. The single unpublished experiment cited as a demonstration of weapon focus (Johnson & Scott, Note 5) is "suggestive . . . but it is far from conclusive" (Loftus, 1979, p. 36). As another example, it is widely claimed (e.g., Loftus, 1979; Woocher, 1977) that stress or arousal experienced by a witness during an event has detrimental effects on the accuracy of the witness's testimony, and this claim is frequently a prominent feature of expert testimony. Unfortunately, there is little basis for this claim. Deffenbacher (1982), in a review of research concerning the effects of arousal on the reliability of eyewitness testimony, lists 19 relevant studies. He reports that 10 of these studies found decreases in eyewitness accuracy with increased arousal, whereas the remaining 9 found that increases in arousal improved eyewitness performance or had no effect.

Deffenbacher claims that these seemingly disparate results conform to the Yerkes-Dodson law, which states that the function relating stress or arousal to performance is an inverted U, such that performance is poorer at very high or very low levels of arousal than at intermediate levels. This claim is unwarranted, however, because Deffenbacher fits the data to the Yerkes-Dodson function simply by assuming that studies showing that performance increased with arousal involved levels of arousal below the optimal arousal level, whereas studies showing impairment of performance with increasing arousal involved arousal levels above the optimal level. Deffenbacher also claims that actual crime situations usually involve arousal levels higher than the optimal level and so concludes that eyewitness performance in these situations is adversely affected. Again, however, the claim that stress in crime situations is above the optimal level is merely an assumption. Deffenbacher's claims about arousal and eyewitness performance may well be correct, but at present there is little empirical basis for these claims.

There may be variables that have well-documented effects that are not obvious to jurors. Biases in identification procedures provide one possible example. However, it is by no means the case that there are a large number of variables with well-documented nonobvious effects. Thus, the argument that expert psychological testimony could almost certainly improve juror discrimination does not appear to be well founded. Testimony that asserts as fact effects that have not been demonstrated (e.g., effects of stress or weapon focus) is clearly inappropriate (and in any event there is no reason to believe that the introduction of undocumented assertions would improve juror performance); testimony limited to documented phenomena, however, may tell jurors little that they don't already know.[5]

It might be argued that expert testimony about obvious variables such as exposure duration, lighting, retention interval and so forth could be beneficial even if jurors understand the effects of these variables, because jurors might not spontaneously think about such variables when evaluating a witness's testimony. However, this argument ignores the fact that the defense attorney in a case involving an eyewitness identification will (in opening and closing statements and in the examination of witnesses) certainly call to the jury's attention any factors (e.g., poor lighting) suggesting that the identification may be inaccurate. Similarly, the prosecutor will point out factors (e.g., long exposure duration) suggesting that the identification is accurate. Thus, expert psychological testimony does not appear to be needed to call the jury's attention to obvious variables.

The Risks of Premature Intervention

We have argued that the available evidence fails to demonstrate that expert psychological testimony will routinely improve jurors' ability to evaluate eyewitness testimony. However, neither do the data rule out the possibility that expert testimony could have beneficial effects.

Clearly, what is needed is additional research concerning eyewitness testimony, juror evaluation of eyewitness testimony, and the effects on jurors of various sorts of expert psychological testimony.[6] If

---

[5] It is worth pointing out here that even if there were a large number of variables with well-documented nonobvious effects, expert psychological testimony concerning these variables would not necessarily improve juror evaluation of eyewitness testimony. The information provided by the psychologist would be probabilistic in nature (Loftus & Monahan, 1980; Pachella, 1981) and would not provide the jury with a basis for deciding that an eyewitness was definitely accurate or definitely inaccurate. Furthermore, the expert testimony generally would not give the jury any basis for deciding how large an effect a particular factor would have in the situation at hand. Thus, the expert psychological testimony might be of little benefit to the jurors and could even have detrimental effects if, for example, jurors grossly overestimated the importance of one or more of the factors discussed by the psychologist.

[6] It is beyond the scope of this article to discuss what form future research should take. However, we note that due to a lack of external validity, many of the studies we have discussed may be limited in the extent to which their results can be generalized to actual situations. We have chosen not to dwell on problems of external validity in our discussion of previous research, but the external validity

this research establishes that jurors are too willing to convict on the basis of eyewitness testimony or that jurors give disproportionate weight to eyewitnesses relative to other sorts of evidence, then expert psychological testimony should be considered as one of several possible methods of improving juror performance. Similarly, if research demonstrates that expert testimony can improve jurors' ability to discriminate accurate from inaccurate witnesses without producing undesirable side effects, such testimony clearly should be employed in the courtroom.

In the meantime, however, what should a psychologist do when asked to testify? When we have discussed our misgivings about expert psychological testimony with our colleagues, the reaction has often been something like this: "Well, maybe you're right when you say that it hasn't been demonstrated that expert psychological testimony helps the jury. However, it might help, and at least it can't hurt, so why not use it?"

We strongly disagree with this argument for several reasons. First, contrary to the claim that "at least it can't hurt," the possibility that psychological testimony has detrimental effects cannot be ruled out. For example, if jurors are already appropriately skeptical about eyewitness testimony, expert psychological testimony might make jurors too skeptical.[7] In addition, in discussing phenomena that are incompletely understood, an expert might give groundless information to the jury (see, e.g., discussion of stress and weapon focus above). Thus, it is even conceivable that expert testimony could decrease the ability of jurors to discriminate accurate from inaccurate witnesses.

A second difficulty with the argument that expert psychological testimony should be used because it might help is that a trial judge would not admit expert testimony on this basis. For expert testimony to be admitted, stronger arguments in its favor would have to be offered. Thus, a psychologist who decided to testify on the basis of the "it might help—at least it can't hurt" argument would in some sense have to misrepresent his or her testimony to the court.

Finally, the use of expert psychological testimony in the absence of clear evidence that it benefits the jury carries risks to the

---

issue should be given careful consideration in future work (see, e.g., Konecni & Ebbesen, 1979).

[7] It is worth mentioning here that the expert testimony in the Wells et al. (1980) study apparently caused subject-jurors in at least some conditions to underestimate the probability that an eyewitness had made an accurate identification. In a condition yielding 50% witness accuracy, subject-jurors who heard expert testimony believed witnesses only, about 32% of the time. Similarly, in a condition producing 74% witness accuracy, the juror belief rate was only about 53%. If we assume that jurors make believe decisions when they estimate the probability of witness accuracy to be greater than .5, these results suggest substantial underestimation of the probability that a witness was accurate. Of course, such underestimation does not necessarily imply underwillingness to convict. Nevertheless, as the Wells et al. results suggest, the possibility that expert psychological testimony may make jurors too skeptical deserves careful consideration.

psychological profession as a whole. Because the effects of expert testimony, are currently unclear, it is inevitable that psychologists will disagree with one another about its use. This disagreement is likely to lead ultimately to a "battle of experts" in at least some cases where attempts are made to introduce expert psychological testimony. The battle of experts could take several different forms. For example, when the defense attempted to introduce expert psychological testimony, the prosecution could use its own expert to argue that the defense psychologist should not be allowed to testify in front of the jury. The prosecution expert could state that many of the assertions that would be made by the defense expert (e.g., about effects of stress or weapon focus) are not firmly established by psychological research and that the expert testimony could conceivably have detrimental effects on the jurors' evaluation of eyewitness testimony. If the judge nevertheless decided to admit the testimony of the defense expert, the prosecution psychologist could also testify in front of the jury, arguing that support was lacking for many of the defense psychologist's claims. The prosecution expert might also attempt to counter the defense expert's arguments about the unreliability of eyewitness testimony, by pointing out factors in the case at hand that would facilitate eyewitness performance (e.g., long exposure duration, good lighting).

A battle of experts could also take more subtle forms. For example, a psychologist could simply serve as an advisor to the prosecutor, helping him or her to prepare an effective cross-examination of the defense expert. In any event, regardless of the form taken by a battle of experts, courtroom confrontation between defense and prosecution psychologists would almost certainly work to the detriment of the psychological profession, creating (or sustaining) the impression of psychology as a subjective, unscientific discipline and of the psychologist as a "gun for hire." The current situation with regard to psychiatric and psychological expert testimony concerning insanity, dangerousness, and the like should serve as food for thought to experimental psychologists.

It may have occurred to the reader that courtroom battles involving members of other professions (e.g., chemists, engineers, physicians) occur quite frequently, but that these professions do not seem to have suffered serious loss of credibility. Perhaps, then, there is little reason to be concerned about the consequences of battles involving experimental psychologists.

Unfortunately, the comparison to professions like medicine, chemistry, and the like may be misleading. We strongly suspect that courtroom battles in which opposing experts positively assert contradictory propositions do decrease public respect for a profession. Nevertheless, professions such as medicine and physics may escape serious loss of credibility because of clear records of past accomplishments and frequent reports of new achievements. Unfortunately, psychology probably does not have the sort of strong public reputation needed to endure battles of experts without significant damage. This may be especially true of the reputation of psychology among members of the legal profession. Consider, for example, the following excerpt from an appeals court decision[8] in which it was ruled that a trial judge had not erred in excluding expert psychological testimony about eyewitnesses:

> How far should the trial judge go in allowing *so-called scientific testimony, such as that of polygraph operators, hypnotists, "truth drug" administrants, as well as purveyors of general psychological theories*, to substitute for the common sense of the jury? Surely the answer is "not in all cases, or even in the ordinary or usual case."

Apart from the possible effects of a battle of experts on the reputation of the field, there is also a question of what the effects of such a battle might be on the outcome of a trial. A battle of experts could conceivably improve juror decision making. On the other hand, both experts might end up being ignored. As with many of the other issues discussed in this article, this one probably should be decided empirically rather than by guesswork.

To illustrate our points about the possible consequences of a battle of experts, we conclude with an example of one of the milder forms that such a battle might take. Specifically, we present a hypothetical cross-examination of a defense psychologist by a prosecutor who has been thoroughly briefed by his or her own expert. We ask the reader to consider whether this sort of occurrence would benefit either the psychological profession or the justice system.

Prosecutor: Are you suggesting that it is impossible for an eyewitness to accurately identify a criminal?

Psychologist: No, but accurate identification is quite difficult.

Prosecutor: In the studies conducted by yourself and your colleagues, do any of the participants do very well at identifying people?

Psychologist: Yes, some subjects do quite well, but others do very poorly.

Prosecutor: Dr. Smith, are you aware of studies showing that subjects made accurate identifications over 90% of the time?

Psychologist: Yes, there are such studies. Usually, however, the performance of witnesses is worse than that.

Prosecutor: Isn't it true that the accuracy rates in identification studies depend heavily on the conditions of the experiment, such as how many faces each subject sees, how long each face is seen, and so forth?

Psychologist: Yes, that is obviously true of any experiment.

Prosecutor: Isn't it also the case that conditions in most experiments are deliberately arranged so that accuracy is low?

Psychologist: Well, yes, in a way that's true. If none of the subjects make any errors we don't learn anything from an experiment. For example, if we wanted to see whether poor lighting makes identification harder, we would do an experiment where subjects see people under good and poor lighting conditions. We would then look to

---

[8] People v. Guzman, *supra*, p. 72, emphasis added.

see whether accuracy was lower with poor lighting. If the task were too easy, most or all of the subjects might make accurate identifications and we wouldn't learn anything about the effects of lighting. To find out whether lighting is important, we have to have a situation in which subjects make some errors. So to ensure that errors occur, we might let the subjects view people for only a short period of time, from some distance away, and so forth.

Prosecutor: Isn't it true, Dr. Smith, that even in tests giving low overall accuracy, some witnesses identify the right person?

Psychologist: Yes.

Prosecutor: Is there any way you can tell beforehand which witnesses will make an accurate identification and which witnesses will be inaccurate?

Psychologist: No, at the present time we have no good way of telling in a particular situation which witnesses will be accurate and which ones will be inaccurate. All we can say is that certain conditions yield lower accuracy than others.

Prosecutor: You have testified, Dr. Smith, that in your psychological tests, the accuracy of witnesses varies widely according to the conditions of the test. You have also stated that in conducting tests, psychologists deliberately create situations that produce low accuracy. Finally, you have said that there is no way you can tell whether a particular individual will make an accurate or inaccurate identification in a particular situation. How, then, can your tests be applied to the present case, in which a bank teller looked at a single bank robber for a much longer time than in most research studies? How can the results of experiments be used to suggest that the witness is inaccurate in his identification?

Psychologist: I cannot comment on the accuracy of any particular witness. All I can do is explain what sorts of conditions lead to a good or poor eyewitness performance.

Prosecutor: I am very interested in what you have called "weapon focus," Dr. Smith. Can you tell us about some of the experiments that demonstrate this effect?

Psychologist: Well, there is one experiment that gives some support for the weapon focus idea, but it isn't really conclusive. Actually . . .

Prosecutor: I am very surprised Dr. Smith, that you are willing to testify about a theory for which there is no experimental evidence.

Psychologist: Well, the idea of weapon focus was developed not so much from experiments but because people threatened with weapons often report having seen the weapon very clearly and often can describe it in great detail.

Prosecutor: That's very interesting. Are you saying that people who are able to give a clear description of, say, a gun, and who claim to have seen it clearly, would be said to have focused on the gun?

Psychologist: Yes.

Prosecutor: Mr. Robinson, the eyewitness in this case, has testified that he saw the robber's face clearly, and he gave a clear description of the robber. Would you say, then, Dr. Smith, that Mr. Robinson must have focused on the robber's face?

Psychologist: Well . . .

Prosecutor: I would like to ask you about your testimony concerning cross-racial identifications. Are you saying that a white person could *never* identify a black person?

Psychologist: No. I merely said that it is more difficult for a white person to identify a black person than a white person.

Prosecutor: Are you suggesting that *most* cross-racial identifications are wrong?

Psychologist: No, I did not say that.

Prosecutor: Well, then, are cross-racial identifications *often* incorrect?

Psychologist: I cannot say exactly how often cross-racial identifications are erroneous, only that cross-racial identifications are less likely to be correct than within-racial identifications.

Prosecutor: How much less likely?

Psychologist: It is difficult for me to answer that question without having the studies in front of me. However, I can say that several studies have found that cross-racial identifications were significantly less likely to be correct than within-racial identifications.

Prosecutor: Does that mean that there might be a difference of about 80% in the accuracy of within- versus cross-racial identifications?

Psychologist: No, the difference in accuracy is not that large.

Prosecutor: Would 50% be a more reasonable figure?

Psychologist: No, the difference is somewhat smaller than that.

Prosecutor: Well, Dr. Smith, can you estimate for the jury just how much less likely a cross-racial identification is to be correct than a within-racial identification?

Psychologist: I can't be sure of the exact figures, but I believe that most studies show about a 10% difference in accuracy between within- and cross-racial identifications.

Prosecutor: That's very interesting. I'm surprised that such a small difference could be considered significant. Would every subject show this effect? In other words, would everyone be very slightly less likely to correctly identify a person of another race?

Psychologist: Not necessarily. In most studies, the results are not exactly the same for every subject. The 10% difference between within- and cross-racial identifications would represent the average performance of a group of subjects.

Prosecutor: So it is probably the case that some people in these studies did just as well at cross-racial identification as within-racial identification?

Psychologist: That's possible.

Prosecutor: So you can't say for any individual that you haven't tested whether that individual is less likely to be correct in a cross-racial or a within-racial identification?

Psychologist: All I can say is that, in general, cross-racial identifications are more difficult than within-racial identifications.

Prosecutor: I would like to ask you a few questions about your testimony on the effects of stress on performance. You testified, I believe, that people under a moderate amount of stress are better at remembering and perceiving than people under very high or very low stress.

Psychologist: That's right. As I said before, the relationship between stress and performance is expressed by what is called the Yerkes-Dodson law, which is a well-known principle of psychology.

Prosecutor: How much stress, Dr. Smith, is moderate stress? That is, what level of stress leads to the best performance, and how much stress must a person be under before his or her performance deteriorates?

Psychologist: That depends on the type of task involved. Some tasks can be performed well under a fair amount of stress, and in other tasks the same amount of stress would impair performance. In general, the more complex the task, the lower the level of stress that gives the best performance.

Prosecutor: I assume that since you have testified about the effects of stress on eyewitness identification, psychologists must have studied this issue extensively.

Psychologist: Yes, there have been a number of studies on stress and identification.

Prosecutor: Do all of these studies show people do poorly when they are under stress?

Psychologist: Well, many of the studies show a detrimental effect of stress.

Prosecutor: Are there also studies in which people under stress did as well as or even better than people who were not under stress?

Psychologist: Yes, there are such studies, but they generally used rather low levels of stress. The studies showing improved performance under stress probably involved stress levels below the point of optimum stress, whereas studies finding impaired performance probably involved stress above the optimal level. So all of the studies fit the Yerkes-Dodson law I described earlier.

Prosecutor: I see. So I guess you are saying that there is some method psychologists use to measure the stress people experience in an experiment, and these measurements show that stress levels were lower in studies where stress helped than in studies where it hurt.

Psychologist: Well, no, not exactly. No single measure of stress was used in all of the studies. But if we look at the procedures that were used, it appears that studies showing improved performance under stress involved lower stress levels than studies showing impairment.

Prosecutor: Are you aware of a study by Clifford and Hollin [Note 6] in which people who were stressed by loud noise did more poorly at identifying faces than people who were not exposed to noise?

Psychologist: Yes, I know of that study.

Prosecutor: So according to what you have said, this study probably involved levels of stress above the optimal level. Is that right?

Psychologist: Yes, that is correct.

Prosecutor: Are you aware of a study by Majcher [1974] in which people exposed to loud noise did better at recognizing faces than people who were not stressed?

Psychologist: Yes.

Prosecutor: So you would say that this study involved stress below the optimal level. Is that right?

Psychologist: Well, yes, I guess so.

Prosecutor: I must admit I am confused, Dr. Smith. Isn't it true that the inducing noise was actually louder in the Majcher study, which you said involved below-optimal stress levels, than in the Clifford and Hollin study, which you said involved above-optimal stress?

Psychologist: Well, yes, I believe that's right.

Prosecutor: Do you know some other details of these studies that lead you to believe that induced stress was higher in the Clifford and Hollin study even though the noise was louder in the Majcher experiment, or are you simply making whatever assumptions are needed to make these studies fit your Yerkes-Dodson law?

Psychologist: I do not know enough of the details of these particular studies to comment on them further.

Prosecutor: Are you aware of a study by Johnson and Scott [Note 5] in which people sitting in a waiting room heard a violent altercation in a nearby room and then saw a person carrying a bloody letter opener come out of that room into the waiting room?

Psychologist: Yes.

Prosecutor: How would you compare the stress experienced by someone facing an apparently violent person who has a bloody letter opener with the stress induced by loud noise?

Psychologist: Well, it's hard to say exactly, but the stress would probably be greater in the situation involving the person with the letter opener.

Prosecutor: So you would say that the stress in this situation was probably above the optimal level?

Psychologist: Again, it's hard to say for sure, but I would say that is likely.

Prosecutor: Isn't it true that men who experienced this stressful situation in the Johnson and Scott experiment did better on several memory tests, including an identification test, than men who were exposed to a nonstressful situation?

Psychologist: Well . . . yes, I believe that is correct. However, I believe that for female subjects in that study, the stressful situation led to worse performance on some tests, including the identification test.

Prosecutor: Wouldn't you agree, Dr. Smith, that the picture emerging from psychological studies of the effects of stress on eyewitness identification is somewhat less than crystal clear?

Psychologist: In any set of studies there are bound to be a few inconsistencies. In general, however, the research shows that high stress impairs eyewitness identification.

Prosecutor: Let me ask you one other thing about stress, Dr. Smith. Would the effects of stress in a task be the same for everyone? In other words, would the level of stress at which performance begins to be impaired be the same for all individuals?

Psychologist: Not necessarily. It is quite possible that a level of stress that impaired performance for one person might have little effect on another.

Prosecutor: According to your testimony, the level of stress at which performance begins to be impaired is different for different situations and for different people. Would you agree, then, that for a particular person in a particular situation, it would be impossible to tell how much stress would be necessary to impair perception and memory without testing that person directly in that situation?

Psychologist: Yes, but as I have said, in general high stress impairs performance.

Prosecutor: How much time have you spent testing Mr. Robinson, the eyewitness in this case?

Psychologist: I have not tested him at all. I have never even met him.

Prosecutor: Then how can you testify about the effects of stress on his ability to identify the person who robbed him?

Psychologist: I cannot make any judgment about whether Mr. Robinson as an individual is an accurate or inaccurate witness. I can only describe the principles concerning eyewitness identifications that have been discovered through psychological research.

Prosecutor: How can these vague principles be of help to the jury, Dr. Smith, when you, with all your knowledge and experience, cannot use them to tell whether a witness was accurate or not?

Psychologist: It is not my function to decide that.[9]

Reference Notes

1. Cavoukian, A. *Eyewitness testimony: The ineffectiveness of discrediting information.* Paper presented at the meeting of the American Psychological Association, Montreal, August 1980.

2. McKenna, J., Mellott, A., & Webb, E. *Juror evaluation of eyewitness testimony.* Paper presented at the meeting of the Eastern Psychological Association, New York, April 1981.

3. McCloskey, M., Egeth, H., Webb, E., Washburn, A., & McKenna, J. *Eyewitnesses, jurors and the issue of overbelief.* Unpublished manuscript, John Hopkins University, 1981.

4. Carr, T. H., Deffenbacher, K. A., & Leu, J. R. *Is there less interference in memory for faces?* Paper presented at the meeting of the Psychonomic Society, Phoenix, November 1979.

---

[9] It is worth reiterating here that the points we have made in this article are meant to apply only to expert testimony. We do not intend to imply that experimental psychologists have no useful role to play in the judicial system. On the contrary, there are probably many useful functions experimental psychologists could serve (e.g., assisting a defense attorney in determining whether there are possible sources of bias in a lineup identification of a defendant). In fact, there may even be special circumstances in which expert psychological testimony would be justified. In particular, expert testimony might be warranted in situations where the psychologist could assert positively that a witness could not have seen what he or she claimed to have seen. Suppose, for example, that a crucial element in a case was whether or not an eyewitness could have noted the color of a sweater worn by a defendant on a clear moonless night (in the absence of any artificial source of illumination). Given that measurements indicated that the illumination was far below the threshold of photopic vision, a psychologist could testify that the witness simply could not have correctly identified the color of the sweater.

5. Johnson, C., & Scott, B. *Eyewitness testimony and suspect identification as a function of arousal, sex of witness and scheduling of interrogation.* Paper presented at the meeting of the American Psychological Association, Washington, D.C., September 1976.
6. Clifford, B. R., & Hollin, C. R. *Experimentally manipulated arousal and eyewitness testimony.* Unpublished manuscript, North East London Polytechnic, 1978.

References

Addison, B. M. Expert testimony on eyewitness perception. *Dickinson Law Review*, 1978, *82*, 464–485.

Chen, H. T. *Disposition of felony arrests: A sequential analysis of the judicial decision making process.* Unpublished doctoral dissertation, University of Massachusetts, 1981.

Deffenbacher, K. A. The influence of arousal on reliability of testimony. In B. R. Clifford & S. Lloyd-Bostock (Eds.), *Evaluating witness evidence: Recent psychological research and new perspectives.* Chichester, England: Wiley, 1983.

Deffenbacher, K. A., Carr, T. H., & Leu, J. R. Memory for words, pictures and faces: Retroactive interference, forgetting and reminiscence. *Journal of Experimental Psychology: Human Learning and Memory,* 1981, *7*, 299–305.

Deffenbacher, K. A., & Loftus, E. F. Do jurors share a common understanding concerning eyewitness behavior? *Law and Human Behavior*, 1982, *6*, 15–30.

Devlin, Hon. Lord P. (Chair). *Report to the secretary of state for the home department of the departmental committee on evidence of identification in criminal cases.* London: Her Majesty's Stationery Office, 1976

Ebbinghaus, H. [*Memory: A contribution to experimental psychology*] (H. A. Ruger & C. E. Bussenues, trans.). New York: Teacher's College. Columbia University, 1913. (Originally published, 1885.)

Ellison, K. W., & Buckhout, R. *Psychology and criminal justice.* New York: Harper & Row, 1981.

Gass, R. S. The psychologist as expert witness: Science in the courtroom. *Maryland Law Review;* 1979, *38*, 539–621.

Goldstein, A. G., & Chance, J. Visual recognition memory for complex configurations. *Perception and Psychophysics*, 1971, *9*, 237–241.

Hatvany, N., & Strack, F. The impact of a discredited key witness. *Journal of Applied Social Psychology*, 1980, *10*, 490–509.

Hosch, H. M., Beck, E. L., & McIntyre, P. Influence of expert testimony regarding eyewitness accuracy on jury decisions. *Law and Human Behavior*, 1980, *4*, 287–296.

Konečni, V. J., & Ebbesen, E. B. External validity of research in legal psychology. *Law and Human Behavior*, 1979, *3*, 39–70.

Laughery, K. R., Fessler, P. K., Lenorovitz, D. R., & Yoblick, D. A. Time delay and similarity effects in facial recognition. *Journal of Applied Psychology*, 1974, *59*, 490–496.

Lindsay, R. C. L., Wells, G. L., & Rumpel, C. M. Can people detect eyewitness-identification accuracy within and across situations? *Journal of Applied Psychology,* 1981, *66,* 79–89.

Loftus, E. F. Reconstructing memory: The incredible eyewitness. *Psychology Today,* 1974, *8,* 116–119.

Loftus, E. F. *Eyewitness testimony.* Cambridge, Mass.: Harvard University Press, 1979.

Loftus, E. F. Impact of expert psychological testimony on the unreliability of eyewitness identification. *Journal of Applied Psychology,* 1980, *65,* 9–15.

Loftus, E. F., & Monahan, J. Trial by data: Psychological research as legal evidence. *American Psychologist.* 1980, *35,* 270–283.

Lower, J. S. Psychologists as expert witnesses. *Law and Psychology Review,* 1978, *4,* 127–139.

Majcher, L. L. *Facial recognition as a function of arousal level, exposure duration and delay interval.* Unpublished master's thesis, University of Missouri, 1974.

Malpass, R. S., & Kravitz, J. Recognition for faces of own and other race. *Journal of Personality and Social Psychology,* 1969, *13,* 330–334.

Myers, M. A. Rule departures and making law: Juries and their verdicts. *Law and Society,* 1979, *13,* 781–797.

Pachella, R. G. The truth and nothing but the truth (Review of *Eyewitness testimony* by E. F. Loftus and *The psychology of eyewitness testimony* by A. D. Yarmey). *Contemporary Psychology,* 1981, *26,* 85–87.

Rembar, C. *The law of the land: The evolution of our legal system.* New York: Simon & Schuster, 1980.

Shepherd, J. W., & Ellis, H. O. The effect of attractiveness on recognition memory for faces. *American Journal of Psychology,* 1973, *86,* 627–634.

Shoemaker, J. 18 months of hell for rapist's lookalike. *Chicago Tribune,* December 28, 1980.

Starkman, D. The use of eyewitness identification evidence in criminal trials. *Criminal Law Quarterly,* 1979, *21,* 361–386.

Wall, P. M. *Eyewitness identification in criminal cases.* Springfield, Ill: Charles C Thomas, 1965.

Weinberg, H. I., & Baron, R. S. The discredible eyewitness. *Personality and Social Psychology Bulletin,* 1982, *8,* 60–67.

Wells, G. L., Lindsay, R. C. L., & Ferguson, T. J. Accuracy, confidence and juror perceptions in eyewitness testimony. *Journal of Applied Psychology,* 1979, *64,* 440–448.

Wells, G. L., Lindsay, R. C. L., & Tousignant, J. P. Effects of expert psychological advice on human performance in judging the validity of eyewitness testimony. *Law and Human Behavior,* 1980, *4,* 275–285.

Woocher, F. D. Did your eyes deceive you? Expert psychological testimony on the unreliability of eyewitness identification. *Stanford Law Review,* 1977, *29,* 960–1030.

Yarmey, A. D., & Jones, H. P. T. Is the psychology of eyewitness identification a matter of common sense? In B. R. Clifford & S.

Lloyd-Bostock (Eds.), *Evaluating witness evidence: Recent psychological research and new perspectives*. Chichester, England: Wiley, 1983.

Chapter 8

Language and Thought

CHAPTER 8: LANGUAGE AND THOUGHT

Humans can be characterized as those animals who make the most extensive use of language. The ability to communicate in a complex and flexible fashion is the singular attribute that clearly distinguishes humans from most other species (with the possible exception of dolphins and other cetacea). Although humans can get along in society without many senses (for example, the blind and deaf), motor control, and even social skills, a person without *any* language is an outcast. Language pervades almost all aspects of human behavior. Many of the higher cognitive functions, such as perception, memory, and logic, are integrated into the language system, to the point where one cannot explain one without the other. The selections included in this chapter point out the importance of language to perception and how the memory and language processing interact during speech production.

8a. Motley, M. (1987). What I meant to say. *Psychology Today, 21*, 24–28.

At a recent meeting of psychologists, a chairperson of one symposium wanted to conclude the meeting and thank her guests (even those who disagreed with her theories.) Much to the delight of the audience and to her own embarrassment, she said, "I would like to spank the theakers. . . ." Freud said that such "slips of the tongue" were signs of hidden thought and emotions. More modern psychologists have said that Freud was wrong and such behavior was due to language-processing difficulties. According to the article, what is the current status of this problem? Use the above example in supporting your explanation.

8b. Brown, R. & Lennenberg, E. (1954). A study in language and cognition. *The Journal of Abnormal and Social Psychology, 49*, 454–462.

Words are so important to humans that if we can find a special name for something, we often think we have "explained" it. This is called the nominal fallacy in science. Yet, having a special name for things does carry some cognitive consequences. According to the Brown and Lennenberg article, what are these consequences? Can you think of examples of special words exclusive to your peer group? Explain what purpose they serve.

What I Meant to Say

Michael T. Motley

It happens quite often. Right before an exam a student calls to ask for a postponement, giving one of several familiar excuses. It is easy to be skeptical when this happens, but I recall one occasion when my doubt was underscored with a curious slip of the tongue. The student said that she wanted the postponement because ". . . last night my grandmother lied—I mean died!"

How should I have interpreted her verbal slip? One possibility is that she had fabricated the excuse, and that her awareness of the lie prompted the error. Another possibility is that she was telling the truth but was afraid I might think that she was lying. Yet another is that she might have been feeling repressed guilt about a lie she once told her grandmother. On the other hand, the slip may have had nothing to do with lies; perhaps it was an innocent slip of the tongue in which the first "d" in "died" simply got replaced by an "l" as the result of some sort of linguistic confusion or articulatory fluke.

These interpretations hint at the wide range of explanations that psychologists, linguists and others have given for verbal slips during nearly a century of study. Almost all researchers who have examined the phenomenon agree on one thing, however: Since slips of the tongue, which we all experience from time to time, represent breakdowns in the normally efficient and error-free process of speech, they might provide a sort of window on the mind.

Linguists and cognitive psychologists investigate verbal slips for insights into how the mind processes information (including spoken language) and controls behavior. One discovery has been that slips of the tongue often seem to be the result of competition between similar verbal choices. These aren't conscious and deliberate choices, such as those that accompany delicate social situations, but are the more automatic and instantaneous choices of casual speech. A colleague, for example, once introduced a point with "Is this a rhetorical question perchaps?" when either "perchance" or "perhaps" would have fit his intention.

Almost any time we wish to express a thought, we must choose from several roughly equivalent verbal possibilities. Sometimes competition between these choices, or indecision about them, results in a slip of the tongue. This explanation has an intuitive appeal, at least in the case of some errors.

At a political event a few years ago, for instance, the featured speaker was introduced as being "as American as mother pie and applehood." Presumably, indecision over two equal choices, "apple pie and motherhood" and "motherhood and apple pie," caused the error. It is easy to imagine verbal competition as the source of numerous slips, such as "hairible" instead of "terrible" or "horrible" and "hairline crackture" instead of "hairline fracture" or "hairline crack."

One reason for such slips could be a lapse in the mental attention normally devoted to resolving competition. Slips of the tongue are more frequent, for example, when we are speaking in public, being interviewed or are confronted with other uncomfortable communication situations. Slips at these times are probably instances of our attention being diverted enough to allow alternate verbal choices to replace intended ones.

There are several ways that verbal competition could cause slips. Some are purely linguistic. When speakers begin to utter one of the choices, they may decide to switch to another after they have passed the point of no return or have uttered a fraction of the first choice. For example, an acquaintance who said "moptimal productivity" might have switched her decision from "maximum" to "optimal" after it was too late to abort the initial "m" of "maximum." But this explanation seems somewhat limited.

A theory known as "spreading activation" offers a more versatile explanation of verbal competition. According to this theory, a person's lexicon, or mental dictionary, is organized so that each word in it is interconnected with other words associated by meaning, sound or grammar—somewhat like the interconnection of points in a complex spider web. When we prepare to speak, the relevant parts of the web are activated, causing reverberation within the system. Activation spreads first to the most closely related words, then to words associated with them and so on. Each word activates an alternate path through the web. The cumulative activation for each word is tallied by checking how often each "point" in the web "vibrates," and the word with the highest accumulated activation (the most vibration, in our web analogy) is selected. Verbal slips would be explained as the result of competing choices that have equal or nearly equal activation levels.

For example, I recently told a colleague who needed information for her son Aaron that she could get it by phoning my wife. I suggested that she "wait for about an hour, because [my wife] is running an Aaron." According to the spreading activation theory, my mental dictionary was receiving activation on the word "Aaron," because he was one of the subjects of the conversation, on "errand" as a topic of the message and on "Aaron," again, because of its association by sound with "errand." Since "Aaron" got a double dose of activation, it won the cumulative-activation competition, so to speak.

Or consider the slip of an older colleague who identified a motion-picture character as "one of the black women in *The Colored Purple*" instead of *The Color Purple*. It is easy to imagine that in this person's mental dictionary, "colored" received activation both as a variation of "color" and as an archaic synonym for "black." Thus, its cumulative activation might have been greater than that of the intended word.

Thus far, spreading activation theorists have not considered the possibility that competing words might be related by something other than meaning, sound or grammar. Sigmund Freud, however, long ago introduced the idea that verbal slips represent the hidden motives and anxieties of the speaker. We still call them "Freudian slips," and, as with the cognitive explanation, there is an intuitive sensibility to Freud's notion, at least for some verbal slips. For example, it would explain a mistake I once made when introduced to a competitor at a job interview. Intending to say "Pleased to meet you," I slipped and said instead, "Pleased to beat you."

Until recently, however, Freud's explanation of verbal slips had been dismissed by most contemporary researchers. The relatively few slips that appear to be related to hidden thoughts were said to be linked by mere coincidence.

There were two arguments against the Freudian explanation. First, there was no known cognitive mechanism by which Freudian slips might operate. It is easy to imagine hidden thoughts that might prompt a local newscaster to proclaim to his voluptuous coanchor that "Bill Cosby is one of the breast bite lights on television," but it is quite difficult to explain the mental operations by which his hidden thoughts could have affected his originally intended utterance "best bright lights." Since it was difficult for many of those interested in the subject to imagine how Freudian slips might occur, it was difficult to believe that they did.

The second criticism of Freud's notion of verbal slips was that his theory was untestable. We can hypothesize, for example, that certain hidden thoughts caused a slip I once heard about a camping trip: "Ron often perks Jackie" instead of "Ron often packs jerky." But it has always seemed difficult to devise methods for testing such hypotheses objectively.

Both of these arguments have been tempered, however, with the development, over the past several years, of laboratory methods for studying of the tongue and Freudian hypotheses in particular.

Freud claimed that hidden thoughts can influence our choice of words, even in everyday speech without verbal slips. To test this claim, my colleagues and I asked men to read aloud and complete a series of fill-in-the-blank sentences. Half of them did this while being mildly sexually aroused—an attractive and provocatively attired woman administered the experiment—while the other half read and completed the same sentences in the presence of a man.

In line with Freud's suggestion, word choices that related to sex as well as completed the sentence were almost twice as frequent for men who were sexually aroused. For example, to complete the sentence, "The old hillbilly kept his moonshine in big. . . ," most men in the nonarousal group answered "vats," "barrels" or "jars," while "jugs" was the overwhelming answer of the aroused group. In another example, given the sentence, "Tension mounted at the end, when the symphony reached its. . . ," most of the men in the nonaroused group responded "finale," "conclusion" or "peak," while those in the aroused group were much more likely to answer "climax."

Spreading activation of hidden thoughts could account for these results. Both groups of men probably experienced activation on words that would complete the sentences, but it seems that in the aroused group another set of items—words related to sex and sexy women—was also activated. For those who were aroused, the double-entendre words, "jugs" and "climax," received double doses of activation and were selected. This suggests that hidden thoughts can activate our mental dictionary, much as Freud suggested.

If hidden thoughts can compete to influence deliberate word choices, might they also create competition that leads to slips of the tongue? It is possible to produce slips of the tongue by asking people to read silently pairs of words that are flashed on a screen at one-second intervals, after being instructed that if a buzzer sounds, they are to pronounce aloud the word pair then on the screen. This process can yield very interesting results. After seeing "let double" and "left decimal," for example, an attempt to say "dead level" will sometimes result in the slip "led devil."

My colleagues and I have used a variation of this procedure to test Freud's claim about verbal slips. One group of men performed the word-pair task believing that they were going to receive an electric shock at some point, while another group of men performed the task with mild sexual arousal—again in the form of a provocative female experimenter. For both groups, the lists and the words to be spoken aloud were identical. Each list contained an equal number of words that could result in slips related to electric shocks or to sexy women.

As Freud might have predicted, the two groups made quite different kinds of mistakes. The men expecting an electric shock were much more likely to make slips such as "damn shock" instead of "sham dock," and "cursed wattage" instead of "worst cottage." Those tested in the presence of the female experimenter were more likely to make slips such as "fast passion" instead of "past fashion," and "nude breasts" instead of "brood nests." Also, men who had been found to be more anxious in general about sexual matters made an especially high number of sex-related slips if they were aroused.

Experiments such as these have given support to Freud's claim that hidden thoughts and anxieties can influence verbal slips. Even more importantly, they are consistent with the spreading activation theory that explains competition between cognitively and linguistically similar choices. Apparently, choices can be activated in the network, whether they originate from the message we intend or from hidden thoughts.

While experiments add to our understanding of slips, another issue remains to be settled: Freud claimed that virtually all slips of the tongue derive from unconscious hidden thoughts. If this were true, however, hidden motives would be responsible not only for slips such as that made by a neighbor who approached a female cocktail-party guest saying, "I don't believe we've been properly seduced yet—I mean introduced yet," but for more innocuous slips, such as saying "chee kanes" instead of "key chains," or "coregaty" instead of "category."

Just as the results of experiments make it unreasonable to insist that no slips are Freudian, the spreading activation theory makes it unreasonable to insist that they all are. For many slips of the tongue, the hidden-motive interpretation seems needlessly circuitous. For example, one of three professors at a recent meeting proposed that funding for a special seminar might be available "once we get underground—I mean under way." One might argue that the "underground" slip shows some sort of guilt or surreptitiousness in the speaker's attitude toward the group's objectives. But one might argue, just as easily, the interpretation that "underground" was the innocuous outcome of competition between "once we get under way" and the colloquial "once we get off the ground," with an extra boost on "underground" coming from similarity to a third alternative "once we're on solid ground," for example.

It seems likely then that the explanation for slips of the tongue lies between the two extremes of those who insist on Freudian interpretations and those who completely exclude them. Most slips probably are the result of verbal competition, with hidden thoughts as the source of the competition in some cases and simple message alternatives providing the competition in others. There is no need to posit hidden motives for slips such as "comprinter puteout" instead of "computer printout," or "offewsional" instead of "occasional." With enough imagination, one might hypothesize hidden thoughts behind these slips, but simpler explanations can be found: "Computer printout" probably competed with "printer output" while "occasional" vied with "few."

On the other hand, hidden motives seem much more likely for slips such as that committed by a lecturer who announced his topic as "Fraud's Theories" instead of "Freud's Theories," or the embarrassing reference to an engagement ring as a "garish cheapsake" in lieu of "cherished keepsake." One might dream up competing message choices for these slips, but the most straightforward explanation is competition from hidden thoughts.

For some slips, the derivation will be impossible to determine. I remember being in an especially inelegant diner, for example, and ordering a "chilled grease sandwich" when I meant to order a "grilled cheese sandwich." While I assumed that the slip came from competition with an alternative verbal choice, "cheese sandwich," the waitress assumed that it had originated with a hidden thought, "greasy-spoon diner." Which interpretation is correct? All that can be said is that both are reasonable possibilities.

A Study in Language and Cognition

R. Brown and E. Lennenberg

A graduate student from Germany recently talked with me about some American English words which seem to him to have no German equivalents. One of these is the verb appreciate, in the sense of "John appreciates classical music; he doesn't appreciate rock." Obviously one easily says in German the equivalents of "John likes classical music," or "John enjoys classical music," but appreciate is not quite the same as enjoy or like or admire or take an interest in. Notice that if someone invites you to listen to a recording of *Tristan and Isolde* the effect of "I don't like Wagner" is very different from "I don't appreciate Wagner." To appreciate x is to be attuned to real virtues x is presumed to have and not to appreciate is to fail to be attuned; it is not to deny that x has virtues. In short, appreciate seems to presuppose in the object qualities deserving admiration in a way that like, admire, and so on do not. It is a verb that enables Americans to talk about differences of taste in a minimally abrasive and rather democratic manner; everything may be presumed deserving of interest but individuals differ in the interests they happen to have developed.

Differences of this kind in the lexicons of languages are always fascinating. If one language has a gap where the other language has a word, does the first language lack also the idea that is the word's meaning? So long as the ideas concern social life we are not surprised that cross-language differences exist. However, the differences extend also to terms that make reference to the physical world; for example, to the names for colors.

In many languages, for instance, there is a single word for both green and blue. This term is also often the name given the sea. But then we begin to understand. Surely the word was used first for the sea and then, by abstraction, for just that range of colors which the sea passes through: the greens and the blues. In a similar way our color terms orange and rose and olive were first object names but have come to be names for the colors the objects exemplify. We can see how differences in the scope of particular color terms might arise in this way. But what we cannot tell, from the linguistic evidence alone, is what such differences signify about the thought and perception of the people who use them. To find that out experiments are needed and this paper describes one such.

It is widely thought that reality exists in much the same form to all men of sound mind. There are objects like a house or a cat and qualities like red or wet and events like eating or singing and relationships like near to or between. Languages are itemized inventories of this reality. They differ, of course, in the sounds they employ, but the inventory is always the same. The esthetic predilections of the Italian lead him to prefer euphonious vowels, while the German is addicted to harsh consonant groupings, but the things and events named are the same in both tongues. We are confirmed in this view by our linguistic education, which requires us to memorize lists of French or German or Latin words and their exact English equivalents.

There are, of course, poetic persons who claim to find in each language some special genius that peculiarly fits it for the expression of certain ideas. But the majority of us are at a loss to understand how this can be, since there is apparently a relationship of mutual translatability among the languages we learn. To be sure, we can see that one language might contain a few items more than another. If the Germans were to invent a new kind of automobile and we had not yet thought of such a machine, their dictionary would have one entry more than ours until we heard of the discovery and named it for ourselves. But these inequalities are in the lexical fringe. They do not disturb the great core of common inventory.

The Whorf Thesis

This linguistic ethnocentrism will be seriously disturbed by the study of languages that lie outside the Indo-European group. It has not prepared us for finding that there is a language in which noun and verb categories apparently do not exist, or that there is another in which the colors gray and brown are called by the same name. Such data from the study of American Indian tongues led Whorf (1950) to reject the usual view of the relationship between language and thought. He suggested that each language embodies and perpetuates a particular world view. The speakers of a language are partners to an agreement to see and think of the world in a certain way—not the only possible way. The world can be structured in many ways, and the language we learn as children directs the formation of our particular structure. Language is not a cloak following the contours of thought. Languages are molds into which infant minds are poured. Whorf thus departs from the common sense view in a) holding that the world is differently experienced and conceived in different linguistic communities and b) suggesting that language is causally related to these psychological differences.

Other authors have believed that the relationship between language and thought is somewhat as proposed by Whorf. Cassirer (1953) maintained that language is the direct manifestation of knowledge; he explicitly denied a form-content relationship between words or language structure and isolates of knowledge. In this he was in agreement with such other German writers as Wundt (1900) and Buhler (1934). Orwell (1949) in his novel *Nineteen Eighty-Four* describes a totalitarian England of the future. The really efficient dictatorship of that day invents a language—Newspeak—in which it is impossible not only to express, but even to think, a rebellious thought. An equally great faith in the causal efficacy of language lies behind the General Semantics movement. Korzybski (1951), for instance, holds that clear thinking and social progress are to be attained through the reform of language.

Cognitive Differences between Linguistic Communities

The first tenet of the Whorf thesis is that the world is differently experienced and conceived in different linguistic communities. The evidence presented in support of this claim is entirely linguistic. It will be helpful to distinguish between the conclusions based on lexical features of two languages and those based on structural features.

Lexical Features. In the Eskimo lexicon there are three words to distinguish three varieties of snow. There are no single-word equivalents for these in English. The word "snow" would be used to describe all three. What psychological conclusions can be drawn from these data? Does the Eskimo see differences and similarities that we are *unable* to see?

Psychologists ordinarily infer perceptual discrimination when a subject is consistently able to respond differently to distinctive stimulus situations. The subject may be rat, dog, or man. The response may be running, salivation, or—speech. Words are used meaningfully when they are selectively employed with reference to some kind of environment—whether physical, social, or linguistic. The linguist in the field may discover the referent of a term by noting the pattern of its usage. The Eskimo's three "snows" are sufficient evidence from which to infer that he discriminates three varieties of snow. These selective verbal responses satisfy the conditions for inferring perceptual discrimination.

What can be said of the English speaker's ability to distinguish the same three kinds of snow? When different stimuli do not elicit differential responses, the stimuli may or may not be discriminated. A subject may be perfectly able to distinguish two situations and still not care to do anything about it. Consequently the fact that English speakers do not have different names for several kinds of snow cannot be taken to mean that they are unable to see the differences. It would seem, then, that all such comparisons are psychologically inconclusive. The Eskimo and American may or may not see the world differently.

There is, however, other evidence to indicate that the speaker of English can classify snows as the Eskimo does. If we listen to the talk of small boys, it is clear that they perceive at least two kinds of snow— *good-packing snow* and *bad-packing snow*. This is a distinction of the greatest importance to anyone interested in making snowballs. This discrimination is evidenced by differential response not to distinct lexical items but combinations of items—good-packing snow and bad-packing snow. Whorf himself must have been able to see snow as the Eskimos did since his article describes and pictures the referents for the words. Since both Eskimo and American are able to make differential responses to snows, we must conclude that both are able to see differences. This seems to lead us to the conclusion that the Eskimo and American world views do not differ in this regard.

Although the three kinds of snow are namable in both Eskimo and English, each of them requires a phrase in ordinary English, whereas single words will do it for the Eskimo. Zipf (1935) has shown that there exists a tendency in Peiping Chinese, Plautine Latin, and American and British English for the length of a word to be negatively correlated with its frequency of usage. This is true whether word length is measured in phonemes or syllables. It is not difficult to find examples of this relationship in English. New inventions are usually given long names of Greek or Latin derivation, but as the products become widely known and frequently used in conversation the linguistic community finds shorter tags for them. Thus the *automobile* becomes the *car* and *television* shrinks to *video* and eventually to TV. Three-dimensional movies are predictably described as *3-D*.

Doob (1952) has suggested that this principle bears on Whorf's thesis. Suppose we generalize the findings even beyond Zipf's formulation and propose that the length of a verbal expression provides an index of its frequency in speech and that this, in turn, is an index of the frequency with which the relevant perceptual judgments of difference and equivalence are made. If this is true, it would follow that the Eskimo distinguishes his three kinds of snow more often than Americans do. It would mean—to cite another example—that the Hopi is less often called upon to distinguish airplanes, aviators, and butterflies than is the American, since the Hopi has but a single name for all three of these. Such conclusions are, of course, supported by extralinguistic cultural analysis, which reveals the importance of snow in the Eskimo's life and the comparative indifference of the Hopi to airplanes and aviators.

We will go further and propose that increased frequency of a perceptual categorization will mean a generally greater "availability" of that category. In the experimental study of memory we are accustomed to think of the methods of recall, recognition, and relearning as increasingly sensitive indices of retention. In the experimental study of categorizing behavior there are two principal methods: (a) Goldstein's (1948) technique of presenting a subject with an array of objects and asking him to group them, and (b) Hull's (1920) discrimination learning technique. Hull's method seems to be the more sensitive of the two. We should guess that when the Eskimo steps from his igloo in the morning and is confronted by a snowy world, these snows will fall into named categories for him in a way that they will not for the American. If however, the American were subjected to a discrimination learning experiment, or if the perceptual structure were otherwise made worth his while, he could see snow as does the Eskimo. We think, really, that more namable categories are nearer the top of the cognitive "deck."

Structural Features. Members of structural categories have no phonetic common denominator. They are grouped together because they have the same structural relations with other forms in the language. In English, nouns constitute a structural category; its members can appear with definite and indefinite articles, can form plurals in certain ways, etc. In French all nouns of the feminine gender belong to one structural category since they all require the feminine articles and suffixes.

Whorf generally assumes that structural categories are also symbolic categories. When he finds structural differences in languages he concludes that there are parallel cognitive differences. There are in Hopi two structural categories showing some similarity to our verb and noun categories, with the difference that one of the Hopi classes includes only the names for such short-term events as lightning, flame, and spasm, while the other includes only such long-term events as man, house, and lifetime. Whorf concludes that the Hopi organizes his world on a dimension we usually overlook. When the structural class has such obvious semantic properties, Whorf's conclusions have a kind of plausibility.

However, very few structural classes have such clear and consistent meanings. In the languages we know best, those of the Indo-European family, there are many structural categories with no discernible meaning. In French, for instance, it is not clear that the gender of a form signifies anything to a speaker. Certainly it is difficult to find any common attributes in the references for French nouns of feminine gender. Not even the majority of them manifest feminine sexuality—even in the extended sense of Freud. The French speak of *le balcon* in spite of their saying, "*Elle a du balcon.*" The linguist Charles Fries (1952) has shown how difficult it is to describe a semantic for the English "parts of speech." If the noun can be defined as "the name of a person, place, or thing," this is only because "thing" is left unexplicated. It serves handily to designate whatever is nominalized and yet neither person nor place.

Even where the ethnolinguist can discover consistent structural meanings, it does not follow that these meanings are present to the native speakers of a language. Suppose that a subject in the laboratory were required to signal his recognition of each of ten different musical chords by raising that one of his ten fingers which has been designated for each chord. If all extraneous sensory information were excluded, his ability to pattern correctly the movements of his fingers would be evidence of his ability to identify the chords. The experimenter might introduce a potential structural meaning by ruling that the fingers of the right hand would always be raised for chords in the major mode and the fingers of the left hand for minor chords. The subject's responses might follow this pattern and yet he need never have detected the major and minor modes. Similarly, even if there were some semantic to French gender, one could speak the language without detecting it. *La fille* and *la femme* could be learned without noticing that both are in the feminine mode. No safe inferences about cognition can be made on the basis of the simple existence of the structural classes described by Whorf. The structural evidence is extremely difficult to interpret, and it seems clear that psychological data are needed to supplement those of the linguist.

Language in Causal Relation to Cognition

The second major tenet of Whorf's thesis is that language causes a particular cognitive structure. In what way can this occur? There seem to be two possibilities. Suppose that the colors red and green are not "given" categories but must be learned. A father who has formed these categories may play a game with his child that will teach the categories. The green blocks are to be used for building a house and the red ones for a barn. The child cannot properly pattern the blocks without learning to make the visual distinctions involved. Notice that the barn and house are not essential here. A father could ask his child to tell him whether each block is red or green. In learning this game, too, the child necessarily would learn to perceive the colors. Because words have symbolic properties, because their usage is patterned with reference to the total environment, language can cause a cognitive structure. To the degree that children are motivated to speak a language as it is spoken in their community they are motivated to share the world view of that community. To be sure, linguistic training is not the only means of procuring cognitive socialization; the house-barn game demonstrates that. The word game has the tremendous advantage that it can be played constantly and concurrently with many other activities. The child and his adult tutor can chatter together whether they are walking or riding, playing or working. In this chatter more is taught than a simple motor skill involving the muscles of articulation. A total culture is internalized.

There is a second, more dubious, avenue for the influence of language on thought. If life is a river, speech is a babbling brook whose course parallels that of the river. The brook is smaller and simpler than the river. A child can learn the phonemic structure of his language fairly easily. He will also realize that as the phonemic patterns he hears spoken change there are important changes in the nonlinguistic world. There is, for instance, an important difference that goes with the shift of speech from *father* to *mother*. When, on the other hand, combinations of phonemes are repeated, two situations are equivalent in some important way. Consider the "strike" and the "ball" in baseball. These are rather difficult categories. The differences between them are subtle and complex. A naive observer of a baseball game would have a difficult time learning these categories by simply observing the game. It makes a great difference that the umpire calls out *strike!* each time a member of that category occurs and *ball!* to identify an instance of the other category. The umpire's shout directs us to look here and now to discover something of importance. The word spotlights a moment of consciousness and puts it in connection with other events similarly spotlighted. The various "strikes" are equivalent in some way and distinct as a category from the events labelled *ball*. The babbling brook can, then, be a guide to the structure of the more complex but also more interesting river.

All of our reasoning cannot be said to prove the validity of any set of psychological conclusions. It does, however, point the direction for such a proof and suggests empirical steps that will advance our knowledge of this problem. We have made a small beginning in this work.

Our findings bear on only one of the claims made by Whorf—that there are cognitive differences correlated with lexical differences. We have developed lexical differences into the variable of "codability" and attempted to determine the relationship between this variable and a single cognitive performance—recognition.

The Experiment

Sensory psychologists have described the world of color with a solid using three psychological dimensions: hue, brightness, and saturation. The color solid is divisible into millions of just noticeable differences; *Science of Color* (1953) estimates 7,500,000. The largest collection (Evans, 1948; Maerz and Paul, 1930) of English color names runs to less than 4,000 entries, and of these only about 8 occur very commonly (Thorndike and Lorge, 1944). Evidently there is considerable categorization of colors. It seems likely to us that all human beings with normal vision will be able to make approximately the same set of discriminations. This ability appears to depend on the visual system, which is standard equipment for the species. Whatever individual differences do exist are probably not related to culture, linguistic or extralinguistic. It does not follow that people everywhere either see or think of the color world in the same way. Cultural differences probably operate on the level of categorization rather than controlled laboratory discrimination.

Our explorations in the Yale Cross-Cultural Index turned up many reports of differences on this level. Seroshevskii (1896), for instance, has reported that in the Iakuti language there is a single word for both green and blue. This is the kind of language difference discussed in the first section of this paper. A region of experience is lexically differentiated in one culture but undifferentiated in another. Color categories differ from such categories as snows in that they have boundaries that can be plotted on known dimensions. Color categories, furthermore, are continuous with one another, sharing their boundaries. Consider for a moment the single dimension of hue taken at a high level of saturation and brightness. Native speakers of English could be shown various shades and asked to give the usual color name for each stimulus presented. For each common color name there would be some shades invariably called by that name. There would be other shades sometimes associated with one name, sometimes with another. When the responses are divided about equally between two or more names, we should have boundaries between categories. If a native speaker of Iakuti were asked to provide the usual color names for the various shades, we should anticipate a somewhat different pattern. English speakers would have trouble naming the hues in the boundary region between green and blue. Probably they would hesitate, disagree among themselves, and sometimes use phrases or such combination names as *greenish blue,* For the Iakuti, on the other hand, this region is right in the center of a category and would be named with great ease.

Of course, our example is greatly simplified over the actual case since we have dealt with the single dimension of hue whereas the color lexicon is actually patterned with respect to all of the three dimensions of visual experience. When these are considered, the range of applicability of a color term is a space within the color solid rather than a distance along a line. The simplification was for expository purposes and does not alter the logic of the argument.

This example of a cultural difference serves to introduce the variable *codability*. Certain colors are differentially codable in the Iakuti and English languages. So long as the data collected are of the usual linguistic variety, this difference of codability will be manifest in only one way—environmental distinctions expressed lexically in one language are expressed with word combinations in another language. Our reasoning led us to expect differential availability of reference categories in such a case. We undertook experimental work to discover additional behavioral indices of codability, and hoped to find one more sensitive than that which can be teased out of linguistic data. If we found such an index, we would go on to explore the behavioral consequences of differential availability of cognitive categories.

There are differences of codability within English itself. Some shades fall safely within the province of a given name while others lie within boundary regions. Here it is a matter of comparing the English codability of one region of visual experience with another region, whereas the ethnolinguist has usually compared the codability of one region of experience in several languages. If we explore the codability variable in English, it seems likely that our discoveries will apply to the cultural differences with which the inquiry began. If a general law can be found relating codability to availability, individual cultures may conform to the law though they differ among themselves in the values these variables assume in particular regions of experience.

Measurement of Codability

The entire series of Munsell colors for the highest level of saturation ("chroma" as Munsell calls it) was mounted on cards in systematic fashion. Five judges were asked to pick out the best red, orange, yellow, green, blue, purple, pink, and brown from these 240 colors. These names are the most frequently appearing color terms in English (Thorndike and Lorge, 1944). For each name the color chip most often selected was added to our test list. Agreement among judges was high, and it is quite clear, therefore, that there is in this series one particular color chip with the best claim to each color name. The number of colors was then raised to 24 by adding chips that would, in combination with the first 8, provide as even a coverage of the color space as practicable. These colors are specified in Table 9-1. One set of the 24 chips was mounted on white 3 x 5 cards, one chip to a card. Another set was arranged randomly on a single large card.

To expose the single small cards a drop shutter was mounted in a 3 x 2-foot gray (Munsell neutral value 6, reflectance 30 per cent) board. The board was about three feet from the subject's eyes and was illuminated from above and behind by a General Electric standard daylight fluorescent lamp.

The subjects were 24 Harvard and Radcliffe students who spoke English as a native language and had no particular training in distinguishing colors. They were screened for color blindness with the standard Pseudo-Isochromatic Plates.

Table 9–1. The Munsell Notation and Scores for Discriminability, Codability, and Recognition for the 24 Test Colors

Munsell Notation*	Discriminability		Codability		Recognition (Group C Table 9–3)	
	Score	Rank	Score	Rank	Score	Rank
2.5R 7/8	38	2	18	9.5	.875	8
2.5R 5/10	27.5	6	7	18.5	.694	11
5R 4/14	23	10.5	19	7.5	1.020	5
7.5R 8/4	18	15	7	18.5	.236	18
2.5R 6/14	38	2	29	1.5	1.499	2
5YR 3/4	24	9	26	3	.972	7
7.5R 5/8	26	7.5	8	16	.736	9
2.5Y 7/10	12	19	3	24	.486	13
5Y 8/12	37	4	25	4	2.450	1
7.5Y 6/8	13	17	4	23	.250	17
3GY 7.5/11.2	23	10.5	14	12	1.222	4
7.5GY 3/4	9.5	23	14	12	0.000	23.5
2.5G 5/8	18.5	14	23	6	.986	6
7.5G 8/4	17.5	16	19	7.5	.167	19
5BG 3/6	4.5	24	12	15	.111	22
10BG 6/6	21	12	7	18.5	.458	14
8.5B 3/6.8	38	2	13	14	0.000	23.5
2.5PB 7/6	19	13	18	9.5	.436	16
5PB 4/10	10.5	21	29	1.5	.695	10
10PB 5/10	12	19	7	18.5	.125	20.5
5P 8/4	12	19	14	12	.547	12
10P 3/10	10	22	24	5	.444	15
5RP 6/10	26	7.5	6	21.5	.125	20.5
8RP 3.4/12.1	31	5	6	21.5	1.464	3

*For conversion to C.I.E. Tristimulus values and Source C, C.I.E. chromaticity coordinates see Nickerson, Tomaszewski, and Boyd (1953).

The subjects were first shown the 24-color random chart for about five minutes. After the chart was removed they were told that each of the colors on the chart would appear individually in the tachistoscope and that the subject's task was to give the name of each as it appeared. "Name" was defined as the word or words one would ordinarily use to describe the color to a friend. The subjects were urged to be both quick and accurate.

The 24 colors were presented in a predetermined random order for each subject. No order was repeated. Each color was exposed until the subject had named it. In our trial procedure we used a voice key and chronoscope to measure the reaction time. The scope was activated by the opening shutter of the tachistoscope and stopped by the subject's first vocalization. This method proved to be unsuitable since subjects would frequently burst out with something other than a color name, which, of course stopped the undiscriminating chronoscope. Consequently, we abandoned this technique and used the stop watch. The watch was started as the experimenter dropped the shutter and stopped at first mention of a color name.

The variable of codability was measured in five ways. (a) The average length of naming response to each color was obtained by counting syllables. (b) The average length was also obtained by counting words. (c) The average reaction time for each color was obtained by ranking all of the reaction times of an individual subject and taking the mean rank across subjects for every color. (d) The degree to which subjects agreed with one another in naming a color was assessed as follows: We counted the total number of different responses to a color (DR) and also the number of subjects who agreed on whatever response was most often given to a particular color (CR). The first value was subtracted from the second and a constant of 20 added to keep the results positive (CR - DR + 20). Color 18, for example, was given the following eight different names: *gray-blue, blue, light gray-blue, light blue, very pale blue, light blue-gray, pale blue,* and *powder blue.* Of these, the single-word response blue occurred most often—six times. Color 18, then, scored 6 - 8 + 20, or 18. (e) The degree to which subjects agreed with themselves from one time to another in naming a color was calculated as follows: Five subjects were recalled after a period of one month and subjected to a repetition of the naming procedure. When a subject gave identical responses to a color on the two occasions, we counted one agreement. We determined the number of agreements for each subject and considered that to be unity. Each individual agreement was then given the appropriate fractional value. Suppose a subject had eight agreements. If he agreed in his name for Color 11, he would add * to the score for that color. The agreement score is, then, the sum of the individual performances weighted for each individual's overall tendency to agreement.

Table 9–2. Correlation Matrix for Five Indices of Codability

Measure	1	2	3	4	5
Number of syllables					
Number of words	.425*				
Reaction time	.387	.368			
Interpersonal agreement	.630*	.486*	.864*		
Intrapersonal agreement	.355	.537*	.649*	.773*	
k from second factoring	.589	.587	.787	.976	.795
Communality from first factoring	.403	.378	.671	.873	.653

*p ≤ .05.

In Table 9–2 the intercorrelations of scores on these five measures appear. All correlations are in the predicted direction and most of them are significant, with .355 the smallest. With a single iteration this matrix yielded a general factor which we call codability. No correlations over .113 remain after the extraction of this single factor. Our fourth index, the degree of agreement between subjects, has by far the largest factor loading. It was selected as the measure of codability for the second phase of the experiment. The obtained codability values for the 24 colors are listed in Table 9–1.

Codability and Recognition

Once the codability variable suggested by Whorf's ethnolinguistic observations had been operationalized, it remained to relate this variable to some nonlinguistic behavior which might be considered an index of availability. We selected the recognition of colors.

From the 240 Munsell chips taken at highest saturation we selected out alternate chips, taking care to include the 24 colors for which codability data had been collected. The resultant collection of 120 colors was systematically mounted on a white card. Hue varied along the vertical dimension of the card and brightness on the horizontal dimension. Since there were 20 steps of hue and only 6 of brightness, we divided the total colors in half and mounted one half above the other so as to make a more manipulable display.

New subjects were screened, as before, for color blindness and language background. The basic procedure was to expose simultaneously 4 of the 24 colors, remove them, and ask subjects to point to the colors just seen, on the large chart of 120. Neither the experimenter nor the subject mentioned any color name during the session. The recognition score for a color was computed as follows: We determined the number of correct identifications made by each subject and considered this number to be unity. Each individual correct identification was given the appropriate fractional value. Suppose for instance, that a subject who correctly identified a total of six colors recognized Color 24. This recognition would have counted as 1/2 on the total recognition score for that color. Another subject for whom Color 24 was one of eight correctly identified colors would have contributed 1/2 to the score for Color 24. In other words, the recognition score for a color is the sum of the individual performances weighted for each subject's overall ability to recognize colors. The scores for the 24 colors appear in Table 9–1.

In trial runs, subjects were asked how they managed to retain the four colors in memory after they were removed from sight. Most subjects reported that they named the colors when they were exposed and "stored" the names. It seemed likely, therefore, that those colors that are quite unequivocally coded would be most likely to be recognized. When a color elicits a considerable range of names, the chances of recovering the color from the name would be reduced. This expectation was fulfilled by a rank-order correlation of .415 between codability and recognition scores.

There is, however, another variable that influenced recognition. The 120 colors used are not perceptually perfectly equidistant. The manufacture of equidistant color chips is technically difficult and expensive and, indeed, above a certain level of saturation, impossible. Since we were unable to control experimentally the variable "discriminability," we must ask whether or not our findings were due to a positive correlation between codability and discriminability. Could it be that our codable colors were so distant, perceptually, from their nearest neighbors that their superior recognizability was actually due to these better discrimination conditions? To obtain an answer to this question we determined the true perceptual distance between each of the colors used from the Newhall, Nickerson, and Judd (1943) charts. These charts convert every Munsell book notation into a renotation which is the specification of a true perceptual locus of each color within the Munsell coordinate system. The difference between two renotations expresses quantitatively the perceptual distance between the colors.

For each of the 24 test colors we computed a discriminability score which describes its distinctiveness from the colors surrounding it. The difference between two renotations yields three numbers, one for each dimension. To make these numbers perceptually commensurable (i.e., to reduce them to a common denominator), the Optical Society of America Subcommittee on the Spacing of the Munsell Colors suggests the values 3, 2, and 1 for hue, chroma, and value, respectively. Since every color has two neighbors on each of the three dimensions, a total of six numbers will express, in a rough way, the discriminability of that color. The sum of these yields the unadjusted discriminability score. Adjustments of this score are necessary (a) because if a color appears on the margin of our chart it has a lower chance of being recognized correctly and (b) because a color that has a very close neighbor on one side and distant neighbors on three others might come out with a good discriminability score although the close contiguity on one side would hinder correct recognition considerably. Consequently, colors appearing on the margin of our chart had the constant 3 subtracted from their unadjusted discriminability score, and colors with a close neighbor had the constant 6 subtracted.

Our scoring method is to a certain degree arbitrary, to be sure, but since the equation of perceptual distances on different visual dimensions is an unsolved problem, there seems to be no more objective method available. In addition, of course, all decisions were made without knowledge of recognition scores.

Table 9–3. Recognition Procedures

Group	N	Number of Colors Originally Exposed	Length of Interval	Content of Interval
A	9	1	7 seconds	
B	9	4	7 seconds	
C	16	4	30 seconds	
D	9	4	3 minutes	Tasks

Note—Exposure time for all groups was 3 seconds.

Since we were unable to control discriminability experimentally, we controlled it statistically. The partial correlation between codability and recognition, with discriminability constant, is .438. Furthermore, the correlation between codability and discriminability is .074, which is not significant. Evidently the relation between codability and recognition is not a consequence of variations in discriminability.

Since the reports of our early subjects indicated that colors were stored in linguistic code, it seemed likely that color codability would increase in importance as the storage factor was maximized in the recognition situation. Discriminability, on the other hand, should remain at the same level of importance or possibly decline somewhat. If, for example, a single color were exposed, removed, and then identified with minimal delay, subjects might retain some direct memory of the color, perhaps as a visual image. In this situation discriminability would be a determinant of recognition but codability would not be. However, when the number of colors is increased and the interval prolonged and filled with activity, the importance of linguistic coding should increase. Table 9–3 describes the experimental variations we used. Groups A, B, C, and D are arranged in what we believed to be an order of increasingly difficult storage of colors. Group C is our major group, for which results have already been described. The tasks which filled the interval for Group D were simple but absorbing—the kind of thing often used in experiments on the Zeigarnik phenomenon.

It can be seen from the data in Table 9–4 that the correlation between recognition and codability scores does increase as the importance of storage in the recognition task increases. The particular order obtained would occur by chance only once in 24 times.

Table 9–4. Correlations Involving Scores on Codability (C), Discriminability (D), and Recognition (R) with Four Experimental Conditions for Recognition

Group	C with R	D with R	C with R, D constant
A	.248	.540*	.248
B	.411	.460*	.426*
C	.415	.503*	.438*
D	.487*	.505*	.523*

*$p \leq .05$.

Table 9–4 also shows that discriminability is most closely related to recognition in Group A, for which the possibility of some direct memory of the color is maximized. The importance of discriminability declines slightly but not significantly as the recognition is made more difficult. Our expectations with regard to both codability and discriminability are generally confirmed.

In the first section of this paper we concluded our discussion of lexical differences between languages with the prediction that a given set of cognitive categories will be more available to the speakers of a language that lexically codes these categories than to the speakers of a language in which the categories are not represented in the lexicon. Lexical differences have been expanded into the variable of codability, and category availability has been operationalized as a recognition score. We found that differences in the English codability of colors are related to differences in the recognition of these colors. We expected these results to apply to the cross-cultural case, and some confirmation of this expectation is available in the results of a study by Lennenberg and Roberts (1953). This study of Zuni Indians used a field adaptation of our methods and apparatus. The Zuni color lexicon codes the colors we call orange and yellow with a single term. Monolingual Zuni subjects in their recognition task frequently confused the orange and yellow colors in our stimulus set. Our English-speaking subjects never made this error. It is a distinction which is highly codable in English and highly uncodable in Zuni. Interestingly, bilingual Zunis who knew English fell between the monolingual Zuni and the native speaker of English in the frequency with which they made these errors.

The Whorf thesis claims more than a simple relationship between language and cognition; language is held to be causally related to cognitive structure. Our correlational evidence does not, of course, establish the direction of causality. If we may be permitted a guess it is that in the history of a culture the peculiar features of the language and thought of a people probably develop together.

In the history of an individual born into a linguistic community the story is quite different. The patterned responses are all about him. They exist before he has the cognitive structure that will enable him to pattern his behavior in the approved fashion. Simple exposure to speech will not shape anyone's mind. To the degree that the unacculturated individual is motivated to learn the language of a community, to the degree that he uses its structure as a guide to reality, language can assume a formative role.

Summary

The Whorf thesis on the relationship between language and thought is found to involve the following two propositions: (a) Different linguistic communities perceive and conceive reality in different ways. (b) The language spoken in a community helps to shape the cognitive structure of the individuals speaking that language. The evidence for the first proposition derives from a comparison of the lexical and structural characteristics of various languages. The linguistic comparisons alone do not establish the proposition. They need to be complemented with psychological data. The second proposition is not directly supported by any data. However, it is clear that language can be described as a molder of thought since speech is a patterned response that is learned only when the governing cognitive patterns have been grasped. It is also possible that the lexical structure of the speech he hears guides the infant in categorizing his environment. These matters require empirical exploration.

An experiment is described which investigates a part of proposition a—the idea that lexical differences are indicative of cognitive differences. Whorf reports many cases in which a given range of experience is lexically differentiated in one language whereas the same discriminations can only be described with phrases in another language. Rather than compare members of different linguistic communities, we chose to work with native speakers of English and to compare their linguistic coding of two regions of experience. Within the realm of color vision there are colors that can be named with a single word and others that require a phrase. This kind of linguistic difference in the length of name (measured by words or syllables) was found to be correlated with the latency of the naming response and the reliability of the response from person to person within the linguistic community and from time to time in one person. A factor analysis of these measures yielded a single general factor—codability. The measure carrying the largest factor loading was the reliability of naming response between individuals who speak the same language. This variable—the codability of a color—proved to be related to the subjects' ability to recognize colors. Codability accounted for more variance in the recognition task as the task was delayed and complicated to increase the importance of the storage factor. Data obtained from the Zuni Indians show a similar relationship between codability and recognition. It is suggested that there may be general laws relating codability to cognitive processes. All cultures could conform to these laws although they differ among themselves in the values the variables assume in particular regions of experience.

References

Buhler, K. *Sprachtheorie.* Jena: G. Fischer, 1934.

Cassirer, E. *The philosophy of symbolic forms.* Vol. 1. Language. New Haven: Yale University Press, 1963.

Doob, L. W. *Social psychology.* New York: Holt, 1952.

Evans, R. M. *An introduction to color.* New York: Wiley, 1948.

Fries, C. C. *The structure of English.* New York: Harcourt, Brace, 1952.

Goldstein, K. *Language and language disturbances.* New York: Grune & Stratton, 1948.

Hull, C. L. Quantitative aspects of the evolution of concepts. *Psychol. Monogr.,* 1920, *28,* No. 1 (Whole No. 123).

Korzybski, A. The role of language in the perceptual processes. In R. R. Blake & G. V. Ramsey (Eds.), *Perception: an approach to personality.* New York: Ronald, 1951.

Kurtz, K. H., and Hovland, C. I. The effect of verbalization during observation of stimulus objects upon accuracy of recognition and recall. *J. Exp. Psychol.,* 1953, *45,* 157–164.

Lennenberg, E. H., and Roberts, J. M. *The denotation of color terms.* Paper read at Linguistic Society of America, Bloomington, Indiana, August 1953.

Maerz, A., and Paul, M. R. *A dictionary of color.* New York: McGraw-Hill, 1930.

Newhall, S. M., Nickerson, D., and Judd, D. B. Final report of the OSA subcommittee on the spacing of the Munsell colors. *J. Opt. Soc. Amer.,* 1943, *33,* 385–418.

Nickerson, D., Tomaszewski, J. J., and Boyd, T. F. Colorimetric specifications of Munsell repaints. *J. Opt. Soc. Amer.*, 1953, 43, 163–171.

Optical Society of America, Committee on Colorimetry. *The science of color.* New York: Crowell, 1953.

Orwell, G. *Nineteen eighty-four.* New York: Harcourt, Brace, 1949.

Seroshevskii, V. R. *Iakuti.* St. Petersburg: Royal Geographical Society, 1896.

Thorndike, E. L., and Lorge, I. *The teacher's word book of 30,000 words.* New York: Teachers College, Columbia University, 1944.

Whorf, B. L. *Four articles on metalinguistics.* Washington: Foreign Service Institute, 1950.

Wundt, W. *Volkerpsychologie.* Vol. 1. Die Sprache. Leipzig: Engelmann, 1900.

Zipf, G. K. *The psycho-biology of language.* Boston: Houghton Mifflin, 1935.

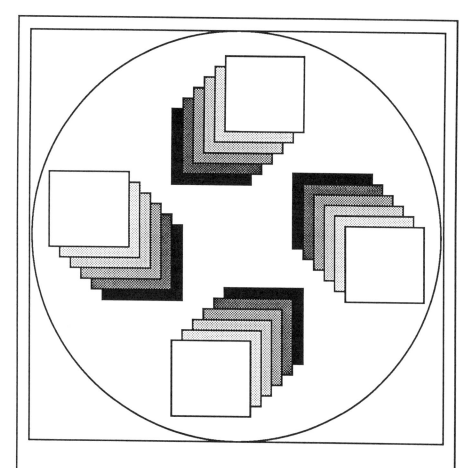

Chapter 9

Intelligence

CHAPTER 9: INTELLIGENCE

Much of the general furor over mental tests has arisen from a 1969 report by Arthur Jensen stating that the majority of one's IQ is inherited. The conclusion Jensen and others jumped to was that there are biologically racial differences in IQ that cannot be altered by education. The similarity of this position with a form of biological determinism is at odds with one of the founding tenets of the United States—"all men are created equal." The selections in this chapter address this problem and present some possible solutions. The intent here is not to provide you with absolute, final, and incontrovertible answers, but to present enough information to allow informed analysis.

9a. Trotter, R. (1986). Three heads are better than one. *Psychology Today*. 20, Aug. 56–62.

Sternberg's personal experiences with IQ tests led to a lifelong interest in different aspects of intelligence and how they can be tested. What are Sternberg's three factors of intelligence? Explain them in your own words. What are some of the problems with old IQ tests and in what way could Sternberg's three factors help solve them?

9b. Scarr, S. & McCartney, K. (1983) How people make their own environments: A theory of genotype → environment effects. *Child Development*, 54, 424–435.

This paper addresses a common contention regarding a major question in IQ research; is IQ inherited? Not only does this paper suggest a novel solution to the controversy but it helps explain some empirical findings that have not fit thus far into prior explanatory frameworks. What are the empirical contradictions, and how do Scarr and McCartney (1983) explain them? Give an example of their evocative and active gene-environment interactions.

Three Heads Are Better Than One

Robert J. Trotter

"I really stunk on IQ tests. I was just terrible," recalls Sternberg. "In elementary school I had severe test anxiety. I'd hear other people starting to turn the page and I'd still be on the second item. I'd utterly freeze."

Poor performances on IQ tests piqued Sternberg's interest, and from rather inauspicious beginnings he proceeded to build a career on the study of intelligence and intelligence testing. Sternberg, IBM Professor of Psychology and Education at Yale University, did his undergraduate work at Yale and then got his Ph.D. from Stanford University in 1975. Since then he has written hundreds of articles and several books on intelligence, received numerous fellowships and awards for his research and proposed a three-part theory of intelligence. He is now developing an intelligence test based on that theory.

Running through Sternberg's work is a core of common-sense practicality not always seen in studies of subjects as intangible as intelligence. This practical bent, which stems from his early attempts to understand his own trouble with IQ tests, is also seen in his current efforts to devise ways of teaching people to better understand and increase their intellectual skills.

Sternberg got over his test anxiety in sixth grade after doing so poorly on an IQ test that he was sent to retake it with the fifth-graders. "When you are in elementary school," he explains, "one year makes a big difference. It's one thing to take a test with sixth-graders, but if you're taking it with a bunch of babies, you don't have to worry." He did well on the test, and by seventh grade he was designing and administering his own test of mental abilities as part of a science project. In 10th grade he studied how distractions affect people taking mental-ability tests. After graduating from high school, he worked summers as a research assistant, first at the Psychological Corporation in New York, then at the Educational Testing Service in Princeton, New Jersey. These jobs gave him hands-on experience with testing organizations, but he began to suspect that the intelligence field was not going anywhere, Most of the tests being used were pretty old, he says, and there seemed to be little good research going on.

This idea was reinforced when Sternberg took a graduate course at Stanford from Lee. J. Cronbach, a leader in the field of tests and measurements. Intelligence research is dead, Cronbach said; the psychometric approach—IQ testing—has run its course and people are waiting for something new. This left Sternberg at a loss. He knew he wanted to study intelligence, but be didn't know how to go about it.

About this time, an educational publishing firm (Barron's) asked Sternberg to write a book on how to prepare for the Miller Analogies Test. Since Sternberg had invented a scheme for classifying the items on the test when he worked for the Psychological Corporation, which publishes the test, he was an obvious choice to write the book. Being an impecunious graduate student, he jumped at the chance, but he had an ulterior motive. He wanted to study intelligence and thought that because analogies are a major part of most IQ tests, working on the book might help. This work eventually led to his dissertation and a book based on it.

At this stage, Sternberg was analyzing the cognitive, or mental, processes people use to solve IQ test items, such as analogies, syllogisms and series. His research gave a good account of what people did in their heads, he says, and also seemed to account for individual differences in IQ test performance. Sternberg extended this work in the 1970s and in 1980 published a paper setting forth what he called his "componential" theory of human intelligence.

"I really thought I had the whole bag here," he says. "I thought I knew what was going on, but that was just a delusion on my part." Psychology comes out of everyday experiences, Sternberg says. And his own experiences—teaching and working with graduate students at Yale—gave him the idea that there was much more to intelligence than what his componential theory was describing. He brings this idea to life with stories of three idealized graduate students—Alice, Barbara and Celia. Alice, he says, is someone who looked very smart according to conventional theories of intelligence. She had almost a 4.0 average as an undergraduate, scored extremely high on the Graduate Record Exam (GRE) and was supported by excellent letters of recommendation. She had everything that smart graduate students are supposed to have and was admitted to Yale as a top pick.

"There was no doubt that this was Miss Real Smarto," Sternberg says, and she performed just the way the tests predicted she would. She did extremely well on multiple-choice tests and was great in class, especially at critiquing other people's work and analyzing arguments. "She was just fantastic," Sternberg says. "She was one of our top two students the first year, but it didn't stay that way. She wasn't even in the top half by the time she finished. It just didn't work out. So that made me suspicious, and I wanted to know what went wrong."

The GRE and other tests had accurately predicted Alice's performance for the first year or so but then got progressively less predictive. And what became clear, Sternberg says, is that although the tests did measure her critical thinking ability, they did not measure her ability to come up with good ideas. This is not unusual, he says. A lot of people are very good analytically, but they just don't have good ideas of their own.

Sternberg thinks he knows why people with high GRE scores don't always do well in graduate school. From elementary school to college, he explains, students are continuously reinforced for high test-smarts, The first year of graduate school is similar—lots of multiple-choice tests and papers that demand critical thinking. Then around the second year there is a transition, with more emphasis on creative, or synthetic, thinking and having good ideas. "That's a different skill," Sternberg says. "It's not that test taking and critical thinking all of a sudden become unimportant, it's just that other things become more important."

When people who have always done well on tests get to this transition point, instead of being continually reinforced, they are only intermittently reinforced. And that is the kind of reinforcement most likely to sustain a particular type of behavior. "Instead of helping people try to improve their performance in other areas, intermittent reinforcement encourages them to overcapitalize on test-smarts, and they try to use that kind of intelligence in situations in which it is not relevant.

"The irony is that people like Alice may have other abilities, but they never look for them," he says. "It's like psychologists who come up with a theory that's interesting and then try to expand it to everything under the sun. They just can't see its limitations. It's the same with mental abilities. Some are good in certain situations but not in others."

The second student, Barbara, had a very different kind of record. Her undergraduate grades were not great, and her GRE scores were really low by Yale standards. She did, however, have absolutely superlative letters of recommendation that said Barbara was extremely creative, had really good ideas and did exceptional research. Sternberg thought Barbara would continue to do creative work and wanted to accept her. When he was outvoted, he hired her as a research associate. "Academic smarts," Sternberg says, "are easy to find, but creativity is a rare and precious commodity."

Sternberg's prediction was correct. In addition to working full time as a research associate she took graduate classes, and her work and ideas proved to be just as good as the letters said they would be. When the transition came, she was ready to go. "Some of the most important work I've done was in collaboration with her," Sternberg says.

Barbaresque talent, Sternberg emphasizes, is not limited to psychology graduate school. "I think the same principle applies to everything. Take business. You can get an MBA based on your academic smarts because graduate programs consist mostly of taking tests and analyzing cases. But when you actually go into business, you have to have creative ideas for products and for marketing. Some MBA's don't make the transition and never do well because they overcapitalize on academic smarts. And it's the same no matter what you do. If you're in writing, you have to have good ideas for stories. If you're in art, you have to have good ideas for artwork. If you're in law. . . . That's where Barbaresque talent comes in."

The third student was Celia. Her grades, letters of recommendation and GRE scores were good but not great. She was accepted into the program and the first year, Sternberg says, she did all right but not great. Surprisingly, however, she turned out to be the easiest student to place in a good job.

And this surprised him. Celia lacked Alice's super analytic ability and Barbara's super synthetic, or creative, ability, yet she could get a good job while others were having trouble.

Celia, it turns out, had learned bow to play the game. She made sure she did the kind of work that is valued in psychology. She submitted her papers to the right journals. In other words, Sternberg says, "she was a street smart psychologist, very street-smart. And that, again, is something that doesn't show up on IQ tests." Sternberg points out that Alice, Barbara and Celia are not extreme cases. "Extremes are rare," he says, "but not good. You don't want someone who is incredibly analytically brilliant but never has a good idea or who is a total social boor." Like all of us, Alice, Barbara and Celia each had all three of the intellectual abilities be described, but each was especially good in one aspect.

After considering the special qualities of people such as Alice, Barbara and Celia, Sternberg concluded that his componential theory explained only one aspect of intelligence. It could account for Alice, but it was too narrow to explain Barbara and Celia. In an attempt to find out why, Sternberg began to look at prior theories of intelligence and found that they tried to do one of three things:

Some looked at the relation of intelligence to the internal world of the individual, what goes on inside people's heads when they think intelligently. "That's what IQ tests measure, that's what information processing tasks measure, that's the componential theory. It's what I had been doing," Sternberg says. "I'd take an IQ test problem and analyze the mental processes involved in solving it, but it's still the same damned problem. It's sort of like we never got away from the IQ test as a standard. It's not that I thought the componential work was wrong. It told me a lot about what made Alice smart, but there had to be more."

Other theories looked it the relation of intelligence to experience, with experience mediating between what's inside the internal, mental world and what's outside—the external world. These theories say you have to look at how experience affects a person's intelligence and how intelligence affects a person's experiences. In other words, more-intelligent people create different experiences. "And that," says Sternberg, "is where Barbara fits in. She is someone who has a certain way of coping with novelty that goes beyond the ordinary. She can see old problems in new ways, or she'll take a new problem and see how some old thing she knows applies to it."

A third kind of theory looks at intelligence in relation to the individual's external world. In other words, what makes people smart in their everyday context? How does the environment interact with being smart? And what you see, as with Celia, is that there are a lot of people who don't do particularly well on tests but who are just extremely practically intelligent. "Take Lee Iacocca," Sternberg says. "Maybe he doesn't have an IQ of 160 (or maybe he does, I don't know), but he is extremely effective. And there are plenty of people who are that way. And there are plenty of people going around with high IQ's who don't do a damned thing. This Celiaesque kind of smartness—how you make it in the real world—is not reflected in IQ tests. So I decided to have a look at all three kinds of intelligence."

He did, and the result was the triarchic theory. A triarchy is government by three persons, and in his 1985 book, *Beyond IQ*, Sternberg suggests that we are all governed by three aspects of intelligence: componential, experiential and contextual. In the book, each aspect of intelligence is described in a subtheory. Though based in part on older theories, Sternberg's work differs from those theories in a number of ways, His componential subtheory, which describes Alice, for example, is closest to the views of cognitive psychologists and psychometricians.

But Sternberg thinks that the other theories put too much emphasis on measuring speed and accuracy of performance components at the expense of what he calls "metacomponents," or executive processes.

"For example," he explains, "the really interesting part of solving analogies or syllogisms is deciding what to do in the first place. But that isn't isolated by looking at performance components, so I realized you need to look at metacomponents—how you plan it, how you monitor what you are doing, how you evaluate it after you are done. [See "Stalking the IQ Quark," *Psychology Today*, September 1979.]

"A big thing in psychometric theory," he continues, "is mental speed. Almost every group test is timed, so if you're not fast you're in trouble. But I came to the conclusion that we were really misguided on that. Almost everyone regrets some decision that was made too fast. Think of the guy who walks around with President Reagan carrying the black box. You don't want this guy to be real fast at pushing the button. So, instead of just testing speed, you want to measure a person's knowing when to be fast and when to be slow—time allocation—it's a metacomponent. And that's what the componential subtheory emphasizes."

THE TRIARCHIC THEORY

Componential
   Alice had high test scores and was a whiz at test-taking and analytical thinking. Her type of intelligence exemplifies the componential subtheory, which explains the mental components involved in analytical thinking.

Experiential
   Barbara didn't have the best test scores, but she was a superbly creative thinker who could combine disparate experiences in insightful ways. She is an example of the experiential subtheory.

Contextual
   Celia was street-smart. She learned how to play the game and how to manipulate the environment. Her test scores weren't tops, but she could come out on top in almost any context. She is Sternberg's example of contextual intelligence.

The experiential subtheory, which describes Barbaresque talent, emphasizes insight. Sternberg and graduate student Janet E. Davidson, as part of a study of intellectual giftedness, concluded that what gifted people had in common was insight. "If you look at Hemingway in literature, Darwin in science or Rousseau in political theory, you see that they all seemed to be unusually insightful people," Sternberg explains. "But when we looked at the research, we found that nobody seemed to know what insight is."

Sternberg and Davidson analyzed how several major scientific insights came about and concluded that insight is really three things: selective encoding, selective combination and selective comparison. As an example of selective encoding they cite Sir Alexander Fleming's discovery of penicillin. One of Fleming's experiments was spoiled when mold contaminated and killed the bacteria he was studying. Sternberg says most people would have said, "I screwed up, I've got to throw this out and start over." But Fleming didn't. He realized that the mold that killed the bacteria was more important than the bacteria. This selective encoding insight—the ability to focus on the really critical information—led to the discovery of a substance in the mold that Fleming called "penicillin." "And this is not just something that famous scientists do," Sternberg explains. "Detectives have to decide what are the relevant clues, lawyers have to decide which facts have legal consequences and so on."

The second kind of insight is selective combination, which is putting the facts together to get the big picture, as in Charles Darwin's formulation of the theory of natural selection. The facts he needed to form the theory were already there; other people had them too. But Darwin saw how to put them together. Similarly, doctors have to put the symptoms together to figure out what the disease is. Lawyers have to put the facts together to figure out how to make the case. "My triarchic theory is another example of selective combination. It doesn't have that much in it that's different from what other people have said," Sternberg admits. "It's just putting it together that's a little different."

A third kind of insight is selective comparison. It's relating the old to the new analogically, says Sternberg. It involves being able to see an old thing in a new way or being able to see a new thing in an old way. An example is the discovery of the molecular structure of benzene by German chemist August Kekule, who had been struggling to find the structure for some time. Then one night he had a dream in which a snake was dancing around and biting its own tail. Kekule woke up and realized that he had solved the puzzle of benzene's structure. In essence, Sternberg explains, Kekule could see the relation between two very disparate elements—the circular image of the dancing snake and the hexagonal structure of the benzene molecule.

Sternberg and Davidson tested their theory of insight on fourth-, fifth- and sixth-graders who had been identified through IQ and creativity tests as either gifted or not so gifted. They used problems that require the three different kinds of insights. A selective-encoding problem, for example, is the old one about four brown socks and five blue socks in a drawer. How many do you have to pull out to make sure you'll have a matching pair? It's a selective-encoding problem because the solution depends on selecting and using the relevant information. (The information about the 4-to-5 ratio is irrelevant.)

As expected, the gifted children were better able to solve all three types of problems. The less gifted children, for example, tended to get hung up on the irrelevant ratio information in the socks problem, while the gifted children ignored it. When the researchers gave the less gifted children the information needed to solve the problems (by underlining what was relevant, for example), their performance improved significantly. Giving the gifted children this information had no such effect, Sternberg explains, because they tended to have the insights spontaneously.

Sternberg and Davidson also found that insight skills can be taught. In a five-week training program for both gifted and less gifted children, they greatly improved children's scores on insight problems, compared with children who had not received the training. Moreover, says Sternberg, the gains were durable and transferable. The skills were still there when the children were tested a year later and were being applied to kinds of insight problems that had never appeared in the training program.

Sternberg's contextual subtheory emphasizes adaptation. Almost everyone agrees that intelligence is the ability to adapt to the environment, but that doesn't seem to be what IQ tests measure, Sternberg says. So he and Richard K. Wagner, then a graduate student, now at Florida State University, tried to come up with a test of adaptive ability. They studied people in two occupations: academic psychologists, "because we think that's a really important job," and business executives, "because everyone else thinks that's an important job." They began by asking prominent, successful people what one needs to be practically intelligent in their fields. The psychologists and executives agreed on three things:

First, IQ isn't very important for success in these jobs. "And that makes sense because you already have a restricted range. You're talking about people with IQ's of 110 to 150. That's not to say that IQ doesn't count for anything," Sternberg says. "If you were talking about a range from 40 to 150, IQ might make a difference, but we're not. So IQ isn't that important with regard to practical intelligence."

They also agreed that graduate school isn't that important either. "This," says Sternberg, "was a little offensive. After all, here I was teaching and doing the study with one of my own graduate students, and these people were saying graduate training wasn't that helpful." But Sternberg remembered that graduate school had not fully prepared him for his first year on the job as an academic, "I really needed to know how to write a grant proposal; at Yale, if you can't get grants you're in trouble. You have to scrounge for paper clips, you can't get students to work with you, you can't get any research done. Five years later you get fired because you haven't done anything. Now, no one ever says you are being hired to write grants, but if you don't get them you're dead meat around here." Sternberg, who has had more than $5 million in grants in the past 10 years, says he'd be five years behind where he is now without great graduate students.

"What you need to know to be practically intelligent, to get on in an environment," Sternberg says, is tacit knowledge, the third area of agreement. "It's implied or indicated but not always expressed, or taught." Sternberg and Wagner constructed a test of such knowledge and gave it to senior and junior business executives and to senior and junior psychology professors. The results suggest that tacit knowledge is a result of learning from experience. It is not related to IQ but is related to success in the real world. Psychologists who scored high on the test, compared with those who had done poorly, had published more research, presented more papers at conventions and tended to be at the better universities, Business executives who scored high had better salaries, more merit raises and better performance ratings than those who scored low.

The tacit-knowledge test is a measure of how well people adapt to their environment, but practical knowledge also means knowing when not to adapt. "Suppose you join a computer software firm because you really want to work on educational software," Sternberg says, "but they put you in the firm's industrial espionage section and ask you to spy on Apple Computer. There are times when you have to select another environment, when you have to say, "It's time to quit. I don't want to adapt, I'm leaving".

There are, however, times when you can't quit and must stay put. In such situations, you can try to change the environment. That, says Sternberg, is the final aspect of contextual, or practical, intelligence shaping the environment to suit your needs.

One way to do this is by capitalizing on your intellectual strengths and compensating for your weaknesses. "I don't think I'm at the top of the heap analytically," Sternberg explains. "I'm good, not the greatest, but I think I know what I'm good at and I try to make the most of it. And there are some things I stink at and I either try to make them unimportant or I find other people to do them. That's part of how I shape my environment. And that's what I think practical intelligence is about capitalizing on your strengths and minimizing your weaknesses. It's sort of mental self-management.

"So basically what I've said is there are different ways to be smart, but ultimately what you want to do is take the components (Alice intelligence), apply them to your experience (Barbara) and use them to adapt to, select and shape your environment (Celia). That is the triarchic theory of intelligence."

What can you do with a new theory of intelligence? Sternberg, who seems to have a three-part answer for every question (and whose triangular theory of love will be the subject of a future Psychology Today article), says, "I view the situation as a triangle." The most important leg of the triangle, he says, is theory and research. "But it's not enough for me to spend my life coming up with theories," he says. "So I've gone in two further directions, the other two legs of the triangle—testing and training."

He is developing, with the Psychological Corporation, now in San Antonio, Texas, the Sternberg Multidimensional Abilities Test. It is based strictly on the triarchic theory and will measure intelligence in a much broader way than traditional IQ tests do. "Rather than giving you a number that's etched in stone," he says, "this test will be used as a basis for diagnosing your intellectual strengths and weaknesses."

Once you understand the kind of intelligence you have, the third leg of the triangle—the training of intellectual skills comes into play. One of Sternberg's most recent books, *Intelligence Applied*, is a training program based on the theory. It is designed to help people capitalize on their strengths and improve where they are weak. "I'm very committed to all three aspects," Sternberg says. "It's really important to me that my work has an effect that goes beyond the psychology journals. I really think it's important to bring intelligence into the real world and the real world into intelligence."

How People Make Their Own Environments: A Theory of Genotype → Environment Effects

Sandra Scarr
Kathleen McCartney

Introduction

Theories of behavioral development have ranged from genetic determinism to naive environmentalism. Neither of these radical views nor interactionism has adequately explained the process of development or the role of experience in development. In this paper we propose a theory of environmental effects on human development that emphasizes the role of the genotype in determining not only which environments are experienced by individuals but also which environments individuals seek for themselves. To show how this theory addresses the process of development, the theory is used to account for seemingly anomalous findings for deprivation, adoption, twin, and intervention studies.

For the species, we claim that human experience and its effects on development depend primarily on the evolved nature of the human genome. In evolutionary theory the two essential concepts are selection and variation. Through selection the human genome has evolved to program human development. Phenotypic variation is the raw material on which selection works. Genetic variation must be associated with phenotypic variation, or there could be no evolution. It follows from evolutionary theory that individual differences depend in part on genotypic differences. We argue that genetic differences prompt differences in which environments are experienced and what effects they may have. In this view, the genotype, in both its species specificity and its individual variability, largely determines environment effects on development, because the genotype determines the organism's responsiveness to environmental opportunities.

A theory of behavioral development must explain the origin of new psychological structures. Because there is no evidence that new adaptations can arise out of the environment without maturational changes in the organism, genotypes must be the source of new structures.

Maturational sequence is controlled primarily by the genetic program for development. As Gottlieb (1976) said, there is evidence for a role of environment in (1) maintaining existing structures and in (2) elaborating existing structures; however, there is no evidence that the environment has a role in (3) inducing new structures. In development, new adaptations or structures cannot arise out of experience per se.

The most widely accepted theories of development are vague about how new structures arise; for example, Piaget (1980) fails to make the connection between organism and environment clear in his references to interaction. Nor is development well described by maturation alone (see Connolly & Prechtl, 1981). Neither Gesell and Ilg (1943) nor contemporary nativists (e.g., Chomsky, 1980) appreciate the inextricable links of nature and nurture in a hierarchically organized system of development.

We suggest that the problem of new structures in development has been extraordinarily difficult because of a false parallel between genotype and environment, which, we argue, are not constructs at the same level of analysis. The dichotomy of nature and nurture has always been a bad one, not only for the oft-cited reasons that both are required for development, but because a false parallel arises between the two. We propose that development is indeed the result of nature *and* nurture but that genes drive experience. Genes are components in a system that organizes the organism to experience its world. The organism's abilities to experience the world change with development and are individually variable. A good theory of the environment can only be one in which experience is guided by genotypes that both push and restrain experiences.

Behavioral development depends on both a genetic program and a suitable environment for the expression of the human, species-typical program for development. Differences among people can arise from both genetic and environmental differences, but the process by which differences arise is better described as genotype → environment effects. Like Chomsky and Fodor (1980), we propose that the genotype is the driving force behind development, because, we argue, it is the discriminator of what environments are actually experienced. The genotype determines the *responsiveness* of the person to those environmental opportunities. Unlike Chomsky and Fodor, we do not think that development is precoded in the genes and merely emerges with maturation. Rather, we stress the role of the genotype in determining which environments are actually experienced and what effects they have on the developing person.

We distinguish here between environments to which a person is exposed and environments that are actively experienced or "grasped" by the person. As we all know, the relevance of environments changes with development. The toddler who has "caught on" to the idea that things have names and who demands the names for everything is experiencing a fundamentally different verbal environment from what she experienced before, even though her parents talked to her extensively in infancy. The young adolescent who played baseball with the boy next door and now finds herself hopelessly in love with him is experiencing her friend's companionship in a new way.

A Model of Genotypes and Environments: Figure 1 presents our model of behavioral development. In this model, the child's phenotype (P_c), or observable characteristics, is a function of both the child's genotype (G_c) and her rearing environment (E_c). There will be little disagreement on this. The parents' genotypes (G_p) determine the child's genotype, which in turn influences the child's phenotype. Again, there should be little controversy over this point. As in most developmental theories, transactions occur between the organism and the environment; here they are described by the correlation between phenotype and rearing environment. In most models, however, the source of this correlation is ambiguous. In this model, both the child's phenotype and rearing environment are influenced by the child's genotype. Because the child's genotype influences both the phenotype and the rearing environment, their correlation is a function of the genotype. The genotype is *conceptually prior* to both the phenotype and the rearing environment.

It is an unconventional shorthand to suggest that the child's genotype can directly affect the rearing environment. What we want to represent is developmental changes in the genetic program that prompt

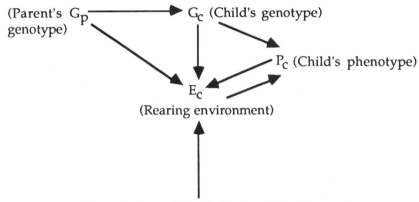

Figure 1: A model of behavioral development

new experiences, before the full phenotype is developed. An example could be found in the development of productive speech; the child becomes attentive to the language environment receptively months before real words are produced. Our argument is that changes in what is "turned on" in the genotype affect an emerging phenotype, both directly through maturation (G_c to P_c) and through prompting new experiences.

The model could just as well specify intermediate phenotypes, such as receptive language in the example of productive speech, but the *idea* that genetic differences (both developmental changes for an individual over time and differences among individuals) affect experiential differences could be lost in a web of path diagrams. The model is designed to present our ideas, not for analysis of variance.

Also clouded by an endless regress of intermediate phenotypes would be the idea that the correlation or the transaction between phenotype and environment is determined by developmental changes in the genotype. We recognize that this is not a popular position, but we propose it to account for data to be discussed in the final sections of the paper.

Thus, we intend the path from G_c to E_c to represent the idea that developmental changes in phenotypes are prompted both by changes in the effective genotype and by changes in the salience of environments, which are then correlated.

The path from the G_c to P_c represents maturation, which is controlled primarily by the genetic program. New structures arise out of maturation, from genotype to phenotype. Behavioral development is elaborated and maintained, in Gottlieb's sense, by the transactions of phenotype and environment, but it cannot arise de novo from this interaction. Thus, in this model, the course of development is a function of genetically controlled maturational sequences, although the rate of maturation can be affected by some environmental circumstances, such as the effects of nutrition on physical growth (Watson & Lowrey, 1967). Behavioral examples include cultural differences in rates of development through the sequence of cognitive stages described by Piaget and other theoretical sequences (see Nerlove & Snipper, 1981).

Separation of Genetic and Environmental Effects on Development: The major problem with attempts to separate environmental from genetic effects and their combinations is that people evoke and select their own environments to a great extent. There may appear to be arbitrary events of fate, such as being hit by a truck (did you look carefully in both directions?), falling ill (genetic differences in susceptibility, or a life-style that lowers resistance to disease?), but even these may not be entirely divorced from personal characteristics that have some genetic variability. Please understand that we do not mean that one's environmental fate is entirely determined by one's genotype—only that some genotypes are more likely to receive and select certain environments than others. A theory that stresses either genetic or environmental differences per se cannot account for the processes by which people come to be the way they are. At any one point in time, behavioral differences may be analyzed into variances that can be attributed more or less to genetic and environmental sources (see Plomin, DeFries, & Loehlin, 1977; Scarr & Kidd, in press). A quantitative genetic approach to estimating variance, however, does not attempt to specify the processes by which individuals developed their phenotypes.

Genotype–environment correlations.—Plomin et al. have described a model of phenotype variation that estimates the amount of variance that arises from genetic and environmental differences. Genotype–environment correlation is a nonlinear component in the additive variance model, included to account for situations in which "genotypes are selectively exposed to different environments." They did not intend to describe developmental processes, as we are doing here. Rather, Plomin and his colleagues were responding to the question, How much of the variation in a phenotype is due to differences among genotypes, differences among environments, dominance effects, genotype–environment interactions, and genotype–environment correlations? Their model addresses sources of individual differences in a population of phenotypes at one point in time. By contrast, our use of the term, genotype → environment effects, is to describe developmental *processes* over time, not to estimate sources of variance in phenotypes. We seek to answer the questions, How do genotypes and environments *combine* to produce human development? and How do genetic and environmental differences *combine* to produce variation in development?

An Evolving Theory of Behavioral Development

Plomin et al. (1977) described three kinds of genotype–environment correlations that we believe form the basis for a developmental theory. The theory of genotype → environment effects we propose has three propositions:

1. The process by which children develop is best described by three kinds of genotype → environment effects: a *passive* kind, whereby the genetically related parents provide a rearing environment that is correlated with the genotype of the child (sometimes positively and sometimes negatively); an *evocative* kind, whereby the child receives responses from others that are influenced by his genotype; and an *active* kind that represents the child's selective attention to and learning from aspects of his environment that are influenced by his genotype and indirectly correlated with those of his biological relatives.

2. The relative importance of the three kinds of genotype → environment effects changes with development. The influence of the passive kind declines from infancy to adolescence, and the importance of the active kind increases over the same period.

3. The degree to which experience is influenced by individual genotypes increases with development and with the shift from passive to active genotype → environment effects, as individuals select their own experiences.

The first, *passive* genotype → environment effects arise in biologically related families and render all of the research literature on parent–child socialization uninterpretable. Because parents provide both genes and environments for their biological offspring, the child's environment is necessarily correlated with her genes, because her genes are correlated with her parents' genes, and the parents' genes are correlated with the rearing environment they provide. It is impossible to know what about the parents' rearing environment for the child determines what about the child's behavior, because of the confounding effect of genetic transmission of the same characteristics from parent to child. Not only can we not interpret the direction of effects in parent–child interaction, as Bell (1968) argued, we also cannot interpret the *cause* of those effects in biologically related families.

An example of a positive kind of passive genotype–environment correlation can be found in reading; parents who read well and enjoy reading are likely to provide their children with books; thus, the children are more likely to be skilled readers who enjoy reading, both for genetic and environmental reasons. The children's rearing environment is positively correlated with the parents' genotypes and therefore with the children's genotypes as well.

An example of a negative passive genotype–environment correlation can also be found in reading. Parents who are skilled readers, faced with a child who is not learning to read well, may provide a more enriched reading environment for that child than for another who acquires reading skills quickly. The more enriched environment for the less able child represents a negative genotype →

environment effect (see also Plomin et al., 1977). There is, thus, an unreliable, but not random, connection between genotypes and environments when parents provide the opportunities for experience.

The second kind of genotype → environment effect is called evocative because it represents the different responses that different genotypes evoke from the social and physical environments. Responses to the person further shape development in ways that correlate with the genotype. Examples of such evocative effects can be found in the research of Lytton (1980), the theory of Escalona (1968), and the review of Maccoby (1980). It is quite likely that smiley, active babies receive more social stimulation than sober, passive infants. In the intellectual area, cooperative, attentive preschoolers receive more pleasant and instructional interactions from the adults around them than uncooperative, distractible children. Individual differences in responses evoked can also be found in the physical world; for example, people who are skillful at electronics receive feedback of a sort very different from those who fail consistently at such tasks.

The third kind of genotype → environment effect is the active, niche-picking or niche-building sort. People seek out environments they find compatible and stimulating. We all select from the surrounding environment some aspects to which to respond, learn about, or ignore. Our selections are correlated with motivational, personality, and intellectual aspects of our genotypes. The active genotype → environment effect, we argue, is the most powerful connection between people and their environments and the most direct expression of the genotype in experience.

Examples of active genotype → environment effects can be found in the selective efforts of individuals in sports, scholarship, relationships—in life. Once experiences occur, they naturally lead to further experiences. We agree that phenotypes are elaborated and maintained by environments, but the impetus for the experience comes, we argue, from the genotype.

Developmental Changes in Genotype → Environment Effects: The second proposition is that the relative importance of the three kinds of genotype → environment effects changes over development from infancy to adolescence. In infancy much of the environment that reaches the child is provided by adults. When those adults are genetically related to the child, the environment they provide in general is positively related to their own characteristics and their own genotypes. Although infants are active in structuring their experiences by selectively attending to what is offered, they cannot do as much seeking out and niche-building as older children; thus, passive genotype → environment effects are more important for infants and young children than they are for older children, who can extend their experiences beyond the family's influences and create their own environments to a much greater extent. Thus, the effects of passive genotype → environment effects wane when the child has many extra-familial opportunities.

In addition, parents can provide environments that are negatively related to the child's genotype, as illustrated earlier in teaching reading. Although parents' genotypes usually affect the environment they provide for their biological offspring, it is sometimes positive and sometimes negative and therefore not as direct a product of the young child's genotype as later environments will be. Thus, as stated in proposition 3, genotype → environment effects increase With development, as active replace passive forms. Genotype → environment effects of the evocative sort persist throughout life, as we elicit responses from others based on many personal, genotype-related characteristics from appearance to personality and intellect. Those responses from others reinforce and extend the directions our development has taken. High intelligence and adaptive skills in children from very disadvantaged backgrounds, for example, evoke approval and support from school personnel who might otherwise despair of the child's chances in life (Garmezy, Note 1). In adulthood, personality and intellectual differences evoke different responses in others. Similarities in personal characteristics evoke similar responses from others, as shown in the case of identical twins reared apart (Bouchard, Note 2). These findings are also consistent with the third proposition.

A Probabilistic Model: The concept of genotype → environment effects is emphasized in this emerging theory for three major reasons: the model results in a testable set of hypotheses for which disconfirmation would come from random association between genotypes and environments, it describes a developmental process, and it implies a probabilistic connection between a person and the environment. It is more likely that people with certain genotypes will receive certain kinds of parenting, evoke certain responses from others, and select certain aspects from the available environments; but nothing is rigidly determined. The idea of genetic differences, on the other hand, has seemed to imply to many that the person's developmental fate was preordained without regard to experience. This is absurd. By invoking the idea of genotype → environment effects, we hope to emphasize a probabilistic connection between genotypes and their environments. Although mismatches between the behaviors of parents and children certainly exist (see Nelson, 1973), we argue that on the average there are correlations of parents' characteristics and the rearing environment they provide.

Waddington (1962) postulated a probable but not determinant connection between genotypes and phenotypes through an epigenetic space in which environmental events deflect the course of the developing phenotype. Figure 2 illustrates Waddington's theory of the probable relationship between genotypic and phenotypic differences. Note that a correlation remains between genotype and phenotype, even though one cannot specify in advance what environmental events will affect phenotypic development. To this conception, we add that genotypes shape many of their own experiences through evocative and active genotype → environment correlations.

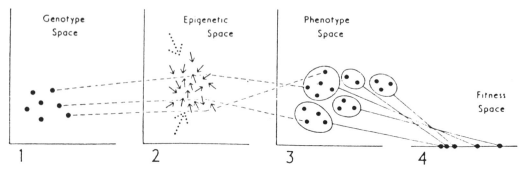

Figure 2: Waddington's epigenetic space

The Role of the Environment Revisited

If genotypes are the driving force behind development and the determinants of what environments are experienced, does this mean that environments themselves have no effects? Clearly, environments are necessary for development and have effects on the average levels of development, but they may or may not cause variations among individuals (McCall, 1981). We argue like McCall that nature has not left essential human development at the mercy of experiences that may or may not be encountered; rather, the only necessary experiences are ones that are generally available to the species. Differences in experience per se, therefore, cannot be the major cause of variation among individuals. The major features of human development are programmed genetically and require experiences that are encountered by the vast majority of humankind in the course of living. Phenotypic variation among individuals relies on experiential differences that are determined by genetic differences rather than on differences among environment effects that occur randomly.

Imposed Environments: In developmental studies, we usually think of environments provided for a child, such as parental interaction, school curricula and various experimental manipulations. In some cases, there are passive and evocative genotype–environment correlations that go unrecognized, as in parent-child interaction and the selection of children into school curricula. In a few cases there may be no correlation of the child's genotype with the treatment afforded an experimental group of which she is a member. On the other hand, it is impossible to ignore the attention and learning characteristics the child brings to the situation, so that the effects of environment manipulations are never entirely free of individual differences in genotypes. Development is not necessarily constrained by genotype–environment correlations, although most often genotypes and environments are correlated in the real world, so that in fact, if not in principle, there are such constraints.

Sometimes, the influence of genotypes on environments is diminished through unusual positive or negative interventions, so that the environments experienced are less driven by genotypes and may even be negatively related to genotypes, as in the passive, familial situation. Examples of this effect can be found in studies of deprivation, adoption, and day care. Studies of children reared in isolation (Clarke & Clarke, 1976) and children reared in unstimulating institutions (Dennis & Najarian, 1951; Hunt, 1961, 1980) have demonstrated the adverse effects of deprived environments on many aspects of development. Such studies usually address average responses to these poor environments. In any case, studies of environments that are so extreme as to be outside of the normal range of rearing environments for the species have few implications for environmental variation that the vast majority of human children experience.

In contrast to the extremely poor environments in the deprivation literature, the adoption studies include only rearing environments in the range of adequate to very good. The evidence from studies of biologically related and adoptive families that vary in socioeconomic status from working to upper middle class is that most people experience what Scarr and Weinberg (1978) have called "functionally-equivalent" environments. That is, the large array of individual differences among children and late adolescents adopted in infancy were not related to differences among their family environments—the same array of environment differences that were and usually are associated with behavioral differences among children born to such families (Scarr, 1981; Scarr & Kidd, in press; Scarr & Weinberg, 1976, 1977, 1978). On the average, however, adopted children profit from their enriched environments, and they score above average on IQ and school achievement tests and on measures of personal adjustment.

Negative Genotype–Environment Correlations: Environments provided to children that are negatively related to their genotypes can have dramatic effects on average levels of development. Extra-familial interventions that provided unusual enrichments or deprivations can alter the developmental levels of children from those that would be predicted by their family backgrounds and estimated genotypes. Intervention theories predict these main effects (Caldwell & Richmond, 1968; Hunt, 1980).

Enriched day-care environments have been shown to enhance intellectual development of children from disadvantaged backgrounds (Ramey & Haskins, 1981; McCartney, Note 3). Similarly, less stimulating day-care environments can hamper children's intellectual and social development, even if they come from more advantaged families (McCartney, Scarr, Phillips, Grajek, & Schwarz, 1981; McCartney, Note 3).

These are, however, rather rare opportunities, or lack of same, providing negatively correlated experiences for genotypes. In the usual course of development beyond early childhood, individuals select and evoke experiences that are directly influenced by their genotypes and therefore positively correlated with their own phenotypic characteristics.

Environmental effects on averages versus individuals: One must distinguish environmental events that on the average enhance or delay development for all children from those that account for *variation* among children. There can be "main effects" that account for variation among groups that are naturally or experimentally treated in different ways. Within the groups of children there still remain enormous individual differences, some of which arise in response to the treatment. It is rare that the variation *between* groups approaches the magnitude of differences *within* groups, as represented in the pervasive overlapping distributions of scores. In developmental psychology, we have usually been satisfied if the treatment observed or implemented produced a statistically reliable difference between groups, but we have rarely examined the sources of differential responsiveness within the groups.

Most often, the same treatments that alter the average performance of a group seem to have similar effects on most members of the group. Otherwise, we would find a great deal of variance in genotype – environment interactions; that is, what's sauce for the goose would be poison for the gander. For the kinds of deprivation or interventions studied most often in developmental psychology, the main effects seem not to change the rank orders of children affected. The main effects are real, but they are also small by comparison to the range of individual variation within groups so treated or not. Some children may be more responsive than others to the treatment, but we doubt that there are many situations in which disordinal interactions are the rule. Very few children lose developmental points by participating in Headstart or gain by being severely neglected in infancy. The search for aptitude–treatment interactions (Cronbach & Snow, 1977) and genotype–environment interactions (Erlenmeyer-Kimling 1972) have not produced dramatic or reliable results.

In studies of adoptive and biologically related families, the correlation of children's IQ scores with the educational level of biological parents is about .35, whether or not the parents rear their children (Scarr & Weinberg, 1977, 1978). Adopted children on the average have higher IQ scores than their biological parents as a result of the influence of their above-average adoptive parents. Taken together, these findings support the claim that treatments can have main effects without overcoming genetic differences in children's responsiveness to those environments. Adopted children have IQ scores above those of their biological parents, yet the *correlations* of adopted children are higher with their biological than adoptive parents (Scarr & Weinberg, 1977, 1978). The average effects of treatments, such as adoption, seem to increase the mean IQ scores, but they do not seem to affect the rank order of the children's scores with respect to their biological parents, and it is on rank orders, not means, that correlations depend. These results imply that the effect of adoptive families is to increase the scores of adopted children above those which would be predicted by their biological parents, but not to alter radically the rank order of individual differences among children they rear. And so it is, we think, with most treatments.

Answering Questions from Previous Research on Twins and Families

Neither extreme genetic determinism nor naive environmentalism can account for seemingly anomalous findings from research on twins and families. Three puzzling questions remain, the first of which concerns the *process* by which monozygotic (MZ) twins come to be more similar than dizygotic (DZ) twins, and biological siblings more similar than adopted siblings on all measurable characteristics, at least by the end of adolescence (Scarr & Weinberg, 1978). The second question concerns the declining similarities between DZ twins and adopted siblings from infancy to adolescence. The third question arises from the unexpected similarities between identical twins reared in different homes.

A theory of genotype–environment correlation can account for these findings by pointing to the degree of genetic resemblance and the degree of similarity in the environments that would be experienced by the co-twins and sibs.

Genetic Resemblance Determines Environmental Similarity: The expected degree of environmental similarity for a pair of relatives can be thought of as the product of a person's own genotype → environment path and the genetic correlation of the pair. Figure 3 presents a model of the relationship between genotypes and environments for pairs of relatives who vary in genetic relatedness. G_1 and and G_2 symbolize the two genotypes, E_1 and E_2 their respective environments. The similarity in the two environments (path a) is the product of the coefficient of each genotype with its own environment (path x) and the genetic correlation of the pair (path b). On the assumption that individuals' environments are equally influenced by their own genotypes, the similarity in the environments of two individuals becomes a function of their genetic correlation.

This model can be used to answer question 1 concerning the process by which MZ twins come to be more similar than DZ twins and biological siblings more similar than adopted siblings. For identical twins, for whom $b = 1.00$, the relationship of one twin's environment with the other's genotype is the same as the correlation of the twin's environment with her own genotype. Thus, one would certainly predict what is often observed: that the hobbies, food preferences, choices of friends, academic achievements, and so forth of the MZ twins are very similar (Scarr & Carter-Saitzman, 1980). Kamin (1974) proposed that all of this environmental similarity is imposed on MZ co-twins because they look so much alike. Theories of genetic resemblance do not speak to how close resemblances arise. We propose that the home environments provided by the parents, the responses that the co-twins evoke from others, and the active choices they make in their environments lead to striking similarities through genotypically determined correlations in their learning histories.

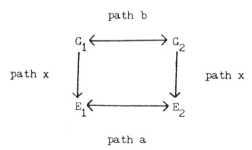

Figure 3: A model of environmental similarity
based on genetic resemblance.

The same explanation applies, of course, to the greater resemblance of biological than adopted siblings. The environment of one biological sib is correlated to the genotype of the other as one-half the coefficient of the sibling's environment to her own genotype, because $b = 0.50$, as described in Figure 3. The same is true for DZ twins. There is a very small genetic correlation for intelligence between adopted siblings in most studies that arises from selective placement of the offspring of similar mothers in the same adoptive home. More important for this theory, however, is the selective placement of adopted children to match the intellectual characteristics of the adoptive parents. This practice allows adoptive parents to create a positive, passive genotype–environment correlation for their adopted children in early childhood, when the theory asserts that this kind of correlation is most important. In fact, the selective placement estimates from studies by Scarr and Weinberg (1977) can account for most of the resemblance between adoptive parents and their children. In addition, adoptive parents, like their biological counterparts, can provide negative genotype–environment correlations that assure that their several children will not differ too much on important skills, such as reading.

Changing Similarities Among Siblings: The second question left unanswered by previous research concerned the declining similarities of dizygotic twins and adopted siblings from infancy to adolescence. It is clear from Matheny, Wilson, Dolan, and Krantz's (1981) longitudinal study of MZ and DZ twins that the DZ correlations for intelligence of .60–.75 are higher than genetic theory would predict in infancy and early childhood. For school age and older twins, DZ correlations were the usual .55. Similarly, the intelligence correlations of a sample of late adolescent adopted siblings were zero, compared to the .25–.39 correlations of the samples of adopted children in early to middle childhood (Scarr & Weinberg, 1978).

Neither environmental nor genetic theories can effectively address these data. How can it be that the longer you live with someone, the less like them you become? One could evoke some ad hoc environment theory about sibling relationships becoming more competitive, or "deidentified," but that would not account for the continued, moderate intellectual resemblance of biological siblings. Genetic theory has, of course, nothing to say about decreasing twin resemblance or any resemblance among young adoptees.

The theory put forward here predicts that the relative importance of passive versus active genotype–environment correlations changes with age. Recall that passive genotype–environment correlations are created by parents who provide children with both genes and environments, which are then correlated. Certainly in the case of DZ twins, whose prenatal environment was shared and whose earliest years are spent being treated in most of the same ways at the same time by the same parents, the passive genotype → environment effect is greater than that for ordinary sibs. Biological and adopted siblings do not, of course, share the same developmental environments at the same time because they differ in age. The passive genotype–environment correlation still operates for siblings, because they have the same parents, but to a lesser extent than for twins. (See Table 1.)

Monozygotic twin correlations for intellectual competence do not decline when active genotype–environment correlations outweigh the importance of the passive ones, because MZ co-twins typically select highly correlated environments anyway. Dizygotic pairs, on the other hand, are no more genetically related than sibs, so that as the intense similarity of their early home environments gives way to their own choices, they select environments that are less similar than their previous environments and about as similar as those of ordinary sibs.

Table 1: The Similarity of Co-Twin's and Sibling's Genotypes and Environments Due to Correlations in the Environments of Related Pairs

	Genetic Correlation	Passive Genotype → Environment Effects in Early Development	Active Genotype → Environment Effects in Early Development
MZ twins	1.00	High	High
DZ twins	.52	High	Moderate
Biological siblings	.52	Moderate	Moderate
Adopted siblings	.01	Moderate	Low

Adopted sibs, on the other hand, move from an early environment, in which mother may have produced similarity, to environments of their own choosing. Because their genotypes are hardly correlated at all, neither are their chosen environmental niches. Thus, by late adolescence, adopted siblings do not resemble each other in intelligence, personality, interests, or other phenotypic characteristics (Grotevant, Scarr, & Weinberg, 1977; Scarr, Webber, Weinberg, & Wittig, 1981; Scarr & Weinberg, 1978).

Biological siblings' early environments, like those of adopted children, lead to trait similarity as a result of passive genotype → environment effects. As biological siblings move into the larger world and begin to make active choices, their niches remain moderately correlated because their genotypes remain moderately correlated. There is no marked shift in intellectual resemblance of biological sibs as the process of active genotype → environment influence replaces the passive one.

Identical Twins Reared Apart: The third question concerned the unexpected degree of resemblance between identical twins reared mostly apart. With the theory of genotype → environment effects, their resemblance is not surprising. Given opportunities to attend selectively to and choose from varied opportunities, identical genotypes are expected to make similar choices. They are also expected to evoke similar responses from others and from their physical environments. The fact that they were reared in different homes and different communities is not important; differences in their development could arise only if the experiential opportunities of one or both were very restricted, so that similar choices could not have been made. According to previous studies (Juel-Nielsen, 1980; Newman, Freeman, & Holzinger, 1937; Shields, 1962) and the recent research of Bouchard and colleagues at the University of Minnesota (Bouchard, Note 2), the most dissimilar pairs of MZs reared apart are those in which one was severely restricted in environment opportunity. Extreme deprivation or unusual enrichment can diminish the influence of genotype and environment and therefore lessen the resemblance of identical twins reared apart.

Research Strategies

The theory we propose can be tested in several ways and prove unable to account for results. First, studies of parental treatment of more than one child would be informative about possible genotype → environment effects. In general, we expect the rearing environment provided for the children in a family to differ in ways that are related to each child's characteristics. Do parents treat all of their children alike, as so many studies of one child per family seem to imply? Can parents be authoritative with one child and permissive with another? Our theory predicts that parents will respond to individual differences in their children, in keeping with Lytton's (1980) research on families with twins. If parent treatment of their children is not related to children's talents, interests, and personalities, the theory is wrong.

Second, studies of responses that individuals evoke from others would test our ideas about evocative genotype → environment effects. The social psychology literature on attractiveness (Bersheid & Walster, 1974; Mursteid, 1972), for example, would seem to support our view that some personal characteristics evoke differential responses from others. Similarly, teachers' responses to children with high versus low intelligence, hyperactivity versus acceptable levels of energy, and so forth provide some evidence for our theory. If others do not respond differentially to individual characteristics for which there is genetic variability, then the theory is wrong.

Third, active niche-building is being studied by the Laboratory of Comparative Human Cognition in their naturalistic observations of children's adaptations to problem-solving situations (Cole & The Laboratory of Comparative Human Cognition, Note 4). Our theory predicts that children select and build niches that are correlated with their talents, interests, and personality characteristics. If not, the theory is wrong.

Fourth, longitudinal studies of adopted children, such as the ongoing work of Plomin and colleagues, can provide valuable evidence of the changing influences of family environments on children. The theory predicts that children's characteristics will be more related to characteristics of the adoptive parents and other adopted siblings in earlier than later development. If adopted children are as similar to their adoptive parents and each other in late adolescence as they were in early childhood, that aspect of the theory is wrong.

Fifth, studies of older adolescents and adults who were adopted in infancy and others who were born into their families can provide evidence on the long-term effects of passive genotype → environment effects within families. Both evocative and active kinds of genotype → environmental effects can be traced through the similarities and dissimilarities of the two kinds of siblings.

In these ways, and others, the theory can be tested. It can fail to account for results obtained, or it can account for the diverse results more adequately than other theories. Given the various results of family studies presented in this paper, we believe that its predictions will be fulfilled. At least, we hope it will encourage more developmentalists to study more than one child per family, genetically unrelated families, and individual differences in experience.

Summary

In summary, the theory of genotype–environment correlations proposed here describes the usual course of human development in terms of three kinds of genotype–environment correlations that posit cooperative efforts of the nature–nurture team, directed by the genetic quarterback. Both genes and environments are constituents in the developmental system, but they have different roles. Genes direct the course of human experience, but experiential opportunities are also necessary for development to occur. Individual differences can arise from restrictions in environmental opportunities to experience what the genotype would find compatible. With a rich array of opportunities, however, most differences among people arise from genetically determined differences in the experiences to which they are attracted and which they evoke from their environments.

The theory also accounts for individual differences in responsiveness to environments—differences that are not primarily interactions of genotypes and environments but roughly linear combinations that are better described as genotype–environment correlations. In addition, the theory accounts for seemingly anomalous results from previous research on twins and families.

Most important, the theory addresses the issue of process. Rather than presenting a static view of individual differences through variance allocation, this theory hypothesizes processes by which genotypes and environments combine across development to make us both human and unique.

Reference Notes

1. Garmezy, N. *The case for the single case in experimental-developmental psychology.* Paper presented at the annual meeting of the American Psychological Association, Los Angeles, August 1981.

2. Bouchard, T. *The Minnesota study of twins reared apart: Description and preliminary findings.* Paper presented at the annual meeting of the American Psychological Association, August 1981.

3. McCartney, K. *The effect of quality of day care environment upon children's language development.* Unpublished doctoral dissertation, Yale University, 1982.

4. Cole, M., & The Laboratory of Comparative Human Cognition. Niche-picking. Unpublished manuscript, University of California, San Diego, 1980.

References

Bell, R. Q. A reinterpretation of the direction of effects in studies of socialization, *Psychological Review*, 1968, *75*, 81–95.

Bersheid, E., & Walster, E. Physical attractiveness. In L. Berkowitz (Ed.), *Advances in experimental social psychology.* New York: Academic Press, 1974.

Caldwell, B. M., & Richmond, I. The Children's Center in Syracuse. In L. Dittman (Ed.). *Early child: The new perspectives.* New York: Atherton, 1968.

Chomsky, N. On cognitive structures and their development: A reply to Piaget. In M. Piatelli-Paimarini (Ed.), *Language and learning*: Cambridge, Mass.: Harvard University Press, 1980.

Chomsky, N., & Fodor, J. Statement of the paradox. In M. Piattelli-Palmarini (Ed.), *Language and learning: The debate between Jean Piaget and Noam Chomsky.* Cambridge, Mass.: Harvard University Press, 1980.

Clarke, A. M., & Clarke, A. D. B. *Early experience: Myth and evidence.* New York: Free Press, 1976.

Connolly, K. J., & Prechtl, H. F. R. (Eds.), *Maturation and development: Biological and psychological perspectives.* Philadelphia: Lippincott, 1981.

Cronbach, L. J., & Snow, R. E. *Attitudes and instructional methods.* New York: Irvington, 1977.

Dennis, W., & Najarian, P. Infant development under environmental handicap. *Psychological Monographs*, 1951, *71* (7, Whole No. 436).

Erlenmeyer-Kimling, L. Gene-environment interactions and the variability of behavior. In L. Ehrman, G. Omenn, & E. Caspair

(Eds.), *Genetics, environment and behavior*. New York: Academic Press, 1972.

Escalona, S. C. *The roots of individuality*. Chicago: Aldine, 1968.

Gesell, A. , & Ilg, F. L. *Infant and child in the culture of today*. New York: Harper & Bros. , 1943.

Gottlieb, G. The role of experience in the development of behavior in the nervous system. In G. Gottlieb (Ed.), *Studies in the development of behavior and the nervous system. Vol. 3. Development and neural and behavioral specificity*. New York: Academic Press, 1976.

Grotevant, H. D., Scarr, S., & Weinberg, R. A. Patterns of interest similarity in adoptive and biological families. *Journal of Personality and Social Psychology*, 1977, *35*, 667–678.

Hunt, J. McV. *Intelligence and experience*. New York: Ronald, 1961.

Hunt, J. Mc.V. *Early psychological development and experience*. Worcester, Mass.: Clark University Press, 1980.

Juel-Nielsen, N. *Individual and environment: Monozygotic twins reared apart*. New York: International Universities Press, 1980.

Kamin, L.J. *The science and politics of IQ*. Potomac, Md.: Erlbaum, 1974.

Lytton, H. *Parent-child interaction: The socialization process observed in twin and single families*. New York: Plenum, 1980.

McCall, R.B. Nature-nurture and the two realms of development: A proposed integration with respect to mental development. *Child Development*. 1981, *52*, 1–12.

McCartney, K., Scarr, S., Phillips, D., Grajek, S., & Schwarz, J. C. Environmental differences among day care centers and their effects on children's development. In E. F. Zigler & E. W. Gordon (Eds.), *Day care: Scientific and social policy issues*. Boston: Auburn House, 1981.

Maccoby, E. E. *Social development*. New York: Harcourt, Brace, Jovanovich, 1980.

Matheny, A. P., Jr., Wilson, R. S., Dolan, A. B., & Krantz, J. Z. Behavioral contrasts in twinships: Stability and patterns of differences in childhood. *Child Development*, 1981, *52*, 579–598.

Murstein, B. I. Physical attractiveness and marital choice. *Journal of Personality and Social Psychology*, 1972, *22*, 9–12.

Nelson, K. Structure and strategy in learning to talk. *Monographs of the Society for Research in Child Development*, 1973, *38* (1–2, Serial No. 149).

Nerlove, S. B., & Snipper, A. S. Cognitive consequences of cultural opportunity. In R. H. Munroe, R. L. Munroe, & B. B. Whiting (Eds.), *Handbook of cross-cultural human development*. New York: Garland, 1981.

Newman, H. G., Freeman, F. N., & Holzinger, K. J. *Twins: A study of heredity and environment*. Chicago: University of Chicago Press, 1937.

Piaget, J. The psychogenesis of knowledge and its epistemological significance. In M. Piattelli-Paimarini Ed.). *Language and learning: The debate between Jean Piaget and Noam Chomsky*. Cambridge, Mass., Harvard University Press, 1980.

Plomin, R., DeFries, J. C., & Loehlin, J. C. Genotype–environment interaction and correlation in the analysis of human behavior. *Psychological Bulletin*, 1977, *84*, 309–322.

Ramey, C .T., & Haskins, R. The modification of intelligence through early experience. *Intelligence*, 1981, *5*, 5–19.

Scarr, S. IQ: *Race, social class and individual differences, new studies of old problems*. Hillsdale, N.J.: Erlbaum, 1981.

Scarr, S., & Carter-Saltzman, L. Twin method: Defense of a critical assumption. *Behavior Genetics*, 1980, *9*, 527–542.

Scarr, S., & Kidd, K. K. Behavior genetics. In M. Haith & J. Campos (Eds.), *Manual of child psychology: Infancy and the biology of development*. (Vol. 2). New York: Wiley, in press.

Scarr, S., Webber, P. L., Weinberg, R. A., & Wittig, M. A. Personality resemblance among adolescents and their parents in biologically-related and adoptive families. *Journal of Personality and Social Psychology*, 1981, *40*, 885–898.

Scarr, S., & Weinberg, R. A. IQ test performance of black children adopted by white families. *American Psychologist*, 1976, *31*, 726–739.

Scarr, S., & Weinberg, R. A. Intellectual similarities within families of both adopted and biological children. *Intelligence*, 1977, *1 (2)*, 170–191.

Scarr, S., & Weinberg, R. A. The influence of "family background" on intellectual attainment. *American Sociological Review*, 1978, *43*, 674–692.

Scarr, S., & Weinberg, R. A. The Minnesota adoption studies: Genetic differences and malleability. *Child Development.* in this issue.

Scarr-Salapatek, S. An evolutionary perspective on infant intelligence. In M. Lewis (Ed.), *Origins of intelligence: Infancy and early, childhood*. N.Y.: Plenum, 1976.

Shields, J. *Monozygotic twins brought up apart and brought up together*. London: Oxford University Press, 1962.

Waddington, C.H. *New patterns in genetics and development*. New York: Columbia University Press, 1962.

Watson, E.H., & Lowrey, G. H. *Growth and development of children*. Chicago: Year Book Medical Publishers, 1967.

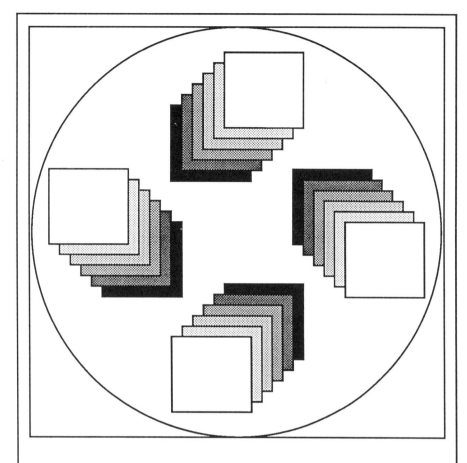

Chapter 10

Social Psychology

CHAPTER 10: SOCIAL PSYCHOLOGY

Social psychology addresses the mechanisms that determine the way we behave in interaction with others. As much as we all wish we were "true to ourselves" and not liable to be influenced by those around us, we all change our behavior in predictable ways in response to group situations. We are, after all, social animals. The articles in this chapter point out some disturbing aspects of human social behavior: our tendency to obey those in authority, and to ignore those in trouble around us. This chapter also includes an interesting theory about a common construct in social behavior, love. Clearly, love plays a role in our most important social interactions, yet there are few theories about what love is and how it functions.

10a. Milgram, S. (1963). Behavioral study of obedience. *Journal of Abnormal and Social Psychology*, 371–378.

At the end of World War II, many Germans were tried and convicted of war crimes because of their roles in Nazi death camps. Their most common defense was that they were just doing their jobs and they were told to commit atrocities on the inmates by those in authority. If you were on the military tribunal and had read Milgram's work, how would you decide the cases? Write an opinion about human obedience based upon Milgram's work.

10b. Shotland, R. L. (1985). When bystanders just stand there. *Psychology Today*, June, 50–55.

This selection discusses the role of bystanders in decreasing crime. Imagine you are an aide to a U.S. senator. Prepare a *brief* position paper for the senator on a bill to enforce "good samaritanism." You may take either the "for" or "against" position but be sure to back up your arguments with elements from the article.

10c. Trotter, R. (1986). The three faces of love. *Psychology Today, 20,* 46–50, 54.

In this selection, many different types of love are differentiated, as well as the three elements that compose "complete love." Try to define your latest "love" in terms of Sternberg's theory. Choose two past "loves," and see if the longevity of the relationship could, if possible, have been predicted from Sternberg's concept of "expected versus obtained" love.

Behavioral Study of Obedience

Stanley Milgram

Obedience is as basic an element in the structure of social life as one can point to. Some system of authority is a requirement of all communal living, and it is only the man dwelling in isolation who is not forced to respond, through defiance or submission, to the commands of others. Obedience, as a determinant of behavior, is of particular relevance to our time. It has been reliably established that from 1933–45 millions of innocent persons were systematically slaughtered on command. Gas chambers were built, death camps were guarded, daily quotas of corpses were produced with the same efficiency as the manufacture of appliances. These inhumane policies may have originated in the mind of a single person, but they could only be carried out on a massive scale if a very large number of persons obeyed orders.

Obedience is the psychological mechanism that links individual action to political purpose. It is the dispositional cement that binds men to systems of authority. Facts of recent history and observation in daily life suggest that for many persons obedience may be a deeply ingrained behavior tendency, indeed, a prepotent impulse overriding training in ethics, sympathy, and moral conduct. C. P. Snow points to its importance when he writes:

"When you think of the long and gloomy history of man, you will find more hideous crimes have been committed in the name of obedience than have ever been committed in the name of rebellion. If you doubt that, read William Shirer's *Rise and Fall of the Third Reich*. The German Officer Corps were brought up in the most rigorous code of obedience . . . in the name of obedience they were party to, and assisted in, the most wicked large scale actions in the history of the world."[1]

While the particular form of obedience dealt with in the present study has its antecedents in these episodes, it must not be thought all obedience entails acts of aggression against others. Obedience serves numerous productive functions. Indeed, the very life of society is predicated on its existence. Obedience may be ennobling and educative and refer to acts of charity and kindness, as well as to destruction.

General Procedure

A procedure was devised which seems useful as a tool for studying obedience.[2] It consists of ordering a naive subject to administer electric shock to a victim. A simulated shock generator is used, with 30 clearly marked voltage levels that range from 15 to 450 volts. The instrument bears verbal designations that range from Slight Shock to Danger:

---

[1] C. P. Snow, "Either/Or," *Progressive*, Feb., 1961, p. 24.

[2] S. Milgram, "Dynamics of Obedience" (Washington, D.C.: National Science Foundation, January 25, 1961), mimeo.

Severe Shock. The responses of the victim, who is a trained confederate of the experimenter, are standardized. The orders to administer shocks are given to the naive subject in the context of a "learning experiment" ostensibly set up to study the effects of punishment on memory. As the experiment proceeds the naive subject is commanded to administer increasingly more intense shocks to the victim, even to the point of reaching the level marked Danger: Severe Shock. Internal resistances become stronger, and at a certain point the subject refuses to go on with the experiment. Behavior prior to this rupture is considered "obedience," in that the subject complies with the commands of the experimenter. The point of rupture is the act of disobedience. A quantitative value is assigned to the subject's performance based on the maximum intensity shock he is willing to administer before he refuses to participate further. Thus for any particular subject and for any particular experimental condition the degree of obedience may be specified with a numerical value. The crux of the study is to systematically vary the factors believed to alter the degree of obedience to the experimental commands.

The technique allows important variables to be manipulated at several points in the experiment. One may vary aspects of the source of command, content and form of command, instrumentalities for its execution, target object, general social setting, etc. The problem, therefore, is not one of designing increasingly more numerous experimental conditions, but of selecting those that best illuminate the *process* of obedience from the sociopsychological standpoint.

Related Studies

The inquiry bears an important relation to philosophic analyses of obedience and authority (Arendt,[3] Friedrich,[4] Weber[5]), an early experimental study of obedience by Frank,[6] studies in "authoritarianism" (Adorno, Frenkel-Brunswik, Levinson, and Sanford,[7] Rokeach[8]), and a recent series of analytic and empirical studies in social power

---

[3] H. Arendt, "What Was Authority?" in *Authority*, C. J. Friedrich (ed.) (Cambridge, Mass.: Harvard University Press, 1958), pp. 81–112.

[4] C. J. Friedrich (ed.), *Authority* (Cambridge, Mass.: Harvard Univ. Press, 1958).

[5] M. Weber, *The Theory of Social and Economic Organization* (Oxford: Oxford Univ. Press, 1947

[6] J. D. Frank, "Experimental Studies of Personal Pressure and Resistance," *J. Gen. Psychol.*, Vol. 30 (1944), pp. 23–64.

[7] T. Adorno, Else Frenkel-Brunswik, D. J. Levinson, and R. N. Sanford, *The Authoritarian Personality* (New York: Harper, 1950).

[8] M. Rokeach, "Authority, Authoritarianism, and Conformity," in *Conformity and Deviation*, I. A. Berg, and B. M. Bass (eds.) (New York: Harper, 1961), pp. 230–57.

(Cartwright[9]). It owes much to the long concern with *suggestion* in social psychology, both in its normal forms (e.g., Binet[10]) and in its clinical manifestations (Charcot[11]). But it derives, in the first instance, from direct observation of a social fact; the individual who is commanded by a legitimate authority ordinarily obeys. Obedience comes easily and often. It is a ubiquitous and indispensable feature of social life.

Method

Subjects: The subjects were 40 males between the ages of 20 and 50, drawn from New Haven and the surrounding communities. Subjects were obtained by a newspaper advertisement and direct mail solicitation. Those who responded to the appeal believed they were to participate in a study of memory and learning at Yale University. A wide range of occupations is represented in the sample. Typical subjects were postal clerks, high school teachers, salesmen, engineers, and laborers. Subjects ranged in educational level from one who had not finished elementary school, to those who had doctorate and other professional degrees. They were paid $4.50 for their participation in the experiment. However, subjects were told that payment was simply for coming to the laboratory, and that the money was theirs no matter what happened after they arrived. Table 1 shows the proportion of age and occupational types assigned to the experimental condition.

TABLE 1
Distribution of age and occupational types in the experiment

Occupations	20–29 years	30–39 years	40–50 years	Percentage of total
	n	n	n	(occupations)
Workers, skilled and unskilled	4	5	6	37.5
Sales, business, and white-collar	3	6	7	40.0
Professional	1	5	3	22.5
Percentage of total (age)	20	40	40	

Note: Total n = 40.

Personnel and locale: The experiment was conducted on the grounds of Yale University in the elegant interaction laboratory. (This detail is relevant to the perceived legitimacy of the experiment. In further variations, the experiment was dissociated from the university, with consequences for performance.) The role of experimenter was played by a 31-year-old high school teacher of biology. His manner was

---

[9] D. Cartwright (ed.), *Studies in Social Power* (Ann Arbor: Univ. of Michigan Institute for Social Research, 1959).

[10] A. Binet, *La Suggestibilité* (Paris: Schleicher, 1900).

[11] J. M. Charcot, *Oeuvres Complètes* (Paris: Bureaux du Progres Medical, 1881).

impassive, and his appearance somewhat stern throughout the experiment. He was dressed in a gray technician's coat, The victim was played by a 47-year-old accountant, trained for the role; be was of Irish-American stock, whom most observers found mild-mannered and likable.

Procedure: One naive subject and one victim (an accomplice) performed in each experiment. A pretext had to be devised that would justify the administration of electric shock by the naive subject. This was effectively accomplished by the cover story. After a general introduction on the presumed relation between punishment and learning, subjects were told:

But actually, we know *very little* about the effect of punishment on learning, because almost no truly scientific studies have been made of it in human beings.

For instance, we don't know how *much* punishment is best for learning—and we don't know how much difference it makes as to who is giving the punishment, whether an adult learns best from a younger or an older person than himself—or many things of that sort.

So in this study we are bringing together a number of adults of different occupations and ages. And we're asking some of them to be teachers and some of them to be learners.

We want to find out just what effect different people have on each other as teachers and learners, and also what effect *punishment* will have on learning in this situation.

Therefore, I'm going to ask one of you to be the teacher here tonight and the other one to be the learner.

Does either of you have a preference?

Subjects then drew slips of paper from a hat to determine who would be the teacher and who would be the learner in the experiment. The drawing was rigged so that the naive subject was always the teacher and the accomplice always the learner. (Both slips contained the word "Teacher.") Immediately after the drawing, the teacher and learner were taken to an adjacent room and the learner was strapped into an "electric chair" apparatus.

The experimenter explained that the straps were to prevent excessive movement while the learner was being shocked. The effect was to make it impossible for him to escape from the situation. An electrode was attached to the learner's wrist, and electrode paste was applied "to avoid blisters and burns." Subjects were told that the electrode was attached to the shock generator in the adjoining room.

In order to improve credibility the experimenter declared, in response to a question by the learner: "Although the shocks can be extremely painful, they cause no permanent tissue damage."

Learning task. The lesson administered by the subject was a paired-associate learning task. The subject read a series of word pairs to the learner, and then read the first word of the pair along with four terms. The learner was to indicate which of the four terms had originally been paired with the first word. He communicated his answer by pressing one of four switches in front of him, which in turn lit up one of four numbered quadrants in an answer-box located atop the shock generator.

Shock generator. The instrument panel consists of 30 lever switches set in a horizontal line. Each switch is clearly labeled with a voltage designation that ranges from 15 to 450 volts. There is a 15-volt increment from one switch to the next going from left to right. In addition, the following verbal designations are clearly indicated for groups of four switches going from left to right: Slight Shock, Moderate Shock, Strong Shock, Very Strong Shock, Intense Shock, Extreme Intensity Shock, Danger: Severe Shock. (Two switches after this last designation are simply marked XXX.)

Upon depressing a switch, a pilot light corresponding to each switch is illuminated in bright red; an electric buzzing is heard; an electric blue light, labeled "voltage energizer," flashes; the dial on the voltage meter swings to the right; various relay clicks are sounded.

The upper left-hand corner of the generator is labeled Shock Generator, Type ZLB, Dyson Instrument Company, Waltham, Mass. Output 15 Volts–450 Volts.

Details of the instrument were carefully handled to insure an appearance of authenticity. The panel was engraved by precision industrial engravers, and all components were of high quality. No subject in the experiment suspected that the instrument was merely a simulated shock generator.

Sample shock. Each naive subject is given a sample shock on the shock generator, prior to beginning his run as teacher. This shock is always 45 volts, and is applied by pressing the third switch of the generator. The shock is applied to the wrist of the naive subject, and has its source in a 45-volt battery wired into the generator. This further convinces the subject of the authenticity of the generator.

Shock instructions. The subject is told to administer a shock to the learner each time he gives a wrong response. Moreover - and this is the key command—the subject is instructed to "move one level higher on the shock generator each time the learner flashes a wrong answer." He is also instructed to announce the voltage level before administering a shock. This serves to continually remind subjects of the increasing intensity of shocks administered to the learner.

Preliminary and regular run. Pretests revealed that the procedure of reading words and administering shocks requires some practice before it can be handled smoothly. Therefore, immediately preceding the regular run, the teacher is given a preliminary series of 10 words to read to the learner. There are 3 neutral words in the practice series (i.e., words that the learner answers correctly), so that shocks are administered for 7 of the words, with the maximum shock at 105 volts (moderate shock). Almost all subjects master the procedure by the time the preliminary run is over.

Subjects are then presented with a second list, and are told that the procedure is the same as for the first list; the experimenter adds, however: "When you get to the bottom of the list, repeat it over again, and continue giving shocks, until the learner has learned all the pairs correctly." The experimenter instructs the subject to "start from 15 volts and increase the shock level one step each time the learner gives a wrong answer."

Feedback from the victim. In all conditions the learner gives a predetermined set of responses to the word pair test, based on a schedule of approximately three wrong answers to one correct answer. In the present experimental condition no vocal response or other sign of protest is heard from the learner until Shock Level 300 is reached. When the 300-volt shock is administered, the learner pounds on the wall of the room in which he is bound to the electric chair. The pounding can be heard by the subject. From this point on, the learner's answers no longer appear on the four-way panel.

At this juncture, subjects ordinarily turn to the experimenter for guidance. The experimenter instructs the subject to treat the absence of a response as a wrong answer, and to shock the subject according to the usual schedule. He advises the subjects to allow 5–10 seconds before considering no response as a wrong answer, and to increase the shock level one step each time the learner fails to respond correctly. The learner's pounding is repeated after the 315-volt shock is administered; afterwards he is not heard from, nor do his answers reappear on the four-way signal box.

Experimenter feedback. At various points in the experiment the subject may turn to the experimenter for advice on whether he should continue to administer shocks. Or he may indicate that he does not wish to go on. It was important to standardize the experimenter's responses to these inquiries and reactions.

If the subject indicated his unwillingness to go on, the experimenter responded with a sequence of "prods," using as many as necessary to bring the subject into line.

Prod 1: Please continue, *or* Please go on.
Prod 2: The experiment requires that you continue.
Prod 3: It is absolutely essential that you continue.
Prod 4: You have no other choice, you *must* go on.

The prods were always made in sequence: Only if Prod 1 had been unsuccessful could Prod 2 be used. If the subject refused to obey the experimenter after Prod 4, the experiment was terminated. The experimenter's tone of voice was at all times firm, but not impolite. The sequence was begun anew on each occasion that the subject balked or showed reluctance to follow orders.

Special prods. If the subject asked if the learner was liable to suffer permanent physical injury, the experimenter said: "Although the shocks may be painful, there is no permanent tissue damage, so please go on." [Followed by Prods 2, 3, and 4 if necessary.]

If the subject said that the learner did not want to go on, the experimenter replied: "Whether the learner likes it or not, you must go on until he has learned all the word pairs correctly. So please go on." [Followed by Prods 2, 3, and 4 if necessary.]

Dependent measures: The primary dependent measure for any subject is the maximum shock he administers before he refuses to go any further. In principle this may vary from 0 (for a subject who refuses to administer even the first shock) to 30 (for a subject who administers the highest shock on the generator). A subject who breaks off the experiment at any point prior to administering the thirtieth shock level is termed a *defiant* subject. One who complies with experimental commands fully, and proceeds to administer all shock levels commanded, is termed an *obedient* subject.

Further records. With few exceptions, experimental sessions were recorded on magnetic tape. Occasional photographs were taken through one-way mirrors. Notes were kept on any unusual behavior occurring during the course of the experiments. On occasion, additional observers were directed to write objective descriptions of the subjects' behavior. The latency and duration of shocks were measured by accurate timing devices.

Interview and dehoax. Following the experiment, subjects were interviewed; open-ended questions, projective measures, and attitude scales were employed. After the interview, procedures were undertaken to assure that the subject would leave the laboratory in a state of well being. A friendly reconciliation was arranged between the subject and the victim, and an effort was made to reduce any tensions that arose as a result of the experiment.

Results

Preliminary notions: Before giving an account of the experimental results, it is instructive to consider how persons predict others will perform when commanded to administer powerful shocks to another person. Fourteen Yale seniors, all psychology majors, were provided with a detailed description of the experimental situation. They were asked to reflect carefully on it, and to predict the behavior of 100 hypothetical subjects. More specifically, they were instructed to plot the distribution of obedience of "100 Americans of diverse occupations, and ranging in age from 20 to 50 years," who were placed in the experimental situation.

There was considerable agreement among the respondents on the expected behavior of hypothetical subjects. All respondents predicted that only an insignificant minority would go through to the end of the shock series. (The estimates ranged from 0 to 3 percent; i.e., the most "pessimistic" member of the class predicted that of 100 persons, 3 would continue through to the most potent shock available on the shock generator—450 volts.) The class mean was 1.2 percent. The question was also posed informally to colleagues of the author, and the most general feeling was that few if any subjects would go beyond the designation Very Strong Shock.

Result of experiment 1: *Subjects accept situation.* With few exceptions subjects were convinced of the reality of the experimental situation, that they were administering shocks to another person, and the most potent shocks were extremely painful. In the postexperimental interview subjects were asked: "How painful to the learner were the last few shocks that you administered to him?" Subjects were instructed to indicate their answers on a printed 14-point scale ranging from "Not at all painful" to "Extremely painful." The modal response was 14 (Extremely painful) with the mean at 13.42.

Signs of extreme tension. Many subjects showed signs of nervousness in the experimental situation, and especially upon administering the more powerful shocks. In a large number of cases the degree of tension reached extremes that are rarely seen in sociopsychological laboratory studies. Subjects were observed to sweat, tremble, stutter, bite their lips, groan, and dig their fingernails into their flesh. These were characteristic rather than exceptional responses to the experiment.

One sign of tension was the regular occurrence of nervous laughing fits. Fourteen of the 40 subjects showed definite signs of nervous laughter and smiling. The laughter seemed entirely out of place, even bizarre. Full-blown, uncontrollable seizures were observed for 3 subjects. On one occasion we observed a seizure so violently convulsive that it was necessary to call a halt to the experiment. The subject, a 46-year-old encyclopedia salesman, was seriously embarrassed by his untoward and uncontrollable behavior. In the postexperimental interviews subjects took pains to point out that they were not sadistic types, and that the laughter did not mean they enjoyed shocking the victim.

Distribution of scores. It had been conjectured that persons would not, in general, agree to administer shocks beyond the level designated as Very Strong Shock. The distribution of maximum shocks for this experiment is shown in Table 2. The obtained distribution of scores deviates radically from the prediction.

Upon command of the experimenter, each of the 40 subjects went beyond the expected breakoff point. No subject stopped prior to administering Shock Level 20. (At this level—300 volts—the victim kicks on the wall and no longer provides answers to the teacher's multiple-choice questions.)

Of the 40 subjects, 5 refused to obey the experimental commands beyond the 300-volt level. Four more subjects administered one further shock, and then refused to go on. Two broke off at the 330-volt level, and 1 each at 345, 360, and 375 volts. Thus a total of 14 subjects defied the experimenter. It is instructive to reprint their remarks at the point of defiance, as transcribed from the tape recordings:

"[0124] I think he's trying to communicate, he's knocking. . . . Well it's not fair to shock the guy . . . these are terrific volts. I don't think this is very humane. . . . Oh, I can't go on with this; no, this isn't right. It's a hell of an experiment. The guy is suffering in there. No, I don't want to go on. This is crazy. [Subject refused to administer more shocks.]"

"[0123] He's banging in there. I'm gonna chicken out. I'd like to continue, but I can't do that to a man. . . . I'm sorry I can't do that to a man. I'll hurt his heart. You take your check. . . . No really, I couldn't do it."

These subjects were frequently in a highly agitated and even angered state. Sometimes, verbal protest was at a minimum, and the subject simply got up from his chair in front of the shock generator, and indicated that he wished to leave the laboratory.

Of the 40 subjects, 26 obeyed the orders of the experimenter to the end, proceeding to punish the victim until they reached the most potent shock available on the shock generator. At that point, the experimenter called a halt to the session. (The maximum shock is labeled 450 volts, and is two steps beyond the designation: Danger: Severe Shock.) Although obedient subjects continued to administer shocks, they often did so under extreme stress. Some expressed reluctance to administer shocks beyond the 300-volt level, and displayed fears similar to those who defied the experimenter; yet they obeyed.

After the maximum shocks had been delivered, and the experimenter called to a bait to the proceedings, many obedient subjects heaved sighs of relief, mopped their brows, rubbed their fingers over their eyes, or nervously fumbled cigarettes. Some shook their heads, apparently in regret. Some subjects had remained calm throughout the experiment, and displayed only minimal signs of tension from beginning to end.

TABLE 2
Distribution of breakoff points

Verbal designation and voltage indication	Number of subjects for whom this was maximum shock
Slight Shock:	
15	0
30	0
45	0
60	0
Moderate Shock:	
75	0
90	0
105	0
120	0
Strong Shock:	
135	0
150	0
165	0
180	0
Very Strong Shock:	
195	0
210	0
225	0
240	0

Verbal designation and voltage indication	*Number of subjects for whom this was maximum shock*

Intense Shock:

255.....................................0

270.....................................0

285.....................................0

300.....................................5

Extreme Intensity Shock:

315.....................................4

330.....................................2

345.....................................1

360.....................................1

Danger: Severe Shock:

375.....................................1

390.....................................0

405.....................................0

420.....................................0

XXX

435.....................................0

450.....................................26

Discussion

The experiment yielded two findings that were surprising. The first finding concerns the sheer strength of obedient tendencies manifested in this situation. Subjects have learned from childhood that it is a fundamental breach of moral conduct to hurt another person against his will. Yet, 26 subjects abandon this tenet in following the instructions of an authority who has no special powers to enforce his commands. To disobey would bring no material loss to the subject; no punishment would ensue. It is clear from the remarks and outward behavior of many participants that in punishing the victim they are often acting against their own values. Subjects often expressed deep disapproval of shocking a man in the face of his objections, and others denounced it as stupid and senseless. Yet the majority complied with the experimental commands. This outcome was surprising from two perspectives: first, from the standpoint of predictions made in the questionnaire described earlier. (Here, however, it is possible that the remoteness of the respondents from the actual situation, and the difficulty of conveying to them the concrete details of the experiment, could account for the serious underestimation of obedience.)

But the results were also unexpected to persons who observed the experiment in progress, through one-way mirrors. Observers often uttered expressions of disbelief upon seeing a subject administer more powerful shocks to the victim. These persons had a full acquaintance with the details of the situation, and yet systematically underestimated the amount of obedience that subjects would display.

The second unanticipated effect was the extraordinary tension generated by the procedures. One might suppose that a subject would simply break off or continue as his conscience dictated. Yet, this is very far from what happened. There were striking reactions of tension and emotional strain. One observer related:

"I observed a mature and initially poised businessman enter the laboratory smiling and confident. Within 20 minutes he was reduced to a twitching, stuttering wreck, who was rapidly approaching a point of nervous collapse. He constantly pulled on his earlobe, and twisted his hands. At one point he pushed his fist into his forehead and muttered: "Oh God, let's stop it." And yet he continued to respond to every word of the experimenter, and obeyed to the end."

Any understanding of the phenomenon of obedience must rest on an analysis of the particular conditions in which it occurs. The following features of the experiment go some distance in explaining the high amount of obedience observed in the situation.

1. The experiment is sponsored by and takes place on the grounds of an institution of unimpeachable reputation, Yale University. It may be reasonably presumed that the personnel are competent and reputable. The importance of this background authority is now being studied by conducting a series of experiments outside of New Haven, and without any visible ties to the university.

2. The experiment is, on the face of it, designed to attain a worthy purpose—advancement of knowledge about learning and memory. Obedience occurs not as an end in itself, but as an instrumental element in a situation that the subject construes as significant, and meaningful. He may not be able to see its full significance, but he may properly assume that the experimenter does.

3. The subject perceives that the victim has voluntarily submitted to the authority system of the experimenter. He is not (at first) an unwilling captive impressed for involuntary service. He has taken the trouble to come to the laboratory presumably to aid the experimental research. That he later becomes an involuntary subject does not alter the fact that, initially, he consented to participate without qualification. Thus he has in some degree incurred an obligation toward the experimenter.

4. The subject, too, has entered the experiment voluntarily, and perceives himself under obligation to aid the experimenter. He has made a commitment, and to disrupt the experiment is a repudiation of this initial promise of aid.

5. Certain features of the procedure strengthen the subject's sense of obligation to the experimenter. For one, he has been paid for coming to the laboratory. In part this is canceled out by the experimenter's statement that: "Of course, as in all experiments, the money is yours simply for coming to the laboratory. From this point on, no matter what happens, the money is yours."[12]

6. From the subject's standpoint, the fact that he is the teacher and the other man the learner is purely a chance consequence (it is determined by drawing lots) and he, the subject, ran the same risk as

---

[12] Forty-three subjects, undergraduates at Yale University, were run in the experiment without payment. The results are very similar to those obtained with paid subjects.

the other man in being assigned the role of learner. Since the assignment of positions in the experiment was achieved by fair means, the learner is deprived of any basis of complaint on this count. (A similar situation obtains in Army units, in which—in the absence of volunteers—a particularly dangerous mission may be assigned by drawing lots, and the unlucky soldier is expected to bear his misfortune with sportsmanship.)

7. There is, at best, ambiguity with regard to the prerogatives of a psychologist and the corresponding rights of his subject. There is a vagueness of expectation concerning what a psychologist may require of his subject, and when he is overstepping acceptable limits. Moreover, the experiment occurs in a closed setting, and thus provides no opportunity for the subject to remove these ambiguities by discussion with others. There are few standards that seem directly applicable to the situation, which is a novel one for most subjects.

8. The subjects are assured that the shocks administered to the subject are "painful but not dangerous." Thus they assume that the discomfort caused the victim is momentary, while the scientific gains resulting from the experiment are enduring.

9. Through Shock Level 20 the victim continues to provide answers on the signal box. The subject may construe this as a sign that the victim is still willing to "play the game." It is only after Shock Level 20 that the victim repudiates the rules completely, refusing to answer further.

These features help to explain the high amount of obedience obtained in this experiment. Many of the arguments raised need not remain matters of speculation, but can be reduced to testable propositions to be confirmed or disproved by further experiments.[13]

The following features of the experiment concern the nature of the conflict which the subject faces.

10. The subject is placed in a position in which he must respond to the competing demands of two persons: the experimenter and the victim. The conflict must be resolved by meeting the demands of one or the other; satisfaction of the victim and the experimenter are mutually exclusive. Moreover, the resolution must take the form of a highly visible action, that of continuing to shock the victim or breaking off the experiment. Thus the subject is forced into a public conflict that does not permit any completely satisfactory solution.

11. While the demands of the experimenter carry the weight of scientific authority, the demands of the victim spring from his personal experience of pain and suffering. The two claims need not be regarded as equally pressing and legitimate. The experimenter seeks an abstract scientific datum; the victim cries out for relief from physical suffering caused by the subject's actions.

12. The experiment gives the subject little time for reflection. The conflict comes on rapidly. It is only minutes after the subject has been seated before the shock generator that the victim begins his protests.

---

[13] A series of recently completed experiments employing the obedience paradigm is reported in S. Milgram, "Some Conditions of Obedience and Disobedience to Authority," *Human Relations*, 1964.

Moreover, the subject perceives that he has gone through but two-thirds of the shock levels at the time the subject's first protests are heard. Thus he understands that the conflict will have a persistent aspect to it, and may well become more intense as increasingly more powerful shocks are required. The rapidity with which the conflict descends on the subject and his realization that it is predictably recurrent may well be sources of tension to him.

13. At a more general level, the conflict stems from the opposition of two deeply ingrained behavior dispositions: first, the disposition not to harm other people, and second, the tendency to obey those whom we perceive to be legitimate authorities.

When Bystanders Just Stand There

R. Lance Shotland

Twenty-one years ago, Kitty Genovese was brutally murdered as her cries in the night went unanswered by 38 of her neighbors. That infamous incident riveted public attention on just how helpless and alone crime victims may be without the support of their fellow citizens.

In fact, bystanders often do play a crucial role in preventing street crimes when they serve as extended "eyes and ears" of the police. Arrests occur more frequently when bystanders are present than when they are not. More than three-fourths of all arrests result from reports by bystanders or victims, while relatively few come from police surveillance alone. In more than half of all criminal cases, bystanders are present when the police arrive. These citizens may be important information sources, potential witnesses and influences on the victim's decision to report the crime.

Bystanders can also help control crime directly. In some cases, they leap in and rescue crime victims, or even form spontaneous vigilante groups that catch and punish offenders. Yet at other times they are peculiarly passive, neither calling the police nor intervening directly. What accounts for these differences? The death of Kitty Genovese intrigued the press, the public and social psychologists, all of whom wondered how 38 people could do so little. In 1968, psychologists John Darley and Bibb Latané started a torrent of research by discovering experimentally that a person is less likely to help someone in trouble when other bystanders are present.

As Latané and Steven Nida have noted, by 1981 some 56 experiments had tested and extended this observation. These studies examined the reactions of unwitting subjects who witnessed a staged emergency—either alone or in the presence of actors instructed to ignore the incident. In 48 of the studies, bystanders helped less when someone else was present. People who were alone helped 75 percent of the time, while those with another person helped just 53 percent of the time. After close to 20 years of research, the evidence indicates that "the bystander effect," as it has come to be called, holds for all types of emergencies, medical or criminal.

The effect occurs, the studies show, because witnesses diffuse responsibility ("Only one person needs to call the police, and certainly someone else will") and because they look at the behavior of other bystanders to determine what is happening ("If no one else is helping, does this person really need help?"). As a result, membership in a group of bystanders lowers each person's likelihood of intervening.

This phenomenon does not completely explain the behavior of bystanders, however. In the Genovese murder, for example, even if each bystander's probability of helping had dropped appreciably, with 38 witnesses we would expect several people to attempt to help. Other factors must be involved.

When the witnesses in the Genovese case were asked why they did not intervene, they said, "Frankly, we were afraid," or, "You don't realize the danger," or, "I didn't want to get involved," and even, "I was tired." In other words, in deciding whether to help, they considered the cost to themselves. When direct intervention might lead to physical harm, retaliation from the criminal or days in court testifying, consideration of such costs is understandable. However, the deterrent effects of other costs, such as intervention time, are more surprising. Some of my own work indicates that if helping is likely to take approximately 90 rather than 30 to 45 seconds, the rate is cut in half.

Ambiguity also lowers the intervention rate. In a simulated rape, many more bystanders intervene if they glimpse a struggle than if they only hear the incident. In a simulated accidental electrocution, researchers Russell Clark and Larry Word found that more people intervene if they see a victim being "electrocuted" than if they see and hear only the flashes and sounds of a presumed victim's electrocution.

At times, people misinterpret rare events such as crimes even if they see them. A young woman recently told me about an incident in which she had intervened. She and her friends had met three young men in a bar. After some friendly conversation, the young men left, and the women left shortly afterwards. From a distance, the woman saw her recent acquaintances in the parking lot and thought they were simply horsing around. It wasn't until she reached her car, which was closer to the scene, that she realized the young men were being assaulted in a robbery attempt.

Even if they interpret the situation correctly, bystanders may still be unsure about what they are seeing. People who see a crime, an accident or other unlikely event may wonder, "Did it really happen?" and freeze while they try to figure it out. Latané and Darley were the first to observe that if people are going to intervene, most do it in the first few seconds after they notice the emergency.

Certain types of crime, such as a man's attack on a woman, have unique features that may particularly invite misinterpretation and inhibit intervention. One Genovese witness said, "We thought it was a lovers' quarrel." Bystanders frequently reach similar conclusions when a man attacks a woman. Nine years after the Genovese incident, this story was carried by the Associated Press:

"A 20-year-old woman who works for the Trenton [New Jersey] Police Department was raped yesterday in full view of about 25 employees of a nearby roofing company who watched intently but did not answer her screams for help. . . . [One witness explained], 'Two people did that up there about a year ago but it was mutual. We thought, well, if we went up there, it might turn out to be her boyfriend or something like that.' "

Some of my own research conducted with Gretchen Straw, a former graduate student, shows that bystanders behave very differently if they assume a quarreling man and woman are related rather than strangers. For example, bystanders who witnessed a violent staged fight between a man and a woman and heard the woman shout, "Get away from me, I don't know you!" gave help 65 percent of the time. But those who saw the fight and heard the woman scream, "Get away from me, I don't know why I ever married you!" only helped 19 percent of the time.

People interpret fights between married people and between strangers quite differently. In our study, the nonresponsive bystanders who heard the "married" woman scream said they were reluctant to help because they weren't sure their help was wanted. They also viewed the "married" woman as much less severely injured than was the woman attacked by the "stranger," despite the fact that the two fights were staged identically. Hence, a woman seen as being attacked by a stranger is perceived as needing help more than is one fighting with a spouse. Furthermore, people expect the husband to stay and fight if they intervene, while they expect a stranger to flee. This makes intervention with fighting strangers seem safer and less costly. Unfortunately, if bystanders see a man and a woman fighting, they will usually assume that the combatants know each other.

What role do individual characteristics play in bystander behavior? Researchers have identified only a few personality factors that differentiate helpers from nonhelpers. Psychologist Louis Penner and his colleagues at the University of South Florida have found that people with relatively high scores for "sociopathy" on a personality test (although not clinically sociopaths) are less likely to help and are less bothered by others' distress than are people with low scores. On the other side of the coin, Shalom Schwartz and his colleagues at the Hebrew University in Jerusalem have shown that people who have a sense of moral obligation to the victim are more likely to help than those who do not.

Psychologist John Wilson of Cleveland State University and his colleagues have found that those concerned with achieving a sense of security are less likely to help than those who feel secure but need to build their sense of self-esteem.

These personality characteristics, combined with all the situational factors described earlier, go a long way in explaining the behavior of bystanders. But there are other factors as well. Consider those rare individuals who intervene directly when a crime is in progress:

Psychologists Ted Huston of the University of Texas at Austin and Gilbert Geis of the University of California at Irvine and their colleagues, who interviewed 32 of these people, found them to be quite different from the ordinary person. Active interveners were very self-assured and felt certain they could handle the situation by themselves. Further, they were likely to have specialized training in police work, first aid or lifesaving, and almost all were male. These people were more likely to have been victimized themselves and to have witnessed more crime in the prior 10 years than were people in general.

From other research, we know that when direct interveners were asked why they did not seek help, they answered that "there wasn't enough time" and boasted that they could "handle the situation." In addition, many either had training in physical defense or boxing or possessed—and were willing to use—a knife.

Not everyone is born or trained to be a hero. Some bystanders help indirectly, by reporting the incident to authorities and/or providing information concerning the crime. Unlike those who leap into the fray, these people do not feel competent to intervene. A typical comment: "I couldn't do anything myself so I went to get help." Such people may also see the potential cost of intervention—injury or death—as too high. A bungled rescue attempt may not help the victim and may harm the rescuer.

Even indirect intervention calls for a quick response. Otherwise the criminal act may be over and the attacker gone. But sometimes the crime happens too suddenly for anyone to comprehend and react in time. The New York *Daily News* reported an example a few years ago.

"A plumber was shot dead on a sunny Brooklyn street last weekend in full view of about 50 of his friends and neighbors. But not a single witness has come forward to tell the police exactly what happened. . . . Treglia was about to get into his truck when a car pulled up alongside him. A man in the car shot him four times and drove off, leaving him dead in the street."

The bystanders were willing to cooperate with the police, but there were no firsthand accounts. Almost every piece of information was based on what the bystanders had heard from others. The police found this hard to believe, but they did not interpret the behavior as a fearful cover-up of mob murder. The bystanders' reactions are understandable if you look closely at how the situation probably developed:

The incident itself must have been over in seconds. Bystanders had no reason to look at the victim until they heard the shots. It would only have taken a second or two to realize that the man was shot, but by then, where was the gunman? Eyewitness testimony would have been impossible for most people. The great majority would not have seen the man fall, or been certain that shots were fired, or known their source. After talking to their neighbors, however, bystanders could have pieced the event together and told the police what they collectively knew.

Another response, a rare one, is spontaneous vigilantism, in which bystanders not only apprehend a criminal but mete out punishment themselves. For example, the Washington *Post* reported:

". . . in the fashion of a Mack Sennett comedy, 29 cab drivers from the L&M Private Car Service and the No-Wait Car Service chased three men who had robbed and stolen one of No-Wait's taxis. Alerted over radio by their dispatcher, the cab drivers chased the suspects from 162nd Street and Amsterdam Avenue through two boroughs, finally cornering their prey in the Bronx. There, they collared two of the suspects, beat them and held them until the police arrived. Both were admitted to Fordham Hospital. One of the drivers, . . . , a Vietnam veteran, said after the incident, 'We've got to stick together.' "

Research shows that spontaneous vigilantism happens only in response to certain types of crimes under definable conditions: First, the crimes generate strong identification with the victim (as in the case of the taxi drivers), leaving community members with a strong sense of their own vulnerability. Second, the crimes are particularly threatening to the local community's standards; bystanders would be especially motivated to prevent any recurrence. Third, bystanders are certain (even if sometimes mistaken) both about the nature of the crime and the identity of the criminal. Although people who resort to spontaneous vigilantism usually do not witness the incident directly, the details seem unambiguous because they are interpreted unambiguously to them by someone they view as credible. Fourth, spontaneous vigilantism usually occurs in neighborhoods that are socially and ethnically homogeneous, factors that enhance communication and trust as well as identification with the victim. Poor areas with high crime rates also breed vigilantes motivated by frustration with crime and by the apparent ineffectiveness of the legal system in deterring it.

When vigilantes join together to take illegal action, each person's share of the responsibility is proportionately lessened. Thus, unlike its usual effects in fostering inaction in bystander groups, the diffusion of responsibility in a vigilante group leads to action.

Bystanders can prevent crime by their very presence on the streets. Interviews with convicted felons confirm that, when planning a crime, they view every bystander as a potential intervener and take steps to avoid being seen by potential witnesses. For example, they avoid heavily traveled commercial districts and favor sparsely used residential streets where potential victims often park. Similarly, victimization on subways is highest when there are few riders, and crime rates are higher in areas that offer the greatest possibilities for concealment.

If bystanders decrease the likelihood of crime, then keeping pedestrians on the street should help to reduce it. Unfortunately, people who fear crime are likely to stay behind locked doors and avoid the streets. The greater their fears, the more they stay off the streets, thereby increasing the risks for those who do venture out.

The prevalence of crime in a community can be viewed as the result of a delicate balance between criminals' fear of bystander intervention and possible arrest and bystanders' fear of criminal victimization. To maintain social control effectively, the balance must strongly favor the citizenry. If fear of crime gains ascendance in a neighborhood, residents lose control of criminals, who then rule the streets.

Districts in which social control has been lost need not remain this way. A major item on the public agenda should be developing strategies to help community members exert social control (see "Should Helping Be Legislated?"), thus returning the streets to law-abiding citizens.

Should Helping Be Legislated?

Given the important role of citizen participation in crime control, Vermont, Rhode Island, Massachusetts and Minnesota have attempted to compel "good samaritanism" through legislation. Other states are considering passing such laws. Under such legislation, citizens who do not respond after witnessing a serious crime against a person could be fined, jailed or sued, depending on how the law is written.

Such laws, if enforced vigorously, might make inaction more "costly" in bystanders' minds than involvement. They might reduce diffusion of responsibility by making bystanders realize that they will be held personally responsible for their inaction. The laws might also tip the balance toward intervention if bystanders find the situation ambiguous, since they may feel it is safer to guard against a penalty by intervening rather than walking away.

Whether these presumed benefits actually occur is unstudied and unknown. But since they require strong enforcement to occur at all, such outcomes are unlikely. In the four states with duty-to-assist legislation, enforcement seems minimal, and to my knowledge, only one person is being or has even been prosecuted.

If such laws were vigorously enforced, the disadvantages might well outweigh the benefits. Consider how bystanders in the Kitty Genovese case might have been affected: The first attack occurred sometime after 3 a.m. The neighbors were in their apartments when they heard the sounds of the struggle and went to their windows. Not all remained passive spectators; some were ineffective helpers, turning on their lights, opening their windows and shouting. They did scare the killer away—twice. But no one went down to rescue her, an act that might have saved her life. One person called the police after considerable soul-searching about what action to take. His response was too late, however. The remainder did nothing.

Would the law have changed anyone's behavior? Perhaps, but not necessarily for the better. These bystanders had an easy escape: the claim that they were sound sleepers and heard nothing. Research shows that a sizable percentage of bystanders will use such excuses. Would they have told the police what they saw and risk a fine, jail or a legal suit for their nonintervention? Will there needlessly be more victims of rape and murder and more criminals going free because witnesses, fearing legal reprisal, will not provide information? Unfortunately, intimidation through such a law seems as likely as enlisting greater bystander participation. In those rare cases having many witnesses, even if some are intimidated, others are likely to report, so little information is lost. But in cases with only one witness, can we afford the risks of intimidation and lost information?

I doubt that a citizen can be effectively prosecuted with such a law, because it has an implicit time frame within which the authorities must be notified. As an example, take the Genovese witness who finally did call the police. How soon should he have acted to avoid prosecution? We know—and a jury trying his case would know—that he did not call in time. But could he have known?

Laws might avoid the specific time question by specifying that a bystander must report the crime within a "reasonable" amount of time, leaving the definition of reasonable up to prosecutor, judge or jury. When did the Genovese helper first become aware of the attack? Could it ever be determined reliably without his cooperation?

A bystander would have to act very quickly to aid in apprehending a criminal. Research conducted in Kansas City suggests that if crimes are reported while in progress, an arrest related to the response occurs just 35 percent of the time. If bystanders report the crime in less than a minute after the event ends, the chance of capture drops to 18 percent. Waiting a full minute to report lowers the capture rate to 10 percent, and delaying by one to five minutes brings it down to 7 percent. Again, what is reasonable?

Or consider the case of the young woman, mentioned earlier, who thought at first that the parking-lot assault she saw was a case of highjinks by friends. Had her car been parked farther from the crime scene, she might have simply ignored it and gone home. With a duty-to-assist law in effect she could have been fined, sued or jailed. Should there be a penalty for an innocent mistake, and how can it be distinguished from deliberate shirking of civil duty? Given the huge monetary and emotional costs of a trial, do we want to leave these decisions to a prosecutor? These are but a sampling of the questions raised by prospective duty-to-assist legislation.

I believe such laws will be unenforceable as part of the criminal code and will create a nightmare in civil court similar to the excesses that have accompanied auto-accident litigation. The basic benefit from such laws, then, is likely to be symbolic, pointing out what society expects of its citizens. But I believe that Americans already know that. Such an unenforced law does a disservice by making people believe that a serious problem has been solved when a viable solution is still desperately needed.

I believe that workable solutions are at hand, but they will take time to institute. Social psychologist Jane Piliavin and her colleagues at the University of Wisconsin suggest that school training at an early age may be part of the answer. We also need more effective strategies for reporting crimes. For example, we know that eyewitness identification has many shortcomings. In a property crime such as burglary, which is likely to have physical evidence, perhaps we should teach people to focus on and report characteristics of the getaway car instead of concentrating on the criminal. Whatever the details of the program, we do desperately need new approaches in order to return the balance of fear to favor the citizenry.

The Three Faces of Love

Robert J. Trotter

Brains and sex are the only things in life that matter. Robert J. Sternberg picked up that bit of wisdom from a cynical high school classmate and appears to have taken it to heart. "I spent the first part of my career studying brains, and now along comes sex," he says, claiming to be only partly facetious.

Sternberg, IBM Professor of Psychology and Education at Yale University, has, in fact, made a name for himself as one of the foremost theoreticians and researchers in the field of human intelligence (see "Three Heads are Better than One," *Psychology Today*, August 1986), but in recent years he has turned a good deal of his attention to the study of love. Why? Because it's an understudied topic that is extremely important to people's lives. "It's important to my own life," he says. "I want to understand what's happening."

Sternberg began his attempt to understand love with a study for which he and graduate student Susan Grajek recruited 35 men and 50 women between 18 and 70 years old who had been in at least one love relationship. Participants rated their most recent significant love affair using the well-tested scales of loving and liking developed by psychologist Zick Rubin and the interpersonal involvement scale developed by psychologist George Levinger. The participants also rated their love for their mothers, fathers, siblings closest in age and best friends of the same sex.

Sternberg and Grajek found that men generally love and like their lover the most and their sibling the least. Women tend to love their lover and best friend about the same, but they like the best friend more than they like the lover. Sternberg thinks he knows why. "Women are better at achieving intimacy and value it more than do men, so if women don't get the intimacy they crave in a relationship with a man, they try to find it with other women. They establish close friendships. They can say things to another woman they can't say to a man."

Sternberg and Grajek concluded that, while the exact emotions, motivations and cognitions involved in various kinds of loving relationships differ, "the various loves one experiences are not, strictly speaking, different." In other words, they thought they had proved that love, as different as it feels from situation to situation, is actually a common entity. They thought they had discovered the basis of love in interpersonal communication, sharing and support.

This research generated a lot of publicity in 1984, especially around St. Valentine's Day, and earned Sternberg the appellation "love professor." It also generated a lot of phone calls from reporters saying things like, "You mean to tell me the way you love your lover is the same as the way you love your 5-year-old kid? What about sex?" Sternberg had to rethink his position.

He analyzed various relationships to figure out what differentiates romantic love from companionate love, from liking, from infatuation and from various other types of love. He finally concluded that his original theory accounted for the emotional component of love but left out two other important aspects. According to Sternberg's new triangular theory, love has motivational and cognitive components as well. And different aspects of love can be explained in terms of these components (see "How Do I Love Thee?").

Sternberg calls the emotional aspect of his love triangle intimacy. It includes such things as closeness, sharing, communication and support. Intimacy increases rather steadily at first, then at a slower rate until it eventually levels off and goes beneath the surface. Sternberg explains this course of development in terms of psychologist Ellen Berscheid's theory of emotions in close relationships.

According to Berscheid, people in close relationships feel increased emotion when there is some kind of disruption. This is common early in a relationship primarily because of uncertainty. Since you don't know what the other person is going to do, you are constantly learning and experiencing new things. This uncertainty keeps you guessing but also generates new levels of emotion and intimacy. As the other person becomes more predictable, there are fewer disruptions and less expressed, or manifest, intimacy.

An apparent lack of intimacy could mean that the relationship and the intimacy are dying out. Or, says Sternberg, the intimacy may still be there in latent form. The relationship may even be thriving, with the couple growing together so smoothly that they are hardly aware of their interdependence. It may take some kind of disruption—time apart, a death in the family, even a divorce—for them to find out just how they feel about each other. "Is it any wonder," Sternberg asks, "that some couples realize only after a divorce that they were very close to and dependent on each other?"

The motivational side of the triangle is passion, which leads to physiological arousal and an intense desire to be united with the loved one. Unlike intimacy, passion develops quickly. "Initially you have this rapidly growing, hot, heavy passion," Sternberg says, "but after a while it no longer does for you what you want it to—you get used to it, you habituate."

Passion is like an addiction, Sternberg says. He explains it according to psychologist Richard Solomon's opponent process theory of motivation, which says that desire for a person or substance involves two opposing forces. The first is a positive motivational force that attracts you to the person. It is quick to develop and quick to level off. The negative motivational force, the one that works against the attraction, is slow to develop and slow to fade. The result is an initial rapid growth in passion, followed by habituation when the more slowly developing negative force kicks in. "It's like with coffee, cigarettes or alcohol," Sternberg says. "Addiction can be rapid, but once habituation sets in, even an increased amount of exposure to the person or substance no longer stimulates the motivational arousal that was once possible.

"And then when the person dumps you, it's even worse. You don't go back to the way you were before you met the person," Sternberg explains. "You end up much worse off. You get depressed, irritable, you lose your appetite. You get these withdrawal symptoms, just as if you had quit drinking coffee or smoking, and it takes a while to get over it." The slow-starting, slow-fading negative force is still there after the person or the substance is gone.

The cognitive side of Sternberg's love triangle is commitment, both a short-term decision to love another person and a long-term commitment to maintain that love. Its developmental course is more straightforward and easier to explain than that of intimacy or passion. Essentially, commitment starts at zero when you first meet the other person and grows as you get to know each other. If the relationship is destined to be long-term, Sternberg says, the level of commitment will usually increase gradually at first and then speed up. As the relationship continues, the amount of commitment will generally level off. If the relationship begins to flag, the level of commitment will decline, and if the relationship fails, the level of commitment falls back to zero. According to Sternberg, the love of a parent for a child is often distinguished by a high and unconditional level of commitment.

Levels of intimacy, passion and commitment change over time, and so do relationships. You can visualize this, says Sternberg, by considering how the love triangle changes in size and shape as the three components of love increase and decrease. The triangle's area represents the amount of love and its shape the style. Large amounts of intimacy, passion and commitment, for example, yield a large triangle. And in general, Sternberg says, the larger the triangle, the more love.

Changing the length of the individual sides yields four differently shaped triangles, or styles of love. A triangle with three equal sides represents what Sternberg calls a "balanced" love in which all three components are equally matched. A scalene triangle (three unequal sides) in which the longest leg is passion represents a relationship in which physical attraction plays a larger role than either emotional intimacy or cognitive commitment. A scalene triangle with commitment as its longest leg depicts a relationship in which the intimacy and passion have waned or were never there in the first place. An isosceles triangle (two equal sides) with intimacy as its longest leg shows a relationship in which emotional involvement is more important than either passion or commitment. It's more like a high-grade friendship than a romance.

Sternberg admits that this triangle is a simplification of a complex and subtle phenomenon. There can be a variety of emotions, motivations and types of commitment in a loving relationship, and each would have to be examined to completely diagnose a relationship. Beyond that, he says, every relationship involves several triangles: In addition to their own triangles, both people have an ideal triangle (the way you would like to feel about the person you love) and a perceived triangle (the way you think the other person feels about you).

Sternberg and graduate student Michael Barnes studied the effects these triangles have on a relationship by administering the liking and loving scales to 24 couples. Participants were asked to rate their relationship in terms of how they feel about the other person, how they think the other person feels about them, how they would feel about an ideal person and how they would want an ideal person to feel about them. They found that satisfaction is closely related to the similarity between these real, ideal and perceived triangles. In general, the closer they are in shape and size, the more satisfying the relationship.

The best single predictor of happiness in a relationship is not how you feel about the other person but the difference between how you would ideally like the other person to feel about you and how you think he or she actually feels about you. "In other words," Sternberg says, "relationships tend to go bad when there is a mismatch between what you want from the other person and what you think you are getting.

"Were you ever the over involved person in a relationship? That can be very dissatisfying. What usually happens is that the more involved person tries to think up schemes to get the other person up to his or her level of involvement. But the other person usually sees what's going on and backs off. That just makes the over involved person try harder and the other person back off more until it tears the relationship apart. The good advice in such a situation is for the over-involved person to scale down, but that advice is hard to follow."

An underlying question in Sternberg's love research is: Why do so many relationships fail? Almost half the marriages in the United States end in divorce, and many couples who don't get divorced aren't all that happy. "Are people really so dumb that they pick wrong most of the time? Probably not," he suggests. "What they're doing is picking on the basis of what matters to them in the short run. But what matters in the long run may be different. The factors that count change, people change, relationships change."

Sternberg can't predict how people or situations will change, but he and his assistant Sandra Wright recently completed a study that suggests what will and won't be important in the long run. They put this question, what's important in a relationship, to 80 men and women from 17 to 69 years old, and divided them into three groups according to the length of their most recent relationship. The short-term group had been involved for up to two years, the mid-term group between two and five years, the others for more than five years.

Among the things that increase in importance as a relationship grows are willingness to change in response to each other and willingness to tolerate each other's imperfections. "These are things you can't judge at the beginning of a relationship," Sternberg says. "In the beginning," he explains, "some of the other person's flaws might not seem important. They may even seem kind of cute, but over the long term they may begin to grate on you. You both have to be willing to make some changes to make the relationship work and you both have to be willing to tolerate some flaws."

Another thing that becomes increasingly important is the sharing of values, especially religious values. "When you first meet," says Sternberg, "you have this love-overcomes-all-obstacles attitude, but when the kids come along you have to make some hard decisions about the religion issue. All of a sudden something that wasn't so important is important."

Among the things that tend to decrease in importance is how interesting you find your partner. "In the beginning," Sternberg says, "it's almost as if the other person has to keep you interested or the relationship will go nowhere. Later on, it's not quite as critical because there are other things in your life that matter."

In addition to asking what is important at different times, Sternberg and Wright asked how much of these various things people had at different times in their relationships. The answers were not encouraging. The ability to make love, for example, often goes just at the time when it is becoming more important. In fact, Sternberg says, almost everything except matching religious beliefs decreased over time. The ability to communicate, physical attractiveness, having good times, sharing interests, the ability to listen, respect for each other, romantic love—they all went down. "That may be depressing," says Sternberg, "but it's important to know at the beginning of a relationship what to expect over time, to have realistic expectations for what you can get and what is going to be important in a relationship."

And Sternberg feels that his triangular theory of love can help people in other ways. "Just analyzing your relationship in terms of the three components can be useful," he says. "Are you more romantic and your partner more companionate? It's helpful to know where you and your partner are well-matched and where you are not and then start thinking about what you can do to make yourselves more alike in what you want out of the relationship."

If you decide to take steps to improve a relationship, Sternberg offers a final triangle, the action triangle. "Often there's quite a gap between thought or feeling and action," he explains. "Your actions don't always reflect the way you feel, so it could help to know just what actions are associated with each component of love."

Intimacy, he suggests, might be expressed by communicating inner feelings; sharing one's possessions, time and self; and offering emotional support. Passion, obviously, is expressed by kissing, hugging, touching making love. Commitment can be expressed by fidelity, by staying with the relationship through the hard times that occur in any relationship or by getting engaged or married. Which actions are most important and helpful will vary from person to person and from relationship to relationship. But Sternberg feels it is important to consider the triangle of love as it is expressed through action because action has so many effects on a relationship.

Citing psychologist Daryl Bem's theory of self-perception, Sternberg describes how actions can affect emotions, motivations and cognitions. "The way we act shapes the way we feel and think, possibly as much as the way we think and feel shapes the way we act." Also, he says, certain actions can lead to other actions; expressions of love, for example, encourage further expressions of love. Furthermore, your actions affect the way the other person thinks and feels about you and behaves toward you, leading to a mutually reinforcing series of actions.

"The point," Sternberg concludes, "is that it is necessary to take into account the ways in which people express their love. Without expression, even the greatest of loves can die."

How Do I Love Thee?

Intimacy, passion and commitment are the warm, hot and cold vertices of Sternberg's love triangle. Alone and in combination they give rise to eight possible kinds of love relationships. The first is nonlove—the absence of all three components. This describes the large majority of our personal relationships, which are simply casual interactions.

The second kind of love is liking. "If you just have intimacy," Sternberg explains, "that's liking. You can talk to the person, tell about your life. And if that's all there is to it, that's what we mean by liking." It is more than nonlove. It refers to the feelings experienced in true friendships. Liking includes such things as closeness and warmth but not the intense feelings of passion or commitment.

If you just have passion, it's called infatuated love—the "love at first sight" that can arise almost instantaneously and dissipate just as quickly. It involves a high degree of physiological arousal but no intimacy or commitment. It's the 10th-grader who falls madly in love with the beautiful girl in his biology class but never gets up the courage to talk to her or get to know her, Sternberg says, describing his past.

Empty love is commitment without intimacy or passion, the kind of love sometimes seen in a 30-year-old marriage that has become stagnant. The couple used to be intimate, but they don't talk to each other any more. They used to be passionate, but that's died out. All that remains is the commitment to stay with the other person. In societies in which marriages are arranged, Sternberg points out, empty love may precede the other kinds of love.

Romantic love, the Romeo and Juliet type of love, is a combination of intimacy and passion. More than infatuation, it's liking with the added excitement of physical attraction and arousal but without commitment. A summer affair can be very romantic, Sternberg explains, but you know it will end when she goes back to Hawaii and you go back to Florida, or wherever.

Passion plus commitment is what Sternberg calls fatuous love. It's Hollywood love: Boy meets girl, a week later they're engaged, a month later they're married. They are committed on the basis of their passion, but because intimacy takes time to develop, they don't have the emotional core necessary to sustain the commitment. This kind of love, Sternberg warns, usually doesn't work out.

Companionate love is intimacy with commitment but no passion. It's a long-term friendship, the kind of committed love and intimacy frequently seen in marriages in which the physical attraction has died down.

When all three elements of Sternberg's love triangle come together in a relationship, you get what he calls consummate love, or complete love. It's the kind of love toward which many people strive, especially in romantic relationships. Achieving consummate love, says Sternberg, is like trying to lose weight, difficult but not impossible. The really hard thing is keeping the weight off after you have lost it, or keeping the consummate love alive after you have achieved it. Consummate love is possible only in very special relationships.

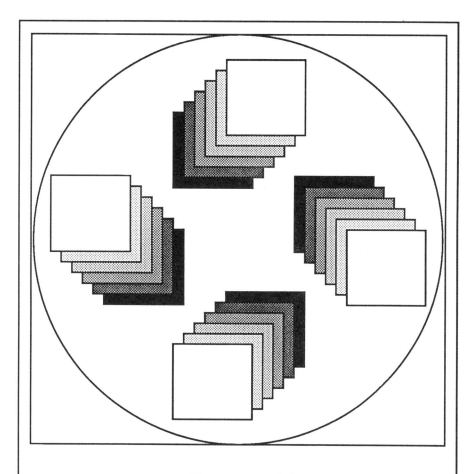

Chapter 11

Personality

CHAPTER 11: PERSONALITY

The field of personality is one of the more misunderstood and scientifically controversial areas of psychology. The term "personality" may be defined as an individual's behavioral trends or set of attitudes that remains relatively constant over time. A person who is "aggressive" may be expected to behave in one consistent way, just as a "paranoid" may be expected to maintain a consistent attitude that others tend to persecute him or her. Some psychologists, such as Darryl Bem, have argued that since all behavior is situation specific there is no such thing as personality at all! Others argue that some aspects of personality and temperament are inherited and fixed at birth. Understanding the nature of personality is made even more difficult by the many preconceptions people have about personality and its applications. Included in this chapter are two articles that discuss socially relevant aspects of predictable behavior traits: criminality and the "Barnum" effect.

11a. Herrnstein, R., & Wilson, J. (1985). Are criminals made or born? *The New York Times Magazine* (Aug. 4) 31, 32, 43, 46.

This selection begins with the premise that criminal behavior has both sociological and biological roots; it goes on to focus on the biological implications. Imagine that you are an "expert" witness involved in a trial. The offender has a history profile that fits many of Herrnstein and Wilson's criminality correlates (that is, a nineteen-year-old male, born prematurely, abused as a child, having a low IQ, poor school performance, and so on). To what extent should such an individual be held responsible for criminal behavior? Use material from the article to back up your answer.

11b. Snyder, C., Shenkel, R. & Lowery, C. (1977). Acceptance of personality interpretations: The "Barnum effect" and beyond. *Journal of Consulting and Clinical Psychology, 45,* 104–114.

The "Barnum effect" concerns the willingness of people to accept interpretations of their personality based on assessment procedures. After reading this article, explain under what conditions you think a client should accept a clinician's evaluation of one's personality. Under what conditions should clients reject these interpretations? Support your answers with ideas from this selection.

Are Criminals Made or Born?

Richard J. Herrnstein and James Q. Wilson

A revolution in our understanding of crime is quietly overthrowing some established doctrines. Until recently, criminologists looked for the causes of crime almost entirely in the offenders' social circumstances. There seemed to be no shortage of circumstances to blame: weakened, chaotic or broken families, ineffective schools, antisocial gangs, racism, poverty, unemployment. Criminologists took seriously, more so than many other students of social behavior, the famous dictum of the French sociologist Emile Durkheim: Social facts must have social explanations. The sociological theory of crime had the unquestioned support of prominent editorialists, commentators, politicians and most thoughtful people.

Today many learned journals and scholarly works draw a different picture. Sociological factors have not been abandoned, but increasingly it is becoming clear to many scholars that crime is the outcome of an interaction between social factors and certain biological factors, particularly for the offenders who, by repeated crimes, have made public places dangerous. The idea is still controversial, but increasingly, to the old question "Are criminals born or made?" the answer seems to be: both. The causes of crime lie in a combination of predisposing biological traits channeled by social circumstance into criminal behavior. The traits alone do not inevitably lead to crime; the circumstances do not make criminals of everyone; but together they create a population responsible for a large fraction of America's problem of crime in the streets.

Evidence that criminal behavior has deeper roots than social circumstances has always been right at hand, but social science has, until recent years, overlooked its implications. As far as the records show, crime everywhere and throughout history is disproportionately a young man's pursuit. Whether men are 20 or more times as likely to be arrested as women, as is the case in Malawi or Brunei, or only four to six times as likely, as in the United States or France, the sex difference in crime statistics is universal. Similarly, 18-year-olds may sometimes be four times as likely to be criminal as 40-year-olds, while at other times only twice as likely. In the United States, more than half of all arrests for serious property crimes are of 20-year-olds or younger. Nowhere have older persons been as criminal as younger ones.

It is easy to imagine purely social explanations for the effects of age and sex on crime. Boys in many societies are trained by their parents and the society itself to play more roughly and aggressively than girls. Boys are expected to fight back, not to cry, and to play to win. Likewise, boys in many cultures are denied adult responsibilities, kept in a state of prolonged dependence and confined too long in schools that many of them find unrewarding. For a long time, these factors were thought to be the whole story.

Ultimately, however, the very universality of the age and sex differences in crime have alerted some social scientists to the implausibility of a theory that does not look beyond the accidents of particular societies. If cultures as different as Japan's and Sweden's, England's and Mexico's, have sex and age differences in crime, then perhaps we should have suspected from the start that there was something more fundamental going on than parents happening to decide to raise their boys and girls differently. What is it about boys, girls and their parents, in societies of all sorts, that leads them to emphasize, rather than overcome, sex differences? Moreover, even if we believed that every society has arbitrarily decided to inculcate aggressiveness in males, there would still be the greater criminality *among* young males to explain. After all, in some cultures, young boys are not denied adult responsibilities but are kept out of school, put to work tilling the land and made to accept obligations to the society.

But it is no longer necessary to approach questions about the sources of criminal behavior merely with argument and supposition. There is evidence. Much crime, it is agreed, has an aggressive component, and Eleanor Emmons Maccoby, a professor of psychology at Stanford University, and Carol Nagy Jacklin, a psychologist now at the University of Southern California, after reviewing the evidence on sex differences in aggression, concluded that it has a foundation that is at least in part biological. Only that conclusion can be drawn, they said, from data that show that the average man is more aggressive than the average woman in all known societies, that the sex difference is present in infancy well before evidence of sex-role socialization by adults, that similar sex differences turn up in many of our biological relatives—monkeys and apes. Human aggression has been directly tied to sex hormones, particularly male sex hormones, in experiments on athletes engaging in competitive sports and on prisoners known for violent or domineering behavior. No single line of evidence is decisive and each can be challenged, but all together they convinced Drs. Maccoby and Jacklin, as well as most specialists on the biology of sex differences, that the sexual conventions that assign males the aggressive roles have biological roots.

That is also the conclusion of most researchers about the developmental forces that make adolescence and young adulthood a time of risk for criminal and other nonconventional behavior. This is when powerful new drives awaken, leading to frustrations that foster behavior unchecked by the internalized prohibitions of adulthood. The result is usually just youthful rowdiness, but, in a minority of cases, it passes over the line into crime.

The most compelling evidence of biological factors for criminality comes from two studies—one of twins, the other of adopted boys. Since the 1920's it has been understood that twins may develop from a single fertilized egg, resulting in identical genetic endowments—identical twins—or from a pair of separately fertilized eggs that have about half their genes in common—fraternal twins. A standard procedure for estimating how important genes are to a trait is to compare the similarity between identical twins with that between fraternal twins. When identical twins are clearly more similar in a trait than fraternal twins, the trait probably has high heritability.

There have been about a dozen studies of criminality using twins. More than 1,500 pairs of twins have been studied in the United States, the Scandinavian countries, Japan, West Germany, Britain and elsewhere, and the result is qualitatively the same everywhere. Identical twins are more likely to have similar criminal records than fraternal twins. For example, the late Karl O. Christiansen, a Danish criminologist, using the Danish Twin Register, searched police, court and prison records for entries regarding twins born in a certain region of Denmark between 1881 and 1910. When an identical twin had a criminal record, Christiansen found, his or her co-twin was more than twice as likely to have one also than when a fraternal twin had a criminal record.

In the United States, a similar result has recently been reported by David Rowe, a psychologist at the University of Oklahoma, using questionnaires instead of official records to measure criminality. Twins in high school in almost all the school districts of Ohio received questionnaires by mail, with a promise of confidentiality as well as a small payment if the questionnaires were filled out and returned. The twins were asked about their activities, including their delinquent behavior, about their friends and about their co-twins. The identical twins were more similar in delinquency than the fraternal twins. In addition, the twins who shared more activities with each other were no more likely to be similar in delinquency than those who shared fewer activities.

No single method of inquiry should be regarded as conclusive. But essentially the same results are found in studies of adopted children. The idea behind such studies is to find a sample of children adopted early in life, cases in which the criminal histories of both adopting and biological parents are known. Then, as the children grow up, researchers can discover how predictive of their criminality are the family histories of their adopting and biological parents. Recent studies show that the biological family history contributes substantially to the adoptees' likelihood of breaking the law.

For example, Sarnoff Mednick, a psychologist at the University of Southern California, and his associates in the United States and Denmark have followed a sample of several thousand boys adopted in Denmark between 1927 and 1947. Boys with criminal biological parents and noncriminal adopting parents were more likely to have criminal records than those with noncriminal biological parents and criminal adopting parents. The more criminal convictions a boy's natural parents had, the greater the risk of criminality for boys being raised by adopting parents who had no records. The risk was unrelated to whether the boy or his adopting parents knew about the natural parents' criminal records, whether the natural parents committed their crimes before or after the boy was given up for adoption, or whether the boy was adopted immediately after birth or a year or two later. The results of this study have been confirmed in Swedish and American samples of adopted children.

Because of studies like these, many sociologists and criminologists now accept the existence of genetic factors contributing to criminality. When there is disagreement, it is about how large the genetic contribution to crime is and about how the criminality of biological parents is transmitted to their children.

Both the twin and adoption studies show that genetic contributions are not alone responsible for crime—there is, for example, some increase in criminality among boys if their adopted fathers are criminal even when their biological parents are not, and not every co-twin of a criminal identical twin becomes criminal himself. Although it appears, on average, to be substantial, the precise size of the genetic contribution to crime is probably unknowable, particularly since the measures of criminality itself are now so crude.

We have a bit more to go on with respect to the link that transmits a predisposition toward crime from parents to children. No one believes there are "crime genes," but there are two major attributes that have, to some degree, a heritable base and that appear to influence criminal behavior. These are intelligence and temperament. Hundreds of studies have found that the more genes people share, the more likely they are to resemble each other intellectually and temperamentally.

Starting with studies in the 1930's, the average offender in broad samples has consistently scored 91 to 93 on I.Q. tests for which the general population's average is 100. The typical offender does worse on the verbal items of intelligence tests than on the nonverbal items but is usually below average on both.

Criminologists have long known about the correlation between criminal behavior and I.Q., but many of them have discounted it for various reasons. Some have suggested that the correlation can be explained away by the association between low socioeconomic status and crime, on the one hand, and that between low I.Q. and low socio-economic status, on the other. These criminologists say it is low socio-economic status, rather than I.Q., that fosters crime. Others have questioned whether I.Q. tests really measure intelligence for the populations that are at greater risk for breaking the law. The low scores of offenders, the argument goes, betray a culturally deprived background or alienation from our society's values rather than low intelligence. Finally, it is often noted that the offenders in some studies have been caught for their crimes. Perhaps the ones who got away have higher I.Q.s.

But these objections have proved to be less telling than they once seemed to be. There are, for example, many poor law-abiding people living in deprived environments, and one of their more salient characteristics is that they have higher I.Q. scores than those in the same environment who break the law.

Then, too, it is a common misconception that I.Q. tests are invalid for people from disadvantaged backgrounds. If what is implied by this criticism is that scores predict academic potential or job performance differently for different groups, then the criticism is wrong. A comprehensive recent survey sponsored by the National Academy of Sciences concluded that "tests predict about as well for one group as for another." And that some highly intelligent criminals may well be good at eluding capture is fully consistent with the belief that offenders, in general, have lower scores than nonoffenders.

If I.Q. and criminality are linked, what may explain the link? There are several possibilities. One is that low scores on I.Q. tests signify greater difficulty in grasping the likely consequences of action or in learning the meaning and significance of moral codes. Another is that low scores, especially on the verbal component of the tests, mean trouble in school, which leads to frustration, thence to resentment, anger and delinquency. Still another is that persons who are not as skillful as others in expressing themselves verbally may find it more rewarding to express themselves in ways in which they will do better, such as physical threat or force.

For some repeat offenders, the predisposition to criminality may be more a matter of temperament than intelligence. Impulsiveness, insensitivity to social mores, a lack of deep and enduring emotional attachments to others and an appetite for danger are among the temperamental characteristics of highrate offenders. Temperament is, to a degree, heritable, though not as much so as intelligence. All parents know that their children, shortly after birth, begin to exhibit certain characteristic ways of behaving—they are placid or fussy, shy or bold. Some of the traits endure, among them aggressiveness and hyperactivity, although they change in form as the child develops. As the child grows up, these traits, among others, may gradually unfold into a disposition toward unconventional, defiant or antisocial behavior.

Lee Robins, a sociologist at Washington University School of Medicine in St. Louis, reconstructed 30 years of the lives of more than 500 children who were patients in the 1920's at a child guidance clinic in St. Louis. She was interested in the early precursors of chronic sociopathy, a condition of antisocial personality that often includes criminal behavior as one of its symptoms. Adult sociopaths in her sample who did not suffer from psychosis, mental retardation or addiction, were, without exception, antisocial before they were 18. More than half of the male sociopaths had serious symptoms before they were 11. The main childhood precursors were truancy, poor school performance, theft, running away, recklessness, slovenliness impulsiveness and guiltlessness. The more symptoms in childhood, the greater the risk of sociopathy in adulthood.

Other studies confirm and extend Dr. Robin's conclusions. For example, two psychologists, John J. Conger of the University of Colorado and Wilbur Miller of Drake University in Des Moines, searching back over the histories of a sample of delinquent boys in Denver, found that "by the end of the third grade, future delinquents were already seen by their teachers as more poorly adapted than their classmates. They appeared to have less regard for the rights and feelings of their peers; less awareness of the need to accept responsibility for their obligations, both as individuals and as members of a group, and poorer attitudes toward authority."

Traits that foreshadow serious, recurrent criminal behavior have been traced all the way back to behavior patterns such as hyperactivity and unusual fussiness, and neurological signs such as atypical brain waves or reflexes. In at least a minority of cases, these are detectable in the first few years of life. Some of the characteristics are sex-linked. There is evidence that newborn females are more likely than newborn males to smile, to cling to their mothers, to be receptive to touching and talking, to be sensitive to certain stimuli, such as being touched by a cloth, and to have less upper-body strength. Mothers certainly treat girls and boys differently, but the differences are not simply a matter of the mother's choice—female babies are more responsive than male babies to precisely the kind of treatment that is regarded as "feminine." When adults are asked to play with infants, they play with them in ways they think are appropriate to the infants' sexes. But there is also some evidence that when the sex of the infant is concealed, the behavior of the adults is influenced by the conduct of the child.

Premature infants or those born with low birth weights have a special problem. These children are vulnerable to any adverse circumstances in their environment—including child abuse—that may foster crime. Although nurturing parents can compensate for adversity, cold or inconsistent parents may exacerbate it. Prematurity and low birth weight may result from poor prenatal care, a bad diet or excessive use of alcohol or drugs. Whether the bad care is due to poverty, ignorance or anything else, here we see criminality arising from biological, though not necessarily genetic, factors. It is now known that these babies are more likely than normal babies to be the victims of child abuse.

We do not mean to blame child abuse on the victim by saying that premature and low-birth-weight infants are more difficult to care for and thus place a great strain on the parents. But unless parents are emotionally prepared for the task of caring for such children, they may vent their frustration at the infant's unresponsiveness by hitting or neglecting it. Whatever it is in parent and child that leads to prematurity or low birth weight is compounded by the subsequent interaction between them. Similarly, children with low I.Q.s may have difficulty in understanding rules, but if their parents also have poor verbal skills, they may have difficulty in communicating rules, and so each party to the conflict exacerbates the defects of the other.

The statement that biology plays a role in explaining human behavior, especially criminal behavior, sometimes elicits a powerful political or ideological reaction. Fearful that what is being proposed is a crude biological determinism, some critics deny the evidence while others wish the evidence to be confined to scientific journals. Scientists who have merely proposed studying the possible effects of chromosomal abnormalities on behavior have been ruthlessly attacked by other scientists, as have those who have made public the voluminous data showing the heritability of intelligence and temperament.

Some people worry that any claim that biological factors influence criminality is tantamount to saying that the higher crime rate of black compared to white Americans has a genetic basis. But no responsible work in the field leads to any such conclusion. The data show that of all the reasons people vary in their crime rates, race is far less important than age, sex, intelligence and the other individual factors that vary within races. Any study of the causes of crime must therefore first consider the individual factors. Differences among races may have many explanations, most of them having nothing to do with biology.

The intense reaction to the study of biological factors in crime, we believe, is utterly misguided. In fact, these discoveries, far from implying that "criminals are born" and should be locked up forever, suggest new and imaginative ways of reducing criminality by benign treatment. The opportunity we have is precisely analogous to that which we had when the biological bases of other disorders were established. Mental as well as physical illness -- alcoholism, learning disabilities of various sorts, and perhaps even susceptibility to drug addiction -- now seem to have genetic components. In each case, new understanding energized the search for treatment and gave it new direction. Now we know that many forms of depression can be successfully treated with drugs; in time we may learn the same of Alzheimer's disease. Alcoholics are helped when they understand that some persons, because of their predisposition toward addiction to alcohol, should probably never consume it at all. A chemical treatment of the predisposition is a realistic possibility. Certain types of slow learners can already be helped by special programs. In time, others will be also.

Crime, admittedly, may be a more difficult program. So many different acts are criminal that it is only with considerable poetic license that we can speak of "criminality" at all. The bank teller who embezzles $500 to pay off a gambling debt is not engaging in the same behavior as a person who takes $500 from a liquor store at the point of a gun or one who causes $500 worth of damage by drunkenly driving his car into a parked vehicle. Moreover, crime, unlike alcoholism or dyslexia, exposes a person to the formal condemnation of society and the possibility of imprisonment. We naturally and rightly worry about treating all "criminals" alike, or stigmatizing persons whom we think might become criminal by placing them in special programs designed to prevent criminality.

But these problems are not insurmountable barriers to better ways of thinking about crime prevention. Though criminals are of all sorts, we know that a very small fraction of all young males commit so large a fraction of serious street crime that we can properly blame these chronic offenders for most such crime. We also know that chronic offenders typically begin their misconduct at an early age. Early family and preschool programs may be far better repositories for the crime-prevention dollar than rehabilitation programs aimed—usually futilely—at the 19-or 20-year-old veteran offender. Prevention programs risk stigmatizing children, but this may be less of a risk than is neglect. If stigma were a problem to be avoided at all costs, we would have to dismantle most special-needs education programs.

Having said all this, we must acknowledge that there is at present little hard evidence that we know how to inhibit the development of delinquent tendencies in children. There are some leads, such as family training programs of the sort pioneered at the Oregon Social Learning Center, where parents are taught how to use small rewards and penalties to alter the behavior of misbehaving children. There is also evidence from David Weikart and Lawrence Schweinhart of the

High/Scope Educational Research Foundation at Ypsilanti, Mich., that preschool education programs akin to Project Head Start may reduce later delinquency. There is nothing yet to build a national policy on, but there are ideas worth exploring by carefully repeating and refining these pioneering experimental efforts.

Above all, there is a case for redirecting research into the causes of crime in ways that take into account the interaction of biological and social factors. Some scholars, such as the criminologist Marvin E. Wolfgang and his colleagues at the University of Pennsylvania, are already exploring these issues by analyzing social and biological information from large groups as they age from infancy to adulthood and linking the data to criminal behavior. But much more needs to be done.

It took years of patiently following the life histories of many men and women to establish the linkages between smoking or diet and disease; it will also take years to unravel the complex and subtle ways in which intelligence, temperament, hormonal levels and other traits combine with family circumstances and later experiences in school and elsewhere to produce human character.

Richard J. Herrnstein is a professor of psychology and James Q. Wilson a professor of government at Harvard. This article is adapted from their book, "Crime and Human Nature," which was published in 1972 by Simon & Schuster.

Acceptance of Personality Interpretations: The "Barnum Effect" and Beyond

C. R. Snyder, Randee Jae Shenkel, & Carol R. Lowery

ABSTRACT

The "Barnum effect" is the phenomenon whereby people willingly give their approval and acceptance of personality interpretations derived from the results of assessment procedures. The research generated over the last 25 years relative to this acceptance phenomenon is reviewed. Characteristics of clientele who accept such interpretations are summarized, with the deduction that it is of questionable usefulness to study such personality characteristics independent of situational factors that elicit acceptance. Situational factors that elicit acceptance are examined, with the conclusion that clientele acceptance cannot be construed as validation of either the clinician or his assessment procedures. Finally, implications of the acceptance phenomenon for the clinical diagnostic process are discussed.

P. T. Barnum's circuses met with wide approval among all types of people. One reason for the popularity of these circuses was that they had "a little something for everybody." Indeed, Donald G. Paterson may have had this general showmanship in mind when he originally warned clinicians about a "personality description after the manner of P. T. Barnum" (cited in Meehl, 1956). The term "Barnum effect," as subsequently labeled by Paul Meehl (1956), refers to the phenomenon whereby people willingly accept personality interpretations comprised of vague statements with a high base-rate occurrence in the general population. In the last 25 years there has been a proliferation of research designed to explore factors that relate to "client" acceptance of personality interpretations. Throughout this research, there has been a remarkably consistent tendency for people to accept the accuracy of personality interpretations. The present article explores this acceptance phenomenon. The first and second sections review the numerous variables that have been investigated in the acceptance research by categorizing these variables into factors in the client and diagnostic situation, respectively. The third section briefly examines the implications of the acceptance phenomenon for the clinical diagnostic process.

Factors in the Client

In general, all the acceptance studies have utilized a similar methodological approach. That is, subjects have followed the same basic four steps—a) completing a personality test; (b) waiting while the test is scored; (c) receiving the interpretation, purportedly derived from their test results; and (d) rating the "accuracy" of the interpretation. It should be noted that all subjects have received the same general "Barnum" interpretation in this paradigm. Although there is relatively little research examining factors "in" people that make them more prone to accept personality interpretations, the first section of this review will explore more closely what might more broadly be labeled the "gullible" personality. The present section examines the following factors: (a) sex of the subject, (b) personality attributes, and (c) clientele "sophistication."

Sex

The term *gullibility* has often been applied to women, the implication being that men are much more logical and, hence, less easily duped. In the first acceptance study conducted by Forer (1949), however, no significant relationships were found between rating of the general personality sketch and sex of the subjects. Additionally, Sundberg (1955) reported that acceptance of a bona fide interpretation as compared to a fake interpretation was equal for males and females. Snyder (1974a), Snyder, Larsen, and Bloom (1976), Halperin, Snyder, Shenkel, and Houston (1976), and Snyder and Shenkel (1976) also have reported no differences in the acceptance of general personality interpretations by males and females. From the results of these studies, therefore, it appears that both sexes are equally susceptible to the Barnum effect.

Personality Attributes

Several measures of personality variables have been examined in relation to the acceptance phenomenon. Sundberg (1955) reported that students who preferred their bona fide interpretations as compared to those who selected the fake interpretations as most accurately describing their personalities scored significantly lower on the Hypomania scale of the Minnesota Multiphasic Personality Inventory (MMPI). However, this single difference in personality as it relates to acceptance may have been due to chance.

Carrier (1963) reported that acceptance of a general personality description was found to be significantly and positively correlated with the achievement, deference, introception, abasement, and endurance variables of the Edwards Personal Preference Schedule. Greater external locus of control as indicated by Rotter's Internal-External (I–E) Locus of Control Scale was also found to be positively related to higher acceptance of the general personality interpretation (Snyder & Larson, 1972; Snyder & Shenkel, 1976). In another study, Snyder (1974a) reported that although the I–E scale correlated positively with acceptance, the correlation did not reach significance. This latter study examined subjects' acceptance as a function of telling separate groups that the interpretation was based on the results of either a projective technique, interview data, objective test, or was "generally true of people." The I–E scale correlated negatively with acceptance only in the projective condition, and this negative correlation appeared to have lowered the overall positive internal–external/acceptance correlation for students in all conditions grouped together.

Measures of response style also have exhibited a relationship with the acceptance phenomenon. Mosher (1965), for example, found that subjects' scores on Couch and Keniston's (1960) Agreeing Response Scale (a measure of acquiescence) were positively related to acceptance regardless of content favorability. (None of the correlations reached statistical significance, however.) Similarly, high scores on the Marlowe-Crowne Social Desirability Scale have been shown to be significantly more acceptant to unfavorable and neutral interpretations (Mosher, 1965). Snyder and Larson (1972) also have reported that higher scores on the Marlowe-Crowne Scale correlate positively, although not significantly, with acceptance of a favorably worded interpretation.

Clientele "Sophistication"

Dana and Graham (1976) have suggested that the Barnum results do not generalize to the actual clinical assessment setting because the college students who serve as subjects are relatively naive and "unsophisticated." Some evidence that acceptance may vary with the "sophistication" of the population is offered by Bachrach and Pattishell (1960). They reported that psychiatric residents were less likely than younger undergraduate and graduate students to accept the general personality interpretations. The number of residents was so small, however, that this finding is highly tentative. Other studies have indicated that "sophistication" does *not* relate to differential acceptance. Forer (1949), for example, found no relationsnip between acceptance and either age or occupational background. Likewise, Stagner (1958) reported that Barnum interpretations generated an equally high level of acceptance from college students, industrial supervisors, and personnel managers.

The influence of client sophistication has not yet been investigated with an actual clinical population. However, this seems inadvisable for at least two reasons. First, there would be serious ethical considerations in delivering the Barnum interpretations to an actual clinical population. Second, any sophistication a person has may be reduced by the situationally caused insecurity that accompanies a visit to a clinician for diagnostic feedback. In this regard, findings in the attitude-change literature suggest that people with low self-esteem are more persuadable than people with high self-esteem (Gollob & Dittes, 1965). Additionally, members of a group who see themselves as less competent than others are more likely to change their opinions to conform to the group (Ettinger, Marino, Endler, Geller, & Natziuk, 1971). Thus in actual clinical practice the person receiving diagnostic feedback is probably situationally insecure and lacks a sense of self-esteem and competence. In such a state, the client may be even more prone to accepting the feedback than the typical college sophomore in the Barnum experimental setting.

In this section, factors in the client that may affect acceptance of a general personality interpretation have been reviewed. Overall, no simple profile can be proposed to define the "gullible" person. This conclusion is similar to that made in the field of attitude change in social psychology, in which efforts to identify a general trait of "persuasibility" have met with very limited success (cf. Hovland & Janis, 1959). At times, Barnum researchers have measured personality characteristics, which, assuming a relationship with acceptance of personality interpretations, would be saying little more than the person who is gullible is easily gulled. For example, it is almost circular to say that a highly acquiescent individual will be more accepting of a personality interpretation than a person low in acquiescence. Finally, the advisability of pursuing personality characteristics independent of situational factors that elicit acceptance is questionable.

Factors in the Clinical Diagnostic Situation

The second section of this article reviews the situational factors that potentially influence clientele acceptance of personality interpretations. In order, the present section examines the following factors: (a) generosity of interpretation, (b) relevance of interpretation, (c) favorability of interpretation, (d) type of assessment procedure, and (e) test administrator and interpreter.

Generality of Interpretation

The earliest research demonstrating acceptance of general personality interpretations was reported by Forer (1949). College students completed a personality test and a week later received the following personality sketch, which was supposedly derived for them from the results of their personality tests:

You have a great need for other people to like you and admire you. You have a tendency to be critical of yourself. You have a great deal of unused capacity which you have not turned to your advantage. While you have some personality weaknesses, you are generally able to compensate for them. Your sexual adjustment has presented problems for you. Disciplined and self-controlled outside, you tend to be worrisome and insecure inside. At times you have serious doubts as to whether you have made the right decision or done the right thing. You prefer a certain amount of change and variety and become dissatisfied when hemmed in by restrictions and limitations. You pride yourself as being an independent thinker and do not accept others' statements without satisfactory proof. You have found it unwise to be too frank in revealing yourself to others. At times you are extroverted, affable, and sociable, while at other times you are introverted, wary, and reserved. Some of your aspirations tend to be pretty unrealistic. Security is one of your major goals in life.

Forer's results demonstrated that students accepted $M = 4.3$ on a 5-point scale in which 1 = poor and 5 = perfect) the general personality interpretation as being accurate for them. The consistency with which individuals accept general personality statements supposedly derived from psychological assessment procedures has been implicated in several subsequent studies (e.g., Carrier, 1963; Lattal & Lattal, 1967; Manning, 1968; Snyder, 1974a; Snyder & Larson, 1972; Stagner, 1958; Sundberg, 1955; Ulrich, Stachnik, & Stainton, 1963; Blumenfeld & Leveto, Note 1).

A related area is that of astrological horoscopes, which frequently bear a strong similarity to the interpretations used in the acceptance literature (Snyder, 1974b). Although astrology has become more popular in recent years, research lends reliable support to the contention that it relates to an individual's personality and behavior (cf. Gauquelin, 1969; Sechrest & Bryan, 1968). Nevertheless, Gauquelin (1969) has reported that 30% to 60% of the population admit to believing that there is some truth in *general* astrology statements. In a related study, a purported astrologer advertised in the newspapers and sent hundreds of inquiring individuals an identical, general horoscope. Over 200 "thank yous" praising his accuracy and perceptiveness were received ("Fraud in Your Future?" 1964). From these findings, it may be suggested that the generality of horoscopes, like the generality in personality interpretations, enhances their acceptability.

The ambiguity of generalized interpretations may even enhance their "accuracy" to the extent that they equal or excel interpretations based on bona fide test data. For example, in a study by Sundberg (1955), MMPIs were obtained from subjects and interpreted by two psychologists experienced with the test. Generalized fake interpretations were then paired randomly with the bona fide interpretations. Each subject was presented with his own test interpretation and the fake interpretation and was asked to indicate which interpretation better described him and which of the two he thought had been written from the test results. Several subjects then gave the pair of interpretations to close friends, who were asked to choose which of the interpretations described the subject better. Results showed that students were able to pick out their own bona fide personality description *only* at the chance level. Likewise, the subjects' friends failed to select the test-based interpretations beyond chance.

Using designs similar to the Sundberg (1955) study, subsequent experiments have shown that subjects perceive the generalized "fake" interpretation as being *more* accurate than interpretations that are actually derived from their personality tests (Merrens & Richards, 1970; O'Dell, 1972). O'Dell explained these results by suggesting that because of their high base rates the fake general interpretations *should* be seen as more accurate than interpretations derived from many of the personality tests currently in use.[1]

In summary, then, studies examining the generality factor have consistently found that global and ambiguous interpretations are seen as highly accurate by the subjects receiving them.

Relevance of Interpretation

Snyder and Larson (1972) noted that in previous studies the psychological interpretations were presented to each subject as having supposedly been *specifically derived for that individual on the basis of his or her test results.* Their study examined whether subjects who were told that the personality interpretation was specifically derived for them (the "for you" relevance condition) accepted the same general personality interpretation any more strongly than subjects who were told that the interpretation was "generally true of people" (the "for people generally" relevance condition). Results indicated that subjects who were told that the general personality interpretation was "for you" rated the interpretation as being a more accurate description of their own personalities than subjects who were told that the interpretation was "for people generally." These results have been replicated in subsequent studies (Snyder, 1974a; Snyder, Larsen & Bloom, 1976). Although a study by Collins, Dmitruk, and Ranney (1977) did not find a significant effect for this relevance variable, the trend was in the same direction as in the aforementioned studies.

To test Forer's (1949) original speculation that individuals accept the personality description for themselves while failing to recognize its applicability to the general population, Ziv and Nevenhaus (1972) utilized a within-subject design. That is, all subjects rated the accuracy of "their" personality description both for themselves and for people in general. As was the case in the other studies using between-subject designs, individuals rated "their" interpretation as being more true of themselves than of people in general. These results were replicated in a similar study by Snyder and Shenkel (1976). Interestingly, however, the relevance effect in the Snyder and Shenkel study was qualified by an interaction between favorability and relevance. This interaction revealed that only those subjects who received a favorable personality interpretation viewed it as being significantly more accurate for themselves than for people in general. Those subjects who received an unfavorable description did not view it as being significantly more or less true of people in general than of themselves. Thus, all of the above

---

[1] A related issue is whether differential acceptance results from the reception of valid or invalid feedback from a personality test. To test this issue, Dies (1972) initially gave subjects the Personality Research Form. In a first study, half of the subjects were given their actual scores on 14 subscales, and half of the subjects were given randomly generated scores. In a second study, half of the subjects received their actual scores, and half of the subjects received scores that were made to be very different from their actual scores. In both studies, no differences were found in acceptance as a function of the validity of test feedback. Subjects rated all profiles as very accurate.

studies support the hypothesis that part of the client's high acceptance of favorably toned personality descriptions results from a belief that the interpretation is specifically derived for him or her (which is the case in actual clinical practice), and that individuals fail to realize that "their" interpretation is just as accurate for the general population. This finding is consistent with recent theory and research suggesting that in certain situations individuals prefer to be unique from others rather than similar to them (Fromkin, 1972; Snyder, 1977b).

Favorability of the Interpretation

Thorne (1961) hypothesized that a favorable interpretation should achieve greater acceptance than an unfavorable interpretation. He called this phenomenon the "Pollyanna effect." Indirect evidence of interpretations containing favorably worded statements being preferred by subjects was first offered by Sundberg (1955). According to two judges' evaluations, there were five times as many favorable as unfavorable statements in the most highly accepted interpretations in his study and twice as many unfavorable as favorable statements in the least accepted interpretations.

Mosher (1965) directly manipulated the favorability of the items in a personality interpretation that supposedly was derived from the results of subjects' projective tests. The first 13 statements were neutral items, and the remaining 24 items were randomly ordered favorable and unfavorable items. The favorable statements produced the most acceptance, the neutral statements were readily accepted but significantly less so than the favorable, and the unfavorable statements were much less readily accepted. In a similar study (Weisberg, 1970), subjects were administered a projective test and received an interpretation that was either favorable, unfavorable, or neutral in description. The degree of acceptance was highest for the positive interpretation and lowest for the unfavorable interpretation.

In a study by Dmitruk, Collins, and Clinger (1973), however, there was no difference in the acceptance of a favorably and of an unfavorably worded interpretation. The different interpretations used by Sundberg (1955), Mosher (1965), Weisberg (1970), and Dmitruk et al. (1973) make a comparison of the studies difficult. Furthermore, unlike the subject self-report measure used in prior acceptance research, Dmitruk et al. utilized judges' ratings of the subjects' subjective comments. Therefore, the dependent variable may not have been sensitive enough to detect differential acceptance as a function of favorability. This explanation is supported by two recent replications of the Dmitruk et al. study in which subjects were asked to self-report their acceptance (Collins et al. 1977; Snyder & Shenkel, 1976). Results from these two studies revealed that the favorable interpretation was accepted more than the unfavorable interpretation.

An important consideration that had been ignored in previous acceptance research is that when the favorability of an interpretation is changed, the relative base-rate truthfulness of those statements may also be altered. That is, the favorable as compared to the unfavorable interpretations may be seen as more accurate or truthful for people in general, and thereby should be seen as more accurate for any particular individual because of a higher base-rate truthfulness. To test this possibility, Snyder and Shenkel (1976) determined the base-rate truthfulness of the favorable and unfavorable interpretations by asking an initial group of people to rate how truthful the favorable and unfavorable interpretations were of people generally. The subjects indicated that the favorable interpretation was significantly more truthful of people in general than the unfavorable interpretation. In a second study (Snyder & Shenkel, 1976), a separate group of subjects responded regarding how accurate the favorable and unfavorable interpretations were regarding their personalities. When the acceptance ratings in this second study were analyzed by controlling for the degree of truthfulness related to the favorable and unfavorable interpretations in the first study, *no* significant acceptance effects were observed. Thus, this investigation raises serious questions for previous acceptance research that has examined the variable of favorability without regard to base-rate truthfulness for people in general. Differential acceptance has been attributed to the favorability of the interpretation, whereas the fact that the "favorable" interpretation was simply more accurate (higher base-rate validity for people in general) may have accounted for the Pollyanna effect results.

Type of Assessment Procedure

Richards and Merrens (1971) administered one of three assessment devices (Bernreuter, Life History Questionnaire, and abbreviated Rorschach) to three groups of college students who later received a generalized personality interpretation. Subjects were asked to rate the interpretation in terms of accuracy, depth, and efficiency. For the three questions asked of the three groups, 70% to 90% of the subjects rated the interpretation as either "excellent" or "good." The Rorschach group had a greater tendency to rate their interpretations as excellent than did either the questionnaire group or the Bernreuter group. The median score for the three ratings (accuracy, depth, efficiency) with the questionnaire and Bernreuter groups was good, whereas the median score for the Rorschach group on each of the ratings was excellent.

Snyder (1974a) also reported data from two separate studies that reveal differential acceptance of the same general personality interpretation as a function of assessment procedure. In the first study, students were given a projective technique, an interview, and an objective personality test. All subjects then received the same handwritten general personality description. Depending on the condition to which the student was randomly assigned, the student was told that the interpretation was derived either on the basis of the projective technique, objective test, interview data, or was told the interpretation was "generally true of people" (a "control" comparison condition). The second experiment was performed by the subjects from the first experiment after being informed that all of "their" interpretations were identical. Each student was randomly assigned to administer one of the four assessment conditions to one subject. For both studies the order of acceptance from highest to lowest was as follows: projective technique, interview, objective test, and control comparison condition.

In each of the aforementioned studies, subjects accepted the interpretation most highly in the projective technique condition. Richards and Merrens (1971) and Snyder (1974a) suggested that the obtained differences may depend in part on the amount of ambiguity in the test presented. The objective tests utilized in these studies may appear to be fairly transparent to the subjects, as well as being easily faked. The projective test, however, is much more difficult for the subject to understand. Thus, the mysteriousness of the interpretation may increase the validity of projective techniques. Furthermore, Snyder (1974a) hypothesized that the interview received higher acceptance than did the objective test because of the individuals' belief in the "intuitive" skills of the diagnostician; that is, some degree of mystery remains.

Recently, Snyder, Larsen, and Bloom (1976) examined the relative acceptance of general personality interpretations that were purportedly based on (a) psychological techniques, (b) graphological techniques, (c) astrological (horoscope) techniques, or (d) statements that were "generally true of people" (the "control" comparison condition). Their study then compared people's faith in these three popular "assessment" procedures. Male and female students served as experimenter diagnosticians. Each experimenter recruited four female subjects and randomly assigned each subject to one of the above four assessment procedure conditions. Results indicated that the order of acceptance from highest to lowest was as follows: psychological technique, graphological technique, astrological technique, and "control" comparison group. The assessment procedures (psychological, graphological, and astrological) were significantly more accepted than the "control" comparison group. There were no significant differences between assessment procedures, however, thus suggesting that these various popular assessment procedures used in our society do not elicit differential acceptance.

It should be noted that Snyder, Larsen, and Bloom (1976) used techniques that were ambiguous in nature: that is, there is a great deal of mystery surrounding projective tests, graphology, and astrology. Nevertheless, Snyder, Larsen, and Bloom (1976) reported that neither the subjects' self-reported contact with nor understanding of the various assessment procedures (psychological tests, horoscopes, graphology) correlated significantly with the acceptance of the personality interpretations. These latter self-report results, therefore, do not support the notion that the mysteriousness of the interpretation may increase subjects' acceptance. Further research is required to clarify what it is about projective techniques that results in greater clientele acceptance.

One potential hypothesis for the varying acceptance of assessment procedures is that clinical clientele perceive differential validity in the tests. Related to this point, Lattal and Lattal (1967) investigated the effect of a negative evaluation of a personality test on students' subsequent ratings of generalized personality interpretations. Students were administered the House-Tree-Person Test and received identical general personality interpretations. One group of subjects was told nothing about the validity of the test, whereas a second group was told that the test was a relatively invalid and questionable personality technique. No significant differences between the ratings of the interpretations for the two groups resulted. It should be noted that no manipulation check was included to insure that subjects who did not receive an evaluation of the House-Tree-Person Test viewed the test more positively than those subjects who received a negative evaluation of the test. Likewise, the favorable nature of the interpretation may have masked any potential effects of perceived test validity upon acceptance. That is, the perceived validity of the test may only begin to have effects on acceptance when the interpretation is unfavorable. These reservations are answered, however, in a subsequent study by Collins et al. (1977). These investigators examined the acceptance of a positively or negatively worded interpretation that was supposedly based on a legitimate test, the Taylor Manifest Anxiety Scale (TMAS), or a satirical personality test, the North Dakota Null Hypothesis Brain Inventory (NDNHBI), developed by the humorist Art Buchwald. (Examples taken from the true-false NDNHBI include: "I think beavers work too hard;" "I am never startled by fish"). Results showed no difference in acceptance between the TMAS and NDNHBI subjects for either the positively or negatively worded interpretations.

Another potential hypothesis is that a longer assessment procedure may be perceived as more thorough and thus may receive higher acceptance than an interpretation based on a *short* assessment procedure. Investigating this hypothesis, Merrens and Richards (1973) gave three separate groups of subjects personality inventories that were either long, intermediate, or short in length. Counterintuitively, results generally showed that the interpretation based upon the short inventory was most favorably evaluated in terms of efficiency, accuracy, and depth. Additionally, upon reviewing interpretations used in another study, Sundberg (1955) noticed that there was a tendency to accept the shorter *personality sketches*. (Unfortunately, no statistical analyses are reported.)

The above studies taken together suggest that although interpretations generated from any one of several different approaches are about equally accepted, among the various types of psychological assessment procedures, the projective technique elicits maximal acceptance. Surprisingly, the shorter the interpretation, and the shorter the assessment procedure from which the interpretation is purportedly derived, the greater the acceptance may be.

Test Administrator and Interpreter

Ulrich et al. (1963) examined whether the prestige of the experimenter was a factor related to acceptance. In the first of two experiments, an instructor administered personality tests to a group of students who later received identical personality interpretations. In the second experiment, the students were instructed to administer the same test to one acquaintance. Results indicated that the interpretations made by inexperienced students were as readily accepted as those made by the instructor. Similar findings have been reported by Snyder (1974a).

Rosen (1975) reported that although subjects indicated that they had more confidence in a psychologist than in an astrologer, the same subjects accepted a personality interpretation equally as high from either source.

Snyder and Larson (1972) studied a variable analogous to the prestige variable. This variable, setting, consisted of a clinician in his office at the university psychological and counseling center and a graduate student in the laboratory at the psychology department. In spite of the effort to maximize the difference in the settings, the results again revealed no differences in the acceptance of the general personality interpretation for subjects in the two clinical settings.

Dmitruk et al. (1973) included both a favorable and unfavorable personality interpretation in a study that examined the effect of clinician status on acceptance. They reported that subjects were equally willing to accept interpretations from either a psychologist or student. In addition, the subjects accepted the negative evaluation as readily as the positive evaluation. As mentioned previously, however, Dmitruk et al. may have used a measure of acceptance that was not sensitive enough to detect differential acceptance. Furthermore, in none of the previously mentioned studies investigating clinician status did the authors report a manipulation check of how the subjects perceived the status of the interpreter.

Halperin et al. (1976) reinvestigated possible intervention effects between favorability and status of the clinician in a more thoroughly controlled study. The authors noted that social psychology has found that the influence of a communicator's status is dependent upon the discrepancy of the message (degree to which it varies from the subject's own beliefs) such that the communicator's status is less influential if the discrepancy is slight (Aronson, Turner, & Carlsmith, 1963; Bochner & Insko, 1966). In an initial experiment, therefore, Halperin et al. empirically established that a negatively worded interpretation was less true of people in general than a positively worded interpretation. Then, either the positively-worded (low-discrepant) or negatively worded (high-discrepant) interpretation was returned to another sample of subjects by either a low- or high-status clinician. A manipulation check verified that subjects did perceive differential status between the presumed clinicians (interpreters). As hypothesized, the interaction between favorability and status revealed that the favorable interpretation (low discrepancy) was equally accepted regardless of the clinician's status, whereas the unfavorable interpretation (high discrepancy) was differentially accepted, such that the higher the status, the greater the acceptance. Thus, the Halperin et al. study provided the first evidence within the acceptance paradigm that the status of a clinician does influence the degree to which subjects accept clinical feedback. Since most clinicians probably have high status in the eyes of their clientele, these results indicate that clinicians may engender high clientele acceptance even when the feedback is rather negative (which is often the case in actual clinical practice).

Could the interpretation source affect acceptance of the subsequent interpretation? Snyder and Larson (1972) addressed this question by examining the degree to which students accepted the results of computer- as compared to human-interpreted personality tests. Results revealed no differences in the acceptance of the general personality interpretation as a function of the subject's being told that the test interpreter was a person or a computer. Thus, subjects appear to place a good deal of confidence in psychological tests regardless of the test interpreter. Interpretation source of the assessment procedure may, however, elicit differential acceptance if examined in the future in conjunction with the favorability of the interpretation.

In this section, factors in the clinical situation that affect acceptance of personality interpretations have been explored. Factors that emerged as being important in eliciting acceptance of the personality interpretation are that the interpretation is (a) general in nature with high base-rate characteristics, (b) presented to the person as being specifically derived for him, (c) comprised of favorably worded statements, and (d) based on short procedures—especially psychologically projective techniques. In the case of unfavorable interpretations, a high-status clinician may enhance subjects' acceptance. From these results, the clinician needs to realize that the acceptance of personality interpretations principally may result from situational factors rather than the validity of the interpretation for any particular client.

Implications of the Acceptance Phenomenon for the Clinical Diagnostic Process

Donald G. Paterson and Paul Meehl (1956) espoused the term *Barnum effect* to stigmatize those personality descriptions that are highly endorsed simply because of the population base rates. The present review has expanded the original Barnum effect definition to include a variety of factors that increase acceptance of a personality interpretation. Acceptance is enhanced by some factors that are inherent in the clinical situation: The interpretation is delivered as being (a) specifically developed for that particular client, (b) derived from the results of psychological assessment techniques, and (c) interpreted by a high-status clinician. Additionally, the interpretation is more likely to be favorably received if the feedback is brief, ambiguous, and does not effectively identify ways in which the client is different from the majority of the human population. Furthermore, subjects not only accept Barnum interpretations, but they also increase their faith in psychological tests and see the experimenter clinician as being more skilled as a result of receiving such feedback (Snyder, Larsen, and Bloom, 1976; Snyder & Shenkel, 1976). Finally, this acceptance phenomenon is amplified when one considers that the insecurity of a typical client in the actual clinical setting may render him or her even more acceptant to diagnostic feedback than the college subjects who served in the Barnum experiments.

Although the aforementioned characteristics associated with the Barnum effect enhance clientele acceptance of feedback, they do not serve the legitimate diagnostic function of identifying problems in order to recommend specific therapeutic interventions. Nor does the Barnum effect allow for an effective discrimination among broadly defined typological conditions such as neurotic, psychotic, or normal (Marks & Seeman, 1962).

Both field and laboratory research have offered evidence that clinicians are often more likely to *attribute* the source of a client's problem to personality-based factors as compared to situation-based factors (Batson, 1975; Carkhuff, 1968; Goffman, 1961; Snyder, 1977a; Snyder, Shenkel, & Schmidt, 1976). If clinicians do have an attributional bias of "seeing" clients' problems in terms of personality-based factors, then it follows that diagnosis generates *personality* feedback for the client. On the basis of the present review, clients may be expected to readily accept such personality feedback. Not surprisingly, then, clinicians are likely to be praised by their clientele. In no sense, however, can such praise be interpreted as "validation" of either the clinician's skill or assessment procedures (Snyder & Shenkel, 1975). One is aptly reminded of P. T. Barnum's alleged statement, "There's a sucker born every minute" (cited in Bartlett, 1968, p. 655). This especially may be true of clinicians who misinterpret clientele praise of personality feedback.

Reference Note

1. Blumenfeld, W. S., & Leveto, G. A. *Gullibility's travels: Or, they just do make them the way they used to.* Paper presented at the meeting of the Rocky Mountain Psychological Association, Denver, May 1974.

References

Aronson, E., Turner, J., & Carlsmith, J. M. Communication credibility and communication discrepancy as determinants of opinion change. *Journal of Abnormal and Social Psychology*, 1963, 67, 31–36.

Bachrach, A. J., & Pattishell, E. G. An experiment in universal and personal validation. *Psychiatry*, 1960, 23, 267–270.

Bartlett, J. *Familiar quotations* (14th ed.). Boston: Little, Brown, 1968.

Batson, C. D. Attribution as a mediator of bias in helping. *Journal of Personality and Social Psychology*, 1975, 32, 455–466.

Bochner, S., & Insko, C. Communicator discrepancy, source credibility, and opinion change. *Journal of Personality and Social Psychology*, 1966, 4, 612–614.

Carkhuff, R. R. The differential functioning of lay and professional helpers. *Journal of Counseling Psychology,* 1968, *15,* 417–426.

Carrier, N. A. Need correlates of "gullibility." *Journal of Abnormal and Social Psychology,* 1963, *66,* 84–86.

Collins, R. W., Dmitruk, V. M., & Ranney, J. T. Personal validation: Some empirical and ethical considerations. *Journal of Consulting and Clinical Psychology,* 1977, *45,* 70–77.

Couch, A., & Keniston, K. Yeasayers and naysayers: Agreeing response set as a personality variable. *Journal of Abnormal and Social Psychology,* 1960, *60,* 151–174.

Dana, R. H., & Graham, E. D. Feedback of client-relevant information and clinical practice. *Journal of Personality Assessment,* 1976, *40,* 464–469.

Dies, R. R. Personal gullibility or pseudodiagnosis: A further test of the "fallacy of personal validation." *Journal of Clinical Psychology,* 1972, *28,* 47–50.

Dmitruk, V. M., Collins, R. W., & Clinger, D. I. The "Barnum effect" and acceptance of negative personal evaluation. *Journal of Consulting and Clinical Psychology,* 1973, *41,* 192–194.

Ettinger, R., Marino, C., Endler, N., Geller, S., & Natziuk, T. Effects of agreement and correctness on relative competence and conformity. *Journal of Personality and Social Psychology,* 1971, *19,* 204–212.

Forer, B. R. The fallacy of personal validation: A classroom demonstration of gullibility. *Journal of Abnormal and Social Psychology,* 1949, *44,* 118–123.

Fraud in your future? *Newsweek,* September 14, 1964, 56.

Fromkin, H. L. Feelings of interpersonal undistinctiveness: An unpleasant affective state. *Journal of Experimental Research in Personality,* 1972, *6,* 178–185.

Gauquelin, M. *The scientific basis of astrology.* New York: Stein & Day, 1969.

Goffman, E. Asylums: *Essays on the social situation of mental patients and other inmates.* Garden City, N. Y.: Doubleday, 1961.

Gollob, H. , & Dittes, J. Different effects of manipulated self-esteem on persuasibility depending on the threat and complexity of the communication. *Journal of Personality and Social Psychology,* 1965, *2,* 195–201.

Halperin, K., Snyder, C. R., Shenkel, R. J., & Houston, B. K. Effects of source status and message favorability on acceptance of personality feedback. *Journal of Applied Psychology,* 1976, *61,* 85–88.

Hovland, C., & Janis, I. (Eds.) *Personality and persuasibility.* New Haven: Yale University Press, 1959.

Lattal, K. A., & Lattal, A. D. Student "gullibility": A systematic replication. *Journal of Psychology,* 1967, *67,* 319–322.

Manning, E. J. Personal validation: Replication of Forer's study. *Psychological Reports,* 1968, *23,* 181–182.

Marks, P. A., & Seeman, W. On the Barnum effect. *Psychological Record,* 1962, *12,* 203–208.

Meehl, P. E. Wanted—A good cookbook. *American Psychologist,* 1956, *11,* 262–272.

Merrens, M. R., & Richards, W. S. Acceptance of generalized versus "bona fide" personality interpretations. *Psychological Reports,* 1970, *27,* 691–694.

Merrens, M. R., & Richards, W. S. Length of personality inventory and the evaluation of a generalized personality interpretation. *Journal of Personality Assessment,* 1973, *37,* 83–85.

Mosher, D. L. Approval motive and acceptance of "fake" personality test interpretations which differ in favorability. *Psychological Reports,* 1965, *17,* 395–402.

O'Dell, J. W. P. T. Barnum explores the computer. *Journal of Consulting and Clinical Psychology,* 1972, *38,* 270–273.

Richards, W. S., & Merrens, M. R. Student evaluation of generalized personality interpretations as a function of method of assessment. *Journal of Clinical Psychology,* 1971, *27,* 457–459.

Rosen, G. M. Effects of source prestige on subjects' acceptance of the Barnum effect: Psychologist versus astrologer. *Journal of Consulting and Clinical Psychology,* 1975, *43,* 95.

Sechrest, L. , & Bryan, J. H. Astrologers as useful marriage counselors. *Trans-Action,* 1968, *6,* 34–36.

Snyder, C. R. Acceptance of personality interpretations as a function of assessment procedures. *Journal of Consulting and Clinical Psychology,* 1974, *42,* 150. (a)

Snyder, C. R. Why horoscopes are true: The effects of specificity on acceptance of astrological interpretations. *Journal of Clinical Psychology,* 1974, *30,* 577–580. (b)

Snyder, C. R. "A patient by any other name" revisited: Maladjustment or attributional locus of problem? *Journal of Consulting and Clinical Psychology,* 1977, *45,* 101–103.

Snyder, C. R. The "illusion" of uniqueness. *Journal of Humanistic Psychology,* 1977, in press. (b)

Snyder, C. R., Larsen, D., & Bloom, L. J. Acceptance of personality interpretations prior to and after receiving diagnostic feedback supposedly based on psychological, graphological, and astrological assessment procedures. *Journal of Clinical Psychology,* 1976, *32,* 258–265.

Snyder, C. R., & Larson, G. R. A further look at student acceptance of general personality interpretations. *Journal of Consulting and Clinical Psychology,* 1972, *38,* 384–388.

Snyder, C. R., & Shenkel, R. J. Astrologers, handwriting analysts, and sometimes psychologists use the P. T. Barnum effect. *Psychology Today,* March 1975, 52–54.

Snyder, C. R., & Shenkel, R. J. Effects of "favorability," modality, and relevance upon acceptance of general personality interpretations prior to and after receiving diagnostic feedback. *Journal of Consulting and Clinical Psychology,* 1976, *44,* 34–41.

Snyder, C. R., Shenkel, R. J., & Schmidt, A. Effects of role perspective and psychiatric history on diagnostic locus of problem. *Journal of Consulting and Clinical Psychology,* 1976, *44,* 467–472.

Stagner, R. The gullibility of personnel managers. *Personnel Psychology,* 1958, *11,* 347–352.

Sundberg, N. D. The acceptability of "fake" versus "bona fide" personality test interpretations. *Journal of Abnormal and Social Psychology*, 1955, *50*, 145–147.

Thorne, F. C. Clinical judgment: A study of clinical errors. Brandon, Vt. : *Journal of Clinical Psychology*, 1961.

Ulrich, R. E., Stachnik, T. J., & Stainton, N. R. Student acceptance of generalized personality interpretations. *Psychological Reports*, 1963, *13*, 831–843.

Weisberg, P. Student acceptance of bogus personality interpretations differing in level of social desirability. *Psychological Reports*, 1970, *27*, 743–746.

Ziv, A., & Nevenhaus, S. Acceptance of personality diagnoses and perceived uniqueness. *Abstract Guide of XXth International Congress of Psychology*, 1972, 605.

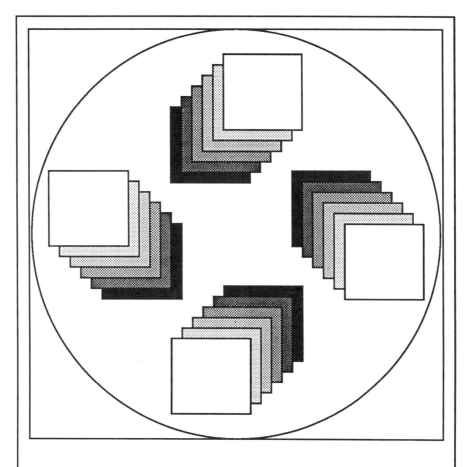

Chapter 12

The Nature of Abnormality

CHAPTER 12: THE NATURE OF ABNORMALITY

To the general public, all psychologists are "shrinks." Thus, at cocktail parties, all psychologists (regardless of their actual training and specialization) are either opportuned for advice ("Hey, you're a psychologist. Maybe you can explain why my boss dresses in a hen suit."), or regarded with great suspicion ("Stop looking at me that way. I know you're analyzing me."). This illustrates the point that "abnormal psychology," which deals with understanding the development and expression of abnormal behavior and its treatment, is the most widely recognized area of psychology. It is not surprising, then, that most students approach psychology because of their fascination with various behavioral problems and not because of an interest in, say, cognitive models of speech production. This chapter deals with issues relating to why some behaviors are considered abnormal. In many cases, how psychologists conceptualize abnormal behavior determines how the problem is diagnosed and treated. The articles by Szasz and Kety address this problem. Further, some new problems are discussed, such as bulimia, that demonstrate the result of unusual behavioral reactions to societal pressures (that is, the need to look thin). The Muuss article reviews this contemporary problem, and summarizes the recent research.

12a. Szasz, T. (1960). The myth of mental illness. *American Psychologist, 15*, 113–118.

12b. Muuss, R. (1986). Adolescent eating disorder: Bulimia. *Adolescence, 21*, 257–267.

One of Szasz's points is that our notion of abnormality is inextricably entwined with current societal values. How might societal values (for example, as expressed in peer pressure), precipitate bulimia? When would you consider a person to be bulimic rather than anorexic? What therapies would you suggest (after reading the Muuss selection) for such a person? Explain your choices.

12c. Kety, S. (1974). From rationalization to reason. *American Journal of Psychiatry, 131*, 957–963.

Both the Szasz and the Kety selections discuss the pitfalls of conventional definitions of mental illness. After reading them, what specific suggestions do you have concerning the operations of mental hospitals? Under what conditions should patients be admitted and released? Remember to cite Szasz's study and Kety's reply to support your points.

The Myth of Mental Illness

Thomas S. Szasz

My aim in this essay is to raise the question "Is there such a thing as mental illness?" and to argue that there is not. Since the notion of mental illness is extremely widely used nowadays, inquiry into the ways in which this term is employed would seem to be especially indicated. Mental illness, of course, is not literally a "thing"—or physical object—and hence it can "exist" only in the same sort of way in which other theoretical concepts exist. Yet, familiar theories are in the habit of posing, sooner or later—at least to those who come to believe in them—as "objective truths" (or "facts"). During certain historical periods, explanatory conceptions such as deities, witches, and microorganisms appeared not only as theories but as self-evident *causes* of a vast number of events. I submit that today mental illness is widely regarded in a somewhat similar fashion, that is, as the cause of innumerable diverse happenings. As an antidote to the complacent use of the notion of mental illness—whether as a self-evident phenomenon, theory, or cause—let us ask this question: What is meant when it is asserted that someone is mentally ill?

In what follows I shall describe briefly the main uses to which the concept of mental illness has been put. I shall argue that this notion has outlived whatever usefulness it might have had and that it now functions merely as a convenient myth.

Mental Illness as a Sign of Brain Disease

The notion of mental illness derives it main support from such phenomena as syphilis of the brain or delirious conditions—intoxications, for instance—in which persons are known to manifest various peculiarities or disorders of thinking and behavior. Correctly speaking, however, these are diseases of the brain, not of the mind. According to one school of thought, *all* so-called mental illness is of this type. The assumption is made that some neurological defect, perhaps a very subtle one, will ultimately be found for all the disorders of thinking and behavior. Many contemporary psychiatrists, physicians, and other scientists hold this view. This position implies that people *cannot* have troubles—expressed in what are *now called* "mental illnesses"—because of differences in personal needs, opinions, social aspirations, values, and so on. *All problems in living* are attributed to physicochemical processes which in due time will be discovered by medical research.

"Mental illnesses" are thus regarded as basically no different than all other diseases (that is, of the body). The only difference, in this view, between mental and bodily diseases is that the former, affecting the brain, manifest themselves by means of mental symptoms; whereas the latter, affecting other organ systems (for example, the skin, hair, etc.), manifest themselves by means of symptoms referable to those parts of the body. This view rests on and expresses what are, in my opinion, two fundamental errors.

In the first place, what central nervous system symptoms would correspond to a skin eruption or a fracture? It would *not* be some emotion or complex bit of behavior. Rather, it would be blindness or a paralysis of some part of the body. The crux of the matter is that a disease of the brain, analogous to a disease of the skin or bone, is a neurological defect, and not a problem in living. For example, a *defect* in a person's visual field may be satisfactorily explained by correlating it with certain definite lesions in the nervous system. On the other hand, a person's *belief* —whether this be a belief in Christianity, in Communism, or in the idea that his internal organs are "rotting" and that his body is, in fact, already "dead"—cannot be explained by a defect or disease of the nervous system. Explanations of this sort of occurrence—assuming that one is interested in the belief itself and does not regard it simply as a "symptom" or expression of something else that is *more interesting*— must be sought along different lines.

The second error in regarding complex psychosocial behavior, consisting of communications about ourselves and the world about us, as mere symptoms of neurological functioning is *epistemological*. In other words, it is an error pertaining not to any mistakes in observation or reasoning, as such, but rather to the way in which we organize and express our knowledge. In the present case, the error lies in making a symmetrical dualism between mental and physical (or bodily) symptoms, a dualism which is merely a habit of speech and to which no known observations can be found to correspond. Let us see if this is so. In medical practice, when we speak of physical disturbances, we mean either signs (for example, a fever) or symptoms (for example, pain). We speak of mental symptoms, on the other hand, when we refer to a patient's *communications about himself, others, and the world about him*. He might state that he is Napoleon or that he is being persecuted by the Communists. These would be considered mental symptoms only if the observer believed that the patient was *not* Napoleon or that he was *not* being persecuted by the Communists. This makes it apparent that the statement that "X is a mental symptom" involves rendering a judgment. The judgment entails, moreover, a covert comparison or matching of the patient's ideas, concepts, or beliefs with those of the observer and the society in which they live. The notion of mental symptom is therefore inextricably tied to the *social* (including *ethical*) *context* in which it is made in much the same way as the notion of bodily symptom is tied to an *anatomical* and *genetic context* (Szasz, 1957a, 1957b).

To sum up what has been said thus far: I have tried to show that for those who regard mental symptoms as signs of brain disease, the concept of mental illness is unnecessary and misleading. For what they mean is that people so labeled suffer from diseases of the brain; and, if that is what they mean, it would seem better for the sake of clarity to say that and not something else.

Mental Illness as a Name for Problems in Living

The term "mental illness" is widely used to describe something which is very different than a disease of the brain. Many people today take it for granted that living is an arduous process. Its hardship for modern man, moreover, derives not so much from a struggle for biological survival as from the stresses and strains inherent in the social intercourse of complex human personalities. In this context, the notion of mental illness is used to identify or describe some feature of an individual's so-called personality. Mental illness—as a deformity of the personality, so to speak—is then regarded as the *cause* of the human disharmony. It is implicit in this view that social intercourse between people is regarded as something *inherently harmonious*, its disturbance being due solely to the presence of "mental illness" in many people. This is obviously fallacious reasoning, for it makes the abstraction "mental illness" into a *cause*, even though this abstraction was created in the first place to serve only as a shorthand expression for certain types of human behavior. It now becomes necessary to ask: "What kinds of behavior are regarded as indicative of mental illness, and by whom?"

The concept of illness, whether bodily or mental, implies *deviation from some clearly defined norm*. In the case of physical illness, the norm is the structural and functional integrity of the human body. Thus, although the desirability of physical health, as such, is an ethical value, what health is can be stated in anatomical and physiological terms. What is the norm deviation from which is regarded as mental illness? This question cannot be easily answered. But whatever this norm might be, we can be certain of only one thing: namely, that it is a norm that must be stated in terms of *psychosocial, ethical, and legal* concepts. For example, notions such as "excessive repression" or "acting out an unconscious impulse" illustrate the use of psychological concepts for judging (so-called) mental health and illness. The idea that chronic hostility, vengefulness, or divorce are indicative of mental illness would be illustrations of the use of ethical norms (that is, the desirability of love, kindness, and a stable marriage relationship). Finally, the widespread psychiatric opinion that only a mentally ill person would commit homicide illustrates the use of a legal concept as a norm of mental health. The norm from which deviation is measured whenever one speaks of a mental illness is a *psychosocial and ethical one*. Yet, the remedy is sought in terms of *medical* measures which—it is hoped and assumed—are free from wide differences of ethical value. The definition of the disorder and the terms in which its remedy is sought are therefore at serious odds with one another. The practical significance of this covert conflict between the alleged nature of the defect and the remedy can hardly be exaggerated.

Having identified the norms used to measure deviations in cases of mental illness, we will now turn to the question: "Who defines the norms and hence the deviation?" Two basic answers may be offered: (*a*) It may be the person himself (that is, the patient) who decides that he deviates from a norm. For example, an artist may believe that he suffers from a work inhibition; and he may implement this conclusion by seeking help *for* himself from a psychotherapist. (*b*) It may be someone other than the patient who decides that the latter is deviant (for example, relatives, physicians, legal authorities, society generally, etc.). In such a case a psychiatrist may be hired by others to do something *to* the patient in order to correct the deviation.

These considerations underscore the importance of asking the question "Whose agent is the psychiatrist?" and of giving a candid answer to it (Szasz, 1956, 1958). The psychiatrist (psychologist or non-medical psychotherapist), it now develops, may be the agent of the patient, of the relatives, of the school, of the military services, of a business organization, of a court of law, and so forth. In speaking of the psychiatrist as the agent of these persons or organizations, it is not implied that his values concerning norms, or his ideas and aims concerning the proper nature of remedial action, need to coincide exactly with those of his employer. For example, a patient in individual psychotherapy may believe that his salvation lies in a new marriage; his psychotherapist need not share this hypothesis. As the patient's agent, however, he must abstain from bringing social or legal force to bear on the patient which would prevent him from putting his beliefs into action. If his *contract* is with the patient, the psychiatrist (psychotherapist) may disagree with him or stop his treatment; but he cannot engage others to obstruct the patient's aspirations. Similarly, if a psychiatrist is engaged by a court to determine the sanity of a criminal, he need not fully share the legal authorities' values and intentions in regard to the criminal and the means available for dealing with him. But the psychiatrist is expressly banned from stating, for example, that R is not the criminal who is "insane" but the men who wrote the law on the basis of which the very actions that are being judged are regarded as "criminal." Such an opinion could be voiced, of course, but not in a courtroom, and not by a psychiatrist who makes it his practice to assist the court in performing its daily work.

To recapitulate: In actual contemporary social usage, the finding of a mental illness is made by establishing a deviance in behavior from certain psychosocial, ethical, or legal norms. The judgment may be made, as in medicine, by the patient, the physician (psychiatrist), or others. Remedial action, finally, tends to be sought in a therapeutic— or covertly medical—framework, thus creating a situation in which *psychosocial, ethical,* and/or *legal deviations* are claimed to be correctible by (so-called) *medical action*. Since medical action is designed to correct only medical deviations, it seems logically absurd to expect that it will help solve problems whose very existence had been defined and established on non-medical grounds. I think that these considerations may be fruitfully applied to the present use of tranquilizers and, more generally, to what might be expected of drugs of whatever type in regard to the amelioration or solution of problems in human living.

The Role of Ethics in Psychiatry

Anything that people *do*—in contrast to things that *happen* to them (Peters, 1958)—takes place in a context of value. In this broad sense, no human activity is devoid of ethical implications. When the values underlying certain activities are widely shared, those who participate in their pursuit may lose sight of them altogether. The discipline of medicine, both as a pure science (for example, research) and as a technology (for example, therapy), contains many ethical considerations and judgments. Unfortunately, these are often denied, minimized, or merely kept out of focus; for the ideal of the medical profession as well as of the people whom it serves seems to be having a system of medicine (allegedly) free of ethical value. This sentimental notion is expressed by such things as the doctor's willingness to treat and help patients irrespective of their religious or political beliefs, whether they are rich or poor, etc. While there may be some grounds for this belief—albeit it is a view that is not impressively true even in these regards—the fact remains that ethical considerations encompass a vast range of human affairs. By making the practice of medicine neutral in regard to some specific issues of value need not, and cannot, mean that it can be kept free from all such values. The practice of medicine is intimately tied to ethics; and the first thing that we must do, it seems to me, is to try to make this clear and explicit. I should let this matter rest here, for it does not concern us specifically in this essay. Lest there be any vagueness, however, about how or where ethics and medicine meet, let me remind the reader of such issues as birth control, abortion, suicide, and euthanasia as only a few of the major areas of current ethicomedical controversy.

Psychiatry, I submit, is very much more intimately tied to problems of ethics than is medicine. I use the word "psychiatry" here to refer to that contemporary discipline which is concerned with *problems in living* (and not with diseases of the brain, which are problems for neurology). Problems in human relations can be analyzed, interpreted, and given meaning only within given social and ethical contexts. Accordingly, it *does* make a difference—arguments to the contrary notwithstanding—what the psychiatrist's socioethical orientations happen to be; for these will influence his ideas on what is wrong with the patient, what deserves comment or interpretation, in what possible directions change might be desirable, and so forth. Even in medicine proper, these factors play a role, as for instance, in the divergent orientations which physicians, depending on their religious affiliations, have toward such things as birth control and therapeutic abortion. Can anyone really believe that a psychotherapist's ideas concerning religious belief, slavery, or other similar issues play no role in his practical work? If they do make a difference, what are we to infer from it? Does it not seem reasonable that we ought to have different psychiatric therapies—each expressly recognized for the ethical positions which they embody—for, say, Catholics and Jews, religious persons and agnostics, democrats and communists, white supremacists and Negroes, and so on? Indeed, if we look at how psychiatry is actually practiced today (especially in the United States), we find that people do seek psychiatric help in accordance with their social status and ethical beliefs (Hollingshead & Redlich, 1958). This should really not surprise us more than being told that practicing Catholics rarely frequent birth control clinics.

The foregoing position which holds that contemporary psychotherapists deal with problems in living, rather than with mental illnesses and their cures, stands in opposition to a currently prevalent claim according to which mental illness is just as "real" and "objective" as bodily illness. This is a confusing claim since it is never known exactly what is meant by such words as "real" and "objective." I suspect, however, that what is intended by the proponents of this view is to create the idea in the popular mind that mental illness is some sort of disease entity, like an infection or a malignancy. If this were true, one could *catch* or *get* a "mental illness," one might *have* or *harbor* it, one might *transmit* it to others, and finally one could get *rid* of it. In my opinion, there is not a shred of evidence to support this idea. To the contrary, all the evidence is the other way and supports the view that what people now call mental illnesses are for the most part *communications* expressing unacceptable ideas, often framed, moreover, in an unusual idiom. The scope of this essay allows me to do no more than mention this alternative theoretical approach to this problem (Szasz, 1957c).

This is not the place to consider in detail the similarities and differences between bodily and mental illnesses. It shall suffice for us here to emphasize only one important difference between them: namely, that whereas bodily disease refers to public, physicochemical occurrences, the notion of mental illness is used to codify relatively more private, sociopsychological happenings of which the observer (diagnostician) forms a part. In other words, the psychiatrist does not stand *apart* from what he observes, but is, in Harry Stack Sullivan's apt words, a "participant observer." This means that he is *committed* to some picture of what he considers reality—and to what he thinks society considers reality—and he observes and judges the patient's behavior in the light of these considerations. This touches on our earlier observation that the notion of mental symptom itself implies a comparison between observer and observed, psychiatrist and patient. This is so obvious that I may be charged with belaboring trivialities. Let me therefore say once more that my aim in presenting this argument was expressly to criticize and counter a prevailing contemporary tendency to deny the moral aspects of psychiatry (and psychotherapy) and to substitute for them allegedly value-free medical considerations. Psychotherapy, for example, is being widely practiced as though it entailed nothing other than restoring the patient from a state of mental illness to one of mental health. While it is generally accepted that mental illness has something to do with man's social (or interpersonal) relations, it is paradoxically maintained that problems of values (that is, of ethics) do not arise in this process.[1] Yet, in one sense, much of psychotherapy may revolve around nothing other than the elucidation and weighing of goals and values—many of which may be mutually contradictory—and the means whereby they might best be harmonized, realized, or relinquished.

The diversity of human values and the methods by means of which they may be realized is so vast, and many of them remain so unacknowledged, that they cannot fail but lead to conflicts in human relations. Indeed, to say that human relations at all levels—from mother to child, through husband and wife, to nation and nation—are fraught with stress, strain, and disharmony is, once again, making the obvious explicit. Yet, what may be obvious may be also poorly understood. This I think is the case here. For it seems to me that—at least in our scientific theories of behavior—we have failed to *accept* the simple fact that human relations are inherently fraught with difficulties and that to make them even relatively harmonious requires much patience and hard work. I submit that the idea of mental illness is now being put to work to obscure certain difficulties which at present may be inherent—not that they need be unmodifiable—in the social intercourse of persons. If this is true, the concept functions as a disguise; for instead of calling attention to conflicting human needs, aspirations, and values, the notion of mental illness provides an amoral and impersonal "thing" (an "illness") as an explanation for *problems in living* (Szasz, 1959). We may recall in this connection that not so long ago it was devils and witches who were held responsible for men's problems in social living. The belief in mental illness, as something other than man's trouble in getting along with his fellow man, is the proper heir to the belief in demonology and witchcraft. Mental illness exists or is "real" in exactly the same sense in which witches existed or were "real."

Choice, Responsibility, and Psychiatry

While I have argued that mental illnesses do not exist, I obviously did not imply that the social and psychological occurrences to which this label is currently being attached also do not exist. Like the personal and social troubles which people had in the Middle Ages, they are real enough. It is the labels we give them that concerns us and, having labelled them, what we do about them. While I cannot go into the ramified implications of this problem here, it is worth noting that a demonologic conception of problems in living gave rise to therapy

---

[1] Freud went so far as to say that: "I consider ethics to be taken for granted. Actually I have never done a mean thing." (Jones, 1957, p. 247). This surely is a strange thing to say for someone who has studied man as a social being as closely as did Freud. I mention it here to show how the notion of "illness" (in the case of psychoanalysis, "psychopathology," or "mental illness") as used by Freud—and by most of his followers—as a means for classifying certain forms of human behavior as falling within the scope of medicine, and hence (by *fiat*) outside that of ethics!

along theological lines. Today, a belief in mental illness implies—nay, requires—therapy along medical or psychotherapeutic lines.

What is implied in the line of thought set forth here is something quite different. I do not intend to offer a new conception of "psychiatric illness" nor a new form of "therapy." My aim is more modest and yet also more ambitious. It is to suggest that the phenomena now called mental illnesses be looked at afresh and more sharply, that they be removed from the category of illnesses, and that they be regarded as the expressions of man's struggle with the problem of *how* he should live. The last mentioned problem is obviously a vast one, its enormity reflecting not only man's inability to cope with his environment, but even more his increasing self-reflectiveness.

By problems in living, then, I refer to that truly explosive chain reaction which began with man's fall from divine grace by partaking of the fruit of the tree of knowledge. Man's awareness of himself and of the world about him seems to be a steadily expanding one, bringing in its wake an ever larger *burden of understanding* (an expression borrowed from Susanne Langer, 1953). *This burden, then, is to be expected and must not be misinterpreted.* Our only rational means for lightening it is more understanding, and appropriate *action* based on such understanding. The main alternative lies in acting as though the burden were not what in fact we perceive it to be and taking refuge in an outmoded theological view of man. In the latter view, man does not fashion his life and much of his world about him, but merely lives out his fate in a world created by superior beings. This may logically lead to pleading nonresponsibility in the face of seemingly unfathomable problems and difficulties. Yet, if man fails to take increasing responsibility for his actions, individually as well as collectively, it seems unlikely that some higher power or being would assume this task and carry this burden for him. Moreover, this seems hardly the proper time in human history for obscuring the issue of man's responsibility for his actions by hiding it behind the skirt of an all-explaining conception of mental illness.

Conclusions

I have tried to show that the notion of mental illness has outlived whatever usefulness it might have had and that it now functions merely as a convenient myth. As such, it is a true heir to religious myths in general, and to the belief in witchcraft in particular; the role of all these belief-systems was to act as *social tranquilizers,* thus encouraging the hope that mastery of certain specific problems may be achieved by means of substitutive (symbolic-magical) operations. The notion of mental illness thus serves mainly to obscure the everyday fact that life for most people is a continuous struggle, not for biological survival, but for a "place in the sun," "peace of mind," or some other human value. For man aware of himself and of the world about him, once the needs for preserving the body (and perhaps the race) are more or less satisfied, the problem arises as to what he should do with himself. Sustained adherence to the myth of mental illness allows people to avoid facing this problem, believing that mental health, conceived as the absence of mental illness, automatically insures the making of right and safe choices in one's conduct of life. But the facts are all the other way. It is the making of good choices in life that others regard, retrospectively, as good mental health!

The myth of mental illness encourages us, moreover, to believe in its logical corollary: that social intercourse would be harmonious, satisfying, and the secure basis of a "good life" were it not for the disrupting influences of mental illness or "psychopathology." The potentiality for universal human happiness, in this form at least, seems to me but another example of the I-wish-it-were-true type of fantasy. I do not believe that human happiness or well-being on a hitherto unimaginably large scale, and not just for a select few, is possible. This goal could be achieved, however, only at the cost of many men, and not just a few being willing and able to tackle their personal, social, and ethical conflicts. This means having the courage and integrity to forego waging battles on false fronts, finding solutions for substitute problems—for instance fighting the battle of stomach acid and chronic fatigue instead of facing up to a marital conflict.

Our adversaries are not demons, witches, fate, or mental illness. We have no enemy whom we can fight, exorcise, or dispel by "cure." What we do have are *problems in living*—whether these be biologic, economic, political, or sociopsychological. In this essay I was concerned only with problems belonging in the last mentioned category, and within this group mainly with those pertaining to moral values. The field to which modern psychiatry addresses itself is vast, and I made no effort to encompass it all. My argument was limited to the proposition that mental illness is a myth, whose function it is to disguise and thus render more palatable the bitter pill of moral conflicts in human relations.

References

Hollingshead, A. B., & Redlich, F. C. *Social class and mental illness.* New York: Wiley, 1958.

Jones, E. *The life and work of Sigmund Freud.* Vol. III. New York: Basic Books, 1957.

Langer, S. K. *Philosophy in a new key.* New York: Mentor Books, 1953.

Peters, R. S. *The concept of motivation.* London: Routledge & Kegan Paul, 1958.

Szasz, T. S. Malingering: "Diagnosis" or social condemnation? *AMA Arch. Neurol. Psychiat.*, 1956, *76*, 432–443.

Szasz, T. S. *Pain and pleasure: A study of bodily feelings.* New York: Basic Books, 1957. (a)

Szasz, T. S. The problem of psychiatric nosology: A contribution to a situational analysis of psychiatric operations. *Amer. J. Psychiat.*, 1957, *114*, 405–413. (b)

Szasz, T. S. On the theory of psychoanalytic treatment. *Int.. J. Psycho-Anal.*, 1957, *38*, 166–182. (c)

Szasz, T. S. Psychiatry, ethics and the criminal law. *Columbia Law Rev.*, 1958, *58*, 193–198.

Szasz, T. S. Moral conflict and psychiatry, *Yale Rev.*, 1959, in press.

Adolescent Eating Disorder: Bulimia

Rolf E. Muuss

ABSTRACT

Bulimia, an eating disorder, recently has emerged as a major mental health problem, especially among adolescent females. The bulimic experiences periods of compulsive binge eating followed by purges to rid the body of unwanted calories. Binges are triggered by intense emotional experiences, such as loneliness, anger, rejection, or stress. Associated features of bulimia are secretiveness, depression, drug abuse, preoccupation with body image and sexual attractiveness, and an awareness that the behavior is abnormal. The physical side effects include dental problems, inflamed esophagus, EEG abnormalities, abdominal or urinary disturbances, and changes in blood sugar level. Cognitive disturbances related to binging and purging are perfectionistic, egocentric, and distorted thinking, misconceptions about nutritional requirements, unreasonable goals and expectations, and disturbed affect. Bulimics resist treatment; however, such methods as cognitive, group, family, behavior, and drug therapy, and hospitalization appear promising.

Bulimia is a Greek word meaning "ox" and "hunger." The disorder was so named because the sufferer eats like a hungry ox, that is, the bulimic indulges in unrestrained eating sprees. During the past decade bulimia has increased dramatically. Some experts claim that it has reached epidemic proportions, especially on college campuses. Bulimia only recently has been recognized as a serious, separate medical and psychological problem, and is listed for the first time in DSM-III. Much is still unknown about the disorder.

Characteristics of Bulimia

A characteristic of bulimia is binge eating. A binge is a period of eating large quantities of food rapidly. It is a gorging process—done usually in secret—that can go on for hours. The bulimic consumes 1,000 to 10,000 or more calories at a time. Often the binge is a response to an intense emotional experience, such as stress, loneliness, depression, or rage, rather than the result of a strong appetite. At the end of the binge the bulimic may feel bloated, nauseated, and physically sick.

The binge is followed by episodes of purging. The fear of keeping a great amount of unwanted calories in the body leads to attempts at rapidly undoing the effects of the binge. The purge may be accompanied by such methods as vomiting, laxatives, diuretics, enemas, compulsive exercising, weight-reducing drugs (e.g., amphetamines), as well as intermittent periods of strict dieting. Eventually, a pattern of alternating periods of fasting and binging-purging develops, which becomes compulsive.

Neuman and Halvorson (1983) and DSM-III (American Psychiatric Association, 1980) list characteristics that are important in identifying the victim of bulimia:

1. Excessive concern with weight gain, and body image.
2. Periods of dieting followed by eating binges.
3. Frequent overeating, especially when distressed.
4. Planning binges or opportunities to binge.
5. Binging on high-caloric, easily ingested, and often sweet foods.
6. Feeling out of control in regard to eating patterns.
7. Guilt or shame following binge-purge episodes.
8. Secretiveness about binges and purges.
9. Awareness that the eating pattern is abnormal.
10. Disappearing after a meal for the purpose of purging.
11. Self-deprecating thoughts and feelings of hopelessness and depression.
12. Resistance to seeking professional help and sabotaging treatment.

Age, Frequency, and Demographics: Bulimia usually begins between the ages of 15 and 18 (Pyle, Mitchell, & Eckert, 1981). Unlike anorexia nervosa, which is more common during early and middle adolescence, the onset of bulimia typically occurs in late adolescence, most frequently at age 18. Bulimia is predominantly a middle- or upper-class white female disorder. It is much more common in affluent, industrialized societies than in developing countries.

Different figures regarding the frequency of bulimia among adolescent females have been reported. On the low side, it has been estimated that at least 5% of college students show occasional bulimic eating patterns. However, Schwartz, Thompson, and Johnson (1985) estimate that 15% to 20% of college women have bulimia or exhibit some bulimic behavior patterns. On the high side, an investigation at the University of Pennsylvania reported that 40% of the female population experienced at least one bulimic episode. At the University of Ohio, 20% of the female students admitted to having at least one bulimic experience, such as gorging and vomiting. The National Association of Anorexia Nervosa and Associated Disorders estimates that over 20% of college women are involved in bulimic behavior.

It must be pointed out that great variations exist in the degree of severity of the disorder, which may explain the differences in the above statistics. Some persons binge and purge occasionally, while for others it becomes an obsession, having many of the characteristics of addictive behavior. Regardless of severity, without treatment the condition tends to become progressively more severe.

Bulimia also occurs in men, but with much lower frequency. Only 5% to 10% of all bulimics are males. The preponderance of female bulimics seems to indicate social causes similar to those for anorexia nervosa (Muuss, 1985). Young, male athletes are most vulnerable, especially those for whom weight is an important factor. In particular, wrestlers are prone to indulge in purging episodes to meet weight requirements before a match.

Bulimarexia

Bulimia is both closely related to and distinct from anorexia nervosa. Bulimia has been referred to as the sister ailment of anorexia, and both disorders share some symptoms and characteristics. The ultimate goal of the anorexic is to lose weight; the aim of the bulimic is to eat without gaining weight.

Some patients move from one disorder to the other. This overlapping condition is sometimes referred to as "bulimarexia." Bulimarexia is characterized by both bulimic eating binges and prolonged periods of anorexic self-starvation. Most bulimarexics start out being anorexic and progress to bulimia; the move from bulimia to anorexia is rare.

Factors Triggering Bulimic Episodes

Binging may follow intense emotional experiences and can emerge as the way of coping with loneliness, anger, depression, or aggression. It commonly starts after an unhappy experience, such as academic or vocational failure, or interpersonal problems. Real or imagined rejection by a male frequently triggers the first binge. During exam time on college campuses, the frequency of binging and purging increases greatly. Binging becomes a symbolic escape from the pressures of life.

In a general sense, bulimia frequently starts as more or less normal voluntary dieting behavior, which later becomes compulsive, uncontrollable, and pathological. An awareness of the uncontrollability of the behavior causes some bingers to seek psychiatric or medical help.

The binge itself may continue unabated for hours and stop only when all available food has been consumed or because of abdominal pain and physical discomfort. Toward the end of the episode, the bulimic feels exhausted.

Vomiting after the binge brings a sense of relief and euphoria. The vomiting episode is sometimes described by the patient in sexual terms, ascribing to it an orgasmic quality: "After vomiting I feel a pleasant release, a warm calmness, a sense of total relaxation and tiredness." However, the initial euphoria is quickly replaced by disgust, guilt, shame, and self-condemnation; for example: "My god, I have done it again, even though I resolved never to do it again. I am worthless," or "I hate myself. I have no control. I'm desperate." Later the binge-purge is followed by more fundamental feelings of hopelessness and depression, and suicidal ideation is not uncommon.

Bulimic Eating Patterns

The foods consumed during the binge are usually high in calories, sweet tasting, and can be eaten rapidly and swallowed easily, such as ice cream, candy, cookies, bread and cheese. Ice cream is preferred because it still tastes good when vomited. When on a binge, bulimics will eat almost anything that is available, including cake mixes and other unprepared foods. It is not a feast, which requires carefully prepared dishes, but a rapid gulping down of enormous quantities of food, often without chewing them properly. The consumption of these masses of food is not a pleasurable pastime, but a compulsion; after the first couple of bites there is very little appreciation for the taste. Binging usually takes place indiscriminately, in secret, alone, and hurriedly.

An account by Mary, a 21-year-old bulimic, reveals the obsessive nature of and loss of control involved in a typical binge.

> It would start to build in the late morning. By noon, I'd know that I had to binge. I would go out . . . and buy a gallon . . . of maple walnut ice cream and a couple of packages of fudge brownie mix—enough to make 72 brownies. . . . On the way home I invariably finished 12 doughnuts. . . . I'd hastily mix up the brownies and get them in the oven. . . . Then, while they were cooking, I'd hit the ice cream. . . . Sometimes I'd finish the whole gallon even before the brownies were done, and I'd take the brownies out of the oven while they were still baking. . . . Seventy-two brownies later, the depression would begin to hit (Chance, 1984).

In extreme cases, bulimics spend as much as $70 to $100 on food, in anticipation of one binge. This may cause financial difficulties or sometimes put them into debt. In some instances, they will steal to support their binges. Some plan their binges in terms of both food purchases and a time when nobody is around. Because of the compulsive nature of the disorder, any interference with the binge plan may be upsetting and arouse anger.

The preparation for the binge and the actual gorging may take priority over everything else, leaving little time and energy for other activities. Bulimic students may have insufficient time for studying, forcing some eventually to drop out of school.

Statistics on binging behavior include:

Binging time: from 15 minutes to 8 hours; average is 1.18 hours.
Frequency: from 1 to 48 episodes per week; average is 12 per week.
Hours per week: from 1 to 43 hours; average is 14 hours.
Calories per binge: from 1,200 to 11,500 and, in extreme cases, up to 30,000; average is 3,500.

A case study of a student's binge-purge behavior shows the compulsive nature of the disorder, the quantities of foods consumed, and the preoccupation with the binge (R. E. Muuss, personal communication).

> The first vomiting period perpetuated itself into a five-year-long habit in which I had daily planned and unplanned binges and self-induced vomiting sessions up to four times daily. I frequently vomited each of the day's three meals as well as my afternoon "snack" of three or four hamburgers, four to five

enormous bowls of ice cream, dozens of cookies, bags of various potato chips, packs of Swiss cheese, two large helpings of french fries, at least two milkshakes, and to top it off, an apple or a banana followed by two or more pints of cold milk to help me vomit more easily.

During the night, I sneaked back into the kitchen in the dark so I would not risk awakening any family member by turning on a light. . . . Every night I wished that I could, like everyone else, eat one apple as a midnight snack and then stop. However, every night I failed, but continuously succeeded in consuming countless bowls of various cereals, ice cream sundaes, peanut butter and jelly sandwiches, bananas, potato chips, Triscuits, peanuts, Oreos, orange juice and chocolate chip cookies. Then I tiptoed to the bathroom to empty myself. Sometimes the food would not come up as quickly as I wanted; so, in panic, I rammed my fingers wildly down my throat, occasionally making it bleed from cutting it with my fingernails. Sometimes I would spend two hours in the bathroom trying to vomit, yet there were other nights when the food came up in less than three minutes. I always felt immensely relieved and temporarily peaceful after I had thrown up. There was a symbolic sense of emptying out the anxiety, loneliness, and depression inside of me, as well as a sense of rebellion to hurt my body, to throw up on the people who hurt me, so to speak.

Associated Medical Features

Prolonged bulimic eating patterns can produce a variety of health problems, depending in part on the purging method. There are several physical side effects. Frequent and repeated vomiting can lead to erosion of the enamel of the teeth, which can contribute to various dental problems; inflamed esophagus, including tears in the esophagus and hiatal hernia; cardiac arrhythmia; EEG abnormalities; and sore throats. Laxative and diuretic abuse contributes to impairment of the natural evacuation process and damage to the colon, urinary infection, impairment of kidney functions, and chronic indigestion. Other medical problems include: bloodshot eyes, facial puffiness, swollen glands, and overexpanded and possibly ruptured stomach. Dramatic changes in blood sugar level can result from binging on sugary foods.

Associated Personality Features

A number of behavior and personality patterns are associated with bulimia. Bulimics tend to be perfectionists, high achievers, and are often academically or vocationally successful. Their predominant fear is not so much one of getting fat, but of being unable to keep eating voluntarily. In other words, the greatest fear is losing control.

Experiencing loss of control leads to lowered self-esteem and sometimes self-hate.

Depression sometimes becomes the presenting symptom for which women seek help; however, some patients experience depressive episodes long before the onset of the eating disorder. In general, bulimics have a very low opinion of themselves and the final outcome of the binge-purge episode is shame, guilt, and depression.

Bulimics frequently show a great deal of egocentric concern with what others think. Their concern with how others perceive them may develop into a belief that others are watching them constantly. The underlying dynamic is a great need to please others, and they may manifest the "good little girl" syndrome, becoming submissive and dependent.

As a result of the binge-purge cycle, bulimic adolescent females look surprisingly normal—neither too thin nor too heavy. They rarely look as thin and emaciated as the anorexic and usually cannot be identified by their physical appearance. Their weight may fluctuate drastically over a short period of time—by as much as 10 to 20 pounds—because of the binge-purge cycle. In extreme cases, weight fluctuates between 80 and 120 pounds. Often, bulimics are attractive; however, they do not perceive themselves as such and show an undue preoccupation with appearance and body image. They have bad feelings about their body and incorrectly evaluate themselves as unattractive and fat. They are extremely concerned with sexual attractiveness, and have an underlying fear of rejection by the opposite sex.

The binge itself is surrounded by a great deal of secretiveness. Bulimics are "closet eaters," whose eating patterns are known by nobody else. Often parents and husbands of bulimics are not aware of their loved one's condition. The bulimics' secretiveness leads to dishonesty, even in primary interpersonal relationships, which precludes referral to mental health professionals.

Nourishment becomes a substitute for tenderness, affection, love, sex, happiness, fulfillment and secret wishes—that is, those things which the bulimic feels life owes her, but which are not forthcoming. Bulimics do not socialize and often have no friends; their preoccupation with food may be a way of shutting out loneliness. Their relationships with others often are superficial, lacking genuine intimacy. Nevertheless, bulimics tend to be more extroverted than anorexics. Their underlying fear is: "If other people get to know me, they won't like me." Low self-esteem prevents them from interacting with other people.

Twenty-five to 40% of those suffering from bulimia use alcohol, marijuana, amphetamines or barbiturates, substances which tend to lower self-control and reduce willpower to stay on a diet. The use of these substances may provide relief from the feelings of guilt and depression that follow the binge-purge, yet ironically also may set off another episode.

Cognitive Deficiencies of the Bulimic

Most bulimic women experience cognitive distortions related to food, weight-loss expectations, eating, and dieting, which in turn influence their thinking in other areas. Correcting this irrational belief system is an essential step toward changing bulimic behavior. The following are common cognitive distortions.

Inaccurate nutritional information: (Loro, 1982). In general, bulimics are not adequately informed as to the requirements for a nutritional, well-balanced diet. They do not understand its importance and often totally eliminate some foods from their diet which they believe to be fattening, e.g., bread, chocolate, potatoes, butter, and meats. They follow one-sided or bizarre dietary guidelines. Often, they jump from one diet fad to another, and may possess a small library of diet books.

Unreasonable, distorted expectations about food and weight reduction: (Loro, 1982). Bulimics hold distorted or incorrect beliefs about foods and eating, i.e., they do not realize that a calorie is a calorie regardless of whether it comes from protein, carbohydrates, or fat. Instead, they may have unrealistic expectations about the "miraculous" benefits of eating large amounts of protein and avoiding carbohydrates. They categorize food as "bad" (cakes, sweets) and as "good" (lettuce, carrots, celery).

Unrealistic goal-setting and adherence to narrowly defined standards: (Loro, 1982). Many bulimics take a restrictive approach to eating. They keep long lists of "forbidden" foods such as ice cream, cookies, chocolate, steak, pizza—often the very foods they especially like. They begin by totally, stoically denying themselves any of these foods. As they deny themselves these items, they experience an increasingly stronger craving for them, which leads to anger and resentment. As feelings of deprivation increase, these foods appear more and more enticing. Eventually, usually under the influence of alcohol, marijuana, or other drugs, or because of anger, depression, stress, or frustration, they break down and consume these foods, not in moderation but in large quantities. The binge leads to a purging episode, which is experienced as failure, triggering guilt feelings, self-condemnation, and often additional binge-purging cycles.

Perfectionistic thinking: (Burns, 1980; Loro, 1982). Bulimics establish rigidly high standards for themselves in terms of dieting or their weight-loss goal, which they want to achieve usually in a short period of time. However, their goals are often beyond reach and reason, making failure inevitable. Furthermore, they perceive even a slight deviation from the weight-loss regimen as a devastating failure; for example: "If I deviated by as much as one slice of bread from my diet, I would have to eat a bag of cookies, two boxes of doughnuts, several candy bars, two bags of English muffins with jam, you name it. Afterwards I vomit." The bulimic is unable to accept a minor transgression for what it is, instead perceiving it as a catastrophe. By having perfectionistic expectations that are impossible to attain, bulimics continuously set themselves up for failure, disappointment, and self-castigation.

All-or-none reasoning (dichotomous thinking): (Burns, 1980; Loro, 1982). Binge eaters tend to think along all-or-none, black/white, yes/no lines. Thoughts and actions tend to be extreme, as in the case of the person above where eating one slice of bread too many led to another binge. Typical of all-or-none reasoning are such statements as, "If I gain any weight, I will be fat," or "If I weigh over 100 pounds, nobody will like me," or "If I can't stick with my diet, I am a total failure." Dichotomous thinking increases the fear of failure and the tendency to overreact when it does occur. Dichotomous thinking also manifests itself when bulimics label foods as "moral" (vegetables, cottage cheese) or "immoral" (ice cream, cookies, steak, pizza). Even in their approach to physical exercise, bulimics either push themselves to the point of exhaustion or do not make any effort at all. They rarely find a workable middle position, and need to learn that moderation is acceptable.

Egocentric view of the world (personalization): (Garner, Garfinkel, & Bemis, 1982). A prevalent belief of bulimics, and also common among adolescents (Muuss, 1982), is that everybody is watching them and can know their thoughts. They become preoccupied with what they believe others think of them and fear that the binge-purge cycle, or any other aspect of their eating behavior, will be discovered. For example: "Two people laughed and whispered something to each other when I walked by. They were probably saying that I looked unattractive. I have gained three pounds" (Garner et al., 1982, p. 16). For the bulimic, self-worth is dependent on the achievement of weight-loss goals and on the opinions of others. The bulimic must learn to "decenter" her thinking (Inhelder & Piaget 1958) and apply the same standards to herself that she applies to others. Her feelings toward others do not depend on their gaining or losing a couple of pounds, and she must learn that the same is true for herself.

Unfounded beliefs and superstitions: (Garner et al., 1982). Bulimics have a particularly strong need for social recognition. They try to please others and are excessively dependent on what others think about them. They are convinced that losing weight will make people like them more, or will help them to solve important problems in their lives. They must learn that popularity, contentment, and happiness are not necessarily dependent on their losing ten pounds or reaching a certain weight. Superstitious behavior can also manifest itself in bizarre behavior and eating rituals.

Overgeneralization: (Burns, 1980; Neuman & Halvorson, 1983). Perfectionists are quick to jump to the conclusion that a negative event will repeat itself endlessly (Burns, 1980). The bulimic who deviates from her dieting and tends to overgeneralize: "I'll never get better. My eating will never improve." As a result of such overgeneralized thinking, the bulimic incorrectly assumes that she has only a narrow margin for success, and fears that she will never improve.

Disturbed affect: Bulimics have problems understanding their emotions and expressing them appropriately. This may be due to social isolation or superficial interpersonal interactions. Their parents may have told them as children what they should feel, thus inhibiting and distorting their true feelings. Out of touch with their feelings, they may suffer from an inability to express appropriately their anger and aggression, and have difficulty asserting themselves. The binge may be a substitute for the expression of anger; in fact, anger-arousing situations often precede the binge episode. Bulimics, however, are not aware of this relationship. For them, binging seems to numb all feeling.

Treatment

There has been very little research on the effectiveness of various treatment modalities for bulimics. The major treatment approaches are similar to those used with anorexic patients (Muuss, 1985). Like anorexics, many bulimics resist treatment. It is important for the therapist not to be coercive, but to be understanding and demonstrate respect for the patient. Without the bulimic's cooperation little can be accomplished. The following are the major treatment approaches.

Hospitalization. Hospitalization is less likely to be necessary for bulimics than for anorexics because they exhibit fewer dramatic and life-threatening symptoms such as emaciation. However, hospitalization may be indicated if the bulimic vomits ten or more times per day or continues to sabotage her treatment plan in secret. In the hospital, the patient's behavior can be regulated and monitored. The patient is denied the opportunity to vomit secretly or to use laxatives.

Individual therapy: Cognitive therapy, in which the therapist identifies and disputes the patient's cognitive distortions, is an especially promising approach. Changing incorrect beliefs is an important step in modifying behavior.

Group therapy: Seeing that others have similar problems, and being able to share their "secret" is a source of relief. The bulimic is highly vulnerable and may not be able to cope alone with the temptation to binge; thus the therapy group provides an important support system.

Family therapy: (Muuss, 1985). For many bulimics family therapy is not possible. Parents may be deceased, unavailable, or refuse to participate in treatment. Often, they have dissociated themselves from their bulimic offspring.

Behavior therapy: Behavior modification has been successful in helping to regulate patients' eating habits. However, it does not get at the root of the disorder.

Drug therapy: Anti-depressant drug therapy is still in the experimental stage. Pope and Hudson (1984) argue that bulimia is closely related to depression: many patients have depressive episodes long before the onset of binging behavior. Eighty percent of their patients responded to anti-depressive drugs. However, other investigators have not been able to attain such high success rates.

References

American Psychiatric Association. *Diagnostic and statistical manual of mental disorders* (3rd ed.). Washington, D.C.: Author, 1980.

Burns, D. The perfectionist's script for self-defeat. *Psychology Today.* November 1980, 34–52.

Chance, P. Food madness. *Psychology Today.* June 1984, *18*, 14.

Garner, D. M. Garfinkel, P. E., & Bemis, K. M. A multidimensional psychotherapy for anorexia nervosa. *International Journal of Eating Disorders*, 1982, *1*, 3–46.

Inhelder, B., & Piaget, J. *The growth of logical thinking.* New York; Basic Books, 1958.

Loro, A. D. *Cognitive problems with social implications in a bulimarexic woman.* Paper presented at the 90th Annual Convention of the American Psychological Association, Washington, D.C., August 1982.

Muuss, R. E. Social cognition: David Elkind's theory of adolescent egocentrism. *Adolescence,* 1982, *17*, 249–265.

Muuss, R. E. Adolescent eating disorder: Anorexia nervosa. *Adolescence,* 1985, *20*(79), 525–536.

Neuman, P. A., & Halvorson, P. A. *Anorexia nervosa and bulimia.* New York: Van Nostrand Reinhold, 1983.

Pope, H., & Hudson, J. *New hope for binge eaters.* New York: Harper & Row, 1984.

Pyle, R. L., Mitchell, J. E., & Eckert, E. D. Bulimia: A report of 34 cases. *Journal of Clinical Psychiatry.* 1981, *42*, 60–64.

Schwartz, D. M., Thompson, M. G., & Johnson, C. L. Anorexia nervosa and bulimia: The sociocultural context. In S.W. Emmett (Ed.), *Theory and treatment of anorexia nervosa and bulimia.* New York: Brunner Mazel, 1985.

From Rationalization to Reason

Seymour S. Kety

The attitude of the public toward the insane throughout all of recorded history has rarely been marked by sympathy and understanding. Rather, it has fluctuated among fear, revulsion, violent hostility or simply isolation and neglect. Among physicians, however, for the past 2,500 years insanity has been thought of as a form of illness with mental, rather than somatic symptoms.

Hippocrates (c. 460–377 B.C.) argued in a compelling way against the prevailing attribution of insanity to supernatural causes:

"And men ought to know that from nothing else but thence [from the brain] come joys, delights, laughter and sports, and sorrows, griefs, despondency, and lamentations. And by this, in an especial manner, we acquire wisdom and knowledge, and see and hear and know what are foul and what are fair, what are bad and what are good, what are sweet, and what unsavory. . . . And by the same organ we become mad and delirious, and fears and terrors assail us, some by night, and some by day, and dreams and untimely wanderings, and cares that are not suitable, and ignorance of present circumstances, desuetude, and unskilfulness. All these things we endure from the brain, when it is not healthy, but is more hot, more cold, more moist, or more dry than natural, or when it suffers from any other preternatural and unusual affection (1, p. 357).

Throughout the Dark Ages in Europe that concept was largely forgotten. It did not reappear until well after the Renaissance. Johann Weyer, early in the 16th century, believed that the insane were sick and could be treated. He was slandered and vilified by the public and the church. Pinel's humanitarian thrust against the atrocious treatment of the insane in 18th-century France was based upon his belief that these patients were suffering from mental illness. He contributed not only to more enlightened attitudes toward the mentally ill but also to the characterization and diagnosis of mental illness. Following the French Revolution and through the age of rationalism that accompanied the 19th century in Europe, science blossomed and permeated all of medicine. It brought knowledge and understanding of the infectious diseases that had plagued the world and paved the way toward their eventual treatment and prevention. The medical model of mental illness was generally accepted by physicians and psychiatrists, becoming the basis for differentiating one form of insanity from another, providing the opportunity to characterize two mental disorders that were widespread at that time, pellagrous psychosis and general paresis, and stimulating research to elucidate their causes and eventually to develop rational and effective methods for their treatment and prevention.

Other forms of insanity remained with us, however, and, despite the gratifying and remarkable progress that has been made in the treatment of schizophrenia and the affective disorders, they still affect five to ten percent of the people in this and every country in the world.

Challenges to the Medical Model

The medical model of mental illness has, in recent times, been seriously challenged. Psychiatric diagnosis has been described as a political judgment, and mental illness has been said to be either a myth or an adaptive and creative response to a hopeless social situation.

Szasz has taken the position that "mental illness is a myth whose function it is to disguise and thus render more palatable the bitter pill of moral conflicts in human relations" (2, p. 53). His arguments to advance that position have been addressed more to the social sequelae of some kinds of psychiatric diagnosis in some places than to the validity of the concept.

Albert Deutsch, a great journalist who worked harder and accomplished more to change the conditions of the mentally ill in the United States than has the whole "antipsychiatry" movement, never found it necessary in doing so to attack psychiatry, science, or the concept of mental illness.

Peter Breggin has undertaken a crusade against biological psychiatry, institutional psychiatry, and behavioral psychiatry which he likens to Hitler's treatment of the mentally ill. He defined biological psychiatry as: "Both the theory that so-called mental illness is biologic and genetic, and the treatment approach which involves drugs, electroshock, and psychosurgery, as well as eugenics" (3). He went on to state: "Clearly, the 'politicalization' of psychiatry is not the responsibility of recent activists, but of traditional biologic, behavioral and institutional psychiatry with their totalitarian politics"(3). I would not previously have believed that admitting a suicidal patient to a mental hospital and prescribing antidepressant drugs or that conducting research on the biochemistry of the brain with the hope of elucidating some of the causes of mental illness could be labeled "totalitarian politics." Dr. Breggin, who seems to be particularly sensitive to criticism against himself, is quite cavalier in his denunciation of entire areas of sober and sincere psychiatric and scientific effort.

The writing of many of the antipsychiatrists is characterized by the broad brushstrokes of diatribe that places blame indiscriminately and inappropriately, by rhetoric and by rationalization rather than by reason. One can apparently do without reason simply by being antiscience. There are valid issues—legal, moral, and public—that are involved in the institutionalization of the mentally ill and that deserve thoughtful discussion and sober adjudication. The complex question of preventive detention is being thoughtfully examined by legal authorities (4) and a distinguished jurist, Judge David Bazelon, has given much thought and substance to the civil rights of the mentally ill as well as their right to treatment (5–7). Each of the drugs that are now highly regarded for the treatment of schizophrenia, mania, or depression has been subjected to the most rigorous kind of critical evaluation in terms of therapeutic benefit and possible risk. Such evidence has not been adduced in support of psychosurgery or mega-vitamin treatment in the therapy of serious mental illness. The scientific and psychiatric communities have shown themselves sensitive and competent to make such discriminations and are likely to continue to do so without throwing out the baby with the bath water.

What is the nature of the evidence and what are the ethical considerations that permit a physician and psychiatrist to deny to his patients those benefits of medical science which have been critically examined and widely accepted, or to promulgate to the public at large their abandonment in favor of alternatives that are poorly spelled out, untested, or illusory? Those who argue most vehemently for the regulation of clinical trials and restrictions on therapeutic drugs apparently see little need for the evaluation or control of their social panaceas.

Among the antipsychiatry movements that Martin Roth has described as "improbable alliances between groups of sociologists, psychologists, psychoanalysts and Marxist critics of contemporary Western society"(8) are those which make sufficient use of stereotyped revolutionary cliches so as to suggest that the state of psychiatry and the plight of the mentally ill are not their major concern.

I appreciate the opportunity I had last June to visit the People's Republic of China, which accorded me an illuminating and refreshing insight into psychiatry there. I was impressed, as every visitor has been, with the important social changes that have taken place—the equalization of wealth and living standards and the great strides that have been made in the relief of poverty and the eradication of major epidemic disease. I also learned something about mental illness in China and the sensible approach to its treatment taken there.

After a few encounters with a doctrinaire denial of the existence of mental illness on the part of those unfamiliar with the problem, I visited the psychiatric department of a large general hospital and a large psychiatric hospital in two of the largest cities. These were very much like their counterparts in the United States. I saw schizophrenic patients humanely and effectively treated with group therapy and phenothiazine drugs, and I learned that the tricyclic antidepressant drugs were highly regarded in the treatment of depression. Schizophrenia was thought of as a mental illness that has both biological and psychological components. For that reason, its most effective treatment depended upon drugs, which could ameliorate the biological disturbances, and reeducation, which might correct the effects of untoward experience. There were fewer hospital beds devoted to mental illness in the large cities of China than in cities of similar size in the West, but it was not felt that the explanation lay in a reduced incidence of mental illness. Instead, it was suggested that Chinese society is more tolerant of mental illness so that patients can be treated in the community and by periodic visits to an outpatient department.

Laing argued against the medical model of schizophrenia in the following way: "There are no pathological anatomical findings *post mortem.* There are no organic structural changes noted in [the] course of the 'illness.' There are no physiological-psychological changes that can be correlated with these illnesses . . ." (9, p. 352). What he could have said is that none of these has yet been found.

Neither Szasz nor Laing denied the reality and validity of general paresis as a disease of the brain. That raises the interesting question of what it was before that was established. Was it a myth, a political judgment, a creative adaptation to an evil society, or simply a mental illness of unknown origin?

The Medical Model as a Process

It should be pointed out that according to the medical model, a human illness does not become a specific disease all at once and is not equivalent to it. The medical model is an evolving intellectual process, consonant with the scientific method, which involves long periods of observation and description, increasingly sharper differentiation, and research rather than wishful thinking.

The medical model of an illness is a process that moves from the recognition and palliation of symptoms to the characterization of a specific disease in which the etiology and pathogenesis are known and the treatment is rational and specific. That progress depends upon the acquisition of knowledge and may often take man years or centuries. Numerous medical disorders and one or two mental illnesses have moved to the final stages of understanding, but many are still at various points along the way. After the recognition of symptoms, there comes the realization that some symptoms occur in fairly regular clusters, which are then described as syndromes. These may ultimately turn out to represent one or several etiological and pathogenetic components, the nature of which may be obscure at earlier stages of knowledge.

The syndromes that are described as schizophrenia, manic-depressive psychosis, or unipolar depression have persisted through several generations of psychiatric experience. Their particular designation may change with time or place, but psychiatrists with different types of training will usually recognize and can agree upon the phenomenologic cluster. The reliability of independent diagnoses, once a standard nosology has been agreed upon, is reasonably high. When we realize that these syndromes have no objective features but are based on subjective evaluation, the reliability becomes even more impressive.

The syndrome too evolves, sometimes breaking up into various subtypes on the basis of new clinical or laboratory information. These may eventually be designated "diseases" when a common pathogenesis or underlying pathology is discovered. Hodgkin's disease and multiple sclerosis are examples of diagnoses based upon recognizable pathology, even though their etiology is obscure, while Parkinson's disease has two quite distinct etiologies. Psychiatrists do not like the term "disease," since it improperly assumes something internal. Instead, they prefer the term "reaction" (which unwarrantedly assumes something external). Of this, Gruenberg wrote:

"The routinizing of the word 'reaction' in our standard nomenclature has accomplished little that is positive—it has given many psychiatrists the false notion that mental disorders are reactions of the organism to circumstances, but that tuberculosis and diabetes and nephritis and measles and mumps are 'things' independent of the patient's nature. For all medical diseases are also reactions of the organism to certain life circumstances and do not exist independently of the people who are sick" (10, p. 368).

The evolution of a medical model from symptoms through syndromes to diseases with specific pathology and, ultimately, with definitive etiologies and rational treatment is an excellent example of the scientific method applied to the alleviation of human suffering. It involves careful observation and study, the generation, sharpening, and testing of hypotheses, and the elucidation of underlying mechanisms, all pointing toward prevention and effective treatment. In many instances throughout medicine, this process has been successful, and there is justifiable concern that the fruits of this knowledge are not available to all the population.

Sometimes the suffering is so great, our understanding so fragile, and the delays in the acquisition of new knowledge so long that we become impatient. Then, not only do we treat with what seems plausible or what we feel offers relief but we attribute to the treatment more effectiveness and value than we can rigorously demonstrate. Instead of developing hypotheses we adopt doctrines, and instead of testing them we rationalize them. Both psychoanalysis and community psychiatry were thus given more confidence than they have been able to justify and permitted more complacency than was reasonable for their ability to treat or prevent serious mental illness. The extravagant claims of those who treat schizophrenia with extraordinary doses of vitamins do not stand up to critical evaluation. Mental illness is indeed different from infectious disease, and the important need is not in the delivery or promulgation of our ignorance regarding its causes, specific treatment, or prevention. Nor does denying the reality of mental illness or calling it a creative and adaptive experience make it disappear. Insofar as any of these beliefs diminish our perception of the problem and placate our need to understand it better, they retard progress.

The medical model of mental illness has been attacked not only on the basis that the underlying mechanisms of mental illness have not been discovered but also that even the syndromes are illusory. Rosenhan (11) felt that he demonstrated this by having eight normal individuals feign hallucinations and thus gain admission to mental hospitals, where they then behaved "normally" (like taking notes on the ward and not insisting on discharge). He also described a follow-up study, in which the threat of sending other pseudopatients to various mental hospitals resulted in ten percent of the actual patients admitted being suspected by a psychiatrist of feigning symptoms. There is no indication that any of these suspicions was strong enough to prevent the admission of an actual patient. Although Rosenhan drew many conclusions from his experiment, this one stands out: "The facts of the matter are that we have known for a long time that diagnoses are often not useful or reliable, but we have nevertheless continued to use them. We now know that we cannot distinguish insanity from sanity."(11).

If I were to drink a quart of blood and, concealing what I had done, come to the emergency room of any hospital vomiting blood, the behavior of the staff would be quite predictable. If they labeled and treated me as having a bleeding peptic ulcer, I doubt that I could argue convincingly that medical science does not know how to diagnose that condition. Rosenhan's pseudopatients received a diagnosis of schizophrenia on admission and schizophrenia in remission on discharge, although we are not told the qualifications that must have accompanied those diagnoses in at least some of the cases. Although that may not justify his rather far-flung conclusions, it could be used to support a statement made some years earlier by another psychologist, Paul Meehl, who has spent many years studying schizophrenia: "Rather than decrying nosology, we should become masters of it, recognizing that some of our psychiatric colleagues have in recent times become careless, and even unskilled in the art of formal diagnosis" (12).

Schizophrenia: Myth or Illness?

My colleagues David Rosenthal, Paul Wender, Fini Schulsinger, Bjorn Jacobsen, and I have recently obtained some results (13) that bear rather directly on the claims of Szasz, Laing, and Rosenhan that schizophrenia is a myth, that it has no biological substrate, and that it cannot be diagnosed reliably. Interestingly enough, we did not carry out the work in order to refute those arguments, since when it began we were either unaware of them or did not take them seriously. Our purpose was to obtain evidence, as free from selective and subjective bias as we could make it, regarding the operation of genetic and environmental factors in the transmission of schizophrenia.

We had surveyed a sample of nearly 5,500 adults who had been adopted early in life by people not biologically related to them and then identified 33 among them who had been admitted to mental hospitals and on whom we could agree in a diagnosis of definite schizophrenia: severe and chronic, mild or latent, or acute schizophrenic reaction. We then picked matching controls for each schizophrenic index patient from adopted individuals who had never been admitted to a mental hospital. The biological and adoptive relatives were then identified: parents, siblings, and half-siblings of the schizophrenic index cases and of their controls—a total of 512 relatives. Of these, 119 had died and 29 had emigrated or disappeared. Of the remainder, more than 90 percent participated in an exhaustive psychiatric interview conducted by Dr. Jacobsen, who had not known the relationship of any subject to a proband. In practically all of the biological relatives, the subject himself did not know of that relationship or did not inform Dr. Jacobsen.

Extensive summaries of these interviews were then prepared, edited to remove any clues that would permit a guess of the relationship of the subject to a proband, and then read independently by each of three raters who were, by training, a clinical psychologist, a psychiatrist, and a physician who had spent a number of years in psychiatric research. Each rater independently recorded his best psychiatric diagnosis for each subject from the transcribed interview. The possible diagnoses covered the entire range listed in the APA diagnostic manual (*DSM-II*) (14) and ranged from no mental disorder to chronic schizophrenia. Since the subject of the study was schizophrenia, the three raters had previously discussed and reached some agreement on the criteria for a diagnosis of the three types of definite schizophrenia employed in the selection of the index cases as well as a diagnosis of uncertain schizophrenia when schizophrenia seemed to be the most likely diagnosis although some doubt existed. A diagnosis of schizoid or inadequate personality, with some schizoid features, was included in what we termed the "schizophrenia spectrum" as being possibly related to schizophrenia.

In all, 365 interviews on as many subjects were independently read and diagnosed by the three raters with the following results:

1. In 324 subjects (89 percent) no rater made a primary diagnosis of schizophrenia or uncertain schizophrenia.

2. On the other hand, in 7 subjects (2 percent), at least one rater made a primary diagnosis of chronic schizophrenia and, in every instance, each of the other raters made a primary diagnosis of definite schizophrenia, usually chronic, sometimes latent, and, in one instance, acute. It is not difficult to recognize independently and reliably the syndrome that Kraepelin described 80 years ago, although there may be disagreement on the severity of the symptoms and the degree of incapacity.

3. In 17 subjects (5 percent), at least one rater made a primary diagnosis of definite schizophrenia, but latent or acute rather than chronic. In all but one of these, the two other raters made diagnoses within the schizophrenia spectrum.

The kappa value for agreement by all three raters on definite schizophrenia in this study was 0.67 and shows a high degree of reliability even when compared with the interrater reliability of only two diagnosticians (15). The kappa values are somewhat lower (0.61 and 0.58, respectively) for definite and uncertain schizophrenia or for the total schizophrenia spectrum. Although the values indicate a satisfactory degree of agreement among these more recent accretions to the original schizophrenia syndrome, there is clearly a need and a basis for sharpening these concepts. The results, however, do indicate that it is possible to distinguish insanity quite readily from sanity, and, in fact, to distinguish a particular form of insanity called schizophrenia.

One could argue that the ability of three raters to agree upon a diagnosis does not give it validity, which can only be derived by reference to some independent criterion. The subjects who have been lumped together thus far are actually divisible into four different populations: the biological and adoptive relatives of schizophrenic adoptees and the biological and adoptive relatives of control adoptees. Of these four populations, one is different from the rest in being genetically related to a person with schizophrenia (with whom they have not lived), i.e., the biological relatives of the index cases. With regard to mental illness other than schizophrenia, these relatives do not differ from the rest (see table 1).

In the case of the schizophrenia spectrum of disorders and for chronic, latent, and uncertain schizophrenia, however, there is a significant concentration in the biological relatives of index cases in contrast to the persons who are not genetically related to a schizophrenic. For chronic schizophrenia, the prevalence in the biological relatives of index cases is 2.9 percent, compared with 0.6 percent in the others: for latent schizophrenia it is 3.5% percent compared with 1.2 percent, and for uncertain schizophrenia it is 7.5 percent compared with 2 percent. For any of these diagnoses of schizophrenic illness, the prevalence in those genetically related to the schizophrenic index cases is 13.9 percent compared to 2.7 percent in their adoptive relatives or 3.8 percent in all subjects not genetically related to an index case (see table 2). These differences between the group genetically related to the schizophrenic index cases and those not so related are highly significant statistically and speak for the operation of genetic factors in the transmission of schizophrenia.

The evidence presented thus far is compatible with a genetic transmission in schizophrenia, but it is not entirely conclusive, since there are possible environmental factors such as in utero influences, birth trauma, and early mothering experiences, these have not been ruled out. However, there are 127 biological paternal half-siblings of index cases and controls among these relatives who can help to settle that question, since the biological paternal half-siblings did not share the same mother, neonatal mothering experience, or postnatal environment, with their adopted half-sibling. The only thing they shared was the same father and a certain amount of genetic overlap. The number of paternal half-siblings is almost identical for index cases and the controls, but the number of those who were diagnosed as having definite or uncertain schizophrenia is markedly different, with 14 among the half-siblings of the index cases and only 2 among the controls (p = .001). There is a similar concentration if we restrict the diagnosis to definite schizophrenia (see table 3). We regard this as compelling evidence that genetic factors operate significantly in the transmission of schizophrenia.

TABLE 1

Consensus Diagnoses Outside the Schizophrenia Spectrum in Biological and Adoptive Relatives

| | Interviewed Relatives in Percents* | | | |
| | Index Group | | Control Group | |
Diagnosis	Biological (N=81)	Adoptive (N=31)	Biological (N=121)	Adoptive (N=41)
Psychiatrically normal	37	36	41	27
Organic illness	9	16	5	15
Neurotic illness	5	10	5	5
Affective illness	2	3	9	7
Personality disorder	33	26	32	37
All nonschizophrenic diagnoses	49	55	51	63

*The Ns represent interviewed relatives, whose consensus diagnoses were outside the schizophrenic spectrum.

TABLE 2

Prevalence of Schizophrenia Spectrum Disorders in the Biological and Adoptive Relatives of Schizophrenic Index and Control Subjects from Consensus Diagnosis on Interview

| Type of Relative | Number of Relatives Identified | Diagnosis of Schizophrenia in Relatives | | | | | | | |
| | | Chronic | | Latent | | Uncertain | | Total | |
		Number	Percent	Number	Percent	Number	Percent	Number	Percent
Biological relatives of schizophrenic adoptees	173	5*	2.9	6	3.5	1.3**	7.5	24***	13.9
Biological relatives of control adoptees	174	0		3	1.7	3	1.7	6	3.4
Adoptive relatives of schizophrenic adoptees	74	1	1.4	0		1	1.4	2	2.7
Adoptive relatives of control adoptees	91	1	1.1	1	1.1	3	3.3	5	5.5

*p < .05 (significances apply to differences between biological relatives of schizophrenic adoptees and controls; other differences were not significant).
**p < .01.
***p < .001.

These data do not permit the conclusion that schizophrenia is a unitary disorder, since they are equally compatible with a syndrome of multiple etiologies and different modes of genetic transmission. They make it difficult, however, to deny the existence of a syndrome that independent raters can agree upon quite reliably and that each rater without knowledge of the relationship finds significantly concentrated only in the biological relatives of schizophrenics. If schizophrenia is a myth, it is a myth with a strong genetic component!

These data do not imply, nor do I believe, that genetic factors and the biological processes involved in their expression are the only important influences in the etiology and pathogenesis of schizophrenia: in fact, we are currently engaged in analyzing these interviews with respect to how experiential factors and their interaction with biological vulnerability make possible or prevent the development of schizophrenia. Environmental factors have always been an important part of medical models of illness, and, in the case of disorders of thought, mood, and behavior, one recognizes the operation of psychological processes and social influences that cannot be described or examined in physicochemical terms (16). They can still be studied scientifically, however, and there are important scientific disciplines devoted to that pursuit.

TABLE 3

Schizophrenic Illness in the Biological Paternal Half-Siblings of Index and Control Groups

| | Biological Half-Siblings of | | | |
| | Index Group (N=63) | | Control Group (N=64) | |
Diagnosis	Number	Percent	Number	Percent
Definite schizophrenia	8	13*	1	1.6
Definite or uncertain schizophrenia	14	22**	2	3.0

*p = .015 (significances apply to differences between index and control groups by Fisher's exact probability law).
**p = .001.

Diabetes mellitus is analogous to schizophrenia in many ways. Both are symptom clusters or syndromes, one described by somatic and biochemical abnormalities, the other by psychological. Each may have many etiologies and shows a range of intensity from severe and debilitating to latent or borderline. There is also evidence that genetic and environmental influences operate in the development of both. The medical model seems to be quite as appropriate for the one as for the other.

Conclusions

The medical model of mental illness has been criticized for the unnecessary and unfortunate social consequences that sometimes accrue to the mentally ill (and that have occurred throughout history, long before there was ever a concept of mental illness). Good sense and logic would require that we address ourselves to the problem of social attitudes. Meanwhile, let us not forget the salutary consequences that are an inherent part of the medical model: the requirements to relieve suffering; to observe, to study, to try to understand the underlying mechanisms of the disorder; to carry out research so that someday we will be able to prevent it and treat it effectively.

The psychiatrist is best equipped to carry out these responsibilities toward the mentally ill on the basis of his broad background in medicine, in clinical psychology and psychopathology, and in the scientific method as it is applied to medicine. Yet psychiatry is in an identity crisis precisely because it has branched out well beyond mental illness into problems it is not especially qualified to handle— community, national, and international affairs; poverty, politics, and criminality. In each of these areas, we have responsibilities as citizens and human beings; we have yet to demonstrate any special competence as psychiatrists. Sir Aubrey Lewis commented on the state of psychiatry thus, "It may be that there is no form of social deviation in an individual which psychiatrists will not claim to treat or prevent the pretensions of some psychiatrists are extreme" (17, p. 189). I am also reminded of a little poem for which I am indebted to Dana Farnsworth:

There was a man named Dr. Peck,
Who fell in a well and broke his neck.
People said he should have known,
To treat the sick and leave the well alone.

The medical model led in another era to the conquest of the psychoses of paresis and pellagra, which were major mental illnesses of their time; for these disorders our efforts today must be applied to the delivery and utilization of the knowledge we have. But there are several million people in our society, and a comparable fraction in every human society that has been examined, who suffer from various forms of serious mental illness that we do not yet understand. The mentally ill do not disappear under the most drastic social changes; their number remains unhappily large under democracy or monarchy, fascism or communism, tyranny or benevolence. Psychiatry has learned to describe their illnesses and to differentiate them into diagnostic categories for the purpose of treatment, which it can sometimes carry out effectively. They suffer from illnesses whose etiology and pathogenesis at the biological, psychological, and sociological levels are still obscure and we have only unsubstantiated hypotheses of how to prevent them. Only research can give us these answers (18). Rationalizations that retard research can only make that goal more difficult to attain.

References

1. Hippocrates: On the sacred disease, in *The Genuine Works of Hippocrates*. Translated by Adams F. Baltimore, Williams & Wilkins Co., 1939, pp 347–360.
2. Szasz, T. S.: Repudiation of the medical model, in *Psychopathology Today*. Edited by Sahakian, W. S. Itasca, Ill, F E Peacock, 1970, pp 47–53.
3. Breggin, P. R.: Pschiatric totalitarianism: Nazi Germany and today. *Freedom Independent* (journal published by the Church of Scientology). May-July 1974 (whole issue).
4. Dershowitz, A.: Preventive confinement: a suggested framework for constitutional analysis. *Texas Law Review,151*:1277–1324, 1973.
5. U.S. vs. Brawner, 471 F 2d 969 (1972).
6. Rouse vs. Cameron, 373 F 2d 451 (1966).
7. Lake vs. Cameron, 331 F 2d 771 (1964).
8. Roth, M.: Presidential address: psychiatry and its critics. *Can. Psychiatr. Assoc. J. 17*: 343–350, 1972.
9. Laing, R.D.: Phenomenological approach to schizophrenia, in *Psychopathology Today*. Edited by Sahakian, W. S. Itasca, Ill. FE Peacock, 1970, pp. 351–358.
10. Gruenberg, E.: How can the new diagnostic manual help? *Int. J. Psy.*
11. Rosenhan D. L.: On being sane in insane places. *Science 179*: 250–258, 1973.
12. Meehl, P. E.: Some ruminations on the validation of clinical procedures. *American Journal of Psychology, 13*:102–128, 1959.
13. Kety, S. S. Rosenthal, D., Wender, P. H., et al.: Mental illness in the biological and adoptive families of adoptive individuals who have become schizophrenic: a preliminary report based upon psychiatric interviews, in *Genetics and Psychopathology*. Edited by Fieve, R., Brill, H., Rosenthal, D. Baltimore, Johns Hopkins Press (in press).
14. American Psychiatric Association: *Diagnostic and Statistical Manual of Mental Disorders*, 2nd ed. Washington, D.C., APA, 1968.
15. Spitzer, R. L., Fleiss J. L.: Unpublished statement cited in Spitzer, R. L., Wilson, P. T.: Classification and nosology in psychiatry and the *Diagnostic and Statistical Manual of the American Psychiatric Association*, in *Comprehensive Textbook of Psychiatry*, 2nd ed. Edited by Freedman, A. M., Kaplan, H. I., Sadock, B. J. Baltimore, Williams & Wilkins Co. (in press).
16. Kety, S. S.: A biologist examines the mind and behavior: many disciplines contribute to understanding human behavior, each with peculiar virtues and limitations. *Science, 132*: 1861–1870, 1960.
17. Lewis, A.: *The State of Psychiatry*. New York, Science House, 1967.
18. Kety, S. S.: The academic lecture: the heuristic aspect of psychiatry. *Am J. Psychiatry, 118*: 385–397, 1961.

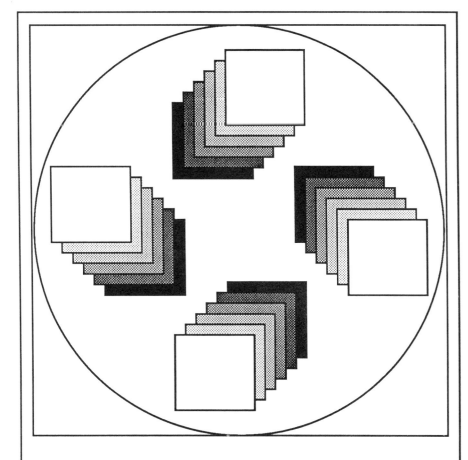

Chapter 13

Psychotherapy

CHAPTER 13: PSYCHOTHERAPY

Some think that the more the underlying brain mechanisms of abnormal behavior are understood, the more we will be able to develop chemical therapies for disturbed patients. Yet, the Frank article in this chapter suggests that the majority of the effectiveness of chemical pain-killers (for example, morphine) is related to the patient's expectation of relief rather than the specific chemical effects. Therefore, the neglect of the "psychological" factors, even in the better-understood treatments (for example, drug treatments for pain), increases the risk of ineffective therapy. Moreover, when treatment centers rely too heavily on the "medical" approach they may make some serious mistakes, such as misdiagnoses and improper treatment. However, because all treatments tend to recruit the patients' own resources to aid the healing process, there is considerable room for different treatments to be effective, as long as the patient believes in the therapy and therapist. The last article by Zilbergeld deals with this subtle issue and its consequences.

13a. Frank, J. (1982). Biofeedback and the placebo effect. *Biofeedback and Self-Regulation, 7,* 449–460.

The Frank selection discusses the placebo response and its interrelatedness to biofeedback. After reading this article, would you recommend biofeedback as a treatment for headaches or tension? Regardless of your support or denial of it, cite evidence from the article to back up your point.

13b. Rosenhan, D. (1973). On being sane in insane places. *Science, 179,* 250–258.

After reading this article, imagine that you are on a board of directors of a psychiatric hospital. What changes would you recommend to avoid the problems outlined in the Rosenhan study?

13c. Zilbergeld, B. (1983). The selling of therapy. In *The Shrinking of America.* Boston: Little, Brown, pp. 87–113.

Whether or not psychological therapy is successful is not the only issue to consider when evaluating different therapies. Psychotherapists work to make a living and those that attract the largest population of clients make more money. Imagine that you have developed a successful technique to reduce stress in working couples. How would you start your practice? Is the marketing of therapy techniques inevitable? Is it wrong? Explain your response.

Biofeedback and the Placebo Effect

Jerome D. Frank

This article reviews the role of positive expectations, including those engendered by placebos, in symptom relief following medical and surgical procedures, and psychotherapy. Viewing biofeedback as instrument-aided psychotherapy, its procedures are considered in the light of their ability to mobilize the same healing forces as all forms of psychotherapy, with some implications for promising directions of biofeedback research.

I have been asked to address the question as to whether nonspecific or placebo variables interact synergistically with active treatment components in such a way that clinical trials which attempt to eliminate the placebo response by double-blind or other techniques give an inaccurate estimate of the clinical value of biofeedback.[1] Realizing after some cogitation that I could not answer this question directly, I have settled for an oblique approach by, first, briefly reviewing what we know and don't know about the placebo effect in bodily healing, then considering its place in psychotherapy, on the assumption that biofeedback is essentially a form of psychotherapy, and, finally, concluding with some possible implications for research, in the hope of stimulating your own thinking.

The Placebo Effect and Expectant Faith

The placebo remedy in itself symbolizes the physician's healing power, and this is reinforced by the physician's direct or indirect message that it will heal. By both these routes, which ordinarily are not separable, the physician seeks to produce a state of mind in the patient which has been termed expectant faith. That this emotion can strongly affect states of subjective distress, such as the report of pain, has long been known. A series of studies have found that on the average the placebo effect accounts for about 60% of the effectiveness of all pain relievers. A puzzling finding is that the proportional effect of placebo is the same regardless of the strength of the active drug—it is 60% as effective as aspirin and also 60% as effective as morphine (Evans, 1974).

That expectant faith as evoked by a placebo can lead patients to reports of reduced pain tells us nothing about the underlying corresponding bodily changes, if any. Many lines of evidence show that expectant faith is associated with acceleration of bodily healing. An example is a study of speed of healing following operative repair of detached retina (Mason, Clark, Reeves, & Wagner, 1969). The sample

---

[1] The current status of the interaction between techniques and the placebo effect in biofeedback is reviewed in Gatchel (1979), and Orne (1980).

consisted of 98 patients in two studies. Patients were interviewed before the operation and their "acceptance" was rated on a paper-and-pencil scale, including such items as trust in the surgeon, optimism about outcome, confidence in ability to cope regardless of outcome, and preparedness to accept the bad with the good. Speed of healing was rated by the surgeon independently and without knowledge of the test scores. A correlation of .61 was obtained between acceptance and speed of healing (p = .001). A similarly strong relationship was found in 100 patients about to undergo open-heart surgery between scores on the acceptance scale pre-operatively and the surgical outcome (Mills, Mimbs, Jayne, & Reeves, 1975). The researchers conclude: ". . . high acceptance and rapid healing occur . . . when the patient has faith in the healer, his methods of healing, and feels that these methods are relevant to the cause of his illness . . . the person seeking to help the slow healer . . . should focus primarily on what variables enhance or destroy the patient's attitude of expectant faith" (Mason et al., 1969, p. 140).

It must be emphasized that the findings of these studies are correlational, which leaves open the question of causality. For example, it may be that both the attitude of acceptance and rapid healing are two aspects of a generally high level of vitality.

To determine whether expectant faith can actually cause acceleration of healing requires that this state of mind be produced by stimuli in the environment. The ability of situational forces to mobilize healing states of mind is strikingly demonstrated by the so-called miracle cures occurring at healing shrines such as Lourdes. These involve rapid healing of gross bodily damage, such as non-union of a fracture or a draining abdominal sinus. Lourdes certifies the occurrence of such an event very rarely—in only two or three pilgrims out of a million—but the evidence for the genuineness of these cures is compelling.

Leaving open the role of supernatural forces, if any, in producing them, two points should be stressed:

1. Since miracle cures are reported by adherents of all religious faiths, their occurrence must depend on the pilgrim's state of mind, not on the validity of the object of his faith; i.e., such cures are irrelevant to the truth or falsity of the belief underlying them. The literature contains reports of 176 cases of cancer diagnosed by biopsy or X-ray that regressed without treatment (Everson & Cole, 1966). Had. they occurred at a shrine of religious healing, they would have been called miraculous.

2. The more important point is that they are not miraculous in the sense that they violate the laws of nature. The consciousness of cure comes instantaneously, to be sure, but thereafter healing occurs through normal reparative processes which are greatly accelerated (Cranston, 1955). No one has grown a new limb or an eye at Lourdes.

The Placebo Effect of Medications, Operations

In the western world, the most salient feature of a healing environment is the physician. His or her role is basically defined by the power to administer medication and perform operations, and we are too easily inclined to think that the healing effects of these procedures are produced solely by their pharmacological or physical effects. Actually, medications and operations are also symbols of the physician's healing role and of the scientific world-view supporting his ministrations, and these symbolic meanings can have striking healing effects.

The healing symbolic component of medication, the placebo effect, is by no means trivial. Actually, until this century, the physician's reputation rested largely on the placebo effect, since most medical remedies were either innocuous or actually harmful (Shapiro, 1959).

If medication can have powerful physiological effects, one would expect surgical interventions to have even stronger ones. As compared to a person seeking medical treatment, someone about to undergo surgery is more apprehensive and is totally dependent on the surgeon—he literally places his life in the surgeon's hands. Furthermore, the operation is a single dramatic act which is expected to produce a prompt cure.

Understandably, there has been little investigation of the noxious or healing psychological effects of surgical procedures because it seems so obvious that all their effects result from the operation itself. Now researchers are looking again, with some startling results.

The healing psychological effects of surgical procedures are clearest with respect to operations on the heart. Of all bodily organs, the heart is most obviously susceptible to emotional influences (it has been called the end-organ of anxiety). Surgery on the heart, the organ of life itself, is an especially impressive demonstration of the surgeon's power, so it should not come as a surprise that psychological effects of heart surgery account for a large part of its effectiveness.

This was first demonstrated by study of an operation for relief of angina which consisted of tying off the internal mammary artery on the supposition that this would increase coronary circulation. The results were impressive. Forty percent of the patients experienced marked symptomatic relief. But then some decided to do a mock operation—that is, to give the anesthesia and open the skin, but not touch the artery—and it proved to be fully as effective as the real one in reducing patients' pain, causing them to reduce their use of nitroglycerin tablets and increasing their exercise tolerance. That is, the placebo effect was sufficiently powerful to affect the actual functioning of the heart (Beecher, 1961).

This operation was therefore abandoned and replaced by coronary bypass, which is currently highly popular. Its rationale is completely convincing—angina is caused by poor circulation to part of the heart muscle, because a coronary artery is partly occluded; therefore it can be treated by restoring the circulation by bypassing the diseased portion of the artery with a segment of vein.

The results have been spectacular. About 90% of patients report reduction of symptoms and improved quality of life. Of these, 82% (76% of total) can tolerate more exercise without pain. Clearly coronary bypass is a very successful procedure for relief of symptoms. It would appear absurd to question that improvement following it is caused by better blood flow to the heart as a result of the bypass. Bypassing the major coronary artery does seem to prolong life. But bypassing the other arteries produces no difference in three-year survival rate as compared with a matched group of patients treated medically. Furthermore, on several objective tests of cardiac function, about 44% showed no change, 38% were actually worse, and only about 20% showed some improvement. In short, symptomatic improvement in 90% was accompanied by improvement in heart function in 20%; so 70% improved symptomatically with heart function the same or worse (Ross, 1976).

Physiological Changes Produced by the Physician's Words

The reports cited so far do not offer direct evidence as to the physiological changes accompanying the favorable mental set created by the physician and his procedures, so it may be worth mentioning two studies focused on such changes.

In a double-blind experiment, asthmatics were given a bronchodilator or a bronchoconstrictor to inhale. With each, they were given two different expectations, one that the inhalant would produce its pharmacological effect, and one that it would produce the opposite. That is, they were told that the dilator would produce bronchodilation on one trial and bronchoconstriction on another, and the same with the bronchoconstrictor. The effect on airway resistance of the dilator was about twice as great when the expectation coincided with its pharmacological action than when they were opposed; a similar, although weaker, result occurred with the constrictor (Luparello, Leist, Lourie, & Sweet, 1970).

In this example, expectations created by the physician's words strongly modified the pharmacological action of a drug. That they can actually reverse it was demonstrated with an emetic, ipecac. A physician gave ipecac to two patients with vomiting of pregnancy through a stomach tube with the statement that it would cure their vomiting. The normal stomach contractions resumed and nausea vanished at the same time interval after administration that stomach contractions cease and nausea starts when ipecac is given as an emetic (Wolf, 1950).

Although the evidence is overwhelming that mental states generated by placebos can produce physiological changes, so far we have only one small clue as to what one of the intervening physiological variables might be. This is the finding that, for patients whose pain following a tooth extraction is relieved by a placebo, the pain recurs if they are given naloxone, a morphine antagonist (Levine, Gordon, & Fields, 1977). Since morphine and endorphins bind to the same receptor sites in the central nervous system, this is evidence that the placebo effect is linked to the release of endorphins.

If the placebo effect can in itself sometimes significantly affect bodily processes and relieve symptoms caused by bodily disease, it would almost certainly also contribute to the alleviation of the kinds of symptoms treated by biofeedback.

The Placebo Effect and Psychotherapy

That the placebo effect also plays a big part in the results of psychotherapy was a startling finding of our early studies. We found, first, that on the average psychiatric outpatients reported the same drop in discomfort after four months of three different forms of psychotherapy (group, individual, and minimal).

Suspecting that this was accounted for by a feature shared by all three therapies, arousal of expectation of help, we tried to evoke the same mental state with another group of psychiatric outpatients simply by giving them a placebo. As a whole, the group reported an identical average drop in discomfort after two weeks as the patients after four months of psychotherapy, About three years later we gave placebos to a sample of both groups of patients (those having undergone psychotherapy and those having received a placebo), and both showed the same average drop in discomfort as they did the first time. A really puzzling finding was that, although the average drop was the same on both occasions, the patients were different. That is, some responded the first time but not the second, and others the second time but not the first (Frank, Nash, Stone, & Imber, 1963).

Along with our failure to find any personality characteristics that were strongly associated with placebo responsivity, this led us to suspect that, as with medical and surgical patients, situational determinants played a large part in the placebo responsiveness of psychiatric patients.

In fact, the determinants of a person's subjective reaction to a placebo prove to be highly complex. Rickels (1967) has listed 14 aspects of patients and eight of physicians, many of which are fleeting, difficult to define, and differ from one clinic and its patients to another.

An experimental demonstration of the situation-bound nature of placebo responsiveness is provided by a study in which obstetric patients were given a placebo to reduce pain created by three different causes—labor pains, after-pains, and self-induced pain caused by contracting muscles whose blood supply had been cut off by a tourniquet (Liberman, 1964). In all three situations the placebo produced more relief of pain than occurred in a control group not receiving placebos, but the number of patients who showed the *same* reaction in all three situations was no greater than would be expected by chance. That is, although the placebo relieved pain on the average, whether it did so for a given patient on a particular occasion seemed to depend on an interaction between the momentary state of the patient and the specific source of the pain rather than on enduring personality attributes.

Although the most important determinants of the placebo response lie in the individual's interaction with the immediate situation, certain enduring personality characteristics which imply responsiveness to other persons may also play a small part. In general, placebo responsiveness seems related to willingness to depend on others for help and ready acceptance of their socially assigned roles. Thus, in a study of patients with surgical pain, a positive response was found to be related to such traits as dependency, emotional reactivity, and conventionality, while failure to respond was related to isolation and mistrustfulness (Lasagna, Mosteller, von Felsinger, & Beecher, 1954), but the relationships were weak. The only consistent predictor of placebo responsiveness was generalized chronic anxiety, especially in patients with pain (Evans, 1974).

In any case, the conclusion seems reasonable that the placebo effect contributes to favorable responses to psychotherapy, as well as to medical and surgical procedures.

Healing Components Biofeedback Shares with Other Forms of Psychotherapy

Turning at last to biofeedback, my view is that it is an instrument-aided form of psychotherapy in which the instrument brings into the patient's awareness the symptom-producing disturbances in organ systems of which he is not conscious, thereby increasing his ability to gain conscious control of them (Lazarus, 1975; Pelletier, 1975).

While the specific technique is clearly relevant and devising the appropriate one for a given symptom often requires considerable ingenuity, the features biofeedback procedures share with all other forms of psychotherapy are also necessary to their success.

Parenthetically, the instrument may not be essential. At least, this is the implication one could draw from the apparent ability of Yogis to achieve the same sort of control of their bodily functions by bringing them to awareness without the benefit of biofeedback apparatus.

At the risk of laboring the obvious, then, let me briefly review what appear to me to be the major healing components of psychotherapy and consider biofeedback in this light. To do this, let me first offer an inclusive definition of psychotherapy. Psychotherapy is a systematic, emotionally charged, confiding interaction between a (1) trained, (2) socially sanctioned healer and a sufferer in which the healer seeks to relieve the sufferer's distress and disability through symbolic communications, primarily words but also therapeutic rituals or procedures.

Survey studies of different forms of psychotherapy have consistently shown, first, that all forms of psychotherapy are followed by more improvement than passage of the same period of time without psychotherapy, but second, that with few exceptions differences in effectiveness of different forms of psychotherapy for most persons are slight, if present at all (Smith, Glass, & Miller, 1980).

A plausible explanation for this finding is that most patients come to psychotherapy, not for symptoms alone, but because they are also demoralized, that this demoralization is a major source of their distress, and that shared features of all forms of psychotherapy cause patients to improve by combating demoralization (Frank, 1974). The core of demoralization is a sense of incompetence, often accompanied by feelings of hopelessness, helplessness, a sense of alienation, and cognitive unclarity as to the meaning of the specific symptoms and what to do about them.

The features common to all forms of psychotherapy, including biofeedback, that combat demoralization are:

1. *An intense, emotionally charged, confiding relationship* with a helping person, often with the participation of a group. Since the therapist represents the larger society, his mere acceptance of the patient as worthy of help combats the latter's sense of isolation and helps to re-establish his sense of connectedness with his group. The patient lets himself become dependent on the therapist for help, because of his confidence in the therapist's competence and good will, his knowledge of the therapist's training, and the congruence of his approach with the patient's expectations.

2. *A healing setting,* which reinforces the relationship by heightening his prestige by symbolizing the therapist's role as a healer. In the case of biofeedback, an important healing symbol is the biofeedback apparatus.

3. *A rationale or conceptual scheme* that provides a plausible explanation of the patient's symptoms and prescribes a *procedure* for resolving them.

4. The *procedure* requires active participation of both patient and therapist and is believed by both to be the means for restoring the patient's health.

The rationale combats demoralization by helping to overcome the patient's sense of isolation through providing a belief system shared by both patient and therapist. Such a shared belief system is essential to the formation and maintenance of all groups. The very existence of a conceptual framework into which the patient's symptoms can be fitted, moreover, implies that they are not unique, thereby overcoming the patient's sense of isolation. Furthermore, the conceptual framework transforms the symptoms from a frightening, mysterious, inchoate experience to one that is understandable, thus reducing the anxiety accompanying it.

In addition to whatever merits specific rituals or procedures may have for combating specific sources of distress, they all share certain healing *functions*. They maintain the patient–therapist bond by giving them something to do together, especially when nothing much seems to be happening. Most procedures also provide criteria for gauging progress, whether it be through gaining insights or modifying behavior, which keep hope alive and provide morale-boosting success experiences. Finally, mastery of the rationale and ritual gives the therapist a sense of competence, which indirectly sustains the patient's faith in him or her.

Viewing biofeedback from this perspective, success, as with all psychotherapies, depends first of all on the patients' *motivation* to participate in the rituals involved which are often disturbing or boring. Thus, biofeedback is more successful with patients suffering from painful tension headaches than with those having asymptomatic hypertension.

Two particularly powerful healing aspects of biofeedback techniques are their ability to inspire the patient's hopes and to enhance his sense of mastery or self-efficacy. Hope—or its relative, expectant faith—not only is a healing emotion in itself, as the studies I have reviewed suggest, but also motivates the patients to stay in treatment, while the sense of mastery, or what Bandura (1977) has termed "self-efficacy," combats demoralization by strengthening the patient's self-esteem.

Biofeedback techniques are especially hope-inspiring for Americans because we love gadgetry and are inclined to expect science and technology to solve all problems. The biofeedback therapist basks in the aura of the applied scientist.

Furthermore, biofeedback maintains the patient's hopes by offering continual, tangible means by which he can monitor his progress in terms of ability to control the auditory or visual stimulus that signals the state of the organ in question. The patient continually sees or hears how well he is doing.

To the extent that patients do progress, they find that they can reduce or eliminate a symptom that they thought was beyond their power to control. Even though they may not be able to alter the environmental stress that gave rise to the symptom, they discover that they can alter their response to it. This is a powerful boost to their sense of self-efficacy. The resulting increased self-confidence may give them the courage to tackle personal problems which they had hitherto avoided that contribute to their symptoms, so that the benefits of biofeedback can generalize over a wide area of their lives. This could explain the finding that the amount of clinical improvement after biofeedback is often much greater than improvement in the special function that has been regulated.

To summarize, biofeedback shares features that combat demoralization that are common to all psychotherapies. The biofeedback therapist's acceptance of the patient for treatment combats the patient's sense of isolation and raises his hopes; the success of the procedure depends on the therapist's ability to convince the patient that it will be helpful; and the treatment itself sustains the relationship and the patient's hopes during periods when not much seems to be happening. Finally, to the extent that it succeeds, it enhances the patient's sense of mastery.

Implications for Research

If this analysis is valid, then the placebo response, or expectant faith, operates synergistically with biofeedback techniques to produce improvement. They cannot be disentangled, so elimination of the placebo component of any technique would lead to an underestimation of its clinic value. In fact, without the placebo component in some sense it wouldn't be the same technique.

Furthermore, experiments directed toward determining how much of the effectiveness of any given procedure is attributable to the placebo effect are hard to design because of the as yet unpredictable differences in patients' susceptibility to the placebo effect at different times. Moreover, to yield a valid finding, the control "pure" placebo technique must arouse the subject's expectant faith as powerfully as the experimental one. Findings of some studies of psychotherapy which showed the experimental therapy to be more efficacious than the placebo control (Paul, 1966) proved not to be replicable if sufficient attention was given to making the placebo control equally plausible to the patient (McReynolds, Barnes, Brooks, & Rehagen, 1973).

A design of some practical utility would be a controlled clinical trial comparing two biofeedback therapies with each other, with determination of the relative efficacy of the two therapies depending on their ratio of cost to benefit. It would not really matter how much of this was due to a placebo effect.

As researchers throughout the field of psychotherapy are painfully coming to realize, neither comparison of therapies with placebos nor comparison of therapies with each other yields very illuminating results. In the absence of better ability to control factors other than techniques that determine the effectiveness of therapy, as already mentioned, differences between the techniques are regularly found not to be great (Smith *et al.* 1980).

A more hopeful approach might be to investigate parameters of the patient–therapist-technique interaction that make certain patients especially accessible to biofeedback and certain therapists particularly skillful in the use of these techniques. One such component is, of course, the organ system involved in the symptom and the symptom itself. Biofeedback techniques most suitable for controlling cardiac arrhythmia differ from those most successful for fecal incontinence. The potentially most illuminating research strategy might well be to hold the procedure constant and seek to determine the specific attributes of patients, therapists, and the patient-therapist dyad related to differential responses of patients with the same symptom to the same procedures. Such information would enhance knowledge, as well as having practical usefulness.

Unfortunately, I have very few suggestions as to where to look, and these can be offered only tentatively. One promising variable, for example, is the extent to which patients see control of their lives as lying within themselves or outside themselves (Rotter 1966; Seeman & Evans, 1962). Biofeedback, one would expect, would appeal especially to patients who see themselves as inner-controlled because implicit in the technique is that they are doing it all themselves. On the other hand, it might appear to those who are externally-controlled because of the use of a machine. The results reported so far are inconsistent (Miller, 1978, p. 385). Further research is needed to identify the conditions that determine which hypothesis applies. Another hypothesis worth exploring is whether therapists and patients who are more practical-minded would use and benefit from biofeedback to a greater extent than those who are more theoretical-minded. From your familiarity with the field, I am sure that you can come up with other pertinent hypotheses.

To summarize, I've tried to show that the placebo effect can strongly influence bodily and psychological processes and that it is inextricably bound up with biofeedback procedures, as with all other forms of psychotherapy. Therefore, research strategies, rather than seeking to eliminate or circumvent it, might do better to grasp the nettle firmly and study the aspects of patients, therapists, and procedures that determine its power.

References

Bandura, A. Self-efficacy: Toward a unifying theory of behavior change. *Psychological Review*, 1977, *84*, 191–215.

Beecher, H. K. Surgery as placebo. *Journal of the American Medical Association*, 1961, *176*, 1102–1107.

Cranston, R. *The miracle of Lourdes*. New York: McGraw-Hill, 1955.

Evans, F. J. The placebo response in pain reduction. *Advances in Neurology*, Vol. 4. New York: Raven Press, 1974. Pp. 289–296.

Everson, T. C., & Cole, W. H. *Spontaneous regression of cancer*, Philadelphia: W. B. Saunders, 1966.

Frank, J. D. Psychotherapy: The restoration of morale. *American Journal of Psychiatry*, 1974, *131*, 271–274.

Frank, J. D., Nash, E. H., Stone, A. R., & Imber, S. D. Immediate and long-term symptomatic course of psychiatric outpatients. *American Journal of Psychiatry*, 1963, *120*, 429–439.

Gatchel, R. J. Biofeedback and the treatment of fear and anxiety. In R. J. Gatchel & K. P. Price (Eds.), *Clinical applications of biofeedback: Appraisal and status*. New York: Pergamon Press, 1979. Pp. 148–172.

Katkin, E. S., & Goldband, S. The placebo effect and biofeedback. In R. J. Gatchel & K. P. Price (Eds.), *Clinical applications of biofeedback: Appraisal and status*. New York: Pergamon Press, 1979. Pp. 173–186.

Lasagna, L., Mosteller, F., von Felsinger, J. M., & Beecher, H. K. A study of the placebo response. *American Journal of Medicine*, 1954, *16*, 770–779.

Lazarus, R. S. A cognitively oriented psychologist looks at biofeedback. *American Psychologist*, 1975, *30*, 553–561.

Levine, J. D., Gordon, N. C., & Fields, H. L. The mechanism of placebo anaesthesia. *Lancet*, September 23, 1977, 654–657.

Liberman, R. An experimental study of the placebo response under three different situations of pain. *Journal of Psychiatric Research*, 1964, *2*, 233–246.

Luparello, T. J., Leist, N., Lourie, C. H., & Sweet, P. The interaction of psychologic stimuli and pharmacologic agents on airway reactivity in asthmatic subjects. *Psychosomatic Medicine*, 1970, *32*, 509–513.

Mason, R. C., Clark, G., Reeves, R. B., & Wagner, B. Acceptance and hearing. *Journal of Religion and Health*, 1969, *8*, 123–142.

McReynolds, W. T., Barnes, A. R., Brooks, S., & Rehagen, N. J. The role of attention-placebo influences in the efficacy of systematic desensitization. *Journal of Consulting and Clinical Psychology,* 1973, *41* , 86–92.

Miller, N. E. Biofeedback and visceral learning. In M. R. Rosenzweig & L. W. Porter (Eds.), *Annual Review of Psychology,* Vol. 29. Palo Alto, California: Annual Reviews Inc., 1978. Pp. 373–404.

Mills, M.,Mimbs, D., Jayne, E. E., & Reeves, R. B. Prediction of results in open heart surgery. *Journal of Religion and Health,* 1975, *14,* 159–164.

Orne, M. T. Assessment of biofeedback therapy: Specific vs. nonspecific effects. In *Biofeedback,* Report of the Task Force on Biofeedback of the American Psychiatric Association, Task Force Report 19. Washington: American Psychiatric Association, 1980.

Paul, G. L. *Insight vs. desensitization in psychotherapy.* Stanford, California: Stanford University Press, 1966.

Pelletier, K. R. Theory and applications of clinical biofeedback. *Journal of Contemporary Psychotherapy,* 1975, *7,* 29–34.

Rickels, K. Anti-anxiety drugs in neurotic outpatients. In J. H. Masserman (Ed.), *Current Psychiatric Therapies,* 1967, *7,* 118–129.

Ross, R. S. The problem of ischemic heart disease: Current approaches and implications. *Johns Hopkins Medical Journal,* 1976, *38,* 217–228.

Rotter, J. B. Generalized expectancies for internal vs. external control of reinforcement. *Psychological Monographs,* 1966, *80,* 1–28 .

Seeman, M., & Evans, J. W. Alienation and learning in a hospital setting. *American Sociological Review,* 1962, *27,* 772–782.

Shapiro, A. K. The placebo effect in the history of medical treatment: Implications for psychiatry. *American Journal of Psychiatry,* 1959, *116,* 298–304.

Smith, M. L., Glass, G. V., & Miller, T. I. *The benefits of psychotherapy.* Baltimore: Johns Hopkins University Press, 1980.

Wolf, S. Effects of suggestion and conditioning on the action of clinical agents in human subjects: The pharmacology of placebos. *Journal of Clinical Investigation,* 1950, *29,* 100–109.

On Being Sane in Insane Places

David L. Rosenhan

If sanity and insanity exist, how shall we know them?

The question is neither capricious nor itself insane. However much we may be personally convinced that we can tell the normal from the abnormal, the evidence is simply not compelling. It is commonplace, for example, to read about murder trials wherein eminent psychiatrists for the defense are contradicted by equally eminent psychiatrists for the prosecution on the matter of the defendant's sanity. More generally, there are a great deal of conflicting data on the reliability, utility, and meaning of such terms as "sanity," "insanity," "mental illness," and "schizophrenia" (1). Finally, as early as 1934, Benedict suggested that normality and abnormality are not universal (2). What is viewed as normal in one culture may be seen as quite aberrant in another. Thus, notions of normality and abnormality may not be quite as accurate as people believe they are.

To raise questions regarding normality and abnormality is in no way to question the fact that some behaviors are deviant or odd. Murder is deviant. So, too, are hallucinations. Nor does raising such questions deny the existence of the personal anguish that is often associated with "mental illness." Anxiety and depression exist. Psychological suffering exists. But normality and abnormality, sanity and insanity, and the diagnoses that flow from them may be less substantive than many believe them to be.

At its heart, the question of whether the sane can be distinguished from the insane (and whether degrees of insanity can be distinguished from each other) is a simple matter: do the salient characteristics that lead to diagnoses reside in the patients themselves or in the environments and contexts in which observers find them? From Bleuler, through Kretchmer, through the formulators of the recently revised *Diagnostic and Statistical Manual* of the American Psychiatric Association, the belief has been strong that patients present symptoms, that those symptoms can be categorized, and, implicitly, that the sane are distinguishable from the insane. More recently, however, this belief has been questioned. Based in part on theoretical and anthropological considerations, but also on philosophical, legal, and therapeutic ones, the view has grown that psychological categorization of mental illness is useless at best and downright harmful, misleading, and pejorative at worst. Psychiatric diagnoses, in this view, are in the minds of the observers and are not valid summaries of characteristics displayed by the observed (3-5).

Gains can be made in deciding which of these is more nearly accurate by getting normal people (that is, people who do not have, and have never suffered, symptoms of serious psychiatric disorders) admitted to psychiatric hospitals and then determining whether they were discovered to be sane and, if so, how. If the sanity of such pseudopatients were always detected, there would be prima facie evidence that a sane individual can be distinguished from the insane context in which he is found. Normality (and presumably abnormality) is distinct enough that it can be recognized wherever it occurs, for it is carried within the person. If, on the other hand, the sanity of the pseudopatients were never discovered, serious difficulties would arise for those who support traditional modes of psychiatric diagnosis. Given that the hospital staff was not incompetent, that the pseudopatient had been behaving as sanely as he had been outside of the hospital, and that it had never been previously suggested that he belonged in a psychiatric hospital, such an unlikely outcome would support the view that psychiatric diagnosis betrays little about the patient but much about the environment in which an observer finds him.

This article describes such an experiment. Eight sane people gained secret admission to 12 different hospitals (6). Their diagnostic experiences constitute the data of the first part of this article; the remainder is devoted to a description of their experiences in psychiatric institutions. Too few psychiatrists and psychologists, even those who have worked in such hospitals, know what the experience is like. They rarely talk about it with former patients, perhaps because they distrust information coming from the previously insane. Those who have worked in psychiatric hospitals are likely to have adapted so thoroughly to the settings that they are insensitive to the impact of that experience. And while there have been occasional reports of researchers who submitted themselves to psychiatric hospitalization (7), these researchers have commonly remained in the hospitals for short periods of time, often with the knowledge fo the hospital staff. It is difficult to know the extent to which they were treated like patients or like research colleagues. Nevertheless, their reports about the inside of the psychiatric hospital have been valuable. This article extends those efforts.

Pseudopatients and Their Settings

The eight pseudopatients were a varied group. One was a psychology graduate student in his 20's. The remaining seven were older and "established." Among them were three psychologists, a pediatrician, a psychiatrist, a painter, and a housewife. Three pseudopatients were women, five were men. All of them employed pseudonyms, lest their alleged diagnoses embarrass them later. Those who were in mental health professions alleged another occupation in order to avoid the special attentions that might be accorded by staff, as a matter of courtesy or caution, to ailing colleagues (8). With the exception of myself (I was the first pseudopatient and my presence was known to the hospital administrator and chief psychologist and, so far as I can tell, to them alone), the presence of pseudopatients and the nature of the research program was not known to the hospital staffs (9).

The settings were similarly varied. In order to generalize the findings, admission into a variety of hospitals was sought. The 12 hospitals in the sample were located in five different states on the East and West coasts. Some were old and shabby, some were quite new. Some were research-oriented, others not. Some had good staff-patient ratios, others were quite understaffed. Only one was a strictly private hospital. All of the others were supported by state or federal funds or, in one instance, by university funds.

After calling the hospital for an appointment, the pseudopatient arrived at the admissions office complaining that he had been hearing voices. Asked what the voices said, he replied that they were often unclear, but as far as he could tell they said "empty," "hollow," and "thud." The voices were unfamiliar and were of the same sex as the pseudopatient. The choice of these symptoms was occasioned by their apparent similarity to existential symptoms. Such symptoms are alleged to arise from painful concerns about the perceived meaninglessness of one's life. It is as if the hallucinating person were saying, "My life is empty and hollow." The choice of these symptoms was also determined by the *absence* of a single report of existential psychoses in the literature.

Beyond alleging the symptoms and falsifying name, vocation, and employment, no further alterations of person, history, or circumstances were made. The significant events of the pseudopatient's life history were presented as they had actually occurred. Relationships with parents and siblings, with spouse and children, with people at work and in school, consistent with the aforementioned exceptions, were described as they were or had been. Frustrations and upsets were described along with joys and satisfactions. These facts are important to remember. If anything, they strongly biased the subsequent results in favor of detecting sanity, since none of their histories or current behaviors were seriously pathological in any way.

Immediately upon admission to the psychiatric ward, the pseudopatient ceased simulating *any* symptoms of abnormality. In some cases, there was a brief period of mild nervousness and anxiety, since none of the pseudopatients really believed that they would be admitted so easily. Indeed, their shared fear was that they would be immediately exposed as frauds and greatly embarrassed. Moreover, many of them had never visited a psychiatric ward; even those who had, nevertheless had some genuine fears about what might happen to them. Their nervousness, then, was quite appropriate to the novelty of the hospital setting, and it abated rapidly.

Apart from that short-lived nervousness, the pseudopatient behaved on the ward as he "normally" behaved. The pseudopatient spoke to patients and staff as he might ordinarily. Because there is uncommonly little to do on a psychiatric ward, he attempted to engage others in conversation. When asked by staff how he was feeling, he indicated that he was fine, that he no longer experienced symptoms. He responded to instructions from attendants, to calls for medication (which was not swallowed), and to dining-hall instructions. Beyond such activities as were available to him on the admissions ward, he spent his time writing down his observations about the ward, its patients, and the staff. Initially these notes were written "secretly," but as it soon became clear that no one much cared, they were subsequently written on standard tablets of paper in such public places as the dayroom. No secret was made of these activities.

The pseudopatient, very much as a true psychiatric patient, entered a hospital with no foreknowledge of when he would be discharged. Each was told that he would have to get out by his own devices, essentially by convincing the staff that he was sane. The psychological stresses associated with hospitalization were considerable, and all but one of the pseudopatients desired to be discharged almost immediately after being admitted. They were, therefore, motivated not only to behave sanely, but to be paragons of cooperation. That their behavior was in no way disruptive is confirmed by nursing reports, which have been obtained on most of the patients. These reports uniformly indicate that the patients were "friendly," "cooperative," and "exhibited no abnormal indications."

The Normal Are Not Detectably Sane

Despite their public "show" of sanity, the pseudopatients were never detected. Admitted, except in one case, with a diagnosis of schizophrenia (10), each was discharged with a diagnosis of schizophrenia "in remission." The label "in remission" should in no way be dismissed as a formality, for at no time during any hospitalization had any question been raised about any pseudopatient's simulation. Nor are there any indications in the hospital records that the pseudopatient's status was suspect. Rather, the evidence is strong that, once labeled schizophrenic, the pseudopatient was stuck with that label. If the pseudopatient was to be discharged, he must naturally be "in remission"; but he was not sane, nor, in the institution's view, had he ever been sane.

The uniform failure to recognize sanity cannot be attributed to the quality of the hospitals, for, although there were considerable variations among them, several are considered excellent. Nor can it be alleged that there was simply not enough time to observe the pseudopatients. Length of hospitalization ranged from 7 to 52 days, with an average of 19 days. The pseudopatients were not, in fact, carefully observed, but this failure clearly speaks more to traditions within psychiatric hospitals than to lack of opportunity.

Finally, it cannot be said that the failure to recognize the pseudopatients' sanity was due to the fact that they were not behaving sanely. While there was clearly some tension present in all of them, their daily visitors could detect no serious behavioral consequences—nor, indeed, could other patients. It was quite common for the patients to "detect" the pseudopatients' sanity. During the first three hospitalizations, when accurate counts were kept, 35 of a total of 118 patients on the admissions ward voiced their suspicions, some vigorously. "You're not crazy. You're a journalist, or a professor [referring to the continual note-taking]. You're checking up on the hospital." While most of the patients were reassured by the pseudopatient's insistence that he had been sick before he came in but was fine now, some continued to believe that the pseudopatient was sane throughout his hospitalization (11). The fact that the patients often recognized normality when staff did not raises important questions.

Failure to detect sanity during the course of hospitalization may be due to the fact that physicians operate with a strong bias toward what statisticians call the type 2 error (5). This is to say that physicians are more inclined to call a healthy person sick (a false positive, type 2) than a sick person healthy (a false negative, type 1). The reasons for this are not hard to find: it is clearly more dangerous to misdiagnose illness than health. Better to err on the side of caution, to suspect illness even among the healthy.

But what holds for medicine does not hold equally well for psychiatry. Medical illnesses, while unfortunate, are not commonly pejorative. Psychiatric diagnoses, on the contrary, carry with them personal, legal, and social stigmas (12). It was therefore important to see whether the tendency toward diagnosing the sane insane could be reversed. The following experiment was arranged at a research and teaching hospital whose staff had heard these findings but doubted that such an error could occur in their hospital. The staff was informed that at some time during the following 3 months, one or more pseudopatients would attempt to be admitted into the psychiatric hospital. Each staff member was asked to rate each patient who presented himself at admissions or on the ward according to the likelihood that the patient was a pseudopatient. A 10-point scale was used, with a 1 and 2 reflecting high confidence that the patient was a pseudopatient.

Judgments were obtained on 193 patients who were admitted for psychiatric treatment. All staff who had had sustained contact with or primary responsibility for the patient—attendants, nurses, psychiatrists, physicians, and psychologists—were asked to make judgments. Forty-one patients were alleged, with high confidence, to be pseudopatients by at least one member of the staff. Twenty-three were considered suspect by at least one psychiatrist. Nineteen were suspected by one psychiatrist *and* one other staff member. Actually, no genuine pseudopatient (at least from my group) presented himself during this period.

The experiment is instructive. It indicates that the tendency to designate sane people as insane can be reversed when the stakes (in this case, prestige and diagnostic acumen) are high. But what can be said of the 19 people who were suspected of being "sane" by one psychiatrist and another staff member? Were these people truly "sane," or was it rather the case that in the course of avoiding the type 2 error the staff tended to make more errors of the first sort—calling the crazy "sane"? There is no way of knowing. But one thing is certain: any diagnostic process that lends itself so readily to massive errors of this sort cannot be a very reliable one.

The Stickiness of Psychodiagnostic Labels

Beyond the tendency to call the healthy sick—a tendency that accounts better for diagnostic behavior on admission than it does for such behavior after a lengthy period of exposure—the data speak to the massive role of labeling in psychiatric assessment. Having once been labeled schizophrenic, there is nothing the pseudopatient can do to overcome the tag. The tag profoundly colors others' perceptions of him and his behavior.

From one viewpoint, these data are hardly surprising, for it has long been known that elements are given meaning by the context in which they occur. Gestalt psychology made this point vigorously, and Asch (13) demonstrated that there are "central" personality traits (such as "warm" versus "cold") which are so powerful that they markedly color the meaning of other information in forming an impression of a given personality (14). "Insane," "schizophrenic," "manic-depressive," and "crazy" are probably among the most powerful of such central traits. Once a person is designated abnormal, all of his other behaviors and characteristics are colored by that label. Indeed, that label is so powerful that many of the pseudopatients' normal behaviors were overlooked entirely or profoundly misinterpreted. Some examples may clarify this issue.

Earlier I indicated that there were no changes in the pseudopatient's personal history and current status beyond those of name, employment, and, where necessary, vocation. Otherwise, a veridical description of personal history and circumstances was offered. Those circumstances were not psychotic. How were they made consonant with the diagnosis of psychosis? Or were those diagnoses modified in such a way as to bring them into accord with the circumstances of the pseudopatient's life, as described by him?

As far as I can determine, diagnoses were in no way affected by the relative health of the circumstances of a pseudopatient's life. Rather, the reverse occurred: the perception of his circumstances was shaped entirely by the diagnosis. A clear example of such translation is found in the case of a pseudopatient who had had a close relationship with his mother but was rather remote from his father during his early childhood. During adolescence and beyond, however, his father became a close friend, while his relationship with his mother cooled. His present relationship with his wife was characteristically close and warm. Apart from occasional angry exchanges, friction was minimal. The children had rarely been spanked. Surely there is nothing especially pathological about such a history. Indeed, many readers may see a similar pattern in their own experiences, with no markedly deleterious consequences. Observe, however, how such a history was translated in the psychopathological context, this from the case summary prepared after the patient was discharged.

> This white 39-year-old male . . . manifests a long history of considerable ambivalence in close relationships, which begins

in early childhood. A warm relationship with his mother cools during his adolescence. A distant relationship to his father is described as becoming very intense. Affective stability is absent. His attempts to control emotionality with his wife and children are punctuated by angry outbursts and, in the case of the children, spankings. And while he says that he has several good friends, one senses considerable ambivalence embedded in those relationships also. . . .

The facts of the case were unintentionally distorted by the staff to achieve consistency with a popular theory of the dynamics of a schizophrenic reaction (15). Nothing of an ambivalent nature had been described in relations with parents, spouse, or friends. To the extent that ambivalence could be inferred, it was probably not greater than is found in all human relationships. It is true the pseudopatient's relationships with his parents changed over time, but in the ordinary context that would hardly be remarkable—indeed, it might very well be expected. Clearly, the meaning ascribed to his verbalizations (that is, ambivalence, affective instability) was determined by the diagnosis: schizophrenia. An entirely different meaning would have been ascribed if it were known that the man was "normal."

All pseudopatients took extensive notes publicly. Under ordinary circumstances, such behavior would have raised questions in the minds of observers, as, in fact, it did among patients. Indeed, it seemed so certain that the notes would elicit suspicion that elaborate precautions were taken to remove them from the ward each day. But the precautions proved needless. The closest any staff member came to questioning these notes occurred when one pseudopatient asked his physician what kind of medication he was receiving and began to write down the response. "You needn't write it," he was told gently. "If you have trouble remembering, just ask me again."

If no questions were asked of the pseudopatients, how was their writing interpreted? Nursing records for three patients indicate that the writing was seen as an aspect of their pathological behavior. "Patient engages in writing behavior" was the daily nursing comment on one of the pseudopatients who was never questioned about his writing. Given that the patient is in the hospital, he must be psychologically disturbed. And given that he is disturbed, continuous writing must be a behavioral manifestation of that disturbance, perhaps a subset of the compulsive behaviors that are sometimes correlated with schizophrenia.

One tacit characteristic of psychiatric diagnosis is that it locates the sources of aberration within the individual and only rarely within the complex of stimuli that surrounds him. Consequently, behaviors that are stimulated by the environment are commonly misattributed to the patient's disorder. For example, one kindly nurse found a pseudopatient pacing the long hospital corridors. "Nervous, Mr. X?" she asked. "No, bored," he said.

The notes kept by pseudopatients are full of patient behaviors that were misinterpreted by well-intentioned staff. Often enough, a patient would go "berserk" because he had, wittingly or unwittingly, been mistreated by, say, an attendant. A nurse coming upon the scene would rarely inquire even cursorily into the environmental stimuli of the patient's behavior. Rather, she assumed that his upset derived from his pathology, not from his present interactions with other staff members. Occasionally, the staff might assume that the patient's family (especially when they had recently visited) or other patients had stimulated the outburst. But never were the staff found to assume that one of themselves or the structure of the hospital had anything to do with a patient's behavior. One psychiatrist pointed to a group of patients who were sitting outside the cafeteria entrance half an hour before lunchtime. To a group of young residents he indicated that such behavior was characteristic of the oral-acquisitive nature of the syndrome. It seemed not to occur to him that there were very few things to anticipate in a psychiatric hospital besides eating.

A psychiatric label has a life and an influence of its own. Once the impression has been formed that the patient is schizophrenic, the expectation is that he will continue to be schizophrenic. When a sufficient amount of time has passed, during which the patient has done nothing bizarre, he is considered to be in remission and available for discharge. But the label endures beyond discharge, with the unconfirmed expectation that he will behave as a schizophrenic again. Such labels, conferred by mental health professionals, are as influential on the patient as they are on his relatives and friends, and it should not surprise anyone that the diagnosis acts on all of them as a self-fulfilling prophecy. Eventually, the patient himself accepts the diagnosis, with all of its surplus meaning and expectations, and behaves accordingly (5).

The inferences to be made from these matters are quite simple. Much as Zigler and Phillips have demonstrated that there is enormous overlap in the symptoms presented by patients who have been variously diagnosed (16), so there is enormous overlap in the behaviors of the sane and the insane. The sane are not "sane" all of the time. We lose our tempers "for no good reason." We are occasionally depressed or anxious, again for no good reason. And we may find it difficult to get along with one or another person—again for no reason that we can specify. Similarly, the insane are not always insane. Indeed, it was the impression of the pseudopatients while living with them that they were sane for long periods of time—that the bizarre behaviors upon which their diagnoses were allegedly predicated constituted only a small fraction of their total behavior. If it makes no sense to label ourselves permanently depressed on the basis of an occasional depression, then it takes better evidence than is presently available to label all patients insane or schizophrenic on the basis of bizarre behaviors or cognitions. It seems more useful, as Mischel (17) has pointed out, to limit our discussions to *behaviors*, the stimuli that provoke them, and their correlates.

It is not known why powerful impressions of personality traits, such as "crazy" or "insane," arise. Conceivably, when the origins of and stimuli that give rise to a behavior are remote or unknown, or when the behavior strikes us as immutable, trait labels regarding the *behaver* arise. When, on the other hand, the origins and stimuli are known and available, discourse is limited to the behavior itself. Thus, I may hallucinate because I am sleeping, or I may hallucinate because I have ingested a peculiar drug. These are termed sleep-induced hallucinations, or dreams, and drug-induced hallucinations, respectively. But when the stimuli to my hallucinations are unknown, that is called craziness, or schizophrenia—as if that inference were somehow as illuminating as the others.

The Experience of Psychiatric Hospitalization

The term "mental illness" is of recent origin. It was coined by people who were humane in their inclinations and who wanted very much to raise the station of (and the public's sympathies toward) the psychologically disturbed from that of witches and "crazies" to one that was akin to the physically ill. And they were at least partially successful, for the treatment of the mentally ill *has* improved considerably over the years. But while treatment has improved, it is doubtful that people really regard the mentally ill in the same way that they view the physically ill. A broken leg is something one recovers from, but mental illness allegedly endures forever (18). A broken leg does not threaten the observer, but a crazy schizophrenic? There is by now a host of evidence that attitudes toward the mentally ill are characterized by fear, hostility, aloofness, suspicion, and dread (19). The mentally ill are society's lepers.

That such attitudes infect the general population is perhaps not surprising, only upsetting. But that they affect the professionals— attendants, nurses, physicians, psychologists, and social workers—who treat and deal with the mentally ill is more disconcerting, both because such attitudes are self-evidently pernicious and because they are unwitting. Most mental health professionals would insist that they are sympathetic toward the mentally ill, that they are neither avoidant nor hostile. But it is more likely that an exquisite ambivalence characterizes their relations with psychiatric patients, such that their avowed impulses are only part of their entire attitude. Negative attitudes are there too and can easily be detected. Such attitudes should not surprise us. They are the natural offspring of the labels patients wear and the places in which they are found.

Consider the structure of the typical psychiatric hospital. Staff and patients are strictly segregated. Staff have their own living space, including their dining facilities, bathrooms, and assembly places. The glassed quarters that contain the professional staff, which the pseudopatients came to call "the cage," sit out on every dayroom. The staff emerge primarily for caretaking purposes—to give medication, to conduct a therapy or group meeting, to instruct or reprimand a patient. Otherwise, staff keep to themselves, almost as if the disorder that afflicts their charges is somehow catching.

So much is patient-staff segregation the rule that, for four public hospitals in which an attempt was made to measure the degree to which staff and patients mingle, it was necessary to use "time out of the staff cage" as the operational measure. While it was not the case that all time spent out of the cage was spent mingling with patients (attendants, for example, would occasionally emerge to watch television in the dayroom), it was the only way in which one could gather reliable data on time for measuring.

The average amount of time spent by attendants outside of the cage was 11.3 percent (range, 3 to 52 percent). This figure does not represent only time spent mingling with patients, but also includes time spent on such chores as folding laundry, supervising patients while they shave, directing ward cleanup, and sending patients to off-ward activities. It was the relatively rare attendant who spent time talking with patients or playing games with them. It proved impossible to obtain a "percent mingling time" for nurses, since the amount of time they spent out of the cage was too brief. Rather, we counted instances of emergence from the cage. On the average, daytime nurses emerged from the cage 11.5 times per shift, including instances when they left the ward entirely (range, 4 to 41 times). Data on early morning nurses, who arrived usually after midnight and departed at 8 a.m., are not available because patients were asleep during most of this period.

Physicians, especially psychiatrists, were even less available. They were rarely seen on the wards. Quite commonly, they would be seen only when they arrived and departed, with the remaining time being spent in their offices or in the cage. On the average, physicians emerged on the ward 6.7 times per day (range, 1 to 17 times). It proved difficult to make an accurate estimate in this regard, since physicians often maintained hours that allowed them to come and go at different times.

The hierarchical organization of the psychiatric hospital has been commented on before (20), but the latent meaning of that kind of organization is worth noting again. Those with the most power have least to do with patients, and those with the least power are most involved with them. Recall, however, that the acquisition of role-appropriate behaviors occurs mainly through the observation of others, with the most powerful having the most influence. Consequently, it is understandable that attendants not only spend more time with patients than do any other members of the staff—that is required by the station in the hierarchy—but also, insofar as they learn form their superiors' behavior, spend as little time with patients as they can. Attendants are seen mainly in the cage, which is where the models, the action, and the power are.

I turn now to a different set of studies, these dealing with staff response to patient-initiated contact. It has long been known that the amount of time a person spends with you can be an index of your significance to him. If he initiates and maintains eye contact, there is reason to believe that he is considering your requests and needs. If he pauses to chat or actually stops and talks, there is added reason to infer that he is individuating you. In four hospitals, the pseudopatient approached the staff member with a request which took the following form: "Pardon me, Mr. [or Dr. or Mrs.] X, could you tell me when I will be eligible for grounds privileges?" (or "...when I will be presented at the staff meeting?" or "...when I am likely to be discharged?"). While the content of the question varied according to the appropriateness of the target and the pseudopatient's (apparent) current needs the form was always a courteous and relevant request for information. Care was taken never to approach a particular member of the staff more than once a day, lest the staff member become suspicious or irritated. In examining these data, remember that the behavior of the pseudopatients was neither bizarre nor disruptive. One could indeed engage in good conversation with them.

Table 1. Self-initiated contact by pseudopatients with psychiatrists and nurses and attendants, compared to contact with other groups.

Contact	Psychiatric hospitals		University campus (nonmedical)	University medical center		
				Physicians		
	(1) Psychiatrists	(2) Nurses and attendants	(3) Faculty	(4) "Looking for a psychiatrist"	(5) "Looking for an internist"	(6) No additional comment
Responses						
Moves on, head averted(%)	71	88	0	0	0	0
Makes eye contact (%)	23	10	0	11	0	0
Pauses and chats (%)	2	2	0	11	0	10
Stops and talks (%)	4	0.5	100	78	100	90
Mean number of questions answered (out of 6)	*	*	6	3.8	4.8	4.5
Respondents (No.)	13	47	14	18	15	10
Attempts (No.)	185	1283	14	18	15	10

*Not applicable

The data for these experiments are shown in Table 1, separately for physicians (column 1) and for nurses and attendants (column 2). Minor differences between these four institutions were overwhelmed by the degree to which staff avoided continuing contacts that patients had initiated. By far, their most common response consisted of either a brief response to the question, offered while they were "on the move" and with head averted, or no response at all.

The encounter frequently took the following bizarre form: (pseudopatient) "Pardon me, Dr. X. Could you tell me when I am eligible for grounds privileges?" (physician) "Good morning, Dave. How are you today?" (Moves off without waiting for a response.)

It is instructive to compare these data with data recently obtained at Stanford University. It has been alleged that large and eminent universities are characterized by faculty who are so busy that they have no time for students. For this comparison, a young lady approached individual faculty members who seemed to be walking purposefully to some meeting or teaching engagement and asked them the following six questions.

1) "Pardon me, could you direct me to Encina Hall?" (at the medical school: "...to the Clinical Research Center?").

2) "Do you know where Fish Annex is?" (there is no Fish Annex at Stanford.)

3) "Do you teach here?"

4) "How does one apply for admission to the college?" (at the medical school: "...to the medical school?").

5) "Is it difficult to get in?"

6) "Is there financial aid?"

Without exception, as can be seen in Table 1 (column 3), all of the questions were answered. No matter how rushed they were, all respondents not only maintained eye contact, but stopped to talk. Indeed, many of the respondents went out of their way to direct or take the questioner to the office she was seeking, to try to locate "Fish Annex," or to discuss with her the possibilities of being admitted to the university.

Similar data, also shown in Table 1 (columns 4, 5, and 6), were obtained in the hospital. Here too, the young lady came prepared with six questions. After the first question, however, she remarked to 18 of her respondents (column 4), "I'm looking for a psychiatrist," and to 15 others (column 5), "I'm looking for an internist." Ten other respondents received no inserted comment (column 6). The general degree of cooperative responses is considerably higher for these university groups than it was for pseudopatients in psychiatric hospitals. Even so, differences are apparent within the medical school setting. Once having indicated that she was looking for a psychiatrist, the degree of cooperation elicited was less than when she sought an internist.

Powerlessness and Depersonalization

Eye contact and verbal contact reflect concern and individuation; their absence, avoidance and depersonalization. The data I have presented do not do justice to the rich daily encounters that grew up around matters of depersonalization and avoidance. I have records of patients who were beaten by staff for the sin of having initiated verbal contact. During my own experience, for example, one patient was beaten in the presence of other patients for having approached an attendant and told him, "I like you." Occasionally, punishment meted out to patients for misdemeanors seemed so excessive that it could not be justified by the most radical interpretations of psychiatric canon. Nevertheless, they appeared to go unquestioned. Tempers were often short. A patient who had not heard a call for medication would be roundly excoriated, and the morning attendants would often wake patients with, "Come on, you m-----f-----s, out of bed!"

Neither anecdotal nor "hard" data can convey the overwhelming sense of powerlessness which invades the individual as he is continually exposed to the depersonalization of the psychiatric hospital. It hardly matters *which* psychiatric hospital—the excellent public ones and the very plush private hospital were better than the rural and shabby ones in this regard, but, again, the features that psychiatric hospitals had in common overwhelmed by far their apparent differences.

Powerlessness was evident everywhere. The patient is deprived of many of his legal rights by dint of his psychiatric commitment (21). He is shorn of credibility by virtue of his psychiatric label. His freedom of movement is restricted. He cannot initiate contact with the staff, but may only respond to such overtures as they make. Personal privacy is minimal. Patient quarters and possessions can be entered and examined by any staff member, for whatever reason. His personal history and anguish is available to any staff member (often including the "grey lady" and "candy striper" volunteer) who chooses to read his folder, regardless of their therapeutic relationship to him. His personal hygiene and waste evacuation are often monitored. The water closets may have no doors.

At times, depersonalization reached such proportions that pseudopatients had the sense that they were invisible, or at least unworthy of account. Upon being admitted, I and other pseudopatients took the initial physical examinations in a semipublic room, where staff members went about their own business as if we were not there.

On the ward, attendants delivered verbal and occasionally serious physical abuse to patients in the presence of other observing patients, some of whom (the pseudopatients) were writing it all down. Abusive behavior, on the other hand, terminated quite abruptly when other staff members were known to be coming. Staff are credible witnesses. Patients are not.

A nurse unbuttoned her uniform to adjust her brassiere in the presence of an entire ward of viewing men. One did not have the sense that she was being seductive. Rather, she didn't notice us. A group of staff persons might point to a patient in the dayroom and discuss him animatedly, as if he were not there.

One illuminating instance of depersonalization and invisibility occurred with regard to medications. All told, the pseudopatients were administered nearly 2100 pills, including Elavil, Stelazine, Compazine, and Thorazine, to name but a few. (That such a variety of medications should have been administered to patients presenting identical symptoms is itself worthy of note.) Only two were swallowed. The rest were either pocketed or deposited in the toilet. The pseudopatients were not alone in this. Although I have no precise records on how many patients rejected their medications, the pseudopatients frequently found the medications of other patients in the toilet before they deposited their own. As long as they were cooperative, their behavior and the pseudopatients' own in this matter, as in other important matters, went unnoticed throughout.

Reactions to such depersonalization among pseudopatients were intense. Although they had come to the hospital as participant observers and were fully aware that they did not "belong," they nevertheless found themselves caught up in and fighting the process of depersonalization. Some examples: a graduate student in psychology asked his wife to bring his textbooks to the hospital so he could "catch up on his homework"—this despite the elaborate precautions taken to conceal his professional association. The same student, who had trained for quite some time to get into the hospital, and who had looked forward to the experience, "remembered" some drag races that he had wanted to see on the weekend and insisted that he be discharged by that time. Another pseudopatient attempted a romance with a nurse. Subsequently, he informed the staff that he was applying for admission to graduate school in psychology and was very likely to be admitted, since a graduate professor was one of his regular hospital visitors. The same person began to engage in psychotherapy with other patients—all of this as a way of becoming a person in an impersonal environment.

The Sources of Depersonalization

What are the origins of depersonalization? I have already mentioned two. First are attitudes held by all of us toward the mentally ill—including those who treat them—attitudes characterized by fear, distrust, and horrible expectations on the one hand, and benevolent intentions on the other. Our ambivalence leads, in this instance as in others, to avoidance.

Second, and not entirely separate, the hierarchical structure of the psychiatric hospital facilitates depersonalization. Those who are at the top have least to do with patients, and their behavior inspires the rest of the staff. Average daily contact with psychiatrists, psychologists, residents, and physicians combined ranged from 3.9 to 25.1 minutes, with an overall mean of 6.8 (six pseudopatients over a total of 129 days of hospitalization). Included in this average are time spent in the admissions interview, ward meetings in the presence of a senior staff member, group and individual psychotherapy contacts, case presentation conferences, and discharge meetings. Clearly, patients do not spend much time in interpersonal contact with doctoral staff. And doctoral staff serve as models for nurses and attendants.

There are probably other sources. Psychiatric installations are presently in serious financial straits. Staff shortages are pervasive, staff time at a premium. Something has to give, and that something is patient contact. Yet, while financial stresses are realities, too much can be made of them. I have the impression that the psychological forces that result in depersonalization are much stronger than the fiscal ones and that the addition of more staff would not correspondingly improve patient care in this regard. The incidence of staff meetings and the enormous amount of record-keeping on patients, for example, have not been as substantially reduced as has patient contact. Priorities exist, even during hard times. Patient contact is not a significant priority in the traditional psychiatric hospital, and fiscal pressures do not account for this. Avoidance and depersonalization may.

Heavy reliance upon psychotropic medication tacitly contributes to depersonalization by convincing staff that treatment is indeed being conducted and that further patient contact may not be necessary. Even here, however, caution needs to be exercised in understanding the role of psychotropic drugs. If patients were powerful rather than powerless, if they were viewed as interesting individuals rather than diagnostic entities, if they were socially significant rather than social lepers, if their anguish truly and wholly compelled our sympathies and concerns, would we not *seek* contact with them, despite the availability of medications? Perhaps for the pleasure of it all?

The Consequences of Labeling and Depersonalization

Whenever the ratio of what is known to what needs to be known approaches zero, we tend to invent "knowledge" and assume that we understand more than we actually do. We seem unable to acknowledge that we simply don't know. The needs for diagnosis and remediation of behavioral and emotional problems are enormous. But rather than acknowledge that we are just embarking on understanding, we continue to label patients "schizophrenic," "manic-depressive," and "insane," as if in those words we had captured the essence of understanding. The facts of the matter are that we have known for a long time that diagnoses are often not useful or reliable, but we have nevertheless continued to use them. We now know that we cannot distinguish insanity from sanity. It is depressing to consider how that information will be used.

Not merely depressing, but frightening. How many people, one wonders, are sane but not recognized as such in our psychiatric institutions? How many have been needlessly stripped of the privileges of citizenship, from the right to vote and drive to that of handling their own accounts? How many have feigned insanity in order to avoid the criminal consequences of their behavior, and, conversely, how many would rather stand trial than live interminably in a psychiatric hospital—but are wrongly thought to be mentally ill? How many have been stigmatized by well-intentioned, but nevertheless erroneous, diagnoses? On the last point, recall again that a "type 2 error" in psychiatric diagnosis does not have the same consequences it does in medical diagnosis. A diagnosis of cancer that has been found to be in error is cause for celebration. But psychiatric diagnoses are rarely found to be in error. The label sticks, a mark of inadequacy forever.

Finally, how many patients might be "sane" outside the psychiatric hospital but seem insane in it—not because craziness resides in them, as it were, but because they are responding to a bizarre setting, one that may be unique to institutions which harbor nether people? Goffman (4) calls the process of socialization to such institutions "mortification"—an apt metaphor that includes the processes of depersonalization that have been described here. And while it is impossible to know whether the pseudopatients' responses to these processes are characteristic of all inmates—they were, after all, not real patients—it is difficult to believe that these processes of socialization to a psychiatric hospital provide useful attitudes or habits of response for living in the "real world."

Summary and Conclusions

It is clear that we cannot distinguish the sane from the insane in psychiatric hospitals. The hospital itself imposes a special environment in which the meanings of behavior can easily be misunderstood. The consequences to patients hospitalized in such an environment—the powerlessness, depersonalization, segregation, mortification, and self-labeling—seem undoubtedly countertherapeutic.

I do not, even now, understand this problem well enough to perceive solutions. But two matters seem to have some promise. The first concerns the proliferation of community mental health facilities, of crisis intervention centers, of the human potential movement, and of behavior therapies that, for all of their own problems, tend to avoid psychiatric labels, to focus on specific problems and behaviors, and to retain the individual in a relatively nonpejorative environment. Clearly, to the extent that we refrain from sending the distressed to insane places, our impressions of them are less likely to be distorted. (The risk of distorted perceptions, it seems to me, is always present, since we are much more sensitive to an individual's behaviors and verbalizations than we are to the subtle contextual stimuli that often promote them. At issue here is a matter of magnitude. And, as I have shown, the magnitude of distortion is exceedingly high in the extreme context that is a psychiatric hospital.)

The second matter that might prove promising speaks to the need to increase the sensitivity of mental health workers and researchers to the *Catch 22* position of psychiatric patients. Simply reading materials in this area will be of help to some such workers and researchers. For others, directly experiencing the impact of psychiatric hospitalization will be of enormous use. Clearly, further research into the social psychology of such total institutions will both facilitate treatment and deepen understanding.

I and the other pseudopatients in the psychiatric setting had distinctly negative reactions. We do not pretend to describe the subjective experiences of true patients. Theirs may be different from ours, particularly with the passage of time and necessary process of adaptation to one's environment. But we can and do speak to the relatively more objective indices of treatment within the hospital. It could be a mistake, and a very unfortunate one, to consider that what happened to us derived from malice or stupidity on the part of the staff. Quite the contrary, our overwhelming impression of them was of people who really cared, who were committed and who were uncommonly intelligent. Where they failed, as they sometimes did painfully, it would be more accurate to attribute those failures to the environment in which they, too, found themselves than to personal callousness. Their perceptions and behavior were controlled by the situation, rather than being motivated by a malicious disposition. In a more benign environment, one that was less attached to global diagnosis, their behaviors and judgments might have been more benign and effective.

The author is professor of psychology and law at Stanford University, Stanford, California 94305. Portions of these data were presented to colloquiums of the psychology departments at the University of California at Berkeley and at Santa Barbara; University of Arizona, Tucson; and Harvard University, Cambridge, Massachusetts.

References and Notes

1. P. Ash, *J. Abnorm. Soc. Psychol.* 44, 272 (1949); A. T. Beck, *Amer. J. Psychiat.* 119, 210 (1962); A. T. Boisen, *Psychiatry* 2, 233 (1938); N. Kreitman, *J. Ment. Sci.* 107, 876 (1961); N. Kreitman, P. Sainsbury, J. Morrisey, J. Towers, J. Scrivener, *ibid.*, p. 887; H. O. Schmitt and C. P. Fonda, *J. Abnorm. Soc. Psychol.* 52, 262 (1956); W. Seeman, *J. Nerv. Ment. Dis.* 118, 541 (1953). For an analysis of these artifacts and summaries of the disputes, see J. Zubin, *Annu. Rev. Psychol.* 18, 373 (1967); L. Phillips and J. G. Draguns, *ibid.*, 22, 447 (1971).
2. R. Benedict, *J. Gen. Psychol.* 10, 59 (1934).
3. See in this regard H. Becker, *Outsiders: Studies in the Sociology of Deviance* (Free Press, New York, 1963); B. M. Braginsky, D. D. Braginsky, K. Ring, *Methods of Madness: The Mental Hospital as a Last Resort* (Holt, Rinehart & Winston, New York, 1969); G. M. Crocetti and P. V. Lemkau, *Amer. Sociol. Rev.* 30, 577 (1965); E. Goffman, *Behavior in Public Places* (Free Press, New York, 1964); R. D. Laing, *The Divided Self: A Study of Sanity and Madness* (Quadrangle, Chicago, 1960); D. L. Phillips, *Amer. Sociol. Rev.* 28, 963 (1963); T. R. Sarbin, *Psychol. Today* 6, 18 (1972); E. Schur, *Amer. J. Sociol.* 75, 309 (1969); T. Szasz, *Law, Liberty and Psychiatry* (Macmillan, New York, 1963); *The Myth of Mental Illness: Foundations of a Theory of Mental Illness* (Hoeber-Harper, New York, 1963). For a critique of some of these views, see W. R. Gove, *Amer. Sociol. Rev.* 35, 873 (1970).
4. E. Goffman, *Asylums* (Doubleday, Garden City, N.Y., 1961).
5. T. J. Scheff, *Being Mentally Ill: A Sociological Theory* (Aldine, Chicago, 1966).
6. Data from a ninth pseudopatient are not incorporated in this report because, although his sanity went undetected, he falsified aspects of his personal history, including his marital status and parental relationships. His experimental behaviors therefore were not identical to those of the other pseudopatients.
7. A. Barry, *Bellevue Is a State of Mind* (Harcourt Brace Jovanovich, New York, 1971); I. Belknap, *Human Problems of a State Mental Hospital* (McGraw-Hill, New York, 1956); W. Caudill, F. C. Redlich, H. R. Gilmore, E. B. Brody, *Amer. J. Orthopsychiat.* 22, 314 (1952); A. R. Goldman, R. H. Bohr, T. A. Steinberg, *Prof. Psychol.* 1, 427 (1970); unauthored, *Roche Report* 1 (No. 13), 8 (1971).
8. Beyond the personal difficulties that the pseudopatient is likely to experience in the hospital, there are legal and social ones that,

combined, require considerable attention before entry. For example, once admitted to a psychiatric institution, it is difficult, if not impossible, to be discharged on short notice, state law to the contrary notwithstanding. I was not sensitive to these difficulties at the outset of the project, nor to the personal and situational emergencies that can arise, but later a writ of habeas corpus was prepared for each of the entering pseudopatients and an attorney was kept "on call" during every hospitalization. I am grateful to John Kaplan and Robert Bartels for legal advice and assistance in these matters.

9. However distasteful such concealment is, it was a necessary first step to examining these questions. Without concealment, there would have been no way to know how valid these experiences were; nor was there any way of knowing whether whatever detections occurred were a tribute to the diagnostic acumen of the staff or to the hospital's rumor network. Obviously, since my concerns are general ones that cut across individual hospitals and staffs, I have respected their anonymity and have eliminated clues that might lead to their identification.

10. Interestingly, of the 12 admissions, 11 were diagnosed as schizophrenic and one, with the identical symptomatology, as manic-depressive psychosis. This diagnosis has a more favorable prognosis, and it was given by the only private hospital in our sample. On the relations between social class and psychiatric diagnosis, see A. deB. Hollingshead and F. C. Redlich, *Social Class and Mental Illness: A Community Study* (Wiley, New York, 1958).

11. It is possible, of course, that patients have quite broad attitudes in diagnosis and therefore are inclined to call many people sane, even those whose behavior is patently aberrant. However, although we have no hard data on this matter, it was our distinct impression that this was not the case. In many instances, patients not only singled us out for attention, but came to imitate our behaviors and styles.

12. J. Cumming and E. Cumming, *Community Ment. Health* 1, 135 (1965); A. Farina and K. Ring, *J. Abnorm. Psychol.* 70, 47 (1965); H. E. Freeman and O. G. Simmons, *The Mental Patient Comes Home* (Wiley, New York, 1963); W. J. Johannsen, *Ment. Hygiene* 53, 218 (1969); A. S. Linsky, *Soc. Psychiat.* 5, 166 (1970).

13. S. E. Asch, *J. Abnorm. Soc. Psychol.* 41, 258 (1946); *Social Psychology* (Prentice-Hall, New York, 1952).

14. See also I. N. Mensh and J. Wishner, *J. Personality* 16, 188 (1947); J. Wishner, *Psychol. Rev.* 67, 96 (1960); J. S. Bruner and R. Tagiuri, in *Handbook of Social Psychology*, G. Lindzey, Ed. (Addison-Wesley, Cambridge, Mass., 1954), vol 2, pp. 634–654; J. S. Bruner, D. Shapiro, R. Tagiuri, in *Person Perception and Interpersonal Behavior*, R. Tagiuri and L. Petrullo, Eds. (Stanford Univ. Press, Stanford, Calif., 1958), pp. 277–288.

15. For an example of a similar self-fulfilling prophecy, in this instance dealing with the "central" trait of intelligence, see R. Rosenthal and L. Jacobson, *Pygmalion in the Classroom* (Holt, Rinehart & Winston, New York, 1968).

16. E. Zigler and L. Phillips, *J. Abnorm. Soc. Psychol.* 63, 69 (1961). See also R. K. Freudenberg and J. P. Robertson, *A.M.A. Arch. Neurol. Psychiatr.* 76, 14 (1956).

17. W. Mischel, *Personality and Assessment* (Wiley, New York, 1968).

18. The most recent and unfortunate instance of this tenet is that of Senator Thomas Eagleton.

19. T. R. Sarbin and J. C. Mancuso, *J. Clin. Consult. Psychol.* 35, 159 (1970); T. R. Sarbin, *ibid.* 31, 447 (1967); J. C. Nunnally, Jr., *Popular Conceptions of Mental Health* (Holt, Rinehart & Winston, New York, 1961).

20. A. H. Stanton and M. S. Schwartz, *The Mental Hospital: A Study of Institutional Participation in Psychiatric Illness and Treatment* (Basic, New York, 1954).

21. D. B. Wexler and S. E. Scoville, *Ariz. Law Rev.* 13, 1 (1971).

22. I thank W. Mischel, E. Orne, and M. S. Rosenhan for comments on an earlier draft of this manuscript.

The Selling of Therapy

B. Zilbergeld

"The biggest big business in America is not steel, automobiles, or television. It is the manufacture, refinement, and distribution of anxiety."

-Eric Sevaried

"There will be more psychologists than people in this country!"

-Edwin Boring

My thesis so far is that deeply ingrained American values, the weakening of traditional sources of meaning and support, and changes in attitudes and expectations have paved the way for acceptance of the therapeutic. But two more factors must be added: our penchant for relying on experts, and the aggressive efforts of these same experts to persuade us that we are in great need of their assistance.

Our belief in the superiority of specialization and our predilection for solutions and perfection pushes us to depend on experts. Even if we have some competence in a given area, we know there are others who know more. Our own efforts seem amateurish and inefficient. Why not let someone with special training do it or at least help us do it? The modern view is well expressed in a recent book: "The key to a successful adult life lies in surrounding yourself with experts, a master person for every need. We have gone beyond taking care of ourselves. We need others to care for our medical, legal, financial, emotional, and even our bodily survival." America is probably the most specialized and professionalized society on earth. We have more experts in more areas than does any other country. Thus, the county of Los Angeles is said to have more lawyers than all of England. Our culture is dominated by professionals who call us clients, tell us what our needs are and how to satisfy them.

Nowhere is our dependence on experts more evident than in the area of personal guidance. With increasing regularity, we look to those whom we assume to have special competence to tell us how to live. Experts in living are not new. There have always been people—witch doctors, wise men and women, astrologers, clerics, and physicians—with whom you could discuss your sins, feelings of unease, bad dreams, physical ailments, and problems with your spouse. There have also been other sources of advice and comfort, from *Poor Richard's Almanac* in the eighteenth century and *The Old Farmer's Almanac* in the nineteenth, to the "Miss Lonelyhearts" newspaper columns of this century, and more recently Ann Landers and Dear Abby. But reliance on experts has mushroomed in recent times. We have more such experts than ever before, we depend on them in more areas, and their presence and advice is ubiquitous.

It is a mistake, however, to think that the therapeutic enterprise flourishes only because we have problems and like to find experts to help us deal with them. Therapists themselves have been very active in promoting a demand for their services. This is not hard to understand once you accept the fact that whatever else counseling is, it is a business. Therapy differs from some other businesses in that what it sells is a want rather than a need. People do not need counseling the way they need food, shelter, and clothing. There could be very little demand for psychological services or a very large demand. Quite logically, mental health workers prefer the latter and have been more than willing to increase it.

Psychiatrist Jerome Frank, one of the wisest observers of the therapeutic scene, thinks that therapy to an important extent generates its own business:

Ironically, mental health education, which aims to teach people how to cope more effectively with life, has instead increased the demand for psychotherapeutic help. By calling attention to symptoms they might otherwise ignore and by labeling those symptoms as signs of neurosis, mental health education can create unwarranted anxieties, leading those to seek psychotherapy who do not need it. The demand for psychotherapy keeps pace with the supply, and at times one has the uneasy feeling that the supply may be creating the demand. The greater the number of treatment facilities, and the more widely they are known, the larger the number of persons seeking their services. Psychotherapy is the only form of treatment which, at least to some extent, appears to create the illness it treats.

Therapy advocates take offense at this kind of statement, arguing that the expansion of mental health services meets existing and previously unmet needs. In other words, therapists deal with already existing problems; they do not create new ones. This argument suffers from a number of difficulties and I think it is specious. Frank's position is closer to the known facts and, if anything, is an understatement. Readers will be in a better place to come to their own conclusions after reading this and the last half of Zilbergeld's book.

The way in which therapists sell their services and therefore contribute to increased demand for them can be broken down like this:

1.   Continue the psychologization of life;
2.   Make problems out of difficulties and spread the alarm;
3.   Make it acceptable to have the problem and to be unable to resolve it on one's own;
4.   Offer salvation.

This formula, or some variation, is applied both by individual clinicians and by organizations. You can hear it when therapists have lunch with those who refer clients to them, when they give lectures and interviews, when they appear in the media, and when they and professional organizations petition agencies, usually those of the federal government, that have money to give away.

Before looking at the formula in greater detail, I want to emphasize that it is not the result of a conspiracy or even consciously arrived at. Neither the outline nor the details are taught in professional and graduate schools, at least not explicitly. But trained therapists obviously want to make a decent living doing work they enjoy and they often find there is no great demand for it. They discover they have to do something to generate consumers for their talks, books, courses, and therapy. I suggest the kinds of things they end up doing, with or without full awareness, are what is described in this formula.

Continue to Psychologize the World

This is simply increasing the size of the pie. The idea is to find more and more places, issues, and events with psychological causes, cures, or implications. Is there unemployment and inflation in the land? Surely they must cause worry, fear, and depression, and therapists need to come to the rescue. In an example perhaps more comical than anything else, *Time* reports that as a result of our current economic problems, counselors are "talking more and more about money in sessions with troubled clients. . . . Some therapists have even taken on the role of financial adviser to their patients." Are there children not learning in schools? Surely this is a result of emotional difficulties such as hyperactivity, and counseling is the appropriate remedy. Are people frustrated, bored, and tense at work? Surely these things, now labeled jobs stress and job burnout to make them sound like official problems, require psychological assistance. Are divorce proceedings adversarial and expensive? Obviously what is needed is a new service provided by therapists: divorce mediation. Are more people exercising these days? Clearly they need help from behavioral experts lest they never discover what one book calls "the profound mental benefits that running offers," or they miss out on, as one article puts it, "the idea that athletics is somehow more than athletics, that it is a way to know ourselves, to balance the feminine and masculine aspects within us all."

To ensure that no one eludes the therapeutic net, counselors divide life into a number of phases or stages, with new ones being discovered all the time, each with its own requirements, problems, and experts. There are now specialists in pediatric therapy, adolescent therapy and, at the other end of life, in geriatric therapy. The portion of life in between is divided up in many ways, a recent addition being something called mid life and its attendant crises, about which there are now countless articles, many books, and a number of experts.

We have barely begun to scratch the surface of the expanding influence of the mental healers. As I believe will become clear, they really do intend that all of life should be included in their sphere of influence. And they don't mind saying so publicly. Howard Rome, one of psychiatry's most prominent spokesmen and former president of the American Psychiatric Association, wrote in 1968 that "actually, no less than the entire world is a proper catchment for present-day psychiatry, and psychiatry need not be appalled by the magnitude of the task." A few years later, he added that "our professional borders are virtually unlimited."

Providing psychological services only for the sick and the seriously distressed was too limiting for many therapists. "Therapy is too good to be limited to the sick," say Erving and Miriam Polster, two highly respected gestalt therapists. They continue: "Psychotherapists who have been used to thinking of the individual, the dyad, and the small group have recently glimpsed the vast opportunities and the great social need to extend to the community at large those views which have evolved from their work with troubled people." Those who are mentally distressed need counseling, and so do those who aren't.

Obviously the role of therapy is being redefined. Some even advocate getting rid of the restrictive term "mental," substituting instead overall health. This would allow counselors to roam freely in all areas now coming under the rubric of health. In line with this vision, therapists have launched a blitzkrieg into areas usually considered the province of medicine. An article in the *American Psychologist* announces that "the most serious medical problems that today plague the majority of Americans are ultimately behavioral, and as such, fall squarely within the province of psychology." What is meant by this is that since the major infectious diseases of the past have been conquered, medical problems today are largely the result of people's behavior: smoking, overeating and overdrinking, too much stress, and insufficient exercise and rest. Psychotherapists rather than physicians are the experts of choice for people whose health is impaired or might become impaired in the future for such reasons. And so a new area of specialization was recently created, usually called behavioral medicine or health psychology. It has its own division in the American Psychological Association and is, I am told, growing by leaps and bounds.

Other definitions of psychology are even more expansive. A book entitled *The Professional Psychologist Today* says that the field is dedicated to "dealing with any problem of less-than-optimal behavior." The idea has gained momentum, and there are now a number of courses and books devoted to the promotion of "wellness," "optimal performance," "peak performance," and "optimal health." A talk in Berkeley was called "Beyond Perfect Health," a state we are told can be reached in "seven easy steps." The assumption here, an engrained part of therapeutic ideology, is that no matter how free of diseases or problems you are and no matter how well you are doing, it's not enough. Who's to say that you're really as well, as efficient, as effective as you could be, or that your performances are truly the best you're capable of. As Lewis Thomas warns, "Once you start on this line, there's no stopping." And that is precisely what makes goals of this kind so attractive to therapists.

Preventing emotional distress is another way of expanding the boundaries of mental health work and it is a topic receiving increased attention. The key assumption is that an ounce of prevention is worth a pound of cure. The idea is unexceptional, being the foundation of public health work. There is, however, an important difference between many medical problems, with which public health is concerned, and psychological problems. As the President's Commission on Mental Health notes, we lack the kind of understanding of the causes of emotional disorders needed for dramatic prevention efforts. Undaunted by this difficulty, many push for more preventative projects. These would include, according to the President's Commission, reducing the stressful effects of life crises such as death of a loved one, marital disruption, unemployment, and retirement, and also creating environments in which people could achieve their full potential.

One of the most vocal advocates of prevention is psychologist George Albee. Starting with the idea that "our social problems are all human problems, and we are the experts on those," he urges mental health workers to become "radical social activists proselytizing for changes in our society." Albee and others think that psychological problems are caused by a dehumanized and unsupportive society, which is tempting enough to believe after you've dealt with the IRS or another bureaucracy, and the way to prevent problems is to change the nature of society. Since society by definition includes all the people, groups, and institutions in the country, adoption of Albee's views would allow therapists to intrude into every single aspect of life.

This seems to be the goal of our mental healers, whether or not they use the rubric of prevention. Evidence supporting this assertion comes from a remarkable book, *Career Opportunities for Psychologists*, published by the American Psychological Association. In a chapter on careers in forensic psychology, we read that "our expectation is that in the future forensic psychologists will roam confidently and competently far beyond the traditional roles of the psychologist in forensic settings." The doing of therapy "need not be viewed as the primary function of the psychologist in the criminal justice system." What else will the confidently and competently roaming psychologists be doing? Among other things, they will be *"reforming* the criminal justice system. Areas suggested ripe for reform are (a) modifications of substantive criminal law; (b) modification of the police role; (c) bail reform . . . (e) prison reform . . . (h) psychologist and psychiatric testimony; and (i) employee selection, job analysis and description, and performance evaluation." There is almost nothing in the justice system that the authors don't see psychologists having a hand in. Undoubtedly social workers and forensic psychiatrists also have plans of their own.

The same book contains a chapter on a new specialty called public affairs psychology. The authors want to be involved in public policy, "especially as it may be proposed or expressed in the form of legislation, defined or clarified through administrative regulations, implemented through government agency actions or operations, or assessed or interpreted by judicial review." In other words, they want to help run the government. If you are wondering precisely what areas they want to help with, the authors supply a handy "minimal list of deserving social problem areas":

> Employment, Social welfare and income maintenance, Human resource development, Energy resource allocation, Environmental degradation, Crime and administration of justice, Transportation, Housing, Education, Urban Life, Technology assessment, Minorities and prejudice, Health Services, Old age and retirement, Population and crowding, Violence and social unrest, and Militarism and war.

As Christopher Lasch, Thomas Szasz, and a few others note, therapists want to diffuse the therapeutic sensibility and therapy itself into every nook and cranny of human existence. Lasch's comment that they "would abolish the hospital only to make the whole world a hospital" does not seem extreme after looking at all the areas they want to encompass in their sphere of influence. To a very large extent, mental health workers have been successful in what Szasz calls the manufacture of madness. The idea of psychotherapy for young people, even infants, old people, and all those in between, for individuals, couples, families, and even whole villages, no longer seems outrageous, and the idea of psychological consultation for businesses, schools, courts, athletic teams, the military, and every other organization you can think of no longer seems strange. Rather, these ideas seem quite reasonable and logical, maybe even necessary.

Make Problems out of Difficulties and Spread the Alarm

We are already incredibly self-conscious and psychologically minded. All the publicity about emotional problems increases both qualities, making many things seem more serious than they are. If you're forty and disappointed because life isn't turning out the way you expected, we have a label for your situation. It's a mid-life crisis, or if you really want to get technical, an adjustment reaction to adult life, an official psychiatric problem. We also have labels if you're recently divorced and feel uneasy about being single again. Perhaps you are suffering from divorce trauma or maybe you're having a life-style transition problem. Whatever your situation and feelings, we have a name for it and therefore you can be sure it constitutes a real and legitimate problem.

What has been created is the psychological version of medical students' disease; everyone sees bits of himself in what any expert says or writes and makes what he or she sees into problems. Yes, it's true I don't always feel in charge of my life, that I sometimes feel guilty, that I'm not using all my potential, that life isn't always joyful. Such commonplace banalities are converted into important, significant issues that demand attention, work, and resolution.

Since there is some resistance to turning every feeling and event into a big problem, therapists feel obliged to spread the alarm, to scare people into giving up their resistances. In *Your Erroneous Zones*, Wayne Dyer informs us that "if you are growing you are alive. If you are not growing, you might as well be dead." Dead? Who wants to be dead? Maybe you better start growing. And here is Joyce Brothers: "The giant marriage wrecker is the most insidious one. Boredom. Sheer spirit-crushing boredom. . . . The chilling fact is that close to 75 percent of all marriages fall short of their potential because boredom creeps in." Where that refrigerated fact comes from is beyond me: I have never seen any data to support it. But surely Brothers's use of it, as well as such terms as "marriage-wrecker," "insidious," and "spirit-crushing," is enough to get many readers wondering if their marriages are in danger of being torn asunder.

While on the subject of marriage, an article in *Reader's Digest* tells us that although only one out of ten marriages achieves its full potential for happiness, every marriage can be enriched. To aid us in our enrichment, a test of marital potential is presented. It yields scores in ten areas, thus assuring that partners will be fully aware of every area where one or both is falling short. The test is to be taken once or twice a year, just in case anyone starts to feel too comfortable. Immediately after husbands and wives share their scores, they should devise "a marital growth plan." Couples are going to have trouble doing nothing about the distressed areas just discovered, a point acknowledged by one of the test's developers: "Once a couple know where their marriage stands . . . they are impelled to do something about it. The test says: Now you know that your marriage can be better. The next step is up to you." By this time, it should be obvious that therapy will be the next step for many of the couples.

Tests on which almost everyone falls short and scare tactics are all part of the selling of therapy. Here is how one therapist spreads the alarm:

> How much of yourself have you really discovered? Are you sure there isn't more? Much more? Are there perhaps some talents you haven't tapped, haven't even realized? Are you using your mind as well as it was meant to be used? Are you still growing?
>
> Yes, I said growing. And by that I mean becoming more of what you really are. Because if you aren't growing, then you can't possibly be satisfied with your life. There are areas of yourself that are crying out for expression.

Sex is a good area about which to make people nervous, since many people already have some doubts about how well they are doing there. Here are a few statements from the experts about this interesting aspect of life:

> The vast majority of us live in a state of sexual deprivation.
>
> Sex is life. . . . If sex is "right," then everything else is right. If sex is "wrong," then nothing else can be right.
>
> The couple that satisfies each other in only three or four ways barely know how to please each other . . . If they don't get past the starting gate and move forward they may not stay satisfied much longer.

If you can't get people worked up about themselves, you can probably succeed in making them worried about their children. Here is how Stanford psychology professor Phillip Zimbardo and Shirley Radl do this in their book for parents on *The Shy Child*. After stating that "shyness does lots of bad things to people"—such as causing "depression, anxiety, low self-esteem, and loneliness," and learning difficulties in school—they conclude with this:

Our primary concern is to help you to minimize the effects of shyness that may keep your children from reaching their full potential as human beings. Even when children are only moderately shy, they still miss out on valuable social experiences. And, when shyness is really severe, living in that psychological prison can ruin a life.

Aside from boredom, deprivation, living in psychological prisons, and having areas that are crying out for expression, there are many other serious consequences to not doing something about your problems, and therapists have been effective in exploiting concerns about them. Publicity for drug and alcohol treatment programs is often not very subtle: ruined careers, health, marriages, and lives are what you can expect unless you get help. Parents are made to feel they are endangering the development of their children unless they deal with them in ways that have to be learned from experts. Couples are told their relationships may deteriorate or end unless something is done to make them better. Sometimes rather strange analogies are drawn in order to make people nervous enough to get into therapy. In an interview at the Fifth World Congress of Sexuality, expert William Masters said that only an "infinitesimal percentage" of those with sex problems were in treatment. He then added, "If they had a broken arm, they'd jolly well seek help right away."

Make It Acceptable to Have the Problem and Be Unable to Resolve It on One's Own

We are constantly told that we are not alone: many, most, thousands, millions, the vast majority, 50 percent, or 75 percent of the population are similarly afflicted. For instance, William Masters and Virginia Johnson, the creators of modern sex therapy, have for more than a decade given wide currency to their idea that "at least half of all marriages in the United States are contending with major degrees of sexual dysfunction or disorder." As far as I know, there is no evidence to support their assertion or similar statements made all the time by other counselors regarding the prevalence of emotional problems. But that is really beside the point, which apparently is to make you feel that you don't have to be ashamed or consider yourself "weird" because of your situation. If millions of other people have similar problems, then it's not so bad that you do too. This is a necessary step in the selling of therapy because many people with problems are embarrassed and might try to hide their shame rather than seek help. But if they can be sold the idea that they are not alone in having the problem and being unable to deal with it on their own, they may be willing to acknowledge their distress and get help for it.

Counselors expend great effort in their public appearances and books not to blame people for having problems. Something else— modern society, religious teachings, repressive upbringing, lack of love or of instruction—is held to be at fault. This is an important part of the selling of therapy, helping potential consumers believe that their distress is not a sign they are bad or mad. They are suffering because others have not given them the right training or adequate opportunities or sufficient support. As I discuss later, however, this notion frequently changes when people get into therapy and they are held responsible for having their problems. Whether or not this happens, one clear message therapists get across to current and prospective consumers is that they and they alone are responsible for doing something about their difficulties. No one else is going to make things better, and problems will not go away on their own. You need not feel guilty or ashamed for having your problem, only for not taking action to correct it. You owe it to yourself and to those around you to get help. This idea fits in nicely with the American penchant for not letting things be and for wanting to *do* something to deal with problems, and is supported by the fear of all the terrible consequences that presumably will ensue if you don't change your ways.

Offer Salvation

All of the above is mainly to set the stage for and make you receptive to the therapy, book, cassette, or course that the therapist has to offer. When it comes to salvation, it seems that every clinician, every book, and every mental health program has a unique and extremely effective way of helping you. Because of the heavy competition, therapists find it useful to differentiate their products and services from those of others. In this sense, the selling of change processes is not much different from the selling of automobiles, detergents, and many other things. The point is to make a distinction even though there is no difference.

Meditation offers a good illustration. All schools of meditation require the student to focus on a constant stimulus, but they use different stimuli—phrases, words, puzzles, breaths, sights, or sounds. However, an impressive body of research indicates that the same results are achieved—what Harvard's Herbert Benson calls the relaxation response—regardless of what the meditator's attention is fixed upon. This strongly suggests that the essential ingredient is the act of focusing and not what is focused on. If all meditation is basically the same, people could be expected to choose the cheapest or most convenient type, or the one that is most aesthetically pleasing to them. If you want them to enjoy your brand of meditation, you have to make it appear special. You need to give it a word, a secret ingredient. Transcendental Meditation, the most aggressive and most successful of the meditation schools, has its secret ingredient, the mantra, a word on which the student focuses. Mantras, we are told, are specially chosen by the instructor for each student and such individually tailored mantras work better than ones the student could select for himself. This despite what the research indicates. So TM sounds different and special. This apparently has been quite an attraction and one of the main reasons for TM's great success. Many people who already knew how to meditate, something that can easily be learned from a book or a brief demonstration, took the TM course thinking they would be getting something better there. And why shouldn't they think this? TM's publicity was aggressive and well done, and TM—not meditation in general but *Transcendental Meditation*—received numerous testimonials from well-known therapists and other public figures. It was easy for those who hadn't derived benefits from other meditation to believe they might reach their goals if only they had the right mantra.

Whatever program, method, or book is chosen, the prospective consumer is led to believe that dramatic changes can be expected, and moreover that they will come in a short time without much effort. Est, for example, says it will "transform the level at which you experience life so that living becomes a process of expanding satisfaction." It's not clear what that means, but it certainly sounds good. Usually the claims are more specific. Adelaide Bry is a therapist who has written books about several change-processes. In one of her books she tells us that life need not be "a time of quiet desperation." Instead, "it can be a time of infinite and joyous possibility" if you make use of her new method, visualization. Here are a few of the things she says you can "realistically expect" from using this method:

•To improve the quality of your life in exactly the areas that need improvement.
  •To be healthier, wealthier, and—believe it!—wiser.
  •To expand your creative talents.
  •To help you get well when you're sick.
  •To deepen your feelings of love.
  •To experience other dimensions of yourself so that you can go beyond all your present limitations.

According to Arthur Janov, whose Primal Therapy created such a stir in the early 1970s, his methods produce "a tensionless, defense-free life in which one is completely his own self and experiences deep feeling and internal unity. . . . People become themselves and *stay* themselves." Clients become more intelligent; are better coordinated; enjoy sex more; work better but do not overwork; lose their depressions, phobias, anxieties, as well as their compulsions to take drugs and alcohol, to overeat, and to smoke; and they are "never moody." There are special benefits for women: increased breast size for flat-chested women and the disappearance of premenstrual cramps and irregular periods. In a way, says Janov, "the post-Primal person is a new kind of human being," one who "is truly in control of his life." (Before readers rush off to sign up for Primal Therapy, I should mention that I am unaware of any independent research demonstrating the validity of these claims.)

Other counselors tell us their approaches are "pleasant," "uncomplicated," and that "the easiest thing to be is yourself." And not much time is required. A book called *Psychological Fitness* offers a "unique three-week psychological shapeup program" that "is the start of your fresh, more exciting life." Clinical psychologist Joseph Bird and his cotherapist promise more in less time. Your life will be changed "almost totally" by their book. "All that is required of you is that you test the formula in its pages—a matter of a few minutes a day for a week or less." But even that sounds like a long time compared to what psychiatrist Robert Goulding, past president of the American Academy of Psychotherapists, has to offer. He told the *San Francisco Examiner* that he "can cure most phobias in 15 to 30 minutes. . . . Therapy doesn't have to be hard or long. It doesn't have to be painful."

Success, effectiveness, and spectacular changes are what we hear about. Successes are big news. Failures are not, unless there is evidence of scandal, e.g., that results were faked. It goes even further than this because, as psychotherapist Albert Ellis notes, the successful cases therapists present are most often "unusually good successes." The modest, partial, and later-relapsing "successes" are not much heard about. Because of this, Ellis observes, the public "may well gain the impression that failures are nonexistent," or at the very least, that the methods discussed are marvelously effective.

Strictly speaking, however, it's not true that therapists don't talk about failures. They do . . . but usually other people's failures. A common theme is that "my" method or genius succeeds where others have failed. Behaviorists heal psychoanalytic failures; family therapists succeed where individual counseling failed; meditation or est works where more traditional methods were of no avail. Counselors gleefully report how many of their patients have been through other programs without benefit. Janov claims that the great bulk of his Primal Therapy clients have had previous treatment ranging from psychoanalysis, gestalt, rational-emotive, to just about every other kind. Masters and Johnson say that 85 percent of their couples have failed in other therapies, and it is becoming increasingly common for weight loss programs to mention how many of their successes failed elsewhere.

The point of such comparison is to demonstrate the effectiveness of the counselor doing the talking or writing. What is easily missed is the fact that a lot of failures are being mentioned.

Another way of discussing failures also leads to viewing therapy as very successful. This is when the therapist's own past failures are mentioned, but only as a contrast to present successes. Thus Heinz Kohut, one of the latest psychoanalytic gurus, in writing about his new treatment methods, which he would have us believe are very effective, says that for some fifteen years he felt "increasingly stumped" by as many as half of his cases. Yet there was no acknowledgment of this fact in his papers written during that period. It is easy to focus on present successes and forget about past failures and just as easy not to ask why the failures weren't admitted when they were relevant.

This pattern has a long tradition in mental healing. Before he developed psychoanalysis, Freud believed in hypnosis and suggestion. In *Studies on Hysteria*, he and his colleague Breuer claimed 100 percent success in treating hysteria with hypnosis. Each hysterical symptom "immediately and permanently disappeared" after the hypnotized patient brought forth the memory of the event which had caused it and expressed the accompanying emotion. Obviously we were well on our way to stamping out hysteria. But the new wonder cure turned out to be not so wonderful after all. Only a few years later Freud was saying that most patients couldn't be hypnotized and that hypnosis rarely resulted in long-term cure. So much for the permanently disappearing symptoms. By this time, however, Freud was using the psychoanalytic approach, the new best way of treating neurosis, and everyone could imagine that all was well.

Clients engage in a similar kind of thinking. Thus Adelaide Bry, therapist, author, and apparently perpetual client, has this to say after taking est:

> I, like so many others, have had high moments after encounter groups, meditation, and other brief or extended mind-expanding experiences. But these feelings were always short-lived.
>
> My own experience with est, and that of the professionals and graduates I interviewed, is that most people continued to experience growth and change over a long period of time.

Bry forgets or never knew that participants in encounter groups and other "mind-expanding experiences" said the same things about them that she is now saying about est. Many reported that while past counseling had resulted in no change or transitory change, whatever it was they had just completed had really done the trick.

It's very easy to overlook the fact that when counselors and clients in 1986 and 1990 discuss past failures, in order to contrast them with the current successes, they will be referring to what we are doing right now.

The exaggerated claims and hoopla that attend the introduction of new therapeutic methods also contribute to the image of therapy's great effectiveness and help bring in customers. Since new methods are added all the time, and since these receive a disproportionate share of publicity, we constantly hear of great things. Every new approach claims unprecedented success. The bad news is longer in coming and the public often doesn't hear about it when it does arrive. The life cycle of new treatment methods has not varied at all in over a hundred years. As an article in the *American Journal of Psychiatry* puts it, "the initial enthusiasm and the report of remarkable results are tempered by the application of more critical study and evaluation resulting in less impressive statistics." As far as I have been able to determine, there has never been an exception to this statement. No psychotherapy's initial claims of remarkable results have stood the test of time and independent investigation. There are a number of reasons for initial successes, including that the innovator's interest and enthusiasm may itself be beneficial. But enthusiasm also seems to put blinders on therapists and researchers so they don't see what they don't want to see. The criteria of success are often too loose, meaning that the results are more a function of the loose standards than of the interventions. Anyone still breathing at the end of treatment is considered to be cured or greatly improved, which tells us nothing at all about the usefulness of the therapy. Enthusiasm also leads to other kinds of errors. For instance, a review of the high recovery rates reported for hospitalized patients in the early 1800s found that the statistics included repeated recoveries of recurring problems in the same patient. Thus one patient who improved and relapsed and then improved again would be counted as two successes. Since some patients relapsed and improved many times, there were more successes than there were improved patients. Needless to say, this does something to the statistics. There is also the fact that enthusiasm is both contagious and intimidating; it may be impossible for many clients to acknowledge to their therapists a lack of progress or a backsliding.

A recent illustration of what often happens with new methods is provided by the issue of controlled drinking. Conventional wisdom has held that total abstinence is the only worthwhile goal for those physically dependent on alcohol, but in the early 1970s two young therapists, Mark and Linda Sobell, published a study apparently demonstrating that their behavior modification approach was very successful in retraining a small group of alcoholic men as social drinkers. Follow-up studies at two and three years after termination of treatment concluded most of the men were "functioning well." The study was hailed as a breakthrough, supplying what was thought to be the first scientific demonstration that controlled drinking worked. The Sobells were accorded widespread publicity and recognition, and their work had a tremendous effect on the thinking of health care professionals regarding the treatment of alcoholism; for many, controlled drinking became a feasible goal, and indeed a more attainable and safer one than abstinence. Then, almost ten years after the Sobells' first report of their results, a reevaluation of their work was published in *Science*. The three researchers who conducted this study carefully reexamined the Sobells' evidence and did a thorough ten-year follow-up. Their analysis showed that the Sobells had misinterpreted their data: the controlled drinking project was an almost total failure from the start. Only one of the twenty patients succeeded in becoming and staying a controlled drinker, and he apparently was mistakenly classified as physically dependent on alcohol in the first place. The sobering conclusion is that there was "no evidence" that the alcoholics "had acquired the ability to engage in controlled drinking safely after being treated in the experimental program."

Another example of the history of new methods concerns biofeedback, the amazing claims for which received widespread and uncritical attention in the 1970s. Here is what Barbara Brown, one of its most visible proponents, had to say:

> Nearly every human being is a potential candidate for biofeedback . . . biofeedback still appears to be the closest thing to a panacea ever discovered. . . . Probably no discovery in medicine or psychology compares, in breadth of applications or in scope of implications to the biofeedback phenomenon.

Biofeedback was thought by some to be an all-purpose treatment, applicable to medical, dental, and psychological problems, especially problems related to stress. Unlike controlled drinking, biofeedback was not an absolute failure. It does have its uses. If nothing else, it can help some people relax, and there's nothing wrong with that. But it has not lived up to most of the claims made in its behalf. As a recent review of the research puts it, "On the whole, the clinical effectiveness of biofeedback-assisted relaxation procedures is not overly impressive." Although positive results have been reported in many studies, biofeedback has not been shown to be superior to other relaxation procedures such as general relaxation training and meditation. In fact, if what people want is a feeling of calm and peacefulness, they would do about as well just sitting in a chair and relaxing, without any formal procedures or training.

But what therapists, clients, and the public usually hear about is the good news. Obviously this is of great help in the selling of therapy.

Therapists are not alone when they set out to sell their services: they have powerful allies. An important group of allies, which one author calls the friends and supporters of psychotherapy, consists of satisfied therapy consumers. They usually miss no opportunity to give testimonials to counseling in general and especially to the specific approach that did so much for them. Even if you are skeptical about the claims made by counselors and public figures, it's easy to become a believer when your neighbor, friend, or colleague reports great benefit gained. Since, as I discuss later in more detail, satisfied clients tend to spread the message while dissatisfied ones tend to keep quiet, chances are that any news you hear will be good news.

The mass media, where most of our beliefs about therapy's effectiveness are learned and nurtured, are another powerful ally. Although the popular media in America have a well-deserved reputation for muckraking, it is also true that in certain areas they are primarily interested in news that is encouraging and optimistic, e.g., in reporting tools for overcoming physical and emotional handicaps. We are regularly offered tidbits about new medical and psychological treatments for all manner of ailments. We are told that experts have discovered a new method for treating cancer, alcoholism, depression, and so forth. Only at the end of the story—if even there—do we hear that the research has so far been done with laboratory animals or on a small and highly select group of people. If one-half, or even one-tenth, of the new cures worked as well as we are told they do, there wouldn't be any disease or problems left uncured or unresolved. Most people are in no position to know that the overwhelming portion of the research will turn out to be useless: that it will be found to be unreproducible, to be inapplicable to the population for which it is intended, or to have terrible side effects.

An illustration of the strength of the media's positive bias is given by Curtiss Anderson, once an editor of *Ladies' Home Journal*. Some time ago, the *Journal* had done a series of articles on women who had dieted, lost lots of weight, and gone on to fulfill their dreams: marriage, children, and homes in the suburbs. Anderson decided to do a follow-up, which was approved by chief editor Beatrice Gould, who thought it would show the women "living happily ever after." But this is not what was found. According to Anderson, "Ninety-nine percent had blown right back up to their old weights. They'd lost their husbands, been divorced, and they were angry again." Anderson thought he had an important story on the meaninglessness of the *Journal*'s stories and of diets. But it was never published. "Mrs. Gould was appalled. She didn't want to hear about it. 'I don't believe it,' she said. 'I don't believe it's true.' " The *Journal*, of course, like so many other of what are called women's magazines, continues regularly to run stories about people who have lost weight, become more independent and assertive, found happiness, and so on. And nary a negative sound is heard.

Mrs. Gould was exhibiting the strong tendency toward cheeriness that characterizes certain parts of the media, especially women's magazines and talk shows. The idea seems to be that people get enough bad news elsewhere which should be balanced with hopeful reports. It's not that depressing and difficult subjects are avoided. Far from it: drug abuse, child-beating, suicide, divorce, sex problems, you name it and you see it or read about it. All of these subjects are acceptable, but the push is to treat them in an uplifting way by presenting suggestions to prevent or resolve them. Therapists who are interviewed are essentially given carte blanche to sell their books and methods however they choose. So no matter how widespread and terrible the problem, we end up on the note that there is something to alleviate or resolve it. It is rare for the therapist's methods and success stories to be questioned, mainly because there is no one to question them. Talk show hosts and reporters are not therapists or therapy researchers. Phil Donahue and Merv Griffin are in no position to say that when they tried the suggested approach with ten people, the results were far less beneficial than what the therapist claims. Even if they or members of the audience doubt the claims, they have no solid base from which to criticize. They can say that it sounds too good to be true, but this does not exactly a strong argument make. Also, time and space limitations encourage absolute statements and work against qualified ones. It is much quicker and easier to say "It works wonders" or "It's very helpful" than to make a thoughtful statement about what kinds of results are obtained by what kind of people with what kind of problem; who benefits most, least, and not at all; and who is harmed.

The pushing of the positive is not restricted to the popular media. It also occurs where you might not expect it, in professional literature. What is wanted is interesting results, meaning positive results. Failures to replicate previous research are published, but not in proportion to their occurrence. Criticism is allowed, as long as it doesn't go too far. As a result, therapists are not forced to think seriously about what they are doing and accomplishing. Reading their own journals, therapists have their positive biases confirmed and reinforced, and then go out with renewed vigor to peddle that optimism to the media and the public, both of which are only too ready to accept it.

Most of the selling of therapy takes place on the local level, on an individual basis, for the prosaic motive of survival. The great majority of counselors I have talked with say they don't like having to sell themselves; they do not necessarily think that therapy is the solution for all the ills of the world and are often embarrassed by the media appearances and claims of other counselors. They wish that without any salesmanship enough clients would show up to keep them in business. But competition is intense and they have to do something. One day I talked with a colleague who was upset about the comments made on television by several forensic psychiatrists. It's disgraceful, he complained: there's no scientific basis for what they do. They're just out to expand the scope of psychiatry and make a quick buck, and in the process they're making a laughingstock of the profession. Yet two days later this colleague was out doing his thing, telling an audience of doctors and nurses that psychological treatment rather than medical care is what most of their patients require. When I ask how this is different from what the forensic therapists do—isn't he also trying to expand the scope of therapeutic work and where is the empirical support for his claims?—he is perplexed; he can see no similarities between what he does and what the forensic experts do. He comes up with many good reasons why his work is important and beneficial, and with as many showing why their work is silly and even harmful. Rationalizations come easily to all of those, including therapists, who have something to sell.

To get a better idea of how the formula for the selling of therapy is actually carried out, let's look briefly at a therapist trying to establish himself in private practice. He must find some way of standing out, otherwise clients will go to already established therapists rather than to him. One way of standing out is to be very good at your work. If the therapist has demonstrated his effectiveness to his teachers or colleagues, they may refer to him. But this route is not open to many, especially in an area with lots of therapists, all of them about equally effective. So what else can be done? One possibility is to specialize. Therapists of all persuasions dealt with their clients' sexual problems, but in the 1970s a new army of specialists arrived, sex therapists, who claimed to be better able to resolve these problems. They received a tremendous amount of publicity, both because of the new methods some of them used and because of the simple fact that they specialized in this interesting area of life. What is true of sex therapists is also true of the many stress specialists who have appeared in recent years. In both the areas of stress and sex, as well as many others, the increased publicity has made people more aware of the issues. For some, this has meant turning hassles and difficulties into problems and for others it has simply meant realizing that help is available. In each case, the result has been more people going to therapy.

If specializing is good, creating a new specialty is even better, for in a new specialty there are unlikely to be many competitors, at least for a while. Creating a new specialty usually means creating a new problem, a new area for which psychological methods are thought appropriate and effective. Some new areas that have been opened up in this way: "learning to love again" after divorce; conflicts in dual-career marriages; transition crises, such as the birth of a child (the crisis of becoming a family) and the children leaving home (the empty nest crisis); and psychological aspects of serious illness such as cancer and even not so serious illnesses. Most of these examples involve the continued psychologization of the world and are attractive for just that reason. A whole industry, for example, has grown up around death and dying as psychological issues. There are now specialists who give therapy to terminally ill clients, their families, and friends. They also conduct training courses for lay people and professionals, especially for physicians and nurses, who are thought not to be sufficiently informed and sensitive about such matters. The media have been very responsive and given much time and space to the new experts because they have basically come up with a new twist to an issue that concerns all of us. Lewis Thomas's observations on the new death business are telling:

There are so many new books about dying that there are now special shelves set aside for them in bookshops, along with the health-diet and home-repair paperbacks and the sex manuals. Some of them are so packed with detailed information and step-by-step instructions for performing the function that you'd think this was a new sort of skill which all of us are now required to learn. The strongest impression the casual reader gets, leafing through, is that proper dying has become an extraordinary, even an exotic experience, something only the specially trained get to do.

A related way of standing out is to come up with a new treatment, presumably more effective than conventional ones, for dealing with familiar problems. Many sex experts and stress experts have done this. Another example is the use of jogging to treat depression, to get in touch with your spiritual side, or "to balance the feminine and masculine aspects" of your personality. Hypnosis can hardly be called a new treatment, having been around for several hundred years, but it is now enjoying one of its vogues, being touted as a useful remedy for almost anything that ails you. Following in the wake of the women's movement, feminist therapies and therapists have become common for women suffering from all kinds of emotional upset. The message is that a feminist-oriented therapist will better understand and be more helpful than someone else. An increasingly popular "new" treatment is the combination of several methods—such as nutritional analysis, guided imagery, gestalt, and movement therapy—under rubrics like "comprehensive" and "holistic." Such combinations have been particularly popular among humanistic therapists. The advantage of combinations is an important one. For prospective clients, and for referral sources and the media, they sound new—after all, gestalt therapy plus Bioenergetic Therapy is not the same as either one or the other—and the labels of comprehensive and holistic are difficult to resist. Closer examination may reveal that what is offered is not substantially new, but since such examinations are rarely done, there is an excellent chance that our therapist will get referrals and publicity he would not otherwise have received.

Publicity is of course all important. Once our therapist decides what he is selling, he needs to get the word around. Probably the most common way of doing this is to make the rounds of possible referral sources—physicians, lawyers, clergy, and other therapists—and tell them of what you have to offer. If you can persuade several lawyers that their work will be easier if their divorce cases spend some time with you for divorce therapy, you are in business. Another common way of selling your services is to advertise publicly by offering courses or workshops, through organizations with large mailing lists. Extension divisions of major universities are a prime target because their catalogues often reach many thousands of people. The point is both to give the course and to use the catalogue to advertise your specialty.

People often come to such events for help with their own problems, and it is not uncommon for some to find they want more help than they can get in the course. If they are impressed by the leader, they may ask for an appointment. Those who have no desire for further assistance from him may remember to mention him to friends or to their own clients. And many more who do not attend the particular course or workshop will nonetheless have been made aware—simply by reading about it in the catalogue—of the leader and his work.

The fortunate few are those who are noticed by the media. Journalists frequently check the mental health listings for newsworthy items. If you are interviewed, you're on your way. The interview is likely to bring referrals and attract the attention of referral sources. Furthermore, media coverage makes you an established expert, leading to requests for more interviews or for talks and more workshops.

So far the discussion has centered primarily on the ways in which individual counselors try to sell their services, but organizations do much the same, and for similar reasons. The media advertisements for programs dealing with problems ranging from drug abuse, alcoholism, obesity, smoking, family relations, depression, and other matters are now so common that no further comment is required. And similar things go on when organizations apply to government and other agencies for money for services or research. Whether at the individual or organizational level, the message is pretty much the same, namely the four-part equation that is the subject of this chapter.

Advertisements for therapy do more than just increase the referrals, fame, and fortune of a particular practitioner or the funding of a particular agency. They redound to the benefit of the entire mental health enterprise. They continue the psychologization of the world, help make problems out of difficulties or things that were barely noticed before, and spread the word that a solution, a psychological one, is available for whatever is troubling you. In short, the promotion of any therapy or therapist reinforces the therapeutic worldview.

The messages we get about therapy, regardless of the source, are seductive. For all the reasons discussed in the preceding chapters, we are receptive to what counselors have to say. When they tell us that we have problems we don't have to put up with, that we could be happier, healthier, and more successful, we listen. They are addressing our main fears and desires. And when they alleviate the guilt we feel for being in the situation and capitalize on our concerns and fears about being there, and then offer a way out, many of us will go for it. The rational parts of our minds may rebel at some of what is said, especially the fantastic claims of therapeutic effectiveness, but for increasing numbers of us there is the suspicion and the hope that maybe there is some truth to what is presented. The counselors usually have impressive credentials and training, and say their work is scientifically validated. They present so many success stories; surely these are not fabricated out of whole cloth. And then there are the testimonials, often from public figures we admire and trust; surely they wouldn't lie. Quickly or gradually, you begin to believe that this book or program can do what it says it can. The questioning, doubting part of you is easily put to sleep or at least told to mind its own business. Hope conquers all and soon you may find yourself enrolling in the program, calling for an appointment, or buying the book. The selling of therapy is one of the most successful examples of salesmanship in modern times.

It is not, I should add, that I have anything against therapists making a living or advertising their services. They have as much right to these things as anyone else. But we should realize that the selling of hundreds of thousands of individual therapists and organizations has a cumulative effect. We are day and night innundated by their messages—indeed, some of the counselors appear so regularly in the media that we think we know them—and the net effect of this over the years is to change the expectations we have of ourselves and the way we look at life.

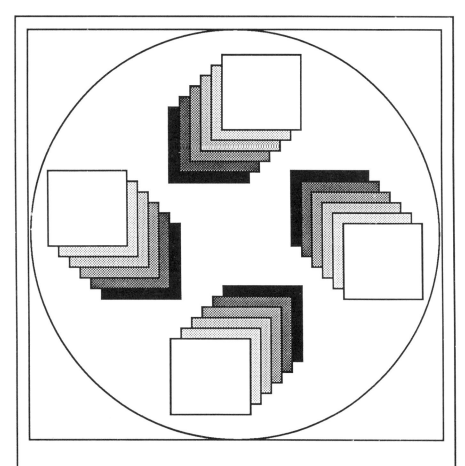

Chapter 14

Applied Psychology

CHAPTER 14: APPLIED PSYCHOLOGY

As previously stated, psychology has been criticized for focusing on behavioral mechanisms not directly relevant to practical applications. The functions that control many lab experiments are only found in those labs and not in the real world. This area of psychology specifically attempts to apply the basic principles of behavior to real-life situations. Applied psychology (engineering and industrial psychology) is one of the fastest-growing fields in behavioral research. The first selection addresses the social psychology of groups with respect to their decision-making behavior and their interaction with individuals and other groups. The second selection concerns the most basic question facing personnel managers: On what basis should employees be selected and evaluated? The third selection discusses various trends and theories of motivation at work.

14a. Janis, I. (1971). Groupthink. *Psychology Today*, 193–201.

In 1986, a group of management people at NASA and Morton-Thiokol decided to launch the shuttle *Challenger*, despite the warnings from their engineers that the engines were unsafe in cold weather. Of course, the shuttle exploded and the space program was set back at least three years. From what you know of that decision, analyze the problem from the perspective of Groupthink. Detail the similarities between Groupthink decisions and the decision to launch the shuttle, *Challenger*.

14b. Dickey-Bryant, L., Lautenschlager, G., Mendoza, J., & Abrahams, N. Facial attractiveness and its relation to occupational success. *Journal of Applied Psychology, 71,* 16–19.

This selection discusses the correlation between physical attractiveness and occupational success. Imagine that you are the personnel manager in an automobile plant and must select, evaluate, and promote the employees under your management. After reading the above article, would you take personal attractiveness into account in these decisions? Why or why not? Could you avoid it, and if so how?

14c. Guest, D. (1984). What's new in Motivation. *Personnel Management,* May, 147–151.

In this selection, various approaches to motivation at work are outlined. Describe two of these theories. Which one would you use if you were a manager in a factory? Explain why. Which of these theories have been used with you when you have worked? Give a specific example from your own experience.

Groupthink

Irving L. Janis

"HOW COULD WE HAVE BEEN SO STUPID?" President John F. Kennedy asked after he and a close group of advisers had blundered into the Bay of Pigs invasion. For the last two years I have been studying that question, as it applies not only to the Bay of Pigs decision-makers but also to those who led the United States into such other major fiascos as the failure to be prepared for the attack on Pearl Harbor, the Korean War stalemate and the escalation of the Vietnam War.

Stupidity certainly is not the explanation. The men who participated in making the Bay of Pigs decision, for instance, comprised one of the greatest arrays of intellectual talent in the history of American Government—Dean Rusk, Robert McNamara, Douglas Dillon, Robert Kennedy, McGeorge Bundy, Arthur Schlesinger Jr., Allen Dulles and others.

It also seemed to me that explanations were incomplete if they concentrated only on disturbances in the behavior of each individual within a decision-making body: temporary emotional states of elation, fear, or anger that reduce a man's mental efficiency, for example, or chronic blind spots arising from a man's social prejudices or idiosyncratic biases.

I preferred to broaden the picture by looking at the fiascos from the standpoint of group dynamics as it has been explored over the past three decades, first by the great social psychologist Kurt Lewin and later in many experimental situations by myself and other behavioral scientists. My conclusion after poring over hundreds of relevant documents—historical reports about formal group meetings and informal conversations among the members—is that the groups that committed the fiascos were victims of what I call "groupthink."

"Groupy." In each case study, I was surprised to discover the extent to which each group displayed the typical phenomena of social conformity that are regularly encountered in studies of group dynamics among ordinary citizens. For example, some of the phenomena appear to be completely in line with findings from social-psychological experiments showing that powerful social pressures are brought to bear by the members of a cohesive group whenever a dissident begins to voice his objections to a group consensus. Other phenomena are reminiscent of the shared illusions observed in encounter groups and friendship cliques when the members simultaneously reach a peak of "groupy" feelings.

Above all, there are numerous indications pointing to the development of group norms that bolster morale at the expense of critical thinking. One of the most common norms appears to be that of remaining loyal to the group by sticking with the policies to which the group has already committed itself, even when those policies are obviously working out badly and have unintended consequences that disturb the conscience of each member. This is one of the key characteristics of groupthink.

1984. I use the term groupthink as a quick and easy way to refer to the mode of thinking that persons engage in when *concurrence-seeking* becomes so dominant in a cohesive ingroup that it tends to override realistic appraisal of alternative courses of action. Groupthink is a term of the same order as the words in the newspeak vocabulary George Orwell used in his dismaying world of *1984.* In that context, groupthink takes on an invidious connotation. Exactly such a connotation is intended, since the term refers to a deterioration in mental efficiency, reality testing and moral judgments as a result of group pressures.

The symptoms of groupthink arise when the members of decision-making groups become motivated to avoid being too harsh in their judgments of their leaders' or their colleagues ideas. They adopt a soft line of criticism, even in their own thinking, At their meetings, all the members are amiable and seek complete concurrence on every important issue, with no bickering or conflict to spoil the cozy, "we-feeling" atmosphere.

Kill. Paradoxically, soft-headed groups are often hard-hearted when it comes to dealing with outgroups or enemies. They find it relatively easy to resort to de-humanizing solutions—they will readily authorize bombing attacks that kill large numbers of civilians in the name of the noble cause of persuading an unfriendly government to negotiate at the peace table. They are unlikely to pursue the more difficult and controversial issues that arise when alternatives to a harsh military solution come up for discussion. Nor are they inclined to raise ethical issues that carry the implication *that this fine group of ours, with its humanitarianism and its high-minded principles, might be capable of adopting a course of action that is inhumane and immoral.*

Norms. There is evidence from a number of social-psychological studies that as the members of a group feel more accepted by the others, which is a central feature of increased group cohesiveness, they display less overt conformity to group norms. Thus we would expect that the more cohesive a group becomes, the less the members will feet constrained to censor what they say out of fear of being socially punished for antagonizing the leader or any of their fellow members.

In contrast, the groupthink type of conformity tends to increase as group cohesiveness increases. Groupthink involves nondeliberate suppression of critical thoughts as a result of internalization of the group's norms, which is quite different from deliberate suppression on the basis of external threats of social punishment. The more cohesive the group, the greater the inner compulsion on the part of each member to avoid creating disunity, which inclines him to believe in the soundness of whatever proposals are promoted by the leader or by a majority of the group's members.

In a cohesive group, the danger is not so much that each individual will fail to reveal his objections to what the others propose but that he will think the proposal is a good one, without attempting to carry out a careful, critical scrutiny of the pros and cons of the alternatives. When groupthink becomes dominant, there also is considerable suppression of deviant thoughts, but it takes the form of each person's deciding that his misgivings are not relevant and should be set aside, that the benefit of the doubt regarding any lingering uncertainties should be given to the group consensus.

Stress. I do not mean to imply that all cohesive groups necessarily suffer from groupthink. All ingroups may have a mild tendency toward groupthink, displaying one or another of the symptoms from time to time, but it need not be so dominant as to influence the quality of the group's final decision. Neither do I mean to imply that there is anything necessarily inefficient or harmful about group decisions in general. On the contrary, a group whose members have properly defined roles, with traditions concerning the procedures to follow in pursuing a critical inquiry, probably is capable of making better decisions than any individual group member working alone.

The problem is that the advantages of having decisions made by groups are often lost because of powerful psychological pressures that arise when the members work closely together, share the same set of values and, above all, face a crisis situation that puts everyone under intense stress.

The main principle of groupthink, which I offer in the spirit of Parkinson's Law, is this: *The more amiability and esprit de corps there is among the members of a policy-making ingroup, the greater the danger that independent critical thinking will be replaced by groupthink, which is likely to result in irrational and dehumanizing actions directed against outgroups.*

Symptoms. In my studies of high-level governmental decision-makers, both civilian and military, I have found eight main symptoms of groupthink.

1 INVULNERABILITY. Most or all of the members of the ingroup share an *illusion* of invulnerability that provides for them some degree of reassurance about obvious dangers and leads them to become over-optimistic and willing to take extraordinary risks. It also causes them to fail to respond to clear warnings of danger.

The Kennedy ingroup, which uncritically accepted the Central Intelligence Agency's disastrous Bay of Pigs plan, operated on the false assumption that they could keep secret the fact that the United States was responsible for the invasion of Cuba. Even after news of the plan began to leak out, their belief remained unshaken. They failed even to consider the danger that awaited them: a worldwide revulsion against the U.S.

A similar attitude appeared among the members of President Lyndon B. Johnson's ingroup, the "Tuesday Cabinet," which kept escalating the Vietnam War despite repeated setbacks and failures. "There was a belief," Bill Moyers commented after he resigned, "that if we indicated a willingness to use our power, they [the North Vietnamese] would get the message and back away from an all-out confrontation. . . . There was a confidence—it was never bragged about, it was just there—that when the chips were really down, the other people would fold."

A most poignant example of an illusion of invulnerability involves the ingroup around Admiral H. E. Kimmel, which failed to prepare for the possibility of a Japanese attack on Pearl Harbor despite repeated warnings. Informed by his intelligence chief that radio contact with Japanese aircraft carriers had been lost, Kimmel joked about it: "What, you don't know where the carriers are? Do you mean to say that they could be rounding Diamond Head (at Honolulu) and you wouldn't know it?" The carriers were in fact moving full steam toward Kimmel's command post at the time. Laughing together about a danger signal, which labels it as a purely laughing matter, is a characteristic manifestation of groupthink.

2 RATIONALE. As we see, victims of groupthink ignore warnings; they also collectively construct rationalizations in order to discount warnings and other forms of negative feedback that, taken seriously, might lead the group members to reconsider their assumptions each time they recommit themselves to past decisions. Why did the Johnson ingroup avoid reconsidering its escalation policy when time and again the expectations on which they based their decisions turned out to be wrong? James C. Thompson Jr., a Harvard historian who spent five years as an observing participant in both the State Department and the White House, tells us that the policymakers avoided critical discussion of their prior decisions and continually invented new rationalizations so that they could sincerely recommit themselves to defeating the North Vietnamese.

In the fall of 1964, before the bombing of North Vietnam began, some of the policymakers predicted that six weeks of air strikes would induce the North Vietnamese to seek peace talks. When someone asked, "What if they don't?" the answer was that another four weeks certainly would do the trick.

Later, after each setback, the ingroup agreed that by investing just a bit more effort (by stepping up the bomb tonnage a bit, for instance), their course of action would prove to be right. *The Pentagon Papers* bear out these observations.

In *The Limits Of Intervention*, Townsend Hoopes, who was acting Secretary of the Air Force under Johnson, says that Walt W. Rostow in particular showed a remarkable capacity for what has been called "instant rationalization." According to Hoopes, Rostow buttressed the group's optimism about being on the road to victory by culling selected scraps of evidence from news reports or, if necessary, by inventing "plausible" forecasts that had no basis in evidence at all.

Admiral Kimmel's group rationalized away their warnings, too. Right up to December 7, 1941, they convinced themselves that the Japanese would never dare attempt a full-scale surprise assault against Hawaii because Japan's leaders would realize that it would precipitate an all-out war which the United States would surely win. They made no attempt to look at the situation through the eyes of the Japanese leaders—another manifestation of groupthink.

3 MORALITY. Victims of groupthink believe unquestioningly in the inherent morality of their ingroup; this belief inclines the members to ignore the ethical or moral consequences of their decisions.

Evidence that this symptom is at work usually is of a negative kind—the things that are left unsaid in group meetings. At least two influential persons had doubts about the morality of the Bay of Pigs adventure. One of them, Arthur Schlesinger Jr., presented his strong objections in a memorandum to President Kennedy and Secretary of State Rusk but suppressed them when he attended meetings of the Kennedy team. The other, Senator J. William Fulbright, was not a member of the group, but the President invited him to express his misgivings in a speech to the policymakers. However, when Fulbright finished speaking the President moved on to other agenda items without asking for reactions of the group.

David Kraslow and Stuart H. Loory, in *The Secret Search for Peace in Vietnam*, report that during 1966 President Johnson's ingroup was concerned primarily with selecting bomb targets in North Vietnam, They based their selections on four factors—the military advantage, the risk to American aircraft and pilots, the danger of forcing other countries into the fighting, and the danger of heavy civilian casualties. At their regular Tuesday luncheons, they weighed these factors the way school teachers grade examination papers, averaging them out. Though evidence on this point is scant, I suspect that the group's ritualistic adherence to a standardized procedure induced the members to feel morally justified in their destructive way of dealing with the Vietnamese people—after all, the danger of heavy civilian casualties from U.S. air strikes was taken into account on their checklists.

4 STEREOTYPES. Victims of groupthink hold stereotyped views of the leaders of enemy groups: they are so evil that genuine attempts at negotiating differences with them are unwarranted, or they are too weak or too stupid to deal effectively with whatever attempts the ingroup makes to defeat their purposes, no matter how risky the attempts are.

Kennedy's groupthinkers believed that Premier Fidel Castro's air force was so ineffectual that obsolete B-26s could knock it out completely in a surprise attack before the invasion began. They also believed that Castro's army was so weak that a small Cuban-exile brigade could establish a well-protected beachhead at the Bay of Pigs. In addition, they believed that Castro was not smart enough to put down any possible internal uprisings in support of the exiles. They were wrong on all three assumptions. Though much of the blame was attributable to faulty intelligence, the point is that none of Kennedy's advisers even questioned the CIA planners about these assumptions.

The Johnson advisers' sloganistic thinking about "the Communist apparatus" that was "working all around the world" (as Dean Rusk put it) led them to overlook the powerful nationalistic strivings of the North Vietnamese government and its efforts to ward off Chinese domination. The crudest of all stereotypes used by Johnson's inner circle to justify their policies was the domino theory ("If we don't stop the Reds in South Vietnam, tomorrow they will be in Hawaii and next week they will be in San Francisco," Johnson once said). The group so firmly accepted this stereotype that it became almost impossible for any adviser to introduce a more sophisticated viewpoint.

In the documents on Pearl Harbor, it is clear to see that the Navy commanders stationed in Hawaii had a naive image of Japan as a midget that would not dare to strike a blow against a powerful giant.

5 PRESSURE. Victims of groupthink apply direct pressure to any individual who momentarily expresses doubts about any of the group's shared illusions or who questions the validity of the arguments supporting a policy alternative favored by the majority. This gambit reinforces the concurrence-seeking norm that loyal members are expected to maintain.

President Kennedy probably was more active than anyone else in raising skeptical questions during the Bay of Pigs meetings, and yet he seems to have encouraged the group's docile, uncritical acceptance of defective arguments in favor of the CIA's plan. At every meeting, he allowed the CIA representatives to dominate the discussion. He permitted them to give their immediate refutations in response to each tentative doubt that one of the others expressed, instead of asking whether anyone shared the doubt or wanted to pursue the implications of the new worrisome issue that had just been raised. And at the most crucial meeting, when he was calling on each member to give his vote for or against the plan, he did not call on Arthur Schlesinger, the one man there who was known by the President to have serious misgivings.

Historian Thomson informs us that whenever a member of Johnson's ingroup began to express doubts, the group used subtle social pressures to "domesticate" him. To start with, the dissenter was made to feel at home, provided that he lived up to two restrictions: 1) that be did not voice his doubts to outsiders, which would play into the hands of the opposition; and 2) that he kept his criticisms within the bounds of acceptable deviation, which meant not challenging any of the fundamental assumptions that went into the group's prior commitments. One such "domesticated dissenter" was Bill Moyers. When Moyers arrived at a meeting, Thomson tells us, the President greeted him with, "Well, here comes Mr. Stop-the-Bombing."

6 SELF-CENSORSHIP. Victims of groupthink avoid deviating from what appears to be group consensus; they keep silent about their misgivings and even minimize to themselves the importance of their doubts.

As we have seen, Schlesinger was not at all hesitant about presenting his strong objections to the Bay of Pigs plan in a memorandum to the President and the Secretary of State. But he became keenly aware of his tendency to suppress objections at the White House meetings. "In the months after the Bay of Pigs I bitterly reproached myself for having kept so silent during those crucial discussions in the cabinet room," Schlesinger writes in *A Thousand Days*. "I can only explain my failure to do more than raise a few timid questions by reporting that one's impulse to blow the whistle on this nonsense was simply undone by the circumstances of the discussion."

7 UNANIMITY. Victims of groupthink share an illusion of unanimity within the group concerning almost all judgments expressed by members who speak in favor of the majority view. This symptom results partly from the preceding one, whose effects are augmented by the false assumption that any individual who remains silent during any part of the discussion is in full accord with what the others are saying.

When a group of persons who respect each other's opinions arrives at a unanimous view, each member is likely to feel that the belief must be true. This reliance on consensual validation within the group tends to replace individual critical thinking and reality testing, unless there are clear-cut disagreements among the members. In contemplating a course of action such as the invasion of Cuba, it is painful for the members to confront disagreements within their group, particularly if it becomes apparent that there are widely divergent views about whether the preferred course of action is too risky to undertake at all. Such disagreements are likely to arouse anxieties about making a serious error. Once the sense of unanimity is shattered, the members no longer can feel complacently confident about the decision they are inclined to make. Each man must then face the annoying realization that there are troublesome uncertainties and he must diligently seek out the best information he can get in order to decide for himself exactly how serious the risks might be. This is one of the unpleasant consequences of being in a group of hardheaded, critical thinkers.

To avoid such an unpleasant state, the members often become inclined, without quite realizing it, to prevent latent disagreements from surfacing when they are about to initiate a risky course of action. The group leader and the members support each other in playing up the areas of convergence in their thinking, at the expense of fully exploring divergencies that might reveal unsettled issues.

"Our meetings took place in a curious atmosphere of assumed consensus," Schlesinger writes. His additional comments clearly show that, curiously, the consensus was an illusion—an illusion that could be maintained only because the major participants did not reveal their own reasoning or discuss their idiosyncratic assumptions and vague reservations. Evidence from several sources makes it clear that even the three principals—President Kennedy, Rusk and McNamara—had widely differing assumptions about the invasion plan.

8 MINDGUARDS. Victims of groupthink sometimes appoint themselves as mindguards to protect the leader and fellow members from adverse information that might break the complacency they shared about the effectiveness and morality of past decisions. At a large birthday party for his wife, Attorney General Robert F. Kennedy, who had been constantly informed about the Cuban invasion plan, took Schlesinger aside and asked him why he was opposed. Kennedy listened coldly and said, "You may be right or you may be wrong, but the President has made his mind up. Don't push it any further. Now is the time for everyone to help him all they can."

Rusk also functioned as a highly effective mindguard by failing to transmit to the group the strong objections of three "outsiders" who had learned of the invasion plan—Undersecretary of State Chester Bowles, USIA Director Edward R. Murrow, and Rusk's intelligence chief, Roger Hilsman. Had Rusk done so, their warnings might have reinforced Schlesinger's memorandum and jolted some of Kennedy's ingroup, if not the President himself, into reconsidering the decision.

Products. When a group of executives frequently displays most or all of these interrelated symptoms, a detailed study of their deliberations is likely to reveal a number of immediate consequences.

These consequences are, in effect, products of poor decision-making practices because they lead to inadequate solutions to the problems under discussion.

FIRST, the group limits its discussions to a few alternative courses of action (often only two) without an initial survey of all the alternatives that might be worthy of consideration.

SECOND, the group fails to reexamine the course of action initially preferred by the majority after they learn of risks and drawbacks they had not considered originally.

THIRD, the members spend little or no time discussing whether there are nonobvious gains they may have overlooked or ways of reducing the seemingly prohibitive costs that made rejected alternatives appear undesirable to them.

FOURTH, members make little or no attempt to obtain information from experts within their own organizations who might be able to supply more precise estimates of potential losses and gains.

FIFTH, members show positive interest in facts and opinions that support their preferred policy; they tend to ignore facts and opinions that do not.

SIXTH, members spend little time deliberating about how the chosen policy might be hindered by bureaucratic inertia, sabotaged by political opponents, or temporarily derailed by common accidents. Consequently, they fail to work out contingency plans to cope with foreseeable setbacks that could endanger the overall success of their chosen course.

Support. The search for an explanation of why groupthink occurs has led me through a quagmire of complicated theoretical issues in the murky area of human motivation. My belief, based on recent social psychological research, is that we can best understand the various symptoms of groupthink as a mutual effort among the group members to maintain self-esteem and emotional equanimity by providing social support to each other, especially at times when they share responsibility for making vital decisions.

Even when no important decision is pending, the typical administrator will begin to doubt the wisdom and morality of his past decisions each time he receives information about setbacks, particularly if the information is accompanied by negative feedback from prominent men who originally had been his supporters. It should not be surprising, therefore, to find that individual members strive to develop unanimity and esprit de corps that will help bolster each other's morale, to create an optimistic outlook about the success of pending decisions, and to reaffirm the positive value of past policies to which all of them are committed.

Pride. Shared illusions of invulnerability, for example, can reduce anxiety about taking risks. Rationalizations help members believe that the risks are really not so bad after all. The assumption of inherent morality helps the members to avoid feelings of shame or guilt. Negative stereotypes function as stress-reducing devices to enhance a sense of moral righteousness as well as pride in a lofty mission.

The mutual enhancement of self-esteem and morale may have functional value in enabling the members to maintain their capacity to take action, but it has maladaptive consequences insofar as concurrence-seeking tendencies interfere with critical, rational capacities and lead to serious errors of judgment.

While I have limited my study to decision-making bodies in Government, groupthink symptoms appear in business, industry and any other field where small, cohesive groups make the decisions. It is vital, then, for all sorts of people—and especially group leaders—to know what steps they can take to prevent groupthink.

Remedies. To counterpoint my case studies of the major fiascos, I have also investigated two highly successful group enterprises, the formulation of the Marshall Plan in the Truman Administration and the handling of the Cuban missile crisis by President Kennedy and his advisers. I have found it instructive to examine the steps Kennedy took to change his group's decision-making processes. These changes ensured that the mistakes made by his Bay of Pigs ingroup were not repeated by the missile-crisis ingroup, even though the membership of both groups was essentially the same.

The following recommendations for preventing groupthink incorporate many of the good practices I discovered to be characteristic of the Marshall Plan and missile-crisis groups:

1 The leader of a policy-forming group should assign the role of critical evaluator to each member, encouraging the group to give high priority to open airing of objections and doubts. This practice needs to be reinforced by the leader's acceptance of criticism of his own judgments in order to discourage members from soft-pedaling their disagreements and from allowing their striving for concurrence to inhibit critical thinking.

2 When the key members of a hierarchy assign a policy-planning mission to any group within their organization, they should adopt an impartial stance instead of stating preferences and expectations at the beginning. This will encourage open inquiry and impartial probing of a wide range of policy alternatives.

3 The organization routinely should set up several outside policy-planning and evaluation groups to work on the same policy question, each deliberating under a different leader. This can prevent the insulation of an ingroup.

4 At intervals before the group reaches a final consensus, the leader should require each member to discuss the group's deliberations with associates in his own unit of the organization assuming that those associates can be trusted to adhere to the same security regulations that govern the policymakers—and then to report back their reactions to the group.

5 The group should invite one or more outside experts to each meeting on a staggered basis and encourage the experts to challenge the views of the core members.

6 At every general meeting of the group, whenever the agenda calls for an evaluation of policy alternatives, at least one member should play devil's advocate, functioning as a good lawyer in challenging the testimony of those who advocate the majority position.

7 Whenever the policy issue involves relations with a rival nation or organization, the group should devote a sizable block of time, perhaps an entire session, to a survey of all warning signals from the rivals and should write alternative scenarios on the rivals intentions.

8 When the group is surveying policy alternatives for feasibility and effectiveness, it should from time to time divide into two or more subgroups to meet separately, under different chairmen, and then come back together to hammer out differences.

9 After reaching a preliminary consensus about what seems to be the best policy, the group should hold a "second-chance" meeting at which every member expresses as vividly as he can all his residual doubts, and rethinks the entire issue before making a definitive choice.

How. These recommendations have their disadvantages. To encourage the open airing of objections, for instance, might lead to prolonged and costly debates when a rapidly growing crisis requires immediate solution. It also could cause rejection, depression and anger. A leader's failure to set a norm might create cleavage between leader and members that could develop into a disruptive power struggle if the leader looks on the emerging consensus as anathema. Setting up outside evaluation groups might increase the risk of security leakage. Still, inventive executives who know their way around the organizational maze probably can figure out how to apply one or another of the prescriptions successfully, without harmful side effects.

They also could benefit from the advice of outside experts in the administrative and behavioral sciences. Though these experts have much to offer, they have had few chances to work on policy-making machinery within large organizations. As matters now stand, executives innovate only when they need new procedures to avoid repeating serious errors that have deflated their self-images.

In this era of atomic warheads, urban disorganization and ecocatastrophes, it seems to me that policymakers should collaborate with behavioral scientists and give top priority to preventing groupthink and its attendant fiascos.

Facial Attractiveness and Its Relation to Occupational Success*

LeAnne Dickey-Bryant, Gary L. Lautenschlager, and Jorge L. Mendoza.
University of Georgia

Norman Abrahams
San Diego State University

ABSTRACT

The relation of facial attractiveness to measured ability was examined for graduates of a military service academy. In contrast to previous research, the present study used criterion measures that were obtained independently of the attractiveness ratings. No relation was found between rated attractiveness and performance in the academy for the entire sample. In addition, no relation was found between rated attractiveness and rank attained 12 years later. However, for those individuals who remained on active duty 12 years postgraduation, a significant relation was found between attractiveness and ability (as measured by academy performance). This result is interpreted as evidence that organizations can foster the development of stereotypes.

Physical attractiveness as a researchable variable has been largely ignored by social scientists. This neglect has been attributed to at least two factors. One is a fear that the results of such investigation would reveal the use of an immutable characteristic in determining a person's destiny (Aronson, 1969). The second is the assumption that estimating facial characteristics from photographs would be very difficult (Cohen, 1973). During the 1970s, however, physical attractiveness was accepted as a research topic. Furthermore, studies of attractiveness using photographic stimuli quickly demonstrated that photographs can yield reliable judgments (Dion, Berscheid, & Walster, 1972; Dipboye, Fromkin, & Wilback, 1975).

Since its debut in research, physical attractiveness has been established as a generally important variable. Of major import was the discovery of the attractiveness stereotype that the physically attractive are perceived as having more desirable personality traits

---

* This article is based in part on a master's thesis completed by the first author at the University of Georgia. The opinions or assertions contained herein are those of the authors and should not be construed as being official or reflecting the views of the U.S. Military.

The authors thank two anonymous reviewers for their helpful comments on an earlier draft of this article.

Jorge Mendoza is now at Texas A&M University.

Correspondence concerning this article should be addressed to Gary Lautenschlager, Department of Psychology, University of Georgia, Athens, Georgia 30602.

than the physically unattractive (Dion et al., 1972). Dion et al. also confirmed the view that the more physically attractive would be expected to lead better (richer, happier, more successful) lives. A positive, linear relation was found between attractiveness and attributed social desirability and expected quality of life. Further, subjects expected more attractive stimulus persons to have more prestigious occupations than their less attractive counterparts. These findings were later strengthened by Gillen's (1981) confirmation that attributed social desirability correlates positively with facial attractiveness in men and women.

Similarly, unattractive persons seem more likely to be perceived as exhibiting negative traits. Unattractive stimulus persons have been targeted as socially deviant (Unger, Hilderbrand, & Madar, 1982), mentally disturbed (Jones, Hansson, & Phillips, 1978), and prone to behavior disorders (Dion, 1972).

Perceived and expected ability seems also to be affected by physical attractiveness. Clifford and Walster (1973) found that teachers' expectations for students' academic futures were positively correlated with attractiveness, and perceived quality of written material has been found to be similarly affected by author attractiveness (Landy & Sigall, 1974).

More disturbing than the mere existence of the attractiveness stereotype is the indication that such perceptions may extend to and have implications for perceived and actual success in the workplace. The results of studies using bogus resumes and applicants of varying attractiveness point clearly to the potential for discrimination in hiring on the basis of physical attractiveness. Attractive candidates have been found to be perceived as more qualified for employment than unattractive candidates (Cash, Gillen, & Burns, 1977; Dipboye et al., 1975), and they were recommended higher starting salaries (Dipboye, Arvey, & Terpstra, 1977; Jackson, 1983).

In summary, research in the last decade has indicated that a physical attractiveness stereotype does exist, whereby desirable qualities are attributed more to attractive people, and that the stereotype may extend to hiring practices. Reported data do not, however, speak to a relation between attractiveness and actual occupational success; the present study explored this relation. Specifically, it was hypothesized that facial attractiveness and measures of occupational success would be positively correlated.

Method

Subjects

Subjects for rating attractiveness were 129 students, 61 men and 68 women enrolled in an introductory course in psychology at a large southern university. Participation in the study was voluntary, in return for which subjects could receive extra points added to their final grades.

Stimulus Materials

Seventy-five black-and-white facial photographs of white men, transferred to slides, were used as stimulus materials. The photographs were obtained from a 1971 military service academy yearbook. To eliminate extraneous effects that might result from differences in sex, hair length, glasses, and facial expressions, these factors were kept constant. Given the appearance code of a military academy, it should be noted that very few photographs were eliminated using these criteria. Selection of photographs was based on judgments of two female and two male graduate students who independently rated each of a larger number of photographs as unattractive, neutral, or attractive. Actual photographs used were chosen on the basis of high interrater agreement as to the judged attractiveness of the stimulus. Interrater reliability estimates ranged from .73 to .84. An equal number of photos depicted attractive, neutral, and unattractive stimulus persons. All photographs were transferred to slides to facilitate administration of the stimulus materials.

Procedure

Subjects were tested in groups of 10 to 25. They were first shown 75 consecutive slides in random order A 15-s viewing time was given for each slide. Participants rated each face on a 5-point scale beginning with very unattractive (1) and ending with very attractive (5). Responses were recorded on an IBM answer sheet for ease of scoring.

Subjects were then asked to view two slides simultaneously, each of which contained one photograph. Twelve different photographs (four each of attractive, neutral, and unattractive targets) were used. These photographs represented the four pictures in each category that had the highest interrater agreement among the original four judges. Each photograph was compared with every other photograph for a total of 66 pairwise comparisons. Pairs were presented for 15-s in random order.

For each stimulus pair the subjects were asked the following questions: (a) How similar in appearance are these two people? (b) Which of these two people do you think is more attractive? (c) Which of these two people do you feel has more leadership ability? and (d) Which of these two people do you think you would like more? The similarity judgments were answered by a mark on a 5-in. line with the end points same and different; answers for other questions were given by checking left or right on a response form.

Results

Attractiveness judgments of the 75 single photographs were combined for each stimulus person, and a mean attractiveness rating for each photograph was obtained. A test of separate regressions of attractiveness ratings on the dependent measures for each sex versus a common regression equation showed that a common regression line fit the data. Therefore, male and female judgments were combined to form the attractiveness measure. The attractiveness measure was then correlated with four success measures (see Table 1), using the Pearson product-moment correlation coefficient. Three of the success measures were obtained at the time the target men graduated from the service academy: (a) standing for course, a final class ranking based on academic and nonacademic factors; (b) cumulative grade point average (GPA) ranking; and (c) aggregate multiple, a weighted combination of military aptitude and academic ability. The fourth measure, rank attained, was obtained at the time this study was conducted. It is the military rank presently held by members of the academy class of 1971 used in the study. Military rank could not be obtained for 4 of the stimulus persons used in this study. All variables were scaled so that positive correlations would reflect the attractiveness stereotype.

Table 1

Comparison of Full Sample with Currently Active Sample Subset and Nonactive Subset

Variable	Military rank	Standing for course	Grade point average	Aggregate multiple
Attractiveness rating				
Full sample	.006	.191	.125	.173
Currently active	−.143	.355*	.306*	.353*
Nonactive	.236	−.021	−.094	−.044
Military rank				
Full sample		−.150	−.161	−.131
Currently active		.014	.051	.048
Nonactive		.100	.057	.098
Standing for course				
Full sample			.927*	.982*
Currently active			.905*	.976*
Nonactive			.943*	.986*
Grade point average				
Full sample				.921*
Currently active				.897*
Nonactive				.934*

Note. For the full sample, $N = 75$; for currently active, $n = 44$; and for nonactive, $n = 31$. For the correlations involving military rank, sample sizes are 71, 42, and 29, respectively.
*$p < .05$.

Correlations of the attractiveness measures and the criterion measures were computed for all 75 target photographs, for targets from the original 75 who are still on active duty (n = 44), for original targets no longer on active duty (n = 31), and for the 12 targets who had been chosen from the 75 on the basis of interrater agreement. For the original group of 75 stimuli, no significant correlations were found.

However, significant correlations were obtained for the targets still on active military duty for three of the four criterion measures. Correlations of attractiveness with standing for course, cumulative GPA, and aggregate multiple were .35 (p < .01), .31 (p < .04), and .30 (p < .05), respectively. However, it is interesting to note that for targets who left the service, significantly different correlations were found. Specifically, for this group the same correlations of attractiveness with standing for course, cumulative GPA, and aggregate multiple were all essentially zero. Additionally, although mean differences in aggregate multiple scores and attractiveness ratings were not significantly different for the two groups, the targets who left the military did have significantly better course standings and grade point averages. The correlation for rank attained with rated attractiveness was nonsignificant for both groups. It should also be noted that none of the academic criteria were correlated with rank attained either.

Significant correlations were also obtained for the group of 12 targets (see Table 2). The correlation for attractiveness rating with standing for course was .66 (p < .01); for attractiveness with cumulative GPA, .56 (p < .05); and for attractiveness with aggregate multiple, .62 (p < .03). Again, rank attained was not significantly correlated with rated attractiveness.

Table 2

Correlations of Measures of Attractiveness with Measures of Occupational Success for Multidimensional Scaling Analysis

Criterion	Standing for course	Grade point average	Aggregate multiple	Rank attained
Rated Attractiveness	.664*	.566*	.622*	.271
Attractiveness Dimension	−.741*	.674*	.739*	.421

Note. For targets chosen for representatives of each category, n = 12.
* p < .05.

The similarities data from the paired comparisons were first analyzed by replicated multidimensional scaling, using the Alternating Least Squares Scaling (ALSCAL) procedure developed by Young and Lewyckyj (1979). One- to four-dimensional solutions were studied. Because the maximum R^2 obtained in the four-dimensional solution (R^2 = .562) was essentially the same as that obtained from the one-dimensional solution (R2 = .559), it was apparent that one dimension accounted for a major proportion of the variance and was clearly interpretable. The paired-comparison data for each of the three additional questions were also used to scale the stimuli following Thurstone's (1927) law of comparative judgment. These scalings were used to aid in interpretation for the multidimensional scaling analysis.

The single dimension from the multidimensional scaling solution correlated significantly with the separate scalings based on each of the three interpretational questions, r = .96 for Question 2 (attractiveness); r = .94 for Question 3 (leadership); and r = .94 for Question 4 (liking); all significant at the .0001 level. This dimension was interpreted as another measure of overall attractiveness. Further evidence for this interpretation comes from the correlation of .93 (p < .0001) between dimension values and attractiveness ratings based on Likert-type scaling of the 12 target photos. In effect, the data collected using the paired comparisons could be described as representing a general evaluative dimension (Osgood, Suci, & Tannenbaum, 1957).

Correlations were therefore computed for the dimension and the criterion measures. Not surprisingly, the dimension was found to correlate .74 (p < .005) with standing for course, .67 (p < .01) with GPA, and .73 (p < .006) with the aggregate multiple. The correlation with rank was nonsignificant.

Discussion

The results of this study suggest that physical attractiveness may well be a determinant of occupational success. The criteria used were actual success measures, which, though they pertain directly to scholastic success, also play an important role in the determination of whether or not a service academy student can or will choose a military career.

The findings of no significant correlations between rated attractiveness (or the attractiveness dimension) and rank attained can be attributed to a severe restriction of range in the latter measure and most notably for those still on active duty at the time of this study. With few exceptions the men used as stimuli had advanced to one of three ranks. For those still on active duty, over 90% were concentrated in a single rank. For those no longer on active duty, 86% were in the rank immediately below that held by those still on active duty. In this situation it would be less likely for an effect to be detected. It should be pointed out that attainment of the ranks presently held by the persons used as stimuli in this study is largely a matter of time. There would have been limited opportunity for superior performance to have had substantial influence on promotions at this stage in an officer's career. A better assessment of the relation may be available in the future when there has been more opportunity for differential advancement.

It is interesting to reflect on the fact that the relation between performance in the academy and rated attractiveness holds for those individuals who remain on active duty some 12 years later The findings of the person-organization fit literature hold that those who remain in the organization are generally those who successfully make an adaptation to it (Porter, Lawler, & Hackman, 1975). The present results suggest that those persons fitting the attractiveness-ability mold are more likely to remain active in the organization. Those persons who remained on active duty had attractiveness ratings and measured academic performance that were consistent with the attractiveness stereotype. Less attractive individuals who remained on active duty were also more likely to have had poorer academic performance than their more attractive classmates, and vice versa. The time lapse between collection of the academy data and current status further suggests that the attractiveness-ability stereotype within an organization may very well be a self-fulfilling prophecy. It does remain to be determined whether later occupational success is itself related to attractiveness, and this question must await criterion maturation for an answer.

In closing there are several points that bear mentioning. The first is a caveat with respect to the stimulus materials. Facial attractiveness may be only one aspect of an overall evaluation of a given person's attractiveness. The further reduction to a single still black-and-white photograph may further limit the usefulness of facial cues in attractiveness judgments. To a certain extent, then, the present study may be criticized from the standpoint of the "paper-people" fallacy outlined by Gorman, Clover, and Doherty (1978). However, an important distinction is that the present study does demonstrate external validity of the attractiveness stereotype. Finally, although one typically expects range restriction to result in decreasing the magnitude of a correlation coefficient, the present study found just the opposite. When the sample of academy graduates was restricted to those still on active duty, results consistent with the attractiveness stereotype were obtained.

References

Aronson, E. (1969). Some antecedents of interpersonal attraction. In W. J. Arnold & D. Levine (Eds.), *Nebraska symposium on Motivation* (Vol. 17, pp. 143–177). Lincoln: University of Nebraska Press.

Cash, T. F., Gillen, B., & Burns, D. S. (1977). Sexism and "beautyism" in personnel consultant decision making. *Journal of Applied Psychology, 62,* 301–310.

Clifford, M. M., & Walster, E. (1973). The effect of physical attractiveness on teacher expectations. *Sociology of Education, 46,* 248–258.

Cohen, R. (1973). *Patterns of personality judgement.* New York: Academic Press.

Dion, K. K. (1972). Physical attractiveness and evaluation of children's transgressions. *Journal of Personality and Social Psychology, 24,* 207–213.

Dion, K. K., Berscheid, E., & Walster, E. (1972). What is beautiful is good. *Journal of Personality and Social Psychology, 24,* 285–290.

Dipboye, R. L., Arvey, R. D., & Terpstra, D. E. (1977). Sex and physical attractiveness of raters and applicants as determinants of resume evaluations. *Journal of Applied Psychology, 62,* 288–294.

Dipboye, R. L., Fromkin, H. L., & Wilback, K. (1975). Relative importance of applicant sex, attractiveness, and scholastic standing in evaluation of job applicant resumes. *Journal of Applied Psychology, 60,* 39–43.

Gillen, B. (1981). Physical attractiveness: A determinant of two types of goodness. *Personality and Social Psychology Bulletin, 7,* 277–281.

Gorman, C. D., Clover, W H., & Doherty, M. E. (1978). Can we learn anything about interviewing real people from "interviews" of paper people? Two studies of the external validity of a program. *Organizational Behavior and Human Performance, 22,* 165–192.

Jackson, L. A. (1983). The influence of sex, physical attractiveness, sex role, and occupational sex-linkage on perceptions of occupational suitability. *Journal of Applied Social Psychology, 13,* 31–44.

Jones, W. H., Hansson, R. O., & Phillips, A. L. (1978). Physical attractiveness and judgements of psychopathology. *Journal of Social Psychology, 105,* 79–84.

Landy, D., & Sigall, H. (1974). Beauty is talent: Task evaluation as a function of the performer's physical attractiveness. *Journal of Personality and Social Psychology, 29,* 299–304.

Osgood, C. E., Suci, G. J., & Tannenbaum, P. H. (1957). *The measurement of meaning.* Urbana: University of Illinois Press.

Porter, L. W., Lawler, E. E., & Hackman, J. R. (1975). *Behavior in organizations.* New York: McGraw-Hill.

Thurstone, L. L. (1927). A law of comparative judgment. *Psychological Review, 34,* 273–286.

Unger, R. K., Hilderbrand, M., & Madar, T. (1982). Physical attractiveness and assumptions about social deviance: Some sex-by-sex comparisons. *Personality and Social Psychology Bulletin, 8,* 293–301.

Young, F. W., & Lewyckyj, R. (1979). *ALSCAL-4 user's guide* (2nd ed.). Chapel Hill. NC: Data Analysis and Theory Associates.

What's New in Motivation

David Guest

We hear less than we used to about motivation at work. No writers on the subject seem to have captured the imagination of managers in the way Maslow, McGregor, and Herzberg did and yet more material on motivation is in fact being published now than ever.

The subject of employee motivation may appear to have lost some of its glamour and novelty to managers, but this has been more than compensated for by gains in utility. Three general trends can be identified which help to explain this. First, there has been a shift away from presenting simplified theories and promising general solutions to the "problem" of motivation towards more careful, more narrowly focused and generally more valid work. The second trend has been to favour consolidation and elaboration of existing theory— improving methods of testing theories in work settings—rather than the development of new theory. And the third trend, and one which most managers would welcome, is a shift away from the development of general theories of motivation at work to a concern for approaches such as job design, leadership, participation and goal setting which can be pursued in different ways according to the underlying motivation theory that informs them.

For management, therefore, many of the most interesting developments lie in the strategies designed to overcome organisational problems by utilising motivation theory.

Meanwhile, new gurus have emerged; they may have moved into different fields, but they are still talking, albeit more indirectly, about motivation at work. Two of the best examples are Ouchi with *Theory Z* (1981), and Peters and Waterman with their more recent best seller *In Search of Excellence* (1982). At the heart of the management strategy which emerges from these studies is some sort of consensus about the need to obtain the involvement, the commitment—the motivation—of employees to their work and to their organisation. The message is over-simplified, but it captures something of the magic of management and most managers are intrigued to know what makes for success. In North America, one by-product has been a marked increase in the importance attached to the broad personnel management field and more particularly to utilising the behavioural sciences, including motivation theory, to ensure effective human resource management. It is an opportunity which does not yet seem to have been recognised or seized to anything like the same extent by personnel management in the UK.

Since developments in motivation cover such a broad field, this relatively brief and inevitably rather sketchy review will examine some of the recent—and in some cases not so recent but nevertheless interesting—work that has yet to make an impact in mainstream management literature.

Needs, Goals, and Orientations

The attempt to classify work-related motives or goals has continued. Research conducted in the 1960s and early 1970s showed little or no support for the theories of Maslow and Herzberg and they have therefore ceased to be a significant focus for further work. Perhaps the most useful work of that time was conducted by Alderfer who adapted Maslow's general classification of needs to the organisational setting. He found three rather than Maslow's five distinct set of needs: the concern for "existence" (including pay and security), for "relatedness" (covering all the social aspects of work) and for "growth" (reflecting job content and personal development).

Power, Achievement and Affiliation

However, while Alderfer has attracted little attention recently (perhaps because his ERG theory seems to offer nothing distinctive or new), there has been a rekindling of interest in the work of Murray, a psychologist working in the 1930s who suggested that people have a set of needs, many of which are latent until stimulated by the environment. Four which have potentially important implications in work settings are the needs for achievement, power, affiliation, and autonomy. McClelland (1975), among others, has conducted extensive research on the first three. Unfortunately the problem of devising acceptable measures of these needs has yet to be satisfactorily resolved, leading to caution in the interpretation of research.

Nevertheless, interesting findings are emerging about the appropriate priorities among these needs for different levels in the management hierarchy. In general terms, it is argued that high need for achievement is particularly important for success in many junior and middle management jobs where it is possible to feel direct responsibility for task accomplishment, but in senior management positions a concern for institutionalised (as opposed to personal power) becomes more important. A strong need for affiliation is not helpful at any level.

The idea that different kinds of motive may be important at different levels in the management hierarchy, and the implied need for flexibility, are useful insights with implications for selection, promotion, and career development decisions. However, those making a bid for power should take note of one of McClelland's findings. In a 20-year follow-up of Harvard graduates who had scored high on the need for power, 58 percent had high blood pressure or had died of heart failure.

Orientation to Work

Sociologists have approached motivation through the study of orientations to work. An orientation is a persisting tendency to seek certain goals and rewards from work which exists independently of the nature of the work and the work context. The initial and by now well-known work by Goldthorpe and his colleagues on *The Affluent Worker* highlighted the "instrumental orientation" of their sample of bluecollar workers, that is, a general view of work as a means to an end, a context in which to earn money to purchase goods and leisure. Unfortunately there has been a tendency to draw a general conclusion from this single study that British blue-collar workers are similarly only likely to be motivated by money.

The orientation approach overlaps quite considerably with the work of Murray and McClelland. Both emphasise the importance of the social environment outside work as the context for the development of motives, an encouraging and important move away from the emphasis of Maslow and others on instinctive needs; and both accept that motivation is subject to modification. This becomes important, for example, in the face of consistent research findings that frustrated career orientations are a major problem in industry. The management of career expectations provides an opportunity to test the feasibility of modifying orientations. At present it is all too common to find that recruitment and management development practices continue to encourage unrealistic expectations of promotion. If they are faced with a motivation problem as a result of this, personnel managers may have only themselves to blame.

Expectancy Theory

Expectancy theory continues to provide the dominant framework for understanding motivation at work. The basic formulation of expectancy theory, which will be familiar to many readers, argues that high effort or motivation will exist when an employee perceives a link between effort, performance, and rewards. In other words, there is a positive pay-off in exerting effort because it leads to higher performance which in turn leads to higher rewards. Whether it actually results in higher performance depends on the extent to which the employee possesses the necessary knowledge and skills and has an accurate appreciation of the appropriate role requirements.

The basic formulation of expectancy theory has been established for some time. Many managers have been put off by its complexity and by its failure to specify the kind of rewards that will prove attractive. For academic researchers, however, its clear propositions have proved irresistible and it has generated a vast amount of detailed research.

A number of reviews have drawn this research together. The most recent lead to the following general conclusions:

1. The predictions about motivation derived from expectancy theory usually hold true at a statistically significant level. In other words, workers do display more effort when they perceive a link between effort, performance, and reward.

2. The predictive power of the theory is greater when the nature of the task and the demands placed on an employee are clear and unambiguous.

3. Expectancy theory assumes that an employee engages in information processing and decision making. This seems more likely to hold true for decisions regarded by jobholders as important or which for some reason attract their attention. For routine day-to-day events at work, habit, derived from previous experience, may well be a more typical basis for motivated behaviour. In other words, workers will not always go through the expectancy theory process before displaying motivation.

4. The research reinforces the view that motivation is an extraordinarily complex process.

As expectancy theory has become more popular, it has attracted criticism—of its underlying assumptions, theoretical propositions, and their measurements; but most important from management's point of view is the practical usefulness of the theory. The nub of the problem concerns the feasibility of testing the theory in work settings where individuals often have limited freedom to make choices due to constraints imposed by their roles, by technology and by established procedures. Only when such tests have been conducted will it be possible to make a more confident assessment about the value of the theory. One way of circumventing this problem is to apply the theory to occupational and organisational choice (Wanous, Keon, & Latack, 1983). The most recent evidence suggests that expectancy theory is an excellent predictor of motivation in this setting. By taking account of the extent to which particular occupations or organisations provide individuals with valued rewards, this research neatly complements the earlier comments about the importance of considering orientations in selection.

Despite a number of problems, expectancy theory still offers an extremely useful basis for understanding and seeking to influence motivation. Many managers may find it most useful as a conceptual and diagnostic framework. In other words, expectancy theory:

Points to the key variables to examine to understand motivation and performance;

Is helpful in diagnosing the causes of problems in motivation and performance;

Points to the steps that need to be taken to improve motivation, i.e., improving the perceived link between effort, performance, and attractive rewards—feasibility or, in cost-benefit terms, desirability of such changes permitting. While it may not make sense to alter technology, at least in the short term, or to incur the wrath of the trade unions, it may be possible to influence perceptions and information feedback.

More specifically, expectancy theory indicates that if management wants a highly motivated workforce it should:

Systematically identify goals and values within the workforce and survey attitudes and perceptions;
.   Provide rewards on an individual basis, tied to performance, rather than on a general basis. An overall pay rise, for example, will have little motivational impact;
Make the selective provision of rewards public, so that all employees can see a link between good performance and higher rewards. This will influence expectations; and
Make sure subordinates have the knowledge, skills and understanding necessary to their role to translate motivation into high performance.

If workers are motivated by the opportunity to achieve attractive rewards, then key tasks for the supervisor are to ensure that subordinates perceive that attractive rewards are available and to clear and clarify the path along which they must pass to achieve these rewards. The supervisor should, for instance, encourage subordinates to value goals which are complementary to organisational goals, and identify and try to remove blocks to goal attainment, such as lack of resources or of skills or understanding of role (in which case the supervisor should provide coaching and explanation).

Expectancy theory predicts that job redesign, which should improve effort-performance-reward links, will have a powerful motivating effect on those with a strong "higher order need" strength, that is, those who value the intrinsic rewards associated with doing an interesting and challenging job.

A final illustration of the application of expectancy theory is Klanderman's work examining the conditions under which union members are likely to engage in militant activity. He shows that members are more likely to participate in strikes, demonstrations, and protests if they perceive that such action is likely to lead to valued goals.

Goal Theory

Locke has developed a relatively simple, and for many people an intuitively appealing, theory of motivation built around the influence of goals. The theory proposes that motivation and performance will be higher when individuals are set specific goals, when goals are difficult but accepted, and when there is feedback on performance. This approach overlaps with some aspects of expectancy theory and even, as a technique, with behaviour modification, but Locke has resisted attempts at integration. There is even more obvious overlap with "management by objectives" (MBO).

Goal theory has generated a considerable body of research, and interest in it shows no signs of abating. The results are generally highly supportive, indicating that individuals are motivated by having a specific goal and they perform better when they are aiming for difficult goals which they have accepted (Latham & Locke, 1979). Participation in goal setting seems to help for some employees, especially at lower levels in the organisation, but mainly as a means of gaining acceptance in the setting of higher goals. Feedback on goal attainment is essential, more particularly in gaining acceptance of subsequent more difficult goals, but it will often have to incorporate social feedback, on the performance and reactions of others, as well as task feedback.

The research on MBO shows that its impact has often been disappointing. This is partly because it has not been effectively "sold' and operated; partly because it has often failed to meet the requirements of goal theory; and partly because difficult goals are not reinforced. The management implications are clear. Higher motivation and performance are likely where specific, difficult but accepted goals are set and feedback is arranged. When goal setting becomes encumbered by bureaucratic constraints, as can sometimes happen with ineffectively operated MBO schemes, then its impact can be swiftly dissipated.

Behavior Modification

Strictly speaking, behaviour modification is not a theory of motivation, but rather a technique concerned with creating the circumstances to ensure appropriate behaviour. It has continued to enjoy some popularity, partly as a reaction to some of the more complex cognitive features of motivation theory.

Typical applications of behaviour modification in industry involve four stages:

1. Pinpoint—specify the behaviour to be changed in precise behavioural terms.
2. Record—establish basic data on current performance.
3. Identify influences on behaviour; these may include prompting, guidance, modelling.
4. Arrange for reinforcement of the desired performance. This typically takes the form of 'social' reinforcement from the supervisor such as praise and useful feedback of results.

One of the most interesting features of this approach is its emphasis on a clear specification of the kind of behaviour sought. Too often attempts to improve motivation are very vague about this. There are some well-known examples of success in obtaining improved performances through behaviour modification. However, recent writing has tended to highlight its limitations. These include the difficulty of precisely specifying behaviour for nonexecutive jobs where "correct" behaviour is hard to predict; the danger of narrowing behaviour to focus only on reinforced tacks; the assumption that extrinsic rather than intrinsic rewards are crucial; and the potentially limited effect of verbal praise, which is nevertheless probably the most feasible form of reinforcement in industry. It seems therefore that in most circumstances we cannot dispense with the concept of motivation.

Reactance Theory

Most approaches to motivation at work go some way towards behaviour modification in suggesting that motivation can be best understood in terms of individual responses to external stimuli, that employees behaviour is, to a considerable extent, moulded by influences such as management policies and practices and the attitudes of co-workers. The key concern is therefore to develop management practices which will have the most positive effect on employee behaviour. However, in much the same way as strategic approaches to the study of organisations emphasise organisational choice and the opportunity for an organisation to exert influence on, rather than merely being controlled by, its environment, so an alternative approach within psychology suggests the same may be true of individuals.

This alternative perspective suggests that individuals are not passive receivers and responders (Staw, 1977). Instead they actively strive to make sense of their environment and to reduce uncertainty by seeking to control factors influencing rewards. Equity theory research, for example, shows how employees can strive for fairness by adjusting their effort or performance in relation to the input/output ratios of other people. There is a growing body of work on "ingratiation," the process whereby subordinates manipulate their superiors' opinion of them to increase their chance of obtaining valued rewards. This helps to explain how some employees appear to be more skillful in obtaining promotion or allocation to attractive work. Some of the research on leadership, most notably the study by Rosen, suggests that subordinate behaviour and reactions influence leadership style as much as leadership style influences subordinates' behaviour (Rosen, 1969). Finally, the evidence from goal theory and from research on the path-goal approach to leadership shows the preference for a reasonably predictable and controllable environment.

Brehm's reactance theory argues that when freedom and control are threatened, an individual is motivationally aroused to reassert freedom and control—the experience of reactance. The work on commitment, intrinsic motivation, and equity shows that if individuals expect to control outcomes for themselves, they devalue outcomes chosen for or imposed on them. Reactance is most likely to occur among employees who perceive that their control is threatened. Therefore middle managers, threatened from below by autonomous work groups or quality circles, are just as susceptible as shopfloor workers. The danger is that any employee who, after many attempts to reassert control, finds that he cannot control factors influencing his rewards may experience "learned helplessness", a process of giving up and ceasing to try. This is more likely when he cannot identify influences on his rewards.

A further important feature of this approach is its analysis of the way in which individuals strive to reduce uncertainty and impose structure and meaning by attributing explanations to events. A first step has been to identify the main types of variable which people use to explain success or failure and four have consistently emerged as the most important. These are ability, effort, luck, and task difficulty. For example, in explaining how they received a large bonus, some workers may attribute it to luck, others to their own efforts. The first are unlikely to display higher effort, since they believe the reward was not subject to their own control; the second, on the other hand, believe the reward was due to effort and may therefore continue to display high motivation. A second step in this research has been to determine what influences the explanation or "causal attribution" that is made. There is some evidence of individual differences in "locus of control". Those with a strong internal locus of control are more likely to believe that they personally control events, whereas those with an external locus of control believe they are controlled by the external environment (Weiner, 1974).

For managers and others concerned to increase motivation, it would appear to be essential to understand the types of attributions made by employees and the influences on them. In this respect, feedback processes and the way in which information is communicated become vital. The more that workers perceive that they are responsible for and can influence their rewards, the greater the likelihood of continued high levels of motivation.

At this point, reactance theory links into expectancy theory. The perceptions of effort-performance-reward links are susceptible to change through feedback and through careful communication of new information. Attribution theory therefore has an important part to play in explaining changes in levels of motivation and in the persistence of high levels of motivation in some workers but not others.

Motivation and Management Policy

Taking some of the main implications of the expectancy and reactance theories together, certain policy choices emerge. On the one hand it may be possible to obtain high and productive motivation through judicious staff selection, by using reactance principles to obtain high commitment to organisational goals, by using goal setting techniques, by careful job design to provide personal or group control over effort-performance-reward links, and by adopting facilitative leadership. On the other hand management may attempt to impose tight control using conventional control systems such as technology, authority structures, and careful allocation of punishment and reward. The result will be a passive, compliant but possibly resentful workforce; the day-to-day work will be done but there will be little enthusiasm, initiative or commitment. Recent research on motivation has helped to make these choices clearer. There are risks in both approaches, but the changing nature of organisational work with its demands for greater autonomy, flexibility, and commitment should encourage many managers to consider how they can use the insights from the more recent work on motivation.

Beginning 40 years ago, and continuing for 20 years, an important theory of human motivation was that of Abraham Maslow. In 1964, Vroom began a revolution in theories of work motivation that has not yet ended. After the revolution began, there was a scramble to develop new theories and, as a result, we went from one or two theories to a dozen or so. That trend has slowed dramatically. As Guest points out in this reading, current research and theory is combining existing theories rather than developing new ones. In addition, there seems to be a movement away from general theories that might explain every aspect of behavior toward more specific theories that might account for limited and specific behavioral events. In this article, Guest provides a broad overview of what is happening currently in work motivation research.